SOCIOLOGY IN USE

A

A

Sociology in Use

Selected Readings for the Introductory Course

DONALD M. VALDES
DWIGHT G. DEAN

Denison University

THE MACMILLAN COMPANY, NEW YORK
COLLIER-MACMILLAN LIMITED, LONDON

© *Copyright*, THE MACMILLAN COMPANY, 1965

Second Printing 1965   51717
Dec. 1965

Library of Congress catalog card number: 65–12153

The Macmillan Company, New York
Collier-Macmillan Canada, Ltd., Toronto, Ontario

Printed in the United States of America

Preface

THE PURPOSE of this anthology is to illustrate for the beginning sociology student what Merton has called the "visibly practical accomplishments" of the discipline.[1] Whatever may be the predilections of an instructor of introductory sociology, the majority of his students will be oriented toward the applied, rather than the pure, aspect of science. To the degree that they fail to see the relevance of the material to the problems of present-day society and their personal lives, they will be less motivated to involve themselves enthusiastically with the subject. Indeed, this book has been compiled to secure for sociology the lasting interest even of students for whom the introductory course may be their only contact with the field.

Because motivation through demonstrated utility has been our primary aim, our major criterion for the selection of articles has been that they demonstrate the actual use of sociological knowledge, rather than the more customary criteria for teaching materials that they have social or theoretical significance. The readings are intended to show how sociology and occasions for its application intrude into everyone's life, pervasively and in quite ordinary circumstances. In a sense, these are case studies showing organizations or individuals utilizing sociological concepts or principles in the attempt to understand or resolve problems.

Many a standard and excellent treatise has been bypassed if its analysis, however excellent, has not been *applied*, if a recommended program has not actually been adopted and evaluated through use. We have attempted to demonstrate the potential of the sociological approach by presenting specific examples of how sociological concepts have been put to work in understanding or resolving problems in a wide range of human activity—e.g., foreign relations, business, religion, medicine, and crime. It is our experience that these programatic or "how-to" examples stimulate the student to explore the subject matter more thoroughly. This selective procedure has yielded a

---

[1] Robert K. Merton, "Social Problems and Sociological Theory," *Contemporary Social Problems*, eds. Robert K. Merton and Robert A. Nisbet (New York: Harcourt, 1961), p. 697.

compilation of articles ranging from simple to complex—from articles written originally for mass publications to those published for specialized groups, and from articles written by lay individuals to those of professional sociologists.

Although the "pure" scientist may tend to consider the practitioner or the popularizer with a degree of scorn, it is nevertheless through him that society at large gains much of its familiarity with and appreciation of research findings. The pure scientist may very well ponder the words of Young: "The expectation of usefulness dominates the popular view of science in the United States in spite of apparently increasing respect for those who contribute to the store of knowledge of man and nature without immediate concern for utility or for reward. This expectation may be accepted as an important aspect of the milieu without interminable and futile argument concerning the extent of acceptance of such a view, its possible dangers for the development of science in both pure and applied form, and its threat to the intellectual integrity of the scientist. Popular expectation need be regarded as simply a condition that sociologists and others concerned with the advancement and utilization of knowledge must take into account." [2]

The "applied" scientist, on the other hand, may well applaud the remark of Maurice Davie that "sociology will stand or fall on the basis of its utility to men as they struggle to live. Applicability is the test for the validity of a science." [3] Furthermore, the distinction between "pure" and "applied" is not so crucial as has been frequently maintained, because, as Stouffer has observed, applied research "stimulates the improvement of known tools and the discovery of better ones" and "provides data and ideas which may speed up the process of generalization." [4]

In the absence of a body of practitioners, sociology can best make its contributions to society "indirectly through the medium of the general culture and climate of ideas." [5] And where, ultimately, do most sociologists have a better opportunity to affect the climate of ideas in our culture than through their own students? The purpose of our volume is to assist the teaching sociologist to make good this opportunity.

For the convenience of students and teachers who will read our book in conjunction with an introductory textbook or other materials all of whose units do not coincide with the chapter headings of our book, we have prepared an extended topical index of the selections. Some are arranged under

2 Donald Young, "Sociology and the Practicing Professions," *American Sociological Review,* **20,** 6 (December 1955), pp. 641–642.

3 Maurice R. Davie, "Theory and Practice in Social Science," *The Papers of Maurice R. Davie,* ed. Ruby Jo Reeves Kennedy (New Haven: Yale University Press, 1961), p. 18.

4 Samuel A. Stouffer, *Continuities in Social Research,* eds. Robert K. Merton and Paul F. Lazarsfeld (New York: Harper, 1950), pp. 198–199.

5 Christen T. Jonassen, "Contributions of Sociology to Marketing," *Journal of Marketing,* **24,** 2 (October 1959), p. 34.

more than one heading, because their content is not fully subsumable under a single area of sociological interest.

DONALD M. VALDES
DWIGHT G. DEAN

Acknowledgment

THE EDITORS wish to thank those who have made this work possible: the publishers and authors who have permitted their work to be included in this volume; J. D. Moore, Editor at The Macmillan Company, for his confidence and encouragement; the staff of the Denison University Library for their assistance in making available the resources of the library; our students, whose questions prompted this compilation illustrating for them and for others the values to be gained by studying sociology; and our families, whose forebearance has been more than generous.

D. M. V.
D. G. D.

Contents

[xi

SOCIOLOGY IN USE

Chapter One

Introduction

NOWADAYS WE WOULD QUESTION the good sense of a farmer who insisted on using a wooden plow, a parent who refused a smallpox vaccination for his child, or a businessman who refused to make a long trip by plane. The practical benefits of science as a problem-solving approach to physical problems confronting man have been quite widely recognized and appreciated. Yet, ironically, solutions to other problems of great public concern, such as delinquency, race relations, maladjusted family life, and international relations, are for the most part sought in terms of ancient folk knowledge. Why have we, as a society and as individuals, been so reluctant to accept the same problem-solving method in regard to human relations that has been so spectacularly successful in understanding and controlling natural phenomena?

Among many reasons for resistance to the use of the scientific method in the solution of social issues is the failure of social scientists to keep open the channels of communication to the ultimate consumers—the public. Whenever men have comprehended the advantages of new techniques and have been convinced of their utility, they have adopted them. Steel plows, immunizations, and air transportation were resisted from their outset until their usefulness was demonstrated. The purpose of this book is to provide, for the beginning sociology student, examples of the practical utility of the sociological approach. Knowledge we acquire is of value, after all, only as we act in accordance with it.

Many of the selections in this book are related to the use of sociology by business. Historically in our society, innovations are more readily adopted when their benefits are

[1

more readily convertible to market value. *Business Week* has stated that sociologists are "invading the business world because business has invited them in through the front door." [1] The contributions of sociologists to knowledge of group behavior, to value patterns, to lines of influence and communication, and to adoption of innovations as well as to the understanding of particular cultures have been helpful to business. The influence of sociologists on business and public administration may be further appreciated when it is noted that in a recent year of *Administrative Science Quarterly* more than 65 per cent of the articles were contributed by sociologists.[2] Two recent books have been devoted principally to the applications of social science to business. One, *Using Social Science Knowledge in Business and Industry,* reported on a seminar planned to "strengthen the bridge between producers and prospective users of social research." [3] The other was produced as a result of a Ford Foundation grant designed to bring together social science scholars and both faculty and graduate students of certain schools of commerce and business.[4]

The medical profession also is increasingly recognizing the value of sociology. By 1960, nineteen sociologists directly responsible for teaching medical students were found on the staffs of fourteen different medical colleges. More than one hundred sociologists, full or part time, were teaching medical personnel, and numbers of others were engaged in cooperative research on medical problems.[5] One physician psychiatrist has utilized the sociological concept of social stratification in his study of mental retardation. He considers low socioeconomic status an intervening variable which, with its attendant inadequate diet and medical care, is likely to produce a premature and/or mentally retarded child. He concluded with a challenging statement: "It is now possible to entertain a new *tabula rasa* theory [hy-

[1] Staff of *Business Week,* "Sociologists Invade the Plant," *Business Week* (March 21, 1959), pp. 95–101.

[2] Kenneth E. Boulding, "Evidences for an Administrative Science: A Review of Administrative Science Quarterly, Vols. I and II," *Administrative Science Quarterly,* **3,** 1 (June 1958), pp. 1–22.

[3] Ruth Leeds and Thomasina Smith (eds.), *Using Social Science Knowledge in Business and Industry* (Homewood, Ill.: Richard D. Irwin, 1963).

[4] George B. Struther (ed.), *Social Science Approaches to Business Behavior* (Chicago: Dorsey Press and Richard D. Irwin, 1962).

[5] American Sociological Society Panel Discussion, "The Sociologist as Medical Educator," *American Sociological Review,* **25,** 1 (February 1960), pp. 95–101.

pothesizing] that at conception individuals are quite alike in intellectual endowment except for . . . quite rare hereditary neurologic defects. It appears to us that it is *the life experience* and *the sociocultural milieu* [italics ours] influencing biological and psychological function which, in the absence of organic brain damage, makes human beings sigificantly different behaviorally from each other." [6]

Further medical acknowledgment of sociological contributions lies in medicine's belated awareness of the significance of the primary group. Many psychiatrists are now beginning to treat mental patients as members of families rather than as individuals—the older method of treating them.[7]

In regard to religious institutions, there has been some interstimulation almost since the beginning of sociology in the United States. Fukuyama points out in his contribution (Selection 2) that it was Laidlaw, a churchman, whose interest in population and social change led to the present practice of the Census Bureau in dividing urban areas into census tracts. Fukuyama traces the development of the relationship between the pure and applied aspects of the sociological knowledge of religion. Continuing use of sociologists is illustrated by the Methodist Church in Ohio,[8] which requested a study of the size and distribution of the population of the state so that adequate plans for new churches might be made. A more specific illustration may be found in the article by Shippey (Selection 43).

The United States Government has utilized the services of sociologists and anthropologists on many occasions. During World War II, George Murdock and others prepared guides, for use by the Navy, on the Marshalls, the Marianas, the Carolines, Okinawa, and other Pacific islands, and their advice on the various cultures is credited with having prevented costly mistakes and saved many lives.[9] Social sci-

[6] Benjamin Pasamanick, "Research on the Influence of Sociocultural Variables upon Organic Factors in Mental Retardation," *American Journal of Mental Deficiency,* **64,** 2 (September 1959), p. 316.

[7] Rudolph Burcotte and Willis H. Ploof, "Use Relative for Therapy," *Science News Letter,* **77,** 22 (May 28, 1960), p. 350; Joseph H. Handlon and Morris B. Parloff, "Family Therapy Works," *Science News Letter,* **77,** 7 (February 13, 1960), p. 102.

[8] John Lane Williams, Director-Editor, *Ohio Area Study and Promotion of the Methodist Church,* Report to the Ohio Annual Conference, Lakeside, Ohio, June 5–10, 1962.

[9] Stuart Chase, *The Proper Study of Mankind* (New York: Harper, 1948), p. 223.

entists were engaged in analyzing the culture of Japan for policy-guiding purposes; that the Emperor be retained after the war was among their recommendations.[10] They served in measuring the effects of strategic bombing upon German morale and production.[11] The sociologist Robert Merton studied the appeals in Kate Smith's 1943 War Bond Drive, and on the basis of his recommendations techniques were prescribed which were followed in the subsequent drives with even greater success.[12]

Perhaps one of the most dramatic examples of the practicality of sociology is furnished by Stuart Dodd in his description of the role of sociologists in the implementation of the highly successful GI Bill of Rights:

After World War I, as after many previous wars, demobilization created a great problem. If it was carried out too *fast,* transportation facilities were glutted, business could not absorb the returning soldiers, and there was much unemployment. If demobilization was too *slow,* there was also resentment among the soldiers over the delay in getting home.

The American government foresaw this problem after World War II. Plans were undertaken to return ten million or more servicemen to civilian life as promptly and smoothly as possible. In addition to organizing the transportation facilities, etc., a major plan for a GI Bill of Rights to provide funds and educational opportunity was proposed to ease the expected unemployment.

No one knew in 1942 or 1943 how to draw up such a Bill of Rights, or what it would cost. How many of the twenty million eligible men would want to go to school instead of marrying or hunting jobs? Estimates of costs varied from three to twenty-four billion dollars.

To solve this problem, more exact facts or observations were needed. The Army requested the Morale Branch, a surveying agency, to ask a representative sample of the troops in all theaters what they intended to do. This sample survey (duly corrected for the intensity of the answers and the probability of married men and men at different levels of schooling actually doing as they said they intended to do) revealed that some 8 per cent of the armed forces would use the GI Bill of Rights, if drawn with certain specifications. This generalization was acted upon and the bill was drawn up. A point priority system was developed for demobilizing, based upon the troops' own weighing of such factors as the individual's number of years in service, number of dependents, combat experience, etc. Trial of the system showed less dissatisfaction with

[10] Meyer Weinberg and Oscar E. Shabat, *Society and Man* (Englewood Cliffs, N.J.: Prentice-Hall, 1956), pp. 99–100.

[11] Stuart Chase, *op. cit.,* pp. 224–226.

[12] Robert Merton, *Mass Persuasion* (New York: Harper, 1946), esp. p. 178.

the demobilization system in this war than in perhaps almost any other war in our history.

The final verification of the whole experiment was dramatic. Here was a case of social scientists making a prediction of how 8 per cent of some twenty million eligible servicemen would behave several years later. The writer was told about a year ago that the outcome had been that some 8.1 per cent of the eligible GI's had used the Bill of Rights since the war. Here is a degree of precision in predicting the behavior of many people well in advance which can compare favorably with predictions in the physical sciences.[13]

There are, of course, many other fields that have profited from the work of sociologists. In part because there is no practitioner role for the sociologist comparable to the relationship between biology and medicine or physics and engineering, and in part because research sociologists generally are pure, not applied, scientists, it has been difficult to obtain reports of demonstrable results in such complex problems as delinquency and crime, unsuccessful marriage, mental illness, and race relations. However, we have included a few: Haskell and Weeks (Selection 13) report on the utilization of the role concept for prerelease preparation of prisoners; Kirby (Selection 15) surveys research on the effect of different ways of treating criminals; Fox (Selection 16) reports on an administrative change in prison that more effectively utilized the services of sociologists; and McCord and McCord (Selection 18) report the effect of early home training on prejudice. Also included is a report of the role played by social scientists in the monumental Supreme Court desegregation decision (Selection 32). An even more vivid presentation is Jackie Robinson's story of his entry into major league baseball. He speaks of how a sociologist coached him and other Negroes in how to behave in order to maximize the chances for acceptance of the first Negro to play major league baseball.[14]

On the other hand, sociology, like any other science, may be used for what may generally be regarded as questionable purposes as well as for acceptable motives. It has been reported, for example, that sociologists were employed by the owner of a huge gambling casino.[15] After gathering data

[13] Stuart Dodd, from "Possible Contributions of Sociology to the Modern Cultural Crisis," *General Studies Report,* University of Washington, 1951, pp. 118–119. Used by permission of the author.

[14] Jackie Robinson, "The Most Unforgettable Character I've Met," *Reader's Digest,* **79,** 474 (October 1961), pp. 97–102.

[15] Keith Monroe, "The New Gambling King and the Social Scientists," *Harper's Magazine,* **224,** 1340 (January 1962), pp. 35–41.

on the social class and the personalities of potential clients, appropriate appeals in advertising, bus service, and other techniques were successfully employed to increase the casino's patronage. Another illustration of what many would call the undesirable use of sociological knowledge is furnished by Schein's article (Selection 21), in which he describes how the Chinese Communists have deliberately used sociological knowledge of the importance of the primary group in order to break down the resistance of American prisoners of war.

For good or ill, the trend in modern life is toward the increased use of all sciences, including sociology. The educated person of today is well advised to become aware of the main viewpoints and findings of the social sciences, whether or not he plans to pursue a career in an occupation for which sociology has traditionally formed a background. Wherever there is human interaction—on the personal or on the societal level—there is utility in sociological understanding.

The five articles in the Introduction give a survey of the sociological approach, whereas later chapters stress the application of particular concepts. One further word: in order to present the readings as concisely as possible, footnotes in the originals have been reduced in number or eliminated. Interested readers may refer to the original source for documentation of specific points. We sincerely hope that everyone who reads these articles will, through them, better understand the value of sociology in contemporary life.

1

Sociological Research on Medical Care

Milton I. Roemer and Ray H. Elling

This brief history of medical sociology is meant (1) to provide an understanding of the contribution of sociology to health, (2) to furnish opportunities for insight into the conditions of the growth of a field, and (3) to exhibit the mutual gains which have been made when two disciplines collaborate. It may also serve to indicate that there are fads in research as well as in matters of popular taste.

The focus of this paper will be on the contribution of social research to the provision of medical care. We will interpret "medical care" to be not coterminous with all health service, but rather to include those health services concerned with the diagnosis, treatment, and rehabilitation of the disabled. Everyone who has studied the field realizes, however, the inseparability of these services from those for prevention of illness or accident, promotion of health, advancement of education and research, and other components of the wide world of health. . . .

DEVELOPMENT OF RESEARCH ON MEDICAL CARE

The earliest recognition and study of the social aspects of illness concerned the mode of occurrence of particular disorders. Contagiousness—a social process—was expounded by the Italian Giroloma Francastoro in 1546, based primarily on observations of plague, typhus fever, and other epidemic diseases. Diseases of miners were studied and described by George Agricola in 1556 and a few years later by Paracelsus. Scurvy, a disease due to nutritional deficiency, found especially among seamen, was claimed by Dutch and British physicians to be preventable by drinking lemon juice in the mid-sixteenth century. These were all observations of social phenomena affecting health and they led eventually to practical actions for disease prevention.

One of the earliest applications of research to the overall problem of health

Reprinted from *Journal of Health and Human Behavior*, **4,** 1 (Spring 1963), pp. 49–67, by permission of the publisher and the authors.

Milton I. Roemer is Professor of Public Health, University of California, Los Angeles.

Ray H. Elling is Associate Professor of Sociology in Public Health and Head of the Social Science Unit, Graduate School of Public Health, University of Pittsburgh.

and medical care in a population was the work of William Petty, an extremely versatile British physician who lived from 1623 to 1687. He believed in measurements and spoke of data on the diseases, educational level, and other attributes of the population as "political arithmetic." In 1662 John Graunt published the first major work on mortality rates according to cause, season, place of residence, and other variables. Based on this type of social data, Petty proposed in 1676 a state medical service of salaried physicians who would serve everyone. Interestingly, he pointed to the greater stability of the military forces, the church, and the courts because their personnel were on public salaries. He put great stress on the importance of hospitals for both patient-care and professional education, and—much ahead of his time—he advocated "hospitals for the accommodation of sick people, rich as well as poor, so instituted and fitted as to encourage all sick persons to resort to them—every sort of such hospitals to differ only in splendor, but not at all in the sufficiency of the means and remedy for the patient's health."

In the period of the enlightenment and the age of revolutions, the social conscience of medicine was expressed in sweeping proposals for health programs. The most important of these was the six-volume comprehensive *System of Medical Policy* (Police), published by the great German physician, Johann Peter Frank, between 1779 and 1817. The emphasis was upon measures of sanitation, protection of mothers and children, accident prevention and—in a later volume—the organization of hospitals and medical care. In England, the early nineteenth century saw the great sanitary awakening, with the issuance in 1842—culminating many years of study and agitation—of the report . . . *On the Inquiry into the Sanitary Conditions of the Laboring Population of Great Britain,* by Edwin Chadwick, a layman, in cooperation with three physicians: Southwood Smith, Neil Arnott, and James Philips Kay. While the modern social scientists may not look upon these works as research, they were by no means pure armchair treatises, but were based on abundant field observations and the use of whatever statistical data were available. In America, a comparable study—based on statistical data from in and around Boston—was issued by the Sanitary Commission of Massachusetts in 1850, under the authorship of the energetic and capable bookseller Lemuel Shattuck. In the early nineteenth century, more than a few important physicians had shown concern for social conditions and their effects on public health.

In the later nineteenth century, building on the collective efforts of trade unions and local friendly societies for many decades before, there arose the social insurance movement, including provisions for the group financing of medical care. The first such national legislation came out of Bismark's Germany in 1883. This was also the period of great discoveries in bacteriology and antisepsis, which changed the whole character of the hospital. The immediate background of these programs of medical care had been the movement for a system of public medical service for the low income groups (not just for paupers, as under the old Elizabethan Poor Laws) led by physicians like Rudolf Virchow and Solomon Neumann in Germany. The research of the later years of the nineteenth century, however, was overwhelmingly concentrated on the discovery of microorganisms and the elucidation of processes in cells which could explain disease. Bacteriology could also provide a scientific grounding for the whole sanitary movement. The practical rewards of such research were so great that it is little surprise that the broad social studies, required for stimulating social action on the improved organization of medical care, had to await the opening decades of the twentieth century.

The major research relating to social action in medical care was bound up with the movement for extension of health insurance in Europe and America. The establishment of the system of Zemstvo medicine in Czarist Russia in 1864—a scheme of public medical care with salaried personnel in rural areas—may not have been ushered in by scientific studies. But the first British health insurance law of 1911 was preceded by a report of the Poor Law Commission in 1909, including the work of figures like Beatrice Webb and William Beveridge. The American Association for Labor Legislation conducted studies which buttressed the movement between 1910 and 1920 for state compulsory health insurance laws. Although none of these passed—under the combined opposition of industry, labor, commercial insurance companies, and medicine—this social research paid dividends in the field of workmen's compensation and in maternal and child health service organization. An occasional physician was deeply conscious of the relations between medicine and society and the need for effective social measures to improve medical care; an example was Dr. James Peter Warbasse, whose collection of essays entitled *Medical Sociology* appeared in 1909.

The halcyon days of the 1920's were not entirely quiet in the field of sociological research, with the Chicago department of sociology under Park, Burgess, and MacKenzie in full swing. The theory of social change and cultural lag enunciated by William Ogburn in 1922 had a clear implication for the analysis of problems of medical care. It is of interest that Ogburn himself used a medical care development—workmen's compensation legislation—as his initial case study for verification of his hypothesis. Studies on the incidence of illness in different socioeconomic groups—showing higher rates among the poor—had been made by Edgar Sydenstrycker and other "medical economists" in the U.S. Public Health Service in the early 1920's. Since 1916, Michael M. Davis had studied and written about the organizational problems of clinics and hospitals. In 1927, there appeared a study that brought together most of the American data then available on health needs and medical care in a volume, structured on the theory of cultural lag. It was entitled *American Medicine and the People's Health* with the subtitle "An Outline with Statistical Data on the Organization of Medicine in the United States with Special Reference to the Adjustment of Medical Service to Social and Economic Change." It was written by Harry H. Moore, a "public health economist" of the U. S. Public Health Service who, in our view, deserves greater recognition in the history of this field than he has received.

The year that Moore's book was published was also the year of initiation of the five years of studies that led to the 28-volume report of the Committee on the Costs of Medical Care. Completed in 1932, at the depth of the great economic depression, this sweeping research project, directed by I. S. Falk (a man trained originally in bacteriology), had an enormous influence on both future research and future actions in the field of medical care financing and organization in the United States. Throughout the 1930's and up to the end of World War II, the model for social research on medical care was set by these studies—at least in America. In Europe, the concept of "social medicine" was enunciated by the great Belgian physician, Rene Sand, and much emphasis was put on the dependence of health on social class, with consequent needs for corrective social action. Alfred Grotjahn in Germany, Arthur Newsholme in England, Jacques Parisot in France, Andrija Stampar in Yugoslavia were medical leaders combining administrative actions with field research, education, and writing on the development of systems of medical care which would effectively meet public needs.

Academic sociologists, however, showed relatively little interest in the problems of medical care with a few exceptions. The major exception was Bernhard J. Stern, whose monograph, *Social Factors in Medical Progress,* was published in 1927. This was a study of resistance to medical innovation, primarily historical, and in his later work Stern applied the same historical approach to analysis of other problems of medical care elucidating current forces by examining their origins and trends. Robert Lynd included a chapter on medical care and the medical profession in his classical study of Middletown. James H. S. Bossard, as a part of the prevailing sociological interest in the dynamics of the big city, reported a study on the location of doctors' offices in Philadelphia done in 1933. In 1936 L. J. Henderson—with shades of Talcott Parsons, 25 years later—wrote of "The Patient and Physician as a Social System." Disease and unmet medical needs were regarded as social problems—symptoms or consequences of "social disorganization"—but the social institution of medicine and the problems within it received little attention from formal sociologists. In 1938, Michael Davis made a plea in the *American Journal of Sociology* that sociologists should address themselves to some of the thorny problems of medical care organization and distribution.

More research germane to social action on medical care came from other academic specialties, especially history, economics, and anthropology. Henry E. Sigerist, the great scholar of medical history, showed how historical study could help to explain not only the genesis of medical knowledge and ideas, but also the patterns of medical care of the population. His work both in Europe and America helped to inspire a whole generation of young physicians to recognize the social role of medicine. Richard H. Shryock was another historian whose contributions were primarily to the sociology of medicine. A number of anthropologists, like W. H. R. Rivers, have found the study of medical beliefs and practices a useful channel to understanding whole cultures, and these studies have in turn given perspective to current problems in medical care.

But it was mainly the economists who in the 1920's and 1930's explored and clarified the problems of medical care, from the setting of both the universities and government. As early as 1919, Sumner Slichter wrote about sickness as a major cause of labor turnover. In 1932, Pierce Williams published an important study on the use of insurance as a method of financing medical care, confined at the time largely to industrial groupings. The Committee on the Costs of Medical Care, mentioned earlier, had mobilized young economists like Maurice Leven and Louis Reed to apply their skills to these problems. Indeed, the whole field of medical care research—even in its strictly sociological aspects—came to be known by the phrase "medical economics." It was the Committee on Research in Medical Economics, for example, which published the interesting empirical study of Gladys Swackhamer on *Choice and Change of Doctors.*

In the latter 1930's, however, there is no question that the major research contribution to action in the field of medical care came from the federal government. At the depth of the depression the U. S. Public Health Service organized the first "national health survey"—providing at the same time work relief by training unemployed workers (under the W.P.A.) as interviewers. This vast field survey provided basic data not only on the extent and types of disease in the American population along with demographic variables; it also demonstrated the relationships of medical care, in all its components, to socioeconomic status. It provided the research support for a wide range of social actions on health insurance, chronic disease control, hospital construction, public medical care for the needy, and other problems. The men and women identified with this far-reaching study came from backgrounds in economics, biostatistics, social work, and even chemical engineering (George Perrott). Follow-up of this medical care research in the later 1930's and the early 1940's came principally from the research arm of the Social Security Board, under the able direction of I. S. Falk.

The war years were obviously preoccupied with critical economic and military mobilization, but they were by no means devoid of research toward action in medical care. Indeed, it was the inspiration of postwar planning for a better world that produced major research documents like the Beveridge Report on *Social Insurance and Allied Services,* the Bhore Commission studies in India, or the Hojer studies in Sweden. In the United States, the immediate postwar years included active and vitriolic debate about national medical care insurance, the effect of which was to produce a great deal of social research in tangential but important problems and issues, like voluntary health insurance, hospital planning, rural health needs, and group medical practice.

If we consider the current period of sociological research on medical care to begin about 1950, we can see that it has acquired a very different set of characteristics from that which preceded it. It seems clear that developments in the general sociopolitical scene of the United States had a strong bearing on the changed approach. As often happens after a war, there was a period of "getting back to normal," when conservative influences became very strong in the United States. With the election of a Republican administration in 1952, the rise of McCarthyism and its inhibiting influence, and the all-pervading influence of the Cold War with Soviet Communism, the direction of social research turned from that geared to broad-scale social-medical reform toward more limited goals. Sociologists, in particular, directed their expanding forces to detailed studies of the internal operation of the whole social institution of medical care.

The convergence of two intellectual developments helps explain the rapid and rich growth of a general field of medical sociology since about 1950. One was the recognition by the medical schools and also the public health agencies and hospitals that social problems required analysis by experts— yet in a manner not identified with the controversial movement toward health insurance and reorganization of medical care. The other was the rapid rise in academic sociology of empirical research methods—an emphasis that favored subjects which were readily quantifiable. Health needs and medical service provided such data, and the centers of medical education and research began to welcome social scientists. The current period since 1950, therefore, has been characterized very largely by contributions to medical care from empirical-theoretical sociologists.

Since 1945, with the publication of such a landmark volume as *The American Soldier,* there has been an effort to interweave theoretical sociology with empirical research on practical problems. With this development sociology has come of age. It has found wide acceptance in the university—the conserver, transmitter, and developer of knowledge. In turn, the broad institutional sectors of our society—family, industry, law, political science, health, education, art, leisure, and religion—have increasingly sought the point of view of the quasi-detached student of society, as the complexity and rate of change within each sector have multiplied.

This has resulted in much specialization in sociology itself, including a focus on health and particularly medical care. Several surveys of the general development of medical sociology have appeared in this country and elsewhere, and interest in the field has blossomed overseas, in England and Germany. Two collections of sociological research relevant to medical care have appeared in recent years.[1] A special section of the American Sociological

---

[1] E. Gartly Jaco (ed.), *Patients, Physicians and Illness* (Glencoe, Ill.: Free Press, 1958); Dorrian Apple, *Sociological Studies of Health and Sickness* (New York: McGraw-Hill, 1960).

Association has been formed. A text has appeared.[2] Behavioral scientists have joined the medical care section of the American Public Health Association. *The Journal of Health and Human Behavior* has been launched and already a special issue on medical care has come out. Let us now examine some of the principal streams of current research, keeping our focus on medical care (as distinguished from prevention, education, research, or other facets of the health field).

PRINCIPAL STREAMS OF CURRENT RESEARCH IN MEDICAL CARE

With this background, it is evident why many different streams of study on the problems of health service should be operating side by side. At least five fields of investigation in medical care can be distinguished today.

First, is the study of the *health needs of the population and the receipt of medical care*—the heritage of studies starting in the 1930's and providing the foundation for programs of health insurance and other methods of improved financing of medical services. Perhaps the most important current work in this field is the continuing National Health Survey being conducted by the U. S. Public Health Service, as authorized by the Congress in 1957. Based on a nationwide sample of some 38,000 households, this systematic and periodic survey of illness and medical services received by the population provides a wealth of useful data on needs for medical care according to age, sex, income level, and geographic location. It is also providing better data than we have ever had on diagnostic categories of disability, acute and chronic. Important also has been the research of the Health Information Foundation, under the direction of Odin Anderson, in surveying family expenditures for medical care in relation to health insurance coverage in 1953 and again in 1958. Being at a different stage of health insurance planning and operation, the Canadians have done important studies on the utilization of services under various types of insurance program. Studies emanating from Saskatchewan, from the Department of National Health and Welfare (under Dr. Joseph Willard), and from the University of Toronto (especially by Dr. Malcolm Taylor) have provided important lessons for medical care planning in the United States. The long-term study of the Windsor Medical Service by the University of Michigan has provided a model for analysis of the dynamics of prepaid comprehensive medical care.

Studies on rural health needs and utilization of medical care—showing continuing deficiencies in relation to urban experience—have continued to flow from the university departments of rural sociology at Cornell, the University of Missouri, the University of North Carolina, and elsewhere. Major

---

[2] Norman G. Hawkins, *Medical Sociology* (Springfield, Ill.: Charles C Thomas, 1958).

contributions of sociologists in this sphere have been the studies of the attitudes of people toward physicians and the medical care system.

In the urban setting, studies have continued to demonstrate the different patterns of need and care among different segments of the population. Particularly notable is the research done in the Boston area showing that those with the greatest medical care needs, as professionally defined (the elderly and other low-income groups), have the lowest recognition of their needs, the least wherewithal with which to meet their needs once recognized, the longest duration of care once it is received, but the least overall care in spite of great need.

These studies of illness and the receipt of or utilization of medical care—of which those mentioned are only a sketchy sample—are providing data of the greatest usefulness in planning improvements in medical care. They answer questions about the needs for health personnel, hospitals, and other resources for providing service. They permit estimates of costs. They elucidate the differentials in need and demand among different demographic groups, like the aged whose needs are such a pressing sociopolitical issue today. They help to clear the air of questions and distortions about underutilization, overutilization, abuse, and other allegations that seem to inevitably complicate the introduction of medical-care innovations. They even offer by-products in the way of epidemiological data on the occurrence and concomitants of specific disorders. They permit the production of comprehensive, interpretive studies on the distribution of medical care like that published by Herman and Anne Somers in 1961. Note must also be made that theoretical contributions to sociology are as likely in the study of this aspect of human endeavor as in others.

A second field of investigation discernible in the medical care world today relates to the *pattern of organization of ambulatory health services* in the community. By organization, we mean not only the structure and functions of complex arrangements—like those in clinics or rehabilitation centers, for example—but also the dynamics of the solo office practice.

Relationships among particular role players is a focus of many studies. One of the most researched problems in medical sociology has been the doctor-patient relationship (one might say over-researched considering the range of other problems and resources available to attack them). Much of the relevant theoretical framework for this work was provided by Hughes. Role expectations were regarded as important in themselves in studies by Apple and Reader. But some investigators, notably Hollingshead and Redlich, broadened this interest in patients' expectations to include background variables such as social class. In this view, expectations and conceptions regarding medical care are variables intervening between one's social position and the differential receipt of medical care. It is not only the availability of care but the patient's willingness to participate in it which is important for the final outcome of treatment. Thus, Elling and others examined family disorganization and reflexive self-concepts as independent variables affecting expectations in an illness and participation in a program of treatment. The expectations and practices of patients from different social positions are articulated with different forms of medical care in a study by Freidson. Work currently under way at Harvard Medical School is throwing new light on the long-recognized patterns of low income and "lower class" people seeking care from general practitioners, while the "middle classes" consult specialists. These studies of relations of patients to health professionals are relevant also to hospital dynamics, to be discussed below.

It is one of the disappointing, even if understandable, facts about medical-sociological research, that so much of it has been focused on relationships within organized group programs (which have been the minority part of health service in the United States) and so little on the pattern of individual-istic office medical care (which predominates in the American scene). One of the few such studies was that carried out by Osler Peterson and his colleagues on the private general practice of medicine in North Carolina. Other work on office practice focuses on the ecological distribution of different types of practices and the relation of practice patterns to medical careers (discussed below).

A number of surveys and analyses of group medical practice in the United States have been made by the U. S. Public Health Service. Studies of the quality of medical care in different group clinics of the Health Insurance Plan of Greater New York were first conducted by Henry Makover, then by others; these have helped to clarify methods of tackling the elusive question of quality measurements. Leonard Rosenfeld and his colleagues applied some of these techniques effectively in their Boston studies on the quality of medical care in hospitals. The whole concept of the "medical audit," developed with the use of hospital records by Paul Lembcke, Robert Myers and Vergil Slee, and others, is now being applied in the evaluation of performance in ambulatory-care clinics. Specialized as this problem may seem to be, it is indicative of the richness of this field that a series of five annual conferences has now been held, under the leadership of Cecil Sheps, on the contributions of research to understanding the problems of ambulatory medical care. To mention only three of the centers tackling this problem, there is the research at Cornell Medical School's comprehensive care and teaching clinic under George Reader, that of Jerry Solon at the Beth Israel Hospital in Boston and that of the University of North Carolina by Kerr L. White. A small but particularly well-designed study of the benefits of a comprehensive—as against specialized and fragmented—approach to the ambulatory patient was conducted in Chicago by A. J. Simon. A more far-reaching study, the "family health maintenance demonstration," by George Silver and his colleagues, has been in process for several years at the Montefiore Hospital and is now available.

British social researchers are also examining the detailed content of ambulatory medical care, under the special conditions of the National Health Service. The studies by Lord Taylor in London, by Gordon Forsyth and Robert Logan in Manchester, and others have helped to clarify the scope and limitations of community general medical practice which has traditionally been rather sharply separated from the hospital and specialty service in Britain (even before the National Health Service). Indeed, comparative international studies of the consequences for patients (and their pocketbooks) of different patterns of medical care organization present invaluable channels for reaching scientific generalizations. Perhaps the ultimate question to be answered—and it has, of course, a thousand subdivisions—is to determine the human consequences of different social organizations of health service. One might hope that these consequences could be defined in terms of health status and survival—as in the peri-natal mortality studies of Health Insurance Plan members and nonmembers in New York City. Even short of this ultimate criterion, a study of results of diverse patterns of care is the soundest foundation for guiding policy decisions.

The Hospital

A third very important sphere of medical care research centers on *the hospital,* both its internal structure and its external relations. As a central link in the medical care chain, considerable work is being done on the hospital, although most of it concerns its internal organization.

In a pioneering work, Smith explored the implications of fractionated authority in the hospital. Since that time there have been only a few comprehensive studies of relationships in the general hospital; notable are those by Wessen and by Burling, Lentz and Wilson. Fox carried through a fascinating study of the system of relationships on a medical research ward. A study by Georgeopolis and Mann, to appear soon, has the virtue of comparing several hospitals as to the relations among internal organizational variables, such as cohesiveness, communication, coordination, and effectiveness. Other studies of this more comprehensive character have focused on the mental hospital.

Role relations among hospital personnel is a major category of internal hospital research. Those involving the nurse have perhaps received the most generous attention. Brown has studied the therapeutic effects of nurse-patient relationships. Her work has since dealt with the entire physical and social milieu of the hospital and its probable effects. Only a few of the other works on the nurse's position in the hospital and her relationship to others are cited here.

There are other hospital personnel on whom a little work has been done. Bates, in examining decision making in the hospital, found the administrator entangled in overlapping spheres of authority involving professional judgments of medical and nursing staffs, on the one hand, and board judgments regarding efficiency and economy, on the other. In a study of the physician as administrator, Goss analyzed his advantages over the lay administrator. Aside from some work on personnel turnover, there is little of relevance to service personnel. With union activity growing in hospitals, this is an important field for further investigation.

Studies of role relations internal to the hospital necessarily involve the patient; however, this concern has usually been secondary. A recent study by Rose Coser focuses primarily on the patient's adaptation to the hospital system. In an insightful summary of the meaning of her work she says, "I found myself analyzing and describing role continuity and discontinuity and those forces that assisted or hindered socialization—the transition from one segment of society to another." [3] She found two main groups of patients: those looking for emotional support and a "home" in the hospital and those looking for technical aid. The support-seekers had much less to look forward to on return to the community, while those seeking technical aid would obviously be "involved" in family and community life upon discharge.

There are few empirical studies of the external relationships of any organization. The hospital is no exception. Various attitude surveys have been conducted. In an important, though unreleased study of attitudes as related to the quality of care, Blum examined public attitudes toward hospitals with high malpractice-suit rates, as compared with attitudes toward hospitals with low rates. He found public attitudes only weakly related, but there were distinct differences between the high- and low-rate hospitals in medical staff composition and other internal features.

Patterns of medical practice, as related to the hospital, is another topic which has received some attention, following the pioneer work of Hall and Solomon. Ethnic and other background variables in relation to forms of practice have received more recent attention from Lieberson and McElrath. The transmission of drug information and the influence of interns and residents have been studied by Katz and others. In an excellent study, Linn compared mental hospitals, making extensive use of tranquilizing drugs, with others making little use of them and found that discharge rates had increased equally in both. The author suggested that changes in community and professional attitudes toward mental illness were more important in explaining discharge rates than were techniques in treatment.

Studies of the hospital's place in the community generally and in its health system are relatively rare. Roemer pointed up the extent to which organized overall health services are fractionated even in a semirural county. Babchuck and others report a study of board composition and the position of hospitals relative to other community organizations. Levine and White have examined transfers of resources among health agencies including the hospital. Ivan Belknap is currently completing a study of hospital systems

---

[3] Rose L. Coser, *Life in the Ward* (East Lansing, Mich.: Michigan State University Press, 1962), p. 147.

in two Texas communities. A study by the authors on factors related to the hospital's receiving support from its environment is nearly completed. As a part of this work, Elling carried out an intensive study of two well-supported and two poorly supported hospitals in a single urban center and the efforts of these organizations to maintain themselves, in the face of demands made by several citizen's hospital planning committees. But generally speaking, there is little research of a sociological nature relevant to hospital regionalization and planning.

A collection of recent sociological research on the hospital, edited by Freidson, will include chapters on the social history of the hospital, patterns of bureaucracy among medical staff, American and foreign hospitals, goals and authority structure, organizational support, teaching atmosphere of hospitals, negotiation of order in the hospital, alienation of labor, physical environment of the mental hospital ward, ecology of an obstretical service, and the timetable of treatment.

A fourth field of work in medical care research may be defined as the study of the *operation of medical care programs for special population groups*. In a sense, these studies cut across the lines of others considered so far, but they are distinguished by the separability of their clientele from the general population. Among these may be mentioned the many studies of the operation of programs of medical care for the indigent, under agencies of government. The Federal Bureau of Public Assistance, the American Public Welfare Association, and the American Medical Association have examined the costs, volume of services, patterns of care, and the administrative difficulties of these state and local public programs. More comprehensive examination of this field is now being made by S. J. Axelrod of the University of Michigan. Likewise, there are studies of the operation of medical services under the Veterans Administration and the more recent "medicare" program for the dependents of military personnel. The medical care needs and services among American Indians have been the subject of a national study. The crippled children's programs in the states are being subjected to repeated critical evaluations, as are the programs of adult restoration under the federal-state program of vocational rehabilitation.

Medical care rendered under the somewhat antiquated workmen's compensation program has also been subjected to fresh scrutiny in recent years. Of special importance also have been the deluge of studies on the needs of and services for the chronically ill, culminating in the four-volume report (already outdated) by the National Commission on Chronic Illness appearing between 1952 and 1959. The care of the mentally ill must also be mentioned under this heading; while most of the studies in this field have been epidemiological or semiclinical, some have analyzed the receipt of diagnostic and treatment services for mental illness in different social contexts.

These studies of person-specific or disease-specific medical care programs all tend to have a highly practical orientation, and they have usually been stimulated by administrative problems of costs, professional relationships, or obvious qualitative defects. At the same time, they do not lack theoretical interest for the social scientist. They tend to provide data in a well-defined population, in which rates can be readily computed. The questions are usually clear and the answers can be applied in corrective social actions. The situation, in a word, tends to be more subject to deliberate action than is the case for medical care studies involving the larger community or national populations.

Health Personnel

The *development of health personnel* adequate in numbers and quality to the tasks which society expects of them is a fifth sphere of important problems with many facets. Clearly, the planning and provision of medical care involve the recruitment, training, and organization of personnel identified with many occupational groups. The sociology of work is involved. The organization of men and women around their occupational identities has received considerable attention under the rubric of professionalization. Yet it is the flux and flow of individual occupational identities, with which we are faced in this rapidly changing technological society, as much as it is the more corporate action of an occupational group.

Part of this development of one's self-identity as a member of one occupation or another occurs in the course of work. A good example of a study of the division of labor at work is offered by Arnold's study of health department personnel. Working back in sequence, another major facet of this "occupational becoming" occurs as adult socialization in professional schools. There are problems of recruitment to a field which Back, Coker, and others examined for medical students considering public health. There is also the less studied problem of exit from a field. The origin of work group members, in terms of life chances in childhood, has been a concern of several sociologists. Once in an occupation, the organization of members for the establishment of their group is a relatively unstudied aspect of occupational becoming, though Garceau's work on the American Medical Association is notable in this regard. The place of an occupation in society and the changing attitudes of the public toward its members is a further problem of occupational groups. Here one must raise questions of occupational mobility, social status and power, and the mandate of the work group. The person's progress through the world of work is his work career. Stages in the career and their recognition are important aspects of occupational sociology. One of the pressing problems of our time is that, with increasing complexity and the accompanying pace of social change, individuals entering many occupations are no longer able to look forward to nicely laid out career patterns. Professional obsolescence and the need for retraining have become important aspects of most work situations.

Many of these general problems of occupational groups have been studied in the health field. Particular attention has been given to the physician. In many ways, because of the extent of his occupational organization and professional development, the physician has served as a prototype for the study of other occupations. Adams has studied changes in the social positions most likely to produce physicians. With increasing emphasis on technical proficiency, rather than philosophy and bedside manner, and with wider access to medical education, it is suggested that more upward-mobile individuals are to be found in the ranks of physicians today. The physician's development in school has received the attention of several researchers. Hall has studied the stages in the career of the practicing physician. Cohn suggests that the physician's exalted status in U.S. society is due to his having "the best of both worlds," service to humanity and the rewards of entrepreneurship. However, some recent trends suggests that other occupations may have recently developed greater drawing power for the very talented student. Glaser has studied the doctor's particular points d'appui in political action.

The nurse too has come in for considerable attention. Hughes, Hughes, and Deutscher have examined the occupation of nursing in general and its changing character. Devereaux and Weiner trace the origins of nursing in the once clearly defined feminine role of nurturance and care, yet find her cut off from "libidinal replenishment" in present-day scientific medicine and caught in an "ill-defined professional, hierarchical, and social position." [4]

Various studies, as noted under the section on the hospital, have been done on the nurse's position and relationships with others at work. . . . Various nursing specialties have received some attention. Stewart and Needham report on the operating room nurse. Willie has examined the preferences of public health nurses for patients of "middle" social class backgrounds. Pearsall has examined supervision and nursing. Greenblatt focuses on research and the nurse. Other work relates to the nursing student.

Some studies of other health occupations exist. More and Kohn have examined motives for entering dentistry. Work has appeared on dental students. Kriesberg and Treiman have examined public attitudes toward dentistry and Barthuli has studied dentists' attitudes. The types of careers and training available to medical care and hospital administrators have been explored. Marginal and emerging health occupations have received some attention in the work of New, McCormick, Wardwell, Lortie, and Friedson. An extensive exploration of public health as an occupational complex is currently underway.

RESEARCH NEEDS AND OPPORTUNITIES

With this broad, if not penetrating, review of sociological research relevant to medical care, we are in a position to discuss future needs for research in this field. There is, first of all, a need for grand designs and courageous

---

[4] George Devereaux and F. R. Weiner, "Occupational Status of Nurses," *American Sociological Review,* **15** (October, 1950), pp. 628–634.

thinking. Sociological research can be a powerful tool for human betterment, as suggested by the President's Scientific Advisory Committee. In this connection, it seems appropriate to quote from the head of a major foundation:

There is urgent need of coordination of the many multiprofessional, social, economic, welfare, and political programs now so conspicuous by their fragmentation, splintering, duplication, ineffectiveness, and skyrocketing costs. New patterns for the distribution of health services, better organization and utilization of facilities and personnel, regionalization of activities, new forms of private and governmental cooperation, and a new approach to the joint financing of the essential services suggest some of the challenges. These are acute problems particularly in view of such plans as the medical care for the aged either under the Kerr-Mills Act or the proposed King-Anderson (Kennedy) Bill under the Social Security System.

This is the most demanding era of our history. The future in medical care must be built as daringly and as energetically as were other aspects of our national economy such as industry, transportation, education, agriculture, and housing. The nation is no longer living in a frontier world, nor even in an individualistic world, but in a world demanding cooperation and interdependency. In each phase of the nation's health program the Federal departments, the universities and the professions, the hospitals, industry, labor, and the public must contribute their share of imaginative leadership in the formulation and execution of new patterns of cooperation adapted to the needs and conditions of present-day American society.[5]

Consequently, we urge broad, comprehensive but well-designed comparative studies of medical care systems and their consequences at levels of the health organization, the community, the nation. Studies of the scope of that currently under the direction of the National Commission on Community Health Services are important. It is our belief, however, that great benefits are to be derived from the interplay of sociological theory, exacting empirical methods, and concern for practical problems. Work in the field of medical care should be guided by this Elysian mixture.

Starting with the macrocosmic, it is time for systematic comparative studies of relations between health systems and the national societies in which they function. One tires of vitriolic attacks or unlimited praise for this national system or that, based on an individual's fleeting "visit" or disappointing work experience. It is time that such questions were considered scientifically with adequate attention to samples, measures, prior questions, and so on. Comparisons of the functioning of medical care systems themselves, as well as attitudes and relations of the public to them, are needed.

On the intranation level, attention to the question of health manpower is needed. What would our knowledge of child development, adolescence, and the maturation of occupational groups suggest to us, if we were to devise a plan for attracting and training 10,000 medical care researchers, planners

---

[5] Willard C. Rappleye, M.D., President, Josiah Macy, Jr., Foundation, "Labor, Management, and Medicine," presented at a meeting of the Section on Occupational Medicine, New York Academy of Medicine, April 5, 1962.

and administrators? How can more physicians be developed to work in settings where community and preventive aspects are fully incorporated in their work? What is the optimal number of physicians and nurses? Can a public health nurse be developed to assume the position of family health counsellor, being vacated by the fast-disappearing "family doctor"?

In line with our earlier comments on the need for social as well as technological invention, leaders might be brought together from the fields of sociology, medical care, health and medicine generally, and the general public for the purpose of defining in ideal form the features of an adequate system of medical care for a community. The problems of personnel, financing, facilities, organization, and community conditions should be considered. A system approximating this ideal might be funded and established in an "average" community. A study team could investigate the process of establishment of such a system and devise adequate measures of its effects, to be compared with the same measures taken in a "control" community of like characteristics. Granted it would be impossible to control every variable— for example, the effect of the study process and normal change in the control community. But through such a comprehensive study, we would learn many lessons.

On the intracommunity level, there are several questions to be examined: *First,* there is the question of the relationship among health service agencies in a community and the need for a better understanding of the factors that inhibit or facilitate interorganizational cooperation. Some notable work on this has been done in recent months, but far more needs to be known before the much-heralded regionalization and planning of health service can become realities. Particularly those factors which inhibit or facilitate the hospital's functioning as a hub of patient-care need further study. Preventive, diagnostic, treatment and rehabilitative services are provided by hundreds of voluntary and official agencies. What affects the hospital's ability or the capacity of other health organizations, like the health department, to coordinate this wide range of services?

Second, it is important to understand the relationship between bureaucracy and individual desires, especially emotional needs. With increasing specialization, there is every likelihood that various forms of group practice will be necessary in order that the full armamentarium of medical care can be available to the individual. But availability is only one part of the receipt of care, and enough work has been done to suggest that the very people who need care most are often least likely to involve themselves in the bureaucratized form of organization. The experience in Detroit, where only 5 per cent of a labor union chose a group practice as opposed to a solo practice when both were prepaid, is only the most recent bit of evidence on this score. How can the bureaucratized form of care be made human enough to be desirable? If bureaucracy is understood, not as "red tape" but as the attempt to organize relationships for the achievement of a goal, then the basic challenge is to rationally organize the technology of modern medical care, while at the same time meeting the infinitely varying needs of individuals. Such organization must find ways of bringing medical care close to where people live, while not sacrificing technical standards.

On the intraorganizational level, there is a desperate need for intensive, comparative studies of clinics and hospitals and their organization as it affects the quality of medical care. Experts in particular medical specialties should be asked to define "good medical care," and organizational forms developed to achieve this—with adequate comparisons of either a before-and-after or a cross-organization nature. Adequate criteria for judging the quality of care will become more and more necessary in the future, so that effective comparisons can be made between different systems of medical care organization—at the agency, the community, the regional, and the national levels.

2

The Uses of Sociology: By Religious Bodies

Yoshio Fukuyama

Even before the turn of the century, some religious bodies were using sociological studies. In this article the author briefly traces the major points in the history of the relationship between organized religious bodies and the field of sociology. He also notes some counterpressures that have inhibited a thorough exploitation of sociological knowledge by religious institutions.

I

Religious bodies, and individuals who have had their roots in the professional leadership of religious organizations, have been both producers and consumers of sociological knowledge since its beginnings in the United States. Albion W. Small, an ordained Baptist clergyman, reminds us in his classic history of "Fifty Years of Sociology in the United States 1865–1915" that

Reprinted from *Journal for the Scientific Study of Religion*, **2**, 2 (Spring 1963), pp. 195–203, by permission of the publisher and the author.

Yoshio Fukuyama is Secretary for Research, United Church Board for Homeland Ministries.

the first course in sociology offered at Harvard in the academic year 1891–92 was taught by the Rev. Edward Cummings, pastor of the South Congregational Church of Boston. Later he writes that

a comprehensive view of the sociological movement in the United States for the last fifty years would include such a survey as Professor Francis G. Peabody of Harvard, or Professor Graham Taylor might supply. . . .[1]

Professor Peabody was a popular speaker at Chautauqua and an early champion of the Social Gospel Movement in this country and Dombrowski in his history of Christian socialism surmises from an examination of records that "it seems probable that Professor Peabody's course at Harvard in 1880 [a decade before the first course in sociology was taught at Harvard College] deserves to be credited as the first course in social ethics to be given in a theological seminary in the United States."[2] Graham Taylor, the founder of the Chicago Commons and for many years a teacher of prospective Protestant ministers at the Chicago Theological Seminary, exposed his students to the full impact of sociological knowledge, particularly as this knowledge was used to make the ministry of the churches more relevant to the social and economic conditions of the times.

The American church historian Sweet notes that Graham Taylor had the title of "Professor of Christian Sociology" at the Seminary before the turn of the century and that "numerous settlements had been established in all the larger cities, not only as institutions for the carrying on of social work *but as laboratories where students of sociology might receive practical training. . . .*"[3] Out of the training center for social workers established by Taylor at the Chicago Commons came the Graduate School of Social Service Administration of the University of Chicago and a division of the Sociology Department of Northwestern University.

Perhaps a more direct consequence of the role of religious bodies in the development of sociological resources surrounds the activities of the Reverend Walter Laidlaw of the New York Federation of Churches in the early 1900's. Dr. Laidlaw is regarded as "the originator of census tracts" by the U.S. Bureau of the Census. It was largely due to his need for comparable census information for areas smaller than the New York boroughs in his work with churches that we have our present system of census tracts for demographic studies.

He used Census Bureau tabulations by assembly districts, and other governmental and private sources of data; and he also collected his own data on families, religious affiliations, nationalities, churches, and church institutions. Since an im-

---

[1] Albion W. Small, "Fifty Years of Sociology in the United States (1865–1915)," *American Journal of Sociology, Index to Volumes I–LII,* p. 203.

[2] James Dombrowski, *The Early Days of Christian Socialism in America* (New York: Columbia University Press, 1936), p. 63.

[3] William Warren Sweet, *The Story of Religion in America* (New York: Harper, 1939), p. 512. [Italics are mine.]

portant part of his plan was to compare data for a given small area with data for the same area at an earlier date, the usefulness of all his information was impaired when in 1905 the State changed the boundaries of the assembly districts.[4]

He thus persuaded the Bureau of the Census to tabulate population data for these areas according to a plan he devised, areas which would remain permanent from census to census. These areas were later called "census tracts" and were extended to other major cities, providing urban sociologists with a basic tool for research.

The later institutionalization of sociological research within religious bodies is rooted in the outgrowth of the Rural Sociological Society from its parent body, the American Sociological Society, in 1912. Among the sociologists who met to organize rural sociology as a subfield were Warren H. Wilson, who was later to become the director of the first town and country church department of any denomination, Edmund deS. Brunner, who also was to be a rural church secretary before embarking on his distinguished career as a sociologist at Columbia University, and Professor Edwin Earp of Drew Theological Seminary. Brunner's comprehensive history of rural sociology refers to Wilson's early surveys of churches in rural counties as being "the most influential" in the development of rural sociology.

Wilson was the first rural sociologist to work extensively in the area of the sociology of a social institution. . . . Out of this work Wilson arrived at the concept of regionalism as of considerable utility to rural sociologists.[5]

At the time Giddings was stimulating interest in rural sociology at Columbia, a Congregational clergyman, Charles Otis Gill, and Gifford Pinchot, undertook the first intensive social study of the rural churches in Vermont and New York. Of their work, Brunner wrote:

Later studies have confirmed some of their findings so consistently as to warrant the claim that they, along with Wilson and his associates, had discovered social laws. The best established of these laws is that in a declining community church membership drops more rapidly than the population, whereas in a growing community its rate of gain lags behind that of the community.[6]

The major themes of this early period in our survey of the uses made of sociology by religious bodies are several. It was a period during which the clergyman and sociologist were in close communication with each other; pulpit and lecture hall were interchangeable for many years in the profession. The raw datum of the sociologist—the changing social scene—was also the parish of the minister, and descriptive studies added to the body of sociological knowledge while they also served to awaken the social conscience of

---

[4] U.S. Bureau of the Census, *Census Tract Manual,* Fourth Edition (Washington, D.C.: U.S. Government Printing Office, 1958), p. 1.

[5] Edmund deS. Brunner, *The Growth of a Science; A Half Century of Rural Sociological Research in the United States* (New York: Harper, 1957), p. 7.

[6] *Ibid.,* pp. 8–9.

the pews. Notable contributions to sociological method and knowledge came from the clergy, and studies of churches laid the empirical foundations for a relatively young but rapidly maturing science.

II

The second period in our survey begins after the end of World War I and the organization of the Interchurch World Movement. The early studies of rural churches by Gill, Pinchot, and Wilson led to the establishment of a Town and Country division within the Interchurch World Movement. This Movement was a massive postwar endeavor of the Protestant denominations to consolidate their resources to evangelize and perform social service at home and abroad. One of its basic purposes, according to its charter of incorporation, was

to make a survey of the home and foreign field in order to ascertain accurately what should be done by the churches and charitable agencies of the country. . . .[7]

Within 18 months, surveys of church and community in 550 counties were completed and 1,600 more were in various stages of completion. Additional surveys had been set up in 357 cities and special studies of new Americans, migrant workers, Negroes, and religious education were undertaken. The Movement ran into serious financial difficulty and became bankrupt in 1920 after spending $8,500,000. The residue of its research was distributed to existing interdenominational agencies and formed the basis of some of the departments which are continued today in the National Council of the Churches of Christ in the U.S.A.

The Institute of Social and Religious Research (originally called the Committee on Social and Religious Surveys) continued the pioneering social research work of the Town and Country division of the defunct Interchurch World Movement. The formation of the Institute in 1921 (financed by John D. Rockefeller, Jr.) marks the beginning of institutionalized research for religious bodies in the United States. The viewpoint prevailed at that time that unbiased studies in the realm of religion and religious organizations could not be competently conducted by the churches and that an agency independent of ecclesiastical control was necessary. Organized "to apply scientific method to the study of socioreligious phenomena," it made over 50 surveys and published over 90 volumes during its 13-year history from 1921 to 1934, encompassing the concerns of both home and foreign missions, rural and urban churches. Perhaps the most lasting of its contributions to sociological literature were the Institute's financing of Lynd and Lynd's classic study of *Middletown* and the collaboration of the Institute's staff with Presi-

---

7 "Notes on the Interchurch World Movement," *Information Service,* **40** (September 16, 1961), p. 8.

dent Hoover's Research Committee in the study of *Recent Social Trends in the United States.*

A contemporary appraisal of the Institute's effectiveness was made in 1929 by an official publication of the Federal Council of Churches as follows:

The Institute has an enviable record among research organizations for the publicity it has received for some of its findings. The work of dissemination has been well done. . . . The Institute's publications are used by professors and students in colleges and professional schools, by officers of religious organizations, and by pastors and local religious leaders. They have also been used by writers for numerous magazines, and are found in many reference libraries. Altogether about 50,000 volumes have been distributed.[8]

The most prominent of the Institute's staff was Harlan Paul Douglass who with Edmund deS. Brunner summarized the research of the Institute in a volume entitled *The Protestant Church as a Social Institution.* Twenty-three years later, Brunner, in inaugurating the memorial H. Paul Douglass Lectures of the Religious Research Association, referred to this final volume published by the Institute as one which brought together the major contributions of Douglass and the Institute to the sociology of the parish. While most of the Institute's studies were wholly descriptive, they provided a sufficient body of repetitive results to form a respectable body of knowledge and laid the foundation for more precise theoretical formulations in later years.

The literature of the period is not clear as to why the Institute of Social and Religious Research came to an end in 1934. Some who have worked closely with Douglass and the Institute suggest that the failure of the churches to take seriously their research findings led Mr. Rockefeller to withdraw his financial support. The hostility of some religious leaders is suggested by the following comment by Brunner in recalling his associations with Douglass:

Douglass was completely committed to the validity, utility, and value of studying the church as an institution by objective methods. . . . It may be difficult today to realize the strength of the resistance to this point of view Douglass and his colleagues encountered. We were, as he wrote under "continuous suspicion." Those who held the church to be a supermundane entity were shocked that such a holy thing could be examined and compared with other institutions and social systems. . . .

Others, who to a greater or less degree admitted the mundane aspects of the church as a divine institution, were extremely sensitive that the Institute studies might exhibit the shortcomings of the church and its professional leaders in such a way as to harm the pursuit of its spiritual mission. . . .[9]

Others who are knowledgeable about the period have suggested that a mood of criticism prevailed within Protestantism which undermined the motivation for continued research. The best known instance of this mood was

---

[8] *Information Service,* **8** (November 16, 1929), p. 3.

[9] Edmund deS. Brunner, "Harlan Paul Douglass: Pioneer Researcher in the Sociology of Religion," *Review of Religious Research,* **1** (Fall 1959), p. 72.

an article in *The Christian Century* by Professor Arthur E. Holt on the theme, "The End of Church Expansion" on May 2, 1934, to be followed a week later by an editorial on "The Passing of Home Missions." These writers believed that the population of the United States had reached its peak and that the work of denominational church extension boards had become obsolete.

Despite this mood, Douglass and his colleagues and students continued their descriptive studies of churches for another decade, concentrating their efforts on city churches and the need for cooperation among them. These studies laid the empirical foundations for the formation of numerous councils of churches and the practice of cooperative church planning (comity) throughout the nation and provided survey methodology for church extension which is continued by the research agencies of denominations and councils of churches to this day.

During this period, in a tradition of social inquiry firmly established a generation earlier at the Chicago Theological Seminary by Graham Taylor, Arthur E. Holt and Samuel C. Kincheloe were guiding their students along fruitful lines of sociological injuiry in the Chicago metropolitan area. Notable among the contributions of the Seminary to the sociology of the church are three of Kincheloe's monographs. Two, which were published in *Religious Education* in the late '20's are still valid typologies of Protestant church behavior in the city: "Major Reactions of City Churches" and "The Behavior Sequence of a Dying Church."The third was a research monograph he wrote for the Social Science Research Council on "Religion in the Depression." He effectively applied the sociological methodology of the "Chicago School" to the study of churches and his work has had a decisive influence on many of his students, who have subsequently assumed important positions in denominational boards and councils of churches, both as researchers and as administrators.

III

The present period in our survey of the use of sociology by religious bodies follows World War II when the nation enjoyed relatively full employment and prosperity. The years since 1945 have been marked by one overriding social fact to which the churches reacted with unprecendented vigor: the increase in population which was highly mobile, and its correlate, the rise of new residential communities in the suburban ring of our cities. The research emphasis of the churches shifted from the problem of adaptation and survival in marginal socioeconomic areas to the problem of institutional conservation within the city and expansion in new residential communities.

This period saw the establishment of numerous offices of "research and survey" and "planning" by national home missions boards of the denominations and by state and local councils of churches. In almost every instance these research units were related to church extension boards and agencies and the methodology of the sociologist—particularly that of the demographer —were called upon to help the denominations establish new churches in new communities under optimum socioeconomic conditions. Spurred largely by the work of H. Paul Douglass and S. C. Kincheloe a decade before, the denominations had agreed upon a program of cooperative church planning —a painful lesson learned by the experience of competitive church locations in rural areas—and hired researchers to bring together relevant population data on the basis of which new church sites were to be allocated.

At the present time research and survey departments are a part of thirteen local and state councils of churches, located in most of the largest cities of the United States.[10] In two states—Oregon and Washington— research direction is given to the state councils of churches on a part-time basis by sociologists from nearby universities.

While this present period may be characterized by a high degree of bureaucratization of research by the religious bodies, it is paradoxical to note that this has also been accompanied by a relative loss of communication with the academic sociologist. It is to be recalled that during the early period of our survey, sociologists and clergymen moved freely between the profession and the churches: churchmen often taught sociology in the universities while sociologists preached the social gospel in the churches. Today, the institutionalized religious researcher is unlikely to have specialized academically in sociology at the graduate level. With a few exceptions, he is more likely to have majored in "social ethics" at the seminary or to have taken a few courses in sociological methods along with his theological education. Nearly all are ordained clergymen. In short, the more institutionalized research became in the churches, the less relevant its work became to the sociological profession.

In surveying denominational use of sociologists, we asked a number of denominational executives, "Does your denomination employ sociologists for the purpose of doing sociological research in the field of religion?" The following response is typical of many we received:

Technically the answer to this question is no. However, the Church and Community Study Research program . . . employs sociological research in their area. . . . In addition, when we want further research than this we take [a denominational seminary professor] who did the study for our Home Missions Societies which resulted in its complete reorganization . . .[11]

---

[10] Councils of churches located in the following cities have research departments at the present time: Boston, Chicago, Detroit, East Orange (N.J.), Indianapolis, Los Angeles, Madison (Wis.), New York, Philadelphia, Portland (Ore.), St. Louis, Seattle, and Washington, D.C.

[11] From a letter to the writer from an executive of a major Protestant home mission board, May 21, 1962.

The National Lutheran Council, representing several Lutheran bodies, is unique in its use of sociologists. Without bureaucratizing the research function, it has drawn on the talents of Lutheran laymen who teach sociology in universities around the nation. In recent years it has called on men of the stature of Charles Y. Glock of the University of California and Gerhard Lenski of the University of Michigan for research services. Two of their seminaries have also employed a management consultant firm to study the possibilities of merger while a market research organization was engaged to study church attitudes in a large midwestern city.

The Lutheran studies have been singularly unique among church-sponsored research. The high caliber of the sociologists they have called upon has insured an enviable level of methodological sophistication for their studies and has had an upgrading effect on the adequacy of the research conducted by other denominations.

This is best illustrated by a recent study of "effective city churches" sponsored by the Urban Church Department of the National Council of Churches. Through the initiative of the National Lutheran Council, several denominations worked together to develop common research instruments to describe various dimensions of religious behavior and beliefs. This study represented a major breakthrough in church-sponsored research, for substantial beginnings were made in the measurement and analysis of such factors as religious ideology, beliefs, knowledge, role expectations of the pastor by parishioners, and devotional life, in addition to the more familiar practice of describing the socioeconomic characteristics of church members and relating the congregation's program to community factors.

Still another kind of contribution made by religious bodies to sociological knowledge is the statistical compilations of the Bureau of Research and Survey of the National Council of the Churches of Christ in the U.S.A. Its *Yearbook of American Churches* remains the most comprehensive source of religious statistics published annually in the United States and is most often quoted by consumers of religious statistics. In 1957 it published church and church membership data for 114 religious bodies (including Catholic and Jewish) by states, counties, and standard metropolitan areas.

We have made some mention of the role of theological seminaries in providing sociological resources to religious bodies. At the present time the more substantial contributions to knowledge continue to come under academic rather than ecclesiastical auspices. An interesting case in point is Paul M. Harrison's study of the bureaucratic structure of the American Baptist Convention which was published under the title *Authority and Power in the Free Church Tradition*. The study was originally a doctoral dissertation at Yale Divinity School and described the distance which prevailed between the normative conception of the church as held by American Baptists and the way it was actually structured within the ecclesiastical bureaucracy. The study itself is a major contribution to the sociology of religion. It also represents a very significant critique of an existing denominational organization. It is quite inconceivable that such a study could have been initiated by the Baptists or any other religious bureaucracy. That it was initiated by the theoretical concerns of a graduate student merely underlines the very critical role that academic institutions continue to play in the increase of our knowledge about the church as a social institution.

There are some major Protestant seminaries which do provide promising contexts in which critical and creative research can be done. Some of the more denominationally oriented seminaries, however, continue to expend most of their efforts, like their denominational board counterparts, in surveys directed toward the conservation and expansion of denominational enterprises. The theoretical sophistication and empirical adequacy of research projects being done in these institutions depend largely on the competence and interest of individual professors rather than on the initiation of ecclesiastical leaders.

During the course of gathering data for this study, we interviewed several non-Protestant sociologists to discover why sociological research was not institutionalized among Catholic and Jewish religious organizations to the extent it is among Protestant bodies. Among Catholics, individual sociologists teaching in universities have made substantial contributions to sociological knowledge, while the research in the field of human relations and civil rights sponsored by such agencies as the American Jewish Committee is among the most sophisticated in the field. In reflecting on differences in practice and use by the three major religious groups, we would make several concluding observations.

The first, suggested by our own survey, is that there still exists, even among Protestants with their bureaucratized researcher, a basic resistance to sociological research when it invades the sacred domain of current program and administrative practices. It is not improbable to suggest that research is not institutionalized in some religious bodies because of a basic fear of what sociological research might reveal of institutional weaknesses. If this be so, how have the Protestant denominations overcome this threat to the *status quo?* Our evidence suggests that they have safely avoided the threat by directing their researchers to concentrate their efforts on the conservation and expansion of the religious institution rather than focusing their research on experimental and critical problems.

The second observation concerns the relatively meager contribution made by present-day denominational and council researchers (with some notable exceptions already mentioned) to the general body of sociological knowledge about the church as a social institution. Part of the reason for this lies in the process of research itself, for it usually originates and ends with the client (i.e., the church extension board), and rarely do the results find their way into the technical literature of the profession. Besides lacking the opportunity and technical training to communicate their findings to the profession, the religious researcher is also limited by the parochial nature of most of the studies he is asked to make.

Thirdly, the major contributions to sociological knowledge continue to emanate from academic institutions rather than from the churches. The academic institution usually enjoys an enviable role in that it tends to be more detached from the vested interests of ecclesiastical bodies than is the researcher who is employed by a denominational board or council. This would suggest that more financial support ought to be found to help the seminaries and universities to direct the research of their more promising graduate students to investigate significant sociological problems in the field of religion which will add new knowledge and suggest new directions and forms of religious behavior. The research talents of a great many graduate students can be channeled to accumulate primary data to test theoretically significant hypotheses and formulate new conceptual tools if funds were made available to encourage them.

In 1956 a study of theological education under the auspices of the American Association of Theological Schools and the Carnegie Corporation discovered "that the clearest directive is to increase the opportunities for able young students to get their advanced training and complete their doctoral work without too much loss of time and too much effort put on outside work. This responsibility does not fall in the first instance upon the schools but upon the churches." The study further noted, "We need some men who are trained both in theology and in psychiatry, both in theology and in law, in sociology . . . The Church could do nothing more significant for the relating of its Gospel to the problems of modern man than to make it possible for a few to achieve mastery in these fields and at the same time develop their theological resources." [12]

We would observe, finally, that the changing role of the sociologist at work for religious bodies—who became less relevant for the sociological profession as he became more bureaucratized within the ecclesiastical organization—reflects in some measure the changing role of the clergy as a whole in American life. There was a time when the village parson was also the carrier of the cultural norms of society. He no longer possesses this role. In the early days when sociology was an infant science, the professor of sociology was quite often an ordained clergyman; traffic between pupit and lecture platform moved in both directions. Today the clergyman is more likely to be merely the consumer of sociological research or if he engages in it, he is more likely to devote his time to purely descriptive studies for administrative decision making.

Yet, there is a need, as Yinger observed a decade ago, for sociologists of religion who are knowledgeable about both sociology and religion, whose

---

[12] H. Richard Niebuhr, Daniel D. Williams, and James M. Gustafson, *The Advancement of Theological Education* (New York: Harper, 1957), pp. 75–76.

commitment to particular religious traditions will give them the necessary interest to pursue real issues facing religious groups but who are also disciplined as scientists so that their findings will be supported by facts which are systematically gathered and scientifically analyzed. According to Yinger,

Competent research in the sociology of religion demands a combination of skills and interests that is not very common. . . . The researcher must, in the first place, have a thoroughly adequate grasp of contemporary sociological theory and research methods. He must be entirely objective in his handling of the data of religion; yet he must be strongly interested in the material and deeply acquainted with it. . . .[13]

IV

In his Preface to the English translation of Karl Mannheim's *Ideology and Utopia,* Louis Wirth dramatically illustrated the difference between technological and sociological knowledge by recalling the rapidity with which Japan opened her doors to the streams of Western influence through technical products and methods, but resisted the social, economic, and political influences of the West. The latter were subsumed under what the Japanese call *kikenshiso* or "dangerous thoughts." According to Wirth,

The authorities regard discussion of democracy, constitutionalism, the emperor, socialism, and a host of other subjects as dangerous because knowledge of these topics might subvert the sanctioned beliefs and undermine the existing order.[14]

There is a sense in which the sociological study of religion and religious organizations continues to be in the area of "dangerous thoughts" in the sense Wirth has used the term, for the sociologist has within his means the opportunity to "subvert the sanctioned beliefs and undermine the existing order" of religious establishment.

---

[13] J. Milton Yinger, "Present Status of the Sociology of Religion," *Journal of Religion,* **31** (July 1951), p. 197.

[14] Karl Mannheim, *Ideology and Utopia; An Introduction to the Sociology of Knowledge* (New York: Harcourt, 1951), pp. xvi–xvii.

3

Contributions of the Social Scientist to Community Development

Otto G. Hoiberg

Communities, like corporations or unions, have become more complex in modern times. The do-it-yourself approach to community problems is as outmoded as Grandmother's poultice. However, just as the psychiatrist necessarily needs the cooperation of the patient, so the social scientist needs the active collaboration of the community if his skills and knowledge are to be realized. He may function as a researcher, a consultant, and/or an educator. Dr. Hoiberg describes many activities typical of these roles and appends a useful list of organizations that have made available materials on community development.

Community life in early America was characterized by a high degree of self-sufficiency. Problems of group living were numerous and pressing, but most of them were handled locally with a minimum of assistance from outside specialized sources. This self-sufficiency can be explained partly in terms of necessity, for local groups often had nowhere to turn for assistance even when it was needed. The agencies were nonexistent that are now available to help community groups with problems ranging from slum clearance to the planning of neighborhood play areas. More important perhaps, was the relative simplicity of life itself. Much of the work considered essential was within the competence of local citizens themselves.

As the generations have passed, new needs have arisen and social life has become more complex. The specialist can often help the contemporary community, urban or rural, when it finds itself in difficult situations. One facet of it, traffic congestion, has been called probably the most serious single problem affecting the future development of cities.[1] It is a problem with many ramifications, and progress toward its solution depends upon contributions from sociologists, economists, statisticians, demographers, and political scientists, among others.

Reprinted from *Community Structure and Analysis*, ed. Marvin Sussman (New York: Crowell, 1959), pp. 129–143, by permission of Thomas Y. Crowell Company, the editor, and the author.

Otto G. Hoiberg is Professor of Sociology and Head, Community Development, University Extension Division, The University of Nebraska.

[1] Miles L. Colean, *Renewing Our Cities* (New York: The Twentieth Century Fund, 1953), p. 158.

The small town likewise finds itself confronted with issues which often require the attention of social scientists. In many such municipalities the merchants have become seriously concerned about the loss of business to larger adjoining trade centers. Why are farmers by-passing their traditional trade centers and now going in considerable numbers to neighboring towns to make purchases? What kinds of goods and services do they buy there? What, if anything, can be done to remedy the situation? Questions such as these are debated perenially by small-town chambers of commerce the nation over, but definitive answers rarely can be reached in the discussion process. Research is needed, and it is the social scientist who is called upon for help.[2]

The open country of rural United States also places increasing reliance upon social scientists in its community improvement efforts. The historic report of Theodore Roosevelt's Commission on Country Life early in the twentieth century pointed up a number of ways in which life on the farm fell short of urban standards. The Commission's findings provided stimulus to rural social research and gave strong impetus to the development of rural sociology as a new discipline. Forward-looking people of rural areas have sensed the relevance of this new body of research data to the problems confronting them. Accentuating their interest in such data have been certain social trends whose impact upon rural social institutions has been felt. To illustrate, one might note how the decline in farm population and the growing tendency of farm people to go to the village for their social, cultural, and religious activities have placed the open-country church in a difficult position. The population base upon which this church can draw for members has dwindled, and even those who have remained on the farms have tended to drop their allegiance to the open-country church in favor of sister institutions in the village. The author was recently approached by a country pastor whose church building would soon have to undergo substantial repairs or be replaced altogether. In deciding whether to repair or rebuild, one question was paramount in the pastor's mind: "What is the future of our church?" A rural sociologist can be of immeasurable benefit to a congregation in its effort to find a realistic answer to such a question.

Let us examine a few of the more common activities through which the social scientist makes his professional talents directly or indirectly available to community groups. Initially, it must be emphasized that his fundamental and distinctive function in relation to community improvement lies in his search for truth, as exemplified in the *research* process.

Joseph S. Himes has stated that research can serve five important functions in social planning.[3] In the first place, "research provides the basis for

---

[2] See, for example, Edgar Z. Palmer, *Some Economic Problems of Clay Center, Nebraska,* College of Business Administration, The University of Nebraska, Business Research Bulletin No. 54 (1950).

[3] Joseph S. Himes, *Social Planning in America* (Garden City, N.Y.: Doubleday & Company, Inc., 1954), pp. 28–31.

precise and accurate definition of the social problem and the occasion of collective action." This may involve quantitative measurement and objective description, as well as the delineation of social issues and value conflicts and, in general, "gives the instigators of planning a measure of the task at hand . . . and enables the leaders to focus their efforts and gear them to the realities of the problem." Second, research serves "to indicate what can and cannot be done." Many action groups have learned to their dismay that the hunch-method for determining feasibility of community projects leaves something to be desired. Where construction of a new school building is being considered, for instance, an intelligent decision requires objective data regarding population trends in the area. A third service of research is "to indicate the experiences of others in similar situations," and here the case study has proved particularly helpful. Fourth, the researcher can help the social planner by assessing "the resources that may be utilized in carrying out the plan." This has reference not only to physical resources but also to personal and social resources of various kinds which are sometimes difficult for the community leader to identify. Finally, it is a function of research "to define the social unit and geographic area of planning." The social planner must know "the nature, size, and limits of the group or area" involved in any given project if effective implementation is desired.

A description of relevant research activity in the various social sciences is beyond the scope of this chapter. A brief reference to the general types of community research, however, may be in order.

Four Southern social scientists [4] conceive of the community as having the following principal components—the ecological, the structural, and the action-interactional—and they conclude that these represent an appropriate basis for classification of research in this field. Among classic examples of research in the first (ecological) category, one might mention the development of the "delinquency area" concept by Clifford Shaw and associates in Chicago. In relation to the second (structural) approach, extensive research has been conducted on major institutions such as the family, church, education, government, and a variety of other social groupings, both formal and informal. The third (action-interactional) approach is of relatively recent origin and holds much promise, both from the theoretical and practical viewpoints. It provides for the study of the community as a social system comprising a network of interacting elements.

It is of interest to community leaders that the research work of the social scientist often relates directly to problem areas in which they are interested from the standpoint of community betterment. The findings of researchers in the field of group dynamics, for example, have been put to good use by people seeking to function more effectively and efficiently as groups. Agricultural

---

[4] Harold F. Kaufman, Willis A. Sutton, Jr., Frank D. Alexander, Allen D. Edwards, *Toward a Delineation of Community Research,* Social Science Research Center, Mississippi State College, Social Science Studies, Community Series No. 4 (1954), p. 3.

Extension agents welcome bulletins like "How Farm People Accept New Ideas" [5] which summarizes pertinent research findings from the fields of psychology, sociology, and social psychology. It points out that people go through the following stages in learning about and adopting new ideas: awareness, interest, evaluation, trial, and adoption; and it then goes on to describe the media of communication which are particularly effective at each stage.

Communities contemplating hospital construction projects have found a volume by Professor Paul A. Miller and associates in Michigan helpful.[6] This publication presents the findings of a research project covering 218 successful hospital construction projects supported by the government under the Hill-Burton Act, and it throws much light upon methods of project initiation, difficulties encountered, publicity and educational questions, the use of consultants, fund raising, leadership, and a number of other problems which are characteristic of this type of endeavor. By way of further illustration, reference might be made to a bulletin by Professors King, Pedersen, and Burrus at the University of Mississippi which summarizes and interprets Mississippi population statistics for the benefit of the interested layman. In their introductory statement they "point out a few ways in which population facts have been or could be used in Mississippi to help us understand and solve our problems." [7] They show how such data have been vital to the operation of the Mississippi Commission on Hospital Care, to the completion of studies of the state's highway and school systems, and to the work of the Agricultural and Industrial Board in its efforts to encourage and plan for industrial development in the state.

Noteworthy also is a recent pamphlet describing research on the impact of new industry moving into a rural community.[8] What problems are likely to confront a small town when an industry suddenly appears? Is there apt to be an integration problem between the old residents and the newcomers who arrive with the industry? What are the major sociological factors to be considered in working out an action program to meet new needs? These are typical questions being asked by citizens in numerous communities. This study by Hoffer and Freeman throws substantial light upon such problems, and while it deals with only a single Michigan community Charles P. Loomis points out in the foreword that the "needs for action and the elements of the action which are described are typical and tend to occur repeatedly in communities that are adjusting to population growth."

[5] Agricultural Extension Service, Iowa State College, North Central Regional Publication No. 1 of the Agricultural Extension Services, Special Report No. 15 (1955).

[6] *Community Health Action* (East Lansing: Michigan State University Press, 1953).

[7] Morton B. King, Jr., Harold A. Pedersen, John N. Burrus, *Mississippi's People, 1950,* Bureau of Public Administration, University of Mississippi, Sociological Study Series, No. 5 (1955), p. 5.

[8] Charles R. Hoffer and Walter Freeman, *Social Action Resulting from Industrial Development,* Department of Anthropology and Sociology, Agricultural Experiment Station, Michigan State University, Special Bulletin 401 (1955).

It seems true, as Hertzler states, that the "social sciences, with their data regarding factors, processes, and structures have developed to the point where they can be of considerable assistance" in social planning; but it must also be admitted that they are "still in a relatively nascent stage" and that there remain "serious deficiencies in contemporary social-science research" which must be overcome.[9]

One of the challenging roads ahead lies in interdisciplinary cooperation. The team approach has been tried at Cornell University where specialists from the fields of psychology, sociology, anthropology, psychiatry, and social work have worked together in a joint research operation.[10] A somewhat less formally structured program has been in existence at the University of Nebraska for a number of years. Through the interdisciplinary Council for Community Study, ten departments of the University have coordinated a number of their research activities, concentrating the efforts of both faculty members and graduate students upon selected communities from time to time.[11]

A second major activity through which social scientists are making their influence felt on community improvement efforts is *consultation*. This type of endeavor has shown considerable growth in the extension programs of American universities during recent years.

In 1955 a new Division of Community Development was created within the National University Extension Association, having equal status with Audio-Visual Aids, Correspondence Study, and other programs of long standing. The Division of Community Development was an outgrowth of a former Committee on Community Organization through which interested NUEA member institutions for some years had shared ideas and engaged in joint projects. This structural reorganization was indicative of a growing emphasis upon community development activities within the NUEA. In a recent study which provided data from forty-five member-institutions of the NUEA, thirty-four institutions stated that they carried on "activities in the area of community development." Of these, eleven indicated that their community development activities were "primarily conducted by a separate bureau of community development set up for this purpose." [12]

Some representative examples of community consultation programs are as follows:

---

9 Joyce O. Hertzler, *Society in Action* (New York: The Dryden Press, Inc., 1954), pp. 387–388.

10 Urie Bronfenbrenner and Edward C. Devereux, "Interdisciplinary Planning for Team Research on Constructive Community Behavior," *Human Relations,* vol. 5 (May 1952), pp. 187–203.

11 See W. K. Beggs, *Community Study as a Vehicle for Interdisciplinary Research in the Social Sciences,* Council for Community Study, University of Nebraska, Community Study No. 1 (September 1953).

12 "Community Development in University Extension," a report by the Administrative Committee, Community Development Division, Norris A. Hiett, Chairman, National University Extension Association, General Extension Division, University of Minnesota (1956), p. 2.

Earlham College, Richmond, Ind.: *Program of Community Dynamics....* In a unique manner, this college conducts a community service program which simultaneously serves as a training opportunity for students in the field of community development.

University of Kentucky, Lexington: *The Bureau of Community Service.* ... With a small staff and limited budget, the Bureau "seeks to carry into the communities of Kentucky the know-how of specialists in the social sciences. The know-how mingles with the goodwill and determination of the dwellers in a community, and constructive developments follow." [13]

University of Michigan, Ann Arbor: *Community Adult Education....* Through its Extension Service and School of Education the University presents a comprehensive program of services to communities, including consultation in program planning, leadership training, organizational problems, and community self-surveys.

Purdue-Indiana Universities, Bloomington: *Community Services in Adult Education....* One of the major emphases has been upon leadership training, the most recent development providing for research and education designed to improve adult religious education in churches throughout the state.

Southern Illinois University, Carbondale: *Department of Community Development....* This is one of the most intensive programs in the nation in terms of time spent in communities by consultants. It stresses community self-analysis through voluntary study groups as a basis for community development.

University of Tennessee, Knoxville: *Municipal Technical Advisory Service.* ... In cooperation with the Tennessee Municipal League, the M.T.A.S. serves as a fact-finding agency of the University established to provide technical advisory assistance, upon request, to city officials in Tennessee.

University of Virginia, Charlottesville: *Community Services....* This is one of the oldest and best-known programs in the United States. A long record of achievement has been described by the Extension Division in its "New Dominion Series" pamphlets.

University of Wisconsin, Madison: *Bureau of Community Development.* ... Half a century ago the "Wisconsin Idea" was introduced which began the task of converting an entire state into a university "campus." Among the important phases of the program is one which provides for consultation between university personnel and community leaders concerning problems of community betterment.

In view of the growing interest along this line among colleges and universities, it is only natural that critical attention should be given to the question of *role*. What are the essential functions of a social science professor who is asked to serve as consultant in a community? What type of relation-

---

[13] See "Community Service in Kentucky," First Biennial Report of The Bureau of Community Service, Sociology Department, College of Arts and Sciences, University of Kentucky (1950).

ship should exist between him and the group with which he is to work? Questions such as these have by no means been fully resolved, but efforts at clarification are being made.[14] In general, it would seem that his tasks are those of helping people (a) to think intelligently and analytically about their community problems, (b) to discover the sources of socially useful knowledge which are at their disposal, and (c) to employ such knowledge effectively in the solution of their problems. Manipulation of people's minds has no more place in a community setting than it does in the university class-room. This, however, does not prevent the consultant from taking a definite stand on local issues or favoring particular types of action programs, but the net effect should be to stimulate action groups to a more careful examination of the problems at hand. If his comments or recommendations tend instead to promote mental laziness and to shift the function of decision-making from the community to himself as an "outside expert," he has forsaken the role of consultant. Care must be exercised not to encourage a feeling of undue dependence upon the consultant which will undermine local initiative and resourcefulness.

Among other problems of consultation programs are those of structure, financial support, and evaluation. As to structure, there seems to be little uniformity. Certain programs are centralized, with most of the community consultation work being channelled through some type of extension office, while others are carried on by academic departments acting independently of each other. Again, some have a minimal superstructure, while others have rather elaborate arrangements with substantial staffs employed specifically to perform this kind of service. Experimentation is continually practiced, and it would be hazardous to characterize any particular form of organization as best.

The financing of community consultation programs reveals a similar lack of uniformity. Funds are variously derived from taxes, subsidies from other extension programs, grants from private benefactors, and fees from the community groups served. In small communities, at least, there is a tendency for universities to provide consultation services free of charge.

The problem of evaluation is difficult indeed because the contribution of the consultant in any given community development project is normally only one of several factors which together determine success or failure. A project may well succeed *despite* the work of a consultant, where the common sense and balanced judgment of local citizens outweigh hasty or ill-considered guidance by the visiting "expert." On the other hand, a project may fail because of schisms, apathy, lack of imagination, poor leadership, or nonsupport, even though the consultant performs in a thoroughly competent professional manner. In other words, a university's community consultation program cannot

---

[14] See the special issue on "The Role of the Community Consultant," *Journal of Educational Sociology* (December 1955). Murray G. Ross, *Community Organization: Theory and Principles* (New York: Harper & Brothers, 1955), esp. p. 8. Blaine E. Mercer, *The American Community* (New York: Random House, 1956), pp. 280–281.

readily be evaluated by tabulating successes and failures among projects on which help has been given. It is even more difficult to attempt an evaluation on the basis of volume of correspondence, number of telephone calls, frequency of field trips, or number of people contacted. Items like these are of interest, to be sure, but they fail to provide data upon which any type of fundamental evaluation can be based. Careful thought should be given to the development of dependable evaluation techniques in the future. Without them the place of community consultation work in the program of the university will certainly be subject to question.

Closely related to community consultation as a channel of communication between social scientist and community is the broad area of *conferences, short courses, institutes,* and *workshops.* Here is perhaps the most vigorous "growing edge" of the modern university program. Nearly two decades ago the University of Minnesota established its Center for Continuation Study, the first building on any university campus designed specifically for work with adult groups. This has been followed by the Kellogg Center at Michigan State University and a similar center at the University of Georgia and by a considerable number of other institutions of higher learning. Even where no special facilities for continuing education exist there are frequently broad programs housed on a catch-as-catch-can basis in classrooms, auditoriums, and dining halls primarily designed for use by the regular student body.

The extensive scope of this type of activity is reflected in the large output of mailed announcements concerning short-term educational programs for business, industry, labor, the professions, and for adults in general who are interested in self-improvement or community betterment.

Speakers, discussion leaders, and consultants who are capable of carrying on a continuing education program are drawn from a wide variety of fields and sources. Wherever any phase of community improvement is involved, the social scientist ordinarily plays a prominent educational role. Through personal give-and-take around the conference table and through lectures, the expert shares his specialized knowledge with adults who have come to learn. Among numerous examples that could be cited are the Second Midwinter Forum on Community Development held at Texas Technological College [15] and the Community Leadership Conference conducted in Wausau, Wisconsin, under the sponsorship of the Bureau of Community Development of the University of Wisconsin.[16] Rolland D. Berger of the latter institution clarified the relation of this type of educational endeavor to community improvement in the following statement about the Wausau meeting:

Out of this conference there have already grown many specific programs of community improvement—a city planning and zoning program for two cities; a community self-study program for two more; a trade area analysis in another;

[15] Proceedings available from Department of Education, Adult Education Program, Texas Technological College (1955).

[16] For a conference summary see the July–August 1949 issue of *Community Development Service,* University Extension Division, University of Wisconsin.

school district readjustment in another; closer understanding between resort operators and businessmen in another; a new industry program for another; and so on.[17]

In the realm of *radio* and *television* there are also encouraging developments serving to establish communication between social scientists, on the one hand, and citizens engaged in community improvement, on the other. For example, an arrangement was made between Indiana University and the Educational Television and Radio Center at Ann Arbor, Michigan, by which a wide variety of half-hour educational television programs was to be distributed on a rental or purchase basis through the National Educational Television Film Service of the Audio-Visual Center at Indiana. Since many of the topics were in the social sciences, they provided a link between research and social action.

An interesting problem-solving approach in educational television has been developed at station WOI-TV, Iowa State College. In a series of programs entitled *The Whole Town's Talking,* television viewers saw actual community groups in the process of solving difficult community problems. Community specialists of various kinds were involved in the production of these programs which proved to have considerable significance in stimulating viewers to undertake action programs in their own localities.

The Family Life Institute of the University of Oklahoma has produced successfully a Family Life Radio Forum, a series of radio broadcasts presenting to the general public the latest scientific information on family relationships and child development. Listening and discussion groups are encouraged as part of the program, and pertinent literature is available in advance of each broadcast. Among other endeavors of this type is the Canadian Farm Radio Forum, a radio broadcast providing for the discussion of rural problems.

An effort to encourage and facilitate community improvement through the use of a *film* has been made at the University of Michigan. In 1952 a 16 mm. sound film entitled *Tale of Two Towns* was produced, which told the story of how two Michigan communities solved their problems. The film was specifically designed as a springboard for the discussion of community development problems in localities throughout the state, and to assure maximum effectiveness a manual for discussion leaders was drawn up for use with the film. The manual gives detailed suggestions as to how the film may be most advantageously used and emphasizes that the primary purpose of the program is to stimulate as many people as possible to future action.

Social scientists also put out valuable *publications* to meet the needs for "some material." It is recognized that costly errors can frequently be avoided, with substantial savings in time, energy, and money, where an examination of relevant literature can precede the initiation of an action program. Many

---

17 *Ibid.,* iii.

of the publications of the social scientists are in technical language; others are popularly written. Some deal with conceptual framework and theory, and others with methods and practice. But whatever their nature and scope, they constitute a medium through which the social scientist can exert a positive influence upon community life.[18]

---

[18] In the original article a list of organizations and agencies which put out printed materials on community development is presented.—Eds.

4

Contributions of Sociology to Marketing

Christen T. Jonassen

> Sociologists have made discoveries of considerable significance to marketing. Specifically, findings have been produced by sociologists in the marketing-related fields of population, collective behavior, motivation, stratification, methodology, research design, measurement, prediction, human ecology, and the family. Much of this knowledge, of course, remains a potential rather than a realized source of information for marketing strategy.

A sociologist is a social scientist who undertakes to isolate, define, and describe human behavior in groups and social settings. He seeks to formulate valid laws and generalizations about human nature, social interaction, social organization, and culture.

Anyone who engages in such activities, seeks such ends, and who in the eyes of other sociologists contributes to these functions is practicing sociology. Therefore, a *sociological contribution* to marketing is anything done by a recognized sociologist that leads to a better understanding of the nature, functions, and processes of marketing.

In what areas and in what ways have sociologists developed materials

---

Reprinted from the *Journal of Marketing,* national quarterly publication of the American Marketing Association, **24,** 2 (October 1959), pp. 29–35, by permission of the publisher and the author.

Christen T. Jonassen is Professor of Sociology, The Ohio State University.

significant for marketing? And what impact has this knowledge had on marketing, and through what channels has this impact been transmitted? This article gives some of the answers.

NATURE OF MARKETING

We have come a long way from the mechanistic, self-regulating approach of the *laissez-faire* economic theorists. They viewed the market in terms of an equilibrium of forces and general, universalistic, immutable, physical-like laws. The classical economist saw the consumer as an "economic man," a creature who exercised free individual choice in a market which seemed to operate in a cultural and social vacuum. This view looked on individual wants and desires as motivating forces, and on individuals as the acting agents.

Sociological influences are most apparent in the modern institutional approach, which sees economic processes as part of an organic whole of the total society. This approach means that marketing activities are not looked on as the individualistic acts of atomistic man, but rather as *functions* operating through various marketing structures which are part of the total social organization.

It views marketing processes as the *activities* of groups of people: buyers, sellers, and marketing functionaries, who are motivated by group pressures as well as individual predilections. It recognizes the influence of culture, custom, heritage, and mores in determining the final outcome.

Its emphasis throughout is not on the individual, but on the *group* . . . not on mechanistic, self-regulating, universalistic forces, but on particularistic *social* and cultural forces . . . not on "rational economic" man, but on men as members of *social* groups susceptible to irrationality and sentiment, as well as social values and pressures generated within such groups. Duddy and Revzan, for example, say that "what the producer is finally confronted with is the forecasting of human behavior," and that "in our modern dynamic society the individual, whether consciously or unconsciously, more often acts as a member of a group." [1]

Such terms as "institution," "group," "society," "mass," "culture," "structure," "structure-function," are found in the institutional approach. These are terms constantly in use by sociologists, and they have had considerable influence on people in other disciplines. Fundamental changes in viewpoint about the nature of man and his marketing behavior have been due largely to the impact of sociological thought and research on economics, psychology, and marketing.

---

[1] Edward A. Duddy and David A. Revzan, *Marketing* (New York: McGraw-Hill, 1953), pp. 124, 125.

SOCIOLOGICAL CONTRIBUTIONS

Population Studies

The statement, "Markets are people with money to spend—and the desire to spend it" [2] points to two additional areas of sociological contribution: *population studies* and *consumer motivation*.

For a long time population studies have been a branch of sociology. In most universities the subject is taught in the department of sociology, and sociological journals contain numerous articles on this subject. Precise knowledge of population factors enables the marketing man to determine how many and what kinds of people there are and where they are. This enables him to predict future populations and thus gives him lead time which helps to adjust the distribution system to future requirements. This is an obvious necessity for a scientific approach to marketing.

Thompson and Whelpton, Hauser, Ogburn, Margaret Hagood, Hawley, Kingsley Davis, Paul Hatt, Kiser, Duncan, Bogue, and Schmid are a few of the sociologists who have made contributions to our knowledge and understanding of populations, processes, and problems. Their publications in this area are so numerous that each would require a bibliography too long to cite here.

Consumer Motivation

In some of the early marketing texts motivation is discussed in terms of the now-discarded instinct theories, emphasizing the individual and largely ignoring the group. But marketing men today are aware that men do not possess "instincts," and that if they have such desires or motives they are the products of group life. This evolution of thought owes much to sociological influences. Knowledge significant for understanding motivation has emerged from sociological research on class, voluntary association, leisure-time activities, and attitude measurement.

Numerous studies of social class—such as those of the Lynds, Davis, Dollard, Hollingshead, Warner, and Kahl—have focused attention on the implications of class and status, and have described differential motivational patterns and styles of life in different classes. Understanding of motivation is also aided by findings from research on participation in voluntary association such as that of Komarovsky, and by studies of leisure and recreation such as the one made by Alfred Clarke.

Men like Bogardus and many of the sociologists discussed below in the section on measurement and scaling were among the first to devise valid and reliable instruments and scales for the measurement of attitudes. Sociologists also have been a healthy counterbalance to the more extreme claims of Freudians and some of their anthropological followers. Rigorous research

---

[2] Duddy and Revzan, *ibid.*, p. 8.

like that of Sewell, Mussen, and Harris has shown that there is little evidence for many of the theoretical pronouncements regarding the effects of early child-rearing on the personality.

Human Ecology

Another area where sociologists have made a considerable contribution is in human ecology which analyzes the processes involved in the spatial and temporal adaptation and distribution of human beings and their institutions. Those aspects of marketing which can most directly profit from a knowledge of ecology are transportation and storage, and the whole area concerned with market-area structures.

In all approaches to marketing, the *area* is an important variable and factor. Sociologists have been concerned with spatial systems for over forty years—in 1915 Galpin brought out *The Social Anatomy of an Agricultural Community,* and in 1916 Robert E. Park published his article "The City" in the *American Journal of Sociology.* Galpin's pioneering study introduced a technique of marketing research which has been widely used since, with certain modifications.

Since then the contributions of sociologists to the description, delineation, and analysis of the dynamics of spatial and temporal systems have been continuous and constitute a vast amount of research too great to analyze here. There should be mentioned, however, the contributions of Odum and Moore, Murkerjee, and Mangus to the study of regional systems; of R. D. McKenzie, Hawley, and Bogue to the analysis of metropolitan community systems; of Park, Burgess, and McKenzie, Schmid, Firey, Wirth, Duncan and Reiss, and Quinn to the analysis of urban systems; and of Galpin, Kolb and Polson, and Brunner to investigation of rural systems.

Most marketing people are familiar with Reilly's law, and equations of retail gravitation. Those interested in the mathematical-model approach to spatial systems would be rewarded by a study of Stouffer's theory of intervening opportunities, of Zipf's equations and hypothesis on intercity movement of persons, and of Dodd's equations describing message diffusion.

Collective Behavior

The realization of distribution specialists that they are dealing with interacting groups, masses, and publics, and the fact that our nation and the world are developing more characteristics of the mass society make the area which sociologists call "collective behavior" ever more important and relevant for marketing. The contributions of sociologists to this area of human behavior have been fairly continuous since Durkheim's early work. Another pioneer in this area was LeBon. Recent contributors are Albig, LaPiere, Lazarsfeld, Merton, Raper, Lee, and Blumer. *An Experiment in Mass Communication* by Otto Larsen and Melvin L. DeFleur contributes to the understanding of the phenomena indicated by the title.

Measurement and Scaling

Another contribution to marketing research made by sociologists is in methodology, measurement, scaling, and prediction. Chapin, Sletto, Bogardus, and Guttman have made basic contributions to scale construction; Burgess, Hornell Hart, Monachesi, and Stuckert to the science of prediction; Chapin and McCormick to the development of models and research design; Parten to sampling; Sletto to the use of control groups in social research; Bowers to methods of studying paths of diffusion in the use of new products; Galpin and Schmid to techniques for mapping quantitative social data; Lazarsfeld and Stouffer to the use of quantitative methods in the study of many areas of human behavior; and Moreno and Lundberg to sociometry.

IMPACT OF SOCIOLOGISTS ON MARKETING

How much impact, if any, have sociological contributions had on marketing? This is difficult to determine. But inferences may be drawn from marketing literature, from an examination of activities of sociologists in the marketing field, and from a look at the structures and processes through which sociological knowledge diffuses into the marketing area.

Publications

Normally one should expect academic channels and textbooks to be an important means of diffusion, but they appear not to be in this instance. Writers of marketing textbooks, while showing evidence of some of the substance of sociology, rarely mention sociology or sociologists. It would require considerable research to determine definitively what emphasis if any is given to sociology in undergraduate courses; but if textbooks are a guide it would seem to be rather negligible. On the graduate level, however, there seems to be more attention given to this subject matter; *The Shopping Center Versus Downtown,* for example, is being used in graduate marketing training programs of some universities.

In marketing and business publications, on the other hand, evidence of sociological influence is more evident. Bartels, for example, in an article in the *Journal of Marketing* in 1951 considers certain aspects of sociology, economics, and some other disciplines, to be part of the area of marketing. *Business Week* of March 29, 1958, reporting on a marketing conference, featured the remarks of sociologist David Riesman. *The Shopping Center Versus Downtown* mentioned above has been reviewed extensively by marketing and business publications. *Consumer Behavior,* published in 1955, has an article by Nelson N. Foote on "The Autonomy of the Consumer," and another by Frederick L. Strodtbeck on "Recent Developments in Attitude Research." An article entitled "A Commercial Application of Guttman Attitude Scaling Techniques" appeared in the *Journal of Marketing* in 1957.

Climate of Ideas

Much sociological influence on marketing, of course, is exerted indirectly through the medium of the general culture and climate of ideas. Another means is through the effect of sociology on other disciplines such as psychology and economics, which in turn produces similar reactions in marketing.

Sociological contributions to the general evolution of thought about the nature and dynamics of man as a consumer and of the market as a social institution and structure have already been discussed. But much sociological material reaches marketing men secondhand, very late, and sometimes in garbled fashion.

Participation of Sociologists in Marketing

Another path of diffusion of sociological knowledge is through direct participation of sociologists in the marketing process as researchers, consultants, and participants in marketing seminars and conventions. The participation of David Riesman in the *Life* [Magazine] sponsored regional round table in Chicago has already been mentioned. Packard would have us believe that there may be sociologists behind the so-called "hidden persuaders," and states that Likert and Stouffer participated in a public-relations conference at Columbia University. Some sociologists are now found in marketing-research organizations and on the staffs of advertising agencies.

Evidence of direct and indirect influence of sociologists is furnished by the results of some recent marketing research. For example, one of the most ambitious pieces of marketing research of recent years, the *Life Study of Consumer Expenditures,* conducted by Alfred Politz Research, Inc., offers much internal evidence of sociological influence in research design, sampling, questionnaire construction, and selection of essential categories of analysis. The "wave" technique of intermittent interviewing of the same households, for example, is very similar to the technique developed by Lazarsfeld in his study of voting behavior.

The study is not of individuals, but of groups, families, and households living in the United States. These families and households are studied by socioeconomic status; education of head of family; stage of "life cycle"; age of household head; and by regions, urban, rural, and different-sized communities.

One category which appears in the *Life* research that is not common in previous marketing studies is "Household's Stage in the Life Cycle." The study credits the development of this concept to the Survey Research Center of the University of Michigan; but the concept of stages in family life cycle has been common coin in sociology for a long time. In their *Systematic Source Book in Rural Sociology,* Sorokin, Zimmerman, and Galpin discussed four stages of family life cycle as early as 1931; and E. L. Kirkpatrick in 1934 wrote an article entitled "The Life Cycle of the Farm Family in Relation to Its Standard of Living." The concept appears in a book of

Waller's in 1938; and it is the organizing theme of Duvall's *Family Development*. Thus, what appeared originally as a concept in sociological literature appears about a generation later in a marketing study as an important category in terms of which data are gathered and analyzed.

Similarly, the use of such categories as "metropolitan" and "nonmetropolitan" owes much to McKenzie, whose writings on the metropolitan region appeared as early as 1924 and 1926, and whose *The Metropolitan Community* was published in 1933. Bogue's *The Structure of the Metropolitan Community* appeared in 1949; and this research monograph as well as the earlier work of McKenzie, Hawley, and other sociologists probably contributed heavily to the decision of the U.S. Bureau of the Census to order its data in terms of Standard Metropolitan Areas.

In Conclusion

Lack of space has made it necessary to omit names of other sociologists and also some relevant work of the sociologists who are mentioned. Many sociologists have made significant contributions to marketing by their impact on the general climate of ideas concerning the nature of man and society and the relations of economic institutions to society. They have also carried out important studies on population, communication, collective behavior, motivation, stratification, methodology, research design, measurement, prediction, human ecology, and the family. Sociological knowledge and methods have diffused into marketing through marketing publications, through participation of sociologists as consultants and researchers, and to a lesser extent through academic channels.

The participants in the *Life* marketing conferences mentioned earlier stressed the necessity of developing basic theories and facts to explain buying behavior. The present article has pointed to some aspects of sociological activity and to some materials that might aid in the solution of this problem.

5

Labor Unions
Find New Use for
Social Research

L. B. Wallerstein

Unions have found that it is a waste of their resources to attempt
to unionize a plant without first appraising their chances of success.
Sociological methods, Wallerstein notes, are currently serving this
purpose.

Social research is now being used by some labor unions to aid their
organizing efforts. Faced with mounting organization costs and reportedly
increasing organizational difficulties, some unions are using the attitude survey, long a social research tool of management, to determine beforehand
whether or not a drive to organize a specific plant will be practicable.

Because of the confidential nature of a preorganizing survey of worker
attitudes toward a union, little is known of such tailor-made surveys. However, a report in the labor press [1] disclosed the procedure which might be
followed by a typical union interested in conducting such a survey.

The union first selects the plant it contemplates organizing. Then, before
distributing literature, sending organizers into the area, and spending much
money on an effort where success may be clouded with uncertainty, the
union calls in a social research agency.

An agency staff man is sent to the plant area. He examines the general
situation. He talks to key union people, among others, in the area. He
investigates the historical background of the plant, including of course any
past organizing attempts. He reads over all union and management literature
available, including the company's house organ and the local labor press.

The advance staff man then conducts pilot interviews with some plant
workers in an attempt to develop key questions the field interviewers will
use in a more detailed interview, with a larger worker sample.

After these key attitude questions are formulated, local field interviewers
are recruited. This may be difficult to do, particularly in a small town, for
these interviewers must be not only skilled in the techniques of interviewing

Reprinted from *Sociology and Social Research,* **42,** 1 (September 1957), pp. 44–45, by
permission of the publisher and the author.
  L. B. Wallerstein is an economist with the United States Department of Labor.
  Any views expressed are the author's own.
  [1] *Labor's Daily,* November 6, 1956.

but also familiar with the area and people. After their initial selection, field interviewers are usually given specialized training by the social research agency.

The crew of field interviewers then query about 1 to 2 per cent of the plant work force. Using the key questions formulated by the advance man as a guide, they probe for feelings about the company and the workers' possible receptivity to unionism. Some interviews may last from two to four hours.

Upon completing his designated interviews, each field interviewer sends a typewritten report of the results of his questioning to the agency head-quarters. (Such field work usually lasts about two weeks.) Then the social research agency's staff members examine the data obtained from the inter-viewers' reports. Themes are extracted, summarized, analyzed, and evaluated from the data.

The results of this analysis and evaluation (which may take as long as three months) tell the union which types of workers will be susceptible to organization attempts, which arguments should be used and which should be avoided in sales talks for the union, which gripes are uppermost in the minds of the workers, what their notion of a union is, and what they think about the company.

Finally, the agency estimates the extent of success possible and predicts just how long a fight will be involved. Where the results of the survey warrant it, the agency will tell the union to save its money and forget about organizing this particular plant. The union, of course, makes the final de-cision. Thus another pragmatic use has been found for a social research tool in yet another field.

The use of this union preorganizing attitude survey is still in its infancy. In the future it may prove to be a source of invaluable research data for the theoretical social scientist, and may well provide the applied social scientist with a livelihood.

Chapter Two

Culture

THE MATURE STUDENT will recognize that there is but a vague line of demarcation between academic disciplines. For this reason, such fields as biochemistry, astrophysics, and social psychology have arisen. The close relationship between cultural anthropology and sociology is another example of overlapping interest. Although it might be said that the anthropologist's chief concern is the concept of culture, the sociologist also finds this concept most useful.

It is no coincidence, then, that our examination of the concept of culture contains illustrations from the work of anthropologists, who have an important role in the application of scientific principles. The administration of UNESCO, Point Four, international relations, and Indian affairs in this country are but a few of the areas in which anthropological assistance has been of much value. At the present time, several excellent books, as well as journals, are devoted to problems of applied anthropology.

Culture, as defined by Clyde Kluckhohn and William H. Kelly,[1] is all the "historically created designs for living, explicit and implicit, rational, irrational and nonrational, which exist at any given time as potential guides for the behavior of men." Notice, first, that the designs are both implicit and explicit—that is, there are *hidden* attitudes, values, and beliefs as well as the more obvious beliefs and actions of a people. That individuals from other parts of the world have attitudes differing from our own is of vital

[1] Clyde Kluckhohn and William H. Kelly, "The Concept of Culture," *The Science of Man in the World Crisis,* ed. Ralph Linton (New York: Columbia University Press, 1945), p. 97.

importance in any interaction between ourselves and those individuals.

Second, notice that only some of these designs are rational; others are nonrational or even irrational. Because of our own tendencies to be ethnocentric, we often perceive the irrational element in the behavior of others more easily than that element in ourselves. We overlook our own nonrational system of weights and measures, for example. We may persist in irrational customs of smoking or overeating in spite of evidence of their harmful effects.

The selections in this chapter illustrate the necessity for understanding culture in general as well as the culture of any particular society with which we may have relationships. In these readings we see the utility of the concept of culture illustrated in the fields of public health and marketing.

6

Our Silent Language

Edward T. Hall

In the late Clyde Kluckhohn's definition of culture, the point is made that culture pertains to both the implicit and explicit guides for the behavior of men. "Our Silent Language" illustrates subtle, hidden differences between different cultures that communicate meanings of which the participants may be unaware.

There are deep and subtle differences between the people of the United States and their South American neighbors. Surface differences can be seen and dealt with. What defeats all of us are the hidden elements in man's psychological make-up whose presence are all too often not even suspected.

I will use the Spanish word *ocultos*—"not seen"—in a new sense to

Reprinted from *Science Digest,* **52,** 2 (August 1962), pp. 19–23, by courtesy of the publisher and the author. Original version from *Américas,* **14,** 2 (February 1962), pp. 5–8, monthly magazine published by the Pan American Union in English, Spanish, and Portuguese. Published in this form by permission of the Pan American Union.

Edward T. Hall is Research Fellow, Washington School of Psychiatry, Washington, D.C.

stand for these hidden psychological patterns that stand between peoples. Like germs that can't be seen, there are many ocultos that cause psychological difficulty. All one sees are the symptoms, the outward manifestation of the oculto.

I will particularize about three specific topics to demonstrate a principle. These are time, space, and friendship. *Ocultos* between the U.S. citizen and his neighbors differ in all three.

I first became aware of space as a patterned aspect of human behavior when I noted that people raised in other cultures handled it differently. In the Middle East I felt crowded and was often made to feel anxious.

"NATURAL" DISTANCES

Fellow U.S. citizens, also, found it hard to adapt themselves to houses and offices arranged so differently, and often commented on how there was too little or too much space, and how much space was wasted. These spatial differences are not limited to offices and homes: towns, subway systems, and road networks usually follow patterns that appear curious to one not accustomed to the culture.

The "natural" way to describe space may be different in two cultures. For instance, I discovered in Japan that intersections of streets were named and the streets were not.

These differing ideas of space contain traps for the uninformed. A person raised in the United States is often likely to give an unintentional snub to a Latin American because of the way he handles space relationships, particularly the physical distance between individuals during conversations.

A conversation I once observed between a Latin and a North American began at one end of a 40-foot hall. I watched the two conversationalists until they had finally reached the other end of the hall.

This maneuver had been effected by a continual series of small backward steps on the part of the North American as he unconsciously retreated, searching for a comfortable talking distance. Each time, there was an accompanying closing of the gap, as his Latin friend attempted to reestablish his own accustomed conversation distance.

In formal business conversations in North America, the "proper" distance to stand when talking to another adult male who is simply a business acquaintance, is about two feet. This distance diminishes, of course, at social functions like the cocktail party, but anything under eight to ten inches is likely to irritate.

To the Latin, with his own *ocultos,* a distance of two feet seems remote and cold, sometimes even unfriendly. One of the things that gives the South or Central American the feeling that the North American is *simpatico* is when he is no longer made uncomfortable by closeness or being touched.

North Americans, working in offices in Latin America, may keep their local acquaintances at a distance—not the Latin American distance—by remaining behind a desk or typewriter. Even North Americans who have lived in Latin America for years have been known to use the "barricade approach" to communication, and to remain completely unaware of its cultural significance.

They are aware only that they "feel comfortable" when not crowded, without realizing that the distance and the desk often create an *oculto* that distorts or gives a cold tone to virtually everything that takes place. The hold of the oculto is so strong, however, that the Latin is sometimes observed trying to "climb over" the intervening obstacles—leaning across the desk for instance—in order to achieve a distance at which he can communicate comfortably.

LATIN TIME LAG

As with space, there are many time *ocultos* that characterize each people. The North American has developed a language of time that involves much more than being prompt. He can usually tell you when his own ocultos have been violated, but not how they work. His blood pressure rises, and he loses his temper when he is kept waiting; this is because time and the ego have been linked.

As a rule, the longer a North American is kept waiting in his own setting, the greater the discrepancy between the status of the two parties. Because of their high status, important people can keep less important people waiting. Also, very important business takes precedence over less important business. The North American has developed a pattern for seeing one person at a time, but individual appointments aren't usually scheduled by the Latin American to the exclusion of other appointments. The Latin often enjoys seeing several people at once even if he has to talk on different matters at the same time.

In this setting, the North American may feel he is not being properly treated, that his dignity is under attack, even though this simply is not true. The Latin American clock on the wall may look the same, but it tells a different sort of time.

By the U.S. clock, a consistently tardy man is considered undependable. To judge a Latin American by the same time values is to risk a major error.

This cultural error may be compounded by a further miscalculation. Suppose the *Norteamericano* has waited 45 minutes or an hour and finally gets to see the Latin American with whom he has an appointment, only to be told, with many apologies, that "there is only five minutes—maybe a meeting can be arranged for tomorrow or next week?"

At this point, the North American's schedule has been "shot." If it is important, he will have to make the time. What he may not understand is an *oculto* common in Mexico, for example, and that is that one is very likely to take one's time before doing business, in order to provide time for "getting acquainted."

First meetings leave the North American with the feeling he isn't getting anywhere. If not forewarned he keeps trying to get down to business and stop "wasting time." This turns out to be a mistake.

In the United States, discussion is used as a means to an end; the deal. One tries to make his point with neatness and dispatch—quickly and efficiently. The North American begins by taking up major issues, leaving details for later, perhaps for technicians to work out.

Discussion, however, is to the Latin American an important part of life. It serves a different function and operates according to rules of form; it has to be done right. For the Latin American, the emphasis is on courtesy, not speed. Close friends who see each other frequently, shake hands when they meet and when they part.

For the Latin American it is the invisible social distance that is maintained, not the physical distance. Forming a new friendship or a business acquaintance must be done properly. The Latin first wants to know the human values of a new acquaintance—his cultural interests, his philosophy of life—not his efficiency. This is all accompanied by elaborate and graceful formal verbal expressions, which people in the United States have long felt too busy to take time for. They tend to assume familiarity very quickly, to invite new acquaintances to their homes after one or two meetings. But the Latin American entertains only friends of very long standing in his home —and never for business reasons.

BRIEF NORTHERN FRIENDSHIPS

Of course, times are changing, because there are an increasing number of Latin businessmen who now demand punctuality even more strictly than in the North. However, there are still a great many times when the old patterns prevail and are not understood. The hidden differences seem to center around the fact that in the North, the ego of the man is more on the surface, whereas in the South preserving institutional forms is important.

It has been observed that in the United States, friendships may not be long lasting. People are apt to take up friends quickly and drop them just as quickly.

A feature influencing North American friendship patterns is that people move constantly (in the 12-year period from 1946–1958, according to U.S. census data, two thirds of those owning homes had moved, while virtually all those renting property had moved). The North American, as a rule, looks for and finds his friends next door and among those with whom he works.

There are for him few well-defined, hard-and-fast rules governing the obligations of friendship. At just what point our friendships give way to business opportunism or pressure from above is difficult to say. In this, the United States seems to differ from many other countries in the world.

WEIGHT OF TRADITION

In Latin America, on the other hand, while friendships are not formed as quickly or as easily as in the United States, they often go much deeper and last longer. They almost always involve real obligations. It is important to stress that in Latin America your "friends" will not let you down. The fact that they, personally, are having difficulties is never an excuse for failing friends. You, in turn, are obligated to look out for their interests.

The weight of tradition presses the Latin American to do business within a circle of friends and relatives. If a product or service he needs is not available within his circle, he hesitates to go outside; if he does so, he looks for a new friend who can supply the want.

Apart from the cultural need to "feel right" about a new relationship, there is the logic of the business system. One of the realities of life is that it is dangerous to enter into business with someone over whom you have no "control." The difference between the two systems lies in the controls. One is formal, personal, and depends upon family and friends. The other is technical-legal, impersonal, and depends upon courts and contracts.

Europeans often comment on how candid the North American is. Being candid, he seeks this in others. What fools him is that the Latin American does not readily reciprocate. One has to be known and trusted—admitted into the circle of friendship—before this happens. Even then, what is not said may be just as important, and just as much noticed, as what is said.

Until we face up to the reality of the *ocultos,* and make them explicit, difficulties in communication are going to continue. *Ocultos* drain the great reservoir of goodwill that the people of the Americas feel in their hearts for each other.

Some Problems
of the Physicians on the
Navajo Reservation

John Adair and Kurt W. Deuschle

The United States Public Health Service maintains responsibility for administering medical care on the various Indian reservations. The following article examines applications of the culture concept that are of particular interest to the young physician or premedical student.

Since World War II there has been a great increase in the number of United States medical personnel working in the so-called "underdeveloped" areas of the world. This expansion in the delivery of scientific medicine is caused by a number of factors. Prominent among these are the great increase in military bases in foreign countries, where the doctors and nurses frequently treat native civilian personnel as well as U.S. troops, and to United States participation in international health programs such as the Pan-American Sanitary Bureau, International Cooperation Administration, and other technical assistance programs.

In addition to these organizations, in 1955 the United States Public Health Service became responsible by Congressional Act for rendering a health service on all U.S. Indian Reservations with a few exceptions, and to the Indians, Aleuts, and Eskimos residing in Alaska. This had formerly been the responsibility of the Bureau of Indian Affairs of the Department of the Interior. Today many young doctors are now recruited through the Universal Military Training and Service Act, for service in the Indian Health Program.

In a recent survey [1] reported to the Surgeon General, Public Health Service, the problem with young physicians in the Indian Health Program was emphasized:

"The youth and short length of service of many of the physicians in the

Reprinted from *Human Organization,* **16,** 4 (Winter 1958), pp. 19–23, by permission of The Society for Applied Anthropology and the authors.

John Adair is Anthropologist, National Institute of Mental Health.

Kurt W. Deuschle, M.D., is Professor and Chairman, Department of Community Medicine, University of Kentucky College of Medicine.

[1] *Health Services for American Indians,* U.S. Department of Health, Education, and Welfare, Public Health Service, 1957, p. 115.

Indian Health Program make for difficulties in program and administration. Over 40 per cent of the medical officers in charge of Indian hospitals are under 30 years of age, and about half are in the Public Health Service, serving their two years under the Doctor-Dentist Draft. These physicians, most of whom are trained and interested primarily in clinical medicine, are expected to assume responsibilities for program planning in both public health and medical care and also to administer hospitals."

In this paper some of the problems which confront these young doctors on the Navajo Reservation are discussed. They are presented in the immediate context of the medical service in that region, but it is believed that many of these same problems and their solution have a broader generality to cross-cultural medical practice which has had such a rapid expansion in other areas of the world.

The physician starting on the Navajo Reservation faces a number of difficulties: learning to work effectively in a government organization; living and working in a relatively isolated social and medical community; comprehending the importance of cultural differences and the language barriers as they are related to the medical program; and recognizing that the pattern of disease and the nature of the clinical work on the Reservation call for a general medical and public health approach.

PROBLEMS RELATED TO GOVERNMENT AND RESERVATION LIVING

Most young doctors assigned to the Navajo Reservation have joined the United States Public Health Service to fulfill their draft obligation. All of these doctors have completed their internship; some have had a year or more residency in medicine: surgery, pediatrics, or another specialty.

Physicians like many other citizens have little knowledge about how the government really operates. They may have no understanding about such matters as the important role of the Bureau of the Budget, the steps involved in obtaining necessary congressional appropriations, the problem of categorized and "earmarked" funds, budget "freezes," and other vital information about government fiscal procedures. Lacking this knowledge the physician may not appreciate the problems which the local administrators encounter in attempting to provide an adequate medical program.

It may take a full year for the most adaptable doctors to adjust to government medical practice; to accept the administrative authority of his chief; to work without undue frustration within established "channels"; to accept the burden of "paper work" as an inherent part of a governmental activity. As a clinician the physician has long been accustomed to looking to his chief or superior as the final arbiter and counselor for his medical diagnoses and treatment. However, in the government health organization, as in any large health program, the physician's chief or superior may well be an able administrator with only secondary interest in the practice of clinical medicine. Some of the more rigid doctors take on the attitude that "government" is a mass conspiracy solely invented to keep them from seeing their patients. . . .

LANGUAGE AND CULTURAL PROBLEMS

A source of considerable frustration to the physician is his inability to talk directly to his Navajo patients. The doctor is unable to judge the patient's subtleties of expression, the tone of voice and inflection, the turn of a phrase which is so important in communicating emotional tone in English. These cues do not come through when working with an interpreter—the whole effect is dulled in the process of interpretation. Moreover, the physician misses the gratification he gets from patients elsewhere when they are able to express their thoughts to the doctor directly. Here what rapport he obtains is again developed through the interpreter. Even a pediatrician treating infants in our society has the satisfaction of talking with the families of his patients. Because of the language barrier, the physician may fall into the habit of addressing himself to his interpreter rather than the patient. This the patients resent, and have been known to complain "these interpreters get between us and the doctors." The importance of the medical history, in fact, becomes secondary to the medical examination in most clinics simply because of the difficulty in getting adequate histories through these interpreters.

All the physician's technical knowledge in explaining the nature of the illness, the plan for treatment and follow-up recommendations must be funneled through the interpreter. The extent to which the physician can communicate with the patient depends on how effective the Navajo interpreter performs his job. Eventually the interpreter who is well used (and has been well trained) becomes, so to speak, the instrument of the physician.

The physician may fail to realize that the literal interpretation usually possible between European languages and English is quite impossible between languages so different structurally as English and Navajo. Even when Italian or Puerto Rican patients cannot speak a word of English they may break through the language barrier to some extent with their volatile and demonstrative expressions. In contrast the behavior of the stolid and undemonstrative Navajo patient serves to magnify the language barrier.

There are numerous other problems which center around the matter of medical interpreters. One of these problems is that of selecting the medical interpreter. Thus far no standard has been set nor systematic screening method devised for the selection of medical interpreters. Usually doctors are attracted to interpreters with whom they have the best rapport, who speak the best English, have the nicest "appearance" yet whose ability in speaking their own language—which may have suffered from years away from the Reservation while in government boarding schools—remains untested.

The consequence of this lack of training for interpreters in the concepts of medicine and lack of experience of the young doctor in how to select, train, and use an interpreter results in a situation which remains highly unpredictable in any given hospital, outpatient clinic, or field health installation.

The failure to select a medical interpreter properly can sometimes result in ridiculous errors as the following incident which occurred at the Fort Defiance Indian Hospital several years ago illustrates:

A doctor hard pressed for an interpreter asked a Navajo kitchen helper to interpret for him one day. She spoke as good English as the regular interpreter and the doctor had no reason to doubt her competence in her own language. The girl was ashamed to confess her ignorance and proceeded to interpret as requested. She told the patient that she would have to have her appendix removed while in reality the doctor had ordered a routine radiograph of the chest.

It should be noted, however, that even in our own urban clinics where there is no language barrier the level of communication between the physician and the patient and of the patient's understanding of his own disease as revealed by the doctor is far from satisfactory. The situation in doctor-patient relations on the Navajo Reservation is not so different in kind, but is intensified in several particulars. Among these are (1) lack of education of the patients in our medicine, (2) the presence of the language barrier which requires funneling all information through an interpreter, and (3) lack of knowledge on the physician's part of those aspects of Navajo culture which have a direct relation to the curing process.

The physician who is unsophisticated in Navajo ways may get into difficulty in evaluating certain situations that occur in the clinic or hospital. For example, the Navajos are so-called "good patients" because they accept and endure certain painful procedures stoically; this may mislead some unwary physician into thinking that the Navajos do not experience pain as sharply as his Anglo patient. Occasionally a physician will continue a difficult venipuncture or other minor surgical procedure because of the patient's seemingly high threshold to pain.

A notable illustration of this point had to do with an obstetrician who administered a minimum of analgesics for his Navajo patients in labor on the assumption that the Navajos had very little pain since they "probably experienced a more natural reaction to childbirth." After this obstetrician completed his tour of duty the physician who succeeded him administered much larger doses of analgesics. Very soon thereafter, the obstetrical patient load at this Navajo hospital increased sharply. When some of these Navajo women were queried as to why they were coming into the hospital they replied: "To have a baby without pain!"

There are numerous other pitfalls for the physician inexperienced in the area. He may ask the ward orderly to take care of a corpse, and get an outright refusal; or if the order is carried out the orderly may request the following day off so that the correct ritual may be performed to cleanse the body of the evil that comes from close associations with the dead.

The doctor may be baffled by the refusal of a patient's relatives to donate blood for indicated surgery or the treatment of anemia. He may not realize that the concepts of sympathetic and contagious magic are still strongly believed in by most of the Navajos. In this instance, if the patient were to die, then the donor of the blood might also sicken and die.

Numerous other points of resistance could be mentioned: the reluctance to take rectal temperatures (probably related to witchcraft usage of feces); the dislike of appearing naked before the doctor (sanctions of modesty are highly developed among the Navajo); the constant series of requests for "time off" on the part of Navajo employees (in order to have the correct counteractive rituals) and requests for medical leave from the sanatoria by a patient who wants to go home for a "sing" which is Navajo healing ceremony.

These points of resistance serve to alert the doctor to the fact that the Navajo patient is certainly very different "from the patient back home." He also comes to realize as a result of his own experience that Indian employees demand in their relationship to the doctor tremendous patience, and the nurturing of a close and sympathetic attitude. The impersonal rigid relations which are traditional to hospitals and clinic management in our own society tend to increase the gap between the doctor and the nurse in their world, and the Navajo patient and employees in theirs.

It is equally easy for the physician to err on the side of being overindulgent in acquiescing to Navajo custom and tradition. This is illustrated by an incident which occurred at the Fort Defiance Hospital several years ago. The surgeon who was treating a patient with severe burns granted the family permission to visit the patient with the medicine man. A curing rite was performed while the patient was unattended by the hospital staff. The herbal infusion which was spat on the patient's wounds during the ceremony resulted in a fatal infection. This incident demonstrates the importance of being highly selective in granting concessions to Navajo tradition when the patient's health status may be compromised. Had the "sing" been performed without the application of the herbal infusion the psychological benefit of the ritual could have been achieved without the danger of infection.

The pity is that each physician must learn most of this for himself. To be certain, those on the job before him may well brief the new doctor in a casual way about the "do's" and "don'ts" of working with Navajo patients; nevertheless, a handbook with relevant cultural materials is needed by the clinician. Many of these data can be found in a few books and monographs, for the Navajo Indians have been the subject of intensive study and research by anthropologists. It is ironical that so often physicians learn by trial and error the complex matters of the cultural differences when there is such a rich literature available. This raises a host of problems not germain to the central theme of this paper, problems concerned with communication between anthropologists and government administrators and anthropologists and the professions. Suffice it to say that this lack of communication is as much, if not more, a failure of the anthropologist as it is of the doctor or public health officer.

The physician who has longer-term bed patients in the hospital or who does service in a tuberculosis sanatorium is in a good position to see the broader context of Navajo disease and health. There, as in sanatoria in our own society, he has an opportunity to get to know his patients and their families who make frequent visits. He gains an understanding of the important part the family plays in the care of the ill in Navajo society. Within recent years there has grown up in the sanatoria a willingness on the part of the doctors to permit their patients leave so they may have their own "sings" at home. This too has a broadening effect on the doctor's thinking, and Navajo traditional medicine becomes relevant to problems of medical care. Furthermore, the physician who deals with tuberculosis has the problem of educating the patient to his illness. If he is perceptive, he soon learns that the germ theory as such has no meaning for the Navajo. They tend to keep their own native theory of disease and are not won over by scientific demonstrations such as looking at microbes under the microscope.[2] While the physician learns that our scientific explanations of the cause of disease fall on deaf ears, he also learns that the Navajo patient takes considerable interest in the progress of his treatment. Radiographs are examined with great interest not only by the patient, but by his whole family.

The physician may recognize the importance of cultural differences when the violation of custom and ensuing resistance on the part of the Navajo are perceived. However, this is just the beginning of cultural awareness. Too often the subtleties of cultural differences are missed altogether or are learned after a harsh experience. For example, the harried physician may be chagrined to discover that the hours of precious time he spent convincing the husband of one of his patients to continue hospital treatment had been completely wasted. The family member who really wielded the power of decision in this matter—the patient's grandmother—had been directed to the waiting room to sit while the parley had taken place. That such events should occur is quite understandable, for the wards and clinics are usually full and the pressing problems of diagnoses and treatment do not allow the physician a great deal of time to investigate such matters. From the moment the physician arrives on the job he is under such heavy work pressure that there is little time to schedule group conferences and workshops for such matters as language and cultural problems. . . .

CONCLUSION

The problems which the physician encounters on the Navajo Reservation are not unlike many challenges in life which we all meet. In effect, the solution depends on the ability of the physician to adapt and adjust his

---

[2] It has been the experience of anthropologists working in other world areas that changing native concepts of disease etiology is most difficult, and not essential to public health programming. William Caudell, "Anthropology and Public Health," in A. L. Kroeber, *Anthropology Today* (Chicago: University of Chicago Press, 1953).

knowledge and skill learned in one situation and to apply the same principles in meeting a markedly different set of circumstances. The imaginative physician will do this instinctively whereas the more rigid physician will probably fail to adapt regardless of how much is done for him. However, the average doctor could probably derive considerably more satisfaction from his work in areas of low technology and different cultural patterns if he received special education, training, and orientation for this work.

8

On the Effective Use of Anthropology in Public Health Programs

Richard N. Adams

Using the 1951 report of George Foster as a basis, Richard Adams discusses the contributions anthropology can make to public health. His recommendations include the following points: (1) administrators of public health programs should have a knowledge of the culture in which they are working; (2) specialists in the social sciences should be assigned to public health field parties; (3) because specialized knowledge must be founded upon basic studies, basic studies should be continued; (4) project action personnel can benefit from training in anthropological concepts and techniques; and (5) anthropological consultants can make a valuable contribution in medium and upper levels of administration and planning.

I. INTRODUCTION

In July of 1951 George Foster published a mimeographed report based on the work carried on by the four anthropologists of the Institute of Social Anthropology of the Smithsonian Institution. (The report, entitled "A Cross-

Reprinted from *Human Organization,* **13,** 4 (Winter 1955), pp. 5–15, by permission of The Society for Applied Anthropology and the author.

Richard N. Adams is Professor of Anthropology, and Assistant Director, Institute of Latin American Studies, University of Texas.

The present article is published with the permission of the Pan-American Sanitary Bureau. The writer wishes to express his gratitude to the following people who read and criticized an earlier draft of this paper: Dr. George Foster, Dr. Guillermo Samamé, Dr. J. L. Garcia Gutiérrez, Dr. Nevin S. Scrimshaw, Dr. Stanford Farnsworth, Dr. Norman Craig. The writer assumes all responsibility for the opinions expressed herein; they do not necessarily represent those of either the readers or the Bureau.

Cultural Anthropological Analysis of a Technical Aid Program," was translated into Spanish and issued by the National Indian Institute of Mexico in 1952, and an article-length summary of it appeared in the same year in the *Boletin de la Oficina Sanitaria Panamericana,* a journal which is distributed through all the countries of the Western hemisphere.) The report consisted of an analysis of the work of the *Servicios* of the Institute of Inter-American Affairs in certain phases of their work in Mexico, Colombia, Peru, and Brazil. The study, as its title indicates, was an attempt to analyze in anthropological terms the efforts of public health personnel to introduce through their regular programs measures of hygiene and sanitation to the populations of selected regions of Latin America.

Foster's report was by no means the first in which opinions were expressed by an anthropologist about public health programs and methods, but it was one of the first to try to present a systematic analysis of some of these programs in anthropological terms and to make recommendations for changes in public health practices on the basis of such an analysis. As such it marked a milestone in the development of the use of anthropology in public health and had a considerable impact on many public health workers in both Latin America and the United States. It provided many public health workers with an excellent example of one way cultural and social anthropology, as the study of human customary behavior, could facilitate the work of public health. Since public health was basically concerned with the changing of human habits, workers in public health could benefit from the aid provided by people whose special study is the field of human habits and habit change. There is little doubt, however, that for many people Foster's report remained merely a preliminary sample. Most public health personnel had little or no contact with cultural anthropologists, nor had they had the opportunity to see in practice the ways in which anthropology might help them. Furthermore, the use of an anthropologist in a public health program was such a new idea that few administrators felt sure enough of the utility of the discipline or knew enough about it to promote its use in specific public health projects.

In the three years that have elapsed since the appearance of Foster's publication, workers in public health and anthropology have had an increased opportunity to discover the most fruitful ways in which anthropology can contribute to public health. In the course of these years, it has been possible to reevaluate the principles and ideas proposed by Foster, to clarify them and to add to them. The purpose of the present article is to present an outline of the ways anthropology can contribute to public health in the light of the experience of recent years, to look at the collaboration between the two fields in the light of Foster's report, and to try to point out what we may have learned since its publication. The general limits of the discussion will be: *How can anthropology be most effectively used as a tool to improve action work in projects of public health?* The point of view is that of a person who has been working in Central America and who has not had access to much of the documentation of work that has been carried on in other parts of the world. As a result, it expresses a bias, both in point of geography and in point of time. Although there is a growing body of literature, much of it in manuscript or mimeographed form, there has been relatively little concern with the way the contributions of anthropology have been made to public health progress, and with what we have learned about collaboration between an anthropologist and members of a public health program.

Foster's principal recommendations may be summarized under three main categories:

1. Administrators of public health programs should have a certain knowledge of the culture in which they are working. Foster mentioned nine phases of society and culture which should be included in the administrator's knowledge (and emphasized that this was by no means a final list). Of these, he put special emphasis on the knowledge of folk beliefs about illness and curing. The other items were economic resources of the population, social organization of the family, education and literacy, political administration, religion, value systems, prestige complex, and motor patterns.

2. Specialists in the social sciences should be assigned to public health field parties, "to gather specialized information (ideally to be pyramided on top of a broad plateau of basic data) to facilitate specific projects." Also, such a specialist could carry on continuing field experiments, varying techniques under different conditions in order to determine more clearly their relative value.

3. Basic studies in both the culture of a specific area and in the theory of anthropology are essential to the effective work of the anthropologist. Foster notes that ". . . it seems obvious that plans should be made to continue the accumulation of generalized basic cultural data not only in Latin America but also in all places where such programs are foreseen. Administratively such work should not be coupled directly with specific action programs, simply because insofar as the research is directed toward too specific problems, the results will be correspondingly of less utility for other types of programs."

Using these three points as a basis of discussion we can now explore some of the problems and issues in the utilization of anthropology in public health.

II. INTRODUCING ANTHROPOLOGY TO THE PUBLIC HEALTH ADMINISTRATOR

Depending upon his knowledge of and attitude towards anthropology, the public health administrator makes the decision as to whether anthropology is or is not to be used in the area under his jurisdiction. In general, it may be said that very few public health administrators have more than a limited knowledge concerning the field; their attitudes towards anthropology vary from over enthusiastic evaluation of the discipline with a corresponding inability to define the limits of its utility, through a neutral lack of interest, to hostility. Rarely has the public health administrator been able to make a critical evaluation or define the limits of utility on the basis of personal experience.

Overenthusiasm towards anthropology usually takes the form of assuming that it can do the "impossible," or that it can introduce changes requiring years in a matter of weeks. Hostility usually takes the form of the medical or public health person claiming that he already knows more than the anthropologist could know about a given culture. In Latin America, occasionally a medical or professional man is found who will claim that because he is a Latin, he knows more of Latin American culture than any foreign anthropologist will ever be able to understand. The peculiarity of such an argument becomes apparent if someone were to claim that an individual who is sick knows more about how to take care of his ailment than does the doctor because the latter, after all, does not have the sickness. For the most part, however, public health officials are so unfamiliar with the possibilities of anthropology that they are neither enthusiastic nor hostile, but merely curious. . . .

III. SOCIAL SCIENCE SPECIALISTS IN FIELD PROJECTS

Foster's recommendation that social science specialists be used in field programs of public health was already in practice at the time his paper appeared. Work in the intervening years, however, has led to a greater clarification of the role that can be played effectively by anthropologists in the public health field. Here we want to discuss the general type of work anthropology can do and certain specific activities: research, consultation, and teaching.

1. Areas of Public Health in Which Anthropology May Help

One of the problems faced by some anthropologists working in public health is that public health personnel usually have so slight a conception of what anthropology is that they have no idea of the ways it may best help. In order that they may see some reasonable administrative order in what is being done, there has at times been a tendency to assign an anthropologist within the established bureaucratic framework of the public health organization, thus greatly limiting the range of effectiveness of the social science work.

The fact that a given subject matter falls within a certain field of public health in itself neither affirms nor denies that anthropology may be of use to it. As a generality, it may be said that the possible utility of anthropology can only be judged in terms of the specific problems that arise (or may be foreseen to arise) when a particular phase of public health work starts in a specific cultural, social, and environmental setting. For example, depending upon the nature of the specific problems involved, setting up a malaria control program, a new water system, a nursing school, or a rural clinic may or may not be benefited by the use of anthropology. In places where malaria is understood to result from the presence of mosquitoes of a certain type, fairly standard methods may suffice for the development of programs; however, where it is thought to be due to chills after one has been perspiring, it may be necessary to use more complicated techniques. Under very difficult conditions, it will help to have an anthropologist available who can interpret the how and why of local beliefs and help establish a meaningful rationale. Many communities around the world will be only too glad to have their water supply improved; however, when a community has peculiar beliefs about the sources of water, it may help to have an anthropologist. On the surface, the establishment of a nursing school does not seem to be the kind of problem where an anthropologist could help. When the country in which it is being established places the nurse in a low social category, however, there may be a real problem of nurse recruitment. Whether or not the establishment of a rural clinic can benefit from the services of an anthropologist again depends upon the nature of the culture and environment in which one tries to establish the clinic; it may also depend upon the nature of the project organization establishing the clinic.

As stated previously, the need or lack of need for social sciences cannot be finally predicted on the basis of the nature of the project alone. There are, however, some indicators which frequently can aid in making an early decision: [1]

(*a*) The greater the cultural difference existing between the project personnel and the members of the subject population, the greater will be the utility of anthropology; (*b*) the greater the social class or caste distinction between personnel and population the more use social science may be; (*c*) those projects concerned with changing human habits learned early in life and/or reinforced often, will find an anthropologist or social psychologist useful. These are not the only situations in which the work of social scientists have been useful, but where they do exist it is a fairly clear indication that such a person may be a valuable addition to the project. Medical, nursing, and sanitary personnel themselves, through their training and interpersonnel professional contact, tend to establish common ideas that may not be shared by other people in the same social and cultural group. To this degree, they differ in culture from those with whom they will have to be working. Lest it be assumed to the contrary, it should be emphasized that the mere

---

[1] George Foster, upon reading this paragraph, commented that it was probably too early to define the range of possible utility of social sciences in public health. The present writer feels that it is important to consider this problem, however, as one means of clarifying our thinking. This paragraph, like the entire paper, should not be considered as fact, but intended to promote further definition and clarification.

presence of formal education in the population is not in itself a satisfactory indication that the culture of that population is similar to that of the project personnel.

On the basis of the above points, there are certain types of populations in which projects may benefit from the use of social science: (*a*) Generally, any segment of a total population with a predominantly low economic and social standing, since such a population usually varies distinctly in culture from that held by medical authorities of that country; (*b*) indigenous populations or those of foreign cultural origin, whether they form a population majority or minority in the total society, may differ in customs from the dominant local populations which produces the medical workers; (*c*) projects to improve nutrition and change basic sanitary and health habits deal with habits which are deeply set in the members of a population and closely related with many activities in daily life that are not easy to change. In general terms, anthropology may be of specific help in programs of nutrition, health education, maternal and child care, certain phases of environmental sanitation, and in the establishment of any integral program of public health. In more general terms, it can be of help in orienting the basic philosophies of such programs as well as in specific research.

2. The Role of Anthropological Research in Public Health

Anthropology has traditionally been a discipline of research. Only in recent years has it gone actively into applied fields and, as a result, its role in these ventures is still in a process of development and definition. Because of their personalities, some anthropologists are also effective in action work, and one school in the United States is promoting a field it calls *action anthropology,* a combination of action and research work. In the writer's opinion, however, the anthropologist's real contribution lies in his capacity as a research investigator and consultant. Few anthropologists have training in general educational techniques, group skills, adult leadership, or social work, which would make their work in action roles particularly effective; consequently, they must act as amateurs in this realm. In the writer's own work, his field team included certain action personnel who put into practice the results of the research as soon as they became available.

There are certainly times when the anthropologist can be of greater long range value to a project by staying out of the action work personally and remaining in a research capacity. This, of course, would vary with the nature of the program, the subject society, and the anthropologist.

If research may be assumed to be an important contribution that an anthropologist can make to public health, it is worthwhile to define more clearly the nature of the research and explore its possibilities in terms of action programs. First, let us define three general types of research anthropology can carry out: problem research, exploratory research, and experimental action research.

a. PROBLEM RESEARCH.   By problem research we mean research on a specific problem occurring in the course of a public health program. For example, if it develops that a project is being slowed up through lack of community cooperation, then the anthropologist can attack this problem and try to determine the causes behind this lack of cooperation and, thereby, provide a solution for obtaining better cooperation. If a project is designed to provide better training for empirical midwives in a region where scientific obstetric practices have never been observed, then an anthropologist can go about studying the situation of the local midwives and try to define the problems the project may expect in dealing with them; in defining these problems, the project can be planned to avoid them. Some of the most useful work to date done by anthropologists in the field of public health has been in or tangential to this realm of problem research. In general, we may define the problem research role of the anthropologist as one wherein he tries to resolve some specific problem standing in the way of the success of the project.

b. EXPLORATORY RESEARCH.   By exploratory research we mean here investigations carried out in a generally unknown geographical region or unknown population group to define in greater or lesser detail the cultural, social, and economic status of a given population so that a public health program may be planned for that region on the basis of its needs and possibilities. The specific things that might be studied in such exploratory research depend upon the size and complexity of the society, the time available for research (including that of learning a language if necessary), and the specific aspects of life that might be affected by the proposed project. Since the object of such a study is to determine which specific areas of the culture might offer problems or warrant consideration in the planning of a future project, the anthropologist must often go into his research somewhat blind as to what he is looking for. He can only try, on the basis of his training and experience, to comb the possibilities. This means a general research through economies, community structure, family organization, other phases of the social organization, and value systems to try to get a general idea of how the people of the society react to one another and to strangers, and how they might react to the various factors a public health program might bring into their community.

Exploratory research is an attempt to avoid future problems, to help provide sufficiently intelligent planning so that a minimum of problem research will be necessary. It cannot be planned out in great detail ahead of time for the simple reason that the anthropologist, unless he is familiar with similar societies, cannot know precisely what he is looking for apart from the fact that he is trying to identify phases of the culture that might later be relevant in some phases of the project work.

c. EXPERIMENTAL ACTION RESEARCH.   By experimental action research we mean research designed to discover the importance or value of specific processes, techniques, or methods in public health work through using certain given natural situations as experimental contexts, and varying certain factors in order to see how they affect the results. In view of the types of problems that have occurred in public health projects in Latin America, this type of research can be extremely valuable. The field of health education can benefit particularly from such experimental research. It is replete with techniques it has inherited from social work, education, and other semiformal disciplines which have seen their development in occidental cultures. In the transfer of these techniques to other cultures and societies, they are often persistently used in spite of obvious indications that they are far from being well adjusted to the cultural context in which they are working. It may be evident from results that such work in health education is not successful, but the only way to determine better ways is to carry on experimental work in the field situation.

It should be apparent that the three types of research mentioned here are not mutually exclusive. Among the most effective type of contribution anthropology can offer to a project is to provide exploratory research, then carry on experimental research, and have constantly available personnel for the investigation of problems as they arise. In practice, the work of anthropologists for various reasons has been limited usually to one of these types of research. The work of the members of the Institute of Social Anthropology—Erasmus, Simmons, Oberg, Kelly, and Foster—was principally problem research. Kelly's more recent work with the Institute of Inter-American Affairs has been more exploratory in nature, while Erasmus had occasion to carry on some experimental research in health education in Ecuador. At present, the degree to which the different kinds of work are carried on depends almost entirely on the anthropologist's choice; few public health administrators have been aware of the varieties of work that can be done.

Another way of looking at the anthropologist's research is in terms of the subject matter on which the investigation focuses. It is convenient to discuss this under three general headings: focus on the subject society; focus on the organization sponsoring the work; and focus on the interrelations between the subject society and the organization.

a. STUDY OF SUBJECT SOCIETY. This has been the most acceptable and successful use of anthropology to date in Latin America. Many persons in the field of public health have witnessed anthropology at work in research on the reasons a given population resisted this change, or reacted as it did to that project, or preferred one clinic to another, etc. The very fact that anthropology classically deals with foreign, aboriginal, or non-Western societies makes it easier for a person not familiar with the field to see its utility in studying these societies. However, whether a subject society can or cannot usefully be studied by anthropology does not depend only upon the fact of its being a member of one of the classical categories of anthropological study. In recent years, anthropology has made some of its most notable advances through extending its study to contemporary Western societies. It has been shown repeatedly that the person who is a member of a society, with the same culture as the members of that society, may be most inept at understanding his own society *unless* he undertakes to study it somewhat systematically. Perhaps 99 per cent of the people lack the means, ability, or desire to study their own society systematically and, consequently, move along as a part of it, without being aware of the many factors operating in their culture. From this point of view, anthropology can also contribute considerably to the study of any contemporary group in which it is proposed to carry on public health work. As it moves further from its area of classical study, however, anthropology merges more and more with the general field of human relations and human behavior, a broad discipline to which the various social, psychological, and biological sciences contribute. Studies of the subject society can include a wide range of research—as wide, indeed, as the culture being studied. Such studies may, as already mentioned, be oriented around a problem, exploratory in nature, or experimental.

b. STUDY OF THE ORGANIZATION. The writer, among others, has found that the organization that plans and carries out a program in public health frequently promotes grave problems for itself. These problems very often stem from the social organization of the administrating group. Depending upon the structure of such an organization, rapidity of decision can be increased or reduced, intercommunication between critical personnel can be facilitated or brought to an absolute standstill, personnel can be relatively free of or constantly subjected to heavy psychological stress, objective self-criticism can be usefully directed or can be completely eliminated; in short, depending upon the social organization of the public health personnel, a given project may stumble along to ultimate failure or at least have an even chance of success.

To use a parallel example, in recent years certain schools of business administration in the United States have been introducing courses given by social psychologists and specialists in group work in order that the budding businessman may better understand the sociopsychological factors that can make a business organization run smoothly at a profit, or hobble it so that it suffers from constant personnel difficulty with a concomitant profit loss. The public health administrator presumably also wishes to see a "profit" in terms of successful public health work. The administrator in a poorly structured organization may find that the success of his project suffers just as much as does a business in which the organizational structure is weak.

This is a field in which anthropologists have not been the leaders, but in which anthropological concepts and methods are very useful. The men who have developed these studies have generally been in the field of communications research, industrial relations, and social psychology. A social scientist familiar with the work in these fields can frequently put his finger on trouble sources in project administration when the administrator and other project personnel are totally unaware of the source of their malfunctioning. This is particularly true of projects where personnel of different nationalities and different cultural backgrounds may be operating.

c. STUDY OF RELATIONSHIPS BETWEEN THE ORGANIZATION AND SUBJECT SOCIETY. When a public health project begins to operate in a given society, from the anthropological point of view there may be a meeting of two different cultures; people with at least two different sets of beliefs and habits have come into direct person to person contact, and one of these sets of people wishes to change the ideas and habits of the other. The most obvious and extreme case of such differences is when a team of Western-trained medical, nursing, and sanitary personnel with an urban background appear in a Mexican, Bolivian, or Brazilian Indian community where they cannot even speak the local language. Most public health workers would probably agree that in such a situation a properly trained anthropologist would be of help. However, it is frequently overlooked that medical, nursing, and sanitary personnel share a subculture of their own which distinguishes them from other members of their own Western society. When a public health officer starts or promotes a change of some condition in a community, he is suggesting that certain of his ideas should be imposed upon that community. From one point of view it makes no difference whether the community is the one in which the doctor was born, or belongs to an entirely different sociocultural group. In both cases, a person who believes and/or practices one habit wishes to impose this habit on a group of people who do not practice it. Hence, whether the public health officer is practicing in his own town or a foreign community, he is still trying to do the same thing: introduce changes in a system of socially shared habits.

In the relationship between a project organization and a subject society a major problem arises from the fact that the members of each group observe the behavior of the members of the opposite group and make judgments concerning them on the basis of the overt characteristics of this behavior. Public health personnel of Western background and training know how a public health doctor should act in our own society; but few know how he should act in a society of Indians speaking an indigenous tongue. It may strike an Indian as being rather peculiar that the doctor acts as if he were performing a favor, when the Indian himself has been feeling that it was he who was doing the favor in bringing his family in to be vaccinated. In Western society the public health officer who closes down a restaurant because it is unsanitary will probably not be thanked. This leads us to a basic problem which arises in the relationships between public health personnel and members of society: that of predicting behavior. To the degree that the public health officer can predict the behavior of the members of the community, he can adjust his methods to be more successful in obtaining his goals. Similarly, to the degree that members of the subject community can predict the behavior of the health officer, they can understand what he wants and adjust their behavior to conform to it or to combat it. When such prediction is impossible, however, the response one makes to the other may have little relation to the intended activity or goals of the other.

To use a current example, the present paper explores some of the relationships that can exist between anthropologists and public health personnel, two types of people who have distinctive subcultures within the framework of Western society. It attempts to make the behavior of anthropologists more predictable to workers in public health, for a certain amount of predictability is an absolute requirement of cooperative work.

Another point of some importance in the use of the social sciences in public health is the integration of such research work into the general planning and structure of a public health project. Thus far we have spoken of "anthropology" and "anthropologist" almost interchangeably. Actually, there can be a good deal of difference in employing anthropology on the one hand and an anthropologist on the other.

Although at one time the writer was of the opinion that the ultimate test of an anthropologist's success in a project would be whether or not his work would be self-eliminating, whether he could solve so many problems and train so many people so well that there would no longer be any problems to solve nor people to train, he is now convinced that this is a mistaken point of view. The anthropologist is a specialist trained to do certain types of work. Some of this work is not difficult to communicate to others and can be taught to other specialists. However, not all the problems encountered in public health programs can be easily solved; if they were, anthropologists might not be needed at all. The fact is that frequently these problems require the anthropologist to bring all his training and facilities to bear on the issue; he cannot easily or rapidly train specialists in other fields to do this.

Perhaps the most practical way of utilizing anthropology would be to provide other specialists—doctors, nurses, sanitarians, and so on—with enough grounding in the field of anthropology and human relations for them to think in its terms. Such a background, especially if strengthened with case work, can help them solve for themselves many of the problems that will confront them, and permit the anthropologist in a project to concentrate his efforts on those more difficult problems other specialized personnel are not trained to solve. Such an arrangement would require fewer services of an anthropologist and give project personnel the satisfaction of having solved their own problems.

This ideal situation, however, of public health specialists with some basic training in anthropology is far from a fact, so it is hardly realistic to base much planning for the immediate future on it. Where available, the anthropologist will, for some time to come, be responsible for carrying on much of the research in the social and cultural problems of specific projects.

Besides those distinctions made earlier between different kinds of research (problem, exploratory, and experimental research), it is also convenient to think of the research capacities of anthropology in terms of certain ways they integrate with the public health project. For this purpose, it is convenient to describe three general categories of investigations: *preliminary, in-service,* and *evaluation.*

a. *Preliminary investigations* are those carried on prior to the initiation of field work of a project within the subject society. It may be used in an exploratory manner in the subject society to obtain general sociocultural data and to search out points in the culture and social organization that might offer problems in the development of the project. It can equally be problem-centered or experimental to solve specific problems that are already recognized with respect to the subject society, or to test certain techniques or methods the project desires to use in the course of its work. Preliminary research cannot be focused practically on the organization since it is unlikely that the project organization exists prior to starting its work. However, an anthropologist with experience can be helpful in avoiding problems that might arise later due to inadequate organization structure.

The main value of preliminary research is that it can help avoid glaring errors at the outset. The public health doctor, nurse, or sanitary engineer has a great many professionally technical problems he must face in the course of the planning and development of a project. In view of the multitude of important factors involved, it is little discredit to the specialist if he fails to take factors of cultural differences, human relations, or other specialties in the social sciences into account in this planning. But such factors can be important. To take a single example, the writer has had occasion to review a number of initial project plans in which the planner had duly taken into account the latest available statistics on population density of the country he was planning for. However, in no case was it noted that the figure for density was based on the entire national territory, and that in some cases up to one half of the national territory was practically unoccupied. This presumably meant that either the figure for density had no meaning to the planner or that he had based his planning on a misleading figure. As an illustration, approximately 94 per cent of the Nicaraguan population is located in a little over one-half the national territory. A figure for density of population based on the entire territory would be very misleading. Also the figure given for density tells you nothing about the relative dispersal of the population in question. Is it concentrated in towns or scattered across the countryside in isolated homesteads?

In the ordinary situation, the planners of a public health program frequently are not allowed the time to make critical inquiries into the nature of the population for which they are planning. Just as often, they are not sufficiently familiar with the type of information that may be available and might be of great importance in their planning. The use of an anthropologist can make preliminary planning more realistic and avoid problems arising from the inability of the public health specialists to gather and analyze the mass of information that should be taken into account.

b. *In-service investigations* refer, as the borrowed term suggests, to research conducted during the course of a project. The most useful in-service research would probably be of a problem-centered or experimental nature. The middle of a project is not the time to be carrying on extensive exploratory studies. In-service investigations are most useful with respect to problems of organizational structure and relationships between the organization and society. Research during the course of a project can discover points of malfunctioning and bring hidden causes of trouble to the surface. In-service research can equally well be carried on with the focus on the subject society, in the solution of problems that arise after the project gets under way, and in the carrying on of experimental work. In practice, most anthropological work done to date in public health projects has been of this type.

c. *Evaluation research* is, as the name implies, research designed to evaluate some activity, phase of work, technique, or method. Evaluation research can be carried on during the course of a project or at its conclusion, but it differs from in-service research in that it is designed to evaluate the relative success or failure of work that has already been done. It is, in this sense, problem-centered. Because of its nature, it must be carried on after the activity in question has started, but it may be planned, and phases of it even initiated, prior to the beginning of the project. Evaluative research is so rare as to be almost hypothetical. The writer knows of no cases within his own experience in Latin America where a project of habit change of any dimension undertook preliminary studies of the habits that were to be the subject of the project, and then carried on periodic and final evaluative research to determine to what degree they had been successful in changing these habits. This has been done in experimental situations, but it has rarely been done consistently in large-scale or long-range projects. Unfortunately it is characteristic of a few workers in public health that they feel the amount of doing required for an activity is a measure of the effectiveness of that activity. An example of this is the evaluation some health educators will give of their work: the number of feet of movie film shown per month, the number of gallons of gasoline used in travel, the number of kilometers or miles covered in visits, the number of people working in the field, the number of meetings held with community members, the number of pamphlets published, etc. All of these are measures of activity, but none are even indices of the success of changing the habits of the population towards which they are directed.

In public health circles, the term "evaluation" has been in popular use for a number of years, but not in the sense of evaluation research. If an administrator feels his job is dependent upon showing results, he may be reluctant to encourage investigation that will show that such results have not been achieved. Also, it is very difficult for a person or team to arrive in the later or last stages of a project and try to evaluate the situation when no preliminary studies have been made. Too often evaluation has been of this nature, and administrators have been reasonably reluctant to have persons unfamiliar with the local situation pass judgment on it. When we speak of evaluative research, we are not referring to investigation committees but to regularly planned research as a part of a project, so that its members may know to what degree their own work is achieving the results it is designed to produce. What is being evaluated is not the capacity of the individuals, a matter of administrative concern, but the effectiveness of the activities, the techniques, and the methods being used in the project.

The subject of research in project work has been discussed at some length, since in the past few years it is in this area that anthropological contributions have been particularly noticeable and, it would appear, that anthropology may make one of its greatest contributions in the future.

IV. ANTHROPOLOGISTS AS CONSULTANTS

Another role anthropologists have played with respect to public health projects is that of consultant or advisor. This is one of the oldest roles of anthropologists in public health and, perhaps, one of the most misused. The author has written elsewhere (*Human Organization,* Vol. 12, No. 2, 1953, p. 12) of his concern with professional anthropologists who have never participated in applied work in the field but who will nonetheless be only too glad to offer advice on the basis of their general knowledge. We are not here concerned with these armchair consultants, however, but with anthropologists commissioned by a public health organization to act as a consultant to specific projects. . . .

To make consultancy services available, public health organizations could profitably begin a list of possible consultants for short-term consultancy in projects where a full-time anthropologist is not available or not needed. Such a list should be composed of persons who have spent some time working in the regions where they may be used, and a standard remuneration rate should be established. Anthropologists who have shown interest in public health work or have had some experience in similar applied work should be informed of the nature of such consultant assignments and be asked whether they would be available for call should such service be needed. With this list available, it would be possible to obtain consultancy service of experienced people for short periods of time at short notice.

It might be added for the sake of completeness that anthropological consultant work at higher administrative levels can also be of considerable value at times, although there has been relatively little use made of such consultants. It may be pointed out in passing that in Mexico anthropologists are serving specifically as administrators on general projects which include public health as one of their phases of work. This is mentioned to point out that in some places such a value is placed on the anthropologist's contribution to administration that he has been made the administrator.

V. THE USE OF SOCIAL SCIENTISTS IN TRAINING PROGRAMS

Earlier we mentioned some problems in the introduction of anthropology to public health administrators. Here we wish to take up another phase in the training of public health personnel with special references to Latin American countries currently carrying on programs to improve their public health services. In connection with the use of an anthropologist as a research person on specific projects it was mentioned earlier that much of the research work could be carried on by the specialized project personnel if they were trained. The training of project personnel in this manner presents a number of problems that need solution.

Theoretically, everyone working in positions in public health which require decisions as to the changing of people's habits should have a reasonably strong background in the social sciences. This background is not merely to make them more capable of carrying out their own work intelligently but, of greater importance, to make them more aware of what they are doing when they decide for one reason or another to change someone's habits. It is pretty presumptuous for one person to say to another that he does not like the way he lives and is going to start a project to change it; but this is precisely what workers in public health do. They say that the members of a certain population are too dirty, don't eat well, have unsanitary habits, or something of this kind, and that they are going to set about to change these habits. We need not go into the rationale behind this, since presumably all public health workers are thoroughly indoctrinated with it. What is needed is rather a tempering of this strong public health bias.

In addition to the people in decision-making positions who can profit by acquaintance with what we might call the philosophy of anthropology, the action personnel in projects and regular public health teams could benefit immensely from knowledge of the techniques of study and analysis used by some of the social sciences. To date, the writer's own concern in this matter has been in Central America, and so the following comments reflect specifically the problems he has met in that region. These problems, he believes, may well be found elsewhere, so they are probably not entirely unrepresentative of difficulties which are to be encountered in teaching anthropology and social sciences to public health workers elsewhere.

Many public health workers with whom the writer has worked have manifested one of two types of backgrounds; some had a very limited training, sometimes no more than primary school; and some received adequate background training, but this background has been very much slanted towards nonempirical, logical methods of thought. Each of these backgrounds offers its own problem. With respect to people who have very weak educational background, the principal problem is one of the complexity of the social sciences. The fields of anthropology, sociology, and related fields rest today on a changing body of theories, and the training of professional personnel in the various fields is principally on the postgraduate level. The people who study to become professionals in one of the specific fields have not only primary and high school background, but have finished their four years of college work. A great deal of what they learn in specialized social science courses becomes meaningful to them because they have been previously subjected to a liberal education. Their study of physics helps them to understand space, time, and motion concepts; a study of astronomy helps them to understand the concept of infinity; a study of philosophy and mathematics helps them to understand the concepts of empiricism, rationalism, logic, the philosophy of science; their study of psychology helps them to comprehend the forces which operate in the human body; their study of history and archaeology helps them to view the past as the antecedent of the present; their study of geography, zoology, and botany help them to comprehend the extensive complexness of the earth and its living creatures; their study of various sciences provides them with the training to draw conclusions, a most important ability; and so on. Each student brings with him to his graduate specialization a broad range of concepts which will help him in his understanding of the concepts used in the social sciences.

What does all this have to do with public health? Just this: a great many workers in the lower echelons of public health are not equipped with a background in liberal education that provides them with the conceptual tools they can use to understand a short course in some phase of the social sciences. Frequently, in order to provide a course which would be meaningful to trainees, the writer has found it necessary to go back so far to fundamental concepts and points of view that it was not possible to get across most of the ideas that would have been most profitable for them in the limited time available.

With respect to the public health personnel who have adequate or extensive educational backgrounds, the problem is considerably different but not less difficult. Whereas the person of poor educational background does not have the basic concepts for understanding much of social science, the educated man frequently shows a remarkable lack of scientific perspective in social situations. In the writer's experience, one particular factor has stood out as an obstacle to the teaching of social science techniques and methods: very few of the people whom he taught could draw a conclusion which was based on specific evidence. Sometimes with a body of written data directly in front of them (and it was often data they themselves had collected), they failed to draw a conclusion that had any relation to the evidence. It should be pointed out that in some cases these men had much broader and more extensive educations and more years of experience than the writer. But there was manifest the very serious defect of assurance to what a conclusion would be without ever needing to gather the data at all. Drawing conclusions, like anything else one tries to do systematically, requires experience and practice; there is nothing magical about it, nor does it require a genius to do so. But it does require training and *doing*.

Of course most professional personnel in public health can draw conclusions that rest on evidence; too often, however, in social and cultural matters, they do not do it. Similarly, it is not a question of whether or not the undereducated personnel of the lower echelons of public health are capable of learning the materials of anthropology and the other social sciences; it is a practical matter of their not initially having in their hands the tools to handle brief courses in the social sciences effectively.

Anthropology and the social sciences have two specific things to offer the worker in public health: a point of view that will promote the worker's understanding of the population in which he is working, and some specific techniques and methods for finding the solutions to particular problems. It is difficult to say which of these is more important, but undoubtedly the second is more frequently requested. Administrators of field projects have asked the writer from time to time if it would be possible for him to give a lecture, a few conferences, or a short course "just to help the field people out." While in sympathy with the desire to provide field personnel with an introduction to anthropology, the writer tries to avoid such requests since he feels that such efforts are almost futile.

There are certain conditions the writer believes must be met before a course in anthropology or some phases of it can be expected to be of any use to field personnel in public health programs:

First of all, the number of hours of the course and the time span over which it is spread must be decided in terms of the educational background of the personnel. This means that we cannot say at the outset that 10 hours or 50 hours of class work is necessary, nor can we say that one month or one year is required. However, except in the teaching of specific techniques to persons already capable of comprehending the theory behind them, we may as well eliminate short courses of a week or two from serious consideration.

Second, the subject matter to be taken up in such a course ought to be carefully planned with the administrator of the training project in order that the specific phases of social science that are included will be of some real utility. Anthropology is a broad discipline in itself, and it is only one of the social sciences. The choice of specific materials to be included is not an easy problem to solve *a priori*. This means that the person who is to give the course should have an introductory period to get to know the general background of the students and the nature of the general problems they will be facing in their work.

Third, there is no doubt that anthropology can make a highly important contribution to field training, but it is not realistic to attempt to give field training without some accompanying theory, discussion, and reading. The writer has encountered the feeling among some administrators that since field experience is very important it can be introduced without loss of time in lectures and discussions. This is like giving a child a series of blocks and telling him to build a toy skyscraper when he has never heard of a skyscraper.

Meeting these conditions would go a long way towards making the training of project personnel in anthropology more successful. One way of making it possible to achieve such conditions is to attach a social scientist to a project for a limited period of time, allowing him sufficient time in advance to learn the needs of the trainees, to plan a course around these needs in consultation with the project administrators, and to coordinate formal course work with in-service training for the personnel. A real advantage to be derived from having an anthropologist attached to such a project is that it permits him to become more familiar with the culture in which the project personnel have to work, and to place more emphasis on those phases of study which will help them to comprehend better the situation in which they find themselves. It should be remembered, however, that if a social scientist is attached to a project in such a capacity, the amount of time devoted to research for the project will be severely restricted.

While training in the course of project work can be of great help to the personnel involved, it must not be thought that it can replace such training provided in schools of public health, nursing, etc., where public health personnel receive their intensive introduction to the problems of public health. Until many of these problems are seen as being connected with human relations and habit change, they will continue to provide problems that cannot be solved by ordinary public health methods. Training and education in such concepts can best be offered at the same time the individual is learning what such problems are from the point of view of their own profession. . . .

9

On the Effective Use of Anthropology in Public Health Programs: A Letter to the Editor

Anne Burgess

This letter to the editor of *Human Organization* appeared after the publication of the preceding article (Selection 8) by Richard N. Adams.

To the Editor:

" 'By experience,' says Roger Ascham, 'we find out a short way by a long wandering.' Not seldom that long wandering unfits us for further travel, and of what use is our experience to us then?" [1] At least it may enable us to cry to those who came after, "This way is good. Use it, I implore you!"

Reprinted from *Human Organization*, **14,** 4 (Winter 1956), p. 2, by permission of The Society for Applied Anthropology.

Anne Burgess is Acting Deputy Director, General Council for Health Education, London.
[1] Thomas Hardy, *Tess of the d'Ubervilles*, Chapter 15.

When, after a "long wandering" in the field of Maternal and Child Health among Malay, Chinese, and Indian peasant and working-class people in a tropical country, I first read Dr. Foster's report, "A Cross-Cultural Anthropological Analysis of a Technical Aid Program," I was astounded at the similarity of so many of the situations and beliefs he describes to those I had encountered in a very different part of the world. Here were the ideas I had found so puzzling—the "hotness" of coffee and the "coldness" of tea, and other foods or medicines; the strange ways that "Wind" could enter the body and create havoc; the need to cover the baby's fontanelle or the toddler's umbilicus (though the rest of the body could be most engagingly naked!); the anxiety about the proper disposal of the placenta; the sympathetic but "superior" attitude of some of the personnel in hospital or clinic. Since then I have read other publications by different anthropologists interested in Public Health, and have always found something that would have been immensely useful to my work, if only I had known it at the right time—ten or fifteen years ago. Certainly if I had seen one description [2] of the position and practices of the traditional midwife in a valley in Peru, my approach to what seems to me now a fantastically similar situation in some of the rural areas of Malaya would have been entirely different, and probably much more effective.

In his thoughtful article, "On the Effective Use of Anthropology in Public Health Programs," Adams points out that the anthropologist can offer the public health worker two things—a point of view, and a knowledge of certain techniques. There is no doubt in my mind as to which is the more important. I can forgive myself for not knowing the anthropological techniques—after all I was medically trained. I find I cannot forgive myself for the lack of "the thoughts of the imagination" which prevented me from respecting a system of medical beliefs which were "foreign" to me, and apparently ineffective as far as child health was concerned.

Luckily, my Scottish upbringing made it easy for me to recognize the mothers as women the same as myself trying to cope with the problems of bringing up a family, pleasing a husband, earning a living, and fitting into life as we found it—and this created a definite bond of sympathy between us which mitigated, to some extent, my regrettable intolerance of blue dye on the wrists as a cure for some childish complaint. But the bond was not strong enough to withstand absence and time, and ten years later I found things being done much the same as they had always been done and that indeed "knowledge without thought is labor lost."

We who have worked without the skilled guidance which the anthropologist has to offer and realize our past inadequacies and failures can, more than anyone, appreciate fully the enormous advantages to be gained from

---

[2] Edward Wellin, "Pregnancy, Childbirth and Midwifery in the Valley of Ica, Peru." Mimeographed Memorandum, Ica Anthropology Project sponsored by WHO and Minister of Public Health and Welfare, Peru, 1953.

such cooperation. I would, therefore say to all my fellow, but younger and more fortunate, workers in Public Health, and particularly in Child Welfare, "use the help of the anthropologists wherever possible. It will save you time, money, energy, disappointment, and frustration. It will also lessen your regrets when you too are 'unfit for further travel.' But like everything else, this knowledge and guidance have their price. No longer will you be able to educate by 'teaching'—confident in your own scientific rightness and the ultimate triumph of proven facts. You will have to use your brains and imagination as well as your factual knowledge to fit this knowledge to the pattern that the anthropologist has disclosed. You will have to behave less like a tram and more like a trolley bus—clinging to your factual lifeline, but maneuvering with patience and skill—and this will take much time and energy. And worst of all, you will have to learn humility, which is difficult for the medical profession—not because we are innately more arrogant than others, but because our training, traditionally and even today, lays tremendous emphasis on the production of 'curers' who tend to rely on the oracular utterance which cannot be questioned. Unhappily, our oracular utterances cut no ice in the countries where most of the world's children live—and have to be replaced by more patient explanations and discussions. The price is high, but not unreasonable. If we would help other people to change their habits, it is perhaps only fair that we should begin by changing our own."

Sincerely yours,

ANNE BURGESS, M.B., Ch.B.,
Formerly Lady Medical Officer,
Malayan Medical Service,
Acting Deputy Director, General
Council for Health Education, London.

10

Changing Markets and Media in Latin America

Leo Bogart

When he was Vice President of the Market Planning Corporation division of McCann-Erickson, Inc., Dr. Bogart, a sociologist, wrote the following study of the problems facing foreign investors with special reference to the problems of those investors facing the mass market. He points out that advertising, in particular, must be specifically geared to a certain audience in spite of the fact that "the normally acute technical problems involved in obtaining valid broadcast ratings are even more difficult in Latin America than they are in the United States." He emphasizes the necessity for understanding not only the existing cultures, but the ways in which the cultures of Latin American are changing.

The foreign marketer, especially the marketer from the United States, is a prime mover in the transformation of Latin-American [1] economic life. He is therefore a significant figure, if not always a beloved one, in relation to Latin-American mass communications media. He is deeply involved in politics, willy-nilly. To circumvent the high tariffs which confront him as an exporter, he is forced to invest in overseas manufacturing operations. But the nationalistic drive for industrial development and diversification often imposes sharp restrictions on foreign ownership or majority control of local companies. He faces a welter of import and currency regulations.

In every aspect of his business, the marketer must weigh political factors to which he would not give a second thought in the United States—in his investments, in his pricing policy, in his plant location, in his employee relations, in the character of his competition with local companies. As a foreigner, he experiences culture clash and conflict in all the human relations aspects of his business—in coping with government bureaucracies which seem even more mysterious and baffling than those which speak his language, in handling employees accustomed to a different pace of work and a different

Reprinted from *The Public Opinion Quarterly*, **23**, 2 (Summer 1959), pp. 159–167, by special permission of the publisher and the author.

Leo Bogart is Vice President, Marketing Planning and Research, Bureau of Advertising, American Newspaper Publishers' Association.

[1] It goes without saying that the term "Latin America" embraces republics which vary widely in their cultural values, their social systems, their ethnic composition, their technological development, and their closeness to the kind of generalizations with which this article abounds.

relationship with their employer, in dealing with a general public suspicious of foreign enterprise, and in winning customers whose values, tastes, and shopping habits differ radically from those with which he is familiar. His customary relationships with wholesalers and retail dealers no longer apply to the local network of distribution, which not only may have distinctive methods of operating but also is apt to be deeply involved with vested political and social class interests.

Any foreign enterprise entering a country with a limited or antiquated economy becomes a force working toward social change. The most striking evidence for such an obvious statement is no doubt to be found in the far-reaching effects of the oil industry on the economies and social patterns of such countries as Venezuela or Saudi Arabia. But foreign marketing institutions have had an influence which, though far less dramatic than that of an extractive industry, is probably far more penetrating and universal in the long run. A basic enterprise like mining or oil production normally affects only a limited number of individuals in a country from the standpoint of direct employment, though the secondary impact, as a result of increased revenues for the state, may be enormous. But a large-scale marketer of goods or services is in constant communication with the broad masses of consumers. Such a company exerts incessant pressure to modernize the system of distribution; its investments in local manufacturing facilities may provide an important spur to economic growth. Marketing activities modify the cultural and social climate by building and changing consumer tastes and patterns of eating, housing, dress, and recreation.

International marketers represent important sources of new ideas, not merely by virtue of the fact that they import and apply the methods of the advanced industrial countries but also because they are in a position to pool their experiences among the less developed countries within which they operate. Each country becomes a test market for a new product, a promotion, an advertising campaign, a new type of packaging, or a new form of retailing.

This essay, then, examines the communications system in Latin America as an aspect of the region's marketing institutions rather than from a political, cultural, or journalistic point of view. We begin by discussing the special characteristics of marketing within Latin America and then see how they are reflected in the media and in media and marketing research.

DEFINING "THE MARKET"

Disraeli once said that there are only two nations in the world, the privileged and the poor. If this is still particularly evident in Latin America,[2] it is by no means clear where one should draw the boundary between the two.

---

[2] At the same time that one normally thinks of Latin America in terms of sharp contrast between opulence and wretched poverty, it must be remembered that since

In the tropical countries with large impoverished rural populations of non-European stock, businessmen sometimes talk of "the market" as though it were confined to those people whose living arrangements are in the Western style and who strive for a Western standard. These may constitute only a fraction of the total population, concentrated in the major cities and within the better residential quarters.

In the absence of a middle class, it is often tempting to the advertiser to intensively cultivate the small segment of the market which can presently afford what he has to sell rather than to go about the thankless and long-range task of building a mass market for his products. This philosophy is summed up in the following statement from a brochure sent out by a large international publication with (of course!) an elite audience:

It is dangerous to spend advertising appropriations attempting to appeal to the millions, most of whom have no buying potential. It is enough of a task for any advertising budget merely to concentrate on those who *do* have the buying power, and to aim *to turn these prospects into buyers of your particular product.* The goal of the advertiser in Latin America, therefore, should be to reach *not* the largest number of people, but the largest number of *prospects.* The advertiser in Latin America should concentrate not on turning *people* into *prospects,* but in turning *prospects* into *customers.*

But the elite group almost never accounts for the total demand for mass-manufactured products. However low the income of the urban worker, if he is regularly employed he must be classified as part of "the market" for branded merchandise. In this respect, he differs from the aborigines in the jungle or the primitive rural folk on the plains or mountains who farm at the subsistence level, almost outside the money economy. Yet even these impoverished masses are not clearly outside "the market."

The rate of urbanization in Latin America has proceeded at such a rapid pace in recent years [3] that there is a never-ending flow of migrants from the rural areas, impelled by poverty and attracted by the economic opportunities of town life. These folk, as yet unaccustomed to city ways, populate the shantytown slums on the fringe of urban society.[4] Their employment is marginal and irregular. As they adapt themselves to the city, they may leave

---

1950, consumption and gross product for the area have each risen by nearly 40 per cent (in constant monetary values), with all that this implies for a rising standard of living. (Population increased 18 per cent in the same period. On the other hand, 40 per cent of the adult population of Latin America is illiterate, with variations, of course, from country to country.)

[3] Urban population as a percentage of the total rose from 39 to 44 per cent in the past decade. The population of cities over 100,000 grew by 31 per cent in Cuba, by 38 per cent in Brazil and Mexico, by 72 per cent in Venezuela, by 94 per cent in Colombia.

[4] Most famous and populous are the *favelas* of Rio de Janeiro, which house hundreds of thousands of people. They cluster ubiquitously on the hills throughout the city, often cheek by jowl with elegant, modern apartment and office buildings.

their squatters' hovels and merge into the settled urban proletariat, to be replaced in turn from the unending trickle of new migrants.

Just as the businessman normally does not consider the rural population to be part of his market, real or potential, so he is apt to ignore the marginal shantytown element in the city. Only rarely do market surveys attempt to include it in their samples. This is partly because of the difficulties involved in applying systematic sampling procedures to streetless clusters of shacks and in getting the cooperation of the inhabitants for successful interviewing. It is usually assumed that the purchasing power of these people is so low that it is impossible to sell them anything, and that they are, moreover, so separated from the main stream of urban life that they are virtually beyond reach of the mass media. But this is by no means necessarily true. A recent survey in Rio shows that a large proportion of the *favela* shanties contain radios and that some even have television sets. Just as an American would find no cause for surprise in TV antennas atop New York tenements or hillbilly shacks in the Ozarks, so the sight of TV aerials sprouting from the tin or thatched roofs of a Latin American slum represents no incongruity for the people who live in it.

THE MASS MEDIA

Significant pressure toward social change comes, inevitably, by way of the mass media. Mass media reflect marketing activity directly in the form of advertising and indirectly in the form of entertainment content whose symbols and settings (almost always drawn from the ideal world whose standards are better than one's own) reinforce advertising goals.

Latin-American newspapers, magazines, radio, and television are strongly influenced by their counterparts in the United States. They reflect the values of the well-to-do, educated minority which controls the mass media. They also show the influence of American trade publications and business organizations which deal with the technical aspects of the media (*Editor and Publisher, Broadcasting-Telecasting, Printers' Ink,* and the like).

In its radio soap operas, its "true romances," and its paperback thrillers, Latin America is in the mainstream of Western popular culture with its fountainheads in Hollywood and Radio City. As a growing influence, television differs from the other media not so much in kind as in degree. American TV programs dubbed into Spanish or with Spanish titles are sold through the international departments of the large package-producing and syndicate firms. Old feature films are staple fare on Latin-American television channels, as on those in the United States. The quiz show, the give-away program, the amateur hour, and other familiar features of American broadcasting are readily adapted to local formats. Leading television personalities are important figures in the daily gossip, the business life, and even the public affairs of the nation.

Television

At most recent count, there were 82 television stations in Latin America (including relay transmitters which do not originate programs) and 1,700,-000 receivers. In most countries of Latin America, television, if it exists at all, is limited to a few channels in the principal cities. This reflects the economics of the medium—the high cost of transmitting equipment, and substantial operating costs.

While television studios and station facilities in some countries may be as modern and lavish as any in the world, in others programs are produced under relatively primitive conditions.[5] In a tour of Latin America, the traveler can actually relive the development of television (now already a matter of history in the United States) as he goes from one country to the next. In the centers of old Caribbean towns like San Juan and Havana, one can look through the enormous open windows with which most houses face the street and see families sitting around the television set of an evening. In Panama, there are the same kind of house and the same interiors, but though the radio may be blaring music the inhabitants are apt to be just sitting and passing away time. Similarly, the visitor to Peru or Chile notes with a jolt that the console radio occupies the same focal position in the living room of an upper-middle-class home as it did in the America of the thirties and forties, or as the TV set does today. (In Lima, UNESCO has an experimental TV station in operation, but only a handful of sets have been sold.) In Montevideo, the television era is in its first dawning. Sets in the windows of radio and department stores draw large crowds of casual promenaders—with the prosperous elements of the community as well represented as any other. Here television is still a fascinating toy, to be observed not because of any interest in what it communicates but because of the miracle that it communicates at all. A hand appears on the screen and over a leisurely ten minutes sketches a cartoon advertising a furniture store. Through it all the audience remains raptly attentive. In Bogotá the crowd which gathers outside the radio shop window is blasé; it knows exactly what programs come on when, and it is interested in the spectacle rather than in the novelty of the medium as such. Here, television is an established phenomenon.

---

[5] In Colombia, for example, the government has a TV monopoly, though it permits commercial sponsorship of programs. Since no funds have been made available for a studio building, programs emanate from a few small rooms in the National Library. The same studio must be used for successive programs. This has its humorous aspects, as when a quiz show featuring a panel of distinguished citizens is followed by another program which provides entertainment by reviewing the hard-luck stories of a selection of particularly pitiable charity cases. The camera turns to the wall to film a succession of still commercials and announcements while the learned doctors rush out of the single exit to make way for large families of barefooted Indians simultaneously rushing in to do their stint.

Radio and the Press

The situation in television is in striking contrast to the tradition of extreme competitiveness within media whose capital requirements are more modest.[6] In the case of radio and the press, the major Latin American cities have a large number of media (by United States standards) in relation to the size of the potential audience. Nicaragua, with 30,000 radios, has 32 radio stations; Ecuador has 100,000 radios and 68 stations; El Salvador has 22 stations competing for the attention of its 24,000 radio sets.[7] In total, there are about 1,000 stations in Latin America (the number has tripled in the past decade) and nearly 13,000,000 radios.

There are also over 900 newspapers circulating 15,600,000 copies, and nearly 600 magazines and other periodicals with a combined circulation of 15,000,000. The proliferation of print media derives at least partly from political tradition. As in Europe, where also there are many parties, each one requires its own organ of expression to maintain contact with its adherents and give them a means of daily reaffirming their own political identity.

It is hard to build up a publishing empire in most Latin American countries (the vast Chateaubriant holdings in Brazil are the notable exception) because there are usually not enough substantial cities to make chain or syndicate operations feasible on a national basis. Since operating expenses are low, it is relatively easy for a marginal publishing or broadcasting enterprise to survive, especially because its claims to an audience receive little critical scrutiny from many prospective advertisers.

The overall effect of having many competitive media fighting over a limited audience and limited revenues is to reduce the audiences, revenues, and resources of all media, a condition which does not improve their professional caliber but which does permit an unusually large number of people to pursue the occupations of journalist and broadcaster.

---

[6] How fierce the competition gets may be suggested by the following anecdote: On a recent visit to one Latin American country, the writer remarked in an interview with a local journalist that about half of all United States advertising goes into newspapers. This remark was headlined in the press as "Newspapers are the best advertising medium, says U. S. expert." This provoked a strong counterattack from the radio broadcasters' association, which demanded the issuance of a new statement affirming the superiority of radio as an advertising medium.

[7] In Cuba, an "old" television country with widespread set ownership in metropolitan Havana, with substantial economic resources and good-sized advertising budgets, the TV pattern follows that of radio broadcasting. There are 6 television channels in the city of Havana and about 30 radio stations, all fighting for a share of the audience's time and of advertising expenditures. (To put the figures on Latin-American media into perspective, it may be pointed out that the United States, with 47,500,000 homes, has 3,344 AM radio stations for about 146,000,000 radio sets, and 522 TV stations for nearly 49,000,000 TV sets.)

International Media

Many of the countries in Latin America are too small, or have too small a literate population within reach of the media, to be able to support publications or broadcasting institutions comparable to those possible in a bigger economy. This adds to the importance of international media, which are further stimulated by the common use of Spanish as the national language in all but two of the Latin American republics.

Although international radio networks have been put together in Latin America at various times, none has been able to obtain the advertising support necessary to operate on a regular and continuing basis. Nothing similar has yet been attempted with television, and the technical difficulties in international broadcasting through this medium will not be surmounted for many years. Because of the vast distances in Latin America and the importance of speed in conveying the news, newspapers have never been able to function on any large scale as an international medium. Radio and newspaper audiences often cut across national boundaries into neighboring countries, but these media are ordinarily aimed at audiences within their own countries.

This leaves magazines as the major field in which media have circulated in substantial numbers across national borders, making it possible for their content to reflect the interests of the area as a whole or broad segments within it. The leading international magazines cover the Hemisphere as a whole. Some, like *Bohemia,* reach into only part of the region. Still others, like *Selecciones* (*Reader's Digest*) offer distinct regional editions to the advertiser.

National borders set limitations on international media in at least three ways, even when (as is the case in Hispanic America) there are no language barriers to overcome:

1. Borders generally interpose some technical obstruction to the free circulation of print media. Duties, licensing fees, or transportation costs usually raise the price of the publication above that in the home country. Postal or other transportation delays may impede the timely appearance of the magazine.[8]

2. Unless a medium sets out deliberately to be international in its outlook, its editorial or programing formula is apt to show a national parochialism which weakens its appeal in other places. The exception occurs where a substantial element in one country consciously or unconsciously incorporates many of the values of another country (as the Latin-American urban middle class does with respect to the consumption values of the United States).

3. Advertising revenues are circumscribed by virtue of the fact that most advertisers market within national territories and do not want their efforts

---

[8] An American living in one South American country subscribed to a magazine which was mailed directly to his office. When this publication did not arrive for a period of several weeks, he got into the habit of buying it at the newsstand in the building in which he worked. One day he bought his own subscription copy.

spread outside their boundaries in the form of waste circulation. For the local (national) advertiser, a medium's circulation beyond the national territory is by definition a loss. Actually the international advertiser has his own problems, since his operations in different countries are apt to be administratively and financially autonomous, and his advertising budgets are accordingly set by different individuals and to different specifications in each country.

AUDIENCE RESEARCH

Audience research in Latin America has been pioneered by American-owned publications like *Life en Español, Selecciones,* and *Visión,* which deal with international (predominantly United States) advertisers accustomed to verification of readership claims.

The traditional reluctance of Latin American media to investigate the size and character of their own audiences has slowly given way in the face of pressure from international advertisers accustomed to developing their schedules on the basis of accurate audience research. Where the media themselves have refused to make a move in this direction, the advertisers have sometimes made it themselves, usually by tacking media exposure questions to the tail ends of market research questionnaires.

Some large American-owned companies have actually conducted radio and television surveys of their own on a continuing basis. In several countries (Cuba, Mexico, Puerto Rico, Venezuela, Brazil) ratings surveys are offered on a regular subscription basis by private research firms.

Where advertising agencies, associations of advertisers, or other interested parties have conducted audience surveys of their own and then gone on to publish the results, the research has not uncommonly met attack from disgruntled media—not on technical grounds, but usually by impugning the honesty of the results.

Local advertisers and broadcasters unfamiliar with modern research techniques and practices often assume that research firms are venal.[9] It is quite likely that some actually are, for in one or two Latin American countries there are rating services which claim to be based on samples of a size that could not possibly be covered by the income from their subscription charges.

It is not uncommon for a radio station to broadcast exhortations to its listeners reminding them of what to reply if they happen to be interviewed in an audience survey. In some cases, the listeners have been told that they might win a prize if they give an interviewer the name of the particular station—whether or not they are actually listening to it.

Unfortunately, there are no professional research associations active in the

---

[9] The director of one rating service reports that when he recently refused a bribe proffered by a radio station owner he was met with hurt indignation: "What have you got against me—when you obviously must be taking money from all the other stations with higher ratings than mine?"

region which might be in a position to suggest, much less enforce, a code of technical or ethical standards. The businessman who is naïve on the subject has no way of distinguishing proper methods from improper ones. And although the bad research cannot really drive out the good, it does at least make its acceptance much more difficult. Paradoxically, one of the very factors that inhibits establishment of professional research associations is the reluctance of the legitimate practitioners to sit down at the same table with some of the more shady pretenders to the craft.

Ethics aside, the normally acute technical problems involved in obtaining valid broadcast ratings are even more difficult in Latin America than they are in the United States. Telephone ownership is not sufficiently widespread to permit telephone coincidental interviewing, nor is literacy high enough to make a diary method feasible. The market is not wealthy enough to support a mechanical measurement system like the Nielsen Audimeter. Coincidental home interviews or some variation of the roster recall technique are therefore most commonly employed. Both methods require many thousands of interviews for a single survey and thereby make it harder to keep the cost of research down to a point which represents reasonable value to the subscriber.

This is, in fact, probably the greatest problem that confronts the researcher in Latin America. It goes without saying that to achieve a given degree of statistical accuracy it is necessary to interview just as many people for a market or audience survey in Tegucigalpa, Honduras, as for one in New York. The American advertiser may spend millions of dollars to get his message across, whereas in Honduras he may spend only a few thousand or even a few hundred dollars. Yet to invest his budget wisely, he needs exactly the same kind of information in the one case as in the other. Therefore, the ratio of his research costs to his total marketing costs must normally be higher in the smaller market than in the larger one.

The problem is often met by doing research with smaller samples than would normally be used in the United States or Europe, and/or by confining the interviewing to the principal city or cities, where interviewing costs can be kept to a minimum, where respondents are most apt to be informed and cooperative, and where, after all, both purchasing power and political influences are apt to be concentrated. This altogether necessary and innocent practice may create problems, insofar as there may be an almost unconscious tendency of the research user to project the findings to the country as a whole.

The impact of survey research upon marketing practices in South America is reflected in a curious tendency on the part of some corporate managements to invest the "A, B, C, D" social class categories of quota sampling with independent reality rather than to consider them as a convenient descriptive device. This simple, if somewhat brittle, view of society is revealed even where research has neither been done nor contemplated. A sales manager may, as a matter of course, refer to a "B" neighborhood or "C" house-wives, without really considering what the terms represent in social status, life style, housing, occupation, income, or education.

CONCLUSION

The enormous expansion of Latin America's capacity to consume carries with it the promise of important social changes in the years to come. Peasant masses are being urbanized and becoming part of the effective market for mass-produced manufactured commodities. Their buying appetites are stimulated not only by constant contact with goods in the expanding channels of retail trade, but also through increasing exposure to the mass media which, through advertising and entertainment content, emphasize consumption values in the North American pattern.

The process of change is accelerated by the rapid adaptation of United States concepts and techniques of retailing, merchandising, advertising, sales promotion, and market research.

The greatest obstacle to the expansion of Latin America's marketing economy stems from the isolation of economic units which follow political boundaries. Latin American countries trade primarily with the United States and Europe, only to a minor extent among themselves. This isolation limits the effectiveness of marketing activities, which can be conducted more efficiently in larger units. The rise of international magazines, and the probable future growth of international radio and television broadcasting, may help to overcome the obstacle and in a small way encourage the creation of a common market which, in Latin America even more than Europe, holds promise for economic expansion.

Chapter Three

Role

ROLE REFERS to the behavior that is expected of an individual occupying a specific social position. Role may be visualized by thinking of a football team. Each play calls for certain actions on the part of each man in each position. Performance in the role may, of course, vary from poor to excellent—and with it, the success or failure of the play. In a sense, though, the play is independent of the specific individual who occupies any certain position—any individual who is at that position has a definite, assigned task on each play.

An individual plays as many roles as he has social positions. *Role conflict* has been succinctly illustrated by Killian in his discussion of the recovery of Texas City from a tornado a few years ago. A state patrolman had to make a choice between his role as a police officer and his role as friend and neighbor to the people of the community in which he was stationed: "As I drove around town after the tornado had passed I realized that the best thing I could do was to try to make contact with the outside and get help from there. I started out to drive to the next town and try to call from there. As I drove out of town people I knew well would call me by name and ask me to help them find their relatives. Driving by and not stopping to help those people who were looking to me as a friend was one of the hardest things I ever had to do." [1]

Seldom does one experience such a sharp conflict of duties. Yet every student is familiar with the choice that

[1] Lewis M. Killian, "The Significance of Multiple-Group Membership in Disaster," *American Journal of Sociology*, **57**, 4 (January 1952), p. 312.

must sometimes be made between "being a good Joe" and making high scholastic marks.

A less dramatic inner conflict may arise from the fact that all individuals and groups do not perceive a given role in the same way. Many types of *role ambiguity* occur. For example, examine the role of public school superintendent.[2] Teachers, school board members, local merchants, parents, and school children each may have somewhat different *role-expectancies* of that superintendent, and each expectancy may call for different actions on his part. Sometimes the same individual will even have contradictory expectancies of the superintendent's role. In addition, a role player may have his own expectancies. Such a situation is described by Campbell and Pettigrew (Selection 11) in their analysis of the Little Rock ministers in that city's integration crisis. When, as in Selection 11, two or more different kinds of behavior are thought to be appropriate action for an individual holding a certain social position, the term *role ambivalence* is sometimes used. A more subtle type of conflict is illustrated in Wispé's article (Selection 12), which analyzes the role problems of salesmen. Which of two or more roles does the individual choose to play? How is his decision reached?

Although perhaps most learning of one's roles is unreflective, certain roles may be quite consciously practiced. Haskell and Weeks (Selection 13) describe the deliberate use of role playing as a device for preparing prisoners to resume life in the community.

[2] See Melvin Seeman, "Role Conflict and Ambivalence in Leadership," *American Sociological Review*, **18**, 4 (August 1953), pp. 373–380.

11

Racial and Moral Crisis:
The Role of Little Rock Ministers

Ernest Q. Campbell and Thomas F. Pettigrew

Role ambiguity comes about when there is more than one set
of expectations for a particular role at a given time; our understanding of human behavior has been increased to the extent that
we recognize this important fact. From the following selection, for
example, we may gain insight into the behavior of clergymen
whose actions might appear "hypocritical" to those who expect
strong moral leadership.

This paper analyzes the conduct of the ministers in established denominations in Little Rock, Arkansas, during the crisis over the admission of Negro
students to the Central High School in the fall of 1957. How do ministers
behave in racial crisis, caught between integrationist and segregationist forces?

One might expect that Little Rock's clergymen would favor school integration. All the major national Protestant bodies have adopted forceful
declarations commending the Supreme Court's desegregation decision of 1954
and urging their members to comply with it. And southern pastors have
voted in favor of these statements at their church conferences—and sometimes have even issued similar pronouncements to their own congregations.[1]
But the southern man of God faces serious congregational opposition if he
attempts to express his integrationist beliefs publicly in the local community.
The vast majority of southern whites—even those living in the Middle South
—are definitely against racial desegregation.[2]

Reprinted from *American Journal of Sociology*, **64**, 5, (March 1959), pp. 509–516, by
permission of The University of Chicago Press and the authors.

Ernest Q. Campbell is Associate Professor of Sociology, University of North Carolina.

Thomas F. Pettigrew is Associate Professor of Social Psychology, Harvard University.

This study was supported by a grant from the Laboratory of Social Relations, Harvard
University. The authors wish to express their gratitude to Professor Samuel A. Stouffer
for his suggestions.

[1] For example, local ministerial groups issued such statements in New Orleans, Loui-
siana; Richmond, Virginia; Dallas and Houston, Texas; and Atlanta, Macon, and Columbus, Georgia. For a review of national church statements see "Protestantism Speaks
on Justice and Integration," *Christian Century*, **75** (February 5, 1958), pp. 164–66.

[2] A 1956 National Opinion Research Center poll indicated that only one in every
seven white southerners approves school integration (H. H. Hyman and P. B. Sheatsley,
"Attitudes toward Desegregation," *Scientific American*, **195** [December 1956], pp. 35–
39). A 1956 survey by the American Institute of Public Opinion showed that in the
Middle South—including Arkansas—only one in five whites approved of school integration (M. M. Tumin, *Segregation and Desegregation* [New York: Anti-Defamation
League of B'nai B'rith, 1957], p. 109).

The purpose of this study is to determine how the ministers of established denominations in Little Rock behaved in the conflict. In analyzing their behavior, we treat self-expectations as an independent variable. This is contrary to the usual course, in which the actor is important analytically only because he is caught between contradictory *external* expectations. The standard model of role conflict treats ego as forced to decide between the incompatible norms of groups that can impose sanctions for nonconformity. This model—which is essentially what Lazarsfeld means by cross-pressures— skirts the issue of whether ego imposes expectations on itself and punishes deviations. Pressure and sanction are external to the actor. Hence the typical model tends to be ahistorical in the sense that a finite number of cross-pressuring groups are used to predict the actor's behavior. It is assumed that the actor cannot have developed from periods of prior socialization any normative expectations for his behavior which would have an independent existence.[3] This additional variable—the actor's expectations of himself— is especially meaningful in the analysis.

Though it is a city of approximately 125,000, Little Rock has much of the atmosphere and easy communication of a small town. It is located in almost the geometric center of the state, and physically and culturally it borders on both the Deep South—like delta country to the east and south and the Mountain South—like hill country to the west and north. Thus Little Rock is not a city of the Deep South. Its public transportation had been successfully integrated in 1956, and its voters, as late as March, 1957, had elected two men to the school board who supported the board's plan for token integration of Central High School. And yet Little Rock is a southern city, with southern traditions of race relations. These patterns became of worldwide interest after Governor Faubus called out the National Guard to prevent desegregation and thereby set off the most publicized and the most critical chain of events in the integration process to date.

Only two ministers devoted their sermons to the impending change on the Sunday before the fateful opening of school in September, 1957. Both warmly approved of the step and hoped for its success. Other ministers alluded to it in prayer or comment. It was commonly believed that a majority of the leading denominations' clergy favored the school board's "gradual"

---

[3] By showing that the actor may have a predisposition toward either a particularistic or a universalistic "solution" to role conflicts in instances where the particularistic-universalistic dimension is relevant, Stouffer and Toby link the study of personality to that of role obligations in a way rarely done (Samuel A. Stouffer and Jackson Toby, "Role Conflict and Personality," *American Journal of Sociology,* 56 [March 1951], pp. 395–406). This study, however, treats the personal predisposition as a determinant of conflict resolution rather than a factor in conflict development. Much the same is true of Gross's analysis (Neal Gross, Ward S. Mason, and Alexander McEachern, *Explorations in Role Analysis: Studies of the School Superintendency Role* [New York: Wiley, 1958], esp. Chaps. XV, XVI, and XVII).

plan. This impression seemed confirmed when immediately after Governor Faubus had surrounded Central High with troops fifteen of the city's most prominent ministers issued a protest in, according to the local *Arkansas Gazette,* "the strongest language permissible to men of God."

When Negro students appeared at the high school for the first time, they were escorted by four white Protestant ministers and a number of prominent Negro leaders. Two of the four whites are local clergymen, one being the president of the biracial ministerial association, the other, president of the local Human Relations Council. Many of the more influential ministers of the city had been asked the night before to join this escort. Some demurred; others said they would try to come. Only two appeared.

On September 23, the day of the rioting near Central High School, several leaders of the ministerial association personally urged immediate counteraction on the mayor and the chief of police. Later, support was solicited from selected ministers in the state to issue a declaration of Christian principle, but dissension over the statement prevented its publication. Indeed, *no* systematic attempts were made by the clergy to appeal to the conscience of the community. Such statements as individual ministers did express were usually —though not always—appeals for "law and order" rather than a Christian defense of the principle of desegregation.

Several weeks after the rioting, plans for a community-wide prayer service began to develop. Care was taken to present this service in as neutral terms as possible. Compromise and reconciliation were stressed: never was it described as organized prayers for integration. And indorsements came from both sides of the controversy—from President Eisenhower and from Governor Faubus. As one of the sponsors put it: "Good Christians can honestly disagree on the question of segregation or integration. But we can all join together in prayers for guidance, that peace may return to our city." The services in the cooperating churches were held on Columbus Day, October 12. All the leading churches participated, with only the working-class sects conspicuously missing. The services varied widely from informal prayers to elaborate programs, and attendances varied widely, too, and totaled perhaps six thousand.

These "prayers for peace" may best be viewed as a ritualistic termination of any attempts by the clergy to direct the course of events in the racial crisis. The prayers had met the national demand for ministerial action and the ministers' own need to act; and they had completed the whole unpleasant business. Despite sporadic efforts by a small number to undertake more effective steps, the ministers lapsed into a general silence that continued throughout the school year.

We began our work in Little Rock in the week after the peace prayers. Following a series of background interviews and a careful analysis of ministerial action as recorded in the press, twenty-nine detailed interviews with ministers were held.[4] Twenty-seven of them are Protestants and two are Jewish; the Roman Catholics did not cooperate.

This sample was not selected randomly; the so-called "snowball technique" was used in order to include the most influential church leaders. This involves asking each interviewee to name the members of the Little Rock clergy that he considers to be "the most influential." The first interview was made with an announced leader of the peace prayers, and interviewing was continued with all the men mentioned as influential until no new names were suggested. We added a number of ministers who were not named but who had taken strongly liberal positions during the crisis. Thus our sample is most heavily weighted with the pastors of the larger churches with the greatest prestige and the pastors of smaller churches who had assumed active roles in the conflict. These two groups, we anticipated, would have to contend with the greatest amount of incompatibility in role.

Most of the interviews were held in the church offices. Rapport, which was generally excellent, was partly secured by the authors' identification with southern educational institutions. A detailed summary, as nearly as possible a verbatim account, was placed on Audograph recording equipment shortly after the completion of each interview. Information in three broad areas was sought, and to this end a series of open-ended questions was developed. A series of questions was aimed at determining whether the respondent was a segregationist or an integrationist. A segregationist here is defined as one who prefers racial barriers as presently constituted; an integrationist is one to whom the removal of legal and artificial barriers to racial contact is morally preferable to the present system.[5]

Each interviewee was asked to give a complete account of what he had done and said in both his parish and in the community at large regarding the racial crisis. If he had not been active or vocal, we probed him for the reason and to learn if he had felt guilty over his failure to state the moral imperatives.

A final set of questions dealt with the pastor's perception of his congregation's reaction to whatever stand he had taken. If pressure had been applied on him by his parishioners, we probed him to learn exactly what pressure had been used and how.

The Segregationist.   Only five of the twenty-nine clergymen we interviewed were segregationists by our definition. None was avidly so, and, unlike segregationist ministers of the sects, none depended on "chapter-and-verse Scripture" to defend his stand. All men in their late fifties or sixties, they

---

[4] Thirteen additional interviews were held with the sect leaders of an openly pro-segregation prayer service. None of these were members of the ministerial association or were in personal contact with any ministers of the established denominations. A detailed report on them will be published.

[5] Using the interview, three judges, the two authors and a graduate assistant, independently rated each respondent as either a segregationist or an integrationist. Agreement between the three raters was complete for twenty-seven of the twenty-nine cases.

did not think that the crisis was a religious matter. One of them was a supervising administrator in a denominational hierarchy. Although all five were affiliated with prominent denominations, they were not among the leaders of the local ministerial body.

These five men have not been publicly active in defending segregation.[6] Each was opposed to violence, and none showed evidence of internal discomfort or conflict. All five cooperated with the neutrally toned prayers for peace. As one of them commented, "You certainly can't go wrong by praying. Praying can't hurt you on anything."

The Inactive Integrationist. Inactive integrationists had done enough— or believed they had done enough—to acquaint their congregations with their sympathy with racial tolerance and integration, but during the crucial weeks of the crisis they were generally silent. These, representing as they do all major denominations, varied considerably as to age and size of church served. Included among them were virtually all the ministers of high prestige, many of whom had signed the protest against Governor Faubus at the start of the crisis and later were advocates of the peace prayer services. Some had spoken out in favor of "law and order" and in criticism of violence. They had not, however, defended the continued attendance of the Negro students in the high school, and they had not challenged their members to defend educational desegregation as a Christian obligation. They were publicly viewed as integrationists only because they had supported "law and order" and had not defended segregation.

Altogether, the inactive integrationists comprise sixteen out of the twenty-nine of our sample. Because it was not a random sample, we cannot draw inferences regarding the division of the total ministerial community or of ministers of established denominations into integrationist and segregationist camps. However, since the sample underrepresents the uninfluential minister who had not been in the public eye during the crisis, we may conclude that a large majority of Little Rock's men of God did not encourage their members to define the issue as religious, nor did they initiate actions or participate in programs aimed at integration.

The Active Integrationist. Eight of our respondents can be designated as active integrationists because they continued to defend integration in principle and to insist that support of racial integration is nothing less than a Christian imperative. They were, on the whole, young men who have headed their small churches for only a few years. Most were disturbed that the churches of the city were segregated; some have urged their churches to admit Negroes.

Most of the active integrationists had serious difficulty with their members because of their activities, evidence of which was lowered Sunday-morning attendance, requests for transfer, diminished giving, personal snubs and in-

---

[6] Again, this is in contrast to the sect segregationists. One sect minister is president and another is the chaplain of the local Citizens' Council.

sults, and rumors of sentiment for their dismissal. One had concluded that his usefulness to his congregation had ended and accordingly had requested to be transferred. By the end of 1958, several others had been removed from their pulpits.

One thing all twenty-nine of the sample had in common was a segregationist congregation.[7] Without exception, they believed that the majority of their members were strong opponents of racial integration. The highest estimate given by any integrationist of the proportion of his congregation which supported his views was 40 per cent; the median estimate for segregation was 75 per cent. Only three interviewees thought that a majority of their members would "accept" a strong public defense of integration by their minister.

Personal integrity, alone, would lead the liberal Little Rock minister to defend integration and condemn those who support segregation. However, the minister is obligated to consider the expectations of his church membership, especially inasmuch as the members' reactions bear upon his own effectiveness.

When an individual is responsible to a public, we distinguish three systems as relevant to his behavior: the self-reference system (SRS), the professional reference system (PRS), and the membership reference system (MRS). The SRS consists of the actor's demands, expectations, and images regarding himself. It may be thought of as what the actor would do in the absence of sanctions from external sources. We have already seen that typically the SRS would support racial integration.[8] The PRS consists of several sources mutually related to his occupational role yet independent of his congregation: national and regional church bodies, the local ecclesiastical hierarchy, if any, the local ministerial association, personal contacts and friendships with fellow ministers, and, probably, an image of "my church." Finally, the MRS consists simply of the minister's congregation. We have already seen that it favored segregation or at least ministerial neutrality.

The net effect of three reference systems seems to favor the cause of integration. Were they equal in strength, and were there no contrary forces internal to any of them, this conclusion is obvious. The minister would then feel committed to support the official national policy of his denomination; his knowledge that fellow ministers were similarly committed would support him, and the local hierarchy would encourage him to make this decision and reassure him should his congregation threaten disaffection. These external influences would reinforce his own values, resulting in forthright action in stating and urging the Christian imperatives. However, internal inconsist-

---

[7] Our study of a modest sample of church members bore out the ministers' estimates of predominantly prosegregation sentiment in their congregations.

[8] Although groups make demands, impose sanctions, and significantly affect the actors' self-expectations and self-sanctions, nevertheless, we treat the self-reference system as an independent variable in role conflict. This system seems especially significant where personal action is contrary to the pressure of known and significant groups.

encies in the PRS and the SRS restrain what on first examination appears to be an influence toward the defense of integration.

The Professional Reference System.   Two overriding characteristics of the PRS minimize its liberalizing influence. First, most of its components cannot or do not impose sanctions for nonconformity to their expectations. Second, those parts of the PRS that can impose sanctions also impose other demands on the minister, inconsistent with the defense of racial integration before members who, in large part, believe in racial separation and whose beliefs are profoundly emotional.

The Inability to Impose Sanctions.   The national and regional associations that serve as the official "voice of the church" are not organized to confer effective rewards or punishments on individual ministers. Especially is this true in the case of failure to espouse national racial policy or to act decisively in the presence of racial tension. This is even more true of the local ministerial association; it does not presume to censure or praise its members. Conversely, the local church hierarchy is an immediate source of sanctions. It has the responsibility of recommending or assigning parishes, and of assisting the pastor in expanding the program of his church.

The probability and the nature of sanctions from fellow ministers among whom one has personal contacts and friends are somewhat more difficult to specify. However, it does not appear likely that he is subject to sanctions if he does not conform to their expectations by liberal behavior on racial matters. Should he indorse and actively support segregationist and violent elements, this would be another matter. If he is silent or guarded, however, it is not likely to subject him to sanction. The active integrationists in Little Rock expressed disappointment at the inaction of their associates while at the same time suggesting possible mitigating circumstances. There is no evidence that personal or professional ties had been damaged.

Among the various components of the PRS, then, only the local ecclesiastica, which does not exist for some, and, to a considerably lesser extent, fellow ministers, are conceivable sources influencing the minister's decision to be silent, restrained, or forthright.

Conflicting Expectations and Mitigated Pressures.   The role of the minister as community reformer is not as institutionalized (i.e., it does not have as significant a built-in system of rewards and punishments) as are certain other roles associated with the ministry. The minister is responsible for the overall conduct of the affairs of the church and is judged successful or unsuccessful according to how they prosper. He must encourage cooperative endeavor, reconciling differences, and bring people together. Vigor and high morale of the membership are reflected in increased financial support and a growing membership, and his fellow ministers and his church superiors are keenly sensitive to these evidences of his effectiveness. His goal, elusive though it may be, is maximum support from all members of an ever-growing congregation.

The church hierarchy keeps records. It hears reports and rumors. It does not like to see divided congregations, alienated ministers, reduced membership, or decreased contributions. Responsible as it is for the destiny of the denomination in a given territory, it compares its changing fortunes with those of rival churches. In assigning ministers to parishes, it rewards some with prominent pulpits and punishes others with posts of low prestige or little promise. However exalted the moral virtue the minister expounds, the hierarchy does not wish him to damn his listeners to hell—unless somehow he gets them back in time to attend service next Sunday. Promotions for him are determined far less by the number of times he defends unpopular causes, however virtuous their merit, than by the state of the physical plant and the state of the coffer.

Now it is especially commendable if the minister can defend the cause and state the imperative with such tact or imprint that cleavages are not opened or loyalties alienated. If, however, the moral imperative and church cohesion are mutually incompatible, there is little doubt that the church superiors favor the latter. One administrator told two of his ministers, "It's o.k. to be liberal, boys; just don't stick your neck out." Indeed, ecclesiastical officials advised younger ministers, systematically, to "go slow," reminding them of the possibility of permanent damage to the church through rash action.

Under these circumstances pressure from the national church to take an advanced position on racial matters loses much of its force. The minister is rewarded *only* if his efforts do not endanger the membership of the church: "Don't lose your congregation." Similarly, the prospect of an unfavorable response from his congregation protects him from the (possibly liberal) church hierarchy; he need only point to what happened to Pastor X, who did not heed the rumblings in his congregation. The higher officials, themselves keenly aware of local values and customs, will understand. And his fellow ministers, too, are, after all, in the same boat. They give him sympathy, not censure, if he says, "My hands are tied." An informal rationale develops that reassures the pastor: "These things take time," "You can't change people overnight," "You can't talk to people when they won't listen." There is strong sympathy for the forthright pastor who is in real trouble, but he is looked on as an object lesson. Thus the ministers reinforce each other in inaction, despite their common antipathy to segregation.

The Self-reference System. We still must reckon with the demands the minister imposes upon himself. It is obvious that the actor has the power of self-sanction, through guilt. A threatening sense of unworthiness, of inadequacy in God's sight, cannot be taken lightly. Similarly, to grant one's self the biblical commendation "Well done" is a significant reward. We have said that the self is an influence favoring action in support of desegregation. Can the inactive integrationist, then, either avoid or control the sense of guilt?

Our data are not entirely appropriate to the question. Nevertheless, four circumstances—all of which permit of generalization to other cases—appear

at least partially to prevent the sense of guilt. These include major characteristics of the ministerial role, several ministerial values and "working propositions," certain techniques for communicating without explicit commitment,
and the gratifying reactions of extreme opposition forces.

The Role Structure.   The church, as an institutional structure, sets criteria by which the minister may assess his management of the religious
enterprise; it does *not* offer criteria by which to evaluate his stand on controversial issues.[9] This encourages, even compels, the minister to base his
self-image, hence his sense of worth or unworth, on his success in managing
his church. Thus, if church members do not share his goals, three types of
institutionalized responsibilities restrain him in reform.

In the first place, the minister is required to be a cohesive force, to "maintain a fellowship in peace, harmony, and Christian love," rather than to
promote dissension. Thus some ministers prayed during the Columbus Day
services that members "carry no opinion to the point of disrupting the Christian fellowship."

Second, he is expected to show a progressive increase in the membership of
his church. Pro-integration activity, lacking mass support, is likely to drive
members to other churches.

Finally, his task is to encourage maximum annual giving and to plan for
the improvement and expansion of the plant. It is hardly surprising that several inactive integrationists who were engaged in vital fund-raising campaigns
shrank from action that might endanger their success.

Working Propositions.   The minister makes certain assumptions about his
work that reduce the likelihood of guilt when he does not defend moral convictions that his members reject. He is, first, a devotee of education, by which
he means the gradual growth and development of spiritual assets—in contrast to his counterpart of an earlier period, who was more likely to believe
in sudden change through conversion. He also believes that communication
with the sinner must be preserved at all costs ("You can't teach those you
can't reach") and for long enough to effect gradual change in attitude and
behavior. A crisis, when feelings run high, is not the time to risk alienating
those one wishes to change. For example, Pastor X acted decisively but, in
so doing, damaged or lost his pastorate: "Look at him; he can't do any good
now."

Communication Techniques.   The minister may avoid committing himself
unequivocally.[10] Some use the "every man a priest" technique, for example,
the stating of his own opinion while expressing tolerance for contradictory

---

[9] Blizzard does not find a "community reformer" or "social critic" role in the ministry
(see Samuel W. Blizzard, "The Minister's Dilemma," *Christian Century, 73* [April 25,
1956], pp. 508–10).

[10] For a full description and illustration of such techniques as used in Little Rock see
our *Christians in Racial Crisis: A Study of Little Rock's Ministers* (Washington, D.C.:
Public Affairs Press, 1959).

ones and reminding his listeners that their access to God's truth is equal with his. Others use the "deeper issues" approach; generalities such as the brotherhood of man, brotherly love, humility, and universal justice are discussed without specific reference to the race issue, in the hope that the listener may make the association himself. Still another course is to remind listeners that "God is watching," that the question of race has religious significance and therefore they should "act like Christians." There is also the method of deriding the avowed segregationists without supporting their opposites. The "exaggerated southerner" technique, which may be supplementary to any of the others, involves a heavy southern draw and, where possible, reference to and aristocratic line of planter descent.

These techniques do not demand belief in integration as a Christian imperative. Further, except for the "every man a priest" technique, they do not commit the speaker to integrationist goals as religious values; the listener may make applications as he chooses. The speaker, on the other hand, can assure himself that the connections are there to be made; he supplies, as it were, a do-it-yourself moral kit.

Reaction of the Opposition. The ministerial body in Little Rock, except for pastors to dissident fundamentalist sects, is defined by agitated segregationists as a bunch of "race-mixers" and "nigger-lovers." For example, the charge was made that the peace prayers were intended to "further integration under a hypocritical veneer of prayer" and that the sect pasors sponsored prayers for segregation "to show that not all of the city's ministers believe in mixing the races." Indeed, ministers of major denominations were charged with having "race on the mind" so that they were straying from, even rejecting, the biblical standard to further their un-Christian goals.

The effect of opposition by segregation extremists was to convince certain inactive integrationists that indeed they *had* been courageous and forthright. The minister, having actually appropriated the opposition's evaluation of his behavior, reversing its affective tone found the reassurance he needed that his personal convictions had been adequately and forcefully expressed.

Were the force of the membership reference system not what it is, the professional reference system and the self-reference system would supply support to integration that was not limited to "law and order" appeals and the denunciation of violence. However, since "Don't lose your congregation" is itself a strong professional and personal demand, the force of the PRS is neutralized, and the pressure from the SRS becomes confused and conflicting. Inaction is a typical response to conflicting pressures within both the internal and the external system.

It is not surprising, then, that most Little Rock ministers have been far less active and vocal in the racial crisis than the policies of their national church bodies and their sense of identification with them, as well as their own value systems, would lead one to expect. Rather, what is surprising is that a small number continued to express vigorously the moral imperative as they saw it, in the face of congregational disaffection, threatened reprisal, and the lukewarm support or quiet discouragement of their superiors and peers.

12

A Sociometric Analysis
of Conflicting Role-Expectancies

Lauren G. Wispé

Whereas the previous article referred to *role ambiguity* as conflicting behavior demanded by outside forces, this article speaks of conflicting behavior demanded by the role itself: Should one be a respected, successful careerist salesman, in terms of sales, at the expense of personal friendships of others in the business? How often does one feel pressured into making such a choice? Must one decide, for example, whether to be a friendly student or to be a successful (dean's list) one?

Sociologists, among them Homans,[1] have advanced the idea that as an individual's behavior actualizes the norms of the group, his prestige in the group rises. And this notion has been implicit in most psychologies of "adjustment." On the other hand, many sociologists, when discussing social disorganization, emphasize the conflict of social norms. These writers not only have designated incompatible demands made upon the individual by society but also have suggested that the conflict in the social system has been responsible for much personal conflict. Riesman's recent provocative analysis of the character structure of the American middle class is a case in point.[2] The latter contends that in the shift from "inner-" to "other-directedness" the individual has become not only an overconformist but at the same time a lonely member of a lonely crowd. Whereas the inner-directed individual

Reprinted from *American Journal of Sociology*, **61**, 2 (September 1955), pp. 134–137, by permission of The University of Chicago Press and the author.

Lauren G. Wispé is Research Social Psychologist, National Institute of Mental Health, Bethesda, Md.

The writer wishes to thank Professor Robert Wherry for his generous assistance with the factorial solution.

[1] G. C. Homans, *The Human Group* (New York: Harcourt, 1950), p. 442.

[2] D. Riesman, R. Denney, and N. Glazer, *The Lonely Crowd* (New Haven, Conn.: Yale University Press, 1950).

internalizes adult authorities, the other-directed person is completely dependent upon peer-group sanctions and is thus in the dilemma of seeking rewards and approbation from the very individuals with whom he is forced to compete. This paradoxical situation has led Riesman to suggest that increase in achievement in the group is made at the expense of peer-group affection.

The hypotheses that prestige in the group is a function of the degree to which one realizes the group(s) norms and that achievement are purchased at the expense of peer-group affection are not necessarily mutually exclusive. Granting that the terms "prestige" and "affection" are not synonymous, a kind of *rapprochement* may be effected by relating it to the concepts of internal and external systems.[3] The admiration in which an individual is held by his group is a function of his ability to realize both the expectancies which apply to the group's attempt to stabilize itself in the community and those which apply to the group's internal interaction. Although groups vary in the importance they attach to the two systems, in general the values of the external system take precedence over those of the internal system. We may thus rephrase our generalization to the effect that an individual's status in the group is a function of the degree to which he realizes, first, the role-expectancies of the external system and, second, those of the internal system. The data presented in this paper provide an illuminating application, if not a crucial test, of these hypotheses.

The data reported here are one part of a larger study of the relationship between individual behavior and group structure. A district of a life insurance company was intensively studied to learn the organization structure, procedures, and values. Several instruments were constructed, pretested, and revised, among which was a seven-item sociometric questionnaire, the results of which are reported here. The entire sales personnel of the district ($N = 43$) were first intensively interviewed about their expectancies toward the three principal positions in the organizational structure. Following the interview, the respondents filled out the sociometric questionnaire themselves.

The interviews were concerned with obtaining the agents' shared expectancies about the various positions. They were asked to consider the functions of a particular position, holding in abeyance, as far as possible, the characteristics of its occupants. These results, reported elsewhere,[4] are impersonal. The sociometric data, by contrast, are highly personal. The items

---

[3] Following G. C. Homans, *op. cit.*, pp. 90–94 and 109–110, the external system refers to the group's interaction with its environment, be this physical or social. The internal system refers to the group's elaboration of behavior deriving from and influencing the external system, but being primarily concerned with the interaction among members.

[4] L. G. Wispé and K. E. Lloyd, "Some Situational and Psychological Determinants of the Desire for Structured Interpersonal Relations," *Journal of Abnormal and Social Psychology*, 50 (1955), pp. 57–60; L. G. Wispé and P. W. Thayer, "Role Ambiguity and Anxiety: An Empirical Investigation," *Journal of Social Psychology*, 46 (1957), pp. 41–48.

were aimed at the agents' most important on-the-job activities. The first four items of the questionnaire asked the respondents to give their first three choices for (1) "an assistant for a day on the debit," (2) "someone to present a new sales plan at their meeting," (3) "house guests for a social evening," and (4) "persons to whom they would turn for insurance information." The next three items required the respondent to identify persons possessing in a high degree the traits of "aggressiveness," "sympathy," and "insurance intelligence." In brief, the sociometric items asked the agents to name the individuals in the group who, in their estimation, best fulfilled certain requirements of the business and to judge particular individuals in terms of certain personal qualities. These data furnished important information indirectly about the role-expectancies of the group.

RESULTS

In order to test the Riesman hypothesis as rigorously as possible, the intercorrelation matrix of the seven sociometric items was factor-analyzed.

Factor A, *insurance intelligence,* has high loadings [correlations] on items 4 and 7, which pertain to "help with an insurance problem" and "technical insurance information," respectively. This factor seems to describe the kind of person to whom the men turn for technical insurance information.

Factor B, *sociability and sympathy,* has loadings on item 3, "choices for a house guest," and item 6, "the most sympathetic man in the district." It is important to note that this factor has practically no loadings on the insurance intelligence items (4 and 7) and negative loadings with item 5, aggressiveness.

Factor C, *aggressive salesmanship,* has high loadings on items 1, 2, and 5. Item 1 refers to "choices for an assistant for a day on the debit"; item 2 refers to "someone to present a new sales plan"; and item 5 is the selection of the "most aggressive man in the district." This factor seems to be the stereotyped aggressive salesman. Significantly, this factor has negative loadings with the insurance intelligence items 4 and 7.

The general factor, g, is the most important factor in terms of explained variance. It has particularly high loadings on items 3 and 6, which pertain to sociability and sympathy. It also has significant loadings on the insurance intelligence items, 4 and 7. Reflected in this factor is a general positive attitude, on which, significantly, item 5, aggressiveness, has the lowest loadings.

DISCUSSION

Clearly, in the agents' definition of the situation, a good salesman should be "aggressive" and "hard-hitting." Items 1 and 5, "an assistant for a day on the debit" and the trait of "aggressiveness," respectively, correlate .57, and they have the highest loadings on Factor C (aggressive salesmanship).

The quality of "sympathy" (item 6) on the other hand, seems to have no place in the respondents' image of a successful salesman, for this item has a negative loading on Factor C, and it is not significantly related to the "choices for an assistant for a day on the debit." "Sympathy" has, however, a significant loading on Factor B, and a very high loading on the general factor, and it correlates .47 with "choices for a house guest" (item 3). Thus the paradoxical situation: the hard-driving agent, who may be a valuable asset on one's debit, may not be the person to invite home for a relaxing evening, while the person with compassionate qualities, who makes a pleasant house guest, may not be the person to select if you have to make your daily quota of sales.

This conflict of expectancies reveals the agents' dilemma. As insurance salesmen these men would like to be successful, and as human beings they would like to be accepted. Yet, according to the analysis, the traits which make for success as an insurance salesman are not related to acceptance as a friend! The issue is not that the respondents perceive sympathy and aggressiveness (as well as aggressiveness and insurance intelligence) as mutually exclusive, since this may be a veridical perception for this situation, but that the role-expectancies applying to the external system are antithetical to those related to the internal system. In order to meet the ideal patterns of the external system, a man must be hard-hitting and aggressive; but to conform to those of the internal system, he must be sympathetic and understanding. The situation thus engenders conflict, since few, if any, individuals can encompass such divergent behavior.

In the interviews there was no verbalized awareness of this conflict. However, these antagonistic expectancies are a potential source of trouble, the more so if they ever engage [5] each other at a conscious level. Although we have no way of knowing how much of the general anxiety permeating this group is a function of this particular conflict, it is very likely that one of the manifestations of it is the widespread personal insecurity and the resulting desire for structured social relationships reported elsewhere.[6] However, since the contrariety is clear, the lack of conscious conflict is itself of considerable interest. The answer to this problem has already been suggested. It is more important to be successful than to be accepted. And, since the men know this, there is, at least on the surface, no conflict.

---

[5] M. B. Smith, "Personal Values as Determinants of Political Attitudes," *Journal of Psychology,* **28** (1949), pp. 477–486.

[6] L. G. Wispé and K. E. Lloyd, *loc. cit.*

13

Role Playing
as Preparation
for Release from a
Correctional Institution

Martin R. Haskell and H. Ashley Weeks

This article describes a deliberate effort to induce prison inmates to prepare for roles they will need to assume if they are to be successful on parole. Many of the behaviors we associate with roles are learned so unconsciously that it may seem a bit awkward to "play" a role. Yet the evidence seems to indicate that this method of resocialization is a most valuable one.

There is general agreement among criminologists that the inmate of a prison, during his period of incarceration, develops a vocabulary that reflects attitudes, beliefs, opinions, and orientations different from and often opposing those of the conventional person. Many inmates, prior to their incarceration, were members of delinquent groups with subcultures deviating materially from that of the dominant culture in our society. Other inmates are subjected to a continuous acculturation and assimilation of the criminal value system and the consequent inability to make a satisfactory adjustment to the world he enters upon release.

The roles played by the inmate of a prison and the roles he is required to play upon his release are dissimilar in many important respects.[1] This is true of most of the important family, occupational, and community roles. In spite of the fact that most inmates work while in prison, the attitudes attached to the role of worker differ materially from the attitudes required for a satisfactory adjustment to a work situation outside the prison. It has been pointed out that workers in the prison labor system are encouraged to be nonproductive, dilatory, and contentious. Prison-developed attitudes affect the indi-

Reprinted by special permission of the *Journal of Criminal Law, Criminology and Police Science*, Vol. 50, No. 5 (January–February 1960), pp. 134–137. (Copyright © 1960, by Northwestern University School of Law.) Also, by permission of the authors.

Martin R. Haskell is Assistant Professor, California State College at Long Beach.

H. Ashley Weeks is Research Associate, Bureau of Public Health Economics, School of Public Health, University of Michigan.

[1] Role is defined as the socially prescribed way of behaving in particular situations for any person occupying a given social position or status. The ability of the individual to perform in a role refers to the relation which his behavior bears to a modal pattern in a given cultural group.

vidual's concepts of the role of job seeker. In prison it is considered to be the duty of the officials to provide a job for the inmate and he comes to feel that he has a right to a job. Foremen and employers outside the prison demand greater productivity and more cooperation than the inmate is accustomed to give.

In order adequately to enact a role the individual must know the rights he acquires as the occupant of a status, the rights of all the others involved in the situation, his obligations, and the obligations of all of the others. This knowledge is usually acquired through experience. Role playing may serve to help individuals adjust to future roles.[2] Cottrell, in listing twelve propositions related to adjustment to any social role, includes two that point to role playing as an aid to adjustment. He writes: [3]

> The degree of adjustment to a future role varies directly with the degree of clarity with which the future role is defined. The degree of adjustment to a future role varies directly with the amount of opportunity for:
> 1. Emotionally intimate contact which allows identification with persons functioning in the role.
> 2. Imaginal or incipient rehearsal in the future role, and
> 3. Practice in the role through play or other similar activity.

To prepare the individual to respond in the socially approved manner in the social situations in which he ordinarily functions, Moreno suggests Role Training, a form of role playing in which emphasis is placed on the reenactment of past performances. This is a technique for differentiating in action those patterns of behavior which may have been inadequate. These inadequacies become obvious to the individual, the director, and the group.

The following questions are raised: In the course of a Role Training Program administered to members of a deviant subculture, will the role playing ability of the subjects improve? Will tendencies toward conformity to the values of the dominant culture increase? Is there a relationship between improvement in role playing ability developed in the course of a Role Training Program and conformity to general social values? Role playing, Role Training, and related techniques have been used to produce attitudinal and behavioral changes in a wide variety of settings in the areas of Mental Health, Industry, and Education. Should not Role Training produce similar changes in inmates of a correctional institution? This study is based on the need for finding answers to these questions.

A Role Training Program was administered to inmates of the Riker's Island Penitentiary between September and December, 1956, as part of their preparation for release on parole. In this paper we shall discuss the nature

---

[2] Role playing is defined as a temporary stepping out of one's own present role to assume the role of another individual or of one's self at another time, in an experimental situation.

[3] Leonard S. Cottrell, Jr., "The Adjustment of the Individual to His Age and Sex Roles," *American Sociological Review,* **7** (October 1942).

of the training administered, changes observed in role playing ability, attitudes toward conformity to general social values, and the relationship between changes in role playing ability and changes in other social values.

The subjects were inmates of the Riker's Island Penitentiary selected from the one hundred and seven whose release on parole was anticipated to be between November 27, 1956, and December 21, 1956.[4] Excluded were (1) those with less than sixth grade reading ability; (2) those under the age of twenty or over forty-one; (3) known homosexuals; and (4) those with major warrants pending. The remaining sixty-six were divided alternatively from alphabetical listing into experimental and control groups. The thirty-three inmates assigned to the experimental group were divided into two training groups of seventeen and sixteen members. Prior to instituting the Role Training each experimental and control group member was given five tests which were repeated after the training was completed. They were:

1. A Role Test. A test of role enactment rated by three judges.[5]

---

[4] The study was conducted with the cooperation of the New York City Department of Correction, the warden of the Riker's Island Penitentiary, and Dr. Paul Benedict, Chief Psychiatrist, Department of Correction.

[5] *A Role Test.* The physical structure of the test situation was as follows: Along one side of the test room, behind individual tables, sat three judges. A few feet from where they were seated was a table on which a tape recorder was mounted. A few feet farther away was another table behind which sat the auxiliary ego, the trained assistant who was to play the same role in interaction with each subject. In another room the subjects, in the company of the Director, awaited the test call. Each subject was conducted into the test room by the Director and given the following instructions:

"You are a truck driver for a moving company. On your way back to the warehouse, after making your delivery, you had a breakdown. You hired a mechanic to fix the truck. It took him two hours. Because of this breakdown you are two hours late getting back. The boss wants to see you. There he is." (Director pointed to the Auxiliary Ego. The Auxiliary Ego then assigned the subject a number, starting with one as the test began, and continuing in rotation until the last man was tested.) The test began.

Neither the judges nor the Auxiliary Ego had any way of knowing which persons were in the experimental or control group. The Director did not follow any set pattern in escorting men into the room. They were escorted into the room in turn as they said they were ready. The judges were all Probation Officers with Master of Arts Degrees in Sociology.

The Auxiliary Ego, in the role of boss, applied four stimuli. He then said: "Now you are the boss and I'll be the driver." They reversed roles and four additional stimuli were applied. The subject was given as much response time after each stimulus as he desired to take. No subject had any knowledge of the role prior to receiving his instructions in the test room. The Role Test administered after the treatment was completed was given in the same manner as the one described above except for the situation selected. In the Post-Test the instructions were as follows:

"You have been a dishwasher in a restaurant for three months. You asked for a chance to become a short order cook. The boss gave you a week's trial. The trial is over. The boss wants to speak to you. There he is." (Director pointed to the Auxiliary Ego and the test began in exactly the same manner as previously reported.)

Prior to the test, the judges were given a rating sheet for each subject. They were asked to familiarize themselves with the twenty possible deficiencies in Role enactment

2. An Empathy Test. Each subject was rated on the accuracy with which he predicted the rating made by the person with whom he interacted.[6]

3. Human Relations Inventory. A projective test designed to measure tendencies toward conformity to social values.[7]

4. Judgment in Social Situations Test.

5. Observation of Human Behavior Test.[8]

The following hypotheses were formulated with respect to the inmates in each group:

1. Members of the experimental group would display greater ability to play roles than members of the control group.

2. Members of the experimental group would display greater ability to take the role of other than members of the control group.

3. Members of the experimental group would show greater tendency toward social conformity than members of the control group.

4. Members of the experimental group would show better judgment in social situations than members of the control group.

---

listed on the sheet. They were instructed to place a check mark on the rating sheet each time a subject made an error indicating a deficiency. Judges were asked to rate each subject while he was performing in the role. They were given on the minute between subjects to complete their ratings. They were further asked to rate without reference to each other so that each rating would reflect the independent evaluation of each judge.

[6] *An Empathy Test.* After completing the Role Test, each subject was handed a form on which he was asked to rate his performance in the Role Test. He was also asked to predict the rating given him by the Auxiliary Ego and by the judges. The Auxiliary Ego had been instructed to rate each subject immediately after his performance in the Role Test. The criteria for rating included five possible deficiencies: Incorrect Response, Display of Impatience, Display of Impoliteness, Lack of Feeling, and Failure to Respond to Others. With respect to each deficiency the subject had to rate himself: Superior, Excellent, Very Satisfactory, Satisfactory, or Unsatisfactory. He also was required to predict which rating he was given by the Auxiliary Ego and the judges.

[7] *Human Relations Inventory.* This test was designed to measure the conformity to cultural and social pressures that become manifest in the acts and attitudes of members of a society. A process of indirect or projective measurement which has been described as the direction of perception technique of attitude measurement is utilized. Bernberg scored the responses obtained from various "conforming" groups in order to provide a normative basis for comparison with a nonconformity group. The test was then submitted to noncomformity groups including one hundred and sixty inmates of a California Prison and subsequently to other prison groups, and in each case a significant difference in the predicted direction was found.

See R. E. Bernberg, "The Direction of Perception Technique of Attitude Measurement," *International Journal of Opinion and Attitude Research,* **6** (1951), pp. 397–406, for validation.

[8] *A Social Intelligence Test.* The Social Intelligence Test was designed to measure certain factors of judgment, information, and memory related to dealing with people and carrying on social relationships. The special edition used in this study consisted of two parts: Judgment in Social Situations and Observation of Human Behavior. Both were administered at the same time. Although the validation of this test has been inadequate, it has been reported to be useful as a rating of ability to deal with people. The two parts were rated separately.

See Frances S. Burks, "The Relation of Social Intelligence Test Scores to Ratings of Social Traits," *Journal of Social Psychology,* **8** (1937), pp. 146–153.

5. Members of the experimental group would show greater ability to observe human behavior than members of the control group.

6. Persons that improved in role playing ability would display greater ability to take the role of other than would nonimprovers.

7. Persons who improved in role playing ability would display greater tendency toward social conformity than nonimprovers.

8. Persons who improved in role playing ability would display better judgment in social situations than nonimprovers.

9. Persons who improved in role playing ability would display greater ability to observe human behavior than nonimprovers.

10. Persons who improved in role playing ability would make a more satisfactory economic and social adjustment after release than would the nonimprovers.

11. Persons who improved in role playing ability would show a lower rate of recidivism than would nonimprovers.

THE ROLE TRAINING PROGRAM

The Role Training Program consisted of fifteen role training sessions each approximately one hour and forty minutes in length. Training was given in each of three major areas, five sessions devoted to each area. The three major role areas around which the training was developed involved occupational, family, and community roles. Within each role area emphasis was placed on certain roles which were considered crucial. These were:

1. *Occupational Roles.* Job Applicant–Employer, Worker–Fellow Worker, Worker–Foreman, Worker–Employer, Worker–Union.

2. *Family Roles.* Son–Mother, Son–Father, Brother–Sibling, Husband–Wife, and Relative, including cousin and nephew.

3. *Community Roles.* Roles played by the individual in his relationships with the School, Church, Neighbors, Public Authority (Parole Officer and Police), and Friends, including former friends and the making of new friends.

The needs of each particular group tended to influence the subject matter of each session as did personality differences of the subjects. Nevertheless, insofar as possible, the above-mentioned roles were stressed. Five sessions were devoted to each role area, and each subject was afforded at least one opportunity to participate as protagonist [9] in each of the three major areas.

INSTRUMENTS AND TECHNIQUES

The five instruments of Psychodrama, the Stage, the Subject, the Director, Auxiliary Egos, and the Audience were used throughout.[10] Since no portion of the room available for the sessions was elevated, the forward portion of

---

[9] The protagonist is the individual whose problem is presented to the group as an active participant.

[10] J. L. Moreno, *Psychodrama,* Vol. I (Boston: Beacon House, 1946), for description of instruments and techniques.

the room was designated as the stage. All action took place in that portion of the room and all the subjects were seated in such a manner as to make the action visible and audible to all. At no time did the group "play at roles." Whatever action took place involved a protagonist who was presenting an actual problem, past or present. The scenes portrayed were reenactments of actual experiences, when initially presented.

The Director was nondidactic, permissive and accepting, viewing the subjects as persons capable of meeting their own problems and of helping one another. At no time did he become analytic, interpretive, or repressive. The Director had a trained assistant who portrayed the roles required by the subjects' world, acting under the instructions of the Director. This person, referred to as an Auxiliary Ego, participated in most of the sessions.

During the first five sessions the Auxiliary Ego played virtually all of the roles required to complement the action of each protagonist. After the fifth session auxiliary egos were frequently drawn from the group. This was done insofar as practicable so that as many members of each group as possible could be involved in the action. The trained Auxiliary Ego was always used when it was necessary to play a feminine role because the subjects resisted portraying such roles. The Audience, or group, participated in a discussion of each problem immediately after the problem was presented in action by a protagonist.

The techniques used included Self-presentation, Soliloquy, Projection, Role-Reversal and Mirror. The double technique was also used extensively.[11] Role-Reversal was used every time a subject played a role so that he might gain practice in playing two roles and further, so that he might have an opportunity of perceiving himself while playing the role of other. Each of the above mentioned techniques was utilized when deemed appropriate by the director.

STRUCTURE OF A ROLE TRAINING SESSION

The Director assumes the leadership role and starts each session with a directed warm-up. This is a technique for focusing the attention of the group around a specific role or role cluster. The warm-up continues until a pro-

---

[11] The techniques referred to above may be described as follows:

Self-presentation. The subject is asked to state his problem, his diagnosis, and his proposed treatment.

Soliloquy. The subject is asked to state what is on his mind. He may be asked to do this when in any role.

Projection. The subject is asked to create a scene as he believes it will be in the future.

Role-Reversal. The subject is asked to change roles with the person with whom he is interacting in a given scene.

Mirror. Someone familiar with the behavior of the subject portrays him.

Double. A trained auxiliary ego plays the role together with the subject, providing stimuli for thought and action.

For detailed description of these techniques see J. L. Moreno, *Who Shall Survive* (Boston: Beacon House, 1953).

tagonist emerges from the group and goes into action. To portray persons required by the protagonist, the Director may assign his Auxiliary Ego or utilize members of the group. After the action portion of the session, the Director encourages the group to discuss the problems raised by the protagonist. Insofar as possible, each session of the Role Training Program administered in the course of this study, followed this pattern.

The Warm-Up

The Director began each session with a warm-up that lasted between ten and fifteen minutes. He started the warm-up with a discussion of the need for training in a particular role. After a preliminary presentation of the problems involved he asked for comments by the members of the group. A discussion by the subjects of their past experiences with the particular role generally developed. In the course of such a discussion a protagonist was moved into action. The sole technique which the Director employed to focus the attention of the group on a particular role was the warm-up.

The Action

Once a protagonist emerged, he was encouraged, with the assistance of the trained Auxiliary Ego, to act out successful and unsuccessful past experiences in which the role was involved. In each scene he was asked to reverse roles at least once so that he could attempt to act in the role of the "other" with whom he had previously interacted. In the role of "other," he was generally asked to soliloquize about himself, frequently with the aid of a double. Other techniques, previously mentioned, were used as they were deemed appropriate.

The Discussion

After the action, the group was encouraged to discuss the problems presented. Suggestions based on past experiences were welcomed. In the course of such discussions, if other members of the group desired to perform in the role presented, they were permitted to do so. Most often another protagonist emerged and went into action. This would result in further action and a broadened discussion.

EXTENT OF PARTICIPATION

In Treatment Group I, ten of the fourteen subjects participated as protagonists in action in occupational roles, family roles, and community roles. Three of the remaining four participated as protagonists in both occupational roles and community roles. Only one member of the group did not participate as a protagonist. All members of the group were active in discussions involving all three role clusters.

In Treatment Group II, twelve of the sixteen members participated as protagonists in action in occupational roles, family roles, and community roles. Two of the remaining four participated solely in occupational roles. The other two did not participate as protagonists at any time. All of the members of the group, including the two who had never participated as protagonists, took active part in discussions and achieved some degree of involvement in all three role clusters.

RESULTS

In order to evaluate changes that occurred in the course of the treatment, scores obtained by members of the experimental group were compared with those obtained by members of the control group, on each of the five tests that were administered before and after the treatment. When compared with the control group, the improvement of the experimental group on the Role Test was significant. The improvement of the experimental group on the Human Relations Inventory was also statistically significant. On the Empathy Test, the Judgment in Social Situations Test and the Observation of Human Behavior Test, the mean post-test scores of the experimental group increased in a favorable direction over the pre-test scores, although the increases were not statistically significant.[12]

Frequency of improvement of the Negro members of the experimental group was compared with frequency of improvement of the White members on each of the five tests and no significant differences were found. Similar comparisons were made between those under twenty-five years of age and those twenty-five and over, between three educational categories, and between drug users and nonusers. No significant differences were found. However, nondrug users had a gain in mean score of 3.0 on the Human Relations Inventory, and a 4.6 gain in mean score on the Observation of Human Behavior Test. Both of these gains were significant at the .05 level. Drug users did not have any gains in mean scores which were statistically significant. Other differences between the various social categories were noted but none was statistically significant.

Eighteen members of the experimental group who improved, five points or more in standard scores on the role test, were compared with ten who did

---

[12] The following table of *t* scores summarizes the results of these tests:

	Role Test	Empathy Test	Human Relations Inventory	Judgment	Observation
t-Score	4.06*	1.03	1.86†	.33	.179

*These differences would occur by chance less than once in a thousand.
†These differences would occur by chance less than five times in one hundred.

not improve. These two groups are referred to as improvers and nonimprovers. The nonimprovers had scores on the post-role test lower than their scores on the pre-test or had an improvement of less than five points. On the Empathy Test, the difference in means between the pre-test and the post-test scores obtained by the improvers was significantly higher than the difference in means of the nonimprovers, ($t = 2.33$).[13] On the Human Relations Inven-

TABLE 1. Relation Between Parole Violation and Improvement on Role Test Experimental Control Group and Combined Groups*

ROLE TEST SHOWED:	NONVIOLATORS	VIOLATORS
Experimental group		
Improvement	16	2
No improvement	3	7
Total†	19	9
Control group		
Improvement	2	2
No improvement	19	9
Total‡	21	11
Combined groups		
Improvement	18	4
No improvement	22	16
Total**	40	20

*At the start of the treatment program there were thirty-three subjects in the Experimental Group and a like number in the Control Group. At the end of the study, there were thirty in the Experimental Group; two withdrew at their own request and one was transferred to another prison. The Control Group was intact. Two members of the Experimental Group and one member in the Control Group refused to take the test.
†Chance would account for this distribution only about once in one thousand times.
‡Chance would account for this distribution about fifty times in one hundred.
**Chance would account for this distribution more than five times in one hundred.

tory, the difference in means between the pre- and post-test was 3.5 for the improvers and —.1 for the nonimprovers. This difference was significant, ($t = 3.78$).[14] There was no significant difference between the mean scores of improvers and nonimprovers on the Observation of Human Behavior Test nor on the Judgment in Social Situations Test.

On March 24, 1957, about three months after the members of the experimental and control groups used in this study were released from the prison, a check was made of parole violations. The relationship between improvement on the role test and parole violation is illustrated by Table 1.

[13] These differences would occur by chance less than two times in one hundred.
[14] These differences would occur by chance less than once in a thousand times.

As can be seen from the table, subjects in the experimental group are much more likely than those in the control group to improve on their role test scores. The subjects in the experimental group who do improve on their scores are much more likely to be nonviolators of parole than those who do not improve. This provides some indication of the value of the Role Test as a possible predictive device. Obviously, those persons least interested in therapy show the poorest results on tests designed to measure improvement. Here we have some evidence that they are also the poorest parole risks. Such conclusions, are, of course, tentative. Follow-up studies in the years to come must provide the true measure of the effectiveness of this treatment program.

CONCLUSIONS

An analysis of the results of this study indicates support for hypotheses one, three, six, seven, and eleven. The results did not support any of the other hypotheses. The fact that the other hypotheses were not supported by the tests used may, in a large part, be due to the inadequacy of the measures. Certainly, it is not likely that all of the change-producing experiences involved in this training program were within the purview of the tests. What is apparent from the results is that a group participating in a Role Training Program improved in skill at playing occupational roles. It is reasonable to infer from this fact that general role playing ability improved. There was also evidence of increased tendencies toward conformity. When the improvers in role playing ability were compared with the nonimprovers, two important findings appeared. First, the improvers in role playing ability showed a significant increase in tendencies toward conformity, when compared with nonimprovers. Second, the improvers showed a substantially lower rate of recidivism after three months of freedom.

PRACTICAL IMPLICATIONS OF THE FINDINGS

This study has demonstrated that Role Training can be used to improve the ability of inmates of a penitentiary to play occupational roles. It is also likely that in the course of this training, role playing ability, in general, was improved. Along with improvement in role playing ability, tendencies towards conformity increased. According to leading experts in penology, a major objective of correctional practice is the increase in the commitment of each inmate to the conventional value system. Role Training should be useful in accomplishing this objective.

It is certainly not unusual for society to use role playing for its ends. Bram in discussing the expansion of role playing by children, in the learning process, points out how this role playing is influenced by society. He writes: "But it is at this point that society steps in and interrupts the free flow of projective fantasies with practical routines, social etiquette, school attendance, and other rituals. Role playing ability is not discarded completely but becomes rechanneled into socially designed functional patterns." [15] Most of the inmates of our penal institutions do not have social agents to rechannel the role playing described by Bram, into socially designed functional patterns. Most of them have never had a successful record of employment in which the essential occupational roles could be learned. Most of them have had very poor family relationships and their community participation has been largely in groups with delinquent subcultures. It has been demonstrated that role training administered to inmates of a prison prior to release on parole improved role playing skill, and that in the course of such training, attitudes were modified in the direction of conformity. If additional studies produce similar findings, correctional institutions should in due course, include a Role Training Program in their rehabilitation plans.

Although the subjects of this study were adult inmates of a penal institution, there is no reason for limiting this training to adults. There were no significant differences on any of the tests administered, between the scores attained by men under twenty-five years of age and those over twenty-five years of age. Thus, it is very likely that a Role Training Program would be effective with the youthful population of a reformatory. It can also be applied in dealing with probationers.

---

[15] Joseph Bram, *Language and Society,* p. 21.

Chapter Four

Socialization

THE HUMAN INDIVIDUAL is not born human. He acquires his "humanness" through group interaction. His ability to speak, his values, his viewpoints are absorbed largely from the groups to which he belongs and therefore reflect their interpretation of the culture in which he lives. From his innermost thoughts and most personal habits to his basic approach to life and his use of logic, he has been made what he is by the groups that have funneled the culture to him. Though it seems fairly well established that the major social-psychological growth, like physical growth, comes early in life,[1] one never ceases to learn and adapt as long as one lives.

A society could not exist were it not for the rather efficient socialization (incorporation, or the taking on of values) that transforms the "bumbling, buzzing confusion" of an infant into the reasonably coherent behavior of an adult member of society. Most taxpayers honestly report their income and pay their income taxes; most husbands and wives are faithful to each other; most employers meet their payrolls promptly; most drivers slow down or stop at the appropriate intersections. In spite of the disrepute in which some hold the term *conformity,* it is a basic requirement of a smoothly operating social group or society. It

[1] A recent survey of 356 young finalists at the 11th National Science Fair-International showed that 95 per cent were science-oriented by the time they were fourteen years old, 63 per cent before they entered the seventh grade. See Shirley Moore, "Origin of the Scientist," *Science News Letter* (September 3, 1960), pp. 177–178. It is of interest to note that although there is still reluctance on the part of some of the science fraternity to accept sociology as a natural science, there is, paradoxically, increasing research by them of a sociological nature.

may be noted that often those who cry loudest about the dangers of conformity are themselves conforming to most social values. The deviant is a felt danger to the existence of the group's values. Whether he is merely a passing nuisance or a harbinger of the social future, he is usually punished in the present. It is not surprising that only a small percentage of the population fails to incorporate the norms of the society; what needs to be explained and understood is why and how so many become the very models of the culture.

The articles in this chapter have been selected to illustrate how an individual obtains an image of the kind of person he is and how this self-image in adult years may in turn operate as a selective tuning mechanism in regard to what that individual sees and hears.

14

The "Good" Boy in a High Delinquency Area: Four Years Later

Frank R. Scarpitti, Ellen Murray, Simon Dinitz, and Walter C. Reckless

In few other situations can the importance of the socialization concept be noted so dramatically as in the situation described by the following article. Although this concept is not applied sociology in the strictest sense, the portent for its application is enormous. Is it not unreasonable to expect the infrequent and casual contact of a parole officer, a court or a boy's club to counteract the hours, weeks, and years of the influence of the home?

This paper reports the results of a follow-up study of the "good" boy in high delinquency areas.[1] In the spring of 1955 an investigation of good boys in the highest delinquency-rate areas of Columbus, Ohio, was undertaken. The focus of the earlier study was an attempt to measure the extent of "insulation" of socioeconomically deprived white youths and to specify the mechanisms—personal and social—through which this insulation was achieved.

In order to identify insulated boys, the investigators interviewed all sixth-grade teachers in schools located in the highest delinquency areas of predominantly white population. The teachers were requested to nominate those white boys in their classrooms who would never, in their estimation, experience contact with the police or courts. One hundred and ninety-one white boys were nominated, comprising approximately one half of all the white boys in the sixth-grade rooms of the elementary schools in the highest (predominantly white) areas of delinquency in the city. When their names were

Reprinted from the *American Sociological Review*, **25**, 4 (August 1960), pp. 555–558, by permission of the publisher and the authors.

This study was made possible by the continuing support of The Ohio State University Development Fund.

Frank R. Scarpitti is Director, Institute Treatment Center, Louisville, Kentucky.

Ellen Murray is Probation Officer, Franklin County Juvenile Court.

Simon Dinitz is Professor of Sociology, The Ohio State University.

Walter C. Reckless is Professor of Sociology, The Ohio State University.

[1] See the two papers by W. C. Reckless, Simon Dinitz, and Ellen Murray, "Self Concept as an Insulator against Delinquency," *American Sociological Review*, **21** (December 1956), pp. 744–746, and "The 'Good' Boy in a High Delinquency Area," *Journal of Criminal Law, Criminology and Police Science*, **48** (August 1957), pp. 18–26.

cleared through the juvenile bureau of the police department and the records of the juvenile court, it was found that in each of 16 instances the boy or a sibling had been known to the police or court for very minor matters; these 16 cases were eliminated. Of the 175 remaining, our field investigator was able to locate and to interview 125 boys and their mothers (or mother surrogates) at home. A structured schedule, containing the De scale of the California Personality Inventory (now called the So scale, which measures a veering toward or away from delinquency) and a series of other scales and items, was administered to each of the boys. A less structured but parallel schedule was administered to each of their mothers.

The results of the earlier study indicate that these 125 good boys, then at the threshold age for entry into delinquency, had developed and internalized law-abiding norms and concepts of self which, as predicted, would protect them from future difficulties. They were isolated from contact with delinquents; they evaluated their home life as satisfactory; they believed that their parents were "fair" and were interested in their sons' welfare; they liked school and their teachers. Above all, they defined themselves as "good" boys —boys who would not become entangled with the law. These concepts were reflected by the evaluation of their mothers and teachers as well as by the very low scores on the delinquency vulnerability (De) scale.

Four years have since elapsed. The good boys are currently about sixteen years of age—the median age of institutionalized delinquents. This paper presents an assessment of the present state of insulation of the original good boys, their interactional relationships, and their concepts of self and others.[2]

METHOD

The present addresses of the original 125 respondents were obtained from such sources as the Columbus Board of Education, the city directory, the post office, and the public utility companies. In all, 103 of the 125 boys were located and restudied. Ninety-nine of the 103 were still in school. The remainder had either left the metropolitan area or the state.

The homeroom teachers of each of the 99 boys still in school were again requested to nominate the boy as (a) one who would not experience difficulty with the law, (b) one who would get into trouble, or (c) one about whom the teacher was unsure. In addition to the nominations, school records were gathered in each of nine high schools and seven junior high schools in which the 99 subjects were students.

As before, each of the 103 boys was cleared through the police and juvenile court files for official or unofficial violation behavior in the intervening years.

---

[2] For a more complete report of this research, see Frank R. Scarpitti, "A Follow-up Study of the 'Good' Boy in a High Delinquency Area" (Master's Thesis, The Ohio State University, 1959).

Each boy and his mother or mother surrogate were interviewed at home by experienced interviewers. The schedules administered to both the boys and their mothers were considerably more involved than those previously utilized. However, every question in the original schedule was included in the later instruments.[3]

FINDINGS

The most striking results in this follow-up investigation are (1) the great amount of stability in the family and school situations of the 103 boys, and (2) their consistency in response and, apparently, in behavior as well, over time.

Stability in Background

There was practically no change in the family situation of the 103 boys in the four-year period, although the parents of one boy had been divorced a year after the initial interview. At the time of the follow-up study, 85 boys were living with both their real parents, three boys with the mother only, 12 with their mother and a stepfather, two with grandmothers, and one with an aunt and uncle.

The families of the respondents, who were found in the original study to be typical of the families in the school areas in terms of father's occupation, were not nearly as physically mobile as anticipated. Forty-seven families had changed residence in the intervening years. Of these, 21 had moved to another residence within the same census tract or to a socioeconomically comparable tract. The other 26 families had achieved some measure of upward mobility and had moved to higher-status areas, generally the newer and modest housing developments ringing the city. A separate analysis comparing the respondents who remained in the high delinquency areas with those who had achieved upward mobility reveals no significant differences on any of the indices included in the study.

Ninety-nine of the 103 boys were still in school, although at least half of them had passed the compulsory school attendance age. Those in school were overwhelmingly enrolled in the academic program (96), with only three in vocational training programs. School records indicate that the boys are by

---

[3] The boys' schedule included 46 items from the De scale (delinquency vulnerability scale of the California Personality Inventory, developed by Harrison J. Gough, but now called the So scale because it tests socialization); a subscale assessing the boy's projections regarding his involvement with the law, consisting of ten items; a subscale consisting of seven items of frequently admitted delinquency taken from Nye and Short (see F. Ivan Nye, *Family Relationships and Delinquent Behavior* [New York: Wiley, 1958], Chap. 2); two subscales assessing the boy's rejection of his mother and his feeling about being rejected by her, 10 items each, also adopted from the Nye schedules (see *ibid.*, Chap. 8); a father rejection subscale; other subscales dealing with the boy's concept of self, friends, school, and so on. So far as possible, these items were duplicated on the schedule administered to the mothers.

no means exceptional in scholastic standing and in school attendance. Scholastically, according to the ratings on their permanent record cards, 11 per cent show scores of excellent, 29 per cent above average, 32 per cent average, 23 per cent below average, and five per cent are rated as poor students. In school attendance, 19 per cent are listed as excellent, 42 per cent as good, 21 per cent as fair, and 19 per cent as poor. These performance records represent no significant change over time.

Teacher Nominations

Of the 99 boys still in school, all but four were nominated by their homeroom teachers as individuals who would avoid future contact with the police and courts. Three major reasons were listed by the teachers in justifying these nominations: the boy's "quietness," coming from a good family, being a good student. Four were nominated as boys who would or might get into difficulty with the law, of whom two were attendance problems, one had "belligerent ideas," and the other a "bad attitude."

Court Clearances

Four boys (all nominated as "good" by their teachers) had become known to the police or juvenile court or both, one time each, during the intervening years. One case involved truancy and was disposed of by the police without referring the boy to the juvenile court. A case involving malicious destruction of property and another involving drunkenness and violation of curfew were held by the police and turned over to the juvenile court. The juvenile court, however, in handling these two cases without official disposition, probably considered them rather petty matters. The fourth boy was arrested for borrowing a neighbor's automobile in the early morning hours to deliver newspapers (he had done this on several occasions, always returning the car to its parking place before the neighbor arose). The police turned this boy over to the juvenile court, which in making an official disposition placed him on probation. None of the four boys had since come to the attention of the authorities.

Delinquency Vulnerability, the Law, and Admitted Delinquency

Table 1 presents, first, the mean score of the original 125 insulated white boys in the high delinquency areas of Columbus, Ohio, on delinquency vulnerability (Gough's CPI De scale, now called So scale); second, the mean score which the 103 boys, revisited in 1959, made in 1955, and, finally, the mean score for the re-test of the 103 boys in 1959. The mean scores have remained stable and even improved (but not significantly). It should be noted that the lower the score (as the De scale was scored in 1955), the less veering toward delinquency and the better socialization—hence, a score of 14.0 is a most favorable one. In fact, none of the criterion groups of "good citizens" in the validation of the De scale (So scale) reached such a favorable figure as the good boys in our original sample of 125. This fact lends additional credence to the continuing nondelinquency or insulation against delinquency of these boys residing in high delinquency areas.

TABLE 1. Mean Delinquency Vulnerability Scores (De) of Sample in 1955 and in 1959

Year	N	Mean	S.D.
1955	125	14.57	6.42
1955	103	14.17	6.17
1959	103	13.64	4.68

As before, each of the respondents conceives of himself as being able to stay out of trouble with the law. Two of the boys, however, believe that possibly they may be brought before the juvenile court or perhaps go to jail. A third states that his mother thinks that he is headed for trouble, and a fourth that his teacher expects him to get into difficulties with the law. These four respondents were the sole nominees as potential delinquents, and none had a record. (Each of the 103 mothers stated that her son would not get into trouble with the law or ever appear before the juvenile court.)

Ninety-four of the boys are favorably disposed toward the police and to the workers at the juvenile court. Perhaps in conformity with contemporary adult attitudes on this matter, 43 per cent of the good boys expressed the view that any real trouble persons have with the law can be "fixed" if they know the right people. Seventy per cent knew no one who had ever been in prison.

On the Short-Nye seven-item scale of admitted delinquent behavior, the good boys appear almost angelic. They generally admit to nothing more serious than occasionally defying parental authority. The mean score on this scale is 1.3, the highest score is 6, and the mode is 0. (These scores, theoretically, could reach a maximum of 14 for those admitting all the behaviors listed.) The reliability of these highly satisfactory ratings should be questioned, however, on the grounds that we have been unable to replicate the Short-Nye scale in any of our other recent studies. In this investigation and in those conducted in New York and Akron, as yet unpublished, it was found that the seven items could not be reproduced in scale form. This is largely attributed to the lack of anonymity of the respondents and their younger age.

Self and Mother and Father

Two Nye scales were used in this study which had not been employed in 1955. One measures the boy's feelings of rejection by his mother, the other his rejection of her. On both scales, the respondents scored almost completely in the nonrejection direction. The boys felt that they were accepted by their mothers or mother surrogates and, in turn, expressed acceptance of them. Their responses on these scales were radically different (P = .001) from those of boys who were held in a detention home (Juvenile Hall) of Alameda

County, California, and on whom we had pretested these instruments.[4] In the same manner, the respondents felt that their mothers were "about right" in severity of discipline, and both less strict and less lax than previously. They also stated that their mothers were somewhat more attentive to them than in 1955.

The boys also expressed acceptance of their fathers, the amount of paternal attention they received, the severity and fairness of paternal punishment, and the amount of interest in them shown by their fathers. There was only one major (favorable) shift in the four year period: the boys conceived of their fathers as being less strict than before.

Self and School and Friends

The respondents' orientations to school remained favorable and almost unchanged in the four-year interval. Of the 103 boys, 98 expect to finish high school, 97 define their relations with teachers as satisfactory, and 92 expect to get a great deal out of school from now on.

Nor was there any apparent shift with regard to their isolation from deviant and law-violating friends. Some 91 of the 103 remained aloof from boys who had been in trouble with the law, and 97 said that they would give up a friend if he was leading them into trouble with the law.

Finally, about 90 per cent of the respondents expect to receive an "even break" from people in the future, believe that adults are usually in their corner, and feel that things have generally gone their way up until now.

SUMMARY AND CONCLUSIONS

This follow-up study confirms our 1955 predictions and those of the teachers and mothers of the respondents, as well as of the good boys themselves, that they would remain law-abiding in the future. At an average age of 16, these boys continue to assess themselves, their mothers, fathers, teachers, and schools favorably. They continue to isolate themselves from law-violating friends and acquaintances; they predict law-abiding behavior for themselves and, in this respect, they reflect their teachers' concepts of them. They again scored lower than any other group on the Gough delinquency vulnerability (De) scale, and do not admit any appreciable amount of previous violation behavior. In sum, they continue to define themselves as good boys and are so defined by others in spite of remaining, for the most part, in high delinquency areas.

The results of this investigation may be interpreted to mean that once a favorable self-image has been internalized by preadolescents with respect to friends, parents, school, and the law, there is every reason to believe that it

---

[4] Judson R. Landis, "Parental Rejection and Delinquency Potential" (Master's Thesis, The Ohio State University, 1959).

is as difficult to alter as a delinquent self-image. In view of their relatively stable and cohesive families, the continued interest in and supervision of their activities by their parents, their school aspirations, and isolation from purveyors of deviant values, it may be predicted that the good boys will persist in their law-abiding behavior.

In process is another follow-up investigation of predelinquents—the counterparts of the good boys followed in this study. It is anticipated that the differences in the "outcome" of these latter cases will justify our belief that the internalization of a favorable self-concept is the critical variable in the "containment" of delinquency.

15

Measuring Effects of Treatment of Criminals and Delinquents

Bernard C. Kirby

Our society spends millions of dollars annually for treatment of delinquents and criminals. What evidence is there that our present methods are effective? Sociological theory would predict that jails and reformatories are not likely to reform, because by the socialization process an individual becomes like those with whom he associates.

This survey of research should be read in conjunction with the Selection 16 (Fox), which reports a study of the effects of counseling within one prison.

The attempt is made here to summarize and classify a number of the more important efforts to measure the results of the various forms of treatment used by courts, social agencies, institutions and other administrative bodies on criminals and delinquents, for either therapeutic or preventive purposes. Several conclusions are reached, and suggestions made which might facilitate such measurement, and presumably improve then the treatment processes used.

To ensure fairly complete coverage of the literature in this field, the leading journals in sociology, social work, and penology were examined, as well

Reprinted from *Sociology and Social Research*, **38**, 6 (July 1954), pp. 368–374, by permission of the publisher and author.
Bernard C. Kirby is Associate Professor, San Diego State College.

as a number of criminology textbooks, proceedings of various annual meetings and conferences, and periodical indexes.

The reports of treatment programs varied within a wide range. However, if one ignores those whose claims to apparent benefits were unsupported, and sometimes not even illustrated by case histories, the more serious ones remaining fall into two main classes. In the first, the subjects are simply divided into two or more subclasses, typically designated success and failure, or improved, doubtful, and unimproved, and then counted. The proportion of successes and failures implies certain conclusions about the treatment. Sometimes the classification is subjective, and if so may or may not be reliability tested, and sometimes it is objective, typically hinging on the question of law violation.

In the second main class are those studies which make use of control groups, whose behavior is compared with that of the treatment groups. The division may be between whole populations of geographical areas, or between populations who, respectively, have and have not received the treatment. Also the populations may or may not be matched, in any one of several ways.

Four different kinds of treatment may be distinguished: (1) probation and parole; (2) correctional institutions; (3) psychotherapy, counseling, and other noninstitutional treatment; (4) capital punishment as deterrent.

PROBATION AND PAROLE

There appears to have been no study of probation in which treatment and control groups were compared. However desirable, it would be hard to arrange to compare two sets of convicted persons, one set released to the community with benefit of probation, and the other set without such benefit.

The usual objection, of course, is that human beings cannot for experimental purposes be deprived of services which might keep them from crime, both for the sake of community protection and because of society's responsibility for all its members, especially the disadvantaged. However, convicted persons are being deprived continually of probation services, because of lack of funds, judicial prejudice, and similar reasons. A minimum amount of planned deprivation, more than matched by abundant services to the experimental group, might be justified by the benefits to later criminals and all society.

In the meantime, probation has produced a few useful studies. Dr. Belle Boone Beard, in her 1934 doctoral dissertation, followed up five hundred Boston Juvenile Court probationers who had been studied by the Judge Baker Foundation Clinic. She found that during a five year period 43 per cent of the boys and 76 per cent of the girls were successful, as defined. She faced the question whether the successes might be attributed to the probation services but did not have the data on which to base an answer. Charles Meyer and Morris Caldwell independently report a recent University of Alabama study of 403 persons who had completed probation from 5½ to 11½ years previously. About 98 per cent were still clear of conviction for felonies, and 84 per cent of convictions of any kind. Other reports, such as the annual reports of most probation departments, cannot go as far as this for their knowledge of their clients' postprobation behavior is scanty and fortuitous.

Much more subjective data were gathered by Bennett Mead in his study of 6,300 federal cases. He asked the probation officers of these subjects to estimate the degree of improvement which the men had experienced under supervision. These estimates were 26.8 per cent "striking improvement," and 34.7 per cent "moderate improvement." But men's judgment of their own labor is notoriously unreliable.

Consideration of parole, as distinguished from probation, is confused because its effects are inevitably commingled with those of the institutions from which the subjects were paroled. One study did however attempt to separate them out. This is *Hepbron's Study of Parole in Maryland,* made in 1935. Because of the practice of releasing some men from prison on parole and others unconditionally, it was possible to compare the later records of the two classes of discharges. The parolees made definitely better records. However the decision as to which men should be released on parole, and which unconditionally, was not made by chance or by a matching plan. On the contrary, the parolees were a group handpicked for their probable success.

There are also the W. C. Jones' study of Illinois parolees and the periodic studies by the New York Board of Parole of the records of men paroled five years earlier. These are suggestive but subject to obvious limitations.

INSTITUTIONAL TREATMENT IN PRISONS, REFORMATORIES, TRAINING SCHOOLS, DETENTION HOMES

Out of the half dozen or so studies of the effects of such institutional treatment, one or two are conspicuously impressive. Vernon Fox has carried out a carefully designed examination of the work of the new Michigan reformatory, called the Cassidy Lake Technical School. Inasmuch as the capacity of the school is only one hundred men, there are ? vs more good candidates for the school than there are openings. It w re possible for Fox to compare the records of Cassidy Lake disc. .n those of men who had been selected as suitable but not admitted . '· of room. From these selected but not admitted candidates, there we 144 subjects who matched with the 144 men who had been admitted. 'ts showed the clear but not pronounced superiority of the minimum c institution at Cassidy Lake. The one flaw, beyond the experimenter's c .ro. ms to be that although all the subjects were selected as suitable for the sch n the final selection the *most* suitable were chosen. A systematic error therefore have been introduced.

L. Wallace Hoffman tells of a radical revision of program in a juvenile detention home, inaugurated on a certain day. Not only did the atmosphere and the general behavior of the children improve markedly, but a count of escapees showed a decline from thirty in the preceding eight months to five in the following fifteen months. No other changes, such as in the population of the institution, were said to have occurred.

The six pioneering studies of Sheldon and Eleanor Glueck of criminal careers of women, children, and men were outstanding in the great care taken to trace down the graduates of the institutions studied. Their findings sharply corrected the generally overoptimistic claims of courts, clinics and institutions of that time. They found, for example, that 88 per cent of one thousand delinquent boys examined between 1917 and 1922 at the Judge Baker Foundation recidivated within five years.

Bowler and Bloodgood, of the Federal Children's Bureau, in 1936 examined the records of 623 boys released from five boys' training schools five to ten years previously. The adjustments of the boys were judged subjectively on the basis of information from a wide variety of sources. The conclusion was that 32 per cent of the boys had adjusted successfully, 33 per cent were doubtful, and 35 per cent were clearly unsuccessful. Similarly, Healy and Alper found that from 50 per cent to 85 per cent of boys released from the various British Borstals were "successes," defined as lack of reconviction.

It is not hard to see why there have been few good studies of the effects of institutional experience. Fox's opportunity is not common and can usually be effected only by an administrative arrangement that is made years in advance. This indeed is probably the biggest hurdle in research in this field. Seldom can observation of material already available suffice. Prior planning by a number of years is usually necessary.

PSYCHOTHERAPY AND NONINSTITUTIONAL TREATMENT

Over half of all the studies found fall into this class, including those of child guidance centers, school-centered plans to prevent or control delinquency, boys' clubs, court-attached diagnostic and treatment units, neighborhood crime prevention programs, and many others.

Outstanding in many respects is the Cambridge-Somerville Youth study. In this long, well-financed experiment, 325 pairs of boys were matched carefully, boy for boy, with respect to over a hundred relevant variables. One of each pair was selected for treatment, by chance, the other for control. The treatment boys were then given the advantage of a variety of services. The control boys had only the usual resources of the community. It was found that the services given the treatment boys were "no more effective than the usual forces in the community in preventing boys from committing delinquency."

The outstanding limitation of the experiment appears to lie in the heterogeneous nature of the services. Friendly interest, inspiration, and simple environmental manipulation were the only techniques used by some counselors, while others used the skills of the psychiatric social worker. The trained social workers, the psychiatrist, and the clinical psychologist were available only part of the time. It is possible for the adherent of any school of thought to maintain that the techniques he favors were not given a fair chance to succeed. How much did the children and the police and parents know of the experiment? What controls could there have been to ensure equal treatment by police particularly, and by parents, playmates, and neighbors, of the treatment and control boys?

No less interesting and significant for research—though negative in its conclusions—is the much older study by Trasher of a boys' club in New York. He measured the increase or decrease in number of offenses charged against boys before and after membership in the club, and observed the trend in offenses as a boy stayed longer in the club. He also compared the offense rates of members with those of nonmembers from the same area and socioeconomic class.

The report by the Committee on Community Interrelations of the American Jewish Congress of the operation of Club Revelation is a good example of an attempt to estimate program effectiveness without large sums of money available for research. The change in the patterns of behavior of the boys is described, with specific notice of the decline in fights.

Shulman used a matched control group in his study of the therapeutic effectiveness of a very permissive activity group. Sixty-five pairs of children were matched. The experimental group played very freely under leaders trained in group therapy. The measure of success was based upon caseworkers' reports of their behavior. The findings showed slight but fairly sure improvement under treatment. The study of Ruth Jacobs Levy on *Reductions in Recidivism Through Therapy,* is somewhat similar.

The St. Paul Experiment of the Federal Children's Bureau relied mainly upon the judgment of its staff in assessing the value of child guidance services to a community. The estimates were that 16 per cent of the children treated had experienced major improvement in behavior, 63 per cent partial improvement, and 9 per cent none. There were also more objective indications of the effect of the services. Juvenile delinquency, as measured by arrests and by juvenile court appearances, decreased very much more during the experiment in the service area than in the entire city or county. Similar differences in arrest rates supported claims of delinquency reduction by the Chicago Area Projects.

CAPITAL PUNISHMENT

This is certainly a subject upon which there is more opinion than knowledge. The usual controlled experiment is impossible, and no one to date has carried out an ex post facto experiment, to use Chapin's term. One can refer then only to such compilations of available material, suggestive rather than conclusive, as have been made recently by Karl Schuessler, utilizing the experience of various American states and certain European countries, and by Thorstein Sellin and Frank Hartung—and longer ago by others. No clear evidence in favor of capital punishment appears in these studies. If carried out, a projected English study by Tadeusz Grygier should throw light on the psychological effects upon prisoners of an execution within the institution, and thus indirectly upon its possible deterrent effects. The November 1952 issue of the *Annals of the American Academy of Political and Social Science,* titled *Murder and the Penalty of Death,* is invaluable to anyone interested in the subject.

CONCLUSION

It is quite clear from this survey that most treatment programs are based on hope and perhaps informed speculation rather than on verified information. One also gets the feeling that people in the correctional field and people in the universities are not making the best possible use of each other. The first group have the acute problem of assessing the effectiveness of their various operations; the second group is interested in good research problems for themselves and their advanced students; yet each seems too often unaware of the other.

We in sociology have certainly not sold our skills to practitioners "outside." For example, a public official recently asked what a sociologist could possibly discover from five hundred cases which the FBI did not already know from its five million. Two or three highly placed penologists questioned whether further work should be done in parole prediction on the ground that a number of studies had already been attempted.

Criminological research has yet barely begun to use the more recent statistical techniques, such as analysis of variance, discriminant function, nonparametric tests, factor analysis, Q-technique, and so forth. As one result, excessive attention may be paid to sheer number of cases and promising opportunities ignored for studies of small populations.

Would it not be feasible for institutional staffs, when considering policy changes, to include in their overall plans some provision for before-and-after or split-half studies of the results of those changes? Similarly, could not a standardized nomenclature be used in case histories or inmates, with terms carefully scaled and their application tested for reliability? This would be a vast improvement over impressionistic judgments of improved or unimproved behavior, good work records, or fair school adjustments, and over the artificial dichotomies of success and failure on parole. Such a more carefully defined vocabulary would be as helpful in individual case work services to subjects as in research with large populations of them.

In these and many other ways the full resources of modern social science may be brought to bear upon the knotty problem of the criminal deviant of our society.

16

The Effect of Counseling on Adjustment in Prison

Vernon Fox

The practical utility of the concept of *socialization* may be illustrated by this account of a change in prison administration policy that permitted one sociologist or psychologist to be a prisoner's counselor throughout his term and to prepare him for release. In spite of the handicap of a caseload of more than one thousand men (the maximum load recommended by professionals is 30 to 35 individuals) and the open ridicule of persons committed to the traditional policy, the results indicate that the new method is more effective. The article also portrays vividly the difficulty of conducting research on criminals, both from a theoretical point of view and from the practical one of the severe understaffing in prisons.

The integration of the professional services into the total prison program is a major problem facing modern penologists. There has been wide disagreement about whether and how assistance from sociology, social work, psychiatry, and psychology can be used advantageously in prisons. Most prisons have accepted assistance from the behavior sciences and arts through the classification committee and the diagnostic depot. These programs gather information about each new prisoner as he arrives, for purposes of diagnosis, research, or compliance with the law. Recommendations are made as to what program he should be given in order that he may in the future select more socially acceptable solutions to his personal problems.

The integration of the professional services with the routine aspects of prisons is not accomplished by classification committees nor by diagnostic

Reprinted from *Social Forces,* **32,** 3 (March 1954), pp. 285–289, by permission of The University of North Carolina Press and the author.

Vernon Fox is Professor and Chairman, Criminology and Corrections, Florida State University.

centers. Neither the classification committee nor the diagnostic center is able to account for the practical interpersonal relationships in the prisoners' contacts with custodial officers, mail office censors, work supervisors, and other inmates, twenty-four hours a day, seven days a week. In the practical situation, professional recommendations from any source are seldom remembered long. The important factors in prisoner placement are often what assignments are filled and what assignments need men.

Traditional classification existed at the State Prison of Southern Michigan prior to 1949. Twelve sociologists and psychologists had prepared social histories and psychological reports on all new prisoners as they arrived. Rough diagnoses were made, cases were presented to the classification committee, and recommendations for institutional, work or school, and custodial placement were made at the end of the inmates' first month at the prison. The recommendations were forwarded to the deputy warden in charge of custody, who made the assignments as he deemed advisable. The recommendation of the classification committee was merely a recommendation. With the exception of one sociologist who specialized in writing preparole progress reports for the parole board three months before the expiration date of each man's sentence, no further formal contact with sociologists or psychologists was provided the inmates. Consequently, the professional services were out of contact with the total prison program except for this highly specialized service.

In order to correct this deficiency, the State Prison of Southern Michigan in 1949 realigned the professional personnel and their work in order to better integrate the professional services into the practicalities of everyday living at the prison. Ten psychologists and sociologists were assigned to the 4,600 men living inside the walls and two were assigned to the 1,200 men living outside the walls. Their title was changed to "counselor," in order to avoid the old prisoners' antipathy toward such titles as "sociologist" or "psychologist." For want of a better system, case loads were assigned to each counselor according to the terminal digits in the prisoners' serial numbers. When prisoners arrived and were assigned numbers by the record office, the counselors were notified, and each prisoner was given the name of his counselor.

The usual information was obtained from the prisoners' relatives, previous employers, schools, and other social agencies. The results of tests for intelligence, achievement, aptitudes, and medical examination were made available. The counselor had also the probation officer's report from the court of sentence when he interviewed any prisoner to prepare the admission summary. This summary outlined the man's major problem and the steps that could be taken within institutional limits to correct it. The counselor then presented his man to the classification committee, recommending a program supported with reasons. The classification committee usually ordered that program to be put in effect, for in Michigan's counselor program the classification committee report had become an order.

Throughout the inmate's incarceration, the counselor interviewed him at regular intervals to help him meet his problems in the prison and to plan for the future. All problems other than custodial discipline were referred to counselors. As sentences expired, the counselor prepared the preparole progress report for each of the men in his case load, outlining the major problems, attempted treatment, progress or lack of progress, with his recommendations for or against parole.

When the counselor system went into effect, many unsympathetic custodial officers refused to answer inmates' questions, but said, "Go see your counselor." For months, the custodial personnel and others unsympathetic to professional service ridiculed it, and "Go see your counselor" echoed through the halls. Many custodial officers assigned counselors to each other on the basis of the terminal digits in their time clock numbers. Facetious as it was, this process helped to spread the idea of counseling so that when the initial malicious intent had been spent, more personnel seriously evaluated it than would have known about it otherwise.

There was a closer interpersonal relationship between the prisoners and professional personnel than had previously existed. For some prisoners the relationship was forced, because the counselor had become the focal point for functions previously handled by others. For other men, the counselor was a welcome contact with a trained man interested in prisoners' problems. For inmates and personnel alike, the realignment of professional personnel from specialized and compartmentalized functions to a generalized integration with the rest of the prison had a telling effect. Assisting each inmate to adjust to living within the institution brought the counselor into contact with work supervisors, custodial personnel, and other people he had never known before. This realignment of sociologists and psychologists had resulted in integration of professional services with the prison program.

The purpose of the study outlined in this paper was to determine to some extent the effect of the use of professional personnel in a counseling program, compared with the use of professional personnel in the traditional classification system. A follow-up study on the basis of success and failure on parole could not be done because not enough time had elapsed to measure such success and failure. The purpose of this study could best be achieved in the practical prison situation by determining the effect of the counseling program on the population which was affected immediately by it compared with the effect of the traditional classification system on a similar population. The tentative hypothesis was that the use of professional personnel in the counseling program, in which cases are followed from arrival in prison to parole, results in better adjustment than does the use of professional personnel in the traditional classification system.

PROCEDURE

To many who observed the counselor program go into effect, there appeared to be a division between the inmates who did not want to accept the counselor program and those who accepted it readily. This division seemed to be based on two factors. The first and most obvious immediate factor was the date of arrival in prison. The group of inmates who had been in the prison a long time and had become accustomed to taking their problems to a captain, deputy warden, or other higher prison official tended to resent being shunted to trained sociologists or psychologists whom they considered to be "youngsters" partially because of their youth and partially because they had been hired a long time after the inmate had begun his sentence. The group of inmates who accepted well the counselor program were those who had arrived for the first time after the counselor system had been initiated. The second factor contributing to the division of acceptance was the differential personality needs in the older inmate group for ego support and reassurance. The difference in attitudes of those who arrived in prison before the counseling program was established and those who arrived afterward was of greater significance than the differential in personality needs. Within any prison system the differences in personality needs will appear and be at least partially satisfied by sympathetic personnel who may be in proximity to the inmate.

The procedure was to compare objectively the adjustment in prison of two groups of inmates with as nearly similar backgrounds as possible, unaffected by previous prison experience, serving their prison terms as close together in time as possible, with one group experiencing the traditional classification system and the other experiencing the counseling program.

The counseling program went into effect on May 1, 1949. The serial numbers of men without previous prison experience who arrived between fifteen months and six months prior to that date were tabulated for the control group, since they served under the traditional classification system. The control group, then, included first-offenders who arrived at the prison between February 1, 1948, and November 1, 1948. Their adjustment in prison was measured until May 1, 1949. The experimental group, or those who had served under the counseling system, was made up of men who had arrived in prison for the first time during the nine months following May 1, 1949. Their adjustment was measured until August 1950. This gave constant time of measurement between the groups temporally as close together as possible.

The cases in each group were individually matched for (1) major type of offense, (2) age, (3) intelligence quotient within five points, (4) length of sentence, (5) marital status, and (6) residential background according to the size of the community. Out of 400 cases, 87 could be matched on all of these factors.

The device selected for measuring adjustment in prison was developed by the writer on the basis of 100 cases in a previous study.[1] The scale was built on the basis of routinely collected reports and records which were tabulated and subjected to statistical analysis to determine the diagnostic weights of

---

[1] Vernon Fox, "The Effect of Juvenile Institutionalization on Adjustment in Prison" (Master's Thesis, Michigan State College, 1943), Chap. 6.

each item. Good, average, and poor adjustment was weighted by multiplying the diagnostic weights of the item according to the criterion of internal consistency by 3, 2, and 1, respectively. Reliability and validity of the instrument were checked by a correlation test with estimation of prisoner adjustment by a sociologist in 27 cases. The final scale with the items arranged in the order of decreasing importance is shown in Table 1. The adjustment scores on the original sample ranged from 60.1 to 117.4, with a mean at 89.9.

TABLE 1. Weighted Scale of Prisoner Adjustment Scores on 11 Items

ITEMS	DIAGNOSTIC WEIGHTS
Work reports:	
Good	24.3
Average	16.2
Poor	8.1
Misconduct:	
No misconduct reports	13.5
Minor reports	9.0
Major reports	4.5
Block officer's reports:	
Good adjustment	13.5
Average adjustment	9.0
Poor adjustment	4.5
Visits from outside:	
10 or more per year	13.2
1 to 9	8.8
No visits	4.4
School reports (prorated if no school):	
Good	12.9
Average	8.6
Poor	4.3
Type of misconduct:	
No misconduct reports	11.4
Rebellion against authority	7.6
Violence against persons	3.8
Correspondence:	
70 or more letters in or out	10.8
40 to 69 letters	7.2
Less than 39 letters	3.6
Chaplain's appraisal:	
Good religious status	9.9
Fair religious status	6.6
Poor religious status	3.3
Financial budgeting:	
Saved $12.00 or more	8.7
Saved $5.00 to $11.99	5.8
Saved less than $5.00	2.9
Work stability:	
6 months or more on one job	8.4
6 months or more on two jobs	5.6
6 months or more on more than two jobs, or less than 6 mos.	2.8
School stability:	
6 months or more	7.2
Less than 6 months, or part-time student	4.8
No school contact	2.4

In order to obtain their adjustment scores, this adjustment scale was applied to the records of the 87 men in the control group, or those who had served under the traditional classification system. The scale was then applied to the records of the 87 men in the experimental group, or those who had served under the counseling system. Means and standard deviations were computed on both arrays of adjustment scores. Comparison was made between the adjustment scores of the two groups by the critical ratio technique.

RESULTS

The results of the comparison of the adjustment scores between the control and experimental groups are shown in Table 2.

The mean adjustment score for the control (classification) group was 93.4, while the mean adjustment score for the experimental (counselor) group was 97.6. The critical ratio between the two distributions was 2.5, which exceeds the 5 per cent level of confidence. The tabulation and computation of the data indicate that a significant difference in adjustment scores exists between the two groups of prison inmates. This difference shows that in this sample the inmates who served under the counseling program adjusted to the prison situation better than the inmates who were processed through and served under the traditional classification system.

TABLE 2. Comparison of Adjustment Scores of Men Serving Under Traditional Classification System and Men Serving Under Counselor System

ADJUSTMENT SCORE	CLASSIFICATION GROUP	COUNSELOR GROUP
Total	87	87
125–9	0	1
120–4	1	4
115–9	3	0
110–4	6	1
105–9	5	10
100–4	10	20
95–9	15	19
90–4	18	18
85–9	15	6
80–4	7	4
75–9	4	4
70–4	1	0
65–9	0	0
60–4	1	0
55–9	1	0

Discussion with the psychologists, sociologists, and social workers who functioned as counselors revealed several practical ways in which the counseling program assisted each man better to adjust to prison routines. Many of the frustrations that present themselves to inmates result from lack of information. Counselors have reported that much of the service rendered some of the inmates is in the reinterpreting for them of a frustrating situation. Some of them, for instance, have suspected that their wives or sweethearts had been unfaithful to them. Many of these fears and supicions had been allayed by discussing the reasons for these suspicions with a counselor who could in many cases reinterpret the evidence for the inmate in a less damaging and more just manner. In some cases, when it appeared that the suspicions may be well founded, the counselor has helped the inmate discuss reasons for it, and what the inmate might have been doing if the situation were reversed. Many such situations have been reinterpreted by inmate and counselor so that either the inmate has considered his suspicions unfounded or could accept their existence without trauma.

The counselor has been called upon to absorb aggression or redirect it in many cases. Frequently the inmate has become enraged at his work supervisor and has come to the counselor for a change of job. The counselor has handled these matters in various ways. Sometimes he just sits and lets the inmate verbalize his aggressions. The counselor has generally been able to reduce the intensity of the aggression in these situations, though it has become sometimes advisable to change the inmate's assignment.

A major contribution that the counselor has been able to make is the creation of an atmosphere that is oriented in the direction of treatment and self-improvement. Knowing that each man he interviews will be his responsibility, the counselor will attempt to orient the man toward self-improvement during the first interview, outline a plan of treatment with the man, and carry it out. The inmate is thereby provided a goal to strive toward, rather than being left to drift into the best ways of getting along in prison. Serving time becomes purposeful.

Most important among these emotionally immature men has been that the counselor provides a source of emotional response. During the therapeutic interview, a transference and countertransference can be built. The relationship in the counselor program can continue long enough to show constructive results. Even before constructive results begin to show, counselors report that many men have said that this was the first time they had found anyone who has been sufficiently interested in them to listen through their stories.

CONCLUSIONS

The counselor system realigned professional personnel so that each inmate had closer contact with a treatment-oriented man trained in sociology, social work, or psychology. For any problem of importance to an inmate, the counselor functioned in some manner. Consequently, case work or counseling services became integrated into the prison program.

The counselors' services to the prison inmates seem to be in (1) reinterpreting frustrating situations, (2) absorbing aggression to extinguish, weaken, or redirect it, (3) giving purpose to prison life by creating a treatment atmosphere and attitude, and (4) providing an emotional object to which the inmate can relate in transference and countertransference in a therapeutic situation.

The counselors' case loads in this study averaged 459 men inside the walls and 600 men outside the walls. This is an absurdly high case load. It is impossible for one man to do any sort of therapy worthy of the name with more than 60 men. In addition, many of the custodial and other personnel openly ridiculed the program. Even with these handicaps, however, integration of professional services through the counseling system showed results significantly improved over the traditional classification system, with the same personnel involved and with the cases in the sample individually matched on background social factors.

The primary conclusion of this study from the administrative standpoint is that if rehabilitation of personalities is to be successfully achieved, the institutional facilities must be organized around the needs of these personalities rather than for the convenience of the institution. While a high degree of specialization gets a specific task done faster, the generalized integration of services is more effective in influencing the adjustment of the personalities within the institution. When attempting to help personalities, the program should be organized in such a way that an inmate may have the same therapist over a long term, preferably his entire treatment period. Further, the therapist should have functions that will insure his integration into the daily routines of the prison.

17

Effectiveness of a Political Telethon

Wilbur Schramm and Richard F. Carter

This article—which is a remarkable confirmation of the findings of Lazarsfeld and others in regard to the 1940 and 1944 elections* —reports that a crash political program is of little effect. When one remembers that for any voter the socialization process has been ongoing for twenty-one years or more, it should not be surprising that a political telethon (or much other campaigning, for that matter) changes few if any voters' opinions. However, campaigning may still be crucial for the politician, for unless he succeeds in getting favorably predisposed individuals actually to go to the polls and vote, he may "snatch defeat from the very jaws of victory."

At 10:40 P.M., Friday, October 31, 1958, Senator William Knowland went before television cameras in Los Angeles in a dramatic effort to carry his campaign for governor to as many as possible of the voters of California. Twenty hours and 20 minutes later, 7 P.M., Saturday, November 1, he concluded the program, still in good voice and fighting mood.

If the telethon did nothing else, it established some kind of a mark for physical endurance. From Friday morning until Saturday night, the candidate went without sleep. He answered, in detail, hundreds of questions which were phoned in to him or picked up by interviewers in remote camera crews. He greeted dozens of nationality groups and other delegations parading through the studio. He helped his daughter celebrate her twenty-first birthday, on television. He talked over campaign issues with guests. From the first hour to the last he hit vigorously at the two main targets of his campaign: "labor bosses" and "crime in California."

The program was carried by a number of television stations throughout California. Knowland's headquarters estimated that 7000 calls came in, asking questions of the Senator, offering encouragement, and pledging campaign

Reprinted from *The Public Opinion Quarterly,* **23,** 1 (April 1959), pp. 121–127, by special permission of the publisher and the authors.

Wilbur Schramm is Professor, Department of Communication and Director, Institute for Communication Research, Stanford University.

Richard F. Carter is Assistant Professor, Department of Communication, Stanford University.

* Paul F. Lazarsfeld, Bernard Berelson, and Hazel Gaudet, *The People's Choice* (New York: Columbia University Press, 1948).

contributions. Vice President Nixon was quoted, in a telegram read on the air, as saying that he had "glowing reports" of the telethon, and was confident that it would "make thousands of new friends not only for your election as Governor but for the entire Republican slate in California."

The telethon was a major effort, inserted late in the campaign in an effort to stem a political tide which was running strongly against Senator Knowland. What did it accomplish?

Because the telethon is a technique which has been successful in other attempts at persuasion by the broadcast media (e.g., the Kate Smith war bond sales [1]), and infrequently tried though often considered as a possible contribution of television to political campaigning, the answer to that question carries importance outside California. In order to get some idea of the effectiveness of the telethon in one of the major communities where it was broadcast, the Stanford Institute for Communication Research made 563 telephone interviews, four days after the program, with a probability sample of telephone homes in San Francisco. Of the 563 persons we talked to, 28 per cent (158) declined to give a party affiliation. Of those who named a party, 65 per cent (263) said they were Democrats, and 35 per cent (142) said they were Republicans. (On November 4, San Francisco voted approximately 70 per cent to 30 per cent in favor of Knowland's Democratic opponent.)

These are the results of the interviews.

WHO SAW THE PROGRAM?

Of the 563 persons we talked to, 11.5 per cent (65) had watched some part of the telethon. These included 31 Republicans, 27 Democrats, 7 who declined to state their party. Comparing them, in terms of percentages, with the total sample, we find a substantial difference:

	REPUBLICANS	DEMOCRATS	WOULDN'T SAY	N
Total sample	25.0%	46.7%	28.3%	563
Viewers	47.7	41.5	10.2	65

It is evident that Republicans were about twice as likely as Democrats 'to see the program. Furthermore, in "Republican homes" an average of 1.87 persons saw at least some part of the telecast, whereas in "Democratic homes" the average number of viewers was only 1.41.

HOW DID THEY LEARN OF THE PROGRAM?

In San Francisco, the telethon was not widely publicized before it took place. Thirty-nine of the 65 viewers (60 per cent) said they tuned in the program *by accident,* 16 (25 per cent) had read about it, and 7 had been told

---

[1] Robert Merton, *Mass Persuasion* (New York: Harper, 1946).

about it. More of the Democrats (67 per cent) than Republicans (48 per cent) came upon it by accident.

WHEN DID THEY VIEW IT?

The program was carried live in San Francisco on a non-network station. Ninety minutes of the program were rebroadcast, from recording, on a network station the following Monday evening. As might be expected, the largest audiences appear to have gathered around the two evening portions of the live broadcast. The following table suggests that it was the Republicans who loyally sat up late to follow the program, and chiefly Republicans who saw the daytime broadcasts. The Democrats, more of whom were probably viewing out of curiosity, tended to catch the evening periods.

	PERCENTAGE OF VIEWING AT DIFFERENT TIMES IN HOMES OF		
	ALL VIEWERS	REPUBLICANS	DEMOCRATS
Friday evening	35.0	30.6	45.0
Saturday, midnight–dawn	4.5	7.1	—
Saturday morning	11.9	15.3	5.0
Saturday afternoon	18.6	23.5	10.0
Saturday evening	22.4	18.8	27.5
Monday evening rebroacast	7.5	4.7	12.5
N	134	85	40

There was no significant difference between the percentage of male and of female viewing at these perids.

HOW LONG DID THEY WATCH THE PROGRAM?

The 56 viewers in 31 Republican homes estimated that they spent a total of 142 hours and 57 minutes with the telethon—2 hours and 33 minutes per average viewer. The 37 viewers in the 27 Democratic homes said they gave a total of 54 hours and 29 minutes—1 hour and 28 minutes each.

HOW MUCH DID THEY TALK ABOUT
THE PROGRAM?

One of the chief reasons why a candidate subjects himself to the physical indignities of a telethon is that he hopes thereby to attract a great deal of attention to his campaign and his arguments. He hopes that viewers will tell others of the telethon, and that the program will be widely discussed. Did the Knowland telethon accomplish this?

Forty-four of the 65 viewers (68 per cent) did not tell anyone of the telecast. Seventeen told friends the program was on the air; 6 told other members of the family (apparently much of the listening occurred with more than one member of the family looking at the set, and therefore there was less need to tell the family). Republicans were more likely than Democrats to tell someone: 42 per cent of the Republican viewers passed the word; only 32 per cent of the Democrats. Since a correspondingly larger percentage of the Republicans reported they heard of the program from a friend, we can assume that Republicans told Republicans about it.

How much discussion did the telethon generate? These are the percentages for the persons in our sample who saw the telethon and for those who did not.

	VIEWERS	NONVIEWERS
Discussed it *with no one*	55.4%	90.5%
Discussed it *once*	15.4	3.2
Discussed it *several times*	24.6	1.8
Discussed it *often*	3.1	.8
Not ascertained	1.5	3.8
N	65	498

It seems therefore that somewhere near half of the viewers did discuss the program, and that more than half of *those* discussed it on several occasions. This discussion, however, penetrated only to about 6 per cent of the nonviewers.

Fifty-two per cent of Republican viewers discussed the program as compared with 37 per cent of Democrats.

WHAT IMPRESSED THE VIEWERS?

About half the viewers came away from the program with definitely favorable impressions.

WHAT IMPRESSED THE VIEWERS	PER CENT	N	EXAMPLES
Nothing	30.7	(23)	
Not ascertained	8.0	(6)	
Program's worth	5.3	(4)	"Educational"; "could learn from it"; "good idea for politics"; "informative."
Program's quality	18		"Interesting"; "well organized"; "terrific"; "good speakers"; "spectacular."
Knowlands' manner			"He answered seriously"; "didn't avoid things"; "fine speaker"; "very impressive that a big man would do this kind of thing."
Negative comments	12.0	(9)	"Too long"; "boring"; "durability overemphasized"; "dictatorial."
Equivocal comments	4.0	(3)	

N = 75 (some made more than one kind of comment)

However, when these comments are divided by party affiliation, it becomes apparent that many more Republicans than Democrats were impressed.

WHAT IMPRESSED THE VIEWERS	REPUBLICANS PER CENT	N	DEMOCRATS PER CENT	N
Nothing	13.5	(5)	45.1	(14)
Not ascertained	8.1	(3)	6.5	(2)
Program's worth	8.1	(3)	3.2	(1)
Program quality	27.0	(10)	6.5	(2)
Knowland's manner	27.0	(10)	19.4	(6)
Negative comments	13.5	(5)	12.9	(4)
Equivocal comments	2.7	(1)	6.5	(2)
N		(37)		(31)

Republicans thus found the program more worthwhile, higher in quality, more impressive generally. It is interesting that the incidence of definitely negative comments should be about the same for members of the two parties.

DID THE TELETHON CHANGE ANY VOTES?

Fifty-five of the 65 viewers said they got no new picture of Knowland from the telethon, and even the other 10 (7 of them Republican) had some difficulty saying just what the new impression was. In general, the comments indicated that existing impressions were reinforced, and existing intentions rationalized, rather than sharply changed. Typical comments were: "Yes, it did. I figure he's pretty wonderful." Or, "No, we were pretty convinced of what we thought of him." Or, "No, my mind was pretty much made up." Or, from a Democrat, "Oh, no, we already knew he was a fine man, but didn't agree with him." And, "I always felt the same way about him; only now he proved what we thought."

As might be expected, then, the telethon apparently did not bring about any wholesale changes in viewers' intention to vote. There was little cognitive change, therefore little attitude change, and, so, little behavior change. *Two* of the 65 viewers said it *helped them make up their minds:* one to vote for, one against, Knowland. *One* Republican said it *changed* his mind; from having tentatively decided to vote for Brown, he returned to the party fold and decided to vote for Knowland.

DISCUSSION: HOW EFFECTIVE WAS THE TELETHON?

These results, of course, are only for San Francisco. They may or may not apply to any of the other cities in which the telethon was broadcast.

Furthermore, the number and kind of questions that can be asked in telephone interview are limited. We could doubtless have found out more by personal interviews, but, considering the small amount of cognitive and attitudinal change revealed in these telephone interviews, the extra cost of personal interviewing was not considered to be justified.

With these limitations, then, we can say that this study of Senator Knowland's telethon supports the generalization derived empirically in Lazarsfeld,

Berelson, and Gaudet's *The People's Choice* [2] and supported theoretically in Festinger's *A Theory of Cognitive Dissonance* [3]—that voters tend to expose themselves to media in order to reinforce their predispositions and reduce the dissonance resulting from challenge to those predispositions, rather than to see what the other side has to offer. Republicans therefore would be expected to hear chiefly Republican speakers, read chiefly Republican materials, and discuss them chiefly with other Republicans; and Democrats vice versa.

This is precisely what seems to have been happening in the case of the Knowland telethon. Republicans were much more likely than Democrats to be in the audiences. Republicans were more likely to have heard about it in advance, to tell others about it, and to discuss it. Apparently they chiefly told other Republicans and discussed it with other Republicans.

The main result of the telethon seems to have been to confirm the impressions of Senator Knowland and the voting intentions which the viewers brought to the program. This is the case although some viewers admired the skill of the program, and Democrats as well as Republicans admired Knowland's endurance, articulateness, and strength of character and personality. It is unlikely that the program changed any large number of votes in San Francisco.

Two elements in the situation may have contributed to this result. For one thing, in San Francisco, at least, the telethon was inadequately promoted in advance. It is astonishing that more than half of the viewers in our sample should come upon this expensive and striking program only by accident. It is somewhat surprising also to find that less than 12 per cent of a probability sample of telephone homes reported viewing the program. The advertising given this program should be compared with the attention directed to such a program as the marathon bond sales program of Kate Smith.

In the second place, the Knowland telethon occurred in the last days of a campaign in which most of the stops of political persuasion had already been pulled, and in which the tide was running strongly against the Republicans. Senator Knowland was trying to hold back the ocean. To judge both from the polls and from our interviews, very few viewers in San Francisco had not made up their minds by the last day of October.

As we try to reconstruct what happened, then, we begin with the fact that most minds were already made up: the Democratic tide was already rolling in. Owing perhaps to inadequate promotion, the audiences were small and disproportionately Republican. The telethon generated less discussion than might have been expected, perhaps because it was so late in the campaign and so many decisions were already made. The people who talked about it were mostly Republicans and they talked mostly to Republicans.

---

[2] Paul Lazarsfeld, Bernard Berelson, and Hazel Gaudet, *The People's Choice* (New York: Columbia University Press, 1944).

[3] Leon Festinger, *A Theory of Cognitive Dissonance* (Evanston, Ill.: Row, Peterson, 1957).

Democrats happened upon the program by accident or out of curiosity, and for the most part read their image of the Republican candidate into what they saw. Republicans came by accident or out of loyalty, and they too found their impression of Knowland confirmed. In retrospect the Democrats who saw the telethon tended to remember it as simply another campaign gadget. To the Republicans in retrospect it took one some of the shape of dramatic tragedy. "I didn't think it was necessary," said one Republican viewer. "He's such a wonderful man. I didn't think he should have to do this sort of thing to be recognized. I was saddened by it."

18

A Follow-Up Report on the Cambridge-Somerville Youth Study

Joan and William McCord

In all organizations, and especially in those dealing directly in the field of human relations, periodic self-appraisal would seem to be as mandatory as it is often neglected. Much labor is expended in voluntary associations to develop certain values among their beneficiaries, for example, but little to measure the effectiveness of the methods being used. In terms of socialization, then, what reforming do reform schools really do? How effective is the church school in guiding the behavior of children who attend? Are family counseling agencies or psychiatric clinics able to prove that individuals really benefit from the contacts? Or must we continue to do all this work on faith?

The following article reviews one of the rare instances of scientific self-study by an organization attempting, in sociological terms, to effect socialization. The results should be a sharp challenge to those who think they know a great deal about human behavior and that "business" may be continued "as usual" simply becacse "we have always done it this way."

One of the most extensive attempts to prevent delinquency and crime was the famous Cambridge-Somerville Youth Study. Founded in 1935 by Richard Clark Cabot, a physician and social philosopher on the faculty of Harvard

Reprinted from The *Annals* of the American Academy of Political and Social Science, **322** (March 1959), pp. 89–96, by permission of the publisher and the authors.

Joan McCord is Research Associate in Sociology, Stanford University.
William McCord is Associate Professor of Sociology, Stanford University.

University, the project aimed at decreasing delinquency in two densely populated, factory dominated cities, Cambridge and Somerville, Massachusetts.

With the aid of a $500,000 grant, Dr. Cabot established a center for the
project. After careful interviews, the staff selected subjects from among hundreds of boys referred by schools, welfare agencies, police, and churches as
difficult children or as ones who were average in behavior and personality.
Each boy was given medical and psychological examinations. Social workers
consulted the families and reported on their homes. On the basis of this information, each boy was matched to another as closely similar in background and in personality as was possible. One in each pair was then selected,
by toss of a coin, to receive the services of the Youth Study. Thus 325 boys
were to be given friendly, regular attention from counselors, as well as whatever medical and educational service seemed needed. A matched set of 325
boys, a control group, was to be left to the usual services of the community.[1]

Beginning in 1939, for an average of five years, the "treatment boys" were
given assistance ranging from academic tutoring to psychological counseling.
The intensity and calibre of treatment varied from counselor to counselor and
boy to boy. In some cases, as Dr. Cabot had hoped, treatment involved an
intimate friendship between boy and counselor. In most cases, however, the
treatment relationship was less close. Treatment had many aspects: talks between the boys and counselors, trips and other recreation for the children,
and medical aid whenever it was required. In addition, many counselors,
focusing on school problems, tutored their boys in reading and arithmetic.
Others acted primarily as coordinators for welfare and family agencies, the
YMCA, and summer camps. Large numbers of boys were encouraged to
participate in shop classes or informal games at the project's center. Religion
formed an important part of the treatment: Boys and their families were
encouraged to attend church, and ministers and priests were alerted to their
problems. Police departments, particularly the juvenile bureaus, kept in close
touch with the project. Counselors often visited the boys' families to offer
advice and general support.

The Cambridge-Somerville Youth Study differed from most social agencies
in three ways: Its subjects were selected by the staff and were therefore, in
a sense, "drafted" into the project. It tried to maintain contact with the boys
and their families until the boys were about seventeen instead of "closing"
cases after shorter treatment. Most importantly, it incorporated a control
group of boys who could later be examined in an objective assessment of
the effectiveness of the treatment program.

The first attempt to measure effectiveness was carried out while the program was in progress. Psychological tests, checks on school adjustment, and
a review of court records failed to uncover significant differences between
the treatment and the control groups.

---

[1] See Edwin Powers and Helen Witmer, *An Experiment in the Prevention of Delinquency* (New York: Columbia University Press, 1950), for a detailed discussion of the
original selection and the treatment of the subjects.

In 1948, almost three years after the project had ended treatment, a second assessment was made by Edwin Powers, the project's Director, and Helen Witmer, a social scientist. At that time it was found that, according to juvenile court and criminal records, the treatment group had committed as many and approximately as serious offenses as had the control group. Dr. Witmer's ratings of the terminal adjustment of the boys also indicated few differences between the treatment and control groups. Since the conclusions of Powers and Witmer are fully presented in *An Experiment in the Prevention of Delinquency,*[2] we will not attempt to duplicate their report.

In 1956 the authors of this article received a grant from the Cabot Foundation to trace the lives of these boys now that they had reached manhood. We dropped from our study those who had died or who had received very little treatment; also, of course, we dropped their matched mates from the control group. We then secured criminal records for the remaining boys who had passed through Massachusetts or Federal courts. By 1948, 90 per cent of a random sample of 200 boys from the study were still living in the Boston area.

We had decided that the presence or absence of criminal behavior would be our criterion of success in treatment and that criminality would be determined through official court convictions. Objections can be made both to the criterion of success and to the method by which we measured it. We might, for example, have attempted to gauge the general mental health, adjustment, or character of the men. Yet since the major avowed aim of the project was the prevention of crime—and since other standards of success seemed relatively difficult to define or measure—we concluded that criminality should be the yardstick of success.

We recognize, of course, the many defects of official criminal records as a standard of criminality. An earlier study made by the Cambridge-Somerville staff revealed that many delinquent acts known to the counselors had gone undetected by the police. Admittedly, official records are incomplete and, in some cases, may reflect a variety of community biases. Nevertheless, no satisfactory substitute has yet been developed. Moreover, we believe that a confirmed criminal is unlikely to pass through the first thirty years of his life without being apprehended at least once. Furthermore, most of our subjects emerged from deteriorated neighborhoods; therefore the usual middle-class biases in court convictions would be equally applicable to all the boys. Thus, for a variety of reasons, court convictions appeared to be the most practical, objective standard of crime.[3]

---

[2] *Ibid.*

[3] Social scientists have attempted to measure criminality through self-reports. Sheldon and Eleanor Glueck, in *500 Criminal Careers* (New York: Knopf, 1930), reported interviews with criminals whom they had questioned on undetected crimes they had committed. A number of the subjects admitted additional crimes. Yet, using this method, one is unable to dissociate bragging or dishonesty from the truth. Ivan Nye, more recently, in *Family Relationships and Delinquency* (New York: Wiley, 1958), used a questionnaire administered to a group of high school students as a measure of

The final group used for this assessment of treatment was made up of 506 men predominantly from lower-class and lower-middle-class backgrounds. Approximately half of these men, divided equally between the treatment and the control group, had been considered predelinquent. Their median I.Q. in childhood was 98; their median age, when treatment began, was 11.

COMPARISON OF TREATMENT GROUP AND CONTROL GROUP

When we compared the court records of the boys who had received treatment with those of the control group, we found that a slightly greater number of treatment boys had been convicted for at least one crime,[4] although their number of convictions was slightly lower. Neither of these differences, however, is statistically significant.

	Number of Boys Convicted	Number of Convictions
Treatment group	107	315
Control group	95	344

Both Professor Gordon Allport, in his foreword, and Edwin Powers had expressed the hope that the treatment boys would evidence better adjustment as they matured.[5] To check this possibility, we grouped the boys according to the age at which they committed crimes. We found that a slightly larger number of treatment boys had criminal records in each of three groups: those convicted only as juveniles, those convicted only after "maturation," and those convicted as both juvenile and as adult criminals. These differences, too, were not statistically significant.

	Number of Boys Convicted	
Age of Criminality	Treatment Group	Control Group
Under 18 only	34	29
18 or older only	35	32
Under and over 18	35	34

Nor was there a significant difference in the number of crimes committed during either the juvenile or the adult period.

---

crime. Yet Nye validated the "reported behavior" questionnaire by showing that it differentiated between incarcerated delinquents and noninstitutionalized high school students—the standard which he attempted to eschew. (Incidentally, the questionnaire failed to tab as delinquent 14 per cent of the incarcerated subjects.)

[4] Twenty-seven treatment boys and 35 control boys had records only for traffic offenses. We did not consider these boys as criminal.

[5] Powers and Witmer, *op. cit.* (note 1 *supra*).

| AGE OF BOY | NUMBER OF CONVICTIONS | |
	TREATMENT GROUP	CONTROL GROUP
Under 18	152	157
18 and over	163	186

Thus again we had failed to uncover evidence that the treatment had successfully deterred criminality.[6] We looked in another direction for such evidence. Although the treatment and control groups had been carefully matched before treatment began, we knew that much had been discovered since the 1930's about the causes of crime.[7] To control against erroneous matching, we held constant the affectional attitudes of the parents, their techniques of discipline, and the neighborhoods in which the subjects had been reared.[8] Nevertheless, we found no statistically significant differences in favor of the treatment group. Nor did we find differences in favor of the treatment group when we held constant the intelligence and the personalities of the boys.

As a result of these various analyses, we were forced to conclude that the treatment program, considered in its totality, had been ineffectual as a preventative of crime.

COMPARISON OF VARIATIONS IN TREATMENT

A comparison of treatment and control groups failed to indicate that the treatment, in general, had been beneficial. One possibility suggested itself as perhaps being responsible for the failure: During World War II, many counselors had joined the armed forces, and the turnover in counselors had been marked. We thought these changes might account for the over-all failure of treatment. Yet when we compared criminal rates—per cent convicted of crimes—we found that they did not significantly reflect this factor.

---

[6] Another criterion of the effect of treatment could be commitment to reform schools, jails, and prisons. A number of biases affect whether a delinquent will go to an institution (judges sometimes consider the home situation or appearance in court). Consequently, we believe that incarceration is less satisfactory than conviction as a standard of criminality. However, the reader may be interested in this aspect of the analysis: Equal proportions of boys from the treatment and control groups were sent to reform schools and equally high proportions, upon release, were convicted for further crimes. Yet only half as many men from the treatment as from the control group were committed to jails and prisons (X^2 5.7; $P < .02$). A number of possible interpretations of this finding are discussed in *Origins of Crime* (New York: Columbia University Press, 1959).

[7] See, for example, Sheldon and Eleanor T. Glueck, *Unraveling Juvenile Delinquency* (Cambridge, Mass.: Harvard University Press, 1950).

[8] See William and Joan McCord, in collaboration with Irving Kenneth Zola, *Origins of Crime* (New York: Columbia University Press, 1959), for a complete description of this analysis.

NUMBER OF COUNSELORS		PER CENT CONVICTED OF CRIMES
One	(*N:* 72)	43
Two	(*N:* 88)	30
Three	(*N:* 47)	53
More than three	(*N:* 46)	48

Despite changes in counselors, the first counselor could be expected to have a degree of influence unmatched by his successors. One of the results of the turnover in counselors was that few boys maintained their relationships with their first counselors for an extended period of time. We anticipated that the duration of treatment by the first counselor would influence criminal rates. Again, we found no confirmation for this view.

LENGTH OF TREATMENT BY FIRST COUNSELOR		PER CENT CONVICTED OF CRIMES
Less than two years	(*N:* 38)	47
2–3	(*N:* 134)	39
More than 3 years	(*N:* 81)	42

Since neither the number of counselors nor the length of treatment by the first counselor seemed to be responsible for the apparent failure of treatment in preventing criminality, we next considered the total duration of treatment. One could argue that programs utilizing the tactics of the Cambridge-Somerville Youth Study must operate over extended periods of time. Length of treatment, to a considerable extent, reflected the staff's estimate of the seriousness of a case. Yet we found no support for the belief that lengthy treatment decreased criminality.

TOTAL LENGTH OF TREATMENT		PER CENT CONVICTED OF CRIMES
Less than 4 years	(*N:* 82)	35
4–6 years	(*N:* 65)	29
More than 6 years	(*N:* 106)	53

In addition to variations in the duration of treatment, there was, of course, wide variation in the intensity of treatment. In almost every case, counselors devoted close attention to family problems. Nevertheless, there were considerable differences in the amount of interaction they had with the boys themselves. Using six months as the minimum time span, we divided the boys according to the greatest intensity of contact they had with any counselor.

Greatest Intensity of Contract		Per Cent Convicted of Crimes
Once a week	(N: 32)	25
Once in two weeks	(N: 84)	51
Once a month	(N: 47)	43
Less than once a month	(N: 82)	33

If we assume that cases considered most serious were seen at least once in two weeks, then the comparison between the group seen every two weeks and those seen every week (for a minimum of six months) gives a measure of the efficacy of intensive treatment. When the criminal rates for these two groups are compared, we find that those seen every week had a significantly smaller incidence of criminality (X^2 6.4; $P < .02$). This finding suggests that frequent contact between a boy and an adult counselor may deter criminality and that sporadic contact has little effect.

Besides reflecting the intensity of treatment, the effectiveness of treatment was found to be related to the age of the boys when they first became participants in the program (X^2 18.9; $d.f.$ 4; $P < .001$).

Age on Nearest Birthday		Per Cent Convicted of Crimes
5–8	(N: 39)	26
9	(N: 35)	29
10	(N: 47)	66
11	(N: 56)	45
12–13	(N: 76)	37

Clearly, early treatment appeared to have been most beneficial; possibly, the drop in crime rate for older boys—over 10 years old—was due to the fact that a higher proportion continued to have guidance through the difficult adolescent period.

We hypothesized that the sex of the counselors, too, might make a difference in the effectiveness of treatment. One might assume, on the one hand, that female counselors would best satisfy a rejected child's desire for maternal care—or, on the other hand, that male counselors would be most effective for they would furnish a masculine model for the boy. To check the relationship between the sex of the first counselor and treatment, we held the boy's age constant.

	Sex of First Counselor			
	Female		Male	
Age of Boy	Per Cent Convicted		Per Cent Convicted	
5–9	(N: 42)	29	(N: 32)	25
10	(N: 6)	67	(N: 41)	66
11–13	(N: 48)	29	(N: 84)	46

The group of boys in the 11- to 13-year age group who had female counselors had a significantly lower crime rate than did those guided by male first counselors (X^2 3.9; $P < .05$). This may be a reflection of independent variables which we were unable to measure, but it appears that female guidance may be more valuable than male guidance for adolescent boys. On the other hand, the very young boy seems to respond equally to male and female counseling. These findings would seem to recommend a reversal in programs which leave adolescent guidance to men and frequently discourage the treatment of very young children by males.

In summary, these comparisons point again to the general ineffectiveness of those forms of counseling which consisted in family assistance plus infrequent interaction with the boy. The analyses suggest, however, that frequent contact with the child—particularly if begun when the child is under ten or by a female after the boy has reached adolescence—may effectively prevent criminality.

A CONTROLLED TEST OF INTENSIVE TREATMENT

One of the greatest difficulties in testing the effects of treatment is the large number of independent factors which may be responsible for variations in results. Having discovered that intensive contact seemed beneficial while the more common "general guidance" approach seemed useless in crime prevention, we sought a controlled test of "the best" treatment offered by the Cambridge-Somerville Youth Study.

Selecting cases which had received the most "intensive" therapy proved to be a rather tangled problem for standards of "good treatment" vary widely. Since the experiment had been initiated by Dr. Cabot, we decided to use his criteria as a basis for the assessment.

In almost every case, as we have noted, counselors worked with the families of their boys. Similarly, there was widespread attention paid to educational and medical handicaps of the boys. Naturally, "good treatment" involved the counselor's alertness to the needs of the family and acceptance by them.

In addition, we established four criteria for judging which boys had undergone the most intensive therapy—standards with which, we believe, Dr. Cabot would have agreed.

First, a counselor had to maintain a relationship with the child for an absolute minimum of two years.

Second, the counselor had to visit the child an average of once a week throughout the two-year period.

Third, the counselor had to have a close relationship with the child. Only if the boy volunteered statements which seemed to indicate his regard and respect for the counselor did we judge their bond as an intimate one.

Fourth, the discussions between the boy and his counselor had, at some point, to touch on the child's basic personality problems: his relation with his parents; his sexual feelings; his attitudes toward authority and his peers; or his feelings of guilt, anxiety, aggression.

After combing the case records, we found, unfortunately, that only twelve cases satisfied these requirements. These boys were some of the most potentially delinquent cases in the project; they had been subjected to a variety of influences which research has shown to be productive of crime. In order to test the effects of treatment on this group, we needed to hold constant those factors which might have some influence on crime but were not directly related to treatment. Therefore each of the twelve boys who received intensive treatment was matched individually to another boy from the treatment group. We matched treated boy to treated boy because information on this group was so much more complete than on the control boys.

Each pair was equated on eight factors: the mother's attitude toward her son, the father's attitude toward his son, the child's personality, method of parental discipline, general home atmosphere, neighborhood, intelligence, and the delinquency prognosis score which had been assigned at the beginning of the experiment.

We were able to find boys who, on these factors, closely resembled the twelve boys who had received the Cambridge-Somerville project's most intensive care.[9] The mothers and the fathers of every pair resembled each other in their attitudes toward their sons. Each pair of boys was of the same general personality type. Except for one set, the pairs matched in terms of the parental discipline which they had received. Eleven of the twelve pairs had similar home atmosphere. Only one set differed by more than a single rating point in neighborhood. Using the Stanford-Binet intelligence scores, we were able to match the boys (within five points) in eight of the twelve pairs. Eight of the twelve pairs had been given a delinquency prognosis within one point on an eleven-point scale.

When we had finished this matching, two groups of remarkably similar boys could be compared with each other. One set of boys had received, for at least two years, the very best attention which the project offered; the other set received the less intensive, and, as we have seen, largely inadequate services of the program.

The results of the comparison are suggestive: While six of the boys who received the most intensive treatment committed at least one crime, eleven of their matched comrades became criminal (X^2 3.9; $P < .05$).

Unfortunately, only a handful of boys underwent the intensive treatment.

---

[9] When difficulties occurred in the matching, we used a "preference" table which gave greater importance to those factors which research had shown to be the most important in delinquency causation. Naturally the matching was done without knowledge of the court records of any of the boys.

The small number of cases makes generalization difficult. Nevertheless, the results seem to indicate that intimate, long-term, "supportive" counseling may help to prevent criminality.

SUMMARY

Three forms of analyses were used to check the efficacy of the Cambridge-Somerville Youth Study in preventing crime. In the first form, we compared 253 boys who had received treatment with 253 boys, carefully matched in personality and family background, who had received no special treatment. In this comparison, we found that the general program—consisting in guidance for the family, medical and academic assistance for the boys, co-ordination of community agencies, and supplementary entertainment of the boys—had been no more effective in crime prevention than other community services: Approximately equal numbers of treated boys and control boys had committed approximately equal numbers of crimes in childhood and adulthood.

In the second form of analysis, we concentrated upon variations within the treatment group. Negatively, we found that neither the change in counselors nor the length of treatment—which, for many boys, was shorter than had been planned—could be held responsible for the failure. On the other hand, we found evidence that the program might have been more successful had a greater number of boys been seen at least once a week by their counselors and had treatment been started during the first decade of the boys' lives. In addition, we found that male counselors were apparently as effective as female counselors with very young boys, although they were less effective with adolescents.

As a final method for assessing the project, we focused upon twelve boys who had received intensive treatment. We matched each of these twelve boys to another who had similar parents, personality, discipline, home atmosphere, and intelligence, yet had received no intensive treatment. We concluded from this closely controlled comparison that intimate, long-term, "supportive" counseling may prevent crime.

Thus, using the standard of "official" criminal behavior, we must conclude that the Cambridge-Somerville Youth Study was largely a failure. Some individuals undoubtedly benefited from the program; but the group, as a whole, did not. Yet even in its failure, the program must be regarded as a magnificent experiment, for its provision of a control group and its careful attention to research have produced a fund of information invaluable to future studies of the causation and prevention of crime.

Chapter Five

The Small Group

IN 1909 CHARLES HORTON COOLEY introduced the concept of the primary group as a group characterized by intimate, face-to-face association and cooperation, and added, "The result of intimate association, psychologically, is a certain fusion of individualities in the common whole, so that one's very self, for many purposes at least, is the common life and purpose of the group. Perhaps the simplest way of describing this wholeness is by saying that it is a 'we'; it involves the sort of sympathy and mutual identification for which 'we' is a natural expression. 'One lives in the feeling of the whole and finds the chief aims of his will in that feeling.' "[1]

Obviously all of us are familiar with the principle of primary groups. Utilizing this principle, however, has only recently been effected. The discovery of the value of primary groups, like many other discoveries, has been made by laymen as well as experts, laymen who saw the value of the principle even if they could not define it. Such organizations as Gamblers Anonymous, Narcotics Anonymous, and Suicides Anonymous have been patterned after the better-known association for alcoholics.[2]

The first article in this chapter (Selection 19) presents the background and the organization of a group that has recently received considerable publicity. It provides an excellent illustration of the small group principle.

[1] Charles Horton Cooley, *Social Organization* (New York: Scribner, 1929), pp. 23–24.
[2] George McGuinness, "Gamblers, Narcotics Addicts Imitate Alcoholics Anonymous," *Wall Street Journal,* **158,** 1 (December 29, 1962), p. 1, p. 13.

The utility of working through relatively intimate association with others has implications in areas beyond personal disorganization. William Karraker (Selection 20) observes the value of the method for training and administering aircraft crews. Other studies have been made along very similar lines for Navy submarine crews, Air Force bomber crews, and Army Infantry units.

Finally, knowledge of small groups was employed by the Chinese Communists in psychological warfare as described in Selection 21.

19

The Anticriminal Society: Synanon

Lewis Yablonsky

Although still in its infancy, Synanon represents one additional attempt to alleviate the drug addiction problem. Dr. Yablonsky points out the theoretical basis for the movement and gives an interesting summary of the operation.

A reader of the *Terminal Island News* of April 12, 1962, would be somewhat surprised to note an unusual statement called "Breaking the Invisible Wall" authored by a former criminal and inmate of the Federal Correctional Institution at Terminal Island, Calif., the U. S. Public Health Service Hospital at Fort Worth, Texas, the State Prison of Southern Michigan, and various juvenile reformatories. James Middleton, the writer of the statement, had served a total of 15 years in these institutions. He has currently been clean of his past lengthy addiction and criminal history for almost 3 years. Middleton is one of a group of seven ex-offenders and former prisoners who go to the Terminal Island institution once a week to run group counseling sessions with about 25 addict inmates. This is the way Middleton described this project in the *Terminal Island News:*

Reprinted from *Federal Probation* **26,** 3 (September 1962), pp. 50–57, by permission of the publisher and the author.

Lewis Yablonsky is Professor of Sociology, San Fernando Valley California State College.

As a former using addict and inmate of Terminal Island and other prisons, having been free from the use of drugs for the past 2½ years by being a resident of Synanon House, I have been aware of the lack of communication between inmates and all those in positions of authority. Perhaps the most difficult problem to overcome for penologists, prison officials, and others dealing with the socially rejected group, the criminal, is the problem of establishing an area of communication, some feeling of rapport. The convict, criminal, or any rebellious delinquent has a defiance of all authority. This he carried to such an extent that he will refuse to even talk to a person in any position of authority whom he considers his enemy. He takes the attitude that "If you are not on my side, you are against me."

On November 26, 1961, six members of the Synanon Foundation were invited to the Terminal Island correctional institution by Chief Parole Officer Frank E. Saunders who believed that the Synanon approach might have something to offer the prisoners who had an addiction history.

Of paramount significance perhaps is the effect synanon has had in bridging this gap in communication between prisoner and official. This has been accomplished by the prisoners being encouraged to verbalize their problem, frustration, attitudes, opinions, etc., in the synanon.

Synanon is a form of intense group interaction. In these meetings synanites and inmate addicts are encouraged to break down this wall and see their problems in a more realistic light. Part of the success of these meetings can be attributed to the fact that an inmate can often lie to the officials and get away with it, however with his fellow inmates, those who know him intimately, and can identify with his problems and his unsatisfactory reaction to them, he can't get away with as much. They see him as he is. Once a person has admitted his failures and inadequacies to others, and as an eventual consequence, to himself, he finds that he can discuss these things with almost anyone.

They are no longer deep, dark secrets which he must hide from others and himself. As Dr. Yablonsky, U.C.L.A. criminologist said, "This is the most significant break-through in the field of criminology in the past 50 years."

It is conceivable to me as an ex-inmate myself that someday Synanon could become an established part of the prison program throughout the United States.

THE BACKGROUND OF SYNANON

The Synanon organization,[1] of which Middleton is a significant member, has been in operation about 4 years. As a result of exposure to this unique social system approximately 100 persons, most with long criminal and addiction records, no longer find it necessary to use drugs or commit crimes. Some Synanon residents have been clean of these deviant patterns for periods of up to 4 years.

This antiaddiction society originated with Charles E. Dederich, a former business executive, who had worked through an alcoholic problem and was motivated to transmit the forces which had led to his own recovery. A strong personality with characteristics of a charismatic leader, Dederich attracted

---

[1] The name *Synanon* was derived from the slip-of-the-tongue of a confused addict attempting to say seminar. It was adopted because it is a new word for describing a new phenomenon.

to his residence by the beach in Ocean Park a coterie of alcoholics and drug addicts who found stimulating and interesting the lengthy philosophical discussions which he led. Many of these persons had no roots and moved into Dederich's "pad." Within a short time a small colony of about 15 addicts moved into the various apartments in the immediate area and emerged as the early core of the Synanon movement. At this point, about 6 months after its inception, there emerged an idealized assumption that no one was using drugs; although this fact was only true for about half the residents at the time.

Two incidents sharply changed the nature of this unusual collectivity and projected the evolution of a clean Synanon community. One was what later became known as the "big cop out." This involved the open admission of occasional use by several key residents. Shortly after this episode the balance of power shifted over to a community with a majority of *clean addicts*. This new situation gave strength and credence to an antiaddiction, anticriminal ethos. To my knowledge, it was the first time anywhere that a group of non-prisoner ex-addicts could be found in one location.

By the summer of 1959 about 40 to 50 men and women, not using drugs, were living in a Synanon colony in one large building. The Synanon movement had become more established and aroused the interest in many significant professionals. *Time* magazine in its April 7, 1961, issue published an extensive description of the Synanon organization at that time.

S. S. HANG TOUGH

Early in August 1959, homeowners along the stylish Pacific Ocean beaches in Santa Monica, Calif., were dismayed to get a new set of neighbors: a bedraggled platoon of half a hundred men and women, who moved into a run-down, three story, red brick building that once was a National Guard armory. White and black, young and middle-aged, criminals and innocents, artists and loafers, the unlikely assortment shared one trait: they were narcotics addicts determined to kick their habit for good.

Scrounging lumber, paint and old furniture, the group converted the top floor of the armory into a barracks-style men's dormitory. They turned the second floor into offices, kitchen, dining hall and living room, and the main floor into women's sleeping quarters. Over the doors in the living room they hung their emblem: a life preserver with the words *"S. S. Hang Tough,"* slang for "don't give up." . . .

Such was the formal dedication of Synanon House a self-run, haphazardly financed experiment in human reclamation whose success has been hailed by Dr. Donald Cressey, University of California at Los Angeles sociologist, as "the most significant attempt to keep addicts off drugs that has ever been made." . . . The technique was patterned roughly after the group-therapy methods of Alcoholics Anonymous. . . . Dr. Cressey describes the psychology: "A group in which Criminal A joins with some noncriminals to change Criminal B is probably most effective in changing Criminal A."

In the often brutally frank personal exchanges, the addicts slowly reveal themselves . . . and through daily contact with similarly beset persons are reinforced in their determination to quit narcotics permanently. Says the founder of Synanon House, 48-year-old Charles E. Dederich . . . , once an alcoholic but never a drug addict: "It is something that works."

The Synanon curriculum is divided into three stages. During the first phase, the emotionally shaken, physically weak addict gradually adjusts to his new surroundings. ... During the second stage, the ex-addict works at a regular job on the outside, contributes part of his wages to the group, continues to live at the house. ... In its final stage, Synanon sends its member out into society.

Interestingly, the potential of this type of an anticriminal society for modifying difficult offenders had been forecast by Professor Cressey in an article published in 1955 in *The American Journal of Sociology*.[2] His projection of the need for this treatment approach was based upon Sutherland's causal theory of criminal "differential association." Cressey logically speculated that, "if the behavior of an individual is an intrinsic part of the groups to which he belongs, attempts to change the behavior must be directed at groups." [3]

Cressey utilizing "differential association" theory as a diagnostic base projected the necessity for an anticriminal society to modify deviant behavior.

The differential association theory of criminal behavior presents implications for diagnosis and treatment consistent with the group-relations principle for changing behavior and could be advantageously utilized in correctional work. According to it, persons become criminals principally because they have been relatively isolated from groups whose behavior patterns (including attitudes, motives, and rationalizations) are anticriminal, or because their residence, employment, social position, native capacities, or something else has brought them into relatively frequent association with the behavior patterns of criminal groups. A diagnosis of criminality based on this theory would be directed at analysis of the criminal's attitudes, motives, and rationalizations regarding criminality and would recognize that those characteristics depend upon the groups to which the criminal belongs. Then if criminals are to be changed, either they must become members of anticriminal groups, or their present pro-criminal group relations must be changed.[4]

Life in the Synanon anticriminal society revolves around a set of educational and apparently group therapeutic procedures developed by Dederich and the group of ex-addict leaders he had personally trained. Synanon by this time had many characteristics of an extended father-dominated family. As Dederich himself described it in an address before The Southern California Parole Officers Association:

We have here a climate consisting of a family structure similar in some areas to a primitive tribal structure, which seems to affect individuals on a subconscious level. The structure also contains overtones of a 19th century family set-up of the type which produced inner-directed personalities. It is the feeling of the Synanon Foundation that an undetermined percentage of narcotic addicts are potentially inner-directed people as differentiated from tradition-directed people. A more or less autocratic family structure appears to be necessary as a pre-conditioning environment to buy time for the recovering addict.

---

[2] Donald R. Cressey, "Changing Criminals: The Application of the Theory of Differential Association," *American Journal of Sociology* (September 1955), pp. 116–120.

[3] *Ibid.*, p. 117.

[4] *Ibid.*, p. 118.

... The autocratic overtone of the family structure demands that the patients or members of the family perform tasks as part of the group. As a member is able to take direction in small tasks such as helping in the preparation of meals, housecleaning and so forth, regardless of his rebellion of being "told what to do," his activity seems to provide exercise of emotions of giving or creating which have lain dormant. As these muscles strengthen, it seems that the resistance to cooperating with the group tends to dissipate.

SYNANON GROUP THERAPY

The daily program for the Synanon resident includes some type of work, a noon educational seminar, the synanon (a form of leaderless group therapy in which all residents participate three times a week), and daily interaction and communication with hundreds of "squares" (nonaddicts) from all walks of life who visit the building regularly.

The synanon, a form of group interaction vital to the overall approach, tends to be a unique form of aggressive leaderless nonprofessional group psychotherapy, directed by what Dederich has referred to as a Synanist. According to Dederich:

The Synanist leans heavily on his own insight into his own problems of personality in trying to help others find themselves, and will use the weapons of ridicule, cross-examination, and hostile attack as it becomes necessary. Synanon sessions seem to provide an emotional catharsis and trigger an atmosphere of truth-seeking which is reflected in the social life of the family structure. The Synanist does not try to convey to another that he himself is a stable personality. In fact, it may very well be the destructive drives of the recovered or recovering addictive personality embodied in a Synanist which makes him a good therapeutic tool—fighting fire with fire.

This form of group therapy is ideally suited for the overall Synanon community. The group sessions do not have any official leader. They are autonomous; however, leaders emerge in each session in a natural fashion. The emergent leader tells much about himself in his questioning of another. Because he is intensely involved with the subject or the problem in the particular session he begins to direct, he is in a natural fashion the "most qualified" session leader for that time and place. In short, the expert of the moment may be emotionally crippled in many personal areas, but in the session where he is permitted by the group to take therapeutic command, he may be the most qualified therapeutic agent.

Synanon, as a side effect, trains persons to become a new brand of therapeutic agent in the correctional field. The system provides the opportunity for offenders to modify their own deviant behavior and then work with other offenders. In this context I view the phenonomenon of Synanon at Terminal Island as a major breakthrough in the field of correction.

Although ex-offenders have been randomly used over the years in the processes of correction, Synanon provides a unique contribution. One can view the seven 2-year-clean Synanon participants in the Terminal Island project as a new type of "therapeutic agent" for dealing with the crime problem. Unlike most professional or ex-offender workers in the field the trained synanist has three levels of experience which uniquely qualify him for work with other offenders.

1. He has a lengthy history of criminal experience. He himself has made the "scene." He knows the crime problem in its many dimensions—at first hand.

2. At Synanon, this individual has deeply experienced the emotional upheaval of rejecting one way of life for another. He has "in his gut" gone through a resocialization process and knows something about the set of experiences and the pain involved in the transition.

3. He knows the Synanon social system. He has a subconscious conception of the processes at work for helping others and he is himself a functional part of this organization. He has been trained at "the Synanon College" for working with recalcitrant offenders.

This triad of experiences qualified the Synanist uniquely for the task at hand. Terminal Island inmates in the Synanon project know they are encountering in the Synanist a new breed of "treatment man." The Synanist is difficult to con or juggle out of position. The Synanist cannot easily be outmaneuvered from his zeal to point up a new direction in life to replace the roles of crime and addiction which he now views as wasteful and stupid behavior. This point of view of the Synanist seems to get across to the inmate seeking a noncriminal mode of existence.

Although the synanon form of group therapy is an important aspect of the method, the basic therapeutic force is the overall synanon social system. The best way to reveal this overall dynamic is to examine its impact on one successful resident.

FRANKIE: A CASE STUDY OF THE SYNANON SYSTEM [5]

Frankie, a 2-year-clean Synanon resident, first came to the author's attention in an unusual fashion. While listening to some tapes being played on the Egyptian King gang killing (an incident studied intensively by the author), Dederich detected a familiar voice. Hearing one King comment, "I kicked him in the head, it was the least I could do," Dederich remarked, "That sounds like Frankie." It was later confirmed that Frankie was this Egyptian King gang member's older brother. It was also determined that Frankie's early case history and violent gang life pattern paralleled his younger brother's. Frankie later turned to using and pushing drugs, a crim-

---

[5] This section is partially derived from a recent volume by the author, *The Violent Gang* (New York: Macmillan, 1962).

inal career, which carried him to the Federal Correctional Institution at Danbury, Conn., New York City's Riker's Island Penitentiary, and finally Bellevue Hospital in New York City. As a result of his experience at Synanon, Frankie was at the time free and clear of drugs and violence for over 2 years.

"Frankie would never use a knife; unless he had to. Mostly with his fists he would beat a guy down and try to kill him right there. They pulled him off this big guy one time—he wouldn't stop punching him in the face." This was a casual observation made by Frankie's ex-"crime partner," the girl with whom he had lived for 5 years in New York. (She is also currently a successful resident at Synanon.)

Frankie's first reaction to Synanon was confusion. "The first thing they hit me with flipped me. This tough-looking cat says to me—'there are two things you can't do here, shoot drugs or fight.'" Frankie said, scratching his head, "I was all mixed up—these were the only two things I knew how to do."

Frankie first came West at the insistence of his parents "to try a new way of life." "The family chipped in, gave me a plane ticket, and told me to straighten out or drop dead." He accepted the plane ticket they gave him and came West under the assumption of continuing his old way of life. In the Los Angeles situation he had trouble getting a good drug connection and stealing enough money to supply his habit. He heard about Synanon, and decided to try it. His initial motives were not pure. His thought was "to get cleaned up a little" and either get organized for a new onslaught on Los Angeles or steal enough to return to New York and his old criminal pattern. Something happened at Synanon to make Frankie stay "clean" for 2 years and later assume the administrative role of "coordinator" at Synanon.[6]

The Synanon environment was interesting and exciting for Frankie. There were, in the addicts' jargon, "lots of hip people." Jimmy the Greek, who at 48 had been an addict for 20 years and a criminal and con-man for over 30 years [7] and Jimmy Middleton who now ran the kitchen at Synanon. In

---

[6] A coordinator works a 4-hour shift, answering phones, catering to visitors and generally handling the House's business as it emerges. It requires some ingenuity and administrative ability.

[7] Jimmy's personal statement in the *Synanon Issue* of the *Terminal Island News* further reveals his criminal background and current view of life: "My addiction history goes back to when I was 12 years old (I am close to 50) but up until the time I came to Synanon, 31 months ago, I never knew what it was to be "clean" on the streets. I have done just about everything illegal to obtain money; work was not a part of this life, for I could not support a habit working. I have spent almost 10 years in county jails, the Lewisburg federal penitentiary, and chain-gangs. I can go so far as to say that I had never met a 'clean' dope-fiend until I came to Synanon. . . .

I have been a resident of Synanon for 31 months. I plan on staying for some time to come. For the first time in my life I like what I am doing—Synanon is growing and I am part of it. There is a group from Synanon attending meetings at Terminal Island every week, for the past 4½ months; I am project director of this group. There are plans in the making to start Synanon meetings on the women's side at Terminal Island —and eventually, men and women together. I am sure with the cooperation we have been getting this plan will come about in the near future."—James (Greek) Georgelas.

the kitchen Frankie received his first job scouring pots and pans and mopping floors. According to Frankie, Jimmy M. could not be conned or manipulated out of position like the therapist Frankie had encountered at Riker's Island Prison. Jimmy M., of course, knew the score and to him Frankie with all his exploits was a "young punk," who could give him no trouble. "I've met kids like this all my life—in and out of the joint."

According to Frankie, "I hated this '. . .' for no good reason. I used to sometimes sit and plan ways to kill him." When Frankie wanted to fight Jimmy over a disagreement about work (no fighting allowed at Synanon) Jimmy laughed and told him if he wanted to fight he would be thrown out of Synanon.

The usual prison situation was reversed and confusing to Frankie. In the "joint" (prison) if Frankie got in trouble confinement became increasingly severe with the "hole" (solitary confinement) as an end point. At the Bellevue Hospital psychiatric ward where Frankie had also "done time" it was a straightjacket. What made Frankie remain, even behave in order to stay at Synanon with its open door?

The fact that Frankie was exported from New York to Los Angeles was a significant force initially in keeping him at Synanon, as he stated it: "At times I felt like splitting (leaving), then I thought it will be hard to make it back to New York. I didn't know Los Angeles and I was afraid to make it it out there—'cause I didn't know the people. Synanon was better than anything else I could do—at the time."

Also, Synanon House was on the beach. The meals were good. In the evening many ex-addict top musicians would play cool jazz.[8] Also there were, according to Frankie, "broads to dance with and get to know." But highly important in this antiaddiction, antidelinquency society there were others who understood him, had made the same "scenes" and intuitively knew his problems and how to handle him. He respected people he could not con. He belonged and was now part of a "family" he could accept.

At Synanon Frankie could also make a "rep" without getting punished or locked up. In prison, the highest he could achieve in terms of the values of "his people" was to become "King" of the sociopathic inmate system, acquire a "stash" of cigarettes, obtain some unsatisfactory homosexual favors, and land in the "hole." In the "inmate system" of Synanon he could achieve any role he was "big enough of a man" to acquire and this carried the highest approval of his fellows. He could actually become a *director* in this organization—which was now in the national spotlight.[9] Articles on Synanon had been published in national magazines like *Time, Life,* and *Nation,* and were coming out daily in the press. For the first time in his life, Frankie was receiving status for being clean and nondelinquent.

---

[8] The Synanon Band recently produced a widely acclaimed professional record album, appropriately called *Sounds of Synanon.*

[9] There are currently 8 directors of the Synanon Foundation. This is the highest and most respected status level of achievement in the organization.

Of course, when he first arrived at Synanon, Frankie attempted to gain a "rep" by conniving and making deals in accord with his old mode of relating. He was laughed at, ridiculed and given a "hair-cut" (a verbal dressing down) by other "old-time con men" members of the organization. He was accused of "shucking and sliding" (simply not performing adequately). The old-time Synanists were ferocious about keeping the organization, which had literally saved their lives and given them a new life status, operating smoothly.

Frankie found that "rep" was acquired in this social system (unlike ones he had known) by truth, honesty, and industry. The values of his other life required reversal if he was to gain a "rep" at Synanon. These values were not goals *per se* which someone moralized about in a meaningless vacuum; they were means to the end of acquiring prestige in this tough social system with which he now intensely identified.

In the small *s* synanons, three nights a week Frankie participated in a form of leaderless group psychotherapy. In these synanons the truth was viciously demanded. Any system of rationalizations about past or current experience were brutally demolished by the group. There was an intensive search for self-identity.

In the process the individual attempted to learn what goes on beneath the surface of his thoughts. For Frankie this was the first time in his life that he discovered others had some idea about what he was thinking underneath. He had individual group therapy in prison—but there he could "con" the therapist and most important, "I said what I thought they wanted to hear so I could hit the street sooner."

Most important Frankie began to get some comprehension of what others thought in a social situation. The fact of empathy or identifying with the thoughts and feelings of others became a significant reality.

Frankie was at first empathic in his usual pattern of sociopathic self-centered manipulation. However, a new force was introduced into the situation—he began to care about what happened to others at Synanon. This was at first selfish. Synanon was for him a good interesting way of life. He had identified with the system and learned "gut level" that if any Synanon member failed, he too was diminished and failed. In Cressey's words which Frankie learned to quote (since after all Professor Cressey was a friend of his) "When I help another guy, it helps me personally."

In the status system, Frankie's rise to the role of coordinator was not quick nor easy. He moved from the "dishpan" to serving food at the kitchen counter.

After several months he was allowed to work outside on a pickup truck which acquired food and other donations. With two other individuals who worked with him on the truck a group decision was made one day "that one shot wouldn't hurt." One individual knew a "connection" on the route. They went to his home. All they could get were some pills.

When they arrived back at Synanon their slightly "loaded" appearance immediately became apparent to the group ("they spotted us right away") and they were hauled into the main office and viciously (verbally) attacked to tell all ("cop out") or get out of the building. A general meeting was called and they were forced to reveal "all" before the entire group.[10] Frankie was back at work on the dishpan that evening.

Such "slips" often come out in the synanon. In a sense, in addition to other forces of growth from the synanon it serves as a form of "first-aid" therapy. If any one reveals a minor "slip," the personal wound is examined and cleaned up by the group before a serious act of misbehavior occurs. (The synanon situation has some of the characteristics of an underground organization operating during wartime. If any member "falls," it may entail the destruction of the entire organization.)

The norms of synanon society are the reverse of the criminal code. On one occasion Frankie, with two other members of Synanon, went for a walk into town. One individual suggested buying a bottle of wine. (No drinking is permitted.) The other two (including Frankie) smashed the idea. However, no one revealed the incident until 2 days later it came up in a synanon. The group jumped hardest on Frankie and the other individual who did not reveal the potential "slip," rather than on the transgressor who had suggested the wine. Frankie and the other "witness" were expected to report such "slips" immediately, since the group's life depended on keeping each other "straight." For the first time in his life Frankie was censured for *"not squealing."* The maxim "thou shalt not squeal" basic to the existence of the usual underworld criminal culture was reversed at Synanon and just as ferociously sanctioned. An individual could get "kicked out" of Synanon for *not* being a "stoolie."

The rule of no physical violence was at first extremely difficult for Frankie to grasp and believe, since his usual response to a difficult situation would be to leap fists-first past verbal means of communication into assault. As a result of the synanons and other new patterns of interaction, Frankie's social ability for communication increasingly minimized his assaultive impulse. Although at first he was controlled from committing violence by the fear of ostracism, he later no longer had a need to use violence since he now had some ability to interact effectively. He could express himself with a new form of communication on a nonviolent, verbal level.

On occasion Frankie would regress and have the motivation for assault—but the system had taken hold. In one synanon session I heard him say, "I was so . . . mad yesterday, I wished I was back at Rikers (prison). I really wanted to hit that bastard Jimmy in the mouth."

Frankie had a sketchy work record prior to Synanon. Other than gang

---

[10] This process known as a "fireplace" may be called at any time, day or night. The "transgressor" is placed at the fireplace in the main living room in front of all other residents. They are ridiculed into an open-honest revelation of their "offense." The group may then decide to evict or give the individual another chance.

fighting, "pimping," armed robbery, pushing heroin, and some forced work in prison, he seldom acted in any role resembling formal work. His theme had been "work was for squares." He learned how to work at Synanon automatically as a side effect of his desire to rise in the status system. He also learned as a side effect of the work process, the startling fact "that talking to someone in the right way made them do more things than belting them."

Frankie's most recent position involves the overall supervision of Synanon's number two building. Here 12 mothers (ex-addicts) in residence at Synanon live with their children. Frankie supervises a budget, the care and feeding of the establishment, and the inevitable daily counseling of his "wards." Although it is not apparent on the surface of his efficient administration, Frankie beneath maintains a state of personal amazement about his new social role in society.

As a consequence of living in the Synanon social system, Frankie developed an increasing residual of social learning and ability. His destructive pattern of relating to others withered away because it was no longer functional for him within this new way of life. Synanon developed his empathic ability, produced an attachment to different, more socially acceptable values, and reconnected him adequately to the larger society within which Synanon functioned as a valid organization.

PRINCIPAL FORCES AT WORK IN THE SYNANON SOCIETY

Involvement

Initially, Synanon society is able to involve and control the offender. This is accomplished through providing an interesting social setting comprised of associates who understand him and will not be outmaneuvered by his manipulative behavior.

An Achievable Status System

Within the context of this system he can (perhaps, for the first time) see a realistic possibility for legitimate achievement and prestige. Synanon provides a rational and attainable opportunity structure for the success-oriented individual. He is no longer restricted to inmate status; since there is no inmate-staff division. All residents are staff.

New Social Role

Synanon creates a new social role which can be temporarily or indefinitely occupied in the process of social growth and development. (Some residents have made the decision to make Synanon their life's work.) This new role is a legitimate one supported by the ex-offender's own community as well as the inclusive society. With the opening of new Synanons and increasing development of projects like the one at Terminal Island, Synanon trained persons are increasingly in demand. Since the Synanon organization is not a hospital or an institution, there is no compulsion to move out of this satisfying community.

Social Growth

In the process of acquiring legitimate social status in Synanon the offender necessarily, as a side effect, develops the ability to relate, communicate, and work with others. The values of truth, honesty, and industry become necessary means to this goal of status achievement. After a sufficient amount of practice and time, the individual socialized in this way in a natural fashion develops the capability for behaving adequately with reference to these values.

Social Control

The control of deviance is a by-product of the individual's status-seeking. Conformity to the norms is necessary in order to achieve. Anomie, the dislocation of goals and means, becomes a minimal condition. The norms are valid and adhered to within this social system, since means are available for legitimate goal attainment.

Another form of control is embodied in the threat of ostracism which becomes a binding force. After being initially involved in Synanon, the individual does not at the time feel adequate for participation in the larger society. After a sufficient residue of Synanon social living has been acquired the individual no longer fears banishment; however, at the same time he is then better prepared for life on the outside (if this is his choice). He no longer fears ostracism and may remain voluntarily because he feels Synanon is a valid way of life for him. In Synanon he has learned and acquired a gratifying social role which enables him as a "coordinator" or a "director" to help others who can benefit from Synanon treatment.

Other forms of immediate social control include ridicule ("hair-cuts," the "fireplace") and the synanon sessions. The individual is required to tell the truth in the synanon. This also regulates his behavior. Real-life transgressions are often prevented by the knowledge that the individual's deviance will automatically, rapidly, and necessarily be brought to the attention of his community within the synanon session. He is living within a community where others know about and, most important, are concerned with his behavior.

Empathy and Self-Identity

The constant self-assessment required in his daily life and in the synanon sessions fosters the consolidation of self-identity and empathy. His self-estimation is under constant assessment and attack by relevant others, who become sensitive to and concerned about him. The process provides the opportunity for the individual almost literally "to see himself as others do." He is also compelled as part of this process to develop the ability to identify with and understand others. A side consequence is the development of self-growth, social awareness, the ability to communicate and empathic effectiveness. When these socialization processes are at work and take hold, the youth becomes reconnected with the legitimate society and no longer finds it necessary to use drugs or assume a deviant role.

SYNANON'S FUTURE

From its unusual beginnings the Synanon Foundation has emerged as a highly efficient organization. The Foundation has federal tax-exempt status and is a corporate entity in the State of California. The State Legislature passed and the Governor signed into law The Petris Bill on June 15, 1961, officially sanctioning Synanon as a "Place" for rehabilitating drug addicts.[11]

Synanon, over the past year [1961], as a partial consequence of donations and the earning power of its residents, has rented four buildings with a total rental of over $1500 a month. Although its budgeting is tight, comparable to other nonprofit organizations, it has met all of its financial obligations as a result of community support. The organization over the past year [1961] has sustained approximately 85 residents in food and clothing, and has

---

[11] The Petris Bill especially passed for Synanon is here presented in full:

Assembly Bill No. 2626 (State of California). An act to amend Section 11391 of the Health and Safety Code, relating to narcotic addiction.

The people of the State of California do enact as follows:

Section 1. Section 11391 of the Health and Safety Code is amended to read:

11391. No person shall treat an addict for addiction except in one of the following:

(a) An institution approved by the Board of Medical Examiners, and where the patient is at all times kept under restraint and control.

(b) A city or county jail.

(c) A state prison.

(d) A state narcotic hospital.

(e) A state hospital.

(f) A county hospital.

This section does not apply during emergency treatment or where the patient's addiction is complicated by the presence of incurable disease, serious accidents, or injury, or the infirmities of old age.

Neither this section nor any other provision of this division shall be construed to prohibit the maintenance of a place [Synanon] in which persons seeking to recover from narcotic addiction reside and endeavor to aid one another and receive aid from others in recovering from such addiction, nor does this section or such division prohibit such aid, provided that no person is treated for addiction in such place [Synanon] by means of administering, furnishing, or prescribing of narcotics. The preceding sentence is declaratory of pre-existing law. Every such place [Synanon] shall register with and be approved by the Board of Medical Examiners. The board may inspect such places [Synanons] at reasonable times and, if it concludes that the conditions necessary for approval no longer exist, it may withdraw approval. Every person admitted to such a place [Synanon] shall register with the police department of the city in which it is located or, if it is outside of the city limits, with the sheriff's office. The place [Synanon] shall maintain its own register of all residents. It shall require all its residents to register with said police department or sheriff's office and, upon termination of the residence of any person in said place [Synanon], it shall report the name of the person terminating residence to said police department or sheriff's office.

entertained approximately 19,000 guests (mostly professional visitors). In addition to the Terminal Island project a Synanon educational and addiction-prevention program has involved most of the 100 Synanon members in over 400 speaking engagements delivered to business, professional, religious, youth, and college and university groups. One evening a week about 40 non-addicts from all segments of society participate in the so-called "Square Synanons." Here the variety of human problems are examined through utilization of the Synanon method involving Synanon residents mixed with "squares." This interaction and cross-fertilization of ideas and insights appear to be of benefit to all.

As a social science research center Synanon is unique. In this open-door environment run by ex-offenders themselves, persons with long addiction and criminal background freely provide important data unavailable in the usual custodial setting. Synanon thus enables the systematic gathering of much useful information about crime, addiction, and the solution of these problems.

The Synanon approach which has emerged under the creative and capable leadership of Dederich and his uniquely trained staff of directors as an effective anticriminal and antiaddiction society, also involves an organization of distinguished citizens from all walks of life called "S.O.S." or Sponsors of Synanon. This supportive organization has a national membership of over 600 persons who donate money, goods, and services. They are currently launching a building program for an ideal Synanon community.

The organization is naturally committed to expansion. Synanon-trained personnel of the type carrying out the program at Terminal Island will no doubt shortly be utilized as the core staff for Synanon Houses planned for other communities. Each new establishment has the potential for "cleaning-up" another hundred offenders.

As viewed by its founder, Charles Dederich, Synanon is still in its infancy. The fact of 100 individuals with long addiction and criminal histories currently clean attests to its effectiveness. However, Synanon, as a social movement or community way of life, appears to have possibilities beyond exclusive application to the addiction problem. As Middleton commented at the outset: "It is conceivable to me as an ex-inmate myself that someday Synanon could become an established part of the prison program throughout the United States."

20

Teamwork and Safety in Flight

William Karraker

The habit of thinking of people as isolated individuals, rather than as groups, is deeply ingrained in our culture. In this article, William Karraker documents dramatically the costliness of this failure to appreciate the concept of the group. He contends that an airline crew will operate more efficiently as a group if it is trained as a group.

Some of the problems of those who manage flight crews are inherent in the organization and scheduling of such crews. Currently, on the airline for which I am a pilot, the basic flight crew, a captain, a copilot, a flight engineer, and two or more cabin attendants, is assembled at a crew base, assigned to a patterned trip away from base, and dispersed at the end of such trip. It will be my thesis that such dispersal at the end of each trip creates or intensifies some of the problems of flight crew management and flight safety with which we shall deal.

In this paper we shall be concerned only with those problems which relate to a crew at work; meaning the crew which has been assembled and which has left its base. We shall not be concerned with hiring policies, at-base management, or record keeping.

It can certainly be agreed that a flight crew is a primary human group, even though present practices sharply limit the life-span of such a group. As a human group, a flight crew may be studied much as other small groups have been studied in other industries and as have air crews in the United States Air Force. It is the primary purpose of this paper to encourage such study.

Before stating the problems under consideration, it will be well to give brief descriptions of the flight crew jobs so that the makeup of the group may be kept in mind as the group itself is discussed.

The *captain* is in command of the aircraft and is responsible for the safety of the passengers, crew, cargo, and the aircraft itself. He is answerable to his company's management, in the person of a chief pilot or flight manager, for the safe, efficient, and otherwise satisfactory conduct of all flights to which he is assigned. His work resembles that of a first-line foreman in industry, in that he supervises no one who supervises anyone else. However, he has no

Reprinted from *Human Organization,* **17,** 3 (Fall 1958), pp. 3–8, by permission of The Society for Applied Anthropology and the author.

William Karraker is a Captain, Pan American World Airways.

power to hire and fire, as most foremen have, and he never has the same work force on successive trips.

The *copilot* is second in command and assists the captain with all pilot duties. He reports to the chief pilot, in general, but, in particular, to the captain of each flight to which he is assigned.

The *flight engineer* is responsible to the captain of each flight to which he is assigned for the airworthiness of the aircraft, the loading of fuel and other fluids, the condition of emergency equipment, and the mechanical operation of engines and other systems in flight. He reports, in general, to a Chief Flight Engineer and to the Maintenance Section of the Operations Department, but, in particular, to the captain of each flight to which he is assigned.

Cabin attendants may be either male or female. There are usually two or three on board. They are generally managed by the Flight Service Superintendent, who reports to a separate section of the Traffic and Sales Department. They report particularly to the captain of the flight to which they are assigned.

It can be seen from these brief job descriptions that each aircraft is staffed by three distinct sections of the Operations and of the Traffic and Sales Departments. The flight crew personnel are responsible, on each flight, partly to the captain of that flight and partly to their respective sections. They are trained and supervised off flight by those separate sections. While these sections appear to make an effort to coordinate their directives, there is occasional confusion, usually as a result of communication breakdown or delay.

FLIGHT SAFETY

With the foregoing job descriptions in mind, we can now examine the categories of problems. Ultimately, everyone concerned with the air transportation industry must relate decisions and actions to flight safety. It is axiomatic that safety must be the prime consideration if any system of flight crew organization is to be installed or maintained.

Examples will best serve to demonstrate the importance to flight safety of crew organization and coordination. Professor Kenneth Andrews of the Harvard Business School, addressing the Bermuda Flight Safety Foundation Seminar, went so far as to say, "Every accident, no matter how minor, is a failure of organization." I venture to suggest that the staffing of an aircraft by three separate "managements," with an aggregate of individuals who have never served as a group before, and who have been trained as individuals— never as a team—is "organization for disaster." The ill effects of this type of organization on flight safety are gradually reduced as each trip progresses, and by intensive training programs, but the fact remains that 70 per cent of airline crashes occur without prior warning.[1] Picture the problem of the ag-

---

[1] "Accident Prevention Bulletin," 56–17, *Flight Safety Bulletin*, September 14, 1956.

gregate crew facing an intense emergency immediately after its first takeoff. Such sudden emergencies have been the most serious when they happened to a flight crew the members of which were not familiar with each other.

A recent example indicates the validity of the foregoing statement. A DC-3 crashed at Burbank, California. In its opinion, the Board said:

This was Captain B's first takeoff with Copilot D. . . . When the malfunction occurred, the captain may have considered his altitude insufficient for safe transition from visual to instrument flight, *or for reliance upon his copilot for much, if any, help on this their first flight together*.[2] (Author's italics)

Consider, also, the more recent case,[3] in which a copilot, being checked for promotion to captaincy, pulled back a throttle on takeoff, due to a fire warning indication not seen or heard by the check captain. This disarmed the autofeathering system, produced a "windmilling" propeller, excessive drag, and a crash. The copilot's action was appropriate for one purpose, but he was prevented from feathering the propeller manually, by order of the check captain, who was conducting a different procedure which he felt to be warranted by *his* conception of the emergency. The Civil Aeronautics Board determined that, "the probable cause of the accident was uncoordinated emergency action in the very short time available to the crew. . . ."

It is noteworthy that the crew, in this instance, consisted of a check captain (acting as copilot) and a senior copilot (acting as captain), both of whom can be presumed to have been well-trained and experienced in standard procedures. Changes were later made in the standard procedures as a result of their demonstrated inadequacy in the case cited.

In a Civil Aeronautics Board accident investigation report, published in full in *Aviation Week,* an accident, which occurred at Tulsa, Oklahoma, was described. A copilot, flying with a captain for the first time, was making a critical instrument approach, through clouds, when the aircraft struck the ground three and six-tenths miles short of the airport.

In determining that the probable cause of the accident was the captain's lack of alertness in allowing the copilot to continue an instrument descent too low for terrain clearance, the Board noted:

This was the first trip Captain M and First Officer J had flown together and . . . it was also First Officer J's first instrument approach into Tulsa. This is not meant to imply that First Officer J was a novice in instrument flying, but rather that his degree of proficiency was unknown to Captain M and, therefore, this approach, being made under rapidly deteriorating weather conditions, should have been monitored with the utmost care.[4]

---

[2] *Accident Investigation Report,* Civil Aeronautics Board, File No. 1-0109.

[3] "Accident Investigation Report," Civil Aeronautics Board reported in *Aviation Week* (October 8, 1956).

[4] "Accident Investigation Report," Civil Aeronautics Board reported in full in *Aviation Week* (February 3, 1958).

Captains rarely permit copilots to perform such approaches on a first flight together, but the case indicates the potentialities.

In 1955, a DC-3 crashed, after hitting a power line pole, during an attempted "go-around" after an aborted landing. According to the Board report:

Captain T advanced the throttles to takeoff power and a go-around was started with the aircraft becoming airborne at 70 knots IAS [Indicated Air Speed] ... as the aircraft passed the south end of the runway at an altitude of approximately 25 feet and an indicated airspeed of 78 knots he (the captain) ordered "gear up." Instead of raising the gear the first officer pulled both throttles back to the closed position. ...

First Officer C testified that he was not advised of the go-around and that the order for gear up was the only thing said by the captain after power was applied and the go-around was started. In accounting for his action of pulling the throttles back, his testimony was:

"At the time the command was given I was expecting an order to reduce power and inasmuch as it looked like a crash was inevitable—when the order came, I moved them by spontaneous action." ...

Since his recall to N Airlines First Officer C had flown three round trips over the route with Captain T.[5] (In a period of one year.)

In this case, something blocked the coordination within a crew of two men, even though they had flown together three times during the year preceding the accident. This is a high rate of return engagements for two men and never occurs in a crew of three or more.

A brief article in *The Aeroplane,* a Canadian publication, contains a description of an accident which occurred when a captain, flying an ILS [Instrument Landing System] approach, descended below established minimum altitudes, both at the outer marker and before establishing visual reference with the ground. The first officer, by hand signs, called these infractions of regulations to the captain's attention during the approach. The Board of Inquiry recognized the first officer's dilemma and said:

the first officer has some hesitation in interrupting the captain to say or do anything which might be taken as criticism of the performance of the captain. Particularly is this the case when the captain is involved in concentrated flying, as during an ILS approach, and it is believed that many first officers have been reprimanded for interrupting the captain at such times. Under the circumstances therefore for a first officer to take over the controls from the captain to avert disaster would be considered a drastic step. Despite this situation, the only reason for carrying two pilots in the cockpit is in order that the load and responsibility can be shared and the safety of the flight increased.[6]

This accident in Canada can be laid side by side with the one discussed immediately before it and, although there are similarities in the two cases,

---

[5] "Accident Investigation Report," Civil Aeronautics Board, File No. 1-0077.
[6] "The Responsibilities of a Second Pilot," *The Aeroplane* (March 18, 1955).

there is sharp contrast in the actions of the copilots. In the latter case, the copilot simply called the captain's attention to the situation, while in the former, the copilot took partial control (by closing the throttles), thus opposing the captain's decision to abort the landing and fly around the airport again. In both cases there was an organizational failure in that the cockpit crews appear to have had insufficient training and experience *as teams*.

Recently, a Boeing 377 was successfully ditched in the Pacific Ocean, without loss of life or serious injury, and the crew members were lauded as heroes. Several years ago, a Douglas DC-4 was ditched off Puerto Rico with heavy loss of life and the captain was suspended and censured. A point of contrast which appears to have been determinative is that, in the case of the Boeing, the captain and crew had the benefit of more than five hours between the time their emergency began developing and the moment they were forced to alight on the water. The captain and crew of the Douglas were afforded less than five minutes. We can agree that the Boeing crew exhibited coordination and competence. But it is safe to say that they had an enormous advantage over the crew of the Douglas, in that a five-hour grace period permits organization and preparation, while a five-minute time interval prohibits any organization and preparation beyond that which has taken place in training and in experience of interaction.

One area of flight safety which does not seem to be getting the attention its importance warrants is that of mental hygiene of flight crews. In some quarters, it is believed that all accidents brought about by "carelessness" are either unconscious suicides, or unconscious expressions of hostility. There is some justification for this belief. Certainly, preoccupations with personal problems, or intra-crew hostilities, contribute to "absentmindedness."

L. I. O'Kelley of the University of Illinois says:

> Since to achieve a safe performance, the pilot must have a highly effective time-sharing between many essential transactions, time devoted to apprehension, self-doubting, and worry means less essential transactions in any given unit of time.... A second effect of stress is a diminished capacity to receive information. While riding as an observer on a crucial checkride of a very experienced, but very worried and anxious pilot, I counted ten instances of relevant information given to the pilot which he did not see or hear in the period from run-up to establishment of cruising altitude. Preoccupation or worry about matters pertaining to the flight or the pilot's personal life operate in the same manner.[7]

Recently, the writer, sitting in at a pilot's "bull session" at a layover point, listened to a conversation dealing with the "difficult" captains with whom copilots and engineers had had to deal. One captain, speaking of an experience during his copilot days, said, "During the second trip with the son-of-a-bitch, if I'd seen we were about to hit a mountain I'd never told him because I'd know no copilot would ever have to fly with him again if we hit."

Preoccupation and intra-crew hostility could each be the subject of an

---

[7] L. I. O'Kelley in *The Air Line Pilot* (September 1954), pp. 11.

extended paper and need only be treated suggestively here. How can team-scheduling of flight crews abate their effects?

As O'Kelley suggests above, worry and anxiety produce the preoccupation which we often call carelessness or absentmindedness. A crew, interacting for a long time, at least longer than is now afforded, would tend to be better apprised of the problems, the anxiety-producing situations of each crew member, and—in the absence of intense intra-crew hostility—would react to alleviate them or to allow for the effects of the preoccupation. This would be done, on the one hand, by sympathy or suggestions for a resolution of the problems and, on the other hand, by "picking up after" the anxious crew member until a temporary situation was remedied. I mention the absence of intra-crew hostility because it indicates the paramount importance of a matching procedure which would allow for personal preference in the choice of flying partners. Intra-crew hostility would, for the most part, cease to exist, presuming proper matching procedures, and presuming a "safety hatch," i.e., provision for voluntary withdrawal from an integrated crew between matching operations.

At present a disturbing amount of complacency exists in flight due, as far as I can see, to the taking-for-granted that each crew member has been trained adequately to cope, not only with routine matters, but with the most extreme emergency. As a long-time observer of flight crews, the writer is convinced that this taking-for-granted is a complete misconception. Individuals cannot be separately trained and then, at a moment's notice, be expected to combine into a smooth-working team when an emergency occurs. "The most amazing thing to a student of aviation psychology is not pilot error, rather it is the excellence of pilot success." [8]

Composed reliance upon selections and training and upon standard procedures is constantly taught, but flight crews are simply aggregates of skilled individuals, skilled in everything except crew-coordination. One needs only to recall the dull spectacles of all-star football and basketball games to realize that long periods of interaction are required to make teams of the most skilled individuals.

One of the characteristics of a team is that the members have, via practices and association, built up a set of conscious and unconscious signals and a pattern of plays in response to these signals. It is this which distinguishes the real team from a simple aggregate of individuals. Crew-scheduling, as it now exists, results in more of a random aggregation of people who share some commonly understood signals as a consequence of training, but probably not as many as they would have were they regularly scheduled to fly together.

Personal observations indicate that there is not currently sufficient communication and interaction between flight crew members to bring about the integration necessary to deal with a sudden emergency in optimum fashion.

---

[8] O'Kelley, *op. cit.*

Jogged occasionally by managers and by check pilots, captains conduct pre-flight and pre-take-off briefings, but these are crude substitutes for integration of coordinated teams.

It is my opinion that many practices of individuals in cockpit crews could be altered or adjusted to if such crews were periodically checked *as teams.* Even a somewhat undesirable practice could be neutralized if it were detected by fellow crewmen in the training and checking process. For example, if a captain were known to be slow in giving directives, his flight engineer could be fishing for the appropriate emergency checklist and his copilot unpacking his oxygen mask, while the captain was gathering himself to give orders on the subject of a simulated cargo compartment fire.

FLIGHT EFFICIENCY

Included for our purposes in this branch of our subject are not only the factors of flight operation at the lowest cost, but also the factors of maintaining schedule, use of every possible flight aid to give passenger and shipper satisfaction, and reporting suggested improvements.

To me it has appeared remarkably anomalous that managers of flight crews have, on one hand, made such strong efforts to standardize and dehumanize the work of flight crew members and, on the other hand, have expressed wonderment that such efforts have produced flight crews which operate at minimum efficiency.

In a stimulating foreword to *Worker Satisfaction and Development,* F. J. Roethlisberger writes:

in the absence of a major constraint, a work group will tend to meet management's minimum expectations as well as provide its members with the minimum satisfaction of their needs. This condition of "frozenness" we should hasten to add, exists not only at the work level. We have "frozen nations," "frozen political institutions," "frozen business," and "frozen social groups" that are capable of elaborating their historical traditions, or waging wars, of surviving, and even of showing a "profit" but that are not free to choose the values that would allow them to enter with maturity into the atomic age.[9]

Substitute "jet age" for "atomic age" in the foregoing quotation and the relevance to this paper becomes apparent. The present-day flight crew is "frozen" within Roethlisberger's meaning, and it can be liberated from this situation only when substantial effort is made at least to study, if not to alter, current practices of crew composition, scheduling, and management. The tragic aspect of the current arrangements is that so little is being asked of persons capable of so much.

It has been a further source of wonderment to me that flight crew managers, aware of their lack of control of flight crews on trips, have abdicated

---

[9] Abraham Zaleznik, *Worker Satisfaction and Development* (Boston: Harvard Business School, 1956).

the control which would be available to them through aircraft commanders by giving those commanders a constantly shifting array of subordinates, and thus making it difficult, if not impossible, to fix responsibility.

The sources of flight crews, as we have said, are two branches of the Operations Department and one branch of the Traffic and Sales Department. From these three departmental branches come different crewmen to staff each trip. It is little wonder, then, that aircraft commanders give up in despair any effort to exercise optimum command responsibility and authority.

As an observer of flight crews I have often wondered at the minuscule interaction between the aircraft commander and the cabin attendants. It is rare, in flight, for this type of communication to proceed beyond the bare essentials required by the departure checklist (purser reports cabin door secure, number of passengers on board, etc.). While we are dealing here primarily with the cockpit crew, the cabin attendants enter into the safety picture by preparing passengers for emergency conditions, preventing passengers from creating emergencies (I once had a passenger-mother warm a baby's bottle by making a bonfire of paper in the aircraft's lavatory basin), and handling passengers during critical situations other than real emergencies.

Optimum cruising control procedures require flight planning, navigation, and engine operation to the end that aircraft proceed the greatest number of miles using the least amount of fuel and in-flight time. This has a profound effect upon the cost of operating aircraft, not to mention its relationship to safety. Examination of flight documents indicates that much could be done to motivate crews to improve this feature of their work.

Captains tend to withdraw into those functions of their jobs not involving leadership or management of crews. This seems to be a source of amazement to flight managers, to the Pilot's Association, and to the captains themselves. It appears not to be recognized by anyone that leadership involves teaching and motivation functions rather than reporting functions. Reporting to a crew member's department manager is currently a captain's only source of control. Naturally in present circumstances he avoids reporting because: (1) he cannot be sure that incidents occurring over the short time of a single trip indicate a pattern; (2) his experiences may indicate that reports are ineffective; (3) he does not wish to initiate a disciplinary action which he may not approve; and (4) under the current system of scheduling, he will not have the difficult or inept crew member in his crew very often. Furthermore, "snitching" (reporting) is not valued in the culture pattern of the United States.

EMPLOYEE SATISFACTIONS

Under present circumstances, the flight crew member is in an impossibly isolated situation. The nearest entity to a primary loyalty target which he has is the local union group, and this fact tends to limit work efforts to the minimum which the union will support in a disciplinary action. This produces a fairly astonishing paradox. Current crew composition and management practices, being disintegrative, have actually limited the alternative loyalty targets of individuals, with the result that collective bargaining agents have been the almost exclusive recipients of employee loyalty. Much of this impulse is wasted in that it cannot be used to lend zest to the work situation and so produce improvement in the actual day-to-day work of the air transport industry.

Employee satisfaction contributes to safety in that satisfied employees tend not to be preoccupied or hostile, but to be interested, effective, and enterprising. Some flight managers seem to suspect some hidden flaw inherent in their subordinates, some mysterious factor producing disloyalty to the total enterprise, at worst, and a lethargy toward it, at best. This whole attitude could be the result of crew composition disorders.

One peculiar problem which has plagued many flight managers has been that of misconduct, especially excessive drinking at layover points. It hardly seems rational that an employee in a highly responsible position would risk his career by "going on a tear" somewhere along his route. But if the atmosphere within each crew is always at the get-acquainted stage, if the employees are always under the impulse to form a group from the current crew assemblage, which impulse is never more than fragmentarily satisfied, then the cocktail party tone will prevail wherever crews take their rest along the way. Also, I would suggest that the more closely knit primary group is apt to be more effective in controlling its members than is the temporary aggregate of individuals.

Employee satisfaction is a highly abstract concept; but it can readily be recognized as valuable by the flight manager who can recall instances of acts done by employees beyond the strict requirements of duty, of acceptance of hardships without complaint, and of indications of a general feeling of enthusiasm for the success of the enterprise.

Let there be no doubt about what is meant by satisfaction here. It does not mean for us a state of self-oriented complacency, but rather something in the nature of what the businessman lists among his assets as good will; but in this case the feeling runs, not from his customers, but from employees toward the enterprise he manages.

Informal leadership has been recognized in industrial research for some time. In a recent study by Zaleznik,[10] it was found, in the machine shop under observation, that the informal leader of the shop was a Negro machinist who knew the job best, most frequently helped other machinists, and freely lent his tools. The formal leader, the foreman, hired, kept records, and furnished communication with higher management. He did little else. Numerous copilots have voiced to me their frustration in working with captains who do not supervise their flights. By supervise we no longer mean the frequent

---

[10] Zaleznik, *op. cit.*

issuance of autocratic orders. What is meant are the helping, teaching, listening, integrating functions of the true supervisor.

With crew integrity, the competent supervising captain will manage the flights he and his crew make with mutual satisfaction. The less-than-competent captain will find actual leadership in the hands of an "informal leader" in his crew. In either case a better situation will prevail than that which frequently occurs now when a competent supervisor meets an incipient informal leader head-on, or a crew with a nonsupervising captain and no informal leader moves listlessly over the routes with no one leading.

CONCLUSIONS

Some time ago I encountered a reprint of an address by Kenneth R. Andrews of the Harvard University School of Business Administration. He raised very important questions:

> I think that none of us doubts that individual (flight) crew members are today well enough trained so that as individuals they are theoretically interchangeable. But can relationships, for example, between first officer and captain, between flight engineer and captain, between stewardess and captain be changed so easily that the team remains strong as its members are shuffled about? The administrative view of safety suggests this question: Is the average crew of a transport aircraft an effective team working under an executive? Is the captain's role defined in administrative terms? Who assigns him his duties? Has the proportion of technical to administrative duties risen helter-skelter over the years? Is the captain supposed to do most of the work with his hands at the same time he commands the crew and considers the comfort and safety of his passengers? Are his duties organized, and is he constantly training his people? We know how to deal with accident-prone individuals, but are crew composition procedures still accident-prone?

This reading, coupled with personal experiences, generated the hunch from which this study stems.

It is my considered opinion, after much reading, observation, and thought, that many of the problems of flight crew managers, relating to safety, efficiency, and employee satisfaction, would be wholly or partially solved, with few side effects of an adverse nature, by scheduling of flight crews as units, as integrated teams for a relatively long time. What I conceive to be important features will be pointed out in the suggested methods for crew composition, scheduling, and management which follow.

Two possible matching procedures suggest themselves. One is the relatively involved one based upon mutual personal preference. This method was used by Moreno [11] in matching roommates at a girls reformatory with outstanding success and has been emulated by the Air Force.[12] Opinion seems to be that

---

[11] G. C. Homans, *The Human Group* (New York: Harcourt, 1950), p. 40.

[12] Leslie D. Zeleny, "Selection of Compatible Flying Partners," *American Journal of Sociology,* **52** (March 1947), p. 424.

personal-preference matching methods are not only simpler, but better. Matching should be a periodic process, not only to realign crews after use of reserves has diluted compatibility, but to permit a graceful change of faces at the end of an appropriate period. Certainly it would not be desirable for a crew to "grow old together" as one objector to the concept has put it.

Another, even simpler matching procedure, would be that which I am informed is used on Braniff Airlines. There, schedule patterns are submitted for bid to captains. After award, the patterns are submitted to other crew members with a captain's name attached to each pattern. In this way, subordinate crew members bid not only for their patterns, but for the captains with whom they choose to fly for the duration of the patterns. For most domestic airlines the period is one month. For an international airline, with longer trips involved, a three-month period would probably serve best.

After the matching process, each crew should be given a number and be scheduled as a unit for the designated period between matchings. Reserve pools (which now exist at some bases), for each category, should be established, not only to provide for sickness, vacations, etc., but for an escape hatch into which a crewman could resign should he find an intolerable personality clash to have developed for him on his crew. A system of measurements of crew excellence should be devised to the end that top crews could be commended or rewarded.

Coordination in groups has been successfully measured in other industries. The most significant work I have heard about has been done by the members of The Technology Project, Yale University, in studying the problems of assembly line workers and their foremen. Their techniques of observation and interviewing appear to be useful in the study of cockpit coordination. Some notable correlations are the difficulty of voice communication due to noise, the high degree of specialization in the presence of complicated machinery, the repetitiveness of activities during long periods, etc.; and contrasting features include immediate contact with the customers during production (a source of satisfaction to the flight crewman), a sense of autonomy for each flight crew, not only as a temporary group, but of each individual within the group, sharp status distinctions, possibilities for serious emergencies, etc.

It is the purpose of this paper to urge an experiment designed to test the present method of crew composition and scheduling against the performance of a group of crews regularly scheduled as units for an adequate period of time for study. The Air Force has made a detailed job analysis of pilot, flight engineer, and radar observed groups, defining the job elements involved in flight crew positions.[13] Perhaps such detailed studies would not be needed, but procedures and techniques have been described and found valid through use.

In civil aviation it would probably be sufficient to match a group of crews,

---

[13] "The Development of Job-Analysis Procedures," *American Institute for Research,* Research Note No. 4, June 1951.

conduct periodic group and individual interviews, and make in-flight observations. Training and proficiency test flights would disclose whether there was significant disparity between performances of the groups in simulated emergency conditions.

It is suspected that such an experiment as has been suggested would reveal that integrated, stable crews, individuals scheduled together for relatively long periods of time, would furnish an overall performance significantly superior to that of the control group.

21

Reaction Patterns to Severe, Chronic Stress in American Army Prisoners of War of the Chinese

Edgar H. Schein

In contrast to the preceding article, concerned with the benefits sought for the individual through creation of primary groups, this selection recites the deliberate reversal of such a procedure. It describes the Chinese Communists' ruthless use of the individual's need for support: by destroying group cohesion, individuals were made susceptible to propaganda.

Although the number of observations (20 cases) is inadequate by the usual scientific criteria, this paper does present a rare and vivid illustration of the importance of the small group to the individual's very life.

In this paper I will outline some of the constellations of stress which prisoners of war faced during the Korean conflict, and describe some of the reaction patterns to these stresses. Rather than presenting a complete catalogue of their experiences, I have selected those aspects which seem to me to throw

Reprinted from the *Journal of Social Issues,* **13,** 3 (1957), pp. 21–30, by permission of The Society for the Psychological Study of Social Issues and the author.

Edgar H. Schein is Associate Professor, Massachusetts Institute of Technology.

This work was completed while the author was a captain, U.S. Army Medical Service Corps, assigned to the Walter Reed Army Institute of Research. He wishes to acknowledge the invaluable help and guidance of Dr. David McK. Rioch and Capt. Harold Williams as well as the staff of the Neuropsychiatric Division of the Walter Reed Army Institute of Research.

some light on the problem of collaboration with the enemy. I will give particular emphasis to the *social* psychological factors, because the Chinese approach to treatment of prisoners seemed to emphasize control over groups, rather than individuals.

My material is based on a variety of sources. I was in Korea during the repatriation, and had the opportunity to interview extensively 20 unselected repatriates. This basic material was supplemented by the information gathered by three psychiatrists, Drs. Harvey Strassman, Patrick Israel, and Clinton Tempereau, who together had seen some 300 men. On board ship returning to the United States, I also had the opportunity to sit in on bull sessions among repatriates in which many of the prison experiences were discussed. Additional details were obtained from the Army dossiers on the men.

The typical experience of the prisoner of war must be divided into two broad phases. The first phase lasted anywhere from one to six months beginning with capture, followed by exhausting marches to the north of Korea and severe privation in inadequately equipped temporary camps, terminating in assignment to a permanent prisoner of war camp.

The second phase, lasting two or more years, was marked by chronic pressures to collaborate and to give up existing group loyalties in favor of new ones. Thus, while physical stresses had been outstanding in the first six months, psychological stresses were outstanding in this second period.

The reactions of the men toward capture were influenced by their overall attitude toward the Korean situation. Many of them felt inadequately prepared, both physically and psychologically. The physical training, equipment, and rotation system all came in for retrospective criticism, though this response might have been merely a rationalization for being captured. When the Chinese entered the war they penetrated into rear areas, where they captured many men who were taken completely by surprise. The men felt that when positions were overrun, their leadership was often less than adequate. Thus, many men were disposed to blame the UN command for the unfortunate event of being captured.

On the psychological side, the men were not clearly aware of what they were fighting for or what kind of enemy they were opposing. In addition, the reports of the atrocities committed by the North Koreans led most men to expect death, torture, or nonrepatriation if captured.

It was in such a context that the soldier found his Chinese captor extending his hand in a friendly gesture and saying "Welcome" or "Congratulations, you've been *liberated*." This Chinese tactic was part of their "lenient policy" which was explained to groups of prisoners shortly after capture in these terms: because the UN had entered the war illegally and was an aggressor, all UN military personnel were in fact war criminals, and *could* be shot summarily. But the average soldier was, after all, only carrying out orders for his leaders who were the real criminals. Therefore, the Chinese soldier would consider the POW a "student," and would teach him the "truth" about the war. Anyone who did not cooperate by going to school and by learning voluntarily could be reverted to his "war criminal" status and shot, particularly if a confession of "criminal" deeds could be obtained from him.

In the weeks following capture, the men were collected in large groups and marched north. From a physical point of view, the stresses during these marches were very severe: there was no medicine for the wounded, the food was unpalatable and insufficient, especially, by our standards, clothing was scarce in the face of severe winter weather, and shelter was inadequate and overcrowded. The Chinese set a severe pace and showed little consideration for weariness that was the product of wounds, diarrhea, and frostbite. Men who were not able to keep up were abandoned unless they were helped by their fellows. The men marched only at night, and were kept under cover during the day, ostensibly as protection against strafing by our own planes.

From a psychological point of view this situation is best described as a recurring cycle of fear, relief, and new fear. The men were afraid that they might die, that they might never be repatriated, that they might never again have a chance to communicate with the outside, and that no one even knew they were alive. The Chinese, on the other hand, were reassuring and promised that the men would be repatriated soon, that conditions would improve, and that they would soon be permitted to communicate with the outside.

One of the chief problems for the men was the disorganization within the group itself. It was difficult to maintain close group ties if one was competing with others for the essentials of life, and if one spent one's resting time in overcrowded huts among others who had severe diarrhea and were occasionally incontinent. Lines of authority often broke down, and with this, group cohesion and morale suffered. A few men attempted to escape, but they were usually recaptured in a short time and returned to the group. The Chinese also fostered low morale and the feeling of being abandoned by systematically reporting false news about United Nation defeats and losses.

In this situation goals became increasingly short-run. As long as the men were marching, they had something to do and could look forward to relief from the harsh conditions of the march. However, arrival at a temporary camp was usually a severe disappointment. Not only were physical conditions as bad as ever, but the sedentary life in overcrowded quarters produced more disease and still lower morale.

What happened to the men under these conditions? During the one- to two-week marches they became increasingly apathetic.[1] They developed a slow, plodding gait, called by one man a "prisoners' shuffle." Uppermost in their minds were fantasies of food: men remembered all the good meals they had ever had, or planned detailed menus for years into the future. To

---

[1] A more detailed discussion of the apathy reaction may be found in Harvey D. Strassman, Margaret Thaler, and Edgar H. Schein, "A Prisoner of War Syndrome: Apathy as a Reaction to Severe Stress," *American Journal of Psychiatry* 112 (1956), pp. 998–1003.

a lesser extent they thought of loved ones at home, and about cars which seemed to them to symbolize freedom and the return home.

In the temporary camps disease and exposure took a heavy toll in lives. But it was the feeling of many men, including some of the doctors who survived the experience, that some of these deaths were not warranted by a man's physical condition. Instead, what appeared to happen was that some men became so apathetic that they ceased to care about their bodily needs. They retreated further into themselves, refused to eat even what little food was available, refused to get any exercise, and eventually lay down as if waiting to die. The reports were emphatic concerning the lucidity and sanity of these men. They seemed willing to accept the prospect of death rather than to continue fighting a severely frustrating and depriving environment.

Two things seemed to save a man who was close to such "apathy" death: getting him on his feet and doing something, no matter how trivial, or getting him angry or concerned about some present or future problem. Usually it was the effort of a friend who maternally and insistently motivated the individual toward realistic goals which snapped him out of such a state of resignation. In one case such "therapy" consisted of kicking the man until he was mad enough to get up and fight.

Throughout this time, the Chinese played the role of the benevolent but handicapped captor. Prisoners were always reminded that it was their *own* Air Force bombing which was responsible for the inadequate supplies. Furthermore, they were reminded that they were getting treatment which was just as good as that which the average Chinese was getting. One important effect of this was that a man could never give *full* vent to his hostility toward the Chinese, even in fantasy. In their *manner* and *words* they were usually solicitous and sympathetic. The Chinese also implied that conditions could be better for a prisoner if he would take more "cooperative" attitude, if he would support their propaganda for peace. Thus a man was made to feel that he was himself responsible for his traumatic circumstances.

Arrival at a permanent camp usually brought relief from many of these physical hardships. Food, shelter, and medicine, while not plentiful, appeared to be sufficient for the maintenance of life and some degree of health. However, the Chinese now increased sharply their efforts to involve prisoners in their own propaganda program, and to undermine loyalties to their country. This marks the beginning of the second phase of the imprisonment experience.

The Chinese program of subversion and indoctrination was thoroughly integrated into the entire camp routine and involved the manipulation of the entire social milieu of the prison camp. Its aims appeared to be to manage a large group of prisoners with a minimum staff of guards, to indoctrinate them with the Communist political ideology, to interrogate them to obtain intelligence information and confessions for propaganda purposes, and to develop a corps of collaborators within the prisoner group. What success the

Chinese had stemmed from their *total* control of the environment, not from the application of any one technique.

The most significant feature of Chinese prisoner camp control was the systematic destruction of the prisoners' formal and informal group structure. Soon after arrival at a camp, the men were segregated by race, nationality, and rank. The Chinese put their own men in charge of the platoons and companies, and made arbitrary selections of POW squad leaders to remind the prisoners that their old rank system no longer had any validity. In addition, the Chinese attempted to undermine *informal* group structure by prohibiting any kind of group meeting, and by systematically fomenting mutual distrust by playing men off against one another. The most effective device to this end was the practice of obtaining from informers or Chinese spies detailed information about someone's activities, no matter how trivial, then calling him in to interrogate him about it. Such detailed surveillance of the men's activities made them feel that their own ranks were so infiltrated by spies and informers that it was not safe to trust anyone.

A similar device was used to obtain information during interrogation. After a man had resisted giving information for hours or days, he would be shown a signed statement by one of his fellow prisoners giving that same information. Still another device was to make prisoners who had not collaborated look like collaborators, by bestowing special favors upon them.

A particularly successful Chinese technique was their use of testimonials from other prisoners, such as the false germ-warfare confessions, and appeals based on familiar contexts, such as peace appeals. Confessions by prisoners or propaganda lectures given by collaborators had a particularly demoralizing effect, because only if resistance had been *unanimous* could a man solidly believe that his values were correct, even if he could not defend them logically.

If the men, in spite of their state of social disorganization, did manage to organize any kind of group activity, the Chinese would quickly break up the group by removing its leaders or key members and assigning them to another camp.

Loyalties to home and country were undermined by the systematic manipulation of mail. Usually only mail which carried bad news was delivered. If a man received no mail at all, the Chinese suggested that his loved ones had abandoned him.

Feelings of social isolation were increased by the complete information control maintained in the camps. Only the Communist press, radio, magazines, and movies were allowed.

The weakening of the prisoner group's social structure is particularly significant because we depend to such an extent on consensual validation in judging ourselves and others. The prisoners lost their most important sources of information and support concerning standards of behavior and beliefs. Often men who attempted to resist the Chinese by means other than *outright* obstruction or aggression failed to obtain the active support of others, often earning their suspicion instead.

At the same time, the Chinese did create a situation in which meaningful social relationships could be had through common political activity, such as the "peace" committees which served as propaganda organs. The Chinese interrogators or instructors sometimes lived with prisoners for long periods of time in order to establish close personal relationships with them.

The Communist doctrines were presented through compulsory lectures followed by compulsory group discussions, for the purpose of justifying the conclusions given at the end of the lectures. On the whole, this phase of indoctrination was ineffective because of the crudeness of the propaganda material used in the lectures. However, its constant repetition seemed eventually to influence those men who did not have well-formed political opinions to start with, particularly because no counterarguments could be heard. The group discussions were effective only if their monitor was someone who could keep control over the group and keep it on the topic of discussion. Attempts by the Chinese to use "progressive" POWs in the role of monitors were seldom successful because they aroused too much hostility in the men.

The Chinese also attempted to get prisoners to use mutual criticism and self-criticism in the fashion in which it is used within China. Whenever a POW was caught breaking one of the innumerable camp rules, he was required to give an elaborate confession and self-criticism, no matter how trivial the offense. In general, the POWs were able to use this opportunity to ridicule the Chinese by taking advantage of their lack of understanding of slang and American idiom. They would emphasize the wrong parts of sentences or insert words and phrases which made it apparent to other prisoners that the joke was on the Chinese. Often men were required to make these confessions in front of large groups of other prisoners. If the man could successfully communicate by a linguistic device his lack of sincerity, this ritual could backfire on the Chinese by giving the men an opportunity to express their solidarity (by sharing a communication which could not be understood by the Chinese). However, in other instances, prisoners who viewed such public confessions felt contempt for the confessor and felt their own group was being undermined still further by such public humiliation.

Various tales of how prisoners resisted the pressures put on them have been widely circulated in the press. For example, a number of prisoners ridiculed the Chinese by playing baseball with a basketball, yet telling the Chinese this was the correct way to play the game. Such stories suggest that morale and group solidarity was actually quite high in the camps. Our interviews with the men suggest that morale climbed sharply during the *last six to nine months* of imprisonment when the armistice talks were underway, when the compulsory indoctrination program had been put on a voluntary basis, and when the Chinese were improving camp conditions in anticipation of the repatriation. However, we heard practically no stories of successful group resistance or high morale from the first year or so in the camps when the indoctrination program was seriously pursued by the Chinese. (At that time the men had neither the time nor the opportunity to play any kind of games, because all their time was spent on indoctrination activities or exhausting labor.)

Throughout, the Chinese created an environment in which rewards such as extra food, medicine, special privileges, and status were given for cooperation and collaboration, while threats of death, nonrepatriation, reprisal against family, torture, decreases in food and medicine, and imprisonment served to keep men from offering much resistance. Only imprisonment was consistently used as an actual punishment. *Chronic* resistance was usually handled by transferring the prisoner to a so-called "reactionary" camp.

Whatever behavior the Chinese attempted to elicit, they always *paced* their demands very carefully, they always required some level of *participation* from the prisoner, no matter how trivial, and they *repeated* endlessly.

To what extent did these pressures produce either changes in beliefs and attitudes, or collaboration? Close observation of the repatriates and the reports of the men themselves suggest that the Chinese did not have much success in changing beliefs and attitudes. Doubt and confusion were created in many prisoners as a result of having to examine so closely their own way of thinking, but very few changes, if any, occurred that resembled actual *conversion* to communism. The type of prisoner who was most likely to become *sympathetic* toward communism was the one who had chronically occupied a low status position in this society, and for whom the democratic principles were not very salient or meaningful.

In producing collaboration, however, the Chinese were far more effective. By collaboration I mean such activities as giving lectures for the Communists, writing and broadcasting propaganda, giving false confessions, writing and signing petitions, informing on fellow POWs, and so on; none of these activities required a personal change of belief. Some 10 to 15 per cent of the men chronically collaborated, but the dynamics of this response are very complex. By far the greatest determinant was the amount of pressure the Chinese put on a particular prisoner. Beyond this, the reports of the men permit one to isolate several sets of motives that operated, though it is impossible to tell how many cases of each type there may have been.

1. Some men collaborated for outright opportunistic reasons; these men lacked any kind of stable group identification, and exploited the situation for its material benefits without any regard for the consequences to themselves, their fellow prisoners, or their country.

2. Some men collaborated because their egos were too weak to withstand the physical and psychological rigors; these men were primarily motivated by fear, though they often rationalized their behavior; they were unable to resist any kind of authority figure, and could be blackmailed by the Chinese once they had begun to collaborate.

3. Some men collaborated with the firm conviction that they were infiltrating the Chinese ranks and obtaining intelligence information which would be useful to the UN forces. This was a convenient rationalization for anyone who could not withstand the pressures. Many of these men were initially tricked into collaboration or were motivated by a desire to communicate with the outside world. None of these men became ideologically confused; what Communist beliefs they might have professed were for the benefit of the Chinese only.

4. The prisoner who was vulnerable to the ideological appeal because of his low status in this society often collaborated with the conviction that he was doing the right thing in supporting the Communist peace movement. This group included the younger and less intelligent men from backward or rural areas, the malcontents, and members of various minority groups. These men often viewed themselves as failures in our society, and felt that society had never given them a chance. They were positively attracted by the immediate status and privileges which went with being a "progressive," and by the promise of important roles which they could presumably play in the peace movement of the future.

Perhaps the most important thing to note about collaboration is the manner in which the social disorganization contributed to it. A man might make a slanted radio broadcast in order to communicate with the outside, he might start reading Communist literature out of sheer boredom, he might give information which he knew the Chinese already had, and so on. Once this happened, however, the Chinese rewarded him, increased pressure on him to collaborate, and blackmailed him by threatening exposure. At the same time, in most cases, his fellow prisoners forced him into further collaboration by mistrusting him and ostracizing him. Thus a man had to stand entirely on his own judgment and strength, and both of these often failed. One of the most common failures was a man's lack of awareness concerning the effects of his own actions on the other prisoners, and the value of these actions for the Chinese propaganda effort. The man who confessed to germ warfare, thinking he could repudiate such a confession later, did not realize its immediate propaganda value to the Communists.

A certain percentage of men, though the exact number is difficult to estimate, exhibited chronic resistance and obstructionism toward Chinese indoctrination efforts. Many of these men were well integrated with secure, stable group identifications who could withstand the social isolation and still exercise good judgment. Others were chronic obstructionists whose histories showed recurring resistance to any form of authority. Still others were idealists or martyrs to religious and ethical principles, and still others were anxious, guilt-ridden individuals who could only cope with their own strong impulses to collaborate by denying them and overreacting in the other direction.

By far the largest group of prisoners, however, established a complex compromise between the demands of the Chinese and their own value system. This adjustment, called by the men "playing it cool," consisted primarily of a physical and emotional withdrawal from the whole environment. These men learned to suspend their feelings and to adopt an attitude of watching and waiting, rather than hoping and planning. This reaction, though passive, was not as severe as the apathy described earlier. It was a difficult adjustment to maintain because some concessions had to be made to the Chinese in the form of trivial or well-timed collaborative acts, and in the form of a feigned interest in the indoctrination program. At the same time, each man had to be prepared to deal with the hostility of his buddies if he made an error in judgment.

DISCUSSION

This paper has placed particular emphasis on the social psychological factors involved in "brainwashing" because it is my opinion that the process is primarily concerned with social forces, not with the strengths and weaknesses of individual minds. It has often been asserted that drugs, hypnotic techniques, refined "mental tortures" and, more recently, implanted electrodes can make the task of the "brainwasher" much easier by rendering the human mind submissive with a minimum of effort. There is little question that such techniques can be used to elicit confessions or signatures on documents prepared by the captor; but so can withdrawal of food, water, or air produce the same results. The point is that the Chinese Communists do not appear to be interested in obtaining merely a confession or *transient* submission. Instead, they appear to be interested in producing changes in men which will be lasting and self-sustaining. A germ-warfare confession alone was not enough—the POW had to "testify" before an international commission explaining in detail how the bombs had been dropped, and had to tell his story in other prison camps to his fellow POWs.

There is little evidence that drugs, posthypnotic suggestion, or implanted electrodes can now or ever will be able to produce the kind of behavior exhibited by many prisoners who collaborated and made false confessions. On the other hand, there is increasing evidence that Russian and Chinese interrogation and indoctrination techniques involve the destruction of the person's social ties and identifications, and the partial destruction of his ego. If this is successfully accomplished, the person is offered a new identity for himself and given the opportunity to identify with new groups. What physical torture and deprivation are involved in this process may be either a calculated attempt to degrade and humiliate a man to destroy his image of himself as a dignified human being, or the product of fortuitous circumstances, i.e., failure of supply lines to the prison, loss of temper on the part of the interrogator, an attempt to inspire fear in other prisoners by torturing one of them, and so on. We do not have sufficient evidence to determine which of these alternatives represents Communist intentions; possibly all of them are involved in the actual prison situation.

Ultimately that which sustains humans is their personality integration born out of secure and stable group identifications. One may be able to produce temporary submission by direct intervention in cortical processes, but only by destroying a man's self-image and his group supports can one produce any lasting changes in his beliefs and attitudes. By concerning ourselves with the problem of artificially creating submission in man, we run the real risk of overlooking the fact that we are in a genuine struggle of ideas with other portions of the world and that man often submits himself directly to ideas and principles.

To understand and combat "brainwashing" we must look at those social conditions which make people ready to accept new ideas from anyone who states them clearly and forcefully, and those social conditions which give people the sense of integrity which will sustain them when their immediate social and emotional supports are stripped away.

Chapter Six

Stratification

"WITHIN SOCIETIES, people classify one another into categories, and rank these categories from higher to lower. The process of defining and ranking such categories is called social stratification, and the resulting set of ranked categories is called the stratification structure. The categories themselves, by analogy with the different layers of rock in a geological formation, are called strata. More popularly, we know them as classes." [1]

"It is the sense of status, sustained by economic, political, or ecclesiastical power and by the distinctive modes of life and cultural expressions corresponding to them, which draws class apart from class, gives cohesion to each, and stratifies a whole society." [2]

The above comments on social stratification offer us insights into related consequences of this phenomenon. From the evidences the editors have been able to gather, it is the businessman who again provides our most direct examples. Martineau (Selection 22) demonstrates that social class operates in what people buy, the particular brand of product they choose, and even the store in which they purchase a product.

That the information on stratification has not been applied to its fullest is the position taken by Dr. Burleigh Gardner (Selection 23). Dr. Gardner points out special features of "working class" membership important to analysis of that group in a market.

[1] Kimball Young and Raymond W. Mack, *Systematic Sociology* (New York: American Book Co., 1962), p. 168.
[2] Robert M. MacIver, *Society: A Textbook of Sociology* (New York: Farrar & Rinehart, 1937), pp. 78–79.

Purchasing behavior is but one area of human behavior in which social stratification has applications. Included in this chapter are demonstrations of the utility of the concept applied to mental health work (Selection 24) and even to the morale of seamen on board an aircraft carrier (Selection 25).

22

Social Classes and Spending Behavior

Pierre Martineau

Although income has generally been the most widely used behavioral indicator in marketing, social class membership provides a richer index. The individual's consumption patterns actually symbolize this class position, which is a more significant determinant of his buying behavior than is income.

There is a social class system operative in metropolitan markets that can be isolated and described. The kinds of things a person will or will not buy are strongly related to his class membership and also to the degree of his mobility or stability. Likewise the individual's loyalties to stores and his propensity to spend or save will in considerable part be class-related.

All societies place emphasis on some one structure which gives form to the total society and integrates all the other structures such as the family, the clique, voluntary association, caste, age, and sex groupings into a social unity.

Social stratification means any system of ranked statuses by which all the members of a society are placed in some kind of a superordinate and subordinate hierarchy. While money and occupation are important in the ranking process, there are many more factors, and these two alone do not establish social position. The concept of social class was designed to include this process of ranking people in superior and inferior social position by any and all factors.

Reprinted from the *Journal of Marketing,* national quarterly publication of the American Marketing Association, **23,** 2 (October 1958), pp. 121–130, by permission of the publisher and author.

Pierre Martineau is Director of Research and Marketing, *Chicago Tribune.*

CLASS SYSTEM

It has been argued that there cannot be a class system existent in America when most individuals do not have the slightest idea of its formal structure. Yet in actuality every individual senses that he is more at home with and more acceptable to certain groups than to others. In a study of department stores and shopping behavior, it was found that the Lower-Status woman is completely aware that, if she goes into High-Status department stores, the clerks and the other customers in the store will punish her in various subtle ways.

"The clerks treat you like a crumb," one woman expressed it. After trying vainly to be waited on, another woman bitterly complained that she was loftily told, "We thought you were a clerk."

The woman who is socially mobile gives considerable thought to the external symbols of status, and she frequently tests her status by shopping in department stores which she thinks are commensurate with her changing position. She knows that, if she does not dress correctly, if she does not behave in a certain manner to the clerks, if she is awkward about the proper cues, then the other customers and the clerks will make it very clear that she does not belong.

In another study, very different attitudes in the purchase of furniture and appliances involving this matter of status were found. Middle-Class people had no hesitancy in buying refrigerators and other appliances in discount houses and bargain stores because they felt that they could not "go wrong" with the nationally advertised names. But taste in furniture is much more elusive and subtle because the brand names are not known; and, therefore, one's taste is on trial. Rather than commit a glaring error in taste which would exhibit an ignorance of the correct status symbols, the same individual why buys appliances in a discount house generally retreats to a status store for buying furniture. She needs the support of the store's taste.

In a very real sense, everyone of us in his consumption patterns and style of life shows an awareness that there is some kind of a superiority-inferiority system operating, and that we must observe the symbolic patterns of our own class.

Lloyd Warner and Paul Lunt have described a six-class system: the Upper-Upper, or old families; Lower-Upper, or the newly arrived; Upper-Middle, mostly the professionals and successful businessmen; Lower-Middle, or the white collar salaried class; Upper-Lower, or the wage earner, skilled worker group; and Lower-Lower, or the unskilled labor group.[1] For practical purposes, in order to determine the individual's class position, Warner and

---

[1] W. Lloyd Warner and Paul Lunt, *The Social Life of a Modern Community* (New Haven: Yale University Press, 1950). Also, W. Lloyd Warner, Marchia Meeker, and Kenneth Eells, *Social Class in American* (Chicago: Science Research Associates, 1949).

his associates worked out a rating index, not based on amount of income but rather on type of income, type of occupation, house type, and place of residence.

Although the Warner thesis has been widely used in sociology, it has not generally been employed in marketing. As a matter of fact, some critics in the social sciences have held that, since Warner's thesis rested essentially on studies of smaller cities in the 10,000–25,000 class, this same system might not exist in the more complex metropolitan centers, or might not be unravelled by the same techniques. Furthermore, many marketers did not see the application of this dimension to the individual's economic behavior, since the studies of Warner and his associates had mostly been concerned with the differences in the broad patterns of living, the moral codes, etc.

SOCIAL CLASS IN CHICAGO

Under Warner's guidance, the *Chicago Tribune* has undertaken several extensive studies exploring social class in a metropolitan city and its manifestations specifically in family buying patterns. The problem was to determine if such a social-class system did exist in metropolitan Chicago, if the dimensions and the relationships were at all similar to the smaller cities which were studied before the far-reaching social changes of the past fifteen years. The studies were undertaken to see if there were any class significances in the individual family's spending-saving patterns, retail store loyalties, and his expressions of taste in typical areas such as automobiles, apparel, furniture, and house types.

It seems that many an economist overlooks the possibility of any psychological differences between individuals resulting from different class membership. It is assumed that a rich man is simply a poor man with more money and that, given the same income, the poor man would behave exactly like the rich man. The *Chicago Tribune* studies crystallize a wealth of evidence from other sources that this is just not so, and that the Lower-Status person is profoundly different in his mode of thinking and his way of handling the world from the Middle-Class individual. Where he buys and what he buys will differ not only by economics but in symbolic value.

It should be understood, of course, that there are no hard-and-fast lines between the classes. Implicit in the notion of social class in America is the possibility of movement from one class to another. The "officeboy-to-president" saga is a cherished part of the American dream. Bobo Rockefeller illustrates the female counterpart: from coal miner's daughter to socialite. As a corollary of the explorations in class, the study also tried to be definitive about the phenomenon of social mobility—the movement from one class to another.

There are numerous studies of vertical mobility from the level of sociological analysis, mostly by comparing the individual's occupational status to that of his father. There are also studies at the level of psychological analysis. This study attempted to combine the two levels, to observe the individual's progress and also to understand something of the dynamics of the mobile person as compared to the stable individual. The attempt was to look both backward and forward: tracing such factors as occupation, place of residence, and religion back to parents and grandparents, and then where the family expected to be in the next five or ten years, what were the educational plans for each son, each daughter, a discussion of future goals.

Because this article is confined primarily to social class, this section may be concluded by saying that the studies show a very clear relationship between spending-saving aspirations and the factors of mobility-stability.

FRAMEWORK OF STUDY

Following are Warner's hypotheses and assumptions for the study:

I. Assumptions About Symbols and Values and About Saving of Money and Accumulation of Objects

Our society is acquisitive and pecuniary. On the one hand, the values and beliefs of Americans are pulled toward the pole of the accumulation of money by increasing the amount of money income and reducing its outgo. On the other hand, American values emphasize the accumulation of objects and products of technology for display and consumption. The self-regard and self-esteem of a person and his family, as well as the public esteem and respect of a valued social world around the accumulator, are increased or not by such symbols of accumulation and consumption.

The two sets of values, the accumulation of product symbols and the accumulation (saving) of money, may be, and usually are, in opposition.

General working hypotheses stemming from these assumptions were: (1) People are distributed along a range according to the two-value components, running from proportionately high savings, through mixed categories, to proportionately high accumulation of objects. (2) These value variations conform to social and personality factors present in all Americans.

II. Assumptions About Product Symbols, Savers, and Accumulations

American society is also characterized by social change, particularly technological change that moves in the direction of greater and greater production of more kinds and more numerous objects for consumption and accumulation.

Hypothesis: New varieties of objects will be most readily accepted by the accumulators, and most often opposed by the savers.

III. Assumptions About the Social Values of Accumulators and Savers

American society is characterized by basic cultural differences, one of them being social status. Social class levels are occupied by people, some of whom are upward-mobile by intent and fact. Others are nonmobile, by intent and fact. The values which dictate judgments about actions, such as the kinds of objects which are consumed and accumulated, will vary by class level and the presence or absence of vertical mobility.

IV. Assumptions About the Personal Values of Accumulators and Savers

The personality components are distributed through the class levels and through the mobility types. By relating the social and personality components, it is possible to state a series of hypotheses about accumulators and savers as they are related to the object world around them, particularly to objects which are new and old to the culture, those which are imposing or not, and those which are predominantly for display or for consumption.

At the direct, practical level, all of these theoretical questions can be summarized by one basic question: *What kinds of things are people likely to buy and not buy if they are in given class positions and if they are or are not socially mobile?* In other words, what is the effect on purchasing behavior of being in a particular social class, and being mobile or nonmobile?

If this is the crucial question, theoretically grounded, then a whole series of hypotheses can be laid out concerning values about money and values about buying various kinds of objects for consumption and for display. Some of these are:

1. *There will be a relationship between values held by a particular subject and the extent to which particular products exemplify those values.*

2. *There is a differential hierarchy of things for which it is worth spending money.*

3. *Veblen's theory that conspicuous expenditure is largely applied to the Upper Class is erroneous. It runs all the way through our social system.*

From these statements certain other hypotheses follow:

4. *At different class levels, symbols of mobility will differ.*

There is a differential hierarchy of things on which it is worth spending money. Class and mobility will be two of the dimensions that will differentiate —also personality and cultural background.

5. *The place in the home where these symbols will be displayed will shift at different class levels.*

The underlying assumption here is that there is a hierarchy of importance in the rooms of the house. This hierarchy varies with social class, mobility, age, ethnicity. The studies also revealed clear-cut patterns of taste for lamps, furnishings, house types, etc.

6. *The nonmobile people tend to rationalize purchases in terms of cost or economy.*

In other words, nonmobile people tend to be oriented more toward the pole of the accumulation of money. Purchases, then, are rationalized in terms of the savings involved.

The basic thesis of all the hypotheses on mobility is this: Whereas the stable individual would emphasize saving and security, the behavior of the mobile individual is characterized by spending for various symbols of upward movement. All of the evidence turned up indicates that this difference in values does exist, and furthermore that notable differences in personality dynamics are involved. For instance, the analysis of how families would make investments shows that stable people overwhelmingly prefer insurance, the symbol of security. By contrast, the mobile people at all levels prefer stocks, which are risk-taking. In Warner's words, the mobile individual acts as if he were free, white, and twenty-one, completely able to handle the world, and perfectly willing to gamble on himself as a sure bet to succeed.

CLASS PLACEMENT

Returning to the factor of social class, in this study placement was based on a multistate probability area sample of metropolitan Chicago, involving 3,880 households. It was found that the matter of placement could not be done by the relatively simple scoring sufficient for the smaller cities. To secure house typings, it was necessary to provide the field investigators with photographs covering a wide range of dwelling types, all the way from exclusive apartments to rooms over stores. Because of the very complexity of metropolitan life, occupations provided the biggest problem. To solve this operational problem, it was necessary to construct an exhaustive list of occupational types involving degree of responsibility and training required by each. The data finally used to calculate the Index of Status Characteristics (ISC) were: (weighted by 5)—Occupation (from 1 to 7 broad categories); (weighted by 4)—Sources of Income (from 1 to 7 types); (weighted by 3)—Housing Type (from 1 to 7 types).

The sum of the individual's weighted scores was used to predict his social class level (see Table 1).[2]

TABLE 1. Predicted Social Class

ISC Scores	Predicted Social Class Placement
12–21	Upper Class....
22–37	Upper-Middle Class
38–51	Lower-Middle Class
52–66	Upper-Lower Class
67–84	Lower-Lower Class

[2] Dr. Bevode McCall helped to solve the ISC scoring problem for Metropolitan Chicago.

The study very clearly shows that there is a social-class system operative in a metropolitan area which can be delineated. Furthermore, class membership is an important determinant of the individual's economic behavior, even more so than in the smaller city. The one department store in the smaller city may satisfy almost everyone, whereas in the metropolitan city the stores become sharply differentiated.

Table 2 shows the social-class structure of Metropolitan Chicago, typifying the transformation of the formerly agrarian Midwestern cities from Pittsburgh to Kansas City into a series of big milltowns:

TABLE 2. Social-Class Structure of Metropolitan Chicago

Social Class	Per Cent
Upper and Upper-Middle	8.1
Lower-Middle	28.4
Upper-Lower	44.0
Lower-Lower	19.5

While the Old Families and the Newly Arrived are still recognizable as types, they constitute less than 1 per cent of the population. A similar study in Kansas City turned up so few that they could not be counted at all. On the other hand, we see the emergence of a seventh class, the Upper-Lower "Stars" or Light-Blue Collar Workers. They are the spokesmen of the Upper-Lower Class groups—high income individuals, who have the income for more ostentatious living than the average factory worker but who lack the personal skills or desire for high status by social mobility.

There is certainly a rough correlation between income and social class. But social class is a much richer dimension of meaning. There are so many facets of behavior which are explicable only on a basis of social class dynamics. For instance, an analysis (Table 3) of the purchase of household appliances in Chicago over a four-year period shows a very different picture by income and by class:

TABLE 3. Purchase of Nine Appliance Types—Four Year Period

By Income	
Over $7,000	36.2%
4,000–6,999	46.0
Under 4,000	17.8

By Social Class	
Upper and Upper-Middle	16.6%
Lower-Middle	29.2
Upper-Lower	45.7
Lower-Lower	8.5

Income analysis shows that the lowest income group represents an understandably smaller market, but nevertheless a market. Social-class analysis highlights a fundamental difference in attitudes toward the home between the two lower classes. The Upper-Lower Class man sees his home as his castle, his anchor to the world, and he loads it down with hardware—solid heavy appliances—as his symbols of security. The Lower-Lower Class individual is far less interested in his castle, and is more likely to spend his income for flashy clothes or an automobile. He is less property-minded, and he has less feeling about buying and maintaining a home.

Several *Tribune* studies have explored the way of life and the buying behavior in many new suburbs and communities. All of them quickly become stratified along social-class and mobility dimensions, and, therefore, differ tremendously among themselves. *Fortune* has reported on Park Forest, Illinois, a Middle-Class suburb of 30,000 and only ten years old. It is characterized by high degrees of both upward and geographical mobility. The people are overwhelmingly those who had moved from other parts of the United States, who had few local roots, and who consequently wanted to integrate themselves in friendship groups. But this was not typical of the new Lower-Status suburbs where the women did relatively little fraternizing. It was not typical of the new Upper-Middle Class mobile suburbs where the people were preoccupied with status symbols, not in submerging themselves in the group.

One new community had crystallized as being for Higher-Status Negroes. This was a resettlement project with relatively high rents for Negroes. Eighty-five per cent of them had come from the South where social class was compressed. But, as soon as they came to Chicago, the class system opened up and they were anxious to establish a social distance between themselves and other Negroes. Almost all of them said they enjoyed the "peace and quiet" of their neighborhood, which was their way of insisting that they were not like the "noisy" lower-class Negroes. They deliberately avoided the stores patronized by other Negroes.

CHOICE OF STORE

All of these studies reveal the close relation between choice of store, patterns of spending, and class membership. In the probability sample delineating social class, such questions were asked in the total metropolitan area as:

"If you were shopping for a good dress, at which store would you be most likely to find what you wanted?"

"For an everyday dress?"

"For living room furniture?"

"At which store do you buy most of your groceries?"

To assume that all persons would wish to shop at the glamorous High-Status stores is utterly wrong. People are very realistic in the way they match their values and expectations with the status of the store. The woman shopper has a considerable range of ideas about department stores; but these generally become organized on a scale ranking from very High-Social Status to the Lowest-Status and prestige. The social status of the department store becomes the primary basis for its definition by the shopper. This is also true of men's and women's apparel stores, and furniture stores, on the basis of customer profiles. The shopper is not going to take a chance feeling out of place by going to a store where she might not fit.

No matter what economics are involved, she asks herself who are the other customers in the store, what sort of treatment can she expect at the hands of the clerks, will the merchandise be the best of everything, or lower priced and hence lower quality? Stores are described as being for the rich, for the average ordinary people, or for those who have to stretch their pennies.

The most important function of retail advertising today, when prices and quality have become so standard, is to permit the shopper to make social-class identification. This she can do from the tone and physical character of the advertising. Of course, there is also the factor of psychological identification. Two people in the same social class may want different stores. One may prefer a conservative store, one may want the most advanced styling. But neither will go to stores where they do not "fit," in a social-class sense.

In contrast to the independent food retailer, who obviously adapts to the status of the neighborhood, the chain grocers generally invade many income areas with their stores. Nevertheless, customer profiles show that each chain acquires a status definition. The two largest grocery chains in the Chicago area are A. & P. and Jewel; yet they draw very different customer bodies. A. & P. is strong with the mass market, whereas Jewel has its strength among the Middle Class.

While the national brand can and often does cut across classes, one can think of many product types and services which do have social class labels. The Upper-Middle Class person rarely travels by motor coach because none of his associates do so, even though there is certainly nothing wrong with this mode of transportation. On the other hand, even with low air-coach fares, one does not see many factory workers or day laborers on vacation around airports. Such sales successes as vodka and tonic water, and men's deodorants and foreign sports cars, were accomplished without benefit of much buying from this part of the market.

COMMUNICATION SKILLS

There is also a relation between class and communication abilities which has significance for marketing. The kind of supersophisticated and clever advertising which appears in the *New Yorker* and *Esquire* is almost meaningless to Lower-Status people. They cannot comprehend the subtle humor; they are baffled by the bizarre art. They have a different symbol system, a very different approach to humor. In no sense does this imply that they lack intelligence or wit. Rather their communication skills have just been pressed into a different mold.

Here again, style of advertising helps the individual to make class identification. Most of the really big local television success stories in Chicago have been achieved by personalities who radiate to the mass that this is where they belong. These self-made businessmen who do the announcing for their own shows communicate wonderfully well with the mass audience. While many listeners switch off their lengthy and personal commercials, these same mannerisms tell the Lower-Status individual that here is someone just like himself who understands him.

Social Research, Inc., has frequently discussed the class problem in marketing by dividing the population into Upper-Middle or quality market; the middle majority which combines both the Lower-Middle and Upper-Lower; and then the Lower-Lower. The distinction should be drawn between the Middle Classes and the Lower-Status groups. In several dozen of these store profiles, there is scarcely an instance where a store has appeal to the Lower-Middle and Upper-Lower classes with anything like the same strength.

It would be better to make the break between the Middle Class, representing one third of the population and the Lower-Status or Working-Class or Wage-Earner group, representing two thirds of metroplitan Chicago. This permits some psychological distinctions to be drawn between the Middle-Class individual and the individual who is not a part of the Middle-Class system of values. Even though this is the dominant American value system, even though Middle-Class Americans have been taught by their parents that it is the only value system, this Lower-Status individual does not necessarily subscribe to it.

WHO SAVES, WHO SPENDS?

Another important set of behavioral distinctions related to social class position was revealed in the "save-spend aspiration" study. The question was asked: "Suppose your income was doubled for the next ten years what would you do with the increased income?" This is a fantasy question taken out of the realm of any pressing economic situation to reflect aspirations about money. The coding broke down the answers to this question into five general categories: (1) the mode of saving, (2) the purpose of saving, (3) spending which would consolidate past gains, meet present defensive needs, prepare for future self-advancement, (4) spending which is "self-indulgent-centered," (5) spending which is "house-centered."

Here are some of our findings.[3] The higher the individual's class position,

---

[3] The saving-spending aspiration analysis was carried out by Roger Coup, graduate student at the University of Chicago.

the more likely is he to express some saving aspirations. Conversely, the lower his class position, the more likely is he to mention spending only. Moreover the higher the status, the more likely is the individual to specify *how* he will save his money, which is indicative of the more elaborate financial learning required of higher status.

Proceeding from the more general categories (such as saving versus spending only) to more specific categories (such as noninvestment versus investment saving and the even more specific stock versus real estate investment, etc.) an increasingly sharper class differentiation is found. It is primarily *noninvestment* saving which appeals to the Lower-Status person. Investment saving, on the other hand, appeals above all to the Upper-Status person.

Investors almost always specify how they will invest. And here in mode of investment are examples of the most sharply class-differentiated preferences. Intangible forms of investment like stock and insurance are very clearly distinguished as Upper-Status investments. Nearly four times as many Upper-Middles select insurance as would be expected by chance, whereas only one fifth of the Lower-Lowers select it as would be expected by chance. By contrast, Lower-Status people have far greater preference for tangible investments, specifically ownership of real estate, a farm, or a business.

To sum up, Middle-Class people usually have a place in their aspirations for some form of saving. This saving is most often in the form of investment, where there is a risk, long-term involvement, and the possibility of higher return. Saving, investment saving, and intangible investment saving—successively each of these become for them increasingly symbols of their higher status.

The aspirations of the Lower-Status person are just as often for spending as they are for saving. This saving is usually a noninvestment saving where there is almost no risk, funds can be quickly converted to spendable cash, and returns are small. When the Lower-Status person does invest his savings, he will be specific about the mode of investment, and is very likely to prefer something tangible and concrete—something he can point at and readily display.

Turning from mode of saving to purpose of saving, very significant class relationships are likewise evident. Consider the verbalization of saving purpose. Lower-Status people typically explain why one should save—why the very act of saving is important. On the other hand, Middle-Class people do not, as if saving is an end-in-itself, the merits of which are obvious and need not be justified.

Spending is the other side of the coin. Analysis of what people say they will spend for shows similar class-related desires. All classes mention concrete, material artifacts such as a new car, some new appliance. But the Lower-Status people stop here. Their accumulations are artifact-centered, whereas Middle-Class spending-mentions are experience-centered. This is spending where one is left typically with only a memory. It would include hobbies, recreation, self-education, and travel. The wish to travel, and particularly foreign travel, is almost totally a Middle-Class aspiration.

Even in their fantasies, people are governed by class membership. In his daydreaming and wishful thinking, the Lower-Status individual will aspire in different patterns from the Middle-Class individual.

PSYCHOLOGICAL DIFFERENCES

This spending-saving analysis has very obvious psychological implications to differentiate between the classes. Saving itself generally suggests foresightedness, the ability to perceive long-term needs and goals. Noninvestment saving has the characteristics of little risk-taking and of ready conversion, at no loss, into immediate expenditures—the money can be drawn out of the account whenever the bank is open. Investment spending, on the other hand, has the characteristics of risk-taking (a gamble for greater returns) and of delayed conversion, with possible loss, to expenditures on immediate needs.

Here are some psychological contrasts between two different social groups:

Middle-Class
1. Pointed to the future
2. His viewpoint embraces a long expanse of time
3. More urban identification
4. Stresses rationality
5. Has a well-structured sense of the universe
6. Horizons vastly extended or not limited
7. Greater sense of choice-making
8. Self-confident, willing to take risks
9. Immaterial and abstract in his thinking
10. Sees himself tied to national happenings

Lower-Status
1. Pointed to the present and past
2. Lives and thinks in a short expanse of time
3. More rural in identification
4. Nonrational essentially
5. Vague and unclear structuring of the world
6. Horizons sharply defined and limited
7. Limited sense of choice-making
8. Very much concerned with security and insecurity
9. Concrete and perceptive in his thinking
10. World revolves around his family and body

CONCLUSION

The essential purpose of this article was to develop three basic premises which are highly significant for marketing:

1. *There is a social-class system operative in metropolitan markets, which can be isolated and described.*

2. *It is important to realize that there are far-reaching psychological differences between the various classes.* They do not handle the world in the same fashion. They tend not to think in the same way. As one tries to communicate with the Lower-Status group, it is imperative to sense that their goals and mental processes differ from the Middle-Class group.

3. *Consumption patterns operate as prestige symbols to define class membership, which is a more significant determinant of economic behavior than mere income.* Each major department store, furniture store, and chain-grocery store has a different "pulling power" on different status groups. The usual customers of a store gradually direct the store's merchandising policies into a pattern which works. The interaction between store policy and consumer acceptance results in the elimination of certain customer groups and the attraction of others, with a resulting equilibration around a reasonably stable core of specific customer groups who think of the store as appropriate for them.

Income has always been the marketer's handiest index to family consumption standards. But it is a far from accurate index. For instance, the bulk of the population in a metropolitan market today will fall in the middle-income ranges. This will comprise not only the traditional white collar worker, but the unionized craftsman and the semiskilled worker with their tremendous income gains of the past decade. Income-wise, they may be in the same category. But their buying behavior, their tastes, their spending-saving aspirations can be poles apart. Social-class position and mobility-stability dimensions will reflect in much greater depth each individual's style of life.

23

The Working Man: Do Marketing Men Know Him?

By the Staff of *Printers' Ink*

> In Selection 22, Martineau argued that the social class concept provides a richer meaning for marketing than does the use of income categories. In the following selection, the staff of *Printers' Ink* reports conclusions of a social research organization that specifically illustrate how deliberate use of the "working class" as defined by social class criteria may be of inestimable value to the business that seeks their patronage.

Marketers may be passing up sales in one of the biggest markets because they don't consider the market's special characteristics. That's the opinion of Dr. Burleigh Gardner, executive director of Social Research Inc., Chicago.

According to Dr. Gardner, the overlooked market is the so-called upper working class, which today has a record amount of money for nonessentials. As a group, this market represents 40 to 45 per cent of U.S. population, and controls about the same proportion of spendable income.

But, Gardner warns, because its members approach middle-class income levels doesn't mean they spend their money in the same way as people of higher social status. Nor do they respond to the same sales appeals.

Gardner says the upper working class is made up primarily of skilled laborers. People in this group work with their hands, or they may be in service occupations that are important to public life but are generally considered of low social status. Policemen, firemen, service station operators and some sales clerks fall into the latter group.

The working-class man and his wife usually have no more than a high school education. They are conscious that they "never had it so good" financially and are anxious to hang on to their prosperity. One of their main ambitions, according to Gardner, is to own their own homes, and a large percentage of them do. When they buy homes they look for "respectable" city neighborhoods or suburban developments where other working-class people live. Even though they may be able to afford to live in more stylish suburbs, they don't feel they would be comfortable among people with more impressive educational or professional backgrounds.

The marketer of consumer goods who tries to use snob appeal to attract

Reprinted from *Printers' Ink*, **277,** 9 (December 1, 1961), pp. 48–49, by permission of the publisher.

working-class people is more likely to antagonize them than create sales, says Gardner. The "good American life" is their goal, and sophistication makes them uncomfortable. They want to be told how a product will fit into their lives, not that the product is used by people of higher status and will, therefore, confer status on them.

In the course of a study of the working class, Social Research Inc. talked with a skilled factory worker who had saved for years to buy a Cadillac. He liked the car but sold it after only a few weeks. It looked out of place parked before his working-class home and he thought the neighbors were laughing at him for "showing off."

THE SYMBOLS THAT COUNT

What is important to the working-class family is visible proof that it can afford all the accouterment of stable, comfortable living. Owning a home is part of it. Other symbols include a late-model, medium-priced car, a houseful of modern (but not extreme) furniture, a well-applianced kitchen, and plenty of up-to-date clothing.

The working-class man and his wife are anxious that the things they buy will be modern and in good taste. But their definitions of both terms differ from those of the middle class.

A study of attitudes toward home furnishings made for Kroehler Manufacturing Co. revealed major differences in taste. The wife of the working man does not care for antiques or traditional furniture; she thinks they are "old-fashioned." Nor is she in the market for the slim-lined style of modern design. To her, good furniture has fairly bulky lines, both because it looks comfortable and because it looks as if it would stand hard use.

She also uses lamps, sofa cushions, draperies and similar accessories in styles that the middle-class woman would consider "fussy."

These attitudes toward furnishings are important to a marketer. For example, sophisticated room settings in furniture advertising and other promotional material will turn the working-class woman away from furniture even when it is a style that would normally appeal to her. She couldn't visualize how the pieces would look in her own living room. Copy, advises Dr. Gardner, should assure her that the furnishings are modern, tasteful, comfortable, durable, and economical.

In buying appliances, however, the working-class wife is more at ease because there is no question of style. She buys all she can in an effort to become less of a slave to her home—and to show her friends that she can afford them.

But she doesn't want to be told that labor-saving devices would give her more time for herself. This would make her feel guilty, because she's afraid she's already too lazy. The wise marketer will appeal to her strong desire to make a good home for her family. He will talk in terms of how the product could help her make a clean, healthy home and give her time to pay more attention to her children and husband.

Several Social Research Inc. studies of women's attitudes toward themselves and each other provide further guides to selling to the working-class wife. She sees herself as a "Cinderella" who is a slave to her home but is always hopeful of transforming herself into a "queen."

And this makes her one of the biggest markets for copies of high-style clothing and the newest in beauty and figure aids. But the type of woman who models the product must jibe with her ideals of femininity. The All-American-girl type, for example, seems too careless about her appearance; so does the "suburbanite," with her fondness for the casual look. Neither one appears to be a good homemaker. On the other hand, the "executive wife" type is admired for her well-groomed appearance and implied ability to manage her home efficiently. The fashion model, too, has strong appeal because she obviously is conscientious about maintaining her appearance.

MAKE THE PRODUCT FIT THEIR LIFE

The high-style model is appropriate for selling clothes and cosmetics to the younger woman who wants to learn the professional tricks of fashion and grooming. The more mature woman responds to cosmetic approaches that imply cleanliness, health, and neatness rather than sex appeal.

Male attire, too, makes its best appeal to the working class if shown in a home setting or a bowling alley rather than in a business office or on the golf course. Here, again, the idea is to show the consumer how the product will fit into his life.

In the past few years boating has become one of the symbols of national affluence. Working-class people buy boats, too. They justify the expense on the grounds that boating—unlike golf, for example—is a sport that can be enjoyed by the entire family.

This is one realm in which they don't feel uncomfortable among people of greater education and social status. During a Social Research interview, one man expressed the reason: "People accept you for what you are. They don't look into you background."

He was talking about equality on the water. The fact that he didn't belong to a yacht club was of no concern, because the working man has no interest in exclusive clubs and swanky restaurants, even though he may be able to afford them.

Marketers who want to sell marine equipment would do well to play up the family-enjoyment concept and play down the idea that a boat is glamorous.

Marketers of any product for the working class should make a careful study of the media they use. The working-class woman wouldn't respond to high-fashion appeals in "class" magazines even if she read them—which she doesn't. She looks to the "family behavior" magazines and her newspaper for information on what is new and what is right for her style of living. She also is susceptible to direct mail. Television doesn't seem as authoritative to her as the printed word.

Mass media are gradually upgrading the tastes and desires of the working class. However, according to Dr. Gardner, it still is important that sales approaches do not set too high standards. Common-man respectability is the goal that the working class strives to achieve and maintain, and publicity, package design, advertising, displays, and other sales techniques must associate a product with this goal if it is to be sold to the working class.

24

Social Class, Mental Hygiene, and Psychiatric Practice

Orville R. Gursslin, Raymond G. Hunt, and Jack L. Roach

This selection challenges the approach of the mental hygiene movement, accusing its directors of "unwittingly enforcing, under the guise of science, a secular version of the middle-class ethic." Class differences are not weighed effectively in mental hygiene's prescriptions, with the result that the lower class is not served by mental hygiene agencies. The authors point out that chances for the early recognition and treatment of mental illness are disproportionately awarded—like so many other valuable things of life— to those of higher status.

Probably two of the most important problems confronting workers in the field of mental health are how to help more adequately those members of the community who seek their services and how to induce even more people who need help and can profit by it to seek them. It might be well for mental hygienists (especially those operating within psychiatric organizations) to

Reprinted from *Social Service Review,* **33,** 3 (September 1959), pp. 237–245, by permission of The University of Chicago Press and the authors.

Orville R. Gursslin is Assistant Professor, State University of New York at Buffalo.

Raymond G. Hunt is Associate Professor of Social Psychology, State University of New York at Buffalo.

Jack L. Roach is Assistant Professor of Sociology, State University of New York at Buffalo.

ponder the paradox implied in the above statements. Inducing more and more people to seek the help of social agencies that are already forced to the wall in attempting to serve those now at their doors poses a dilemma.

It is hardly the purpose of the present discussion to offer any resolution of this question. Instead, the writers have set the more realistic goal of discussing certain factors that bear directly upon the problems stated above.

In the first place, the two problems—how to help more effectively and how to induce people to seek help—are not unrelated. Similar considerations are involved in both. For instance, it has been becoming increasingly difficult to ignore the fact that psychiatric agencies are not serving all members of the community in equal fashion. As more and more empirical analyses emerge, it becomes increasingly evident that marked class-linked inequalities exist in the treatment of mental illness. The recent appearance of Hollingshead and Redlich's volume, *Social Class and Mental Illness,* seems to provide ample documentation for this proposition.

Clearly this proposition bears upon the issues noted. Something is happening either in the community or in social agencies, or perhaps in both, with the result that patient populations are in no way representative of the larger populations from which they derive. The Hollingshead-Redlich study in the New Haven community is one demonstration among many of the extent to which social-class membership operates in patient selection to bring relative exclusion of lower-class persons from psychiatric services.

What is to be done? Certainly if the ideal is service to the community, not just to the middle class, some action is called for. Hollingshead and Redlich have in fact outlined what will unquestionably become a controversial program aimed at insuring a wider spread of psychiatric service within the community. No doubt the social conscience of professional workers and of interested laymen will dictate vigorous discussion of this issue (one national magazine has already devoted a sizable amount of space to a review and discussion of the Hollingshead-Redlich book and the problem which it highlights). It is likely that whatever action ensues will be oriented more toward the problem per se than to some of the basic reasons which may have created it. Indeed, Hollingshead and Redlich hardly touch upon them in terms here considered.

It is the conviction of the present writers that the phenomenon is not simply a result of an insufficiency of psychiatric facilities and trained professional workers (though neither of these is denied) or of simple ignorance of members of lower strata of society about the existence and value of psychiatric services. Rather, it is our thesis that the problem is rooted in the relationship between the American stratification system with its correlated value orientations, on the one hand, and the philosophic underpinnings of psychiatric practice, on the other. As a consequence, the bare problem posed by the work of the New Haven group and of others is in reality far more difficult to resolve than may initially appear.

This paper, then, is an attempt to explore some fundamental aspects of the relationship between social status and psychiatric treatment as it pertains to mental hygiene and psychiatric practice in social agencies and to discuss certain implications of our analysis for social action. The discussion will center mainly on the urban child-guidance clinic, both because it is the type of agency with which the writers are most familiar and because the convergences of mental hygiene and psychiatric practice are perhaps clearest there. It is presumed, however, that the discussion to follow is generally applicable to other psychiatric agencies.

It appears to be fairly well established that child-guidance clinics seem to be serving a largely middle-class clientele. Not only do family members from this group find representation in child-guidance clinic case loads disproportionate to their numbers in the population, they tend to be seen for longer periods, to be seen more frequently, and to reap whatever benefits accrue from being seen by more prestigeful staff members. In addition, they are much more likely to be receiving psychotherapy than are their lower-class counterparts.

How are these phenomena to be understood? In attempting to come to grips with this question, we shall pose three general queries which represent key problems of understanding bearing upon the issues stated at the outset of this paper. These are:

1. Who feels the need for the services of child-guidance clinics?
2. How do potential clients learn about and get to such clinics?
3. What are some of the conditions determining case selection?

In answering these questions we shall highlight significant sociocultural dynamics that appear to play a forceful role in the determination of these issues and that may very easily be overlooked.

MENTAL HYGIENE AND THE MIDDLE CLASS

Who does feel the need for the service of a child-guidance clinic? The obvious answer is, "Anyone who is having trouble with a child and cannot cope with it himself." Undoubtedly this reply is true, as far as it goes. The difficulty is that it is too simple and categorical. It neglects more than it answers. How does one decide when one is "having trouble"? When does one stop trying to handle such "troubles" one's self?

It does not seem feasible to attempt an answer to this question until some satisfactory answer has been given to the question of how potential clients learn about and get to child-guidance clinics. Clearly no one can feel the need for a service until he knows of its existence and has available channels for seeking it out. In order, however, to answer even this question one has to look at certain characteristics of most child-guidance clinics.

In general, these clinics seem to have what has been loosely referred to as the "mental-hygiene orientation." This orientation involves an adherence to the mental-health philosophy identified with the mental-hygiene movement. As is well known, this movement derives from the reforms initiated by Clifford Beers some fifty years ago and is now closely associated with such policy-making agencies as the National Institute of Mental Health.

Twenty years ago, Kingsley Davis formulated a penetrating analysis (which has even now received too little attention) of the intimate relationship between the guiding philosophy of the mental-hygiene movement and the middle-class ethic.[1] It was Davis' argument that the mental hygienist was in reality unwittingly enforcing, under the guise of science, a secular version of the middle-class ethic. As a result, the mental hygienist becomes, in effect, an extension or agent of the middle class.

As provocative as is Davis' argument, it cannot stand on assertion alone. Some empirical demonstration of the correlations he posits is necessary. It needs also to be shown that the relation between mental-hygiene philosophy and the middle-class ethic is exclusive—that there is a contrasting lower-class ethic to which it may be opposed. The raw material for such comparisons is readily available to anyone who wishes to devote the time and energy to seeking it. The sociological literature is replete with descriptions of the ethical codes of both the lower and the middle classes. By the same token, there is no dearth of "official" mental-hygiene literature to which ethical codes may be placed in apposition.

To illustrate this thesis, a sampling of statements drawn from mental-hygiene literature and representing mental-health advice is presented in Table 1 (p. 216). Alongside each statement are listed the coordinate middle-class and contrasting lower-class value orientations related to that statement.

Two conclusions are apparent from Table 1. First, that this mental-hygiene material is based upon propositions involving an admixture of cultural "common sense" along with tidbits of psychiatric "knowledge." Second, that these propositions are smoothly blended into the middle-class cognitive and evaluative frame of reference. The writers do not wish to suggest that this is all that comprises the mental-hygiene orientation. Nor is any derogation intended. It is sufficient to note the apparent derivation of the mental-hygiene evaluative tone from the middle-class ethic.[2]

With this framework in mind one may recall that there has been a traditionally close, supportive relationship between the mental-hygiene movement and the urban child-guidance clinic. The support which the mental-hygiene movement receives from the child-guidance clinic is, at least partly, a function of the vital role it has played in the founding and growth of these clinics.

Consistent with this relationship is the strongly prophylactic interest of the child-guidance clinic. It appears to be a commonly accepted notion that, as an

---

[1] K. Davis, "Mental Hygiene and the Class Structure," *Psychiatry,* I (February 1938), pp. 55–56.

[2] Using a similar approach, the authors have prepared a more exacting analysis of mental-health mass-media literature. It will appear in a forthcoming publication.

integral part of their community services, clinic staff members play an appreciable part in mental-health education efforts. Typically this involves such activities as participation in family-life and child study groups and presenting talks on emotional health and illness among children, in addition to interpreting the functions of the clinic. These activities play a part in promoting "receptivity" in groups which might include potential clients. One measure of the success of this direct influence is the substantial number of self-referred

TABLE 1. Mental Health Propositions and Coordinate Middle- and Lower-Class Value Orientations

MENTAL-HEALTH STATEMENT*	MIDDLE- AND LOWER-CLASS ORIENTATIONS
1. Plan for tomorrow, but don't worry about it.	Middle-class future orientation vs. lower-class present orientation.
2. Everybody needs love, especially children.	Child- and affection-centered family of middle-class vs. laissez-faire and parent-centered lower-class system.
3. Face up to your responsibilities.	Middle-class personal responsibility emphasis vs. dependency on friend, relative, or social agency among the lower class.
4. Set goals you can reach.	Goal orientation (see 1) and importance of striving (but "within attainable limits" is apparently a mental-hygiene modification, as against the old ethic of "reach for the sky") vs. "if you set goals you'll only be disappointed" orientation of lower class.
5. Control your emotions; don't let them run you.	Middle-class restraint vs. lower-class freer display of grief, anger, love, etc.
6. Do something about your troubles; don't engage in self-pity.	Middle-class emphasis on initiative and active problem-solving vs. lower-class stress on luck and fate; feeling of futility and fear of taking chances.

*Quoted or paraphrased from *Mental Health Is for Every Day* (Albany: New York State Department of Mental Hygiene, 1952).

clients who have been made aware of the clinic through its educational activities.

The significant point here is that these educational services become channeled predominantly to a middle-class population. The types of organizations concerned about such problems are composed mostly of middle-class people. Indeed, such formal organizations are a characteristically middle-class phenomenon. There would be little in the way of similar access to the lower-class population with its informal and closed group structure.

Furthermore, if the general propositions developed concerning the middle-class–mental-hygiene relationship are even more broadly correct, it follows that groups most likely to be receptive to mental-hygiene educational efforts will lie within the middle class. It is this segment of society that will most easily understand the tone of the "message" transmitted because of the congruence of values and cognitive dispositions suggested. For the same reasons middle-class individuals will be more likely to find themselves in agreement with the mental hygienist as to the types of behavior to be defined as "problems" and with their preferred modes of solution of these problems.

Work with formal organizations dealing with child and mental-health problems is, of course, only one means of access to people. But use of other means of communication is influenced by other features of the life of the several social strata. For example, the vast bulk of mental-hygiene "propaganda" disseminated through the mass media is found in middle-class sources (e.g., women's magazines, "middle-brow" fiction, etc.). The reading habits of members of the lower class are not such as to bring them into contact with mental-hygiene material with anywhere near the frequency found in the middle class. Analogous conditions would hold for other communication and entertainment media.

In addition, middle-class persons have closer relationships with physicians, school officials, and other referral sources favorably regarded by child-guidance clinics. Hence it is more likely that members of the middle class will be far more familiar than lower-class persons with the presence and functions of child-guidance clinics (and probably of other similar agencies as well) and will be better acquainted with and will have more available channels of access to these facilities.

This is not to imply that there is any formal attempt by mental-hygiene advocates to direct their message only to the middle class. On the contrary, the message is purportedly directed to all. What is suggested is that, because of the content of the message and the mechanisms by which it is disseminated, it reaches, and is palatable to, mainly middle-class individuals.

DYNAMICS OF PATIENT SELECTION

Who feels the need for child-guidance clinic services? The greater familiarity of middle-class persons with such facilities has been indicated. This familiarity, coupled with the dispositional alignment of these persons with the mental-hygiene message, will probably lead middle-class persons to seek out such services for help with "problems" of a nature "appropriate" to the clinic.

There are other characteristics of the middle class which will reinforce this tendency. Among these are the child-oriented nature of the middle-class family, in which concern for the child's future is especially marked, and the possession of comparative socioeconomic stability and leisure which allows time to have parent-child problems and to do something about them.

Through all of this it must be borne in mind that the middle-class ethic is closely tied to the conditions of middle-class life, just as the lower-class code is rooted in the conditions of life peculiar to the lower class. Given the correlation between mental-health values and middle-class ethical strictures, it would seem unlikely that mental-hygiene propositions, while possibly "adjustive" for middle-class persons in a context of middle-class behavior settings, would be equally "adjustive" for lower-class persons operating within the contraints of lower-class life. Such values might even be "negatively adjustive" for lower-class persons, and there seems no reason why they should not recognize this fact, if only implicitly.

In any event, the probability seems high that it will be essentially a middle-class group which reaches the clinic to make even an initial contact.[3]

What happens, however, after the patient reaches the clinic? Evidence has accumulated indicating that a comparable sort of selection operates during the intake phase, further reducing the proportion of lower-class patients accepted for treatment. Moreover, we have already noted that, if accepted for treatment at all, the lower-class patient is likely to be treated for a shorter time, less intensively, by different methods, and by staff members lower in the hierarchy of professional prestige. Hollingshead and Redlich, probably correctly, offer tentative explanations of these trends couched in terms of the convergence between middle-class standards and the frames of reference of clinic personnel. In particular, Hollingshead and Redlich emphasize the communication problems created by the differential value and cognitive orientations of middle-class practitioners and lower-class patients.

It seems fairly apparent, then, that a significant portion of the variance in selection of patients in child-guidance clinics is attributable to characteristics of the mental-hygiene philosophy propounded by these agencies in relation to features of American class structure. It is also probably true that a similar situation exists in other psychiatric agencies.

IMPLICATIONS FOR POLICY AND PRACTICE

Should a more vigorous effort be made by child-guidance centers to "reach" and give service to the lower-class clients? A definite answer to this question is contingent in the first instance on whether or not the present situation can be appreciably altered. To the writers this would seem to be rather doubtful in view of the almost inevitable consequences of some of the pervasive forces discussed.

It may be that the similarity of class backgrounds of patients and staff resulting from the kind of selection processes indicated may be a favorable circumstance in the process of giving and receiving help. There is, for example, the point of view that the most efficacious use of relationship-oriented therapeutic services may be within the framework of closeness of client and therapist with regard to such considerations as values, norm patterns, and general ways of living.

If this is true, it might well be desirable for child-guidance clinics to pro-

---

[3] It is also likely that the greater competitive strains of middle-class life will contribute to this fact. However, a treatment of this thesis would take us too far from the main theme of the present paper. The reader is referred to A. Green, "The Middle-Class Male Child and Neurosis," in *Sociological Analysis,* ed. L. Wilson and W. Kolb (New York: Harcourt, 1949), pp. 236–248.

ceed with their present mode of operations, and to take even more advantage of the present level of articulation between client needs and nature of service given. Thus the task at hand would be to concentrate on gaining greater understanding of middle-class culture and its relationship to parent-child problems, and, when necessary, to alter present services in order to bring about more efficient dovetailing with the needs of such a clientele.

It can be safely assumed, however, that social work and the community at large would scarcely tolerate the consideration or carrying out of such a program. In other words, the expectation would be that necessary steps should be taken to insure greater extension of appropriate services to persons other than those of the middle class. As indicated in the body of this paper, however, far more drastic changes will be required than a "simple" policy change at the intake stage. In this connection the experience of Coleman and his colleagues has some relevance. They found that, despite a change of orientation in their clinic to that of a community agency with an open intake system, "class position" was still the most important factor determining who received psychotherapy.

The New Haven project points to the need for a basic overhauling of the whole concept of mental illness and of present modes of treatment and their applicability to the lower class. In particular, the New Haven investigators question the feasibility of utilizing existing psychiatric personnel for services to lower-class individuals. Formidable obstacles in communication, difficulties in determining what is normative and what is deviant behavior, especially when viewed against a middle-class frame of reference, marked variation in perception of problems by therapist and client, among other factors, are cited in support of their view.

Hollingshead and Redlich urge the development of a new kind of psychotherapist specifically equipped to work with lower-class individuals. In addition to a psychiatric grounding, such counselors, or whatever they might be called, would ideally possess an intimate understanding of lower-class culture which would be gained largely through an educative process based on what available knowledge the social sciences can offer regarding this segment of the population. Hollingshead and Redlich believe that social workers are one of the professional groups that possess some of the characteristics favorable for successful work with lower-class clients, and consequently that social workers could well form the vanguard of such therapists.

The present authors have considerable reservation about how adequately social workers might "fill the bill." It is likely that status insecurity, upward striving, and in general the middle-class identification which seems to characterize the bulk of social workers may make for as much social distance between lower-class clients and social workers as exists between such clients and psychiatrists. Two more considerations that need to be taken into account in weighing social work as suitable clay out of which this particular therapist protoype can be fashioned are (1) social work's heavy reliance on the psychiatric orientation and (2) the growing tendency in casework agencies to serve a middle-class clientele. Not to be overlooked also is the interesting question as to how receptive social workers, or for that matter any other "helping group," would be to such a plan.

AN ALTERNATIVE APPROACH

There is, of course, good justification for distress over the unequal distribution of psychiatric services to the disadvantage of the lower class. Sufficient concern should be exercised, however, that the concentration of efforts toward expanding treatment facilities should not obscure consideration of a basic question that needs to be dealt with, namely, to what degree (and in what way) psychotherapy can be regarded as a major approach to the problem of mental illness in the lower class.

Granted that the whole question of the etiology of mental illness in the lower class may be an uncharted region, the probability seems strong that the severe socioeconomic deprivation that characterizes a large portion of the lower-class population can be considered as directly involved in the exacerbation of psychiatric disorders, if not a major "underlying" determinant. Whatever the actual extent of causation may be, submarginal living circumstances are hardly conducive to a state of mental health, as usually defined in our culture. Especially with regard to lower-class persons who are members or products of multiproblem families that eke out a bare existence, a primary effort should be directed toward mitigation of such conditions rather than concentrated on repair of the resultant personality damage.

What is the significance of all of this for the mental-health movement? In only peripheral ways has the movement come to grips with the issue of mental illness in the lower class.[4] As indicated in this paper, the movement's educational efforts are not appropriate to lower-class culture. Rather than attempt to devise ways and means of getting to the lower class with a preventive mental-health message, those centrally associated with the mental-health movement might better proceed by taking greater advantage of their strategic position to influence legislation aimed at eradicating some of the social problems that help bring about the apparent high incidence of psychiatric breakdown in the lower class.

---

[4] For instance, improvement in care of patients in public hospitals for the mentally ill, which are heavily populated by lower-class individuals.

25

Environment, Communication, and Status Change Aboard an American Aircraft Carrier

James F. Downs

Here is an interesting observation of unanticipated social consequences of modified architecture and military functions. The kinds
of problems and situations presented here in the context of a military stratification system are useful in analyzing many types of
organizational difficulties. The application of the knowledge of the
stratification (status) concept, for example, may very well alleviate
or eliminate the types of tensions described in this article. Unfortunately, there is abroad a vulgarization of the idea, developed
in the classic Hawthorne studies, that "change is always good." *
It should be carefully noted that change only under certain conditions may increase productivity, which can depend on such things
as the employee's personal involvement in decision making versus
felt threat to status, and so forth. Administrators aware of the status
implications of any organizational change can minimize many tensions and frustrations.

In the spring of 1951, the aircraft carrier U.S.S. *Dauntless,* operating
against Communist forces in Korea, developed problems in feeding her crew
and disembarking the liberty party. At sea, the chow lines were long, slow
moving, and in a state of confusion. Because it kept men from their jobs, this
was a potential threat to the efficient operation of the ship and contributed to
lowered morale. In port, the process of disembarking the liberty party de-
generated into a confused melee which hindered in-port routine and further
contributed to lowered morale.[1] The second problem was resolved rather
simply but, in the period of the writer's service aboard the *Dauntless,* no solution was found to the chow line situation.

This paper will analyze the two problems in the light of three factors which

Reprinted from *Human Organization,* **17,** 3 (Fall, 1958), pp. 14–19, by permission of
The Society for Applied Anthropology and the author.
James F. Downs is Assistant Professor of Anthropology and East Asian Studies, Uni-
versity of Rochester, New York.
* See Delbert C. Miller and William H. Form, *Industrial Sociology* (New York:
Harper, 1951), pp. 43–51, for a discussion of some of the Hawthorne studies.
[1] This assessment of the state of the ship's morale may be criticized as subjective but
it is the result of comparisons made by the writer between the *Dauntless* and five other
vessels in which he served during five years' duty as an enlisted man in the United States
Navy and Naval Reserve.

appear to have been the most important in affecting the behavior of the men involved in the chow line and liberty party and will compare the two problems in an attempt to see why, in consideration of the forces at work, one was solved simply and the other seemed insoluable.

The three areas which will be examined are

1. *Naval Architecture:* To relate the structural uniqueness of an aircraft carrier to certain behavior patterns which appeared in the *Dauntless'* sailors.

2. *Social Communication:* An analysis of the working of communication systems, particularly in the area of feedback to superiors, and how this affects the problems under consideration.

3. *Changing Status Relationships:* To consider the changes in technology and naval policies which affected established status relationships and symbolism.

In general the *Dauntless* could have been described as a "happy ship." There appears to have been no unusual number of courts-martial or other disciplinary actions, usual criteria of lowered morale. The ship's officers, particularly the captain, the executive officer, and department heads displayed unusual concern for the welfare, comfort, and happiness of the crew. There was, however, a distinct trend toward lowered morale from a high point during the period when the vessel was recommissioned in the summer and fall of 1950.

The lowered morale did not find expression in resentment of commissioned officers. With the exception of officers who made reputations as incompetents or martinets, enlisted-commissioned relationships were very good.

The relationships between senior petty officers and their juniors, however, were strained. Bickering, arguments, personal feuds, "soldiering" on the job, accusations of favoritism or persecution were common. It was extremely difficult for senior petty officers to get work carried out without constant supervision and threats of coercive action.

The personality of the captain was an important factor in maintaining morale and efficiency despite the tensions among enlisted personnel. The captain was extremely popular with the men who looked on him as their active protector against higher authority. It was not uncommon to hear men say a certain distasteful job had to be done "because Captain Jack wants it." There was a common attitude that "if Captain Jack knew about this he'd square it away," whenever an unpleasant or annoying situation developed. Although many of the 3,000-plus men aboard seldom saw their captain, there was a growing body of lore concerning his disregard of naval formalities and his concern for enlisted men.

THE LIBERTY PARTY: PROBLEM AND SOLUTION

When the liberty party was called away, the quarterdeck was a scene of extreme confusion. Half-formed ranks of men wavered uncertainly across the hangar deck and dissolved into clumps of shoving, cursing, impatient sailors.

The officer of the deck and the master-at-arms force made hurried and harried inspections. During the period the liberty party was on deck it was virtually impossible to conduct routine business across the bow. Men left the ship disgusted, impatient to make up for lost time and filled with truculence which not infrequently was expressed in brawls in the garish night clubs, beer halls, and brothels of Yokosuka. Further conflicts were engendered because some men, with or without permission of their superiors, "knocked off" before liberty and loitered around the quarterdeck in dress uniforms waiting for liberty call so they could be first off before the rest of the men had time to change uniforms.

The situation was brought to an abrupt end and order was restored by adopting a seniority system for releasing the crew on liberty. Chief petty officers, as always, were allowed to go ashore without standing formal inspections. All other men fell into ranks according to military seniority. First class petty officers formed the first rank, second class petty officers the second rank, etc. If a first class petty officer was late on the quarterdeck he fell in with the front rank and went ashore regardless of the number of junior men who may have been waiting longer than he.[2]

Among the lower rated petty officers and nonrated men there was a great deal of vocal complaint about such an undemocratic system. The complaints died out when it became apparent that the system would not be changed and that the complainers were getting ashore sooner than they would have under the old first-come-first-off system. Naturally enough the system had the immediate and unanimous support of the senior petty officers.

THE CHOW LINE: THE UNSOLVED PROBLEM

The problem of the chow lines revolved around the feeding of "early chow" men; those people who because of continuing work assignments or watch standing schedules were fed before the main body of the crew. Passes were issued to each division to dole out to an early chow detail. Because the main chow line was long and slow moving, division officers and senior petty officers received a great deal of pressure from their people to enlarge the early chow lists. Soon the early chow lines were as long and as slow moving as the regular chow lines.

The lines were scenes of extreme confusion. Men allowed their friends to crowd into line ahead of them. Individuals and groups crowded or tried to crowd into line. Often two groups appeared on the end of the line at the same time and formed branching lines which jockied for position in the main line. Arguments were regular, fist fights not uncommon, resentment and anger the order of the day. As the lines became almost immobile, other men tried

---

[2] Navy enlisted men are divided into rated (noncommissioned officers) and nonrated men. Ratings are twofold, inasmuch as they represent a nonmilitary specialty, such as yeoman, and a military rank, such as first class. A first class yeoman, therefore, is expected to have greater professional competence than a third class yeoman as well as to have greater command responsibilities.

to by-pass the lines by requesting that the master-at-arms in charge of the mess decks admit them directly. Not infrequently these men were accompanied by a distraught division officer who backed their request on the grounds of urgent work assignments.

Numerous attempts to correct the situation were made. Requirements for early chow details were stiffened, a closer watch kept on early chow passes, men without passes were refused entrance to the mess decks, but none of the attempts were successful for more than a few days.

PRESTIGE SYMBOLS: SLEEPING, LIBERTY, AND MESSING

The relationship between the two problems is not simply one of handling a large number of men. Other occasions, when it was necessary for men to fall into lines or formation, were generally orderly. The relationship can be seen more clearly if one examines the prestige and status symbolism of the Navy.

In addition to the obvious differences between ranks in pay and uniforms, status is most often expressed in three areas: the amount and ease of obtaining liberty time; the elaborateness of sleeping accommodations; and the elaborateness of eating accommodations.

Without detailing the gradations between ranks, the situation is best illustrated by comparing the facilities of the captain and an apprentice seaman. The captain lives in a suite of cabins. In addition he has a sea cabin near the bridge. A special detail of mess attendants and cooks prepare and serve his meals and bring him snacks on the bridge if he requests them. He eats alone, at a time he decides, although he may, by tradition, invite a junior officer to dine with him. In port, the captain can leave his ship at will and remain ashore until the vessel sails.

The apprentice seaman lives in a bunkroom. If his bunk is coveted by a senior enlisted man he can be demoted to a less desirable bunk. He must maintain his own possessions in a small locker. His hunger is assuaged at regular mess times during which he must stand in line, be served on a tray, eat at large tables, and wash his own mess gear. His snacks are limited to night rations issued to night watches by the galley, candy and other "gee-dunk" [3] purchased after a long stand in a ship's store line. His liberty is rigidly controlled by a rotation system and, except in emergency, he has little chance to get more free time. Between these extremes are a number of gradations in cabin size, number of cabin mates, type of bunk and locker, and messing facilities.

Within this framework, particularly on the enlisted level, great importance has been attached to the ability to get early chow, early liberty, or a more

---

[3] "Gee-dunk" is one of the few distinctly nautical words remaining in naval jargon. Originally it meant candy but it has been extended to cover Cokes, malted milk, sundaes, and other foods sold in a ship's service facility.

comfortable sleeping place. With the problems and general background in mind, we can examine the main factors in the specific situations under consideration.

1. Naval Architecture

An aircraft carrier represents a number of important departures from traditional naval vessel design which have resulted in alteration of spacial relationships among groups of enlisted men.

The uppermost deck of a carrier is the flight deck, which is surveyed by the "island" where the underway quarterdeck is situated. The officer of the deck, who has operational control of the vessel cannot see the hangar deck, which would be the main deck on a conventional ship. Thus, the confusion in the chow lines was not personally observed by the officers of the deck, as it would have been on a conventional vessel. To spot and control such situations is one of the responsibilities of the Officer of the Deck and on conventional vessels there is little doubt that the O.O.D. would have taken immediate action. The most probable course would have been to issue orders to the chief master-at-arms to bring the situation to order. This failing, reports would have been made to the executive officer and to the supply and commissary officer. Such reports coming from the O.O.D. would take priority over complaints from junior division officers filtered up through "proper channels."

In contrasting the liberty party and chow lines problems, we see that the liberty party was under the direct eye of the O.O.D. at the in-port quarterdeck and that it also formed directly under the captain's suite and was very close to the officers' accommodation ladder. When noted directly, the situation was corrected with immediate and direct action.

On conventionally designed vessels the maindeck is in the charge of the boatswain's mates, specialists in seamanship and ship maintenance. Their efforts are under the eye of the captain, other ship officers, visitors, other ships, and superior commands. A great deal of the ship's reputation for smartness rests on their ability to maintain the cleanliness of the main deck. Rails, stanchions, awnings and standing rigging provide opportunities for applying decorative rope, string and canvas work, traditional sailors' "folk craft." On a carrier the hangar deck and flight deck are devoted to the handling and maintenance of aircraft. The deck divisions are relegated to a number of interior spaces in the lower decks and forecastle. The only topside spaces for which they are responsible are the small areas on the forepeak and fantail, one given over to anchor cables and winches, the other, more often than not, to trash and garbage. These spaces seldom come under the eye of superior officers except during inspection. The interior spaces are compartments and passageways requiring swabbing, chipping, and painting, each maintained by a small detail. The job of swabbing, scrubbing, and holystoning the maindeck has been eliminated and with it the central operation of the deck division for which it functioned much as close order drill. The boatswain's mate no longer supervises a half a hundred men with swabs or holystones, chanting in unison as they move up the deck behind the "hose men." Instead he moves from one small group to another checking on their progress, most of his authority delegated to junior petty officers or leading seamen in charge of each group. This provides little opportunity for creating *esprit de corps* among the seamen of the deck divisions and weakens the prestige of the boatswain's mates, officially the senior petty officers aboard ship.

Because space has always been a prime design factor, the amount allotted to any working group became a subtle symbol of that group's importance and prestige. The demands of flight operations forced naval architecture to reduce drastically the space allotted to certain working groups. This not only created distinct practical problems of working in reduced space but threatened the groups affected with a loss of an unrecognized, but important prestige symbol.

An important factor in the chow line problem may have been the fact that the ammunition hoists ran directly through the mess decks. Bombs and other ammunition were discharged on the mess deck and moved to another hoist which took them to the flight or hangar deck for arming aircraft. During World War II, the hoists would have been used largely when the crew was at general quarters during a battle. In the Korean campaign, the continuous flight operations meant that the mess decks would be used as a working space during mess hours. This not only interfered with the chow lines physically, but created an air of confusion and bustle which was foreign to that which sailors have come to expect at mealtimes.[4]

2. Social Communication

An aircraft carrier, like any other capital ship, is a network of communication systems. Old-fashioned voice tubes connect various important working spaces, pneumatic tubes are used to carry written messages, a telephone exchange connects virtually any two compartments, a sound power system carries operational and battle information, a public address system broadcasts to every corner of the vessel, and messengers are always on hand. This system is admirably designed to carry orders from senior to junior and reports from junior to senior. There is, however, no real provision for senior officers to discover actual conditions on lower levels except through the reports of juniors.

These reports become formalized and are of little real value in determining actual reactions and attitudes. Juniors, furthermore, are extremely reluctant to bring problems to a senior because it reflects on their own ability to handle the situation.

---

[4] Officially and unofficially, mealtimes are periods of rest and formality. Men are not allowed in messing areas wearing hats or dirty clothes. Officers and men passing through on duty are required to remove head coverings and official calls, requiring special formations on deck, are never made during mealtimes.

There is little direct contact between senior officers and enlisted men in working or informal situations. Officers seldom enter enlisted men's quarters except during an inspection, and enlisted men are permitted in "officers' country" only on duty. In addition, senior officers are isolated from junior officers by the fact that they live separately and by the formality of wardroom dining. The captain, of course, does not dine in the wardroom and is even more isolated from upward communication.

In a situation such as the chow line, junior officers who received complaints from their men hesitated to bring the problem to department heads. If they did, the department heads were equally reluctant to bother the executive officer. Only when the problem became one of major importance actually affecting the operations of the various departments did it receive serious attention on levels of higher ship-wide authority.

As we have seen earlier, the liberty party problem did not have to traverse the slow channels of upward communication but came directly to the attention of officers of high authority.

This problem of adequate feedback is endemic in the naval service and a great deal of enlisted lore is concerned with attempts on the part of captains to "find out what's going on." Stories of captains who disguise themselves as enlisted men are common. One of the favorites is a story in which a captain befriends an enlisted man, inviting him to the captain's cabin for secret conversations about the problems among the crew (always over a few drinks). While these stories appear to have occasional basis in fact, the majority of them seem to be a symbolic expression of the desire of enlisted men to communicate upward through the official channels which seem to block knowledge of their attitudes and reactions from reaching officers on the highest level.

3. Changed Status Relationships

The confusion in the chow lines and liberty parties and the tensions between enlisted men might be credited to inadequate training or leadership. Under examination, neither explanation is valid.

A large part of the crew were reservists with from one to five years active wartime duty to their credit. The rest, except for apprentice seamen directly out of recruit training, were career enlisted men in the regular Navy. The commissioned personnel presented a similar picture of experience.

In actual operations, arming, landing, and launching aircraft, transferring stores at sea, etc., the performance of large numbers of men was often record-breaking in its efficiency. In sick line, large numbers of men waited patiently without confusion. On the occasions when the supply department held bazaars of Japanese souvenir goods, hundreds of men waited just as patiently in slow-moving lines, even though there was definite economic advantage in getting an early selection of the merchandise offered.

As suggested earlier, the two problems appear to be related in the field of prestige and status because eating and going on liberty are status symbols of the first order among naval enlisted men.

The architectural features and the lack of feedback, while they contributed heavily to the intensification of the problems, cannot be considered the factors which created the confusion.

Since World War II, sweeping changes have taken place in the Navy, paralleling the changes which occurred in the late nineteenth century when the Navy shifted from wood and sail to steel and steam. These changes have had a direct impact on the traditional status relationships among enlisted men. Technological changes have been supported by a number of personnel policy changes no less important in upsetting status relationships.

Ever since the adoption of the cannon as a primary weapon of naval war in the sixteenth century, the men who have maintained and operated the guns have had high status aboard ship. In the modern Navy, gunners' mates, fire controlmen, turret captains, torpedo men, seamen gun-pointers, gun captains, etc., have been given high status. Their efforts are basic to victory in battle. In peacetime their excellence is a primary criterion for judging a ship's efficiency and a captain's ability.

The introduction of aircraft threatened the offensive role of the rifled gun. The threat was reflected in the intense conflicts between "battleship" and "carrier" admirals before World War II. However, the major importance of the carrier in the war did not seriously damage the prestige of the gunnery group because of the importance of the gun in antiaircraft defense. A certain conflict existed between gunnery people and aviation people on aircraft carriers but the gun was still a primary weapon in both offensive and defensive action.

The postwar development of supersonic aircraft which fly too fast to permit accurate training of guns and render short-range, rapid-fire weapons totally useless, drastically upset the traditional prestige patterns. During the Korean War, it was tacitly admitted that the guns of an aircraft carrier were of little defensive value. Officially, the guns were maintained and scheduled sessions of target practice held, but often operations deemed essential by the gunnery department were set aside to accommodate requests of the aviation department. In addition, the Navy was already looking forward to the adoption of rockets and missiles which would totally eliminate the use of guns.

Faced with lowered usefulness and a corresponding loss of prestige in the eyes of the rest of the crew and in their own opinions, gunnery personnel tended to fight stubbornly for the symbolic privileges of the past, insisting on a place in the early chow line, resenting it if aviation people were allowed ashore before them. On the other hand, aviation people felt that their activities were vital to the ship and that they deserved the prestige privileges of the gunners' mates.

A further example of changing technology is in the area of visual communications. Prior to World War II, the primary means of short-range communication were semaphore, flashing lights, and flag hoist. The latter technique, in which distinctive flags are hoisted in prearranged combinations, is extremely rapid, almost foolproof, and secure from enemy interception. It was a primary system used in maneuvering ship formations, issuing battle and operation orders, etc. To conduct flag hoist communications, all, or a large part, of the signal gang was required, each man working at an assigned station as part of a team.

The smartness and speed with which a signal gang handled flag hoist messages was considered a measure of a ship's efficiency. Thus the captain was always interested in the activities of the signal bridge, not only as a communication center, but as an important part of his own career. In assigning seamen to the signal gang, every attempt was made to obtain men superior in intelligence and education. Because signalmen stood watches in and out of port, they were traditionally granted extra liberty privileges. Because they worked closely with the highest ranking officers aboard, other enlisted men believed signalmen were "in the know" and looked to the signal bridge as a center of information about future operations. Signalmen were very much aware of their status and competed fiercely with other signal gangs in actual operations and in flag hoist drills which were held regularly. Signalmen were able to communicate with other vessels on an unofficial basis, a service which they rendered to their shipmates in exchange for favors.

The development of radar during World War II made night battle maneuvers possible on a scale impossible in previous years. Flag hoist, of course, was useless at night and other visual systems were slow, and limited by the requirements of security.

At the same time there were great advances made in the field of short-range, high frequency radio which could be used for voice communication. In addition, the war years saw an increasing number of officers trained in aviation techniques assigned to shipboard duties. The result was a gradual increase of the use of voice radio both night and day which placed flag hoist in a secondary position. Frequent wartime and postwar transfers of personnel made it difficult to train the close-knit, smooth-working signal teams of the past and efficiency dropped from its prewar peak. This lowering of efficiency confirmed in the minds of aviation-trained officers that the flag hoist system was old-fashioned and unable to compete with modern electronics. As more dependence was placed on the voice radio, captains tended to have less interest in the activities of the signal bridge. The prestige of signalmen began to drop.

In the *Dauntless* and other aircraft carriers, the problem was complicated further by the fact that all radar screens had to be crowded on the single mainmast which made it difficult to hoist clear flag signals, adding to the frustration of the signalmen who saw the situation as another indication of their loss of importance.

The loss of prestige and utility was reflected in a loss of morale among signalmen. Nonrated men no longer tried to get signal bridge assignments. There was less care in selecting personnel for the bridge and men assigned to the signal gang more often than not protested the billet and aspired to a billet in a rating specialty group involved in electronics or aviation. Signalmen petty officers tended to feel that they were at a dead end and that their chances for promotion were much less than in the newer rating specialties. Many petty officers began casting about for other specialties into which they could transfer.

The situation on the signal bridge was not improved by the change in uniform regulations which abolished the distinctive signalman rating badge and combined signalmen with quartermasters and buglers.

The technological changes being carried out in the Navy brought about similar prestige problems throughout the service. Old rating groups found their importance waning before specialists in new techniques and they fought hard to retain the prestige symbols which had represented their status in the past. The new rating groups, sensing their own importance, attempted to obtain the symbols which would reflect this importance. Often the new men, trained in electronic and other new techniques, had educational backgrounds vastly different from men working the older rates. Because civilian enterprise was experiencing a shortage of their skills and was actively seeking to recruit service-trained specialists, these men also tended to have aspirations different from other sailors. The older rating groups resented the new men and often called them "bum sailors," "college boys," "queers," and "lazy bastards." In return, the new groups spoke of the traditional ratings as "boneheads," "swab jockies," and "skivvy wavers." [5]

During World War II, a number of changes in personnel policy, designed to correct inequities which had grown up, to improve efficiency, or to reduce expenditures, were introduced. These policies, logical in themselves, had rather far-reaching effect in social relationships among enlisted men.

In the years prior to the war, laundry and barbering were conducted as private or semiprivate enterprises aboard Navy vessels. Men willing to take on the duties of launderers or barbers were relieved of other duties and worked full time at the jobs. Because this work took up most of their time, they had little opportunity to study for advancement in rating, so the jobs traditionally belonged to nonrated men. Because they were paid for their services by their shipmates, barbers and laundrymen often made several times as much money as did senior petty officers and the jobs were considered desirable billets.

During the war, this system was felt to be inequitable and a new rating established which included laundrymen, barbers, the attendants of the ships store and other service personnel. Soon ship's servicemen, in every rank from third class to chief, were serving ashore and afloat. The older ratings tended

---

[5] "Skivvies" is a naval term for underwear, used in this context to refer to signalmen who used hand signal flags to transmit semaphore messages.

to resent the assignment of petty officer rank to jobs which had been considered assignments for nonrated men in the past.

Another serious disarrangement of traditional enlisted relationships occurred when new regulations governing the wearing of rating badges were promulgated. Since the introduction of steam in the 1840's, enlisted personnel had been divided into two groups: the deck or seaman group and the engine room force. When formal uniform regulations were introduced this division was recognized by permitting the deck ratings to wear their badge on the right arm. At the close of World War II, there were eight right arm rates: boatswains' mates, gunners' mates, torpedomen, turret captains, quartermasters, signalmen, fire controlmen, and mine men. Precedence was accorded these groups in the order listed, but any right arm rate was considered to have precedence over any left arm rate of equal rank. In actuality, it was not uncommon for a right arm rating to be put in charge of temporary details even though left arm ratings with higher rank were present.

In 1948, new uniform regulations directed that all rating badges were to be worn on the left arm. The action was justified on economic grounds but appears to have been part of an overall plan to reduce indications of rank and precedence in the military.

There is no indication that the order was intended to erase the actual precedence standings of the various ratings, but this is essentially what did occur. The absence of the right arm-left arm symbolism clouded the previously clear ranking of enlisted men. Right arm ratings found their authority challenged by left arm ratings who pointed to the new regulation in support of their argument that "you guys ain't no better than anybody else." Right arm petty officers resented bitterly what they considered a demotion into the ranks of the "black gang," while left arm ratings who had long supported the myth that right arm sailors were less intelligent than left arm sailors protested the change as vigorously as did the right arm men. Because a great number of the petty officers in the *Dauntless* had been on inactive duty since before the new regulation was promulgated, they were extremely bitter at having been recalled into service and finding that their precious status symbol had been erased.

SUMMARY

The problems of confusion and discipline in the chow lines and liberty party appear to be related inasmuch as they are expressions of a prestige competition between groups of men with formerly high prestige, based on their importance to the mission of the service, and groups of men exercising new and extremely important skills.

It has been shown that in areas where no prestige symbol was involved or where the prestige and mission of the ship transcended that of the specialty groups, men were orderly, disciplined, and efficient. As the chow lines and liberty party were no better or worse than can be found on any large ship, it would appear that the confusion and lack of discipline which developed were not a direct result of individual impatience with a slow-moving line or long wait for permission to leave the ship.

The tensions which developed into chow line and liberty party confusion can be traced to the unstable prestige situation in enlisted ranks which caused men to try to assert themselves to obtain or retain the high status symbols which revolve around eating and liberty.

Contributing factors were the design of an aircraft carrier which permits situations to develop unobserved by the officer of the deck and other officers of high authority and the lack of upward communication from enlisted men to high ranking officers. Another factor in this area is the one of altered spacial relationships between the various rating groups which reflected changes in role importance.

CONCLUSIONS

The major contrast between the two problems discussed is that the liberty party situation was solved quickly and permanently while the chow line confusion seemed insoluble.

It is significant, considering not only these specific problems but all military administration, that the officers who set out to solve the liberty party problem utilized the military rank of enlisted men as a determinant of who would leave the ship first. While there was a good deal of uncertainty when the relative prestige of various specialty groups was considered, the system of ranking went unchallenged. Thus by design or accident, the liberty party confusion, stemming from prestige-competition between specialties, was brought to order by bypassing the disputed area. Military rank became more important in this situation than specialty mark. Petty officers of whatever specialty shared in common the privilege of leaving the ship before nonrated men. This tended to break up group solidarity along specialty lines and to create new alignments along lines of military ranking. In a number of cases, the writer believes, there was a distinct improvement in discipline among enlisted men after this concrete symbol of noncommissioned officer status was utilized.

The chow line problem, however, was never treated other than as a problem of conflicting specialty groups. Efforts to correct it revolved around ascertaining who was more important to the ship and thus rated early chow. Any decision created resentment in one quarter or another.

The questions asked in this paper transcend the problems of feeding and disembarking on liberty large numbers of men. The Navy is undergoing a vast change in technology, greater perhaps than that of the 1890's, which is affecting traditional enlisted men's relationships. The uncertainty of the situation is reflected in the high percentage of men who leave the service after one enlistment, despite increased pay and allowances and great efforts to make their lives more comfortable. One is led to ask if it is not possible that an emphasis on military rank and a de-emphasis on specialty prestige might not give the individual sailor a feeling of social stability which he does not have at present.

It is certainly possible that naval architects who have been forced to consider the problem of "livability" aboard naval vessels should also consider the problem of "sociability" in designing vessels of the future, which will undoubtedly depart drastically from traditional naval design.

How to solve the twin problems of maintaining military rank distinction between officers and enlisted men, which is necessary for discipline, and improving upward communication which is equally necessary for intelligent command, is an important but unanswered question.

Chapter Seven

Social Organization

THE CONCEPT of *social organization* is particularly broad, encompassing the "coordination of social norms, sanctions, and action systems." [1] It may be regarded as the patterned relationships that exist between men, either as individuals or in groups. Society, through its various organizations, provides the means by which the basic human needs may be satisfied. The terms *social organization, institutionalization, social system,* and *social structure* are distinct though closely related concepts describing how a group or society organizes to get the necessary work done. We have chosen here not to distinguish between them, but rather to treat them as one might a camera with turret lens, which focuses on objects of study of varying scope.

Although there is a tendency toward equilibrium, forces may disrupt an existing organization. This disruption would be the case when new groups come into contact with each other or when unique situations develop for which old rules do not apply. [2] An illustration of the latter can be found during such natural disasters as cyclones, earthquakes, or other calamities. "In disaster, suddenly the customary machinery of community living breaks up." [3] Even in these disrupted circumstances, it has been discovered that new

[1] George A. Lundberg, Clarence C. Schrag, and Otto N. Larsen, *Sociology* (3rd ed.; New York: Harper & Row, 1963), p. 369.

[2] Because what is often classified as *collective behavior* (fads, crowds, mobs, social movements, etc.) is, in our view, simply a situation where the norms and rules are undeveloped or disrupted, we treat such phenomena as cases of underorganization or disorganization.

[3] Ellsworth Bunker, "The Voluntary Effort in Disaster Relief," The *Annals* of the American Academy of Political and Social Science, **309** (January 1957), p. 110.

patterns of interaction develop very quickly. Indeed, because of the inevitability of unforeseen emergencies, specialized organizations have been developed whose specific task it is to deal with these crises and to restore order.

Less dramatic but no less real are those disruptions brought about by rapid social change associated with industrialization and urbanization. Old family and community controls are difficult to sustain in highly mobile twentieth-century society. Reflections of old values may still be observed in the occasional outburst against the working mother—even though research has indicated that families in which the mother works are no more delinquency-prone or tension-prone than are other families. New courtship patterns are developing, though our society has not yet accepted either the "lonely hearts club" or a scientifically oriented service for finding mates. These new patterns, as well as organizations such as Parents Without Partners (which was formed to aid divorced or widowed parents in the rearing of their children), will probably continue to grow in numbers and influence. "Let's get organized" is a cry familiar to all of us when we are in situations where the old ways of doing things prove inadequate.

At the opposite end of a theoretical spectrum, the desire for continued conditions of uniformity may lead to overorganization, with the consequent "red tape" so commonly deprecated today. What is disparagingly called "bureaucracy" (the sociologist uses the term to refer to social organization within a specific association) is the ultimate end of getting organized. Complete lack of predictability (a condition of underorganization) is intolerable; yet the effort to reach predicability frequently leads to undesirable restraints on the freedom of individual action (a condition of overorganization). This development, in turn, leads to a demand to reconceptualize the functions on various organization charts and to redirect tasks and assignments. Organizations, like individuals, develop habits which are difficult to change. Adaptation to new circumstances may be slow.

The selections in this chapter were chosen to illustrate these three aspects in the organization, or *institutionalization,* process.

26

The Role of the Police Officer in Crowd Control

Joseph D. Lohman

As indicated in the introduction to this chapter, some of the disruptive effects of emergencies can be curtailed, or even eliminated, if adequate plans are developed in advance. Fire drills are a common example of successful pre-emergency planning. Other types of emergencies do not lend themselves to such well-established forms of preparatory countermeasures. To deal with those situations where no norms exist (tornadoes, floods, riots, and so on), an outline of organizational action, drawn from a variety of comparable situations, must be developed. By this means, the disruptive forces may be minimized.

The steps in the development of an aggressive and destructive crowd can be identified. The first stage in the transformation of a collection of separate individuals into a mob is the occurrence of some exciting incident. Whatever the nature of the incident, if it is sufficiently exciting and commanding of attention, it will attract a group of onlookers who will mill about the scene of the incident and who may have occasion to take sides. In the early stages of the gathering of crowds, it is often possible for the police officer to isolate an incident by making a quick, yet adequate, determination of the facts. Then, by taking immediate action—e.g., the taking of the parties into custody—he may avoid the involvement of many onlookers. The speed with which the police officer operates in these situations is the measure of the extent to which onlookers can accumulate. By cutting short such an accumulation, he can prevent an incident from becoming an affair which it will be impossible for him to handle. The following incident, related by one of the supervisory officers, illustrates the way in which incidents can be expeditiously handled in such a manner that more serious developments are avoided:

A cab load of white sailors were having an argument with a cab driver over the payment of their fares. This argument took place in a Negro area at 47th and Michigan, and a crowd of curious onlookers began to gather. The sailors, who were under the influence of liquor, began to hurl insults at the Negro bystanders.

Reprinted from Joseph D. Lohman, *The Police and Minority Group* (Chicago: Chicago Park District, 1947), pp. 80–86, by permission of the author.

Joseph D. Lohman is Dean, School of Criminology, University of California, Berkeley.

An ugly situation was in the making when a police officer appeared on the scene. He immediately ordered the cab driver to take his cab with the load of sailors to a point several blocks distant. The removal of these sailors from the crowd which had collected made it possible for the officer to deal with the dispute between the cab driver and the sailors and prevent what otherwise might have been a dangerous race incident.

Many times an officer does not arrive upon the scene of an incident until after a crowd has assembled and achieved a degree of aggressive unity. As an incident proceeds to attract numbers of individuals, they are pressed together. They quite naturally begin to brush and contact one another, even to initiate conversation with utter strangers. This activity is somewhat akin to the behavior of sheep crowded together in a corral. They move around and about in rather aimless fashion, all the while communicating to each other the collective excitement of the situation. This is known as the milling process.

This process creates among the members of the crowd an internal rapport, a kind of collective hypnosis in which the individual loses his self-control and responds only to the dictates of the crowd as a whole. Here is an important fundamental fact which every police officer who has dealt with a crowd has had occasion to experience. In the mob the individual loses his ability to act in terms of cool and rational considerations. He is swayed by the moods and sentiments of the mob. He begins to act in quite different terms than if he were alone or out from under the influence of the mob. In this fact exists the immense potentiality for evil behavior which crowds often exhibit. Quite often individuals find it difficult to understand how they could possibly have acted as they did while part of a crowd or mob.

Notwithstanding the increasing difficulties which confront a police officer in coping with a milling crowd, there are control measures which can be employed at that stage. One effective handling of a milling crowd is indicated in the following incident related by one of the supervisory officers.

A relief agency had sent out notices that it would employ men at a certain hour at Humboldt Park field house. When an officer arrived on the scene, a crowd of several thousand had gathered in front of the field house. The officer was confronted by a sea of heads milling about the doors. Excitement was rising, men pushed against one another, and there was danger that a protecting rail would collapse from the weight of the pressure against it. If left to its own devices, the crowd would soon have broken the railing, with resultant injuries, and might have stormed the building. The officer took a position where he could command the attention of the crowd and told them that if they would form an orderly line, they would all be registered in due course. He selected four men as the first elements in a column and began to march them in zig-zag fashion around and away from the field house. Soon he had the whole crowd arranged in a column of fours stretched around and away from the field house.

In this incident the officer acted in terms of a practical understanding of the potentialities of the milling crowd. He realized that the milling must be broken up before the crowd became hysterical and aggressive. He introduced the regular formation in order to isolate individuals from each other in groups of fours. Thus, he transformed the crowd and potential mob into an orderly assembly.

In many cases, however, the crowd or mob has already achieved a degree of unity and purpose that makes it unresponsive to this kind of suggestion. When this is the case, it becomes necessary for police officers to remove the most excited individuals from the crowd. The most excited individuals are always a focus of attention in the organization of an aggressive mob. Their removal will contribute to, and make possible, the dissolution of the remaining less excited individuals. In the removal of these individuals, the police officers must make a *show of force*. However, it does not necessarily mean that they should *use* force. The difference is an important one, and a failure to make the distinction may result in unnecessary bloodshed. The mere presence of sufficient numbers of men in uniform is what is meant by a *show of force*. This awes the crowd so that it becomes unnecessary to *use* force in removing key persons. The idea of individual heroic police action is not only unnecessary, it may be positively damaging and foolhardy. A police officer who attempts single-handed to subdue a mob or grapple with individuals puts his own safety in jeopardy. In the violence that then is bound to ensue, he merely stimulates the ugly tendencies of the crowd. It is of prime importance that such situations be avoided. It can be done if supervisory officers so arrange and instruct their personnel that reinforcements can be mobilized at any point in the shortest possible time and in numbers appropriate to the situation.

In the following incident related by one of the supervisory officers unpleasant results followed an *inadequate* show of force:

A mob had gathered who were being harangued by an inflammatory soapbox orator. The officers drove up in a squad car and decided to place the speaker under arrest. Drawing their clubs, they made their way to the center of the crowd, where the speaker stood. The speaker, however, was surrounded by sympathizers. So were the two police officers. The members of the crowd set upon the officers, wrested their clubs from their hands, knocked them down, and kicked them. They were unable to arrest the speaker. Only with the arrival of reinforcements and a considerable *use of force* were arrests made and the mob dispersed.

In this instance the law was represented in too little strength. There was an *inadequate* show of force, with the result that the crowd was not overawed. The mere presence of a larger group of uniformed men would have made unnecessary the later resort to the *use of force*.

Tension in a crowd is usually highest at a point-front and center. Here the excited individuals who exercise such unusual influence on all the others are located. These are the points upon which police attention should be centered and the approach made if the exciting influence of strategic individuals needs to be checked. A tactic used in the Harlem riots by the New York police and also by the Milwaukee police in the dispersal of dangerous crowds met with considerable success. It is that of directing the crowd from its outer edges to "break up and go home." This was done by means of a public-address system mounted on a sound truck. The blare of the speaker and the authoritative tone of the commands attract the attention of the individuals in the crowd. In so doing, it turns them away from the excited individuals and breaks up their influence. This technique is unquestionably helpful in breaking up crowds in their early stages and can be useful in penetrating the consciousness of a group which is already well organized.

The final stage in the development of a mob has been called the phase of social contagion. In this period, the small original crowd is swelled by numbers of bystanders. They usually have little, if any, knowledge of the precipitating incident. They are impelled by curiosity and are merely attracted by the sight of gathering people. Innocent as they are of the incident, they are, nevertheless, quickly captured by the mood of the crowd and begin to share its collective excitement. A supervisory officer furnishes the following incident to indicate that innocent bystanders are drawn to and become a part of the mob:

A crowd had collected in Douglas Park and were being incited by questionable leadership. It began to collect people passing by and before long it became necessary to break it up by positive police intervention. Considerable force was used, and later it was found that the greater proportion of those who received injuries were innocent bystanders who had drifted into the crowd from 12th street.

In the early stages of the formation of the crowd, a cordon of police would have been effective in minimizing such injuries. By means of the police cordon, individuals could be permitted to escape from the crowd, but not to enter it. In the handling of mob situations, the police cordon prevents the riotous infection of great masses of individuals by preventing social contagion. In the Harlem riots, the cordon was used with great success. By throwing police cordons around danger areas, thousands of curiosity seekers were prevented from being exposed to the mob situation and in that way becoming infected with its spirit. Letting people out means freeing them from the excitement of the mob; keeping them out of the area means that the mob spirit will not be able to possess them.

27

Interinstitutional Conflict as a Major Impediment to Delinquency Prevention

Walter B. Miller

Despite their avowed concern with juvenile delinquency, the organizations mentioned in this article were unwilling or unable to modify their beliefs and methods sufficiently to institute any action whatsoever to effect their announced hope of reducing delinquency. Here is a case study of failure to achieve stated goals caused, in part, by a lack of realization of the need for reorganization or for modification of present social organizations by synthesizing the divergent views, aims, and methods of several social systems into a new, unified social institution. You may wish to contrast this failure with the results reported in Selection 28.

Can you see comparisons between the situation discussed in this article by Walter B. Miller and the conflict between business and labor, nation and nation? Can the universal, stated desire for peaceful relations between groups be frustrated by the same unwillingness or inability to modify beliefs and practices, to take stock, and to reorganize?

Juvenile delinquency is a major area of concern in the United States today. Although there is evidence of some increase in the actual incidence of juvenile crime, it is equally evident that the intensity of public concern over this issue has increased far more rapidly than the demonstrated statistical increase. This paper will focus, not on juvenile crime as such, but on the larger adult community, and, in particular, on that segment of the community which maintains explicit responsibility in this area.

It is the thesis of this paper that the nature of current concern over juvenile delinquency serves important latent functions for substantial segments of the adult community. If this thesis is true, we would expect to find, as in all areas where a significant discrepancy exists between the overt or recognized aspects of a phenomenon and its covert aspects or latent functions: (1) discrepancies and contradictions between officially stated policy and actual operating procedure; (2) recurrent failure to follow through on plans whose objectives

Reprinted from *Human Organization*, **17**, 3 (Fall 1958), pp. 20–23, by permission of The Society for Applied Anthropology and the author.

Walter B. Miller is Director, Midcity Delinquency Project, Boston University.

conform to officially stated positions but whose execution would in fact run counter to the latent functions; (3) much conflict over goals and methods both between concerned institutional systems and between subunits within these systems. The net result of these forces would be to produce action stalemates both through failure to take action and through mutual blocking of efforts to the end that the latently functional status quo is preserved.

That public concern over juvenile delinquency serves *psychological* functions for adults as individuals has been maintained by several investigators. This paper will attempt to show that the nature of current institutional practice regarding delinquency serves important *structural* functions as well; that is, for the great majority of organized institutions which maintain programs directed at juvenile delinquency, the adoption of operating procedures and philosophies which would be effective in reducing juvenile crime would, in fact, pose severe threats to the viability of the institution. The focus here will be on the area of delinquency *prevention* rather than on methods of dealing with the adjudicated delinquent. Since the area of prevention is far less structured and has developed fewer established operating procedures than the area of treatment or disposition, the dynamics of institutional functioning in this area are revealed in much sharper relief.

It has been established that there is far more law-violating behavior by adolescents than is officially acted on; according to one study, the actual number of potentially arrestable delinquents is three times that of those actually arrested. Once an individual is officially apprehended for the commission of a delinquent act or acts, a whole series of established procedures are set into motion; the individual may be released with a warning, put on probation, or sentenced to undergo a variety of corrective measures ranging from a citizenship course through psychiatric treatment to straight confinement. But in the area of "prevention" things are much less well established. There is growing sentiment to the effect that "prevention" of juvenile crime would be a much sounder procedure than attempting to deal with the individual once he has already committed a crime, and would be much more economical in the long run. But then the question becomes—how does one "prevent"? Once something has happened you can take steps as a consequence of that occurrence, but what steps should you take for something that has not happened yet, but which might? Thus, while there are many well-established institutions—courts, police, correctional institutions, psychiatric agencies—whose operating procedures and philosophies are geared to handling individuals who have committed delinquent acts and been apprehended, there are, with a few exceptions, *no* established institutional structures whose major responsibility is delinquency prevention, and whose institutional values and operating philosophies are geared to that objective. Existing organizations undertake prevention, if at all, as a relatively minor adjunct to major institutional responsibilities which lie elsewhere—a fact which has important bearing on the potential effectiveness of prevention programs.

Following sections will describe very briefly the experience of one large Eastern city in attempting to institute and maintain a "preventive" program on the community level. In 1950, rising public apprehension over juvenile delinquency in general, and gang violence in particular, produced demands for action from many quarters. Since gang activity was a focus of concern, and much gang delinquency is undetectable or undetected, traditional approaches based on restriction or treatment were seen as unfeasible, and pressures to institute some sort of community-based preventive program were exerted on the major institutional structures with assumed or assigned responsibility in the area of juvenile crime.

I

The city contained scores of intricately interrelated organizations, both public and private, varying widely in size, scope, and method of operations, and in assigned or claimed area of jurisdiction or concern with juvenile crime. Of these, about a dozen public and private organizational groupings maintained major responsibility in the area of juvenile crime. The principal public agencies were the municipal government, the recreation department, the police department, the courts, the public schools, and the state youth corrections division. Major private groupings were medical and psychiatric clinics, social work agencies, churches, unive   and various special cause groups, such as ethnic associations and crim   tion societies.

Initial pressures produced a   of statements as to the desirability of a preventive program, but no ac   complex set of maneuvers was carried on for about three years, usu   volving the appointment of special committees which then appointed   group which turned in a set of recommendations strongly affirmi   rability of a preventive program, and at the same time explaining   program was not the responsibility of that particular organizatio   continuing stalemate was finally broken early in 1953, primarily t   combined pressure   two ethnic groups, the Jews and the Negr   ter a prominent   clergyman had been murdered, allegedly   gro teenage gang.   acting through their organized represntaive groupings, inf   ed the Negroes with antisemitism; the Negroes, through th   anized groupings, intimated that this charge indicated anti-Negro sentir   he part   the Jews. Two other groups whose interests were being   ng activity—the public schools and the settlement ho   ures to those of the Jews and Negroes, and, in the spr   delinquency committee was created, comprising represe   hundred youth-concerned groupings in the metropolitan ar   ne major groups cited above. At the time this committee wa   ny statements were made by all groupings—police, courts, the municipal administration, churches, private agencies—pledging their fullest mutual cooperation in this enterprise aimed at coping with the city gang problem.

Despite the sense of urgency and crisis which attended the organization of the central committee, no concrete action was taken for more than a year. This year was filled with indecision, groping for direction, and constant mutual blocking and conflict, sometimes veiled, sometimes overt, among the agencies represented on the central committee. A great variety of proposals was forwarded and debated, reflecting many divergent conceptions of the causes and proper treatment of juvenile crime, and the group seemed unable to reach any agreement on a positive course of action. After six months, a sociology professor at a local university was persuaded to accept responsibility for formulating a plan of action, and in June of 1954—four and a half years after the initial moves, and a year and a half after the murder which had broken the stalemate—a special demonstration project in delinquency prevention was set up in one district of the city. By this time, several of the major organizations originally represented on the central committee had terminated active affiliation—principally, the police and the Jewish clergy. The Jews lost interest rapidly when it developed that anti-semitism had played a relatively small role in gang attacks on Jews.

The prevention project, which was to operate for three years, was staffed primarily by social workers, and included three service programs—a program of direct service to selected "delinquogenic" families, a community organization program, and, as a major effort, a program of direct work with delinquent corner gangs. Although it was the creation of the central committee, once project operations actually started, the committee became progressively disenchanted with its offspring. As the project took action in more definite and visible ways, it became clear that many of its methods and the operating philosophies behind them were in radical conflict with the institutional ideals of the various groups represented on the central committee. This was evidenced in responses ranging from passive non-participation, through withdrawal, to active opposition.

During the three years of the project's existence, the executive board of the central committee became a battleground for its component organizations, with the project and its methods serving as a pawn in these conflicts. After the first meeting, at which a project social worker presented a report on his activities, the representative of the Catholic Archdiocese resigned in indignation from the executive board. Following this incident, a watchdog committee was set up to oversee the project. The head of this committee was a Protestant clergyman who was strongly opposed to the methods of the project. About a year later the project became involved in direct conflict with the state division of corrections, with such sufficient intensity that the corrections division issued an order forbidding its parolees to participate in project activities, and, in fact, jailed a parolee who defied this order. The social agencies initially regarded the program with great suspicion, as did the schools. During the latter part of the program the city recreation department representative on the central committee, incensed by a report issued by the project, demanded that no further reports be issued unless approved by the central committee. During the second year, funds to support the project, which were raised by the central committee, became increasingly difficult to obtain, and about this time the committee's original chairman, who had been active in initiating and supporting the project, was replaced, without his prior knowledge, by another man who was far less assertive.

Shortly after the start of the project's third year, its director resigned, partly because of increasing difficulties in obtaining financing, and no attempt was made to replace him with a person of equivalent status. Before the director left, he formulated a detailed proposal for the establishment of a permanent delinquency prevention agency under state and municipal auspices, using the project's experience as the basis of recommendations. The three-man committee chosen to present this program to the mayor and governor consisted of an amiable but aged chairman and the two most outspoken opponents of the project on the central committee. The recommendations for a state-municipal program presented under these auspices were rejected both by the mayor and governor. Once the program was officially terminated, the central committee appeared eager to forget that it had ever existed. Although federal support for post-project research had been obtained, members of the central committee were most reluctant to permit such continuation and questioned the right of the project to have sought these funds, despite the fact that authorization had been officially voted.

During the period when the project was subject to increasing opposition by its parent organizations on the central committee, these agencies were also engaged in attacking one another both in the arena of central committee meetings and through other media. A judge accused the police of inefficiency in dealing with delinquents and in keeping adequate crime statistics; a police chief accused the social welfare agencies of coddling delinquents; the director of a medical group accused the corrections division of increasing the delinquency of those in their care; a Catholic prelate accused the social work agencies of neglecting religion in their dealings with delinquents; a psychiatric agency head accused the police of harmful advocacy of punitive measures; the Archbishop accused enforcement agencies of politically motivated laxness in prosecuting delinquents; a group of legislators attempted to oust major officials of the youth corrections department over the issue of personnel qualifications. In addition, subunits within these larger organizations feuded with one another; a judge accused other judges of excessive leniency in dealing with juvenile offenders; a committee of the school department claimed that some teachers were fostering delinquency by being unable or unwilling to cope with school behavior problems; the Police Commissioner castigated and demoted a sizable group of patrolmen, charging them with inefficiency in dealing with juveniles in their area of jurisdiction; a Protestant clergyman claimed that some Protestants sects were failing in the fight against delinquency by remaining too aloof from community involvement.

II

We have, then, a situation which involves these elements: first, a social phenomenon—gang violence—which is universally condemned; a crisis incident which arouses deep feelings and provides a spur to direct action; the mobilization and pledged cooperation of all the major concerned institutional groupings of a major American city; and then—much delay and misdirected energy by these institutions in setting up a project to which they become progressively more hostile; constant interinstitutional conflict over a variety of issues; and finally a virtual stalemate in launching any sort of effective action to cope with the problem. This situation is by no means unique; it is found in many cities faced with similar problems; in particular, conflicts between the police, churches, courts, social agencies, and schools in the New York City gang situation have been widely publicized. This prevalent phenomenon—apparently universal agreement on a basic objective, gang control, coupled with mutual conflict leading to almost complete blocking of action, may be explained by focusing on the *means* proposed to secure the end—means which derive from the operating philosophies of the various concerned organizations. This paper suggests that operating philosophies may be *non*functional for the purpose of reducing juvenile crime, and that a consequence of differences in institutional philosophies is that a significant proportion of energy potentially directable to delinquency reduction is instead expended in conflict between institutions.

The nature of these differences may be illuminated by specifying six dimensions along which conflict takes place: these relate to differences in conceptions of the *etiology* of delinquency; of the *disposition* of the delinquent; of the *approach priority;* of the appropriate *organizational method,* and of the proper *status of personnel.*

Morality-Pathology

A major difference in assumptions as to the etiology of juvenile crime, as well as other forms of behavior, involves fundamental concepts of human nature. According to one school of thought, deviant or criminal behavior must be viewed in terms of morality and immorality; an individual is morally responsible for his own behavior, and failure to conform to norms and standards represents a triumph of evil forces over good in an inner struggle for which the individual is held personally responsible. The opposing school maintains that deviant or criminal behavior should be viewed in terms of sickness and health; that an individual who violates social and legal norms is, in fact, driven by inner forces over which he has relatively little control, and which have their origins in pathological conditions of the organism.

Individual Locus-Social Locus

A second important difference involving etiological concepts relates to the locus of deviant behavior. One school attributes criminal behavior to forces within the *individual*—moral or physical-psychological—which may be dealt with by corrective measures directed at the individual; the other school finds the significant factors in the nature of the *social milieu*, and sees basic alterations in social conditions as the necessary course of action.

Restriction-Rehabilitation

This dimension relates to the proper method of dealing with offenders. The restrictive school of thought advocates the separation or isolation of the individual from normal social intercourse on the assumption, first, that the *protection of society* is the paramount necessity, and second, that punishment both serves as a deterrent to future violation and is merited in consequence of transgression. This dispositional prescription is generally forwarded by those espousing the morality concept of etiology. The treatment or rehabilitative school, basing procedure on the "pathology" conception of etiology, postulates "cure" or directed efforts to modify behavior patterns of the offending individual as of prime importance, with his restoration to normal social interaction a desired objective.

Action-Research

This dimension relates to consideration of priority in approaching the problem. One school maintains that the urgency of the situation, or the intensity of need, demands immediate action, based on the best knowledge currently available; the other maintains that far too little reliable information exists as to the nature of the involved phenomena and methods of treatment, and that the most productive expenditure of energy can be made by undertaking systematic research to gain essential knowledge.

Localization-Centralization

This dimension concerns the issue of the most desirable method for organizing preventive programs; one school believes that programs should be undertaken within and by the local community, on the grounds that only local people are sufficiently familiar with the special conditions of the local situation for adequate understanding, and that local autonomy must be maintained; the centralization school maintains that the nature and magnitude of the problem demand mobilization of resources which local groups, operating independently, could not afford, and that, to be effective, resources must be pooled and efforts coordinated to avoid duplication and overlap.

Lay-Professional

This dimension relates to the qualifications and status of personnel who are to implement preventive programs. One school holds that only those who manifest characteristics similar to those of the subject population—either through similarities in class or locality status—can be effective, and that attributes essential to effectiveness, such as warmth and sympathy, are independent of training; the other school maintains that work in so difficult an area demands that practitioners be exposed to a course of professional training which both imparts knowledge as to specialized procedures and eliminates those whose personality characteristics would be detrimental to this kind of work.

The various institutional structures related to delinquency tend to maintain characteristic syndromes of these etiological and procedural positions. The described positions are seldom maintained in the "pure" form, since they are presented here as polar extremes which define variable dimensions—and "middle positions," such as equal stress on action and research, may be taken, but most institutions involved do maintain definitely identifiable positions of varying intensity along these dimensions. Conflicts along the varying dimensions take place, both *between* and within, concerned institutions, but intra-institutional differences are generally concealed from public notice. The most severe conflict occurs between institutions which take extreme opposing positions on all or most of these dimensions; conflict is less severe when there is disagreement on only one or two. For example, the major juvenile court of the city described above strongly supported the "morality" and "individual locus" concepts of etiology: the restrictive dispositional method, action priority, and localized organization. The major child psychiatry clinic supported the "pathology" etiological concept; rehabilitative treatment method, centralized organization, and use of professional implementary personnel. These positions put the two organizations in direct conflict in four of the six dimensions; in agreement over one—individual etiological locus—and in minor opposition over the action-research issue. Similar comparisons could be made between each set of involved institutions.

SUMMARY

The argument of this paper may be summarized as follows: There is much conflict over the issue of proper procedure among the different groups which maintain varying orders of responsibility for delinquency prevention. This conflict results in a lack of coordination and mutual blocking of efforts leading to a stalemate in reference to a community-supported objective. But these conflicts over method derive from the basic institutional philosophies of the several institutions; although these philosophies may be effective in facilitating achievement of the stated objectives of the institution, their maintenance is vital to the institution's continued existence and this latent objective has greater priority than the achievement of the institution's explicit objectives, and much greater priority than achieving objectives only peripherally related to the institution's primary explicit aims.

This situation would appear to have important implications for delinquency prevention. It would imply that the major impediment to effectiveness in this field relates more to the nature of relations among the various concerned institutions than to a lack of knowledge as to effective procedure. Much is now known about the causes of delinquency and promising ameliorative techniques have been developed. The principal difficulty lies in the *application* of these techniques, and any realistic possibility of such application depends almost entirely on existing institutional structures. This would suggest a shift in emphasis in current research and action efforts, from a primary focus on the relations between implementing institutions and the subject population, to the relationships among the institutions themselves. Both research and action efforts involve severe difficulties since they will touch on areas intimately related to the viability of the institution—areas all the more charged and sensitive, since they are frequently unconscious or implicit.

28

The Application
of Social System Analysis to
a Labor-Management Conflict:
A Consultant's Case Study

Delbert C. Miller

In this account, Dr. Miller discusses one aspect of his work as a consultant to a corporation. Here we may observe the systematic use of the concept of *social organization* (or a *social system*). The article presents a central position of a sociologist: examining social organizations with their aims and objectives in a society made up of many similar organizations—cooperating, competing, accommodating each other, much as individuals do.

Contrast this approach to problem solving, and particularly the role of the consultant, with the unsystematic methods described in Selection 27.

In April, 1957, the writer was engaged as a consultant to an industrial relations director of a large flour-milling company in order to assist with the solving of a pressing labor-management problem. The problem is significant to social science because it reveals a linkage of various systems of group relations which have importance to decision-making. The case itself provides an opportunity to observe the application of social system analysis *within* a social process as it progresses through the following stages: (1) beginning with a social conflict and the disruption of an established bargaining pattern, (2) extending through the period when the consultant and industrial relations director were analyzing the problem and the possible actions to be taken, (3) embracing the action taken by the general manager and the immediate outcomes, and (4) ending with the resolution of the conflict as consummated by the signing of a new labor contract.

The company, the two unions, and the persons involved must remain anonymous. Fictitious names have been given to all parties, but the details of the case are described accurately.

Reprinted from *The Journal of Conflict Resolution*, **3**, 2 (June 1959), pp. 146–152, by permission of the publisher and the author.

Delbert C. Miller is Professor of Sociology and Business Administration, Indiana University.

THE ORGANIZATIONAL COMPLEX OF LABOR-MANAGEMENT RELATIONS IN COMPANY X

When the labor contract was opened for negotiation in the spring of 1957, there was an established pattern of labor-management relations of ten years' standing. The company contained two unions with which it bargained. One was Local 68, an AF of L union composed of 220 workers in the mill headed by leaders whom the company had found "easy to deal with"; the other was Local 3 of the International Long Shore Workers' Union (ILWU) representing 90 workers in the warehouse and headed by aggressive leaders who had been "driving hard bargains" and had been trying constantly to increase their power. The company was a member of a Trade Association, which bargained for an area contract with the AF of L Council representing Local 68. At the same time, the company bargained independently with Local 3 of the ILWU. A parity agreement covering general wage increases and working conditions had been signed with Local 3 each time a new agreement had been negotiated with Local 68. The established bargaining system is shown in Figure 1.

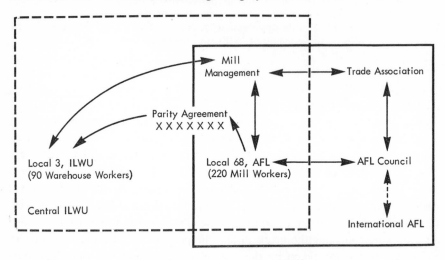

FIGURE 1. The established bargaining system of the labor-management parties of Company X.

A LABOR-MANAGEMENT PROBLEM AND THE DISRUPTION OF A SOCIAL SYSTEM

The following account is described as it happened:

The established bargaining system became disrupted about 18 months prior to the entry of the consultant. The disruption occurred when differences over expulsion of some international union officials arose between the AF of L Council and its constituent member, Local 68. Since then, a feud has been going on between them and getting ever more bitter. The precipitating factors giving rise to the present labor-management problem are now these: Local 68 has withdrawn from the AF of L Council and asks the company to bargain independently with it. The AF of L Council refuses to recognize this right of secession and demands that Local 68 return immediately so that a new labor contract may be negotiated. The council has notified the company that it must bargain with the council in writing a new contract for Local 68.

The Trade Association is disturbed because Company X is its largest member and it may no longer be needed if the company should recognize Local 68 as an independent union. Moreover, the association may face increasing difficulties in holding its other members, especially if new labor contracts in Company X should put its remaining members at a competitive disadvantage. The association feels that its very survival may now be at stake. The company is equally disturbed lest it lose control of its position of maintaining similar contract provisions with its area competitors, and it is especially concerned about its future competitive position if the plant were to be struck. Under its trade-association agreement members agree to deliver flour from their own supplies to fill orders for a struck plant. The company feels that it may lose these important advantages because of an interunion organization "squabble" for which it is not responsible in the slightest degree. This is why the general manager has been putting pressure on the industrial relations director and on the leaders of Local 68 to see that the local gets back into the AF of L Council.

Local 68 is disturbed because of pressure coming from the company, the association, and the council to reassume its membership in the council. It feels that everyone is asking them to surrender their principles of justice and to humiliate themselves. After all the bitter feeling, the leaders cannot see themselves "crawling back to those dirty four-flushers in the Council." They are determined to resist every pressure to get them back and to insist upon an independent bargaining role with the company. The time for reopening the contract is now. Every day that goes by means that they are working without a contract.

The general manager has told the industrial relations director to get a contract signed. His words are: "Tell 68 they are going back into the AFL Council. We are going to sign a contract with the Council and 68 can take it or lump it. We must act this week." The industrial relations director has said, "You'll have a strike on your hands!" The consultant has been asked, "What should the company do?"

AN ANALYSIS OF ALTERNATE SOCIAL SYSTEMS FOR THE PARTIES

Up to this point the consultant had secured the patterned bargaining relationship of the parties and had a factual picture of the factors precipitating the problem. He took the view that an understanding of the interlocking character of the social system was of critical importance, since a resolution of the problem involved the possible necessity of establishing an alternate social system in place of the traditional bargaining social system. Figures 2 and 3 show two alternate social systems that might be instituted if the traditional system were permanently disrupted. An analysis of all three systems follows.

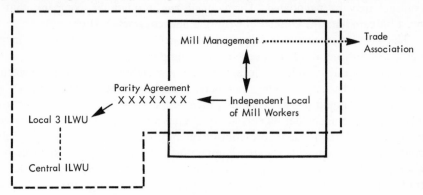

FIGURE 2. Alternate Social System II.

FIGURE 3. Alternate Social System III.

A. The Established Social System I

This is the social system (Figure 1) which had included the management of Company X, Local 68, Local 3, the AF of L Council, Central ILWU, and the Trade Association. Each party had functioned within an established pattern for ten years and had derived mutual benefits. Now, even though disrupted by the feud of Local 68 with the AF of L Council, the former economic advantages would be retained if harmony could be restored to the system.

B. Alternate Social System II

This social system would include the management of Company X, Local 68 (independent), Local 3 (ILWU), Central ILWU, and the Trade Association (see Figure 2). This system would involve recognition of the demand of

Local 68 for independent status. It would involve a new arrangement with the Trade Association, since it would no longer function to negotiate the contract with the AF of L Council. The Trade Association might be dropped entirely unless a new role could be developed for its services.

C. Alternate Social System III

This system would include the management of Company X and a single new independent union composed of former Local 68 and Local 3 (see Figure 3). Such a new union might be created through a National Labor Relations Board election. The company would cut ties with the Trade Association, and the two unions would disaffiliate from their international union.

The problem of analysis now becomes one of weighing the possibility of creating a new social system or reestablishing the traditional pattern. The goals to be met include in each instance such objectives as long-run industrial peace and high levels of productive efficiency in plant operations. It is interesting to note that alternate systems II and III involve a loss of identification with central organizations. These are identifications which had been built up over the years for protection of the parties against adverse market conditions for goods or labor.

APPRAISING ALTERNATE ACTION PATTERNS

Three alternate action patterns were presented by the industrial relations director. The consultant, working with the industrial relations director, analyzed each action pattern as to possible repercussions upon the *values of each participant, pattern of control,* and *social costs incurred.* The appraisal work sheet is shown.

APPRAISAL WORK SHEET

Alternate Action Patterns
1. *Reconstruct Established Bargaining Pattern.* Company will refuse to bargain outside the Trade Association and insist that Local 68 go back into the AF of L Council.
   A. Values of Each Participant.
      Local 68 is humiliated by being forced to return to the council. Company is satisfied to establish tried and successful area of bargaining; fear of competitive disadvantage in future strikes is dispelled and the power of Local 3 is diminished. Association is satisfied as desire to maintain area bargaining is achieved.
   B. Pattern of Control.
      Require Local 68 to return to council by NLRB decision.
      Company will work with council and Association to get Local 68 to go back to council. Association puts pressure on council to achieve reestablishment of traditional pattern.
   C. Social Costs.
      Local plant relations which have been very good may be seriously weakened if Local 68 is coerced to return to the council. A strike may result.

2. *Institute a New Bargaining Pattern with Recognition of the Mill Workers in an Independent Union.*

A. Values of Each Participant.

Local 68 is highly pleased to achieve an independent social and bargaining position. Local 3 is pleased and believes that it may now have more influence over Local 68 and the company. Company wants to keep area bargaining conditions inside the new arrangement. Association wants to keep the company in the association and maintain area bargaining rates and working conditions; however, association is very displeased with the company and the unions for disrupting the established pattern.

B. Pattern of Control.

Local 68 is weakened slightly but feels secure as long as Local 68 and Local 3 maintain parity agreement. Local 3 senses it will be stronger because of its aggressive leadership and it may capture Local 68 for its union. Company loses association as bargaining agent. It will need to establish new controls over Local 68 lest Local 3 become real power. Association puts pressure on council and on company to reestablish the traditional pattern.

C. Social Costs.

Company is afraid of the growing potential power of Local 3 in bargaining. There is the danger to the company of their sales being pirated during a future strike if they should leave the association. Association may lose Company X as member and thus lose strength. It faces future difficulty with association members in the likelihood of inequities in agreements within the area.

3. *Institute a New Bargaining Pattern with Recognition of a Single Independent Union of Mill and Warehouse Workers.*

A. Values of Each Participant.

Local 68 wants independence and fears militant leadership of Local 3, especially when backed by Central ILWU. Local 3 is strongly opposed to a combined union and fears company is trying to weaken Local 3 by absorbing it in the larger mill workers union. Company would be able to bargain with only one union. Association would be satisfied if company continues to use association as a bargaining agent.

B. Pattern of Control.

Mill workers could be weakened by aggressive leadership power of warehouse workers; warehouse workers could be weakened by voting strength of mill workers. Company might find it harder to control a stronger single union, especially if mill and warehouse workers should get together for their mutual advantage; association bargaining might be made difficult or impossible by demands from a single strong union.

C. Social Costs.

Mill workers placed in weaker position with possible loss of independence from aggressive leaders among warehouse workers. Warehouse workers placed in a weaker position unless their leaders can compensate for loss of voting strength. Company may have serious in-plant labor trouble if the new, single, independent union is created under pressure from the company and from the government.

CONCLUSION REACHED BY INDUSTRIAL RELATIONS DIRECTOR

At the termination of consultation, the industrial relations director reached a preliminary recommendation. The consultant made no recommendations because he took the view that a responsible official could do this best within the context of the situation. He knew that the industrial relations director would have to persuade the general manager on the wisdom of any course of action. It was the industrial relations director who feared that Local 68 could not be forced back into the AF of L Council and, if attempted, would bring a strike action. His conclusions based on the social analysis prepared by the consultant were now as follows:

1. Recognize right of Local 68 to bargain independently. Do not put pressure upon the local to affiliate with the AF of L Council against its will.
2. Seek to reconcile the AF of L Council to the necessity of inducing Local 68 to return. Failing this, seek authorization of Local 68 as independent bargaining unit. NLRB would be petitioned to hold globe election in which Local 68 would vote in secret election for continued affiliation with council or independent status.
3. Secure a parity agreement clause that states no strike action will be taken without vote of both unions. This will put power of strike in hands of Local 68, a less aggressive union.
4. Maintain associate membership in the Trade Association. Use it as clearing house for information and to secure bargaining help when needed.

MANAGEMENT ACTION

The industrial relations director reported his recommendations to the general manager. The manager maintained that everything must be done to restore the traditional bargaining pattern and get Local 68 back into the council. Strategy was carefully discussed, and the two managers agreed now to put the *pressure on the AF of L Council rather than on Local 68.* The general manager called the international vice-president of the AF of L, located in a regional city center, and told him that the local council would have to "come off its high horse and get 68 back into the Council" or the AF of L was going to lose one of its strongest unions. The international vice-president made a hurried trip to the big city. The vice-president convinced the AF of L Council leaders that they must effect a reconciliation. The vice-president and the AF of L Council president were quietly admitted by management upon the company grounds, and for some days they browsed about talking with Local 68 leaders and members. Finally, Local 68 voted to stay in—the council had "eaten crow" and members of 68 were satisfied. (Local 68 leaders said "the big boys admitted their mistakes and practically got down on their knees and asked us to come back.")

A contract was later negotiated with high satisfaction to all parties. The result was a reestablishment of the traditional pattern. The established social system became reconstructed as it was of old, when Local 68 leaders became active in the council, and all parties resumed their habitual roles. Here we have a validation of the principle that social systems tend toward equilibrium. The values of the established system were strong enough to maintain the "boundaries of the system" in the face of a strong threat to the survival of the system. Boundary maintenance resulted because the external economic and social environment remained relatively constant, and to regain equilibrium, the system needed only the redefinition of role expectations between Local 68 and the AF of L Council.

INTERPRETATION OF MANAGERIAL AND CONSULTANT ROLES

The industrial relations director can be seen to serve as a buffer and mediator between the union leaders and the general manager. He is the person who must relate what Roethlisberger calls the "logic of worker sentiments" with the "logic of managerial cost and efficiency." This was especially borne out when the parity agreement was drawn between Company X and Local 3 of the ILWU. Health and welfare provisions had been included for the first time in the contract with Local 68. The general manager tried to cut down these provisions in the bargaining with Local 3, since health and welfare are not part of the parity agreement. The industrial relations director, knowing intimately the feelings of Local 3 members (and, perhaps, respecting their aggressive leaders), insisted upon a parity package for Local 3 and convinced the general manager of its importance.

The general manager is seen as a person who had the practical knowledge of expediting action as demonstrated in his dealings with the international vice-president of the union. His more immediate responsibility for economic results may have prompted him to pursue his goal of restoring the established bargaining pattern. His action in bringing the international vice-president into the situation was the catalyst that excited the reactions which restored the equilibrium.

The consultant's role may be seen as one of assisting in defining the alternate actions and their possible repercussions more sharply than they might otherwise have been and, perhaps, giving the industrial relations director more influence in resisting direct coercion of the local union. If this be true, then social diagnosis proved itself useful, because a wrong decision could easily have involved a large loss to the company and to the workers. In addition, labor relations may have been worsened for an indefinite period.

CONCLUSION

Social system analysis may prove to be a powerful tool in solving many problems of labor-management relations. The problem discussed in this paper is patently a case in which social relations (in contrast to economic relations) are crucial to the resolution of the conflict. Without careful analysis of alternate systems, including value orientations, patterns of control, and, especially, social costs incurred, it is literally impossible to weigh consequences of action. Perhaps other concepts could be fruitfully introduced.[1] The beliefs and sentiments of the actors, the norms of groups, sanctions, systemic linkage, and the boundaries of the systems are all basic to a full understanding. In the case described it was important that the concepts used should be as few as possible and put so simply that a person like the industrial relations director, untutored in systemic theory, might participate in the analysis. The problem required immediate action, and it was necessary that the consultant rely upon the industrial relations director for all the factual knowledge necessary to analyze the problem and the alternate social systems involved. The roles of the industrial relations director and the consultant need to be judged by other labor-management experts. If the verdict should be that they acted wisely, then the theory of social system analysis has demonstrated its validity and a wider field of utility.

EPILOGUE—ONE YEAR LATER

The parties named herein assembled in April, 1958, and made a contract highly satisfactory to all members of the established bargaining system. The industrial relations director reports that labor relations are in a more harmonious state than he has observed them in his ten-year history with the company. Local 68 appreciates the fact that the company did not try to force it back into the council against its will. The council and Local 68 have healed their former breach. The company is pleased that it has negotiated a difficult health and pension program that is within its ability to pay. Local 3 is satisfied that it has achieved all the collective-bargaining advantages of Local 68 through its parity agreement without having to take bargaining responsibility.

These attitudes of satisfaction reflect an institutionalization of a set of role expectations. The stability of interaction, in turn, describes a condition in which particular acts of evaluation on both sides are oriented to common standards.[2]

---

[1] Talcott Parsons, *The Social System* (Glencoe, Ill.: Free Press, 1951); Talcott Parsons and Edward A. Shils, *Toward a General Theory of Action* (Cambridge, Mass.: Harvard University Press, 1951); Charles Loomis and J. Allan Beegle, *Rural Social Systems* (Englewood Cliffs, N.J.: Prentice-Hall, 1950); Charles P. Loomis, "Talcott Parsons as Systemic Sociologist" (mimeographed paper, Michigan State University, 1958).

[2] Talcott Parsons, *The Social System*, pp. 37–39.

Chapter Eight

Social and Cultural Change

JUST AS THE LINE between culture and society is subtle and abstract, so it is with the difference between cultural and social change. We may distinguish between the two by noting that a change in culture is a change in the way people do things, their values, their way of life. Social change, on the other hand, refers to change in the interrelationships among people. Here, the existing patterns of interpersonal relationships undergo an alteration, variation, or modification.

Neither cultural nor social change is new. From his beginning, man has adapted to his environment by means of variations in his way of doing things. The key to the unique power of man among all the other animals lies in his ability to achieve cultural change rather than to rely on biological variation in order to meet the demands of his environment. Although in isolated societies new methods must develop as a result of invention, diffusion (the spread of ideas as well as material objects) is an important source of social change in situations where there is contact between societies. It is with change from factors external to the society that we shall be concerned in this chapter.

A general principle may be noted at this point: The people of any society generally believe that their way of doing things—i.e., their culture—is superior to that of others. This belief is called *ethnocentrism* by social scientists. It was in this context that the Conquistadores "helped" the Aztecs by imposing Christianity upon them. Whereas blunt force was employed to effect social change in the sixteenth century, today more sophisticated methods are usually preferred. The first two selections (29 and 30) illustrate the part the anthropologist plays in bringing about social change and the difficulties he faces in attempting to do so.

Much of the early history of sociology and some of the early but substantial contributions to the field came as a result of a conscious effort to change existing forms of interpersonal relations. The community survey is one such venerable technique for instituting social change. Central to the effort to effect change is a body of facts, and the community survey was employed for just that purpose. John Howard and his concern for prison reform, Frederic Le Play's interest in the effects of industrialization on the French worker, and Charles Booth's study of the impoverished people of London are but a few examples.

Contemporary surveys involve not only the fact-gathering aspect, but also bring into focus the central problem in the minds of the community members involved. The third selection (31) illustrates the work of a fact-finding committee under the guidance of and in consultation with sociologists. On the basis of the objective appraisal, a program of action was instituted and, eventually, the results were evaluated.

The remaining selections (32–35) demonstrate the application of the social and cultural change concept in such diverse areas as interracial housing, agriculture, and religion.

29

An Experiment
in Applied Anthropology

John Collier Jr. and Mary Collier

How can the social sciences enable a poverty-stricken people to improve its condition? In this article, the work of United States and Peruvian anthropologists is described. In contrast to this example, you may wish to recall the situations described in *The Ugly American,* by William J. Lederer and Eugene Burdick.

In a beautiful mountain valley in the high Andes of Peru, inhabited by some 380 families of Indians, an eventful social experiment has been under way during the past five years. It is an experiment in "applied anthropology" [or "applied social science"]. Under the guidance of scientists a "backward" population has been stirred to break away from the hopeless traditions of centuries and raise itself to a more abundant life. The way in which this has been accomplished makes the experiment significant for millions of people in the underdeveloped areas of the world.

In the decade since World War II the U.S. has found itself assuming, partly from necessity and partly as a matter of wise long-range policy, responsibility for aid to peoples all around the globe—in the Pacific, in Asia, in Europe, in Africa, in South America. This experience has made plain that aid raises problems which reach beyond money and technology. There is the problem of persuading a backward people to accept not only technological innovations but also the economic and social changes made necessary by these innovations. Even more important, there is the problem of giving help without making them dependent. Benevolence all too often defeats its basic purpose by destroying a people's self-reliance.

It was these considerations that prompted a group of social scientists to undertake their experiment in applied anthropology in the Peruvian valley. Their aim was to learn how an impoverished population might be stimulated to lift its standard of living by its own efforts and within the framework of its own culture. The scientists undertook to acquire a thorough understanding of the people's customs and tradition and then to assist the community as "participating interventionists."

From *Scientific American,* **196,** 1 (January 1957), pp. 37–44. Reprinted with permission. Copyright © 1957 by Scientific American, Inc. All rights reserved.

John Collier Jr. is Instructor in Education and Anthropology, San Francisco State College.

The originator of the project was Allan R. Holmberg of Cornell University, an anthropologist who had studied Indian groups in Peru for the Smithsonian Institution and later in association with the University of San Marcos. Holmberg enlisted his Peruvian colleagues and students in a search for a laboratory in which to study how a backward group would respond to the introduction of modern technological change. On a field trip with his students Holmberg found an ideal community for such a program. It was an ancient estate, called Hacienda Vicos, on the upper slopes of a long, narrow valley paralleling Peru's highest mountain range, the Cordillera Blanca. The hacienda was in decay, its lands eroded, its more than 2,000 Indians living in hunger and disease. Holmberg conceived the bold idea of renting the hacienda and operating it in the conventional way, but under a scientific group instead of the usual private patron. With a grant of funds from the Carnegie Corporation of New York, the Cornell department of sociology and anthropology rented the hacienda from the Peruvian Government and launched a five-year experiment, known as the Cornell-Peru Project, in cooperation with Peruvian scientists and government agencies.

Hacienda Vicos is an estate of some 35,000 acres at an altitude of from 9,000 to 12,000 feet in a valley called the Callejón de Huaylas. Its history goes back to the Spanish Conquest. Legend says that nearly 400 years ago its then owner, a very wealthy Spanish woman, on her deathbed gave the hacienda, complete with its Indians, to a hospital in Lima. Whether or not this story is true, Hacienda Vicos has been in public custody since the early 17th century, first under Spanish authorities and later under the Peruvian national government. For hundreds of years the estate, with its lands and peonage system intact, has passed from one lessee to another, recently by public auction to the highest bidder.

The hacienda system, established by the Spanish conquerors, is maintained by rigid traditions which even the patron is often powerless to change radically. The Indians who live on a hacienda are its serfs, and the owner or lessee is their lord—their benefactor and exploiter. One member of each serf household must work for the hacienda three days a week without pay. In return the Indians are allowed to farm a few acres of land, drink water from the streams, gather faggots for their fires and graze their animals in allotted pastures. They turn to the patron for assistance and advice in times of trouble and leave every important decision in his hands. Within the hacienda they attend chapel, bury their dead, celebrate their fiestas, and remain bound for generation after generation.

The Cornell-Peru staff's decision to operate the hacienda under the traditional rules was the core of their anthropological approach. They wished to avoid disrupting the community or creating confusion and anxiety. Their purpose was to acquire a full understanding of the Indians and their problems in the customary pattern of their lives, to persuade them to improve their farming methods, to plow back the higher returns into a better life for the community and eventually to lead the Indians to a free and self-reliant life. The change would develop from the bottom up, not be imposed from the top.

Peru is a land of the Indian. Its leaders have long been aware that the country is held back by the traditional prejudices and fetters of its Indian masses, and they therefore welcomed the anthropologists' project, hoping, with the scientists, that it would be a practical demonstration of wide benefit. The Cornell-Peru experiment received enthusiastic cooperation from the country's universities, scientists, educators, and authorities in agriculture and public health.

At Vicos the anthropologists found a clear epitome of Peru's problems. Its Indians were almost completely illiterate: only 2 per cent could read and write, and most spoke only the Indian language Quechua. Hunger was their chronic condition, and drinking almost their only recreation. Epidemics brought death to nearly every home. They were little better than slaves, despised by their neighbors. Between the hacienda Indians and the *mestizos* (mixed Spanish-Indian breeds) of surrounding communities there was strong hostility. *Mestizos* look down on Indians, considering them biologically inferior; the Indians are submissive but fear and distrust the *mestizos*. Nevertheless, the Project scientists had to hire *mestizos* for skilled work on the hacienda, and they took advantage of the necessity to study the relationship between the groups. They were confident that cooperation would eventually improve the relationship. The Project even kept on the administrator who had been in charge of the hacienda for several years under the former lessee.

The first task was to increase the food crop. Most of the Vicosinos were living at a level of bare subsistence. A blight had hit the potato fields in the two preceding years, and the corn crop also had failed. Food was so scarce and costly that the Indians were eating the seed grain, digging up seed potatoes as soon as they were planted, selling their cattle to buy food, and stealing as much of the hacienda crop as they could.

The Project staff had an agricultural survey made and took steps to rebuild the potato culture. It obtained blight-resistant potato seed, fertilizer, and insecticides from agricultural experiment stations, and then offered them to the Indians at cost.

Few came to buy. Days passed and the Indians paid no attention to the announcement. Recognizing that most of the Indians could not pay for the seed even if they had wanted to, the Project then worked out a credit plan. It proposed to advance the seed, fertilizer, and insecticide on a crop-sharing arrangement—half of the crop to the hacienda, half to the farmer.

This plan was first presented to a meeting of the *mayorales,* the Indian leaders of the community who served as foremen in directing the work of the other peons. The *mayorales* listened, and shook their heads. They declared the plan would never work. But it became plain that the leaders were hostile to the proposal because vested interests were at stake. They feared that improvement of the prospects of the other peons would undermine their own favored position.

Notwithstanding this discouraging opposition by the leaders, the Project staff decided to offer the plan directly to the community as a whole. At the peons' weekly meeting (the *mando*) for assignment of the week's work, the scientists described their proposal. It evoked excited discussion among the peons. They appeared to approve it at first, but after one of the *mayorales* spoke against it, the approval seemed to cool. Only nine of the 125 peons present came forward to sign up for the plan at the end of the meeting. Later 22 more did so privately, but a majority of the community hung back, and active opposition grew. Rumors, perhaps initiated by landowners and *mestizos* in the area, spread among the distrustful and suspicious peons. Why had the *gringos* come to the valley? What were their reasons for offering help to the Indians? The *mestizos* whispered that the fair-appearing scheme surely hid some plan to cheat and exploit the peons. One rumor went so far as to suggest that the Americans had come to Vicos to fatten the Indians on potatoes and then boil down their bodies for oil for American machinery! The credulity that accepted such lurid tales was fed by the Indians' fear of change—of what the unknown might bring.

Mario Vásquez and other Peruvian scientists in the Project worked hard to allay the Indians' fears. Vásquez visited scores of Indians in their homes and in the fields and signed up nine more peons to participate in the program. But of the total of 40 who agreed to take part, only 17 actually took the seed and entered into the farming project when the planting season began. Most of these were the poorest of the poor; against the disapproval of their wives in some instances they decided to take the chance to save themselves from starvation and improve their position.

The participating Indians were required to carry out to the letter instructions from Peruvian Government agricultural specialists. They had to disinfect the seed potatoes and the land, to plant the seed at 18-inch intervals in rows three feet apart, to apply guano as fertilizer, to spray insecticides at set times, and to remove blossoms from the plants. They were instructed in techniques of cultivation, irrigation, and so on.

Besides supervising every step of the cultivation—the fumigating, the planting, the harvesting—the Project staff also kept a careful watch on the farmers' working relations and social behavior. By doing so, they were able to forestall small frictions and points of resistance that often defeat a whole program. For example, at one point the staff employed a young, intelligent Vicosino as a supervisor. Their close observation at once disclosed that this was a mistake. Taking orders from a young member of their own group hurt the vanity of the older Indians; they preferred to be directed by outsiders.

This delicate pride was illustrated by another incident. A peon whose plots had somehow been overlooked during a routine inspection of the participating fields turned up at the hacienda highly agitated. He complained: "If you don't pay as much attention to my field as you do to the others, people will think it is because my field isn't being cultivated correctly and that you are displeased!" Incidents such as these demonstrated how important it is to enlist the perceptions and skills of social science (applied anthropology) in any aid program among a proud and sensitive people.

Throughout this first season the other Vicosinos felt sorry for the 17 Indians who had been foolish enough to be taken in by the Project. They would surely lose everything, and have thrown away their season's labor. But at harvest time the nonparticipants were taken aback. The 17 participants harvested more than double the usual crop of potatoes. Each of them divided his crop into two piles, one to be taken by the Project, the other to be kept by himself. The Project staff then invited the farmer to take his choice of the piles. The Indians were deeply impressed. This was something foreign to their experience: the *gringos* did not cheat; they kept their word!

The following season 87 Indians, including one of the *mayorales* who had opposed the program, took advantage of the seed. Even some of the *mestizos* asked to be included in the experiment. By the third year 135 Indians took part, and they accounted for nearly 80 per cent of the total potato crop raised on Hacienda Vicos. In that year some of the Indians bought the seed and other materials on credit, instead of sharecropping. All but one of the borrowers paid his debt in full at harvest time. Consequently the sharecropping system was dropped entirely in 1955. The Indians proved in that season that they were sufficiently skilled in the new farming techniques to take the full risk and responsibility of buying the seed and to realize a yield adequate to support themselves at a higher level than they had known.

Economic reforms sowed their own seeds of social reform. For example, the hacienda Indians had constantly stolen cattle from one another and fought over the ownership of animals. The Project staff suggested that they brand their cattle. The Indian leaders showed no enthusiasm for this, but when one of them observed bitterly that the wealthiest had built their herds by rustling, the owner of the largest herd began to brand his cattle to prove his innocence. The other Indian families followed his example, and cattle rustling stopped.

Along with the rehabilitation of their agriculture, the Indians also began to rehabilitate the collapsing ruins of the hacienda. Under the direction of skilled craftsmen they rebuilt their crumbling dwellings, erected storage buildings for the crops and soon were able to turn to the construction of a school.

Although school attendance is theoretically compulsory in Peru, fewer than 5 per cent of the eligible children in Vicos were enrolled, and these came only sporadically. As Vásquez observed, even these few Vicosino families treated schooling like their forced labor for the patron: so long as one child of a household was in school, it didn't matter whether the child who sat on the school bench on Monday was the same child who had sat there Friday. School was kept in an open porch, where a woman instructor tried to teach about eight children of assorted ages something of reading, writing, and arithmetic in Spanish, a language almost totally foreign to most of the Quechua-speaking Vicosinos.

Soon after the Project began in 1951, the Indians were invited to a meeting to discuss the possibility of a new school. They agreed to provide all the labor, and the Project offered to buy needed materials. Plans were drawn for a modern schoolhouse, and ground was broken in May, 1952. The Indians made thousands of adobes (clay bricks), quarried great piles of rock for the foundations and felled tall eucalyptus trees to make the doors, window frames, and roof beams. The only materials that had to be purchased were glass for the windows, lime for the plaster, cement for the floor, and tiles for the roof. Although much of the building project was at first quite beyond the Indians' limited skills, the work was accomplished, under the direction of the contractor and a few *mestizo* craftsmen. In 1953 the first unit of six classrooms was opened, and the following year saw the completion of a second unit with three more classrooms, a spacious auditorium, a dining room and kitchen for the hot-lunch program. Later living quarters for teachers were built.

The Peruvian educational authorities, who operate the school, have staffed it with eight teachers, and more than 200 children are now enrolled. Most of these are boys, who receive vocational instruction, including carpentry and agriculture. A small group of girls attends a technically separate primary school in the same building.

This beautiful school has become a symbol. It has given new confidence to the community, for the building is notably finer than any other rural school of the region. And it has inspired the Indians with the pride of achievement. Visitors have come even from Lima to see the modern school the Vicosinos have built with their own hands.

Hacienda Vicos has seen a third major improvement—its first health program. With the cooperation of the Cornell-Peru Project, the regional Peruvian public health agency has set up a clinic which serves not only the hacienda but also the neighboring *mestizo* town of Marcará. Twice a week a truck, supplied by the United Nations International Children's Emergency Fund, arrives at Vicos with a doctor and nurses and public health specialists. Though their program is chiefly concerned with child and maternal welfare, the clinic at Vicos gives attention to all, dispensing medicine and advice on the full range of ailments from itches to tuberculosis. The doctors visit critically ill patients in their homes, though this sometimes means an hour's ride on horseback on the rocky mountain trails. The clinic gives a thorough physical examination to all the children attending the school. It keeps careful medical records which supply an invaluable body of data for studying the health of Peruvian Indians. The clinic is gradually educating the Indians to combat their ailments with modern medicine rather than with native religious methods or magic. . . .

Along with the basic projects—food, education, health—there have been special programs, one of which deserves particular mention. All young Peruvian men who have not served in the army are required to attend military drill every Sunday for a two-year period. This had been a hateful service for the Vicosinos and a further exploitation of their status, for the politicos of the town where they drilled, five miles from the hacienda, had merely used the pretense of the Sunday drill to make the Indians do community work. The Cornell-Peru Project arranged for the young men to be drilled right at the hacienda, not only conforming to the national law, but providing an exercise in working together and fostering pride in their own group, which they had sadly lacked. The Project also used the Sunday gathering to provide classes in Spanish, reading, writing, and arithmetic. Two years ago the Indians of Vicos, marching in sandals with wooden guns and wooden bayonets, won a citation at the annual military review of their province.

Foremost among all the purposes of the Project has been a calculated endeavor to develop the Indians' self-reliance and change their own image of themselves—an image of serfs destined to poverty and endless unrewarding work. The Project ended tyrannical exploitation of the Indians, not only by the hacienda but also by outside employers. The peons no longer are sent out to work without pay in mines or factories. No longer do neighboring communities come to the hacienda to conscript crews for construction of bridges and public buildings. The weekly meetings of the *mayorales* and of the peons have been turned into discussion sessions at which both the foremen and the peons can air their grievances and take part in decisions. The goal of the entire program is to enable the Vicosinos themselves to continue their progress toward a higher level of living when the Project staff withdraws from the community.

Beyond all this, the Project's broader concern has been to develop a body of scientific experience which will serve to establish equations for work in other underdeveloped areas—in Peru itself and in the world at large. In the Vicos research U.S. scientists have teamed up with scientists of Peru. Indeed, a great part of the detailed research has been carried out by Holmberg's Peruvian student and assistant Mario Vásquez. He lived with an Indian family on the hacienda and was largely responsible for dispelling distrust and enlisting the Indians' cooperation. As a research project the Vicos experiment has also attracted dozens of other students from the University of San Marcos and from Cornell and other universities.

Perhaps the biggest single lesson the Project has demonstrated is that, by working within the existing structure of a society, with sufficient understanding of both its limitations and its potentialities, it is possible to accomplish basic social changes without a staggering budget or swarms of personnel. The anthropologists at Hacienda Vicos have shown that in the field of social reform, understanding may be a far more important tool than money or power.

30

The Case of the Hungry Calves

William W. Stein

An understanding of the social structure of the family—an important aspect of any culture—is necessary to any attempt to induce cultural change. In this account from the Cornell-Peru Project, we can observe the relationship between culture and the acceptance or rejection of new methods in animal husbandry.

Note that even an anthropologist—with far more training in objectivity than the average individual—may, because of ethnocentrism, unconsciously assume that people of another culture will react like those in his own society.

THE COMMUNITY OF HUALCAN

Hualcan is a Quechua-speaking Andean Highland Indian village in the District of Carhuaz, Department of Ancash, Peru. The settlement is located in a narrow valley, the Chucchun, which opens into the Callejon de Huaylas just south of the town of Carhuaz, a little over six miles west of the village. The Hualcan lands belong to the Indians who live there, and on the basis of this fact the settlement is locally classified as an *estancia,* an independent landowning community, as distinguished from an *hacienda,* or estate, which is often in the hands of an overseer appointed by an absentee landlord.

The Hualcan houses are dispersed over the valley bottomlands and on the

Reprinted from *Human Organization,* **15,** 1 (Spring 1956), pp. 15–21, by permission of The Society for Applied Anthropology and the author.

William W. Stein is Assistant Professor of Anthropology, University of Alberta at Calgary.

The material presented in this paper was gathered while the writer was in Peru as an Area Research Fellow of the Social Science Research Council and a Pre-Doctoral Fellow in Anthropology of the Wenner-Gren Foundation for Anthropological Research during 1951–1952.

low slopes of the hills which surround the village on three sides. The bottom-lands, at an altitude of 9–10,000 feet, are irrigable and in use throughout the year: in the dry season, from May to October, and the rainy season, from November to April. Other Hualcan lands, both single-crop fields and pastures, extend up to the "puna" at about 13,000 feet. The territory of Hualcan actually goes beyond this altitude to the lakes and glaciers of the Cordillera Blanca, a mountain range with peaks of over 20,000 feet.

The economic condition of Hualcan is somewhat better than that of many other *estancias* in the area mainly because the Hualcainos, the people of Hualcan, have a source of water: several small glacial lakes from which water is carried to the fields in the dry season by means of a system of irrigation ditches. Moreover, Hualcainos own both bottomlands for intensive agriculture and higher, nonirrigable slopes for hardy grain crops and pasture. Larger tracts of pasture land on the hills and the "puna" are also brought into use. Subsistence activity is thus fairly well distributed between farming and herding.

The agricultural capital of Hualcan is not really sufficient to produce adequately for the more than 700 Hualcainos. About half of the households in the village find it necessary to maintain a status of dependency on the Mestizo *haciendas* across the valley. Such households are obligated to furnish *hacienda* labor on three or four days per week in return for fields and pasture which they can use for their own needs. Almost all of the "free" households, the other half of the community, send members to work for periods ranging from a week or two to several months on the Peruvian coastal plantations, a day's journey away. Coastal wages are good and regular migrations of male laborers to centers such as Paramonga and San Jacinto occur during lulls in the agricultural cycle when household supplies can be reduced. Only a very few households are self-sufficient, in the sense of not having to depend on one outside agency or another to supplement production. Even these few fortunate families, however, must trade their surplus products outside the village for the household necessities and luxuries which cannot be produced in Hualcan. In this context, self-sufficiency and accumulation are such highly desirable goals for the Hualcaino that he can seldom bring himself to part easily with even a poor and inferior item of property.

All Hualcainos are agriculturists and herders, although many of them practice some specialty: ceramics, weaving, tailoring, petty trading, or curing. Every Hualcaino owns at least a small piece of land. Without this minimum there is little self-esteem for the individual and no social status in the community. Similarly, every person who belongs to Hualcan, including even infants, will own at least one grazing animal. The fields furnish a variety of grain, root, and garden produce: maize, wheat, barley, quinoa, potatoes, oca, ullocu, squash, pumpkin, cabbage, peppers, and many other minor food plants and herbs. The animals (chickens, guinea pigs, sheep, goats, burros, and cattle) furnish meat almost incidentally, except for the excessive quantities which are consumed at fiestas. The sheep is one of the most important animals in Hualcan, since it provides wool for most of the clothing. Cattle, too, are important: they serve as draft animals in agriculture. Cattle also furnish milk which, when it is available, the Hualcainos regard as an interesting if not a staple dietary item.

Getting a living in Hualcan is at best a difficult art. Agricultural capital, land and livestock, is constantly threatened by a host of natural and human forces. Crops are attacked by blights, hail, frost, heavy rains, or drought. Animals are pest-ridden and malnourished because good lands simply cannot be spared for fodder crops. Humans steal from each other and involve themselves in expensive litigation over property. The result is that Hualcainos do not get enough to eat for most of the year. Food is consequently an important item in Hualcan, a source of gratification, anxiety, and violence. Food figures in ritual gift-giving. It is consumed in enormous quantities at fiestas which are periods of food "license." Damages to crops, animals, or food stores, and counteraccusations are bases for verbal and physical aggression.

In Hualcan terms, man is enjoined to seek his living with all the force he can muster. An important principle, or "theme," [1] of Hualcan culture affirms that all gratification is to be achieved only with effort and that man therefore has to exert himself. The Hualcan approach to the world, especially in the subsistence sphere, is frenetic. Man's relations with nature and with his fellow man are tinged with violence. At the same time, peace and harmony do exist as important goals for the Hualcaino.

THE "EXPERIMENT"

The field work on which this paper is based was carried on in Hualcan for six months, from December, 1951, to June, 1952. Residence was established in the household of Miguel Paucar, a Hualcaino of about 55 years of age who had passed through a long series of ritual offices and thus commanded considerable respect throughout the community.

Miguel Paucar's household was one of the more self-sufficient family groups in Hualcan. It was not among the community's three richest households, the members of which owned large amounts of property and carried on extensive trade outside Hualcan with their surplus produce. However, both Miguel and his wife, Nicolasa, owned enough fields to furnish an adequate diet for most of the year. They owned enough sheep to clothe themselves. Miguel was a specialist in weaving and tailoring. He owned a loom and one of Hualcan's half-dozen sewing machines. With these he was able to add some grain or potatoes to the household income now and then, and even

---

[1] Morris E. Opler ("Themes as a Dynamic Forces in Culture," *American Journal of Sociology*, **51** [1945], p. 198) defines "themes" as follows: "The term 'theme' is used here in a technical sense to denote a postulate or position, declared or implied, and usually controlling behavior or stimulating activity which is tacitly approved or openly promoted in a society." Hualcan themes have been discussed at length in William W. Stein, "Hualcan: An Andean Indian Estancia" (Ph.D. Thesis, Cornell University, 1955), pp. 360–398.

occasionally a few coppers. Nicolasa raised a surplus of hot peppers in her garden and collected the eggs from the household chickens. She would take these to the market in town on Sundays to sell for cash which she then used to buy salt, matches, and sweetening. When Miguel had a free day, he would go to town to work for a townsman in the fields or in construction. With his earnings he purchased coca and, once in a while, a new blade for an agricultural implement. The surplus wool from the flock of about 40 sheep was sold for cash or bartered for coastal products when the traders came to Hualcan every year in July.

Miguel's son, Manuel, and daughter-in-law, Victoria, did not own as much property as their elders but were gradually accumulating things. They expected eventually to inherit from their parents. When Miguel was a young man he made several trips to the coast to earn money for the purchase of much of his present property. He had not been on the coast for several years, however, because his agricultural and ritual responsibilities did not give him the time. Manuel, on the other hand, had been going to the coast from time to time, although since Victoria had had a baby the frequency and duration of these trips were diminishing.

Early during the writer's stay in Hualcan, two of Miguel's cows calved: one early in January and the other toward the end of that month. Shortly after the second calf was born, the two young animals were brought down to the house from the pasture. This action coincided with the onset of a rather cold and rainy period with frequent afternoon and evening hail storms. Miguel explained that keeping the calves at home would protect them from the weather and would give them a chance to suckle peacefully. They were tethered under a shelter in the courtyard of the house. The sows were kept with the other animals in a pen, about 100 yards removed from the house. Each morning, the women whose job it was to herd the animals would bring the cows to the calves, let them suckle for a while, and then drive all the animals together up to the pasture where they spent a good part of the day. They often called upon Modista, Miguel's daughter of about eight years, and Deunicia, an older girl whose mother was a poor dependent in the household, to take charge of the animals while the older women went about their other duties.

About a week after the calves were first brought to the house, a change in the morning routine was observed. When the cows were brought from the animal pen they were staked in front of the house. The two girls, Modista and Deunicia, would get the calves from the courtyard and hold them in front of the cows while Nicolasa and Victoria milked. After the women had got perhaps two or three quarts the calves were let loose and allowed to suckle for a while. Then the animals were taken to the pasture. When this morning milking began, the household diet changed. The milk was used often for the evening meal in the preparation of grain pudding. Immediately, too, the women began to set aside a quantity of milk each day for making into cheese.

When the cheese was ripe it was used as a condiment in the flavoring of soups and stews. Both pudding and cheese, incidentally, are considered great dietary luxuries and indices of economic well-being.

The calves, on the other hand, appeared to be receiving an inadequate diet. Hualcan animals are in poor condition to begin with. There are many animal parasites, and fodder is scanty and of poor quality. Hualcainos' knowledge of animal husbandry is not "scientific" but traditional. Folk remedies, charms, divination, and prayers to the Saints are all parts of the Hualcan herding complex. The idea of human control would not apply. Often Hualcainos watch their animals die and are impotent to take any course of action beyond the philosophic comment that at least they will be able to have a little fresh meat for a few days.

The household milking was observed for two weeks. At the end of that period the writer suggested to Miguel that stronger animals might be raised if the calves were allowed to suckle freely for a while. The writer pointed out to Miguel that perhaps one of the reasons for the poor quality of the local cattle was that their milk was taken away from them too soon. He explained that he was no animal doctor but that the additional milk might conceivably produce a better animal in the end. The writer also offered to take the responsibility for the loss of the milk supply to the household by purchasing the cows' milk production for six weeks. At the end of that time, an assessment of the calves' development was to be made. Miguel did not appear too enthusiastic about the idea, but he agreed to go along with it mainly because of the extra cash income which it would afford.

THE PROBLEM

When a new technical idea is presented to the members of a community, it is assessed in terms of a field of the relevant features of the way of life of that community in the innovative situation. A wide range of cultural "facts" structures the situation for the culture-carriers. Similarly, such "facts" place certain limits on the action of the innovator and on the nature of the innovation. The new idea has to be conceived on the basis of a preexisting system of thoughtways. Its meaning to the culture-carriers becomes, therefore, something quite different from its meaning to the foreign innovators who present the idea, who view the technique or the tool from the standpoint of their own cultural system of logic. The problem would appear ultimately to rest in uncovering and understanding the meanings behind differing systems of premises relating to the nature of man and the universe which are to be found among both donors and recipients. On such a groundwork it might be possible to predict what both donors and recipients will do in the situation. This approach would appear to have significance for even so mundane a problem as getting milk to feed hungry calves in the village of Hualcan.

The calf "experiment" was no experiment. Beyond the methodological considerations of supervision and measurement of both experimental and control groups, no control was achieved over situational factors of human relationships and meanings. A trait, such as calf-breeding, may be taken as a kind of point around which are focused a variety of cultural patterns. The system of logic which is inferred to underlie these more immediate systems of belief and action connects them with patterns relating to other avenues of life which appear to be based on the same set of fundamental cultural principles. Thus, from the trait, which is itself a nexus of immediate patterns, it appears to be possible to trace relationships throughout the cultural system, to view the whole culture as a matrix for the trait. The innovative situation in a sense furnishes a challenge to the culture-carriers to assess the new trait in terms of all relevant features which can be defined from the totality of past experience.

It is the aim of this paper to describe and interpret the failure of an attempted technical innovation. The course of events will be shown to involve a network of cultural factors which ramify into all important aspects of the life of the community. Spicer's recent casebook [2] of attempted technical innovations and their successes and failures has clearly pointed out the role of cultural factors which lead to unanticipated consequences in programs of technical "aid."

In the case to be described here, the problem was initially viewed as one of demonstrating the economic consequences of furnishing calves with a better diet. No attempt was made to ascertain the probable social consequences of the manner in which this goal was to be achieved. The human subjects were not consulted with regard to the desirability of such consequences. Fortunately for the household and the community there were no significant consequences, since the attempted innovation was patently unfeasible in terms of the viewpoint of the Hualcainos. The observer was able to take a relatively objective position due to the nature of his role in the field: that of an anthropologist who had no strong emotional or economic investment in the outcome of the proposed change in dairying practices. There was neither hostility toward the innovator nor social disruption as by-products of the "experiment." Rather, the subjects were furnished with a humorous subject for leisure-time conversation.

This case illustrates some of the types of problems which a technician might have to face in Hualcan were he to inaugurate a serious attempt at technological change. It will also serve to point out how ignorance of local conditions can lead to an unrealistic demand on people when an innovator from another culture brings with him little more than his own cultural premises to help him assess the situation.

---

[2] Edward H. Spicer (ed.), *Human Problems in Technological Change; A Casebook* (New York: Russell Sage Foundation, 1952).

THE HUMAN FACTORS

For a week the cows were not milked in the writer's presence and they were allowed to suckle their calves freely. Suddenly, the women resumed their morning milkings and no explanation was volunteered. When the family members were asked about it a few days later, they explained that the children of the household were taking the milk while the animals were pastured on the hills, and that they also were stealing into the animal pen at night to get it. Moreover, they added, the women of the household needed it.

It did not seem at the beginning that the proposal was an unreasonable request, except with regard to the fact that no veterinarian had given an opinion on its validity based on technical knowledge. It was unknown whether or not more milk for calves was a significant variable in such an attempt to improve livestock quality. Cattle diseases and parasites plus poor fodder for grown animals appeared to be mainly responsible for the condition of the Hualcan livestock. However, it was hoped that more milk for calves might help a little. There could, of course, be no way of prediction of success or explanation of failure of the milk to produce better animals. Furthermore, the writer understood that while he could take the responsibility of paying for the milk, others would have to take responsibility for the supervision of the "experiment." Even if the family did not believe in a successful outcome, the writer felt that they would accept the money and wait for proof.

The writer ignored practically all of the factors which invalidated the whole "experiment." First, the milk was not paid for in advance. He assumed that a payment could be made weekly for the milk production. However, in this way no compact was made with Miguel. In Hualcan there appears to be an idea or premise which is basic to interpersonal relations and which may be called the principle of compactual responsibility. In practically all transactions which partake of the nature of a contract, a situationally-structuring gift, the DERECHUN,[3] is made in advance. This negotiation is a necessary preliminary. If the subject of a DERECHUN, that is, the one who is approached by another who has a request to make, wishes to avoid responsibility he has but to refuse the gift. If he accepts the DERECHUN he is thereby obligated to perform according to the agreement which is made. This kind of preliminary gift structures the situation for planting a field on shares, for betrothals, for accepting a politico-religious office, and even for relations with demons who cannot get power over one until one accepts the DERECHUN. In effect, then, the writer did not really force anyone to accept compactual

---

[3] The orthographic convention used here is suggested by John H. Rowe ("Inca Culture at the Time of the Spanish Conquest," *Handbook of South American Indians,* ed. Julian Steward. Bureau of American Ethnology Bulletin No. 143, Vol. 2, pp. 183–330. Washington, 1946, pp. 185–186.) The use of capitals for Quechua material distinguishes it from Spanish, which is written in italicized lower-case letters.

responsibility for the supervision of the "experiment," since no preliminary and situationally-structuring gift was made. Miguel was free to promise to *try* to feed the calves more milk but he did not obligate himself to superintend the "experiment" and, indeed, he was not free to perform in accordance with the writer's proposal, as was later discovered. Miguel put as much pressure as he could reasonably be expected to exert on the older members of his household. However, in Hualcan a household head functions in this type of situation more as a mediator than as a director.

Had the writer attempted to make a compact with Miguel he would have been told, as he later found out, that Miguel actually owned only one of the cows. The other belonged to Nicolasa. The writer had assumed that Miguel, as head of the household, had control over the other household members. While this was an essential fact of Hualcan family organization, based on principles of age and maleness as validations of status, there were at least two other important principles involved as regulators of the household economy. Individuals are enjoined to be self-sufficient. They are also enjoined to share with others with whom they have "holy" relationships, that is, relatives. Personal property is inviolable but has to be shared with those who "count." The resources and income of all the members of a household, although they are owned separately, are pooled. A field, for example, is always owned by an individual but the other members of his household help him operate it. The products from the field are divided at the harvest and each individual has his own section of the household storeroom and his own storage jars to hold his share. While it might be said theoretically that Miguel "owned" his cow's milk supply, it belonged to the whole household in fact.

Had Miguel been asked he would have explained further that he really had no say at all in the disposal of his cow's milk since the women of the household were pasturing them. Hualcan women, as "gatekeepers" of gratification, have a general control of the household larder and dispose of the products as they see fit. While Miguel "owned" a number of grain jars, for example, Nicolasa always saw to it that Miguel's grain was used proportionately in the preparation of meals. In the case of the milk, Nicolasa and Victoria were using that product in their cooking. Some of the cheese they made was taken to town to be sold for cash which was then used for the purchase of household items like salt, matches, aspirin, and sweetening.

Also, it was observed that a good portion of the milk was being given away. The women were sharing it with the relatives of every other member of the household. It would be unforgivable for a family to have a milk supply and not share it with relatives. Although the family relationship is a "holy" relationship and a source of stability for the individual, family status has to be validated constantly. In Hualcan perhaps the most important type of status validation is by contribution. Thus Nicolasa and Victoria were validating the status of the other household members as well as their own as relatives to other persons by utilizing the means at their disposal to share something good with those others. In this way, too, the household members affirmed their own dependence on their relatives by offering a symbol of honor and respect, and they fulfilled their obligations for past favors given by those to whom they gave the milk.

Had Nicolasa been approached with the proposal, and had a formal attempt been made to obligate her, she would have pointed out that she could only assume responsibility for her "own" cow, which was really Miguel's. She had lent the cow which was technically hers to Victoria to care for and to milk. In a broad sense, the second cow "belonged" to Victoria while she was taking care of it. It was Nicolasa's alone, with regard to ultimate disposal, since Nicolasa held formal title to it. However, if it had been possible to approach both Nicolasa and Victoria properly, they would no doubt have repeated that the children would take milk from cows in the pens and on the hills, in any case, and that little could be done about it.

Unattended property in Hualcan appears to be "fair game" for any passerby. Hualcainos are constantly on guard against theft. Their expectations are fulfilled frequently when valuable portions of their crops are taken. The people are poor, and many steal because of necessity. Others steal maliciously, in order to hurt their victims in return for real or supposed wrongs. Still others steal because they have been stolen from, and this method is the only way of assuring a return for their labors. A few, perhaps, steal "habitually" because they have always done so.

Hualcainos are not without protective devices against stealing. Houses, for example, are built in such a way that the courtyard cannot be seen from the outside. The would-be thief often does not know whether or not someone is at home. Every family owns one or more dogs which set up a tremendous racket at the approach of someone other than a neighbor and will go on to the attack unless called off by one of the household members. Both harvests and animals are protected by means of CUKLLA, little portable brush huts, which may be moved from a harvested field to one which is ripe or from one pasture to another. Few families, of course, have the personnel to install a guard in a CUKLLA in every field, but it is hoped by the Hualcainos that the presence of such a hut will indicate to the thief the possibility that someone *might* be inside.

If Nicolasa and Victoria had thought about the problem objectively, they would have had to admit that the idea of guarding property, such as the milk supply, from violation was indeed precedented in Hualcan. A family member always takes a turn regularly at staying with the animals when they are pastured on the hill, far away. An arrangement could have been made with a responsible adult to watch over the cows and their calves to see that the latter received their milk.

It must be remembered that the milk thieves were children, not malicious strangers. While children are cherished, in Hualcan terms, they are not in a favorable status of life. Since they are not great contributors they are consequently able to assert no greater status than that of dependents. The infant is fondled and loved demonstrably as long as he is helpless. At the age of about one year, property is heaped upon him at his haircutting ceremony, at which time he becomes a property-holding mèmber of the community. As soon as he passes beyond the toddler stage, however, especially when another baby has entered the household, he is thrust into the care of his siblings or other household children. As quickly as possible he is introduced to the hard business of getting a living. Emphasis is placed on making the individual self-sufficient early. Until children are strong enough to "count" in agricultural production, they are generally accorded a scant share of the products. They are clothed in ragged castoffs in a community where clothing is an important status symbol. They often have to be satisfied with scraps and cold leftovers from meals where food patterns are also integrated with status. Sometimes, children are even sent off on errands when there is something good in limited quantity to be divided among the older members of a household.

Hualcan children, like the dogs, are always hungry. As a consequence, patterns of stealing food are included in childhood activities. Children raid their own and neighbors' household larders for food, just as their parents steal from their *patrones,* the Mestizo landowners. These patterns of stealing are expected and householders do their best to guard against the raids of children. In the case of the milk supply, Nicolasa and Victoria were satisfied as long as they took a reasonable quantity of milk from the cows each morning. However, it would have been difficult to protect the milk supply from more serious violation from time to time if the women had not been measuring it daily.

Another set of factors relating to herding practices must also be taken into consideration. Children often have sole charge of the household animals away from the house. One of the tasks which is given to children as early as possible is that of herding. While this is generally considered women's work, the women are not always free of other responsibilities in the household economy. Consequently they assign herding tasks to the children. When there is a milk supply among the cows, it is expected that the herders, children or even adults, will take some during the day as a kind of *temple,* a form of additional compensation for labor, like a "tip." *Temple* is always expected 'o accompany exchange transactions which involve the payment of goods or cash for services. In effect, then, the herders would be denied their *temple* if the milk were forbidden them.

When the scheme for more milk for calves was proposed, the writer had begun to achieve a vague conception of the importance of the principle of the necessity for self-sufficiency in Hualcan. This principle was unconsciously used as a part of the presentation of the argument for the "experiment" to Miguel when the proposal was phrased in terms of allowing the calves to have their due and not withholding from them the means to cope with the world on their own terms. However, the writer did not adequately understand the female principle in Hualcan. As has been pointed out, the female is the "gatekeeper" of gratification. If this principle can be applied to cows, then the cows themselves were the "gatekeepers" to their own milk supply. In no sense could the milk be said to "belong" to the calves. Rather, by applying the principle which enjoins sharing with those who "count," the cows were obligated to their human caretakers who protected them from predatory animals, nursed them when they were sick, and furnished them with food in the form of pasture. Cows, after all, do not own land. Consequently, if anyone is "due" the milk, it is the people who take care of the cows.

Yet the principle of self-sufficiency is not without applicability to the growth and development of calves. It is simply applied in a way which was unanticipated. The call to action is applied to calves as it is to humans, parallel with self-sufficiency, and calves are enjoined to seek independence early. As the calves grew older, it was observed that the household members made systematic and successful attempts to wean the calves. For the first weeks the calves were allowed free access to their mothers. At the end of this period morning milkings were begun. At the same time, the calves were encouraged to eat more grass, and choice leaves and blades were offered to them. It cannot be said that Hualcainos are lacking in concern for the well-being of their cattle. The family members pointed out that it was advisable to get the calf used to taking care of itself early, that it was not good for it to be too dependent upon its mother. Anything can happen to a cow. For the calf ultimate satisfaction and service lies precisely in self-sufficiency within the rules of the system.

In the context of Hualcan culture, the proposal as it was originally stated was meaningless. The subjects of the "experiment" worked out a resolution of the problem which was set before them: they ignored it. Miguel and his family were frank in explaining, to the best of their ability, why they did not wish to continue attempting the impossible. While the writer had some prestige in their eyes he had no power. If coercion had been possible and had been attempted, the family would have conformed openly but they would have continued their traditional practices in secret, and they would have been amused at the trick they were playing on the outsider. The Hualcan ethical system does not apply completely to the outsider and Hualcainos feel their greatest solidarity in many situations where relationships with outsiders are involved. Since they fear outsiders and feel themselves to be powerless and ineffective in dealings with them, Hualcainos find it difficult to be direct. Instead, they tend to assume confusion and lack of understanding.[4] They try to take advantage of the outsider, stealing from him if possible.

This type of behavior is in conformity to another organizing principle of Hualcan culture, that of the supernatural danger of the outside world. Some of this evil power adheres to the Hualcaino who visits the outside. An out-

---

[4] As a case in point: Once one of the writer's colleagues in the field came to Hualcan for a visit. When he presented himself at the house, the family at first denied all knowledge of the writer. When pressed, they denied knowledge of his whereabouts. Finally they sent the visitor off in the opposite direction from the house where they knew the writer to be.

sider brings it into the community. While outsiders effectively control Hualcan and the Hualcainos, as *hacienda*-owners who control the household economies of their *peones,* as townsmen who exact labor tribute, or as political authorities with the means of physical coercion, they are also believed to be dangerous in a supernatural sense. Many outsiders are conceived as demons of one type or another, or they are thought to bear evil powers which make people sick with tuberculosis or syphilis. It is only after social interaction has gone on, when the stranger is no longer strange, that most Hualcainos are able to assess the outsider as a fellow human being who, if slightly contaminated, is not particularly dangerous.

Matters relating to the supernatural are not irrelevant to the context of animal husbandry. God is conceived in Hualcan as the supreme power who has arranged the world in its present form for His own reasons. He has placed good and evil forces in the world in a kind of balance. His relatives, the Saints, are more approachable and are in fact the mediators between man and God. The Hualcaino therefore prays not to God but to Santa Ursula, the patroness of Hualcan. The household economy of any family depends upon destiny which is equated with God's will. If the fields produce well, for example, it is a sign that one has fulfilled one's obligations to the supernatural powers and has achieved harmony with the field of forces of the universe. Bad luck in agriculture is a sign that something is lacking in one's obligations or that one has become contaminated with evil power. Blasphemy brings as a supernatural sanction contamination with holy power. Therefore, if one's animals are poor, the matter is between oneself and God, to be mediated by God's representatives, the priests, or by Santa Ursula. The condition of the livestock varies according to God's will and not according to man's efforts. Livestock can be protected and one's herds can become numerous and healthy through devotion to God's will, by serving Him and His relatives through ritual practices and labor. It would be presumptuous for a human to pretend to assume control over the destiny of his own livestock. It is man's duty to accept the destiny which God gives him and to try to achieve harmony within these limits. At the same time, if one fulfills the letter of one's compact with God, if one devotes oneself to labor and to the honor of God and the Saints, one's destiny can be changed. However, this is a matter of appeal to the supernatural and not one of human action. In a religious sense, therefore, the avenue to the control over the condition of the livestock is defined as supernatural. God, not more milk, is the deciding factor in the maturation of calves.

CONCLUSION

The "experiment" failed because of the lack of control over a multitude of human factors which have been outlined in the preceding section. These factors make sense in Hualcan terms, despite superficial inconsistencies. It would be apparent in terms of Western logic that one cannot be at the same time self-sufficient economically, a good relative who shares his things freely, and an honorable man in terms of compactual responsibility. The principle of the call to action is hardly compatible with the idea of the acceptance of destiny, or God's will, and the principle behind the procedure of enlisting God's aid through service and ingratiation is a contradiction of both. Yet in the Hualcan system these principles are not contradictory; rather, they are applied in any real situation in different ways. No Hualcaino senses tension or feels disturbed.[5]

There is little conflict or ambivalence in the decisions which are made with regard to problems of milk supply for Hualcan calves. Similar assessments of situations occur regularly in Hualcan, based on the Hualcan system of thought. It is not so much a matter of *which* principles are applied to a situation but *how* they are applied. Such integration is dynamic: situations can change, and some principles may become emphasized, while the integrative significance of others diminishes.

The terms of the original proposal which called for a change in Hualcan dairying practices would have created conflict by bringing about an abnormal situation, or series of situations, relating to the several aspects of milk-handling and calf-care, had the Hualcainos accepted the goal and the means. Fortunately, they accepted neither. The Hualcainos might have been favorably influenced in their assessment of the new idea if the potential conflicts which accompanied the proposed means could have been resolved. In daily life Hualcainos dispose of countless complex problems in terms of their own definitions of the nature of the social and physical world. If an innovator had introduced the idea of more milk for calves and had made the goal of greater control over the destiny of livestock understandable, attractive, and feasible, and if objective evidence of the utility of the means could have been furnished, many Hualcainos would no doubt have made the attempt to incorporate the new trait into their lives. If the innovator had been equipped to phrase the proposal in accord with the principles of Hualcan culture the "experiment" would have had more chance of success. This would have meant the achievement of an understanding of Hualcan principles and their integration in order to gain some basis for making reasonable predictions of how the situation would be assessed by the Hualcainos. The evidence sug-

---

[5] The criteria of tension and disturbance are used in a definition of cultural integration by Albert K. Cohen as follows: ". . . integration, in the cultural sense, is a matter of tension on the level of action . . . whether or not two norms [give] rise to felt disturbances or tensions [is] a function of situations. That is, if norm "A" prescribes a certain mode of action towards objects and situations with the characteristic "a," and norm "B" prescribes a different mode of action towards objects and situations with the characteristic "b," the consistency of the two norms or their capacity to generate tension depends on the extent to which the social system generates situations which combine both characteristics "a" and "b"." ("On Definitions of Integration," Social Science Research Council Social Integration Seminar. MS., 1952, p. 4.)

gests that some substitute for milk would have been required in the relevant contexts in order to avoid disruptions of patterns of milk production, distribution, and consumption, and repercussions in the wider social context. The writer, with limited means, would not have been able to furnish a milk substitute had he understood its necessity. Therefore, from both methodological and ethical standpoints, the "experiment" should never have been attempted.

31

The Use of Survey Methods in a Citizens' Campaign Against Discrimination

Claire Selltiz

This article presents a report of the efforts of a committee to reduce interracial discrimination. A significant aspect of the report is its description of three stages in an attempt to effect social change: (1) the fact-finding procedure, (2) the method of effecting social change, and (3) the evaluation of the effectiveness of the campaign to change the existing forms of interpersonal relations in one narrow sphere.

In 1950 a group of citizens of New York City, working with limited and unpaid professional assistance, organized and carried out a campaign to reduce discrimination in restaurants in an area around the United Nations building. The event is of interest to social science because the group evaluated its suc-

Reprinted from *Human Organization,* **14,** 3 (Fall 1955), pp. 19–25, by permission of The Society for Applied Anthropology and the author.

Claire Selltiz is Research Scientist, Research Center for Human Relations, New York University.

The project reported here was carried out by a group of citizens, all volunteers. Limitations of space make it impossible to give credit to all those who participated. Among the lay participants, however, special mention should be made of Mr. Snowden T. Herrick and Mrs. Edna A. Merson, who served as chairmen of the Committee. A number of social scientists served as technical consultants: Drs. Kenneth B. Clark, Dan Dodson, Samuel H. Flowerman, Herbert Hyman, Patricia Kendall, Sophia M. Robison, and the author.

cess by a systematic comparison of restaurant practices before and after the campaign. While a number of communities have undertaken "self-surveys" of discriminatory practices, this is the only case known to the writer in which the results of the undertaking have been objectively measured.

The project was carried out by the Committee on Civil Rights in East Manhattan. The Committee was organized in the spring of 1949, "to compare public practices now existing in East Manhattan and those principles upon which our democracy was founded." The Committee is composed of representatives of 23 affiliated organizations, plus a few individual members-at-large. About half of the member groups represent specific minorities or have as their primary concern the reduction of discrimination and prejudice. The others represent broad community interests; they include such groups as branches of the American Association of University Women, of Americans for Democratic Action, of the Welfare and Health Council of New York City, and the Uptown Chamber of Commerce.

Both the organizational representatives and the members-at-large are more or less ordinary citizens. Although above average in education and in concern with problems of civil rights, they are not especially prominent in the community. They include, for example, housewives, schoolteachers, a public relations consultant, an editor, a photographer, a salesman, a biochemist, a group worker, a personnel director, an attorney, and a few persons working professionally in the field of intergroup relations. In addition to these "ordinary citizens," CCREM enlisted a number of prominent persons as sponsors and several social scientists as technical consultants.

In selecting its first project, CCREM recognized two criteria: the importance to the life of minority group members of practices in the area, and feasibility of investigating them.

Employment and housing were considered more important than public accommodations in their effects on the lives of minority group members, but they presented serious problems by way of gathering accurate information. Committee members were generally skeptical of the trustworthiness of information from interviews with persons responsible for policy and practices. Nor were they more favorably inclined to basing their conclusions on information from people opposed to discrimination and presumably in a position to know the facts. They wanted to come out with findings which could not be successfully challenged. Thus, they wanted to test practices—specifically, by determining whether majority group and minority group members, matched in all other relevant respects, would be treated alike in a given situation.

The fields of housing and employment seemed too formidable for such testing by the as yet inexperienced Committee. Public accommodations seemed to be much easier to tackle by this approach. The Committee recognized that this field is less crucial than others in its bearing on the lives of minority group members, but nevertheless it seemed sufficiently important to merit investigation. It was, therefore, decided that the Committee's first survey would deal with the practices of eating places—with the further simplification of limiting the study to one minority group, Negroes.

To reduce the scope of the project still further, the Committee decided to cover only the eastern half of midtown Manhattan, with its high concentration of restaurants. At the time, it seemed likely that a similar group would investigate the practices of eating places in west midtown. An area of about 150 square blocks was selected—from Fifth Avenue to the East River, and from Thirty-fourth Street to Fifty-ninth Street. This neighborhood was especially interesting because it includes the site of the United Nations building, with its personnel from many lands.

PREPARING FOR THE INITIAL SURVEY

Development of the Measuring Instrument

In the course of the discussions which led to the selection of eating places as the subject of the first survey, it had been decided that two teams—one consisting of two Negroes, the other of two white persons—would go to each restaurant, ostensibly as ordinary diners. Starting from the assumption that democratic practice requires the giving of equal service to all persons regardless of race, discrimination was defined as any inequality between the treatment accorded the two teams, unless there seemed reason to believe that the difference in treatment was due to some factor other than the difference in race.

The measuring instrument, then, must be such as to provide accurate comparison of the treatment given the two teams. It took the form of a questionnaire report to be filled out separately by each team after they had left the restaurant. Emphasis was placed on objective information which could easily be subjected to statistical analysis rather than on subjective or narrative reports.

The first step in preparing the questionnaire was to list the possible ways in which discrimination might be shown. The most obvious, of course, would be refusal to serve the Negro team. In view of the New York State Civil Rights Law, such refusal might be expressed deviously rather than forthrightly, by claiming, for instance, that reservations were necessary, or by simply keeping the Negroes waiting indefinitely. Short of refusal to serve the minority team, the following possible milder forms of discrimination were listed:

1. Evidences of confusion at the appearance of the Negro team or of hesitation about admitting them, such as a hasty conference between headwaiter and waiter, shifting of waiters, etc.

2. Directing the Negro team to a table in an undesirable location: one which would be considered poor by most customers, regardless of race (tables near the kitchen, near a lavatory, etc.); or one which placed the Negroes

out of view of other diners (tables in a back corner, on a balcony, in a separate room, etc.).

3. Poor service: markedly slower than that given other customers; markedly faster than that given other customers, in an apparent attempt to get the Negroes out of the restaurant as quickly as possible; rudeness by restaurant employees; statements that items of food ordered were not available when in fact they were.

4. Inferior food: excessive amounts of salt or other spices added to the food served the Negro team; decayed food; etc.,

5. Overcharges.

Questions were framed to get the information necessary to judge whether or not each form of discrimination had been practiced. Wherever possible, the questions called for short factual answers: "When did you enter the restaurant?" "When were you seated?" "Did you pick your own table, or were you assigned by a restaurant employee?" "Was the table assigned to you located in any of the following places . . . ?" A few questions called for evaluations or subjective impressions; for example, "Did you feel you were being hurried as compared with other persons served by the same waiter?" Such questions were followed by attempts to get the evidence on which such judgments were based: "What made you feel that way?" or "State your reasons" or "Please describe."

In order to make possible an analysis of characteristics of resturants which might be related to discrimination, the questionnaire called for information on the following points: price of dinner, nationality of cuisine, location of restaurant, number of employees, race of employees, extent of occupancy at the time of the test.

Pilot Survey of Luncheonettes

At about the time the questionnaire was being put into final form, two students from the New York School of Social Work of Columbia University volunteered to conduct a pilot survey. Luncheonettes and drugstores serving food were selected for this pilot study, which took place in the period May 8–29, 1950. The procedures and findings have been reported fully by the two students who took responsibility for this part of the survey; [1] only a brief summary will be given here. Forty-nine of the 227 luncheonettes and drugstores in the area (that is, approximately one fifth of the total number) were tested. No discrimination of any kind was found in any of the places tested; in every case the treatment given the Negro team was substantially the same as that given the majority team.

This pilot test indicated the need for only minor revisions in the testing

---

[1] Phyllis Landa and Gerard Littman, "A Pilot Study to Test Discriminatory Practices against Ethnic Minority Groups in Public Eating Accommodations: An Audit to Determine the Degree of Discrimination Practiced against Negroes in Luncheonettes" (unpublished thesis, New York School of Social Work of Columbia University, 1950).

instructions and report form. However, it revealed serious organizational and administrative problems—in recruiting testers, making assignments, filling out and returning report forms, supervising progress, etc.—and led to much more careful planning of these aspects in the survey of restaurants proper.

Selecting the Sample of Restaurants to Be Tested

Since no complete list of restaurants was available, a complete enumeration was made during the winter and spring of 1950 by volunteers who walked through every block in the area, recording each eating place—its name, address, price range, and any other relevant information which could be secured. The enumeration produced a list of 771 eating places within the area—including restaurants proper, luncheonettes, drugstores, cafeterias, bars and grills, cocktail lounges and night clubs.

In view of the findings of the pilot study, the 227 luncheonettes and drugstores were removed from the list. As the Committee proceeded in its deliberations, its originally ambitious plans were gradually whittled down by realistic considerations. It was finally decided that limitations of personnel and funds made it impossible to test an adequate sample of the remaining 544 eating places; some categories would have to be omitted from the survey. Cafeterias were dropped on the ground that their practices were probably quite similar to those of luncheonettes, in which no discrimination had been found. It was decided also to omit bars and grills, cocktail lounges, and night clubs, on the grounds that these were not primarily eating places and that they presented special problems in testing.

Hence, the survey concentrated on restaurants proper, of which there were 364 listed in the area, ranging in price of an average meal from 75¢ to $10.00. It was decided to stratify on the basis of price, the variable most suspected of being relevant to the likelihood of discrimination.

The cards on which the data about each restaurant had been entered were arranged in order of the estimated price of an average meal. At the beginning of the week scheduled for testing, teams were available for 47 tests. It was decided to reduce the population about which statements were to be made, rather than to reduce the accuracy of the findings, by using less than a 25 per cent sample. This was done by narrowing the price range to be covered, focusing on restaurants in the middle of the range. The median card was selected as the first case in the sample; the other cases were selected by taking, alternately, every fourth card above and every fourth card below the median. As additional teams were set up during the week, the sample was expanded. The final sample consisted of 62 restaurants, constituting 25 per cent of the 248 restaurants with average prices from $1.30 to $3.75.

Recruiting and Training the Testers

The volunteers who carried out the tests were recruited from the member organizations of CCREM, from other interested organizations, and from among friends of Committee members. There were 153 testers in all: 68

Negroes and 85 white persons, from 25 different organizations. All the testers were of pleasing appearance, quiet in manner, well but not ostentatiously dressed. All the minority group members were judged to be recognizably Negro; persons so light-skinned that they were not likely to be identified as Negroes by restaurant personnel were asked not to participate.

In both the minority and the control groups, there were twice as many women as men. More than 80 per cent of each group were between the ages of 21 and 45. The testers were distinctly above average in education and socioeconomic status. The great majority (90 per cent of the control testers and 76 per cent of the Negro testers) had attended college. Only one (a member of the control group) had not attended high school. Of the minority group, 34 per cent were engaged in professional or semiprofessional work, 25 per cent had clerical or sales jobs, and 16 per cent were students. Of the control group, 49 per cent were engaged in professional or semiprofessional work, 21 per cent had clerical or sales jobs, and 14 per cent were housewives.

An intensive training session was held the evening before testing began. The training instructions had four main themes: an injunction that all testers approach the situation open-mindedly, without preconceptions that they would either find or not find discrimination; the need for all teams to follow the same standardized procedures so that the results would be comparable; the importance of remaining passive regardless of the treatment given the minority team in order not to affect the practices of the restaurant and thus invalidate the test results; and the necessity for careful but unobtrusive noting of details of time, location, etc.

THE INITIAL SURVEY

The testing took place on six nights during the period June 16–23, 1950, omitting Saturday and Sunday. All tests were conducted during the dinner hour, with teams entering the restaurants between 6:30 and 7:30 P.M.

The basic procedure was very simple: a Negro team and a white team went to each restaurant, and the treatment given the two teams was compared. The white team had two functions: first, to serve as a control against which the treatment given the Negro team could be measured; second, to observe, insofar as they could, the treatment given to the Negro team.

As far as possible, the two teams were matched except in skin color. If the Negro team consisted of two men, the white team going to the same restaurant consisted of two men; similarly, both teams might consist of two women, or of a man and a woman. With few exceptions, both teams were of about the same age. Since the entire group of testers was quite homogeneous in socioeconomic level, in dress, and in general social behavior, no special effort was made to match teams on such factors as these.

The two teams assigned to a given restaurant separated before reaching the vicinity of the restaurant they were to test. The minority team entered the restaurant first so that there could be no question as to which team was entitled to be seated first and no possibility that the white team might be given a more desirable table simply because they had arrived first. The minority team was followed closely—less than a minute later—by the control team. All testers had been given general instructions as to the type of meal to order, to eliminate possible differences in time needed to prepare food or possible differences in treatment related to the prices of the meals ordered within a given restaurant.

Each team left the restaurant as soon as its two members had finished eating, still without giving any indication of acquaintance with the other team, and returned to the Committee's headquarters. There the two members of each team jointly filled out the team's report form, without discussing their experiences with the opposite team or indeed with anyone else until the form had been completed. The questionnaire was checked for completeness and clarity by a member of the Committee. Then the two teams who had tested a given restaurant came together, and a member of the Committee compared the two reports, asking for details on any points which were not clear or where the reports differed. At this time, most disagreement between the teams (and there were very few) were resolved by discussion; in the two or three cases where there was genuine disagreement as to what had happened or why it had happened, the supervisor wrote a detailed report of the versions given by each team. Final judgment as to whether the two teams had in fact been given approximately equal treatment was left to a committee of eight coders.

Description of the Restaurants Tested

As stated earlier, 62 restaurants were tested, constituting 25 per cent of all the restaurants within the geographic area and price range previously described. The sample was checked against the enumeration in terms of price and location and was found to be representative, except for a slight under-representation of one corner of the area.

Of the 62 restaurants tested, 39 served American food and 23 specialized in foreign dishes (11 French, 8 Italian, 2 French-Italian, 1 German, 1 Swedish). At the time the teams entered, 42 per cent of the restaurants were less than half full, 21 per cent were about half full, 21 per cent were about three-quarters full, 11 per cent were about full but with no people waiting, and 5 per cent had people waiting for tables. About one third had less than five waiters or other visible service staff, another third had from 5 to 9, and another third had 10 or more. About three fourths of the restaurants had a headwaiter or hostess. Only 9 of the 62 had any nonwhite employees who were visible, that is, waiters, bus boys, etc.

Deciding Whether Discrimination Had Occurred

As has been stated, the questionnaire, the training of testers, and the testing procedures were all designed to secure objective information and to minimize the effects of possible bias on the part of the testers. The judgment as to whether the treatment reported actually showed inequality, and hence discrimination, was left to eight members of the Committee who served as coders. Preliminary classification was done by coders working in pairs; finally the whole group of coders, acting as a committee, reviewed all the tests and made the final decisions as to whether or not there had been clear inequality of treatment.

The decisions of the coders as to whether the minority team had received discriminatory treatment in a given restaurant were based on their judgment as to whether the facts reported indicated clearly that the minority team was treated less well than the control team and that the inferior treatment could not reasonably be considered accidental. In reaching their decisions, the coders took into account such factors as whether discriminatory treatment was manifested in more than one way (thus lessening the likelihood that any given action might have been accidental), whether both teams reported the treatment as unequal, etc. The final decision rested on the convincingness of the evidence reported. Whenever there was reasonable ground for believing that inferior treatment given the minority group might have been accidental, the case was not considered one of discrimination, even if both teams reported that the minority was given less good treatment.

Findings

In no resturant was the minority team refused service, nor was there any attempt to avoid serving them by such devices as saying that reservations were needed or by making them wait indefinitely without being given a table. However, in 26 restaurants (42 per cent of those tested; $Op = 6.3$) the minority team was given treatment so clearly inferior to that given the control team as to be considered discriminatory. In no case was the control team treated less well than the minority team.

Types of Discriminatory Treatment. Unequal treatment was of two general types: assignment of the Negro team to a table in an undesirable location, and giving poorer service to the Negro team than to the control team. Table 1 shows the number of restaurants in which each of these types of discriminatory treatment was encountered.

In about 70 per cent of the restaurants, the testers were assigned to tables by a headwaiter or other restaurant employee. In these restaurants where tables were assigned, there was a marked tendency to give the minority team a less desirable table than the control team. The control teams were given undesirable tables in 9 of the 62 restaurants tested, whereas the minority teams were given undesirable tables in 28 of the 62 restaurants. In each case, in addition to rating the desirability of the table given each team, the testers rated the comparative desirability of the two tables. In only one case was the control team reported as having a less desirable table than the minority team. In 17 restaurants the minority teams were given clearly less desirable tables than the controls, even though other tables were available.

In no case did the control team report being treated rudely, being made to wait out of turn for a table, receiving unduly slow service, or other evidence of reluctance to serve them. In contrast, there were 21 cases in which the minority team was given such clearly inferior service that the restaurants were classified as discriminatory. In 19 of these cases, the minority team was treated rudely by one or more restaurant employees; in 7 of these 19, they were also made to wait considerably longer for service than diners at nearby tables. In three restaurants the minority team was hurried to the point of inconvenience, although nearby diners were not hurried.

TABLE 1. Types of Discriminatory Treatment, Initial Survey

Types of Discrimination	Number of Restaurants
Less desirable location only	5
Poorer service or rudeness only	9
Both less desirable location and poorer service	12
	26

Characteristics of Discriminatory Restaurants. The only observed characteristic in which the restaurants which discriminated differed significantly from those which did not discriminate was price.[2] As shown in Table 2, discrimination was encountered in one seventh of the restaurants in the $1.30–$1.99 price range, and in slightly more than half of those where the average price of the meal was between $2.00 and $3.99.

TABLE 2. Frequency of Incidents of Discrimination in Restaurants in Various Price Ranges—Initial Survey

Price of Average Meal	Number Tested	Number with Incidents	Per Cent of Incidents to Number Tested
$1.30–1.99	21	3	14
$2.00–2.99	26 ⎫ 41	15 ⎫ 23	58 ⎫ 56
$3.00–3.99*	15 ⎭	8 ⎭	53 ⎭

*The prices actually paid differed slightly from the estimates based on the enumeration. This is why the upper price limit here is higher than that reported in the selection of the sample.

---

[2] Where the number of cases and the lowest expected theoretical frequencies were sufficiently large, probabilities were calculated by Chi-square. Where the number of cases or the theoretical frequencies were too low to justify the use of Chi-square, probabilities were calculated by Fisher's exact test for fourfold tables and multiplied by two to make them comparable to a two-tailed test such as Chi-square. The differernce in the frequency of discrimination between restaurants in the $1.30 to $1.99 price range and those in the $2.00 to $3.99 range, as shown in Table 2, is significant beyond the one per cent level ($p = .003$). With regard to all of the other characteristics considered, as described in the following paragraph, the statistical tests indicated that the obtained differences in frequency of discrimination between restaurants in different categories might be expected to occur by chance more than 8 times in 100 (p's ranged from .09 to .70).

When price was held constant, no significant differences in frequency of discrimination were found between American and foreign restaurants, between restaurants with and without headwaiters, nor among the geographic sections of the survey area. There was no relation between the size of the visible staff and the occurrence of discrimination, nor between the occupancy of the restaurant and the occurrence of discrimination.

THE ACTION PROGRAM

The next question was: What steps should be taken to reduce—or, hopefully, eliminate—discriminatory practices? CCREM enunciated two principles: that its approach would be "educational" and persuasive rather than militant, and that it would attempt to enlist broad community support for a change in practices. There was no assumption that this approach would necessarily be the most effective one under all circumstances, but it seemed promising, and it seemed the one most appropriate for a group representing such a range of organizations as CCREM's affiliates.

Activities Directed Toward the Restaurant Field

The Committee turned its attention first toward the organizations of persons with responsibility for policies and practices in restaurants; associations of restaurant owners and unions of restaurant employees. There were 9 such organizations operating in the area at the time: 7 management associations, and 2 union groups (one of which was a Joint Board representing 12 hotel and restaurant unions). Representatives of CCREM held one or more conversations with the officers of each of these organizations. Within four months after the first contact, all of the groups had signed pledges of equal treatment to all patrons both in seating and in service.

The next step was to send a letter to the owner or manager of each of the 364 restaurants in the area, informing him of the survey findings and of the organizational pledges, and enclosing an individual pledge for his signature. This letter was followed by three others during the next year. A total of 127 pledges were signed and returned, representing approximately one third of the restaurants in the area. Eleven of the owners added notes expressing their sympathy with the campaign and offering to help.

A more direct personal approach seemed called for in the case of restaurants which had been found to discriminate. A fundamental policy of the Committee was that no individual restaurant would be named in any public discussion of the survey findings, since the sample had been selected randomly and was assumed to be representative of all restaurants in the area. This did not, however, rule out the possiblity of individual conferences with the managers of restaurants where discrimination had been encountered.

The Committee planned to talk individually with the managers of each of the restaurants in which discrimination had been found. This program was not completed, largely because of lack of personnel; most of the Committee members have full-time jobs and are not able to visit restaurants at the odd daytime hours when restaurants are free. The interviews which were carried out, however, were of considerable interest and showed a wide range of reactions. At one extreme was the manager of a small relatively inexpensive hotel restaurant. She seemed completely cooperative, expressed surprise at the Committee's report of the treatment received in her restaurant, and volunteered to issue instructions to her employees that all patrons were to be treated alike. At the other extreme was the owner of a small "exclusive" French restaurant in the upper price bracket, who denied that discrimination had occurred in his restaurant and was generally hostile toward the Committee members. There were two conversations with this owner, and two follow-up tests of his restaurant; the final one showed no discrimination.

Activities Directed Toward the Community

The decision to adopt a persuasive approach toward the restaurant industry had entailed a decision not to publicize the survey findings until some progress could be reported—or until the Committee was satisfied that no progress was going to be achieved through persuasion. The Committee's first press release was issued immediately after the signing of pledges by all the restaurant unions and management associations; it reported not only the survey findings but the restaurant industry's pledge to eliminate discrimination. This story was carried in three major New York City newspapers and in two Negro papers with national circulation; it led to mention of the survey or personal appearances of CCREM members on five broadcasts over four radio stations. Later, 10,000 copies of a popular pamphlet about the survey and the follow-up action program, entitled "Have You Heard What's Cooking?", were distributed.

CCREM's conception of its work with the community, however, focused on direct appeals to individuals in organizations rather than on broadside appeals thorugh the mass media. The first step along these lines was a meeting, in April 1951, of those who had participated in the initial test, to inform them of the success in securing pledges from the restaurant organizations and to discuss further plans. This was followed by reports and sociodramatic presentations at meetings of 10 groups affiliated with CCREM or interested in its work.

THE FINAL SURVEY

A retest was carried out in the spring of 1952 to determine what changes, if any, had taken place in the almost two years since the initial test.

Selecting the Sample

The major question in planning the resurvey was whether to retest the same restaurants used in the first audit or to select another representative sample of restaurants in the area. Retesting the old sample had great research advantages because of the greater confidence that any changes found would not reflect chance sampling variations, and because of the possibility of detailed analysis of the characteristics of restaurants which had changed their practices. On the other hand, taking a new sample was attractive for a number of practical reasons. Information about a new sample, when added to that from the original audit, would give data about the practices of a larger total number of restaurants; this was particularly important if subsequent action was to be taken with regard to those which discriminated. Further, testing a new sample would increase the number of restaurants which had at least once had the experience of serving Negro customers. And, incidentally, the members of the Committee would find a new batch of restaurants more interesting.

Resources were not great enough to allow for retesting the entire old sample and a sufficiently large new sample to give reliable results, so a compromise was adopted. It was decided to retest all the restaurants which had been found discriminatory in the first survey and half of those which had been found nondiscriminatory, and to test a new sample of 50 restaurants. In the analysis, the nondiscriminatory restaurants would be weighted so that they would account for their proper proportion of an original sample.

No sampling procedure was needed, of course, to identify the old discriminatory restaurants; all 26 of them were to be tested. The cards of the 36 which had not discriminated in 1950 were arranged in order of price, and every other one selected. One of these turned out to have gone out of business, leaving 17 to be tested. The enumeration cards which had been prepared in the winter and spring of 1950 were used as the basis for selection of the new sample. After the cards for the 62 restaurants in the original sample and those of a few which were known to have gone out of business were removed, there were 175 cards within the price range covered by the initial survey. From these cards, arranged in order of price, a sample of 50 restaurants was selected by taking every fifth card, then every tenth one of the remaining cards.

Procedures

The tests were carried out at the dinner hour during the period of March 21 to April 1, 1952, omitting Saturday and Sunday. Training, testing, reporting, and coding procedures were essentially the same as in the first audit, except for minor changes designed to insure greater clarity in the reports.

In this second audit there were 272 testers: 130 minority group members, 142 in the control group. They came from about 40 different organizations. Although only 37 of the 272 had taken part in the initial survey, as a group they were very similar to the 1950 testers in age, sex, education, and occupation.

Description of the Restaurants Tested

A total of 93 restaurants was tested. The old sample, of course, remained the same in such characteristics as geographical location, nationality of food, size of staff, and character of staff. The new sample differed slightly in some of these characteristics.

The geographic distribution of the restaurants tested again differed slightly from that of the total population of restaurants within the area. Again about two thirds of the restaurants tested served American food, one third specialized in foreign dishes, mostly French or Italian. Again, about one third of the restaurants had less than 5 waiters or other visible staff, one third had from 5 to 9, and one third had 10 or more. Approximately 80 per cent had a headwaiter or hostess. Again, only a very few restaurants had any visible nonwhite employees.

As might be expected, prices had risen; whereas the prices paid per meal in the first test had ranged from $1.30 to $3.99, they now ranged from $1.37 to $4.77. Since the percentage increases were fairly consistent, it was possible to set up new categories which included approximately the same proportions of restaurants as those in the first survey. The two sets of categories are shown in Table 3.

TABLE 3. Price Categories, 1950 and 1952

CATEGORIES	1950	1952
"Lower priced"	$1.30–1.99	$1.37–2.27
"Medium priced"	$2.00–2.99	$2.28–3.37
"Higher priced"	$3.00–3.99	$3.38–4.77

Although no relation between the occurrence of discrimination and the fullness or emptiness of the restaurant had been found in the first survey, the hypothesis had been offered that restaurant business might be worse (or better) in 1952 than it had been in 1950, and that this might account for any difference found in the prevalence of discrimination. The extent of occupancy during the two audits, however, was found to be almost identical.

TABLE 4. Types of Discriminatory Treatment, Final Survey [3]

TYPES OF DISCRIMINATION	NUMBER OF RESTAURANTS
Less desirable location only	6
Poorer service or rudeness only	2
Both less desirable location and poorer service	7
	15

[3] This table, as well as all subsequent discussion which deals only with the discriminatory restaurants, is based on the 15 restaurants in which discrimination occurred; in view of the small number of cases, the two formerly nondiscriminatory restaurants which now showed discrimination have not been weighted.

In summary, the second sample was similar in all major aspects to the one originally tested, both being fairly representative of all restaurants in the given price range within the geographical area bounded by Fifth Avenue, the East River, 34th Street, and 59th Street.

TABLE 5. Frequency of Incidents of Discrimination in Restaurants in Various Price Ranges—Initial and Final Surveys

	1950	1952 (TOTAL SAMPLE, WEIGHTED)
PRICE RANGE	PERCENTAGE WHICH DISCRIMINATED	PERCENTAGE WHICH DISCRIMINATED
Lower	14	14
Middle	58	17
Upper	53	15

Findings

As in 1950, in no restaurant was the minority team refused service. More important, there was a marked reduction in the number of restaurants where the minority team encountered discriminatory treatment. In only 16 per cent of the restaurants was the minority team given treatment clearly inferior to that of the control team.[4] This figure (16 per cent) was the same both for the restaurants which were being retested and for the new sample. The difference between this proportion and that found in the first survey—42 per cent—is significant at the 1 per cent level.

Types of Discriminatory Treatment. Again the two major types of discrimination encountered centered around location of tables and quality of service. Table 4 shows the frequency of occurrence of these two types of treatment.

Characteristics of Discriminatory Restaurants. The initial survey had shown markedly greater incidence of discrimination among the restaurants in the middle and upper part of the price range tested than among those in the lower part of the price range. Table 5 shows the percentages of restaurants in each price range which dicriminated in 1950 and in 1952.

Obviously there was no decrease in the proportion of lower-priced restaurants which discriminated; however, the original low frequency of discrimination in this price range left relatively little room for improvement. The drop in discrimination for both the middle- and upper-priced restaurants is significant at the 1 per cent level.

The small number of restaurants in which discrimination occurred during the retest makes it impossible to carry out any statistical analysis of characteristics related to discrimination. Factors such as nationality of cooking,

---

[4] In one case the reporting was not sufficiently clear to permit a decision as to whether there had been discrimination. This case was dropped from the analysis. The present figure is based on the 92 cases which could be coded, with the nondiscriminatory cases from the original sample weighted (doubled) to account for their proper proportion.

presence of headwaiter, size of staff, geographic location, and occupancy were inspected, but no trends sufficient to establish significance in such a small number of cases appeared.

COMMENT

The drop in discrimination between the first and second surveys provides interesting evidence of the ease and speed with which discriminatory practices can be changed under favorable conditions. There is no assumption that the work of CCREM was exclusively responsible for the marked reduction of discrimination in Manhattan restaurants. The period between the two tests was marked by a general liberalizing of practices with regard to minority groups in many areas of living. Moreover, just before the second survey there had been a change in New York State law, providing for more effective enforcement of the law forbidding discrimination in public accommodations which had long been in existence. Although the new law had not yet gone into effect at the time of the resurvey, it is possible that the news of its passage may have affected restaurant practices. It remains to be seen whether a program of objective fact-finding, followed by educational and persuasive action directed toward the persons responsible for policy and practices in the area and an attempt to enlist community support for the change in practices, can be effective in areas where discrimination is more strongly supported by economic considerations and personal prejudice. CCREM intends to put this question to the test as it turns its attention to the field of private housing.

32

Desegregation Background: The Role of Social Scientists

Kenneth B. Clark

A 1953 issue of the *Journal of Social Issues* was devoted to an appraisal of the evidence presented to the Supreme Court prior to the decision of 1954 regarding desegregation in the public schools. This article, a portion of that issue, presents a summary of the relationship between the lawyers and the social scientists, the latter serving as expert witnesses. Here, then, is a view of the legal profession making direct use of the knowledge of the social scientists.

I. THE BACKGROUND: THE ROLE OF SOCIAL SCIENTISTS

In May 1951, the first of the cases dealing with the problem of the constitutionality of state laws which require racial segregation in public, elementary and high schools was argued in the Federal District Court in Charleston, South Carolina. This case represented the culmination of a series of cases in which the Legal Staff of the National Association for the Advancement of Colored People sought to eliminate various forms of racial discrimination and segregation through court action. In the previous cases which dealt with the problem of discrimination and segregation in state-supported graduate and professional schools, the Legal Staff of the NAACP was successful in having Negro students admitted to these schools which had previously excluded them by proving that the facilities provided by the states for Negroes were inferior to those for whites or that no facilities were provided for Negroes.

In the *Sweatt v. Painter* and the *McLaurin v. Oklahoma State Regents* cases the NAACP for the first time presented an attack on the constitutionality of segregation *per se*. While these cases were decided within the 1896 *Plessy v. Ferguson* "separate but equal" framework, the standards of equality were set so high by the court as to make it difficult, if not impossible, to maintain racial segregation at the state-supported graduate and professional school level. These decisions, however, were so narrowly drawn—they were specifically related only to graduate and professional education—that they could not be considered determinative of the general issue of the constitution-

Reprinted from the *Journal of Social Issues*, **9**, 4 (1953), pp. 2–12, by permission of The Society for the Psychological Study of Social Issues and the author.

Kenneth B. Clark is Professor of Psychology and Director, Social Dynamics Institute, C.C.N.Y., City University of New York.

ality of segregation in education. The Legal Staff then decided to raise this constitutional question at the elementary and secondary schools level. A decision at this level would be considered crucial to the perpetuation of segregation.

The South Carolina case in 1951 reflected this legal decision to approach the specific problem of racial segregation in education in elementary and secondary schools. This case was not argued within the legal framework of the Plessy doctrine. The lawyers of the NAACP asserted as their primary legal argument that the fact of state-imposed racial segregation itself is a violation of the constitutionally guaranteed rights of the Negro as an American citizen. In developing this argument in this and the subsequent cases, these lawyers relied primarily upon the "equal protection" and "due process" clauses of the Fourteenth Amendment. In establishing this point before the courts, it was necessary to show not only that the educational facilities provided for the Negro students were inferior to those for whites, but also that compulsory racial segregation in elementary and high schools inflicts injuries on these Negro pupils. Evidence in support of the contention that the facilities were unequal was presented by professional educators and was not contested by the State of South Carolina or in a subsequent case by the State of Virginia. This evidence was the type presented in the earlier graduate and professional school cases.

Proof of the arguments that segregation itself is inequality and that state-imposed racial segregation inflicts injuries upon the Negro had to come from the social psychologists and other social scientists.[1] Because of this fact, it was necessary in the trying of these public school cases to develop an extensive collaboration between social psychologists and the legal profession, particularly the legal staff of the NAACP. This collaboration began before the trial of the first case at the Federal District Court level and continued through the argument (December 1952) and reargument (December 1953) before the United States Supreme Court. The details and extent of this collaboration are presented here for the record and in order to serve as a guide for future collaboration between social psychologists and other social scientists and the legal profession.

In their work with the lawyers, the social psychologists assumed the following responsibilities:

1. They testified in the Federal District Courts and in one State Court as expert witnesses on the effects of segregation on personality development, the effects of school segregation in lowering of motivation and impairing

---

[1] For a preliminary discussion of the role of social scientists as expert witnesses in these public school segregation cases and a consideration of some of the general problems which social scientists must solve as they seek to function in this area see: Clark, K. B., "The Social Scientist As An Expert Witness in Civil Rights Litigation," *Social Problems,* **1,** 1 (1953), pp. 5–10.

ability to learn, the social and psychological significance of a state-imposed racially segregated society, the consequences of desegregation, and the relationship between desegregation on the graduate and professional school level and the possibilities of desegregating the elementary and high schools. One social psychologist examined the Negro children involved in three of these cases with appropriate projective techniques and interviews in order to determine whether they showed evidence of personality distortions related to racial discrimination and segregation.

2. They prepared an *Appendix to Appellants' Briefs* entitled "The Effects of Segregation and the Consequences of Desegregation: A Social Science Statement." This appendix was submitted to and accepted by the United States Supreme Court during the October term, 1952, and was considered in conjunction with the legal briefs submitted in the South Carolina (*Briggs v. Elliott*), Kansas (*Brown v. Board of Education of Topeka*), and the Virginia (*Davis v. County School Board*) cases in the first argument before the U.S. Supreme Court in December 1952.

3. They collected and analyzed relevant data on actual incidents of racial desegregation. This material was made available to the lawyers for their use in answering one of the five questions which the U.S. Supreme Court posed as the basis for the reargument in December 1953.

4. One social psychologist, the present author, acted as general social science consultant to the Legal Staff of the NAACP. In this capacity, he served as liaison between the lawyers and the social psychologists who participated in these cases either as expert witnesses or in helping to prepare the social science brief or both. It was his responsibility, further, to advise the lawyers on such matters as the special areas of competence of prospective expert witnesses; to suggest competent individuals who might accept the responsibility of testifying as expert witnesses; to approach such individuals when so directed by the Legal Staff; to attend certain conferences of the Legal Staff of the NAACP in order to become familiar with the legal issues, arguments, and terminology involved in these cases and in order to offer suggestions concerning the limits and scope of available and relevant social psychological data. He and others aided in the preparation of these cases for presentation both at the trial and at the appellate level; and in the Virginia case he and others helped in analyzing the testimony of expert social science witnesses called by defendants so that inconsistencies and weaknesses in their testimony could be brought out in cross-examination.

Social Scientists and Psychologists as Expert Witnesses in the Segregated School Cases

In each of the cases which challenge the validity of state laws requiring segregated schools, a number of educators testified on the educational inequalities between the white and Negro schools and the educational and social consequences of these inequalities. In addition to these educators, social scientists and psychologists gave expert testimony on the social and psychological implications and consequences of segregated schools.

In the South Carolina case, David Krech of the University of California, Helen Trager of Vassar, and Kenneth B. Clark of the College of the City of New York were the psychologists who testified for the plaintiffs. The court also granted permission for the testimony (which was originally given in the Sweatt case) of Robert Redfield of the Department of anthropology of the University of Chicago to be included in the record of this case.

The psychologists and social scientists who testified for the plaintiffs in the Kansas case were Horace B. English of Ohio State University; Wilbur B. Brookover of Michigan State College; Louisa Holt of the University of Kansas and Menninger Clinic; John J. Kane of the Sociology Department at the University of Notre Dame; and Bettie Belk of the Workshop in Human Relations at the University of Kansas City in Missouri.

The following psychologists and social scientists testified for the plaintiffs in the Delaware case: Jerome S. Bruner of Harvard University; Otto Klineberg of Columbia University; George Gorham Lane of the University of Delaware; Kenneth B. Clark; Kenneth Morland of the Department of Sociology and Anthropology at the College of William and Mary; and Frederick B. Parker of the Department of Sociology at the University of Delaware. Dr. Frederick Wertham, a psychiatrist, also testified in this case on the psychiatric consequences of segregated education.

The most extensive use of the testimony of psychologists and social scientists was found in the Virginia case. The attorneys for the defendant and the State of Virginia in this case sought to counteract the effect of the psychological testimony of the NAACP's—plaintiffs—witnesses by presenting their own witnesses who were qualified as experts in psychology and psychiatry. They presented a psychiatrist, Dr. William H. Kelly, and two psychologists: John Nelson Buck, a clinical psychologist, and Henry E. Garrett of Columbia University. The following psychologists appeared as expert witnesses for the plaintiffs in this case: Isidor Chein of New York University; Mamie P. Clark of Northside Center for Child Development (rebuttal testimony); Horace B. English of Ohio State (rebuttal testimony); Alfred McClung Lee of Brooklyn College (rebuttal testimony); M. Brewster Smith, then of Vassar College; and Kenneth B. Clark. Elsa Robinson of New York University assisted in this case but did not testify.

Preparation of the Social Science Brief

The original draft of the social science brief was prepared by a special committee of SPSSI under the chairmanship of Gerhart Saenger, which collected and analyzed the available data and theory on the effects of segregation on personality development. Immediate practical use of this material was not contemplated initially by this committee. As the committee continued to meet, it became apparent to those of its members who were also involved with the work of the Legal Staff of the NAACP that much of the work of the committee would be relevant to the segregated school cases and could be made available to the lawyers in these cases if they felt that they could use it.

The specific responsibility for preparing a preliminary draft of the report was given to Gerhart Saenger, Isidor Chein, and Kenneth B. Clark. The final form of this report which was printed as the *Appendix to Appellants' Briefs* [2] resulted from the collaboration of Isidor Chein, Stuart Cook, and Kenneth B. Clark in revising and rewriting the preliminary draft. Thirty-two social scientists, psychologists, and psychiatrists endorsed this statement which was submitted to the United States Supreme Court over their signatures.

The Nature of the Collaboration

Throughout this collaboration between social scientists and lawyers which was essential to the trial of these segregated school cases, it was necessary to maintain effective communication between the two approaches to social problems. The fact that this type of extensive and intensive collaboration is not common required the development of specific techniques for collaboration, a sensitivity to the many intangibles which might interfere with the most effective interchange of ideas, and an ability of each discipline to be willing to learn the limits and scope of the other and the degree to which the other could be effective in attaining the desired goals.

One of the most effective means of communication was through the legal conferences which were attended by a social scientist. Through these conferences, it was possible for the social scientist to become familiar with the fundamental legal issues and problems involved in the cases and to understand the place of social science data within the larger legal structure of the case. As valuable as were these legal conferences, frequent informal discussions with individual members of the legal staff were equally valuable. In these informal discussions, a more genuine interchange of ideas, concepts, and terminology could occur. In fact, there were times when the lawyers could speak as social psychologists and the social psychologists began to sound like lawyers. In spite of this mutual accommodation, however, a clear distinction of roles and responsibilities had to be maintained for effective collaboration.

In view of the fact that a systematic and empirical approach to the study of society is relatively new and the fact that legal arguments and decisions depend to such a large extent on precedent, the introduction of social science testimony in these cases was an extension of the legal frontiers. There was understandable concern on the part of some of the lawyers about whether

---

[2] This document has been reprinted as "The Effects of Segregation and the Consequences of Desegregation: A Social Science Statement," *Minnesota Law Review,* **37,** 6 (1953), pp. 427–439.

this type of evidence would be admissible in the courts and how it would be evaluated within the normal framework of the legal discipline.

The intensity and duration of this collaboration, furthermore, required a sensitivity to the intangibles of interpersonal relationship. It was necessary for the social scientists and the lawyers to be aware of the fact that the importance of these cases placed a personal stress on the human beings involved. It was essential for these individuals to be flexible and casual in their relations while at the same time capable of expressing mutual respect and appropriate warmth and friendliness as each made his contribution. Fortunately, these conditions were not difficult to obtain in this situation since the liaison person between the social scientists and the lawyers had known many of these lawyers on a friendly basis for many years before assuming this specific role.

Social Science–Legal Collaboration, June to December, 1953

In preparation for the reargument before the United States Supreme Court, it was necessary to continue and broaden the scope of social science collaboration with the Legal Staff of the NAACP. This was so, since the five questions posed by the Court as the basis for this reargument seemed primarily social science rather than legal questions. Of these five questions, two were concerned with the history of the adoption of the Fourteenth Amendment, one was concerned with the power of the Court, and two were concerned with the method of transition from segregated to nonsegregated schools.

The first three questions were clearly within the province of those historians who were specialists in the post Civil War period of American history and in constitutional and legal history. The responsibility for obtaining the historical answers to these questions was, therefore, given to those individuals who were competent in these areas of knowledge and who were willing to contribute their skills and knowledge. The responsibility for the most effective use of this material and the decision as to how it would be used remained, as always, with the Legal Staff of the NAACP. The task of coordinating the work of the many individuals involved in extra legal research at this stage of these cases was assumed by John Davis, a political scientist, now of the College of the City of New York.

An attempt was made to answer Question IV by collecting and analyzing instances of change from a segregated to a nonsegregated situation. It was decided that this task was primarily the responsibility of the social psychologists. The author of this issue was assigned the responsibility for developing a research plan within the limits of the available time and budget in order to obtain empirical answers to this question.

Otto Klineberg and Robert K. Merton of Columbia University aided in the development of the plan and were consulted by the author during the early stages of the actual collection of data. Many other outstanding social scientists contributed to the collection of data in this research. All of the individuals who signed the social science *Appendix to Appellants' Brief* were sent letters requesting help in the search for specific instances of desegregation. The majority responded immediately. Many of those who did not respond at that time could not do so because they were out of the country. It is not possible to list the many individuals who helped in the collection of data for this monograph. In many cases the cited references to unpublished memoranda, reports, and letters in the body of this report reflected those who have helped us in the collection of these data.

Acknowledgements

Special acknowledgement, however, must be made in appreciation of the help and support which have been given by those mentioned above as well as the following: Gordon Allport, Viola W. Bernard, M.D., Alfred McClung Lee, Gardner Murphy, and Goodwin Watson. Robin M. Williams, John Dean, and Robert Johnson of Cornell University Social Science Research Center were generous in making available their time and their extensive research experience. In addition, they made it possible for us to study much of their relevant data by sending us a summary memorandum. Stuart W. Cook and Isidor Chein were most helpful in evaluating the analysis of the empirical data in terms of the specific principles which emerged. In the light of the available evidence, they suggested revisions, additions, and other modifications in the preliminary statement of these principles. The author, however, assumes full responsibility for the final form of this report and the form of the statement of the principles. Brewster Smith contributed more than his skills as an editor to the publication of this manuscript. He was involved in these data from the beginning of the study and contributed his counsel and advice from that time up until the last reference was checked.

Special acknowledgement is also owed to June Shagaloff of the Field Staff of the Legal Division of the NAACP. Miss Shagaloff was assigned to work with the author in the collection of data relevant to the answering of Question IV. She worked indefatigably from the beginning of the project until the completion of the preliminary draft of the manuscript which was presented to the lawyers at their final conference. Miss Shagaloff assumed a major responsibility for the determination of sources of data and much of the responsibility for the actual collection of data in many areas, particularly in the area of public schools, housing, unions, and industry. This research could not have been completed within the allotted time were it not for the quantity and quality of work contributed to it by Miss Shagaloff.

It is necessary also to express my gratitude to my wife, Mamie P. Clark. Her constant encouragement and her practical help contributed significantly to the completion and publication of this issue.

The major credit for the collection and use of these and other relevant data must go to Thurgood Marshall and Robert L. Carter and the other lawyers of the Legal Staff of the NAACP for having the foresight to recognize the need for this type of evidence and testimony, for making the decision to obtain it, and above all, for having the courage to push forward the frontiers of constitutional law and legal precedence by using this testimony at the trial and appellate level of these cases. In doing so, these lawyers made it possible for social science to have a more direct contact with this immediate practical problem of society.

II. THE QUESTION POSED AND THE STRATEGY OF THE REPLY

The Question—Its Implications

Among the questions posed by the United States Supreme Court as the basis for the reargument of the five cases which challenge the constitutionality of state-imposed racial segregation in public elementary and high schools was the following:

(Question IV) Assuming it is decided that segregation in public schools violates the Fourteenth Amendment,
(a) Would a decree necessarily follow providing that, within the limits set by normal geographic school districting, Negro children should forthwith be admitted to schools of their choice, or
(b) May this court, in the exercise of its equity powers, permit an effective gradual adjustment to be brought about from existing segregated systems to a system not based on color distinctions?

In attempting to answer this question, it is necessary to make certain assumptions concerning the intent of the Court in asking it. A basic assumption which must be made is that this question suggests a concern that there might be important social problems which would arise if the Court were to decide that segregation in public schools is unconstitutional and on the basis of this finding were to issue a decree requiring that "within the limits set by normal geographic school districting, Negro children should forthwith be admitted to schools of their choice." Part (b) of the question, therefore, may be seen as an attempt on the part of the Court to reconcile the legal and constitutional rights of Negroes with some "effective gradual adjustment" from the "existing segregated systems to a system not based on color distinctions." Implicitly this part of the question suggests that this approach is less likely to lead to social disruptions and, therefore, would be more socially desirable, provided it is possible to reconcile it with judicial powers, precedence, and procedures.

The Specific Role of Social Scientists

Although the specific legal issues inherent in this question are outside of the province of social science, the social scientists may provide the facts which would contribute to concrete answers to the above question and its implications. What are the facts and how do they compare with the speculations?

The following are some of the questions which social scientists may seek to answer in the light of empirical evidence:

1. In what areas of American life have there been significant recent changes from racially segregated to nonsegregated patterns? (a) How were these changes brought about? What were the actual mechanics of change? What type of preparation was made for the change? (b) What were some of the problems which arose in the transition from segregated to nonsegregated systems? (c) How were these problems effectively dealt with? (d) What were the immediate and long range consequences of the change?

2. Does a direct and immediate order to change from a segregated to a nonsegregated situation in itself lead to major social disruptions?

3. Is a "gradual adjustment" or change from "segregated systems" "to a system not based on color distinctions" likely to be more "effective" than a direct and immediate change?

4. What are the conditions which determine the effectiveness of a change from racially segregated to nonsegregated systems?

The task of the social scientists in this phase of the litigation was (1) to attempt to answer the above questions through collecting and analyzing all of the available evidence, particularly in the South, as to whether and how a change from a segregated to a nonsegregated situation can be smoothly and effectively accomplished: and (2) to present this evidence in a specific and concrete way in order to make clear the conditions under which nonsegregation has been and, therefore, can be accomplished without severe or permanent disruption of a community.

Relevant information was obtained in the following ways: (1) examining of the available literature in social science journals, general periodicals, and newspapers which described or analyzed specific examples of changes in patterns of American race relations; (2) obtaining direct reports from individuals who observed directly or participated in situations which changed or were changing from a segregated to a racially nonsegregated pattern; (3) reading of relevant unpublished research manuscripts and unpublished research data.

Limits and Scope of Results

In view of the fact that changes from segregated to nonsegregated patterns do not always occur voluntarily and at the same rate in the southern states as in other regions of the country and in view of the fact, also, that when such changes do occur in the South they are not as likely to be widely publicized, it was not possible to amass a substantial amount of evidence on this issue without including information from northern and border states. A similarity in the prior racial mores and customs of such areas as southern Illinois, Missouri, Kansas, New Mexico, and Arizona to those of the South makes the data obtained from these areas significant indicators of what would generally be expected from southern states if they were required to undergo similar changes in pattern. Furthermore, some direct examples in southern states of changes from segregation to nonsegregation in Army camps, in schools run by the Army, Navy shore installations, churches, industrial plants, and labor unions were found and indicate in general that these states do not differ significantly from northern and border states in their ability to accommodate to a specific change in social situations.

In the *Appendix to Appellants' Briefs—the Effects of Segregation and the Consequences of Desegregation: A Social Science Statement* [3] a summary of the contributions of contemporary social science on the consequences of segregation and some of the factors involved in changing from segregated to nonsegregated practices were presented. On pages 13 through 17 of this *Appendix,* an evaluation of the available evidence dealing with known instances of desegregation is presented. Upon the basis of the studies examined, the following conclusions are stated:

desegregation has been carried out successfully in a variety of situations although outbreaks of violence had been commonly predicted [p. 14].

Under certain circumstances, desegregation not only proceeds without major difficulties, but has been observed to lead to the emergence of more favorable attitudes and friendlier relations between races [p. 15].

The specific conditions under which effective desegregation had taken place were described (p. 17) in this summary.

The present report does not deal with the problem of the nature and consequences of racial segregation, but it does present a more detailed picture of the process of desegregation. It describes in detail the areas and social institutions in which desegregation has recently taken place, the methods by which this has been effectively accomplished, and the consequences of desegregation.

The data presented are not intended to prove that patterns of change from segregation to desegregation are widespread throughout the United States. These specific instances of the process of desegregation are described and analyzed in order to illustrate the fact that such changes can and do take place and to clarify the social conditions within which they occur smoothly, effectively, and without severe social disruption.

The term *desegregation* is used in this report to describe the process of change in social situations or institutions from a system of organization in terms of separate facilities for whites and Negroes, exclusion of Negroes, or a deliberate restriction of the extent or area of participation of Negroes to a system wherein distinctions, exclusion, or restriction of participation based upon race no longer prevail. *Desegregation* seems a more descriptive term for the actual process with which this report is concerned than is the term *racial integration. Desegregation* is a more objective and empirical term and does not imply the complexity of social and individual adjustments and attitudinal factors which are inherent in the more evaluative term *integration. Desegregation* is also preferable to *nonsegregation* in that it connotes a process rather

---

[3] See pp. 13–68 of the original. Sources and documentation for statements made in Sections II and III of this report are given in notes that are gathered at the end of Section III, pp. 64–68. [Here omitted.—Eds.]

than a single act. Desegregation is considered *effective* in this report if it fulfills the following conditions: (1) was accomplished; (2) there was relative ease in overcoming initial resistance; (3) there was no loss, or there was an increase, in the general efficiency of functioning of the institution involved; or (4) any initial disruption or loss in efficiency was overcome as the desegregation process continued.

Forms of Present Report

An analysis of the specific instances of racial desegregation revealed that some general principles operated in the desegregation process and are related to the success or failure of desegregation. These principles emerged from an initial examination of all of the available cases of desegregation. This report presents each principle and then illustrates the principle by appropriate specific cases of desegregation. A given principle is generally supported by many illustrative cases and a given case may support two or more principles.

33

Integration of Racial Minorities in Public Housing Projects

Edward Rutledge

Although this article does not cite the contributions of sociology in framing a how-to-do-it plan of action for integrating public housing, the necessity for such a policy position came from a sociological source. It is suggested that prior to reading the Guide for Local Housing Authorities the reader examine "Postscript" (Selection 33A), which acknowledges the part played by a well-known study of interracial housing.

PURPOSE OF GUIDE

Local Housing Authorities in various part of the United States, from New York City to Seattle, Washington, have demonstrated how racial minorities can be integrated successfully in public housing projects. Integration of racial

Reprinted from a pamphlet of the same title issued by the Public Housing Administration, United States Government.

Edward Rutledge is Housing Director of the New York State Commission for Human Rights (formerly known as the New York State Commission Against Discrimination).

minority families with white families in the public housing projects of some communities such as New York City and Seattle has been in operation for more than a decade; in communities such as Newark, New Jersey, and Youngstown, Ohio, it occurred within the last few months of 1950. In all instances, whether they be large cities or small cities, or whether a policy of integration was arrived at by choice or by compliance with legislation or ordinance, various racial groups have lived as neighbors in adjacent apartments, in the same stairwells, in the same buildings, and in the same courts. Experience has taught us there is only one way to integrate: DO IT!

When a racial minority family is accepted on the basis of need and referred to a vacant dwelling unit regardless of the race of his next door neighbor, the act in itself marks the end of discrimination and segregation which is what most State laws or local ordinances on nondiscrimination in housing require. Experience has shown, however, that to eliminate or prevent discrimination and segregation, further steps are necessary, and these can be best described by the term *intergration*. The effort toward integration is the central theme of this guide.

The integration of racial minority families in public housing projects does not stop at the specific act of housing them in the dwelling units. It is a continuous operation which necessitates full understanding—sometimes special efforts—by the Commissioners and staff of the Authority, the project tenants, and the community in which the project is located.

The "doing it" takes some know-how, but for the most part it takes a wholehearted, sincere, and firm interest on the part of the Local Housing Authority to make integration succeed. Once that interest exists and a forthright position is taken by the Commissioners and Executive Secretary of the Authority, integration then becomes another phase of management operation and is treated with the same judgment as other major management functions.

Some 150 Authorities throughout the United States are now required by state law or local ordinances to conform to policies of nondiscrimination and nonsegregation of families in their existing projects or new programs. A number of other Local Housing Authorities, on their own initiative, have adopted resolutions to build housing which would be open to all people without regard to race, creed, color, national origin, or ancestry. These and other Authorities will, in the future, want to derive the benefits of the combined experience of Authorities that have been engaged in the integration of Negro families. It is for them that this Guide has been written.

THE GUIDING PRINCIPLES OF INTEGRATION

Out of the experience of the past ten years, at least ten fundamental principles have emerged which may be used as guides to accomplish integration:

1. The Local Housing Authority must commit itself to a policy of nondiscrimination and nonsegregation.

2. The Executive Director must put this policy into effect in all projects under his jurisdiction at the earliest possible time.

3. The Executive Director must take a firm and forthright position in declaring this policy to the staff.

4. The Executive Director and his Management staff must assume full responsibility for putting into effect the program of integration.

5. All applicants and tenants should be made fully aware of the Authority's policy and its practices.

6. A continuous public relations program should be carried on by the Authority, and public interest groups should be made aware of the policies and practices and problems of the Authority.

7. The selection and placement of tenants must be carefully observed especially in the initial stages of integration. Need must become the objective criterion upon which selection is finally made.

8. The public facilities of the Authority's projects must be open to all tenants regardless of race, creed, color, or national origin.

9. The staff of the Authority must put into practice a policy of employing personnel in all job classifications based solely on qualifications and without regard to race, creed, color, or national origin.

10. The entire Housing Authority must demonstrate a wholehearted interest in making the program of integration succeed.

These guides may be used as a yardstick in the measurement of whether or not integration has been accomplished. Obviously, in dealing with the various factors inherent in the operation of public housing projects there can be no single blueprint which is applicable to any and all operations. Such factors as (1) the type of program, (2) the history of its operation, (3) the legislative climate in which it operates, (4) the background and attitudes of its personnel, (5) prevailing community attitudes determine largely how the job can be done.

We have studied and participated in the experiences of Authorities which have established one interracial project and at the same time have maintained others exclusively for whites. Still, other Authorities have established integrated policies and practices in all but one or two projects which they have maintained exclusively as white. In addition, there are Authorities that have attempted to practice integration but by the selection of sites and the policy of permitting tenants to show preference for certain projects, have facilitated the creation of all-Negro projects. The ten principles outlined earlier are derived from the experiences, both negative and positive, of Authorities which have attempted to institute or have accomplished integration.

Each community will have its special conditions. But no matter what its special conditions are; whether the community is large, medium, or small; whether it is a new program or an old program or a combination of both; whether its projects consist of 50 or 10,000 units, the only one way really to integrate is to "do it."

A CASE IN POINT

That is exactly what we told the Housing Authority of the City of Newark in 1950. This Authority already had an existing program of 3,008 units and 1,360 other units scheduled for construction in 1951. Three thousand and eight families were living in eight different projects in different neighborhoods and different conditions in an industrial city of about a half million people of all races, religions, and national origins.

Thirteen years ago when the first low-rent development program was proposed in this city, the issue of establishing an all-Negro project was debated vigorously. A compromise was reached whereby it was decided to build a project which would house whites and Negroes, but in separate buildings. As a result, the first project allocated one building to Negro families, and the other three buildings to white families.

And after seven additional projects were built in this city immediately before and during World War II, the Authority wound up with: four projects all white; two projects which segregated whites and Negroes by buildings where the proportions were approximately 25 per cent Negro to 75 per cent white; one project which segregated Negroes not only by buildings but, in addition, by a playground separating these buildings with a fifty-fifty allocation of units by race; and one project which segregated Negroes from the whites by buildings and a heavily trafficked one-way street, Negroes constituting 70 per cent of the population.

This Authority was now faced with the necessity of complying with the State laws which require that all existing housing projects conform to practices of nondiscrimination *and* nonsegregation. In addition, important community groups, all of whom were supporters of public housing, insisted that the Housing Authority comply immediately. Confronted with these pressures, in addition to developing a new program, the Housing Authority director now wanted the answers on "how to do it?" No actual blueprints were available, but there were experiences of other Authorities which could be helpful so long as there was the will to achieve integration.

To do it now or wait until the new program was developed no longer was debated. It was a question of *when* to announce the new policy, *when* to put the policy into practice, and on *which* projects to begin with integration.

The ten principles provided the Director of the Authority with the essential guides he needed to embark on a program of integration. Using these guides he could accomplish integration. This is how the Authority did it:

1. Policy Statement

After a series of meetings with various community organizations, the Director of the Authority agreed at a final meeting with these groups that the Authority would commit itself to a policy of integration on all existing projects. Shortly after this meeting the Authority unanimously adopted a strong resolution stating that a policy of nondiscrimination and nonsegregation "shall take effect immediately." This resolution was widely publicized in the local press and in newspapers throughout the State and nearby states.

2. Putting Policy into Effect—When and Where

The question of when to announce the policy had now been resolved. It was already an accomplished fact. Now arose the question of precisely when and where to begin. It was determined on the basis of an evaluation of the effects on the tenants of the newly announced policy that the Authority ought to DO IT IMMEDIATELY in order to avoid misleading rumors and opportunity for agitation by those tenants opposed to the new policy of the Authority. But still unresolved was the question of which project to select for the introduction of this policy. Should it be introduced in one of the projects with segregated buildings, or all four of them, or should it begin with an all-white project? The advisability of introducing families in all eight projects at approximately the same time became clear once it was recognized that some project managers might feel penalized in bearing the brunt of this program. It was also recognized that white tenants would resent the singling out of their particular projects while others remained untouched.

Thus, after careful deliberation, the Executive Director decided to put the new policy into effect in all projects within two weeks after its announcement.

3. The Executive Director's Forthright Position

When the Executive Director had decided *what, when,* and *where,* he held a meeting with all his housing managers, tenant selection staff, and other key personnel. At this meeting he outlined the background of the decision of the Housing Authority to abolish segregation and the reasons for establishing a policy of integration. He made it celar to all that he expected full and whole-hearted cooperation from every member of his staff and that no obstruction of any type would be permitted; that he did not want the "buck passed" to "upstairs"; that he expected the managers to "carry the ball" and assume full responsibility for carrying out the program as they had in carrying out all other management functions; that those who could not go along with the program should submit their resignations now; and that if they treated this program lightly and shrugged it off, he would consider it insubordination. His whole thesis was: This job has to be done. He expected it to be done with their full cooperation.

4. Staff Responsibilities

After the Executive Director held the meeting with his staff, plans were drawn up for an intensive staff training program aimed toward having the managers apply their trade skills and know-how in the introduction of the program of integration on their projects. Meetings with each manager were arranged at his project to be attended by the Director of Management, representatives of the PHA Racial Relations Branch, and the Authority Tenant Selection Supervisor. At each of these meetings the characteristics of each project were analyzed informally, the manager being encouraged to set forth his ideas and plans for introducing integration. As a result, concrete suggestions were developed about each of the projects and other suggestions or techniques were developed to be used in all the projects.

For example, it was decided that in the first few months of this new program the manager should concentrate on interviewing all prospective tenants, white and nonwhite, who had been referred and cleared by the Tenant Selection Office. In addition, he should take it upon himself to show these families the apartments available to them. In the course of personally escorting the tenant, he should introduce him to the neighbors.

It was also decided at these conferences that once the policy had been clearly presented to prospective tenants and applicants, if an apartment adjacent to a Negro family were offered to a white family and it was refused on that ground, or vice versa, the refusing family should not be accorded the opportunity to choose another apartment if such were available. The manager had performed his obligation when he offered the apartment to the family.

It was further established at these conferences that the manager wanted the full responsibility of undertaking this program after the tenant had been referred to him. As part of that responsibility he felt it necessary to instruct his entire staff, his watchman, laborers, maintenance men, bookkeepers, and interviewers that he expected full compliance from them in regard to the spirit and letter of the Authority's policy. The general feeling of the manager was that if any questions were raised with his staff by neighbors or tenants, they should not get involved in any discussion of the policy but should refer all inquiries to him.

The managers also felt that there should be close liaison with Tenant Selection, particularly in the initial stages, to aid in the selection and placement of the proper type of tenants. In this connection the managers agreed that a control chart should be maintained, in order to avoid congregation of Negro families in any one building.

These individual meetings culminated in a meeting of all the managers and other key personnel to review the general conclusions drawn and also to hear a talk given by a housing manager with long experience in interracial management practices with another Authority. His general conclusions were that once you decide not to discriminate you don't discriminate and that if you are going to integrate, you just go ahead and integrate.

5. Tenant Orientation

The managers found that much gossip and rumor were spreading among the tenants in regard to the policy of the Housing Authority. Ever since the State law had been enacted there had been expectations among the tenants that some change would occur, but they did not know when, how, or where. Therefore, it was decided to post a bulletin in the management office which recited the State law and Housing Authority resolution. However, in a few days, upon further checking, this was found to be inadequate. Therefore, it was agreed to use the unusual expedient of addressing a letter directly to the tenant, attaching a copy of the law and Housing Authority resolution, together with a highly favorable editorial in a major newspaper praising the Authority "for a forward, progressive action."

In addition to this direct approach which had extraordinarily satisfactory results in tenant relations, it was deemed advisable to incorporate the Housing Authority policy statement in the preliminary application just above the applicant's signature and also to have the Tenant Selection stationery carry this policy as part of the letterhead. These measures were designed to facilitate the operations of the Tenant Selection staff and to more fully acquaint the tenants with the policy of the Authority before they were referred to the manager's office for assignment to apartments.

6. Community Relationships

When the Authority announced its policy publicly, it immediately received not only wide publicity in the press but received commendation from all the public interest groups which had been concerned with its former segregated program. The Executive Director also kept in frequent touch with key representatives of these groups informing them of progress made. Immediately before initiating the program of integration, representatives of intergroup organizations arranged jointly with the Executive Director to hold a conference with the Department of Public Safety. At this conference, attended by representatives of the intergroup organizations, the Executor Director and Chairman of the Authority, and the Racial Relations Officer of PHA, the program was explained to the Commissioner so that in the event difficulties were to arise when Negro families arrived at the projects where agitation had been heaviest, the police would be available to handle the situation. Agreement was reached whereby proper arrangements would be made to alert the police. Suffice it to say, their intervention was not found necessary, but the patrol cars were readily and deliberately available at the time of some of the first move-ins.

Only one or two of the eight projects contained the possibility of racial difficulties. These projects were all white and were located in neighborhoods which had resented and resisted the building of the public housing projects in their respective areas.

Another example of how closely the intergroup organizations worked with the Local Housing Authority was a conference with the Superintendent of Schools about breaking down the barriers on the segregated project where the preponderant Negro population was separated by a one-way street from the white tenants. Here it was found that the school districting followed by coincidence the racial lines, so that most of the Negro children went to a school on one side of the project and white children walked in another direction to another school. Both schools, however, were interracial, yet the *districting* separated the project children along racial lines. The Authority and the intergroup representatives recommended that the School Board consider the possibility of redistricting so that the project would not remain so artificially divided. This proposition was considered favorably by the School Board which was at that time drawing up plans for redistricting the city. In addition, the Authority and community groups have considered plans which would eliminate the one-way street to make it a play street and faciliates movement back and forth, particularly of children. This is in view of the fact that the playground is on one side of the street located in the area occupied by Negroes and thus automatically used only by Negro children.

Thus, in various joint efforts and through good public relations, the Authority has let the public interest groups know that it is interested in their cooperation. It kept them informed of the progress made toward integration.

7. Tenant Selection

Initial steps taken by the Authority in tenant selection were reflected by the nature and characteristics of the projects to which tenants were to be referred.

The Authority was faced with a variety of occupancy patterns and a variety of neighborhoods. In regard to the project located in the most "unfriendly" neighborhood, unfriendly both to Negroes and public housing, the Authority took exceptional care in the selection of the first tenants. This project was occupied by a heavy preponderance of members of one religious faith in a neighborhood of the same religious character. Many of these tenants were early in-migrant war workers and seemed to feel that the Authority breached an agreement with them. It was at this project that the tenants' association had threatened a march on City Hall and had also held some provocative meetings. This was the one project where the Executive Director had felt compelled to call in the tenant association representatives and spell out in unequivocal language the policy of the Authority, reminding the tenants that they were expected to cooperate fully.

Therefore the first two Negro families selected were GI students attending the college administered by this faith. A number of the GI students' colleagues were living in this project also. Shortly before the first Negro family moved in, a window was broken in their apartment. This was repaired by the management without comment. The Negro housewife was aware, however, of some mishap, for she observed the newness of one window pane as compared to the others. She made no comment on this matter until some time later, when a tenant selection staff member talked with her.

Apparently no special situation developed as a result of this first move-in. Shortly after the family was established there, however, the president of the tenant association visited the family and warmly welcomed them to the project. A few weeks later, on Hallowe'en, the Negro family prepared a table full of candy, nuts, etc., and when a few white children knocked on the door, they were invited into the apartment. Soon, about ten white children were there enjoying themselves, playing with the young Negro child. They remained about an hour. The next day a neighbor dropped in, told the Negro housewife that her child had reported to her about how good a time he had at their home. She asked whether the Negro woman's child could be allowed to go upstairs to play with her child. During the same period one neighbor walked over to her at the washline, informed her that she had not wanted to appear obnoxious or obvious by visiting her too soon, but she wanted the Negro housewife to know that she was happy to have her as a neighbor. Meanwhile, another Negro GI family with a small baby moved in. The same day a neighbor knocked on the door, greeted her, and invited her to use her phone in case of an emergency, such as if the baby got sick. By Christmas, three Negro families had been moved into this project in three different buildings in different parts of the project. All three families attended the Christmas party and were accepted freely.

Another project which presented a completely different situation was the one which was segregated on a 70 per cent Negro to 30 per cent white ratio. This project was located in a mixed neighborhood, yet the color line had held fast only on the project until the new policy was put into effect. In this instance a greater effort had to be exerted by Tenant Selection and Management to secure the type of white families which would move into vacancies in the Negro buildings. By careful selection and good judgment this situation was overcome. Within a period of several months, five white families were moved into several formerly all-Negro buildings, and four Negro families were moved into four different white buildings on the other side of the project. The facility with which this was accomplished could be attributed not only to the excellent management and tenant selection practices in this initial stage, but also to the fact that the tenants were aware of the over-all interest of the Authority and the community groups as expressed in their meetings with the Local school and civic officials.

The experience was repeated in one form or another in the other six projects. Only carefully selected tenants were housed during this initial period, so that in a period of three months it had begun to put its policy into practice in all eight projects. The Authority realized that this crucial period should be short and not prolonged. Now that the eight projects have moved toward full integration, the need for high selectivity has lessened.

8. Public Facilities

The Authority has accepted fully the principle that the public facilities of the public housing project must be open to all tenants without regard to race, creed, color, or national origin. It has reviewed the use of its public facilities with the view toward establishing these facilities for the full use of all tenants. In this regard, the public interest groups and the Authority have expressed interest in securing recreational supervision on these projects.

9. Staff Integration

The Authority is in the process of analyzing its job classifications. During 1950 a Negro economist was appointed to the staff. Another Negro has been assigned to training for management operations. One of the recent Negro employees is a civil engineer. The Authority has one Negro manager, and one Negro is a member of the Authority itself. A Negro is in the key position of Tenant Selection Supervisor. The Executive Director is conscious of the need to carry out this phase of the Authority's operations and obviously is actively putting the policy into practice.

10. Wholehearted Interest of Housing Authority

The staff members of the Authority expressed their wholehearted interest in a meeting held early in 1951 of all tenant selection personnel and management personnel, including the Executive Director and the PHA Racial Relations Officer. At this meeting, each manager reported on the success the program had achieved on his project; the tenant selection people referred to the positive attitudes expressed by prospective tenants and applicants to this program. The staff asked for more regular meetings to review the programs and the progress made on each project.

The Executive Director urged acceleration of the program, pointing out that all the groundwork laid in the early months probably was responsible for the smooth operations. He noted further that as a result of the positive steps taken, public housing had won the strong friendship and support of more groups than it had before, that the Housing Authority had won state and nationwide acclaim for doing a job honestly and forthrightly, and that all groups recognized the Authority's sincere interest in achieving full integration by going ahead with the job and doing it.

APPLICATION OF GUIDING PRINCIPLES TO ALL AUTHORITIES

Our review of this Local Housing Authority's experience in some detail reveals clearly the necessity to deal forthrightly and honestly with the staff, the tenant, and the community. Obviously the successful execution of the Guiding Principles of Integration in any Authority is reflected in how effectively the staff, the tenant, and the community are orientated.

All authorities, therefore, might well bear in mind the following considerations in introducing a program of integration to the staff, the tenant, and the community.

The Staff

Once the Authority has announced its policy and the Executive Director has taken a forthright position on integration, doing the job of integration is conditioned by the most effective use of the staff.

1. It may be necessary to take into consideration personalities and activities in the assignment of individuals to key operations.

2. Special effort should be made to employ and utilize at their highest level of skill and training various racial groups as a visual demonstration of a policy of integration.

3. Periodic staff meetings should be held and exchange of experiences and ideas encouraged.

4. Spot maps (for staff use only) indicating the location of families by various racial groups may be utilized as a check against segregation.

The Tenant

All applicants and tenants should be made fully aware of the Authority's policy of integration.

1. A prospective tenant should be informed of the Authority's policy at the initial interview.

2. A statement of the Authority's policy might well be incorporated in the application form.

3. The Authority's policy might well be incorporated in the lease.

4. In those Authorities which are undergoing changes of policy, it may prove desirable in most instances to inform tenants by letter of the Authority's policy of nondiscrimination and nonsegregation.

5. Furthermore, in those Authorities which are undergoing changes of policy, Management should make it a point to introduce the prospective tenant to his neighbor on as casual a basis as possible at the time the tenant is being shown the apartment allocated to him.

6. Special attention should be given to the assignment of tenants on a selective basis during the relatively short crucial period of effecting changes in policy.

7. In Authorities with more than one project, tenant selection should be centralized and referrals of tenants should be made to vacancies existing or occurring in all projects, thus facilitating the selective process in the assignment of applicants to the various projects.

8. In those Authorities undergoing changes of policy to integration, definite consideration should be given to the intratransfer of families on the basis of their need for different-sized apartments. Management might well consider some of these families in the initial stages of integration.

9. All public services, utilizing project space, should be open to all families regardless of race, creed, color, or national origin. This is a basic principle.

The Community

A continuous public relations program should be conducted by the Authority.

1. Maximum cooperation of all municipal officials and departments is an essential element in effecting the policy of integration.

2. A continuous cooperating relationship should be maintained with the churches, labor unions, minority group, and intergroup organizations; and all other groups and individuals interested in housing and the general welfare of the community.

3. The beneficial use of the local newspapers, radio, and television will often stimulate an atmosphere favorable to integration.

4. Periodic consultation with these various forces tends to point up the community's stake in the operation of a housing program and to stimulate a feeling of community participation and responsibility.

33A

Postscript

Louis Danzig

A new policy for locating tenants is now in effect in Newark's eight public housing projects and will also apply to the three skyscraper developments soon to be constructed. That policy, one long favored by many of us, provides that henceforth all apartments are to be allocated on a basis of need, regardless of race, religion, and color. As a result, the partial segregation which has characterized public housing in Newark will no longer obtain. Instead of Negroes and whites being kept in separate buildings, they are being assigned to apartments in the same buildings without regard to their race.

In large measure, this change in fundamental policy reflects the impact of the study reported in this book. The study has served as a catalyst to the reexamination of our basic interracial policies in housing and as a stimulus to their change. Many of us have long felt that the artificial separation of Negro and white families was an unwholesome procedure. However, until the study of Dr. Deutsch and Mrs. Collins, we had no scientific evidence

From page 130 *Interracial Housing*, A Psychological Evaluation of a Social Experiment by Morton Deutsch and Mary Evans Collins, Research Center for Human Relations, New York University, The University of Minnesota Press, Minneapolis.

Louis Danzig is Executive Director, Housing Authority of the City of Newark.

to substantiate our feelings. In supplying us with an objective picture of race relations in our projects, a picture which is faithful to our own impressions, their study dramatically focused our attention and that of the community at large on matters which, under the press of other business, we had tended to ignore.

The study did more than help to focus attention on the basic question of segregation in housing. Perhaps its most important consequence was its usefulness to those community groups concerned with intergroup relations and civil rights, such as the Essex County Intergroup Council. To such groups the study was an invaluable tool in creating the atmosphere which made it possible for the housing authority to adopt and execute a policy of nonsegregation. I don't know how many meetings of such groups I attended, but invariably the Deutsch-Collins study was referred to and quoted. All these meetings were necessary and helpful. Without active support from community groups and the new state law prohibiting discrimination in public housing, it would have been extremely difficult for us to adopt a change in policy.

A word about the change. Naturally, as we undertook the process of integrating our projects, we were beset by some anxieties. If, however, our Newark experience may serve as a guide, the changeover to a policy of nonsegregation is not so difficult and troublesome as one anticipates. Some of our tenants (these are by far in the minority) have complained to us vociferously, but there has been no disruption of our projects. When the complainants met a firm, calm response from housing management, they invariably subsided. Our experience leads me to believe that if a housing authority, its executive director and his staff, show complete sincerity in the change and never retreat from their announced position with respect to nonsegregation, the change will be successful. This, in any case, is what we have found to be true in Newark.

Even in this short time we have already observed significant changes in attitudes, as a consequence of which we shall undoubtedly find that as we break down the physical barriers between Negroes and whites in our projects, many of the social barriers will also disappear. We have been pleasantly surprised to find that some of the white tenants who were loudest in their objections to living next to Negro families have come to accept as *neighbors* the Negro families living next to them.

34

How Research
Can Improve Practice:
A Case Study

Everett M. Rogers

This case study of the Agricultural Extension Service shows how the implementation of research findings has affected one social-process field.

The Agricultural Extension Service is often regarded as one of the most effective adult educational agencies in the United States. It is one of the oldest and probably the largest and most fully developed. In the past fifty years, it has helped transform United States agriculture from a traditional way of life into an efficient and productive business. The purpose of the Extension Service, as stated by federal law, is to diffuse new ideas in agriculture and home economics.

Elite landowners had realized the need for improved agricultural technology as early as 1785, a date which marked the founding of the first "agricultural society" in the United States. Gentlemen farmers met in these societies to debate the merits of new crop varieties and livestock breeding methods. It was not until soon after 1900, however, that the average farmer felt a similar need for an educational service in agriculture. Starting in 1911, farmers organized by counties to contribute funds in order to hire a county agent. Many counties had already employed agricultural agents by 1914 when the Smith-Lever Act was passed, which provided federal funds to state Extension Services in order to develop further the county-agent system. In later years, county home-economics agents were hired to diffuse new ideas to homemakers, and county 4-H agents were employed to assist youth in their 4-H club work.

The Federal Extension Service provides annual federal grants to each state Extension Service, but does not have direct administrative control over the state units. In addition to administrators at the state level, there are Extension "specialists" representing each academic department (such as agronomy, agricultural economics, human nutrition, and poultry). These specialists form

---

Reprinted from *Theory into Practice*, **1**, 2 (April 1962), pp. 89–93, by permission of the publisher and the author.

Everett M. Rogers is Associate Professor of Rural Sociology, The Ohio State University.

an intellectual bridge between research workers and the county agents in the subject matter of the specialists' particular disciplines.

County agents are "generalists" rather than specialists, and act as consultants on all kinds of local problems in their county. They may call upon a specialist for the answer to some problem, or they may ask a specialist to address a county meeting on a particular topic. Because the county agent's funds are provided by county (as well as state and federal) tax funds, he is somewhat responsive to local conditions. He usually involves several hundred local people on his county Extension committees to advise him on the nature of local educational needs and to plan his program.

DIFFUSION RESEARCH

Rural sociological research on the diffusion of innovations actually began in response to a need for Extension workers to understand the relative effectiveness of the various educational methods available to them. In the 1920's administrators in the Federal Extension Service instigated evaluation studies of their program's effectiveness. One handy evaluation measure was the adoption of farm and homemaking innovations that had been recommended and promoted by the Extension Service. In one of the early studies in 1925, Wilson and his associates determined the ratio of innovations adopted by farmers to the relative costs of diffusion.

Little other research was completed in this tradition until the early 1940's when Kollmorgen's investigation of the adoption of new ideas by German-Swiss farmers in Tennessee, Hoffer's study of the adoption of innovations by Michigan celery growers of Dutch descent, and Ryan and Gross's analysis of the diffusion of hybrid seed corn in Iowa were published. The last is the classic study in the diffusion of innovations, and is undoubtedly one of the most widely known rural sociological studies of all time. Since these studies, the amount of rural sociological research on diffusion has proliferated rapidly until a review of the tradition in 1962 indicated a total of 284 research publications on this topic.

APPLICATION OF RESEARCH FINDINGS

The purpose in all of these studies was to improve the effectiveness of the Extension Service (and other agencies) in diffusing new ideas. Some of the major findings that have been successfully used by Extension workers [1] are described as follows:

---

[1] The fact that these research studies were mostly completed by rural sociologists in agricultural universities who were geographically removed and organizationally separated from county Extension workers suggests that a diffusion problem existed for the results of diffusion research. A popular summarization of sociological research on diffusion was presented to many Extension workers at their state conferences by two

1. Individuals appear to pass through a series of steps in the adoption process as they first become *aware* that an innovation exists, then gain *interest* in the idea and seek further information about it, *evaluate* its potential for their farm or home, *try* it on a small scale, and then decide to *adopt* or reject the innovation. It was found by Ryan and Gross that the period from awareness to adoption averaged about nine years for all respondents in their hybrid-corn study.

One generalization which has emerged from several rural sociological analyses is that *impersonal information sources are most important at the awareness stage and personal sources are most important at the evaluation stage in the adoption process.* This finding provides a strategy for Extension workers seeking to diffuse an innovation: if an audience is not yet at the awareness stage, mass media are the most appropriate channels for communicating the innovation. However, if most of the audience is at the evaluation stage for the new idea, personal contacts and group meetings may be the most appropriate Extension method to use.

2. Another general finding from diffusion research is that the rate of adoption of a new idea closely approaches a normal distribution over a period of time. At first, only a few individuals adopt an innovation; these first 2.5 per cent are the "innovators." The next 13.5 per cent are the "early adopters," followed by the "early majority," 34 per cent; the "late majority," 34 per cent; and the "laggards," 16 per cent.[2] The social characteristics, values, and communication behavior of each adopter category have been determined. It is often useful to county Extension agents to plan a somewhat different (but interrelated) "diffusion campaign" for an innovation on the basis of each adopter category. For example, it has been found by diffusion researchers that innovators often travel directly to agricultural scientists in order to secure new ideas. Early adopters seek information mainly from local Extension agents, and are less cosmopolite in their communication behavior. Early and late majority depend heavily upon discussions with neighbors and friends to convince them of innovations, and have somewhat less contact with county agents. Laggards are often suspicious of county agents' recommendations, seldom seek them for advice, and secure their farm information from their neighbors. By knowing the differences in communication channels among

---

rural sociologists, George M. Beal and Joe M. Bohlen. Their presentations, plus a popular bulletin (North Central Rural Sociology Subcommittee for the Study of Diffusion of Farm Practices, *How Farm People Accept New Ideas* [Ames, Iowa: Agricultural Extension Service, Iowa State College, Special Report 15, 1955], which summarizes this research, have done much to increase Extension workers' "adoption" of diffusion-research findings.

[2] This method of adopter categorization on the basis of innovativeness is discussed by Everett M. Rogers, "Categorizing the Adopters of Agricultural Practices," *Rural Sociology*, **23** (December 1958), pp. 345–354. The percentage included in each adopter category is somewhat arbitrary, but is based on standard deviations from the mean year of adoption (which result in standard-sized categories when the adopter distribution approaches normality).

adopter categories, a county Extension agent may utilize the most appropriate communication channel to reach each adopter category.

3. Research findings indicate that Extension workers possess low source credibility for the laggards. This generalization implies that county agents need to work through opinion leaders in their farm audience in order to reach the laggards indirectly via the "trickle-down" process. County agents have been widely trained by sociologists on how to select farmer opinion leaders by sociometric and other techniques.[3] The efforts of over 14,000 professional staff members in U.S. Extension Services are supplemented and extended many times by a corps of about one million unpaid voluntary leaders. Of course, it makes a great deal of difference whom the Extension worker selects as leaders to receive special educational assistance. For example, diffusion research shows that innovators, while eager to adopt new farm ideas, are not respected by their neighbors as sources of farm information and advice. Early adopters possess greater opinion leadership than any other adopter category in most communities.

These three illustrations show some important ways in which the results of diffusion research have improved the effectiveness of the Extension Service.[4] There are many other possible examples of ways in which programming and teaching have been improved. As suburbanization, improved transportation and communication, farm specialization, and other social changes affect the role of the Extension Service in the United States, even greater reliance may be placed upon the results of sociological and educational research. The intellectual interrelatedness of theoretically oriented rural sociologists and practically oriented Extension workers in the past two decades has resulted in advantages to both.

---

[3] County agents were certainly using a leader approach to adult education for years before the diffusion-research studies were begun, but the current emphasis on selection and use of opinion leaders stems, at least in part, from the rural sociological investigations.

[4] A generally similar contribution of diffusion research to Extension Service effectiveness may be observed in the Netherlands. See A. W. van den Ban, "Research in the Field of Advisory Work," *Netherlands Journal of Agricultural Service,* **9** (May 1961), pp. 122–123.

35

Social Changes and the Church

Truman B. Douglass

The church, as a social institution, is affected by every social and cultural change which occurs in its environment. Of all social institutions, however, the church is probably the most conservative. The current awakening of religious interest throughout the United States presents the church with many opportunities and confronts it with potential dangers.

An adequate review of ecological changes as they affect the Church would include consideration of nearly all the major sociological changes that have occurred in American life in recent years. These changes constitute important aspects of the environment with which the Church interacts. There is scarcely any feature of human society which does not influence the estate of the churches. Economic conditions, population shifts, family life, class structure, race relations, education, leisure, changes in the distribution of age groups, the condition of the general culture, the definition and redefinition of social goals—all have their consequences for the Church.

Because the Church is in many respects a conservative institution, these ecological changes frequently present themselves to the Church in the form of problems and dilemmas for those who shape its policies, plans, and program.

There are, of course, churchmen who adopt what is essentially a transcendentalist view of the Church. They would claim that in its essential characteristics the Church is untouched by outward change. They feel that the lines of the Doxology which read, "As it was in the beginning, is now and ever shall be," apply equally to the teachings of the Christian Gospel and to the primary features of the Church. If, however, one believes, as does this writer, that in addition to its divinely given attributes the Church bears the marks of a human institution, then every change occurring in society and its culture has implications for and effects upon the Church.

Reprinted from The *Annals* of the American Academy of Political and Social Science, **332** (November 1960), pp. 80–88, by permission of the publisher and the author.

Truman B. Douglass is Executive Vice President, United Church Board for Homeland Ministries.

QUANTITATIVE CHANGES

Some conspicuous quantitative changes have had major effects upon the life and activity of the churches. The population upsurge and increased mobility constitute such obvious features of twentieth-century American society that the Church, even in its most conservative expressions, has not been able to ignore them.

A quarter of a century ago the Protestant churches were persuaded that the period of church extension—of establishing new churches—was virtually ended in the United States. This conviction was articulated at a congress of home mission boards held in Washington, D.C., under the sponsorship of the Home Missions Council of North America. At this meeting the conviction was expressed that the settlement of the country had been completed, that the population had reached a point of stability, that the nation was adequately provided with churches, and that, therefore, the home mission boards could turn their energies and resources to other tasks.

The prognostications were completely negated by subsequent events—primarily by the population explosion, the wartime and postwar migrations of the American people, the continuing suburban trend, and the creation of multitudes of new communities. As a consequence, the intimation that the churches would refrain from major efforts in the field of church expansion has proved to be far from correct. For a number of years the churches have been organizing new congregations at the rate of approximately 10,000 per year. The value of new construction of religious buildings rose from $117,-000,000 in 1923, to $863,000,000 in 1958 and will closely approach a billion dollars in 1960.

Thoughtful church leaders are beginning to realize that these expansionist phenomena have their dangers. There is danger that the denominations will be more interested in reaping a statistical harvest than in making certain that the religious needs of communities are well served. Churches are likely to give more attention to quantitative growth than to the improvement of the qualitative excellence of their programs. There is danger that in the vast reshuffling of our population, and in the attendant concentration of the churches upon numerical increase, individuals will be lost to view. A mobile population requires more mobile forms of pastoral care than the Protestant churches have yet devised. It is more impressive for the minister's record to add ten new members to the rolls of his church than to make certain that ten old members who have moved to new places are established in churches in their new homes. There is danger that with all the building and rebuilding of church edifices, churches will be known for the comfort and modernity of their structures rather than for the Gospel they preach and for the quality of Christian life exhibited by the congregation.

THE RELIGIOUS REVIVAL

Church members now constitute 63 per cent of the population of the United States. This compares with 16 per cent in 1850 and 22 per cent in 1900. There is much debate about the accuracy of these figures. One variable which is not taken adequately into account in comparing the statistics reported by the churches is the changing conception of a church "member." For example, in the case of the Episcopal Church, in 1916 only 1 per cent of its members were children under 13, as compared with 26 per cent in 1926. Efforts have been made to standardize the statistics by calculating the percentage of people aged 13 and over who are recorded as church members, since denominations vary greatly in their practice of enrolling children. When this correction is made the figures do not show, as is frequently assumed, a steady rise in the proportion of church members in the total population since the beginning of the century. They show, rather, a decline from 1916 to 1940—55 per cent in 1916 and 50.7 per cent in 1940—and a notable rise thereafter. "In other words the American revival dates not from 1900 or before, but from 1940 or shortly after." [1] The growth since 1940 has been impressive—from 50.7 per cent to 63 per cent of the population in 1958. Today the membership of religious bodies in the United States exceeds 110,000,000.

There is a question whether this increased popularity represents a success or an embarrassment for the churches. It has produced, according to Martin E. Marty,[2]

the erosion of particularity, the smoothing of the edges of witness, the loss of religious content. Particularity is challenged by a blurry, generalized religion; distinctive witness is confronted by amiable syncretism; theological content is often replaced by sentiments about religion. There are intimations that many churches represent a kind of American Shinto and that their popularity is gained by their identification with the "American way." They have tended to become simply one aspect of the general culture rather than being in tension with it and exercising a critical function toward it.

CLASS AND RACE

The effects upon the churches of changes in the class structure of American society are largely indeterminate.

Evidence is abundant that a revolution is occurring in the racial and class composition of our nation. One relevant set of facts pertains to the composition of the labor force. The number of farmers, for example, declined from 16.5 per cent of the labor force in 1910 to 7.3 per cent in 1950. The proportion of farm laborers declined from 14.5 per cent in 1910 to 4.3 per cent in

---

[1] Michael Argyle, *Religious Behavior* (Glencoe, Ill.: Free Press, 1958), pp. 28–29.

[2] Martin E. Marty, *The New Shape of American Religion* (New York: Harper, 1958).

1950. During the same forty year span, professional persons increased from 4.4 per cent of the labor force to 8.5 per cent, and the proportion of clerks, salespeople, and those in similar occupations increased from 10.2 per cent to 18.9 per cent. White-collar workers increased in number from 5,115,000 in 1900 to 21,600,000 in 1950. They now constitute 36.6 per cent of the labor force as compared with 17.6 per cent in 1900. There has been a parallel change in the distribution of income. In 1929, 65 per cent of the population had incomes under $3,000 per year. In 1951 this portion was reduced to 46 per cent. The proportion receiving incomes between $3,000 and $7,500 rose from 29 per cent in 1929 to 47 per cent in 1951.

Little is known of the effects of these changes upon the Church. No significant amount of research has been done in this field. It seems evident, however, that some of the widely held presuppositions regarding the relationship between social class and the churches have not been substantiated. For example, it might have been expected that with the virtual disappearance of an American proletariate, the so-called pentecostal sects—churches which allegedly drew their membership primarily from the economically disadvantaged groups —would have ceased to flourish. This has not been the case. The Assemblies of God increased their membership from 6,700 in 1916 to 148,000 in 1936; they continued this growth and reached a membership of more than 505,000 in 1958. The Pilgrim Holiness Church had 5,300 members in 1916, 20,100 in 1936, and 32,600 in 1958. The Pentecostal Holiness Church had 5,600 members in 1916, 20,100 in 1936, and 32,600 in 1958.

Conversely, the churches which might have been expected to benefit from the number of what Vance Packard calls "the strivers for upward mobility"— namely, such denominations as the Episcopal, Congregational, and Presbyterian Churches—have exhibited no gains which are disproportionate to those made by other denominations which presumably offer fewer social advantages.

At least three factors seem to have contributed to the failure of church members to behave according to anticipated formulas. First, church affiliations seem to be more stable than other social affiliations and do not seem to be affected—at least not immediately—by a change of status. Second, some of the Pentecostal sects have steadily grown more respectable, have changed their character to conform to the changed class status of their membership, and have taken on more of the ways of the conventional "old-line" churches. For example, the General Conference of the Seventh Day Baptist denomination has joined the National Council of the Churches of Christ in the United States of America. Third, the evangelizing zeal of the Pentecostal groups has not waned as their members have acquired economic advantage and social status—nor has the zeal of such denominations as the Episcopal, Congregational, and Presbyterian notably increased, it would seem, as changes in the class structure of the nation have presented them with the sociological bases of larger opportunity.

One of the anomalies in this area of class-race relationships is the fact that the denominations which have been known as churches of the proletariat have made slower progress toward the integration of Negroes into their membership than have some of the longer established and presumably more socially conservative bodies. In 1950 a survey of Presbyterian, United States of America churches disclosed that out of 2,706 reporting congregations, 832 were integrated. A 1958 study of Congregational Christian churches in metropolitan areas found that 12 per cent included Negro members and that 49 per cent were willing to accept Negroes as members. The Protestant Council of New York City asserts on the basis of a recent study that half the churches in that city have an interracial membership. Liston Pope estimates that about 10 per cent of the total number of Protestant churches in the nation are interracial. This figure is five times as large as the corresponding figure for ten years ago. There is no evidence that the Pentecostal sects have shown any similar disposition toward integration. This is probably due, in the first place, to their tendency to make a radical separation between faith and social ethics and, in the second place, to the fact that many of these sects have their greatest strength in the South.

The most intensive study yet made of the attitudes and practices of a single denomination respecting racial integration covered the Congregational Christian churches in standard metropolitan areas. Questionnaires were sent to all the churches of that denomination in such areas. When congregations showed themselves willing to participate in the study, interviews were held with the minister and at least one lay official. Of the 1,500 churches of the denomination located in standard metropolitan areas, 1,054 took part in the study.

Two significant and encouraging facts were disclosed. First, some modest gains in racial inclusiveness were revealed. The survey showed that 26.6 per cent of the churches in metropolitan communities included in their membership representatives of at least one minority group. A less thorough study made twelve years previously revealed that only 17 per cent of these churches could be classified as inclusive.

Second, in the opinion of ministers and lay leaders, well over half the congregations studied—63.4 per cent of them—would support their pastors in implementing a policy of racial inclusiveness.

There were some disheartening findings. Nearly half the local churches that were studied had no definite policy for receiving members of racial minorities. Approximately 70 per cent said they had never confronted a situation that required decision in that area of policy. Since the study was limited to highly urbanized communities where the size of racial minorities has rapidly increased in recent years, it is evident that the churches are not aggressively pressing toward a policy of racial inclusiveness.

In the opinion of a large number of lay officers of churches, the pastors would have more support for programs of desegregation in the community than in their own churches. Dr. Herman Long, the director of the study, considered this the most negative finding.

A majority—51.4 per cent—of the lay respondents from the Midwest believed that there are exceptions to the denomination's announced policy of unconditional hospitality to members of all racial groups. It is alarming that what has been considered the southern pattern may also be the midwestern pattern.

A general result of the study was to indicate that in a period of history when events in the realm of human relations move with lethal swiftness the churches proceed with glacial slowness. The extent of integration in the churches compares unfavorably with accomplishments in other areas such as employment in federal and state governments, the armed services, professional sports, labor unions, institutions of higher education, and so on.

CITY AND SUBURB

The city and the suburb are obverse sides of a primary problem-area for the work of the churches. Nearly every denomination has acknowledged publicly that from the standpoint of institutional strength it is losing ground in the inner city. Most denominations also acknowledge that with the whole nation coming under the influence of a predominantly urban culture, the failure of the Church to find its place in the city raises questions concerning the relevance of its message and program to modern society.

Curiously, some denominations are troubled almost as much by their successes in the suburbs as by their failures in the inner city. This seems strange, for in a number of instances denominational programs of suburban expansion were undertaken as a deliberate plan for compensating losses of institutions and members in the central metropolitan areas.

Meanwhile, the "exploding metropolis" continues to explode. The 168 standard metropolitan areas have steadily increased their share of the country's population. In July 1958 these areas included 59 per cent of the total population of the United States. Within these areas, the suburbs continue to grow at a faster rate than the central cities. Between April 1950 and July 1958, about 12.4 million people were added to the population of communities adjacent to our larger cities, giving an average annual increase of 3.7 per cent annually. This is almost three times the rate of growth within these cities and more than double the rate for the country as a whole. While, for example, there has been no appreciable population change in New York City, Jersey City, and Newark, the adjacent communities have increased at the rate of 3.9 per cent a year. A gain of 1.6 million persons has occurred in the New York-Northeastern New Jersey standard metropolitan area. This gain is exceeded only by the increase in the Los Angeles area.

The embarrassment of the Church concerning its suburban prosperity has been mentioned. The Church does not minimize its responsibility for providing religious ministries to the millions of people who have moved to the burgeoning suburbs, nor does it ignore the fact that many of these people occupy positions of strategic influence in American society. The Church is ill at ease over its success because of the relative simplicity of its adaptation to a suburban environment. Church leaders are beginning to recognize that the task of establishing a successful church in a new, rapidly growing suburb is scarcely more difficult than the problem of establishing a filling station on a new superhighway. The Church is disturbed at finding itself too readily at home in a one-class community. It is haunted by the consciousness of its essential nature as an inclusive fellowship in which distinctions of "Greek and barbarian, wise and simple, bond and free" are transcended.

On the other hand, the problems of the Protestant churches in the central city are not simply functions of population increase or decrease. There appears to be something in the urban community and its culture which is alien, if not hostile, to the Church. For example, during a period when 200,000 people were moving into New York City in the area below Fourteenth Street, seventeen Protestant churches moved out.

One probable cause of the Church's alienation from the city is the fact that a large proportion of ministers come from rural and small-town communities. A recent study of the sources of the Protestant ministry revealed that in a sampling of 1,709 ministerial students only 36 per cent came from cities of more than 25,000 population. Because of their rural and small-town origins, many ministers bring to their work in a city church a distaste for city ways. Facing the life of the city, the average Protestant minister's dominant emotion seems to be not the "love that casteth out fear," but the fear that excludes love. He is terrified by the vast agglomeration of human beings, by the city's monstrous vitality, myriad forms, restless energies, and by the impudent way in which it deals with the proprieties which a polite, middle-class Protestantism identifies with a "Christian culture." The minister is likely to be disabled from dealing with city people by his moralistic approach to their problems. He looks with disapproval upon an institution of such importance as the neighborhood tavern. He is appalled by the extravagance, late hours, and alcoholic excesses of city people and judges these "sins" far more harshly than small-town snooping, gossip, philistinism, and cruelty toward the nonconformist.

OTHER CULTURAL CHANGES

Other changes in the culture are presenting the Church with problems and with opportunities only partially realized.

There is, for example, the growth of leisure. More and more the attention of the individual American and the family is centered on the use of the hours and days away from productive work. Approximately 15 per cent of total consumer expenditures are annually spent on leisure-time activities. With the arrival of the five-day week, and with the prospect of the four-day or even three-day week, the Church must reconsider its program in the light of a three-day or four-day "sabbath." The inviolability of the hour of eleven o'clock on Sunday morning and the universally observed time for corporate worship is brought into question. One church in New York City has had some success in its experiment with holding its weekly service of congregational worship on Friday evening in the summertime. Many churches are developing programs of adult education—often in the form of small groups engaged in the study of theology and biblical subjects—as ways of providing constructive leisure-time activities.

Another major cultural change is what Peter Drucker calls the educational revolution. Education today, instead of removing people from the productive enterprise into a leisure class as it often did in the past, has become almost a prerequisite to effective participation in the productive process. This fact constitutes an authentic revolution.

What does this revolution mean for churches that have set mediocre standards for the education of their ministry? What does it mean for churches whose outlook has been essentially anti-intellectual? The presence in their congregations of large numbers of persons who have been trained in the principles of critical thought constitutes a new situation which the churches have only begun to face.

DENOMINATIONAL IRRELEVANCE

Finally, a general observation that must be made about the changed situation of the churches is that the denominational system which characterizes religious affairs in America is becoming increasingly irrelevant to the actualities of our society and culture. While this irrelevance is becoming more clearly visible, the denominations, with their enlarged memberships and increased financial prosperity, become more self-assertive and tend to dominate the religious scene.

All churches in the United States, including the Roman Catholic Church and the "undenominational" association of Community Churches, are also sects. As the sectarian system becomes stronger and its constituent denominations become increasingly powerful, it also becomes less and less pertinent to the realities of American life. The so-called religious revival of the last decade has to be appraised in the light of the increasing irrelevancy of the fundamental structure of the Church in this nation.

The irrelevancy has been produced by some of the social and cultural facts that have been considered in this article.

One of these facts is the mobility of the American people. No church, not even the largest, is ubiquitous. When people are moving to the extent that the American people have been moving since 1945, many of them settle in places where no church of their traditional denominational affiliation is present. In consequence, many of them change their denominational associations. They discover that this can be done without impairing—often, indeed, enriching—their religious experience. Many pastors of urban churches annually receive by transfer from congregations of other denominations three or four times as many members as they receive by transfer from congregations of their own denomination. It is evident that for many persons denominational loyalty ranks low among the considerations which influence their choice of a local church. Convenience of access, good Sunday School facilities for the children, the general excellence of the church's reputation and program, even availability of parking space may be more important factors than the continuance of an existing denominational affiliation.

A recent survey which included interviews with 4,100 members of Congregational Christian churches in all parts of the country, revealed that only one member out of three was originally a Congregationalist. The churches studied derived over one half of their present membership from four other denominations: Methodist—18 per cent; Presbyterian—15 per cent; Baptist—11 per cent; and Lutheran—8 per cent. Two per cent of the members included in this study originally were Roman Catholics.

On the point of the historic theological and ecclesiological controversies which produced the separated denominations, the indifference of the laity is monumental. It has increasingly come to be recognized by both clergy and laity that many of the persons who avoid the Church do so not because of the "offense of the Cross," but because they are repelled by the offense of competing denominations.

DENOMINATIONAL DILEMMA

Can anyone seriously believe that these separated clans and tribes of the Christian family have any relevance to the real problems that humanity confronts in our time, or that their prosperity or lack of it provides any standard for judging the advance of the Christian movement? The statistical records of the denominations are not only notorious examples of the do-it-yourself craft of "how to lie with statistics," but are virtually meaningless as measurements of Christian accomplishment. One reads the recruiting literature of almost any denomination and tries vainly to find some resemblance to the criteria of the New Testament. The motivations to which appeal is made are not essentially different from the apologetic for the Junior Chamber of Commerce or the Neighborhood Improvement Association. They say, in effect:

Join us because we are a great organization with so many million members and so many thousand congregations. We have a noble tradition; we were brought to this country by passengers on the Mayflower. We have spawned the following well-known personalities. In this nuclear age, when the whole world is a neighborhood, we have missions from northern Greenland to Tierra del Fuego. Furthermore, through the influence of our great personalities and our spiritual teaching we are one of the chief bastions for the defense of the American way of life.

When a denomination is asked what is the relationship of this type of publicity to Christ's summons to "leave all and follow me," or to "do the things I command you," the answer is, "None whatever." This discontinuity is widely recognized. The response of intelligent persons to the typical forms of denominational propaganda is worse than incredulity; it amounts to boredom.

Thus the movement toward the overcoming of denominational disunity is generated not only by religious considerations but also by sociological factors. At the present moment it is being somewhat retarded by the economic prosperity of the denominations and by the illusions of omnicompetence which this prosperity produces. While there are some four hundred state and local councils of churches representing the cooperative tendencies of Protestantism, the denominations are reluctant to assign to them any real responsibilities except statistically unproductive functions such as work with agricultural migrants, sharecroppers, and American Indians.

The dilemma of denominationalism gives a significance far greater than their quantitative dimensions to the movements toward actual unions of denominations—particularly those movements which aim at a reconciliation of fundamental differences of polity such as the differences between the episcopal, presbyterian, and congregational systems. Such unions are far more important than the reunion of separated branches of the same denominational family. One such union—the union between the Evangelical and Reformed and the Congregational Christian Churches—has already been accomplished in this country. Others are under consideration.

Chapter Nine

Public Opinion

LIKE SO MANY OTHER TERMS used in sociology, *public opinion* is taken from the English language rather than newly coined from Greek or Latin. Because it is also a term in the English vernacular, it is subject to misinterpretation when used technically. "A public," according to Broom and Selznick, "consists of people who (1) regard themselves as affected by an event or activity, (2) can in some way register that concern, and (3) are taken into account." [1] Examples of a public, then, would be the sports public (or even more accurately, football fans), the advocates or opponents of birth control, and the conservationists and others who wish to preserve the Indiana Dunes as a national park.

Some authorities insist that, in addition to the characteristics mentioned above, there must be the element of controversy. The editors look upon controversy, however, as simply one stage in the formation of public opinion. Mention should be made of the qualifying fact that, except in elections, one person's "vote" is not as good as another's: the prestige and power of the individual or group are certainly factors to be considered. An additional factor is the intensity with which views are held. It is also well to bear in mind that the opinion of a specific public is not necessarily rational. For example, at one time, public opinion about the desirability or utility of world exploration and about the revolution of the earth was undoubtedly quite different from the present one, and present public opinion

[1] Leonard Broom and Philip Selznick, *Sociology* (New York: Harper, 1963), p. 274.

about both of these matters may be quite different from that concerning the desirability or utility of the current race to put a man on the moon.

The first three articles (Selections 36–38) in this chapter were selected to demonstrate that a precondition of winning friends and influencing people is a thorough knowledge of the opinion of the public to which one is addressing a message—whether this message be concerned with newspaper sales, product advertising, or the advantages of democracy over communism.

If men define things as real, they are real in their consequences, as W. I. Thomas pointed out a generation ago. The fourth article (Selection 39), by Dr. Gillette, is included to enable us to examine reality. But public opinion is not necessarily consistent with reality; 50 million Frenchmen can be wrong, and in the fifth article (Selection 40), Alfred Balk testifies to the cost of erroneous public opinion.

Finally, and on a more positive note, the concluding article (Selection 41) enables us to see how modern technology and mathematical theory may be combined together and interpret existing public opinion. The article helps us understand a little better how opinion is formulated.

36

How Editors Use Research
on the Minneapolis Dailies

Sidney S. Goldish

In the colorful words of the author, "It was necessary for the
Wright brothers to fly by the seat of their pants when they took out
the Kitty Hawk in 1903; but the pilot of a 1960 jetliner doesn't
fly by the seat of his pants, and none of us would want him to."
The author describes in detail how social researchers have been
hired and utilized by the Minneapolis newspapers. He shows how
anyone in a position of authority must have information obtained
by scientific social research in order to know how to appeal to his
clientele, his territory, his "publics." Note that the author, as a social scientist, seeks in his research to discover what exists, not what
he might prefer things to be.

Since 1944, *The Minneapolis Star* and *Tribune* have been maintaining a
research program—originally in our promotion and public service department;
then, in 1947, as an adjunct of our news department; and, since 1956, as a
separate department of our company. Our commitments of manpower and
money to research have been substantial in past years, and they are growing.

The implication is clear: We believe newspaper research is worthwhile . . .
useful . . . necessary.

Research is a *service* department at the *Star* and *Tribune*. It exists to serve
other departments—news, editorial, advertising, circulation—and also to serve
management. We use research as a tool, to augment our knowledge of the
readers and markets served by our newspapers, and to assist in decision-
making processes.

The kinds of research we do deal with people, with communication, and
with markets. (You will note the omission of any reference to research for
our production departments—composing room, pressroom, mailroom, stereo-
type, and engraving. The reason is that our department doesn't do any. We
lack the technical skill and knowledge to undertake it. That kind of research
is done, but under other auspices, and in other quarters.)

The methods we use are those which social scientists on this and other
university and college campuses, here and abroad, have developed—and
continue to develop. We utilize sampling and interviewing procedures in most

Reprinted from *Journalism Quarterly*, **37**, 3 (Summer 1960), pp. 365–372, by permission
of the publisher and the author.
Sidney S. Goldish is Director of Research, *Minneapolis Star and Tribune*.

of the work we do. Among the seven people in our department on a regular, fulltime basis (plus 70 to 80 interviewers throughout the state of Minnesota who do field work for us as occasion arises), we need people who have had training in statistics, in probability theory, in sampling design, in psychology and sociology—and in journalism.

Certain ground rules govern the research we conduct:

1. It should produce *relevant* facts bearing on practical problems confronting some department, or combination of departments.

2. It should produce *reliable* facts, of measurable accuracy.

3. The prospective *uses* for the research findings should be planned in advance. We should know the "why" of the study before we begin it, so that we do not overlook or ignore important considerations.

4. The costs of every study we make are assigned directly to the department for which the study is made. That is one way of making reasonably sure that a study, once completed, will be put to use—not pigeon-holed.

While I want to concentrate here on research which is done at the behest of, and for, the editors of our newspapers, I might outline quickly some examples of the other kinds of research activity in which we are involved at the *Star* and *Tribune*.

For our national advertising department, since 1953, we have been making annual studies which we call the "Minnesota Homemaker Surveys." These are studies in which we interview 2,400 women in statewide households to learn which types of products—in various categories—they are using, and which specific brands they have on hand or last purchased. The results, with year-to-year comparisons, are published each year by our promotion department, and distributed to advertisers, advertising agencies, manufacturers, and distributors from coast to coast, to help tell the story of the "Minnesota market."

We have made a score or more of shopping-center studies for our retail advertising department. Interviewers are assigned to specific shopping centers to question people about the frequency with which they shop at the particular center, about the nature of their shopping that day, about the newspapers— daily and weekly—which they read regularly, and—most important—about their place of residence. These enable our retail staff to determine the areas from which shoppers come to patronize the particular centers.

Once a year we prepare, for our circulation department, a careful series of population and household estimates of the governmental subdivisions which make up the Minneapolis ABC city zone. These data become the basis for percentage-of-coverage figures for circulation and advertising department use.

Periodically we examine our public relations—the way in which our readers, and the public, view the "image" of the Minneapolis *Star* and *Tribune*.

The list of examples can be a long one, but these will suffice to suggest the diversified nature of the reseach department's work in the market, consumer, and opinion fields.

A considerable amount of staff time and effort goes, however, into research on our newspapers themselves, and it is on this phase of our work that I want to dwell.

These studies can be divided readily into three areas:

1. Public opinion and attitude studies for publication.
2. Readership studies.
3. Audience and competitive media studies.

Our company's entry into research came with the establishment of the Minneapolis *Tribune*'s Minnesota Poll of Public Opinion in March 1944. The poll is conducted on a statewide basis, regularly, year in and year out— during and between election campaigns. We view the public opinion poll as a form of news reporting—a means of learning public reactions to major issues, to parties and candidates, and to current problems. Every Sunday, two Minnesota Poll reports are published in the *Tribune*—one on the Open Forum page, opposite editorial, and the other in the news sections. We endeavor to deal with different kinds of topics in each pair of reports.

The Minnesota Poll has, we believe, performed a unique public service for Minnesotans during its 16-year history. It has enabled people to discount the claims of special-interest groups which purport to represent what the public wants, but which frequently represent only fractional segments of the public. It has reflected the people's mood on state legislative proposals while those proposals have been very much in the news. It has thrown light on the relative importance of campaign issues, on the personal popularity of public officials and candidates, and on people's thinking about national and international crises.

Its record of evaluating and assessing the temper of the electorate in the biennial elections which come our way has been respectably good. On the Sunday preceding election day we publish a summary of what the so-called "likely voter" group in Minnesota is disposed to do about their choices among parties and candidates; and, except for "electing" the losing candidate for governor in 1954, the Minnesota Poll's diagnoses of election day results have been quite good. Even in 1948's classic test of fire, the Minnesota Poll correctly tied the Truman fate in Minnesota to the outcome of Hubert Humphrey's first campaign for a United States senate seat. (We claim to have batted only .800 in the 1948 election, but obviously this is a case of excessive modesty.)

Twice within the last year we have used the Minnesota Poll machinery to make special studies of statewide samples of high school teen-agers, and from those studies we have produced, respectively, a seven-part and a six-part series of Sunday feature articles which have been well received, both by our editors and our readers.

All of the Minnesota Poll surveys are carried out, in the field, by an interviewing corps of some 65 to 70 interviewers, who call on households in predesignated areas to question adults about their opinions in interviews which average 25 to 30 minutes.

Through the Poll, and through many of the market and consumer surveys we send into the field, we collect a rather steady flow of factual information about our readers—and about our competition. We ask about the daily and Sunday newspapers which respondents "regularly read"; we inquire into their magazine-reading habits; we ask about television viewing and radio listening; we make inquiries about the regularity with which *weekly* newspapers come into the home—and how often they are read.

From these kinds of data, we prepare reports which indicate to our editors the extent to which our newspapers are the sole papers received in the home, and the extent to which they compete with other daily or weekly papers—or with each other. We determine the characteristics of our reader households —the number of people in the household, their ages, their educational levels, the occupational status of the chief wage-earners, their labor union ties, their political preferences, their religious affiliations, and so on. We are able to describe, more fully and more accurately, our audiences and our competition, for our editors and advertising departments, than circulation records alone can do.

But the richest and most fruitful research we do for our editors is centered in readership and reader-interest surveys. These are carried out for us by the Research division in the School of Journalism at the University of Minnesota, after joint planning by our department and the University researchers. Under our research contract, which comes up for review and renegotiation every two years, we not only pay for the costs of the surveys but also contribute to basic journalism research at the University. We are thoroughly aware of the necessity for developing and strengthening the basic knowledge and techniques which our applied researchers use in solving specific problems.

There are advantages to both sides in an arrangement such as we have had these 16 years with the University of Minnesota:

1. The University School of Journalism is able to provide practical experience to graduate students in communications research; the readership reports and data become teaching aids in undergraduate courses; the funds help to keep a journalism research facility in operation at the university.

2. The *Star* and *Tribune* benefit from having readership studies conducted by an outside organization; we gain the advantage of regular consultation with academic experts in research on our surveys; and our own staff is freed of the detailed work which a readership survey requires.

In these readership surveys, interviews generally are made—for convenience—with readers living in the Minneapolis metropolitan area; but we ourselves have conducted enough studies elsewhere to feel assurance that the findings are generally indicative of what readers *outside* the metropolitan area also are interested in. Moreover, we are not content in any of these studies with merely learning what readers have done about reading the survey issue; we also collect data, in supplemental questionnaires, about readers' opinions, habits, and characteristics—all of which are extremely useful in the analyses we make.

What are some of the major lessons we've extracted from these studies?

(1) Readers consume our newspapers—in a reading sense, of course—with a high degree of selectivity. No news story, or picture, or column, or comic, or advertisement attracts or appeals to *all* readers. Selection is influenced by readers' jobs, income levels, educational background, sex, economic status, age, and place of residence—among others.

(2) Apart from Page 1, any given item of news content has a one-in-five chance of being read by the typical adult reader. The expectation norm we use for adult readership is approximately 20 per cent, and we use the 20 per cent figure as a crude yardstick of performance when we examine readership scores in a survey paper.

(3) During the 1950's, when television was growing rapidly throughout the United States, our readership surveys provided us with continuing assurance that readership was *not* going to hell in a hand-basket, contrary to the claims of TV competitors. Except for a small but measurable decline in comics reading in the evening newspaper, readership ratings were maintained, or improved, over their levels prior to the widespread entry of TV sets into homes. And if you will recall the "Videotown" studies made by a New York advertising agency, Cunningham & Walsh, in New Brunswick, N.J., for a 10-year period, you'll remember that the findings there likewise confirmed that newspaper reading remained relatively unaffected by the arrival of TV sets in the households.

(4) Reading interests of *men* tend to focus on news of politics and government, taxes and business—and sports. They read comics to a slightly lesser degree in the morning newspaper than do women, but to a somewhat greater degree in the evening paper. They have a greater interest than women do in editorials, and in columns offering comment and opinion on major issues of the day.

(5) Women are more likely to read articles that deal with human interest themes, with health and family care, with children. They read the obituary columns, vital statistics, food and fashion material, church and school news, the social columns, tips on home decorating and flower gardens, and recipes. And women are greatly interested in the advertising content of the newspapers. There are women who readily concede that they find the ads as "newsy" as other parts of the paper.

(6) Large numbers of readers have interest in accident stories and crime news.

(7) Young people—the teen-age set—read comics, sports news, advice

columns, fashion notes—and news of movie and TV celebrities. And the higher their grade in school, the more likely they are to be using the newspaper as an informational resource.

(8) If proof were needed, the surveys have shown, over and over, the wide-ranging appeal of pictures for readers of both sexes and all ages.

(9) Short, crisply-written news items, assembled under stock headings—like "News of the World" or "People in the News"—are well read. Readership scores of 50 per cent to 60 per cent frequently are recorded for such columns.

(10) Best-read stories are rarely the Page 1 play stories, and often are not even on Page 1.

But these are "generalizations"; what are some of the specifics? Let me tick off some of them:

In a typical household, our daily papers are read by 2.8 persons; our Sunday paper, by 3.1 persons.

The average adult reader pays attention to about 65 items in the *Morning Tribune;* about 75 items in the evening *Star.* (The *Star* carries a larger newshole than the *Morning Tribune.*)

Approximately half of the readers who start a Page 1 story which jumps, follow the story to the jump page.

About three out of five—60 per cent—of the adults read something on the editorial page; and about half of these—approximately 30 per cent—read one or more of the editorials.

Reading of comics is widespread; comics attract highbrows and lowbrows alike. In the morning, about 7 out of 10 men and women read comics; in the evening, nearly the same proportion of men read comics, but women readers drop to around 6 out of 10.

A combination of events—the broadening of the stock-ownership base in the American public, a growing awareness of the local-impact importance of news of business and finance, *and better reporting*—appears to account for an increase in the reading of our business and financial pages during the last decade.

More than 80 per cent of the people who consult any schedules of television programs as an aid to the selection of programs they want to watch, use newspaper TV listings for guidance.

About four out of five men, and one woman in five, read sports news in the morning paper. About 7 out of 10 men, and 30 per cent of the women, read the sports section of the evening paper.

There is widespread acceptance in Minnesota, we find, of the belief that the newspapers are superior to television and radio in presenting the news most satisfactorily and most accurately, and also in providing better background and interpretation of the news.

During the period 1949–59, we found a gradual improvement in the ratings which people assign the *Star* and *Tribune* for the kind of job we do in reporting events in the areas of labor union news, business and market news, and political news.

About three out of five adults confine their reading of our daily papers to a single reading session, but the rest pick up the paper to read at least two different times.

As you may surmise by this time, there are relatively few areas of reader behavior or reader reaction to our newspapers which, over the years, we have left unexplored.

The important question remains: What's the *practical* effect of all this? How do our editors *use* this kind of information—or *do* they?

The answer is: They *do* use it—and in a variety of ways.

We've strengthened our reporting of news in the business world in recent years because of our recognition of growing interest among readers in that type of news.

We carry detailed TV program schedules—daily and Sunday—because we know that readers turn to the papers for the latest information on what TV offers.

The *Morning* and *Sunday Tribune* and the evening *Star* carry several different kinds of news-shorts columns, assembled under "News of the World" or "On Worldwide News Fronts" labels, because we have found that the readership of these brief items is vastly increased when they are grouped in such roundups.

Last year, in the course of an opinion survey centering on our papers, we learned that readers in appreciable numbers fail to distinguish between the opinion-and-comment columns of the newspapers' *editorial* pages, and the news pages themselves. Many people are unaware of a distinction which is crystal-clear to us who are involved in newspaper operations, and which too often, apparently, we take for granted. The reaction of Wilbur Elston, editor of our editorial pages, is expressed in the intermittent but fairly regular appearance nowadays on those pages of a box, set in one- or two-column measure, boldface, which reads like this:

This is the *Star*'s [or *Tribune*'s] OPINION PAGE. This editorial page offers the newspaper's own opinions on matters of current interest in the editorial column at the left. It welcomes the opinions of readers in the Everybody's Ideas column [that is, the letters column]. It publishes opinions of columnists and other contributors elsewhere on the page.

And, along the same line, on the two or three days each week on which the page OPPOSITE the editorial page carries editorial material—columns, interpretive pieces or letters—there's a boxed caption at the top of the page which reads: "Second OPINION Page"—further underscoring the point.

One of the better illustrations of how our editors have put readership research findings to use goes back four years, when we introduced a wholesale redesign of the evening *Star*—based in good part on research—after a newsroom task force had spent more than nine months on the job. These were some of the consequences:

1. We went to five-days-a-week use of news-color pictures on Page 1 and on the Picture Page inside, because of our findings that *good* news-color art stops four out of five readers. It's dramatic; it lends impact; it's eye-stopping.

2. We opened up inside pages for news holes, because of our findings that a mixed-content page—that is, a page carrying both news and advertising—gained 30 to 35 per cent in readership when there was adequate space on the page for some display of the news. Our rule now is that the news space on the page should contain at least 15 column inches, spread preferably over three adjacent columns, and at least five inches deep, *or* over two adjacent columns of greater depth.

3. We combined reader interest in news shorts with the service function of an index, by creating a Page 1 news summary which has a color block under its heading, contains a series of news digest items—each of which keys to the page where the full account of that story may be found—and also jumps to Page 2 or Page 3, thereby stimulating the reader to turn the page. Readership of that column has been running from 35 per cent to 45 per cent since it was started.

4. We introduced a larger body type in our papers because, in the course of the *Star* redesign study, we determined through research that more than 7 out of 10 adults wear eyeglasses—and most of them regularly wear glasses when reading. So we switched from 8-point type on a 9-point slug, to a 9-point body type on a 9½-point slug—to make our papers easier to read.

5. We departmentalized and stressed our suburban news coverage because of research findings that suburban news not only was being read by more than 7 out of 10 adults who live in the suburbs, but also by 6 out of 10 men and women living in Minneapolis itself—the central city.

What we did, in the phrase applied by our executive editor, W. P. Steven, was to employ "editorial engineering" in giving the *Star* a new look. And, in terms of reader satisfaction, advertising gains and circulation growth, it appears to have worked out very well.

Having sought to make a case for the fact that our editors use research data, and having indicated some of the ways in which they do use it, I'd like now to tackle one of the central problems that seem to bother many publishers and editors when one talks of newspaper research. Their position can fairly be summarized, I believe, like this:

1. "Everything you've found out through research, I've known all along; this merely confirms it."

2. "You can't edit a newspaper successfully by slide rule."

3. "The research that is done isn't practical; it doesn't tell me the things I *want* to know."

4. And, finally, "I know my readers and what they want; after all, I've been in this business now for umpty-nine years; and I don't need statisticians to tell me what to do."

That's the case as I've heard it, at home and elsewhere, on quite a few occasions during the dozen years I've been engaged in *Star* and *Tribune* research.

This is our point of view:

1. Information about readers and what they choose to read is a form of military-type intelligence which editors need as their audiences grow and as the society in which those audiences exist becomes more complex. It was necessary for the Wright Brothers to fly by the seat of their pants when they took off at Kitty Hawk in 1903; but the pilot of a 1960 jetliner doesn't fly by the seat of his pants, and none of us would want him to. And it's not necessary for the 1960 editor to do any seat of the pants flying, in *his* difficult assignment, either.

2. An editor can assess his audiences, through research, without abdicating one iota of editorial responsibility or judgment. Readership statistics are not controlling. They never can be an adequate substitute for professional training, experience, and insight—nor are they intended to be—but they *can* enable him to make his moves more informedly, more intelligently.

If we were to treat readership data as binding, or if we were to produce newspapers limited to "best-read" types of content, we'd have the most flamboyant, sensational and frivolous newspapers ever published—because the best-read stories, day in and day out, are usually those heavily vested with violence, sex, controversy, and so-called human interest qualities. Readership data are not, and cannot be, replacements for the editor's professional judgment of what is important, consequential, significant, in the day's news—and we would have it no other way.

The point is that readers' interests and demands on their newspapers are widely varied; that readers are people with diverse backgrounds and equally diverse informational and entertainment needs; and the editor whose responsibility is to provide them with the news fare they require should know wherein, and how, they do differ. Editing from the strength of knowledge is to be preferred to editing by hunch, intuition, or calculated guess.

At the same time, there are a number of limitations on our ability to inform our editors of things they should know:

In the first place, readership findings reflect only what the reader has selected for consumption out of that which the editor makes available to him—not necessarily what he would *prefer* to read if he had unrestricted choice. Therefore, each study is a measure only of what the reader has culled from the newspaper as it is, not his "ideal" newspaper.

Second, the reader is incapable of telling the editor what that "ideal" should be.

Third, all readership data are relative values. They are a reflection of what readers exposed themselves to, in a single issue of a single newspaper which carries a unique array of news and entertainment items. No other newspaper ever is precisely the same, before or after. And because of the rapidly changing nature of the news, and therefore the newspaper product, his reading of specific content items will change from day to day, or from paper to paper. Hence, one would be unwise to accept a single newspaper readership study as a basis for saying, "Now I know what our readers read." It takes an accumulation of studies to develop trends and patterns of reader behavior, before one may say with reasonable confidence, "*Now* I begin to know."

Fourth, there are many areas of reader behavior which are still unresearched. We are forced to infer or deduce the motivations that prompt a reader to give his attention to specific news items; we don't *know* with assurance what the motives are. We have taken some preliminary passes at studies of the extent to which we are successful in *communicating* ideas and facts to readers—but there is a great deal to be done in ascertaining which techniques are more successful and which less successful. We don't know how much the reader *retains* of what he finds in the newspapers. We don't know enough about that lightning-fast process in the reader's mind which causes him to read an item at the top of column 2 on page 47—but reject, or skip, adjacent news items in columns 1 and 3.

We think such things about readers should be known; and I am confident that the years ahead will produce far more insights into these aspects of the behavior of the people who make up our audiences than we now find it possible to achieve.

But, even under present conditions, we believe that research has enlarged considerably the editor's awareness of the public he serves, and that—whether we can measure the result with precision or not—our newspapers *are* doing a more effective job of communicating to readers the kinds of information they want or need.

A federal budget story which is a recital of dreary—if staggering—dollar totals, for example, is of considerably less value when it comes to *informing* people than the story which tells the budget story in terms of "you and your family," because the latter type of report will command the larger audience. And a newspaper's job is to be read.

The Minneapolis *Star* and *Tribune* publish great quantities of news material each day whose readership scores we know will be low but which are of compelling interest to various publics within our region—stock tables for investors and business executives; speech texts for "eggheads" who want to know exactly what the man said, and how he said it; box scores for the baseball addict; the Washington columnists' weighty pontifications for the opinion-leader elites which demand constant stimulus, whether they agree or disagree. And we propose to continue doing so.

Readership research is a procedure that enables both editors and advertisers to gauge the impact of their offerings to readers, and also makes it possible to try out new ideas—to test the kind of reception a new or different approach will get from readers.

A few years back, we introduced a "home and hobby" section in the Minneapolis *Sunday Tribune* with marked success—a success which was predictable because survey data had shown great interest among readers in that type of information and feature material.

Anything that helps to take the guesswork out of the editing process is worthwhile. Research is capable of providing a strong assist. If you will grant that a decision supported by provable fact is more likely to be correct than one based on conjecture, surmise or tradition, then—so far as Minneapolis *Star* and *Tribune* editors are concerned—research has justified itself.

37

Opinion Research and Marketing

Leo Bogart

The interrelationship of the contributions to knowledge of human behavior by different academic disciplines is well illustrated in the field of public opinion. To the study of public opinion—whether regarding political issues, moral issues, or market preferences—sociologists, social psychologists, psychologists, political scientists, and businessmen have made contributions. Here the author details the development and present status of public opinion research as it relates to commercial endeavor. This and the preceding article (Selection 36) should convince even the most skeptical that any organization that sells to the general public must be constantly aware of the current state of public opinion.

In practice and in the popular conception, market research and opinion research are connected so closely as to be indistinguishable. Both employ the interview as the principal method of collecting data, and both borrow from the social sciences the theories by which they interpret data.

Because techniques of field work and analysis are in large measure identi-

Reprinted from *The Public Opinion Quarterly*, **21**, 1 (Spring 1957), pp. 129–140, by special permission of the publisher and the author.

Leo Bogart is Vice President, Marketing Planning and Research, Bureau of Advertising, American Newspaper Publishers' Association.

cal for the two fields, most research organizations generally consider the appropriate skills to be interchangeable. The same project director who in the morning designs a questionnaire, lays out a sample, or prepares a tabulation plan for a study of attitudes toward the Baghdad Pact may in the afternoon go through identical procedures in organizing a study of the market for chlorophyl toothpaste. And it is likely that he will employ the same interviewers and the same coding and tabulating personnel.

The best-known figures in the field of political polling—George Gallup, Elmo Roper, and Archibald Crossley—are also leading practitioners of marketing research. Such leading research firms as the Psychological Corporation, the Opinion Research Corporation, and International Research Associates conduct both opinion and market surveys. Market research organizations like Alfred Politz Research, Willard R. Simmons, Audits and Surveys, National Analysts, and the major advertising agencies frequently measure opinion on subjects with only a tangential relationship to marketing.

The general public probably identifies market research as a form of opinion polling. Indeed this is in the market researcher's interest, for he can introduce every interview—whether it deals with chewing gum or plumbing fixtures—with the familiar and (to the respondent) flattering refrain, "I'm making a *survey* to find out what people *think* on various subjects, and I'd like very much to have your *opinions* on a few questions."

Like the opinion survey, market research has in the last two decades become part of the public domain. Full-page newspaper advertisements regularly detail the results of audience surveys for rival magazines. The broadcast measurement rating services are a common subject of articles in the press and jokes by television personalities. In popular literature, the market researcher occupies a position of almost sinister infallibility, although he, like the political pollsters, strongly felt the effects of the mistaken 1948 electoral forecast. The research man portrayed in John Schneider's *The Golden Kazoo* is an icy creature, molded of the same material as the slide rule and the calculator. He can come up with almost instantaneous reports on the public temper, and is therefore an indispensable adjunct of the ad man who "merchandises" a presidential candidate like a tube of toothpaste.

Schumucker knew that figures do lie. So his kids—all of whom were of one wholesome clean-cut friendly type—brought back from the field more than mere figures. They brought back also complex mental drives and deep emotional urges, the hidden reasons behind the unreliable figures.

After his Flying Survey Squad took samplings from the bedrock opinion in a half-dozen representative states, and from the many strata representing income, race, religion, geography, sex, and indefinitely so on, Schumucker put the samplings into a battery of electronic calculating machines which sorted, counted, and analyzed the stuff. Then Schumucker knew. He *knew*.[1]

---

[1] John G. Schneider, *The Golden Kazoo* (New York: Rinehart, 1956), p. 78.

To say that the researcher "knows" is to see him as a scientist, albeit something of a "mad scientist." And some market researchers are not loath to don white laboratory robes on occasion. (In the presentation of one recent study, methodological details were withheld on the grounds that only "the skilled research doctors" were qualified to review them.)

Kenneth D. Hutchinson has described the broader field of marketing (distinct from marketing research) as scientific in no greater a degree than carpentry, dry cleaning, or poultry raising:

> There is a real reason . . . why the field of marketing has been slow to develop an unique body of theory. It is a simple one: marketing is not a science. It is rather an art or a practice, and as such much more closely resembles engineering, medicine, and architecture than it does physics, chemistry, or biology. The medical profession sets us an excellent example, if we would but follow it; its members are called 'practitioners' and not scientists. It is the work of physicians, as it is of any practitioner, to apply the findings of many sciences to the solution of problems. Among the sciences which the medical man employs are biology, physiology, chemistry, physics, psychology, and many more. . . . It is a characteristic of a practice that the solution of each problem faced calls for a different and distinct combination of techniques and approaches. The fact that each problem is different, however, does not deter practitioners from approaching them in the scientific manner and spirit.[2]

Practitioners of opinion research might be reluctant to admit that such a restricted definition applies to their own field. Most of them would insist that the study of public opinion may be regarded either as a science or as an art. As a science it seeks to formulate ever more precisely the principles that underlie the formation and expression of social values and individual attitudes. As an art it perfects and practices techniques for penetrating and describing systematically the beliefs and behavior of large numbers of people.

INTELLECTUAL TOOLS OF MARKETING RESEARCH

The market researcher deals with a restricted range of problems, to which he may apply the whole body of public opinion theory and technique, but to which he must also apply other types of knowledge. Insofar as he is concerned with what goes on inside of people's minds he is squarely in the realm of opinion research. To the extent that he is concerned with what people *do* he may find himself heavily involved in other branches of social science, or even in engineering. He resembles an opinion researcher most when he looks at human beings in two of their aspects: (1) as consumers actively exercising their economic force in the market, and (2) as members of audiences for marketing strategies and advertising media and messages. In the first respect, he is concerned with their potentialities, tastes, and habits as customers. In

---

[2] Kenneth D. Hutchinson, "Marketing as a Science: An Appraisal," *The Journal of Marketing*, **16**, 3 (January 1952), pp. 286–293.

the second respect he considers them as recipients of the manufacturer's efforts to sell goods and services; his research seeks to determine with what media they can best be reached, and with what appeals they can most successfully be attracted to the product.

Essentially, opinion research is field research. The student of public opinion derives most of his knowledge of how people think and why they think as they do by actually going out and talking to them. The theorists of public opinion, whether they write texts like William Albig or critiques like Herbert Blumer, must constantly refer back to those empirical studies in which someone has asked respondents what they believe or feel or want.

By contrast, market research uses the results of original field work only as part of an array of data acquired in a number of ways. This reflects the different origins of the two fields. While opinion research is concerned only with people, market research also deals with commodities and with the material resources of distribution. It therefore necessarily uses traditional forms of business record-keeping. Market research began as desk research, and to a large extent it still is that, though it has increasingly used field methods. It makes extensive use of statistics which are not compiled from interviews.

Much of today's desk research entails the secondary or tertiary use of data originally acquired by the survey or questionnaire method—e.g., government census data or trade association reports. A great deal of the research used to evaluate advertising media has the same character. A broadcast rating service may question thousands of television viewers every month about their program preferences. The percentages resulting from this field investigation are presented as ratings in reports to advertisers and agencies. But the ultimate user converts the ratings into comparative cost-per-thousand figures or classifies them according to levels of station coverage. Thus, at the final point of use, the data are manipulated on a purely mathematical level and altogether apart from questions of popular taste, socioeconomic differences in viewing habits, and the like. For printed media, too, comparative audience information may be placed on punch cards, to enable selection according to a formula based on the extent of penetration. In such cases the figures have acquired a quasi-reality of their own; they, rather than the original interviews or observations, are the raw material of research.

Something like this happens also in the case of store and pantry auditing, which borrows its sampling and analytical techniques from opinion research while at the same time rejecting any exercise of opinion or perception on the part of the "respondent." In the presentation and interpretation of such studies, the "share-of-market" commonly achieves the same disembodied status as the television program popularity rating.

Sales analysis, which is at the vital center of marketing research, employs methods of reasoning analogous to those used by the opinion researcher in his statistical breakdowns and cross-tabulations, although it deals with very different kinds of data. Sales records yield significant diagnostic information when they are broken down in terms of such variables as geographic regions, sales territories, city sizes, types of outlet, or distributors. Experimental sales tests, an important part of marketing research, apply ordinary scientific methods to the comparison of sales results under controlled conditions. Each variable is studied separately, whether it is a product characteristic, pricing, advertising, or type of distribution.

Forecasting sales, or broader economic trends, demands the use of mathematical techniques of extrapolation and projection. Recently, similar techniques have been used to apply operations research to the study of distribution systems, although personal observation and analysis of records are the methods commonly used to describe a distribution structure schematically. In the study of distribution costs, break-even points, dealer margins, and salesmen's compensation, the economist does not ordinarily need the help of the opinion researcher.

TRENDS IN MARKETING RESEARCH

The field methods of opinion research have been applied to marketing problems only in the recent past, although the historian of market research can reach far back to cloak his profession with the aura of antiquity. The late Lawrence C. Lockley [3] points out that "even the children of Israel sent interviewers out to sample the market and the produce of Canaan." [4] Be that as it may, today's marketing research seems to have emerged as part of the same wave of rationalization that has produced, since Frederick Taylor, several generations of industrial efficiency experts. The drive toward "scientific management" has emphasized research in marketing much as it has revolutionized cost accounting, perfected time and motion study, and automated manufacturing.

In 1879, N. W. Ayer wired state officials and publications throughout the country in order to get local information on grain production for a client who manufactured agricultural machinery. Shortly before the turn of the century, Harlow Gale at the University of Minnesota investigated advertising effects with the aid of a mail questionnaire. But in spite of these pioneer efforts, developments came slowly. By 1910 less than $50,000 a year was being spent on all forms of market research. [5] At about the same time, modern media research received its first major application when R. O. Eastman, then advertising manager of the Kellogg Company, persuaded 40-odd members of the Association of National Advertising Managers to sponsor a cooperative postcard magazine readership survey.

---

[3] In "Notes on the History of Marketing Research," *Journal of Marketing*, **16** (April 1950), pp. 733–736.

[4] One might reach even farther back than Lockley did. Adam and Eve conducted the first taste test, with unforgettable consequences.

[5] This was the estimate of J. George Frederick who had helped found the Business Bourse in the previous year. By contrast, such expenditures today may be in the quarter-billion dollar category.

The Bureau of Business Research was founded at the Harvard Graduate School of Business Administration in 1911, and Charles Coolidge Parlin came to the Curtis Publishing Company to head up a new research division in the same year. The first attempts of these pioneer research organizations were devoted to analysis of distribution practices rather than to the study of consumer wants and preferences. The Harvard research bureau started by studying the operating expenses of retail stores, while Curtis surveyed the marketing structures of a number of major industries.

In 1916 the Chicago *Tribune* published a market study of Chicago based on returns from a sample of house-to-house interviews using a fixed questionnaire. It became increasingly apparent that an understanding of customer buying, habits, wants, and expectations was essential to efficient marketing practice. As this happened, market research techniques underwent increasing refinement and marketing men began to borrow more self-consciously from their colleagues in the social sciences.

The methods used in these early investigations have a kind of archiac charm to an observer of today's era. Harry Dexter Kitson, writing in the November 1923 issue of the *Annals,* a number devoted entirely to "Psychology in Business," is critical of basing business decisions on the (apparently prevalent) practice of asking a college class, "Which of these 10 appeals would be most likely to make you buy?" But Kitson himself believed that the correct solution to a marketing problem could be found by following prevailing practice. As a case in point he cited a decline since 1900 in the percentage of full-page magazine ads with borders around them.

On the assumptions of the historical method, that trends of practice show the pathways to profitable practice, the present-day advertiser will be in accord with other successful advertisers if he lays out his full-page advertisments without borders.

In defining the characteristics of "the modern consumer," Kitson lists four attributes: he is "impersonal," "exists in the mass," "is widely distributed," and "is a many-sided individual." One may question the inclusiveness or accuracy of these descriptive phrases, but the concepts clearly reflect the influence of social science. This is a very different kind of outlook from that expressed in the compilation of trade statistics.

Kitson's description of the purchase decision, as it takes place in the mind of the consumer, is borrowed from behaviorist psychology: [6]

The energy of the brain may be distributed in various amounts over different systems, the amount in each system depending on the strength of the corresponding idea. In the case of a purchase, if the main idea is to grow in strength, its brain system must draw off from the other systems the brain energy resident within them, until the energy of the brain is all drained off into the one system, which means the triumph of the idea.

---

[6] This may have been rather astute, after all. John Watson did very well in the advertising business.

The literal meaning of this quotation is much less interesting than the way in which it illustrates the emergence of an "applied psychology" focused on fundamental marketing questions.

Nothing better illustrates the progress made in the following decade than the contrast between Kitson's analysis of the purchase decision and the one made by Paul Lazarsfeld in an article on "The Psychological Aspect of Market Research" in the *Harvard Business Review* of October, 1934.

The "time of deliberation," the "anticipated features of the purchase," the "relation to previous purchases" are only examples of what we could call the psychological "coordinates" of a purchase. It seems to us that one of the outstanding contributions of the psychologist to the problem of market survey is the careful, general study of the structure of the purchase, in order to prepare us to find in a special study what could possibly be characteristic for the investigated commodity.

Lazarsfeld saw two functions of the psychologist in market research: (1) to interpret the data and (2) to supply more and better knowledge of the structure of the purchasing act. The connection between these two separate functions he found in the term "motive." In the details of any purchase he saw some of the happenings bearing what he called "an accent of motivation" whereas others did not. He writes: "It is mainly the procedure of interpretation, and the formal analysis of the act of purchase, which the psychologist can and ought to contribute to market research." (In today's vocabulary, we might substitute "opinion researcher" or "social scientist" for "psychologist.")

In the early 1920's such psychologists as Daniel Starch and Henry Link had turned their talents to the study of markets and advertisements. The following years were especially fruitful in methodological progress, principally in sampling and interviewing. By the mid-1930's market research practices had already assumed a form very similar to those of the present day, and social scientists were exercising an important—though by no means dominant—influence on them.

It is no accident that the *Public Opinion Quarterly* and the *Journal of Marketing* were both established in the same year, 1936. Since that time, the two fields have grown closer together, as students trained in the social sciences have increasingly found their way into market research organizations. The American Association for Public Opinion Research and the American Marketing Association alike include members of both the academic and business communities. At the time that AAPOR was founded in 1946, it consisted about equally of "commercial" and "noncommercial" members. Today a substantial majority of the membership is drawn from business.

MARKETING TURNS TO THE SOCIAL SCIENTISTS

The closer ties between opinion research and market research arise from two broader trends. First, social scientists have become more curious about the operation of the business system. Growing disparity between academic and business salary scales has strengthened the material incentive for many university teachers and researchers to switch careers. A change in the intellectual climate has also led social scientists to focus increasingly on business problems. The development of social science in the United States was originally linked with various social reform movements and a strong skepticism about the prevailing economic system. Not many years ago, a social scientist who worked for business was considered (in the grand sense) to have "sold out" to the devil or (in a petty way) to be entering "trade." The political events of the postwar years have shaken much of this ideology. Since social scientists generally no longer recognize any viable alternative to existing economic mechanisms, they have become more willing to consider business problems as worthy of serious study.

A second broad trend is that businessmen have increasingly turned with greater expectations toward social science. As they have used more research they have become more sophisticated about its methods, and the methods themselves have become more sophisticated. Market research, which began by collecting data, has devoted increasing effort to analyzing it.

More searching analysis, in turn, has made for greater demands on theory drawn from the social sciences. It has also created a demand for skills which would not have been found in the traditional equipment of market research. Qualitative methods long familiar to social scientists were applied in the 1930's to the study of mass media effects, and in the '40's to the investigation of advertising and marketing subjects. In the '50's these methods were given a new name—motivation research—and encountered some stiff resistance from the defenders of unqualified quantification. Controversy rages not over the permissibility of qualitative research, but as to its proper use—as to whether it is in itself a means of understanding,[7] or whether it should be merely preliminary or illustrative, with the "real" answers emerging from proper statistics. The internecine quarrels of the research fraternity may have shaken some faith in the business community, but they may also have strengthened an awareness that the explanation of consumer behavior is a complex job that requires specialized talent and training.

Motivation research and qualitative advertising copy research have brought wider use of techniques extraneous to the original basic core of market research practice: the depth interview, qualitative content analysis, projective techniques for the diagnosis of personality. A single large market research organization may include sampling statisticians, clinical psychologists, survey analysts, and economists. The "all-around" market research man of yesterday's vintage could himself perform any of the tasks necessary to plan a study, collect and process the data, and present the findings. Today his principal skill may be that of knowing which experts to call on for assistance.

It must be remembered that most practitioners of market research come from a business school or general economics background rather than from

---

[7] Used in the sense that Max Weber used the German *"Verstehen."*

the social sciences. In many companies, advancement in marketing research may come through the clerical ranks, and a college education may not be considered necessary. Differences in academic training are probably reflected in the theoretical reference points and the general design of a study, rather than in any startling difference of technique. In most ordinary market survey work, little if any distinction is visible between the methods of a social scientist and those of a business school graduate. By and large, the quality and usefulness of the research depends on the researcher's ability and temperament rather than on the character of his original training. This may simply result from the fact that the social scientist who applies himself full time to business problems quickly acquires work patterns similar to those of other toilers in the same vineyard. His research is aimed at pragmatic objectives. There is rarely time to pursue truths which are irrelevant to the job in hand.

Of the enormous aggregate amounts of market research data relevant to theories of human behavior, very little has been brought to the level of generalization. One obvious reason is that studies are made for clients or for management on a confidential basis. Research results are normally revealed to a wider audience only when the client or research organization can use them for some special purpose. This may happen when the study shows the sponsor in a favorable light, or when the findings have such general interest that he wins recognition from releasing them as a public service. The research organization may press to publish a study to illustrate the quality of its work.

Furthermore, the commercial researcher usually lacks the opportunity for leisurely reflection on the theoretical principles which underlie the pattern of his findings. Too often he even lacks the time to read his colleagues' reports, or to cast more than a casual glance at the scholarly literature in his field. Once completed, a study is rarely looked at a second time with an eye to determining whether its contents have long-range interest.

It would be wrong, however, to assume that market research has failed to make noteworthy contributions to social science, and to the study of public opinion. Three different types of contribution may be cited:

1. Audience studies for the national magazines have provided pioneer opportunities for the large-scale application of new techniques, such as probability sampling. Since these studies are invariably intended to serve promotional ends, they often are published and available to all comers.

2. Studies originally prepared for special purposes have been turned back to university research groups for reanalysis and have thereby enriched the literature of social science. *Personal Influence* by Paul Lazarsfeld and Elihu Katz and *They Went to College* by Patricia West and Ernest Havemann are eminent illustrations.

3. Miscellaneous survey findings, reported in press releases or brochures, have been used as data by students of mass communication.

It would be mistaken to conclude, however, that social scientists in the universities have become as interested in marketing problems as market researchers are in social science. The study of industrial psychology and of "human relations in industry" are accepted parts of college curricula and research programs, but no such place has been won by the social psychology of consumption and marketing, although they surely are no less important than the social psychology of work.

THE MARKET AS A SOCIAL PHENOMENON

The market researcher borrows the techniques and lore of opinion research to understand the consumer, but he must also use other forms of social research. It is not always necessary to question people directly in order to investigate their buying habits. Observation may be an equally valuable instrument. The market researcher knows this when he makes a pantry audit or store audit to tell how much and what kinds of merchandise are on hand, instead of expecting customers or dealers to give him an accurate report.

In recent years some research firms, for instance, Alderson and Sessions, and Arthur D. Little, Inc., have begun to use an experimental approach to the study of the purchase decision, setting a panel of housewives to play a "game" in order to find out what products they will "buy" in different types of outlets and under various competitive conditions. This interesting technique has its antecedents both in the mathematics of von Neumann and Morgenstern and in the conditioned reflexes of innumerable white rats, trained to make economic choices. Studies of this sort should prove to be increasingly important and productive in the future, especially as hypotheses based on field research become more and more refined, and demand the test of laboratory experimentation.

Whether or not he is consciously aware of it, the market researcher is constantly making use of those other branches of social science which describe the structure and processes of society as a whole. Studies of demographic and social trends, and of urbanism, furnish the market analyst with a basis for understanding and predicting the changing character and wants of the consumer. He must turn to the accumulated knowledge about social movements to explain (and thus abet or combat, according to his allegiance) product fashions and developments such as the creation of markets for vodka and quinine water, or the shift to king size and filter cigarettes.

Students of stratification have shown a strong interest in the differences of life styles and consumption patterns which provide the outer symbols of social status. W. Lloyd Warner and Burleigh Gardner have used the concept of social class to explain a wide variety of consumption habits, ranging from the choice of greeting card designs to the selection of merchandise for listing in mail order catalogues. Gregory P. Stone has used status symbolism as a key to differentiate among women who shop at neighborhood and chain stores and to analyze clothing preferences. In a review of the sociological literature on "Careers and Consumer Behavior" [8] David Riesman and Howard Rose-borough have related buying behavior not only to social class but also to stages in the human life cycle.

Students of marketing have drawn freely from the great reservoir of social research in order to understand the mind and behavior of the individual consumer, but they have made considerably less use of social research to increase their understanding of marketing institutions. Too many market surveys are made or interpreted with the tacit assumption that people's opinions of various products and brands will automatically express themselves in buying behavior. Actually, the positioning of a product in the market depends not only on what people think about it (if they think about it at all), but on the kind of distribution it receives. The study of distribution channels and mechanisms has never particularly fascinated social scientists, and except in the form of occasional retailer surveys it is a realm which many working market researchers rarely frequent.

Yet the past few decades have witnessed revolutionary changes in merchandising. Supermarkets have become the dominant force in the grocery field, with the result that one sixth of the food stores do 70 per cent of the business. The drive for efficiency in retailing favors major nationally advertised brands which are "presold" to the customer and have higher turnover. Prepackaging of meats, vegetables and dairy products eliminates the last vestiges of interpersonal contact between shopper and sales clerk. The growth of suburban retail centers further changes the social character of shopping and threatens to affect urban downtown areas radically. Distinctions among the merchandise lines of grocery, hardware, drug, notion, and department stores have begun to blur.

These developments, and those yet to come, carry significant social implications. They also make it imperative that the market researcher concern himself with the distribution process and the people at work in it. Salesmen have been studied by sociologists (for example, Raymond Mack) and by personnel psychologists (such as those at the Life Insurance Agency Management Association), who seek to isolate the ingredients of success or failure in order to improve selection and training. This kind of study might be profitably extended to cover the characteristics and occupational roles of sales or marketing executives, or to store managers, buyers, and other retailing personnel.

The market researcher also has much to learn from the study of bureaucracy and institutional organization. He must examine the relation of a company's sales organization to its key distributors, of distributors to wholesalers or jobbers, and so on through the sales process. Too often, the market researcher's job is considered completed when he has reported consumer reactions to a product, even though consumer acceptance may mean far less for ultimate sales than the willingness of dealers to stock, display, and promote the merchandise. Realistically, market research should be concerned not only

---

[8] In the second volume of *Consumer Behavior* (New York: New York University Press, 1955).

with the preferences and purchasing habits of customers, but also with the characteristic interpersonal relationships of the people who handle it at the intermediate levels between the manufacturer and customer.

This point is well documented in a special report in *Super Market Merchandising* (February 1957), which deals with the "buying committee," a small executive group which selects merchandise for retail food chains:

No product, no promotion can gain admission to at least 88 per cent of the nation's Super Markets without the express consent of the buying committee.

Yet no more than 800 of these buying committee members pass judgment on products that go through 7241 stores involving annual sales of $7.5 billion according to the research sample studied by *Super Market Merchandising*.

It requires little further arithmetic to establish how few are the number of men who decide what groceries 40 million shoppers will roll out in a $23-billion-a-year industry.

Such a development should fascinate the social scientist who is interested in the concentration of power over public taste; it should also be an urgent subject of investigation by professional students of marketing.

Though a better understanding of marketing phenomena will increasingly come from other areas of social science, the interdependence of opinion research and market research will certainly remain evident. Improvements in sampling, questioning and analytical techniques will continue to have common interest to both fields. Such technical progress will be speeded by the vastly increased expenditures on survey research.

Students of marketing will also continue to look to the field of public opinion research for more precise knowledge in several major areas:

1. *The Measurement of Communications Effects.* Evaluating the impact of advertising messages and media represents much the same problem—though on a different scale—as determining attitude changes induced by a college course on race relations or by an Army film on the Battle of Britain. But commercial research cannot be limited to a classroom laboratory, and in the field the results even of well-designed studies are often disappointingly inconclusive, because of the enormous number of uncontrollable variables.

2. *The Study of Personal Influence.* Major purchases are preceded by considerable discussion within and outside the family, and choices of even minor products reflect a brand imagery developed in part from casual conversation and observation of others. Interpersonal influences are difficult to define and measure within the framework of the consumer survey, particularly since respondents often confuse them with advertising messages.

3. *The Description of Personality.* The appeal of a particular product or brand is in many instances clearly related to characteristics of individual personality. Such characteristics can be broadly defined by clinical psychologists working with standardized diagnostic instruments. Projective tests can often be introduced as part of a small-sample consumer motivation study, and some tests (such as the house-tree-person test) can even be administered by an interviewer whose skills are only moderately above average. But in a broad-

scale survey the interpretation of projective material becomes prohibitively expensive. This makes urgently desirable the development of valid—and standardized—psychological indicators which can be quantitatively analyzed.

Finally, it is apparent that market and opinion research resemble other branches of social science in that their agenda of outstanding problems can be expected to grow rather than diminish in the coming years.

38

Measuring the Effectiveness of an Overseas Information Campaign: A Case History

Leo Bogart

This scientific study was carried out in the classical "before-after" research design. It is of interest, however, not only for the careful research procedures described but for the substantive findings as well. One can only wish that this kind of critical research had accompanied every effort in every country that the United States has tried to influence. It is important to keep a finger on the pulse of every country as a potential "customer" of democracy.

As to the specific findings, there is confirmation of previous research so strong that it might be said to yield two laws: (1) In a free situation, individuals expose themselves to propaganda or education on the basis of their present values, and such efforts are more likely to strengthen present beliefs than to modify them. (2) There is differential response to communication by age, sex, and social status.

The measurement of communications effects is by now the subject of a considerable literature.[1] The first significant research in this field took place a generation ago, with the college classroom typically used as a laboratory

Reprinted from *The Public Opinion Quarterly*, **21**, 4 (Winter 1957), pp. 475–498, by special permission of the publisher and author.

Leo Bogart is Vice President, Marketing Planning and Research, Bureau of Advertising, American Newspaper Publishers' Association.

[1] For comprehensive summaries of this literature, see Arnold M. Rose, *Studies in the Reduction of Prejudice* (1st ed.; Chicago: American Council in Race Relations, 1947). Also Joseph T. Klapper, *Effects of Mass Communication* (New York: Free Press, 1960).

and the subject of experiment commonly being the effects on prior attitudes of a course in sociology or psychology.

This tradition of research culminated in the carefully designed studies performed during the war for the Army's Information and Education Division, and subsequently described by Hovland and his associates.

Studies of students and of troops are similar in that they utilize as subjects a captive audience which lacks the option to avoid or suppress the message if it so desires. Serious questions may still be raised as to how communications effects take place in a normal situation, one in which the audience controls its exposure to the media of communication, in which the effects of any particular message are diluted by the pressure of a myriad of competing or irrelevant messages, and in which words are reinforced or contradicted by the impact of events.

The attempt to measure communications effects in the field has been most frequently made in the subject areas of politics and marketing, where the stakes are high and where substantial research budgets can be met. In their studies of the 1940 and 1948 election campaigns Paul Lazarsfeld, Bernard Berelson, and their associates relate changes in voting intention to mass media effects (among other things). Large corporations have sometimes made similar studies of the effectiveness of advertising or marketing campaigns, but these remain unpublished.

Two notable community studies have utilized the familiar scheme of interviewing cross-sections of a population before and after large-scale public information efforts. In Cincinnati in 1949, Shirley Star and Helen Hughes found that the effects of an information campaign on behalf of the United Nations were untraceable in the light of the problems which the organization itself faced during the same period. A study of a venereal disease information program in Columbus, Ohio, made by the Bureau of Applied Social Research, also showed disappointing results. Those who were most apt to expose themselves to VD were least apt to expose themselves to the media which carried information on the subject.

The present study is presented as a case history in the same area of research. It was planned not with theoretical objectives in mind but with the immediate objective of evaluating a test campaign.

BACKGROUND OF THE STUDY

The communications campaign in this case was conducted in Greece in the later part of 1952 as part of the U.S. information program in that country. The U.S. Information Agency has used a wide variety of communications techniques; the test campaign represented an experimental use of paid newspaper advertising as a means of conveying ideas to a wide overseas public. A series of 14 advertisements was prepared for insertion in Greek newspapers and a booklet, "The March of Freedom," was offered free to the readers of the ads. The appearance of the advertisements, both in their size and styling, was such as to make them stand out in the newspaper.

The research was organized and timed as an integral part of the campaign itself.[2] The objectives were to determine (1) whether or not these materials succeeded in attracting the attention of a wide popular audience; (2) what kinds of people they reached; (3) what the readers thought of them; (4) what kinds of information the ads and the booklet managed to convey to their readers; and (5) what political attitudes they modified, if any.

The newspaper advertisements aimed to create or reinforce the conviction that the U.S. and Greece are joined together in the cause of freedom and that their common ideals are those embodied in the Universal Declaration of Human Rights. The advertisements used large photographs and brief texts to illustrate and discuss the rights enjoyed by citizens in a democracy.

These freedoms were visualized in terms of the "rights of children" which might be expected to gain warm acceptance virtually everywhere. The underlying point of view is expressed in the following quotation from one of the ads:

We believe it is important to the U.S.A. that this child and every child in every land shall have these basic human freedoms.

We believe this because we deeply love the freedoms we are building in our own life ... and we know that our own freedoms are not fully safe until freedom is safe for anyone, born anywhere.

This does not mean, of course, that we want Greece and other countries to try to be like the U.S.A. Each free people will always have its own way to build its own use of freedom.

But the goals we seek are common.

Emphasis in the ads was not on the present *threat* to freedom; only the last ad in the series referred directly to the Soviet Union and the "cold war." They were, rather, focused on the positive aspects of human liberty.

One ad mentioned the Declaration in its headline, and another focused on the booklet offer. All the rest referred to individual rights, covered in nine of the Declaration's Thirty Articles. All the ads except one featured large photographic illustrations of children.

"The March of Freedom" was a 32-page booklet illustrated with two-color drawings which showed significant stages in the development of human rights from Hammurabi's Code to the United Nations. It contained no di-

---

[2] The writer assumed responsibility for this project after the completion of the field work. The original research design was prepared by Herta Herzog and Donald B. Armstrong, Jr. The field work was under the direction of William Reynolds. Ben Gedalecia headed the Office of Research and Evaluation of the U.S. Information Agency at the time the study was made. The interpretations and statements made in this article are solely those of the writer and in no way reflect either the official position of the Information Agency or that of the writer's own organization.

rect references to communism. Its objective was rather to show the historical continuity of the democratic tradition.

Between November 16, 1952, and January 3, 1953, the 14 advertisements were run on a twice-a-week alternating schedule in all four Salonica newspapers. (These papers claim a combined total daily circulation of about 50,000.) Every ad appeared once in each paper, but no ad ever appeared in more than one paper on the same day. Approximately 17,000 copies of "The March of Freedom" booklet were distributed by the U.S.I.S. Library in Salonica directly and by mail.

METHOD OF STUDY

The study was designed to permit comparison of the attitudes of a cross-section of adults in Salonica, who were interviewed shortly before and again immediately after the advertisements ran in the press. To overcome any possible "panel effect," the second wave of interviews (after the ad campaign) was conducted not only with the *same* people who had been in the original sample, but also with *another* parallel cross-section of the population, a sample whose members had not been interviewed previously.

Changes in opinion between the first and second survey periods might have occurred quite independently of the advertising campaign, through the impact of world events or of political developments in Greece.[3] For example, attitudes toward the United States might have become more favorable between the first and second wave of the study because of a general improvement in opinion throughout the country rather than as a result of the ad campaign. Or opinion might have remained about the same in Salonica, while it became less favorable elsewhere in Greece (that is, the ads might produce their effect not by *improving* attitudes but by preventing a decline which was evident elsewhere).

To take these possibilities into account, a simultaneous before-after survey had to be run in *another* Greek city in which no advertising or information campaign was conducted. In the control city selected, Patras, two identical random samples (consisting of separate individuals) were interviewed in two waves corresponding with the two waves of the Salonica survey.[4] The survey

---

[3] During this period, elections were held both in Greece and in the United States, truce negotiations were bogged down in the Korean War and the Soviet bloc continued to spar with the West in the U.N. General Assembly.

[4] Both cities surveyed are major ports—though Salonica is a larger and more prosperous one than Patras. In Macedonia, only 50 or 60 miles from the Bulgarian and Yugoslav borders, Salonica became a part of modern Greece only in 1913. It is the country's second largest city, with 300,000 inhabitants (and another 150,000 in the surrounding area). More cosmopolitan, and because of its size, position and history, more internationally minded than Patras, Salonica was closer to the centers of Communist rebellion during the Greek civil war. Patras, with a population of 67,000, is a provincial city in the Northwestern Peloponnesus.

was completed by the addition of a special sample of persons in Salonica who had sent or called for "The March of Freedom" booklet at the U.S.I.S. Library. The first wave of interviews took place between September and October, 1952. The second wave took place immediately after the ad campaign ended, during the week of January 4–11, 1953.

To summarize, the study plan was carried out in terms of the following design (Table 1):

TABLE 1. Summary of Study Design

| | NUMBER OF INTERVIEWS[5] | |
	BEFORE	AFTER
Patras	246	—
Salonica	—	266
Panel (same persons interviewed twice)	352	285
Cross-section	—	794
Requested booklet	—	254

A total of 2,238 interviews was conducted.

All the interviewers employed were especially recruited and trained for this study. In making contact with a respondent, the interviewer identified himself as being from a "Statistical Research Corporation from Athens." If the respondent was uncooperative, he was told that the "Statistical Research Corporation" in Athens was affiliated with an American research organization and that the findings of the study would be sent to the United States for analysis. This was presented in such a way as to reassure him of the complete anonymity of his responses.

The fact that in about half the cases it was necessary to identify the survey with American sponsorship undoubtedly introduced some bias, particularly on those questions directly referring to the United States. However, had the survey *not* been presented as being under American auspices, many respondents would have assumed that it was being conducted by the Greek government. This might well have produced an even more serious bias and a greater refusal to respond.

To get identical cross-sections, systematic random samples of names were drawn from the central files of official identity cardholders. This appeared to be the best available means of developing true cross-sectional probability samples in a country where census statistics were very limited and not very reliable, and where opinion research was virtually unknown.

In carrying out this project, it became evident that the police files were

---

[5] Except where noted, all percentages reported in this article are based on the sample sizes given here. The actual number of cases is given in the tables where the base is smaller for some reason. The statistical significance between percentages at the .05 level has been computed by the method described by Cuthbert Daniel, "Statistically Significant Differences in Observed Per Cents," *Journal of Applied Psychology,* **6,** 24 (December 1940), pp. 827–828.

kept erratically. Although a considerable effort was made to trace the missing persons, many of the names originally listed had to be replaced by new names drawn at random from the official files. Repeated call-backs were made in order to interview persons who were not at home at the time of the first call. These call-backs continued until the person was found (and for several days after the regular interviewing period).

Apparently the police files were much more complete for women in the smaller city than in the larger one. Since no correction was made for this in the actual field work, 47 per cent of the respondents in Patras and 72 per cent of those in Salonica were male on the first wave, and similar disproportions were found on the second wave. To overcome this bias and to make the statistical findings for the various samples comparable, all tabulations used in analysis were made separately for men and women. Since separate percentages for men and women would have added greatly to the complexity of the presentation, a new set of total percentages has been computed in which men and women are assigned equal sampling weights. The percentages thus obtained hardly differ from those that might be computed from a 48 per cent male–52 per cent female weighting, and with few exceptions they differ but slightly from the total percentages based on the actual sample sex distributions.

THE CLIMATE OF OPINION

To understand what the ad and booklet campaign accomplished we must first look at the *existing* pattern of public opinion and information which the campaign sought to influence. We must also note the points on which opinions in the test city and in the control city (Patras) were similar and different.

Economic problems were most on people's minds at the time of the survey; 60 per cent in Patras and 46 per cent in Salonica referred in general to economic problems and an additional 13 per cent in Patras and 16 per cent in Salonica specifically mentioned employment problems. With such a focus of attention, other subjects received relatively few mentions. Virtually no one discussed the threat of communism. Only 9 per cent (P) and 7 per cent (S) thought the preservation of peace was an important problem. It appears therefore that the U.S. information campaign, centering as it did on *political* rights and freedoms, faced a challenge in the form of a widespread public preoccupation with the immediate day-to-day problems of making a livelihood.

In answer to the question, "Does the attitude position of a little country such as Greece influence the future shaping of international events?", the great majority of those answering said that Greece's attitude mattered a great deal. Most of the answers stressed Greece's strategic geographic position, and its potential importance as a military base.

Political conditions in Greece in 1952 made it inadvisable to raise direct questions about political convictions and sympathies in an opinion survey. Some indications of where sympathies lay could, however, be gleaned from responses to an indirect question like this one: "When Communists become powerful in a particular country, do you think this is the result of a national movement brought about by economic conditions or is it stimulated by Russia?"

While the choices presented are not mutually exclusive, it might be surmised that those who were most sophisticated about the aims and methods of Communism (and therefore most strongly anti-Communist) would point to the Russian influence. The first alternative paraphrases an explanation which Communists themselves would find acceptable; it might therefore be an indication—not of pro-Communist thinking, but of a certain measure of vulnerability.

In both cities, communism's growth was attributed much more often to a national movement caused by economic conditions than to Russian stimulation. In Salonica this was the prevailing opinion by a larger margin (39 per cent, as against 12 per cent) than in Patras (42 per cent against 28 per cent) perhaps showing greater Communist influence in the larger city.

Although many Greeks thought communism arose independently of Russian imperialism, this by no means placed them in the Communist camp. The survey findings showed the United States to be the most popular and respected nation in Greek eyes, while the Soviet Union was widely criticized and disliked. Almost nine out of ten mentioned the United States as a country eager to protect the personal freedom of its citizens. Virtually no one named the U.S.S.R. in this connection. On the question of which country today comes closest to being a democracy, the U.S. was far in the lead; the Soviet Union and Greece were each named by only a small number. The Soviet Union was often named as the country most guilty of meddling in the affairs of others (in general and of Greece in particular).

The preponderant hostility toward the Soviet Union took the form of a general belief that Soviet power was on the wane. To the query, "Ten years from now do you think Russia will have increased or decreased its following among other nations?", virtually all of those replying said that Russia would decrease her following and almost everyone said this was a good thing. Conversely, the overwhelming majority said the United States would increase its following in the next ten years and that this was good.

Overall feelings toward the U.S.A. were described as being *very* favorable by most of the respondents (more so in Salonica than in Patras). No one ventured to say that his feelings were unfavorable, and only a few claimed to have neutral feelings. Judgment was almost unanimous that the U.S. is sincerely interested in protecting the rights and freedoms of its citizens. Only about one person in five had no opinion on this point. The generally favorable outlook toward America was reflected in an overwhelmingly affirmative response to the question, "Do you think the U.S. is doing all it can to help Greece?" and in a strong belief that the U.S. wants to help Greece remain free and independent rather than to dominate it.

Although the ultimate purpose of the U.S.I.S. campaign was to influence opinion, its immediate objective was to increase knowledge of democratic rights and freedoms. How much awareness existed to begin with?

When respondents in both cities were asked to name the rights and freedoms which citizens enjoy in a free country, their response was similar, with freedom of opinion and expression far in the forefront, and references to working men's rights strong in Patras. An average of 1.4 rights was mentioned in Patras and 1.1 rights in Salonica; 18 per cent and 27 per cent were unable to name any rights at all.

The Universal Declaration of Human Rights which was emphasized in the ads and booklet was unknown to all but a tiny minority. In the interviews made before the campaign began, 8 per cent (P) and 26 per cent (S) claimed to have heard of it, but only 2 per cent (P) and 6 per cent (S) were able to explain what it was. The democracies rather than the Communist countries were named as the ones who signed it. In other words, the campaign was designed to inform its audience on a subject with which they were not too familiar. There was considerable room for expanding knowledge of democratic freedoms in general, and of the Declaration of Human Rights, in particular.

THE INFORMATION CAMPAIGN AND ITS AUDIENCE

The campaign was based on the assumption that newspaper advertising is an effective means of reaching the public in Greece, as it has proven to be in the United States, though Greek newspapers do not have the mass circulation of the American press. In Salonica, for instance, the four daily papers, with a total city circulation of 21,000, must serve the needs of 300,000 residents (about 190,000 adults over 18) in the city, and additional thousands in the surrounding region.

However, the survey indicates that Greek newspapers reach a much greater audience than might be guessed by American readership standards. In both cities 75 per cent reported that they read newspapers. It may be estimated that in Salonica each copy of the newspaper reaches approximately five adult readers represented by pass-along readership, reading in coffee houses, and the practice of paying the news vendor a small sum for the privilege of looking at the paper. About one in five in the sample proved to be illiterate.

How many people were reached by the ads and the booklet? How did they react to what they read? Were people who had not been directly exposed to the campaign aware of it in any way? These questions were answered by the second wave cross-section of Salonica residents who were interviewed after the campaign. Their answers closely parallel those given by members of the panel who were interviewed on both waves.

The ads were seen by a large proportion of the reading public. When asked, "Have you seen or heard about any ads lately which have been published by a foreign country?", 54 per cent said they had seen such ads, and 2 per cent more said they had heard of them. All but a handful of those who said they had seen the ads associated them with the United States. Four out of five of those who said they had seen the ads could answer a question on the main point.

Readership of the ads was estimated in two ways: (1) by asking the respondent directly how many ads he had seen, and (2) by actually taking him through the ads one by one, in each case asking whether he had previously seen it or read it. With this aided recall question the average number of ads recalled was 4.8 apiece for all who saw any, or 3.0 apiece for the public as a whole—36 per cent of the public claimed to have read at least one ad. The average ad was reported as read by about a third of those who remembered noting it. The individual advertisments varied considerably in the degree to which they captured attention and interest. The most successful ad was noted by 45 per cent of the public and read by 17 per cent. The least popular one was noted by only 23 per cent and read by 8 per cent.

There were notable differences in the degree to which various groups in the population came into contact with the campaign. Since literacy was higher among men (92 per cent in Salonica) than among women (73 per cent), men read more newspapers every day (55 per cent compared with 28 per cent). More of them, therefore, claimed to have seen at least one ad (66 per cent against 47 per cent of the women), and of those who saw at least one, more ads were noted (5.1 per noter) by men than by women (4.6). More men were also aware of the booklet (48 per cent against 26 per cent).

The expected differences may be found when we compare exposure for different socioeconomic groups, as in Table 2.

TABLE 2. Exposure to the Campaign, by Socioeconomic Status*

| | SALONICA BOOKLET SAMPLE | SALONICA CROSS-SECTION, WAVE II | | |
	GOT BOOKLET	SAW BOOKLET	SAW OR READ ADS	NOT EXPOSED
Well-to-do	12%	14%	8%	5%
Middle class	66	68	56	29
Poor	22	18	36	66
Total	100%	100%	100%	100%
$N(100\%) =$	(254)	(62)	(493)	(235)

*Percentage not weighted by sex.

Of those who were known to have called or written for the booklet, 84 per cent were men, and 30 per cent were under the age of 20. They were considerably better educated than the average; at least 34 per cent of them (probably more) were students.

Of those who claimed to have seen the ads, 21 per cent were unable to recall the main idea, 24 per cent described the ads as being about human rights, and 17 per cent mentioned freedom of the individual. An almost equally large number of responses were expressed not in terms of human rights in general but of *children's* rights. One fourth said the ads were about the freedoms and rights of children. An additional 5 per cent said the ads were supposed to teach people to give their children rights and privileges; 6 per cent said that the ads were supposed to teach young children about freedom. Only 1 per cent referred to "The March of Freedom" booklet.

Thus for a good many of those who saw the ads, *attention* was drawn from the *ultimate* point (U.S.-Greek unity in support of universal human rights) to the *immediate* appeal. The ads visualized human rights in terms of the rights of children in order to capture reader interest and to arouse a favorable sentiment for the *underlying* message. Apparently this is what happened, since the ads were (by American standards) extremely successful—not only in reaching an enormous part of their potential audience, but in impressing their central theme upon the memory of the people who saw them. Of all those who saw or heard of the ads, 80 per cent commented favorably on them, while only 5 per cent had critical reactions. Comments on production and format outnumbered those on the content of the ads, 4 to 3. The ads were liked precisely because their readers accepted them at face value: they were *not* thought of as propaganda serving a selfish interest. Everyone who had seen or heard of the ads was asked what their purpose was. They answered with references to the ads' literal meaning rather than with any sophisticated inferences about their underlying political objectives; 22 per cent said the purpose was to enable people to learn their rights and freedoms ("To teach people their rights"; "To make known the liberties of the individual").

Another 11 per cent said the purpose was to educate and inform people on the subject of freedom ("To propagate the idea of freedom among people"; "Teach the world truth"), and 8 per cent said it was to show the life of the free world ("Show the liberties of the individual in the democratic governments"). Significantly, 22 per cent of those answering said the purpose of the ads was to help youth ("For the freedom of children"; "To learn child's rights"). While this is a favorable judgment, it suggested that the pictures of children, while they attracted interest, distracted some readers from the ads' main message and purpose.

Of those who knew of the ads 88 per cent thought it was a good thing for the U.S. to publish them. Only 1 per cent said they thought it was a bad thing and 11 per cent gave no answer. When asked *why* it was a good thing for the U.S. to publish the ads, 25 per cent replied that it is good for people to learn about their freedoms and rights; 17 per cent said the ads were generally educational and useful; 9 per cent believed they were educational for children or young people; 12 per cent gave generally favorable replies.

Although, when asked directly, readers did not indicate that the *purpose* of the ads was to gain support for the United States, one in three thought the ads were good because they worked to this end! 23 per cent said the ads were good because they made friends for the U.S. An additional 9 per cent said they were good because they informed people about America. Thus at the same time that readers did not consciously think of the ads as propaganda designed to win their friendship, a good many of them volunteered the same idea to justify their approval.

The purpose of the ads was, of course, not merely to create a favorable impression, but to influence the thinking of the Greek people. A majority of those who saw the ads had the impression that they were influenced (whether or not they actually were). 54 per cent replied affirmatively to the question, "Would you say the ads contributed in any way to your knowledge or attitudes?" 36 per cent said that they hadn't—a substantial minority which probably includes not only the critical and the apathetic, but a great many people who felt already as much convinced as they could possibly be.

Since attitudes were so predominantly favorable to begin with, the major potential for change was on the part of a small minority of critics. If all those who said the ads affected their attitudes and knowledge had really been influenced, the campaign might be considered spectacularly successful.

A principal objective of the ads was to stimulate interest in "The March of Freedom" booklet. Of the public as a whole, 28 per cent said they had noticed the statement about the booklet in the *ads,* and 9 per cent had heard about the booklet in some other way; 63 per cent had not heard about it. Eight per cent of the public claimed to have read the booklet (21 per cent of those who knew of it). Of these, a third had gone to get it at the U.S.I.S. Library, and 37 per cent had sent for it. The remainder had read a copy obtained by another family member or by a friend.

Of all those who read the booklet, more than two out of five said it described the *historical* growth of freedom or liberty. Another two out of five said it was about human rights or freedom in general. As in the case of the ads, comments concentrated on production and format rather than on content. Like the ads, the booklet seems to have been accepted at face value, and not thought of as propaganda. Half said its purpose was to teach people about the idea and meaning of freedom. One in every five or six said its aim was to show the development and evolution of freedom in a historical sense. About as many believed it had a general educational mission. Only a small number said its purpose was to win friends for the United States.

Among those who had read the booklet, opinion was virtually unanimous that it was a good thing for the U.S. to publish. This was explained most often by the argument that it informed and educated people about their rights and freedoms. A sizable proportion explained that it was a good thing because it was beneficial to the United States. Thus in the case of the booklet as in the case of the ads, the information campaign won approval for doing the very job of propaganda which its audience did not *think* it was designed to do.

OPINION CHANGES IN THE TEST AND CONTROL CITIES

Thus far we have described the climate of opinion in Salonica and Patras before the U.S. information campaign began, and the audience which the campaign reached in Salonica, the test city. To determine what effect the campaign had on public opinion, we must make a series of comparisons between those who were and were not reached, before and after the campaign took place. The design of the study makes it possible to look for effects in three distinct ways: (1) by comparing results before and after, for the test and control cities; (2) by comparing results, before and after, for exposed and unexposed groups within the test city; and (3) by internal analysis of changes within the test city panel.

Let us first consider whether changes in opinion or knowledge took place in Salonica as a direct result of the campaign, but not in Patras. There was no significant shift of opinion in either city in the proportions who:

1. Felt very favorably toward the U.S.
2. Thought that the U.S. was interested in dominating Greece.[6]
3. Thought that Russia was the country most guilty of meddling in Greek affairs.
4. Thought the U.S. was doing all it could to help Greece.
5. Thought that communism was mainly caused by economic conditions.

On a number of points, opinions changed between the first and second waves of the study, but it generally changed the same way in *both* Salonica and Patras, apparently as the result of attitude trends throughout Greece:

1. There was an increase in the proportion who felt that the U.S. was sincerely concerned with the freedom of its citizens.
2. There was an increase in the percentage who thought the U.S. would increase its following among the nations within the next 10 years.
3. Similarly, there were more who thought that Russia would decrease its following within the next 10 years.
4. There was a general shift in the mention of problems as most important for Greece. Fewer named political forces or problems (perhaps because ex-

---

[6] As opposed to those who said the U.S. wants Greece to remain free and independent.

citement generated by the Greek and American elections had been dissipated by the second wave), and relatively more people in both cities mentioned employment and economic problems and problems of reconstruction.

5. In both cities there was an increase in the percentage mentioning free elections among the rights and freedoms which citizens enjoy in a democracy. This is understandable in the light of the interest generated by the election campaigns.

In a number of respects, however, the campaign appeared to have had an effect in the test city. The number who claimed to have heard of the Declaration of Human Rights was greater on Wave II than on Wave I, in both cities. In Patras, there was a small increase in the percentage who could demonstrate that they knew what the Declaration was. However, in Salonica the proportion familiar with the Declaration jumped from 6 per cent of the public before the campaign to 27 per cent afterwards. (See Table 3.)

TABLE 3. Knowledge of the Declaration of Human Rights

	PATRAS		SALONICA	
	BEFORE	AFTER	BEFORE	AFTER
Say they have heard of it	8%	28%	26%	35%
Explain what it is	2	10	6	27
Unable to explain	6	18	20	8
Say they haven't heard of it	92	72	73	64
No answer	—	—	1	1
Total	100%	100%	100%	100%

Knowledge of the countries that had signed the Declaration and knowledge of the rights and freedoms which citizens enjoy in a democracy increased in Salonica but not in Patras between Wave I and Wave II. There was a major drop in the percentage who could not answer the question, and *more* individual rights and freedoms were named. (See Table 4.)

TABLE 4. Knowledge of Rights and Freedoms

	PATRAS		SALONICA	
	BEFORE	AFTER	BEFORE	AFTER
Per cent who can name no rights and freedoms	18%	15%	27%	4%
Average number of rights mentioned	1.4	1.4	1.1	2.0

There was an increase in Salonica of those who mentioned the right to free choice of employment, the right to own property, and freedom of religion, while fewer persons mentioned these rights on the second wave in Patras. (See Table 5.) Freedom of opinion and expression was mentioned more often on

Wave II in both cities, but the increase was significantly greater in Salonica.

On one other major point there was a clear-cut change of attitude in Salonica only. Although there was no change in the proportion who said the U.S. was sincerely interested in keeping Greece free and independent; the proportion able to support this point of view with *reasons* increased enormously in Salonica. It remained the same in Patras. The "don't know's" declined in Salonica, and the kind of reasons given seemed to show the effect of the points made in the ads and in the booklet, with far more people mentioning the general attitude of the U.S. as a supporter of freedom. (See Table 6. The most heavily exposed in Salonica give this answer most often.)

In addition to the points just mentioned on which the campaign clearly seems to have been influential, other changes of opinion took place which

TABLE 5. Rights and Freedoms Enjoyed in a Free Country*

	PATRAS		SALONICA	
	BEFORE	AFTER	BEFORE	AFTER
Right to:				
Opinion and expression				
(free speech, free press)	47%	55%	41%	66%
Thought or conscience	11	12	23	24
Free elections	9	28	11	22
Life, liberty, and security				
of person	18	12	14	20
Work—free choice of				
employment	29	14	6	21
Action	4	5	5	9
Religion	7	5	1	15
Will	1	1	5	1
Own property	1	1	2	9
All others	8	5	5	4
Don't know	18	15	27	4
No answer	—	—	—	—

*Percentages do not add to 100% because more than one answer was possible.

TABLE 6. Reasons Why U.S. Wants Greece to Remain Free*

	PATRAS		SALONICA	
	BEFORE	AFTER	BEFORE	AFTER
General attitude of U.S.	39%	32%	30%	57%
Selfish attitude toward				
Greece	28	33	18	17
Ideological relationship				
between U.S. and Greece	22	14	8	8
Feeling that Greece is				
mother of civilization	—	14	1	9
Other reasons	—	—	—	10
No answer	14	7	46	2
$N(100\%) =$	(155)	(197)	(312)	(702)

*Percentages do not add to 100% because more than one answer was possible.

may be attributable to it. In Salonica there was a slightly greater tendency to mention the U.S. as a country eager to protect personal freedoms, and as the country which comes closest to being a democracy. There was a decline, from 8 per cent to 4 per cent in Patras and from 13 per cent to 7 per cent in Salonica, in the proportion naming Great Britain.

On the second wave in Salonica there were somewhat fewer who did not answer the question about whether Greece's attitude influences international events. There was also an increase in the proportion who said Greece's attitude mattered somewhat or not at all. This change of opinion may have been due to the trend of international events rather than to the campaign.

EXPOSURE AND ATTITUDES

Thus far we have seen that *opinions* underwent only slight changes in Salonica, the test city, compared with Patras, while knowledge of the subjects stressed in the ads underwent major increases. Were these changes due to the direct influence of the campaign, or did they occur independently? We can answer this question best by seeing how those who were *most* exposed compare in knowledge and attitudes with those who had *no* contact with either the ads or the booklet.

To do this, a comparison has been made of the special booklet sample (the people who actually *went* or *sent* for the *booklet*) with those members of the Salonica cross-section who *saw* the *booklet,* those who *saw* or *read* at least one *advertisement,* and those who were completely *unexposed.* The evidence indicates that not only knowledge, but some important attitudes, were different among these different exposure groups.

Those who were least exposed were least able to answer the question as to whether Greece can influence international events. Less than half of those who saw neither the ads nor the booklet—the least literate, educated and politically active part of the public—offered an opinion on this point. Considering only those who express opinions, it is apparent that, the greater the exposure, the greater the feeling that Greece's opinion matters in world affairs. This is a political sentiment (that is, an expression of patriotism and of conviction that thinking about current events is important). It may also be a reflection of the respondent's personal pride and dignity, of the feeling that his views matter. It is probably a good index of political interest and activity (See Table 7).

While there was no direct indication of anti-American feeling, and very little neutrality, one indication of real opinion about the United States is the distinction between "very favorable" and merely "favorable" views.[7] By this criterion, the people who read the booklet were most strongly pro-American

---

[7] Anti-American respondents who feared to express their views openly might be expected to give the weaker of the two responses.

TABLE 7. Does Greece's Attitude Shape International Events? (By Exposure)

| | SALONICA BOOKLET SAMPLE | SALONICA CROSS-SECTION | | |
	GOT BOOKLET	READ BOOKLET	READ OR SAW ADS	OTHERS
% not answering	7%	10%	12%	52%
N(100%) =	(254)	(62)	(494)	(238)
(Based on those who give an answer)				
Great deal	73%	64%	64%	50%
Somewhat	20	30	25	29
Little or not	7	6	11	21
Total	100%	100%	100%	100%
N(100%) =	(236)	(56)	(436)	(115)

(68 per cent), and those who saw the ads more pro-American (55 per cent) than the nonexposed (39 per cent).

Of those who read the booklet 87 per cent said they were familiar with the Declaration of Human Rights, while 45 per cent of those who saw the ads, and only 9 per cent of the unexposed, made this claim. The greater the exposure, the more familiarity was shown with the rights enjoyed by citizens of a democracy, as Table 8 indicates.

TABLE 8. Knowledge of Rights or Freedoms in a Free Country (By Exposure to the Campaign)*

| | SALONICA BOOKLET SAMPLE | SALONICA CROSS-SECTION | | |
	GOT BOOKLET	READ BOOKLET	READ OR SAW ADS	OTHERS
Property	14%	13%	11%	6%
Culture	4	3	2	—
Opinions	74	68	70	61
Equal justice	6	10	1	2
Life, liberty	20	28	22	17
Elections	26	25	26	16
Work	21	15	22	21
Thought	30	43	27	11
Action	9	8	9	11
Will	1	3	1	†
Religion	23	22	18	11
All others	5	7	5	6
Don't know, no answer	1	—	2	11
N(100%) =	(254)	(62)	(494)	(238)
Average number named	2.4	2.4	2.2	1.6

*Percentages add up to more 100% because more than one answer was possible.
†Less than half of 1%.

As Table 9 demonstrates, knowledge of democratic rights was greatest among the well-to-do and least at the bottom of the socioeconomic ladder. Could this not by itself be the explanation of the pattern shown in Table 8, with the well-to-do and most educated (whom we have already seen to be most apt to have read the booklet or the ads) best able to answer this information question?

TABLE 9. Knowledge of Rights and Freedoms in a Free Country (By Income)*

	SALONICA CROSS-SECTION		
	WELL-TO-DO	MIDDLE	POOR
Property	10%	13%	6%
Culture	2	2	1
Opinions	65	68	66
Equal justice	8	2	1
Life, liberty	23	23	18
Elections	28	25	19
Work	20	20	23
Thought	28	29	18
Action	13	10	9
Will	2	2	†
Religion	17	20	11
All others	12	7	5
Don't know, no answer	2	3	8
$N(100\%) =$	(60)	(386)	(344)
Average number of rights named	2.3	2.2	1.7

*Percentages add up to more than 100% because more than one answer was possible.
†Less than half of 1%.

Table 10 indicates clearly that this is *not* the explanation, since within each social level, the higher the exposure, the greater the average number of rights mentioned.

TABLE 10. Rights and Freedoms in a Free Country Average Number Mentioned, by Social Status and Exposure (Salonica Cross-section)

	WELL-TO-DO		MIDDLE		POOR	
	AVERAGE No.	BASE N	AVERAGE No.	BASE N	AVERAGE No.	BASE N
Read booklet	2.9	(9)	2.4	(42)	1.9	(11)
Saw ads	2.3	(39)	2.3	(276)	2.0	(178)
Others	1.9	(12)	1.8	(68)	1.5	(155)

If we consider only a group which is quite homogenous to begin with—the *men* (only) who went or sent for the booklet, the most intensely exposed audience won by the campaign—we find that attitudes toward the U.S. do not vary with social status, whereas knowledge of democratic rights is lowest among the poor respondents, those under 21 years, and those without relatives in the United States.

Did the campaign tend to select for its audience people who were already predisposed to be favorable toward its objectives? By comparing the responses given before and afterwards by the same individuals in the Salonica panel, we can see to what extent people who started out with a particular opinion (on Wave I) became exposed to the campaign, and compare them with those who initially held other opinions.

It has already been noted, for example, that the most heavily exposed were most apt to say (on Wave II) that Greece's attitude matters a great deal in shaping international events. Of the panel respondents who felt this way before the campaign, 56 per cent subsequently read the ads or the booklet, compared with only 40 per cent of those who started out with a different view. Similarly, the ads and booklet were read by 57 per cent of those who originally thought the U.S. was interested in the freedom of its citizens, but only by 29 per cent who did not have this opinion before the campaign.

In these cases, the differences may be accounted for in terms of the personal characteristics which influenced attitude and exposure independently. What happens when these characteristics are held constant in the analysis, so that the influence of initial attitude on exposure may be traced among people who are fairly much alike? To some degree, the campaign tended to select an audience which was friendly at the outset. In the panel, persons who originally felt "very favorable" to the United States read the ads or the booklet more than did those who originally felt merely "favorable" or "neutral," or who gave no indication of how they felt. (54 per cent of the former, compared to 42 per cent of the latter group, were heavily exposed.) This may be accounted for by the difference in exposure between those men and women who were not "very favorable" to begin with, and reflects the larger number of women who had no opinion on this question.

While half the young persons of 30 and under became exposed, whether or not they were initially very favorable, the middle-aged and older people who were *less favorable* before the campaigns were *less likely to read* the ads or the booklet. The initial attitude held by upper and middle income respondents did not influence their exposure.

There was, in short, remarkable similarity in the degree of exposure found among people who were initially very favorable, regardless of their social characteristics. About half the people who were predisposed to be friendly to the U.S. read the ads or the booklet—and this was true regardless of what kinds of people they were.

Of those who claimed to have heard of the Declaration of Human Rights on the first wave of interviews, only a minority were actually able to explain what it was. These few became a very highly exposed group. Whatever their personal characteristics, 18 of the 23 cases (79 per cent) read the ads or the booklet.

THE EFFECTS OF EXPOSURE ON ATTITUDES IN THE SALONICA PANEL

We have seen (1) that attitudes and knowledge, as well as exposure, differed among different kinds of people, and (2) that though exposure was widespread, it was greatest among those who were most friendly at the start. With these findings understood we can consider whether exposure *changed* information or attitudes. Table 11 shows the shifts which took place in the per cent feeling "very favorable" toward the United States.

TABLE 11. Per Cent Very Favorable to U.S. (By Exposure to the Campaign, Salonica Panel)

Very Favorable	Read Booklet	Read Ads	Saw Ads	Unexposed
Both waves	46%	50%	32%	24%
Before campaign only	17	17	23	29
After campaign only	17	18	26	13
Neither time	20	15	19	34
Total	100%	100%	100%	100%
N(100%) =	(24)	(116)	(90)	(55)
Net change	0	+1	+3	−16

There are several points to be noted:

1. The less the exposure, the less favorable was the original attitude on Wave I.

2. Regardless of exposure, between a third and a half of the respondents shifted in their response on this important question. Among those who had read the ads or the booklet a smaller percentage (35 per cent) shifted opinion than among those who were less exposed (47 per cent).

3. In spite of the fairly large fluctuation of opinion within the panel, shifts in one direction cancelled out shifts in the other direction—except in the case of those who were completely unexposed. This group was less favorable (by 16 percentage points) *after* the campaign, suggesting that exposure to the campaign offset a generally unfavorable trend. Although this difference is not statistically significant, there appears to have been a very marked pattern in the shift of opinion. Regardless of exposure, the groups which on Wave I were most apt to give no answer to this question (women, older persons, and the low-income group) became more favorable on Wave II, or at least showed no change. Their move from "no answer" to "very favorable" may have been due to the effect of being interviewed twice, rather than to any real modification of attitudes attributable to the campaign.

By contrast with the considerable shift of opinion on this general attitude question, there was relatively little change of judgment as to whether or not the U.S. was helping Greece all it could, with about three fourths of the respondents holding to the affirmative both times. There was also no real shift of opinion—either among the heavily exposed or the lightly exposed—as to whether Greece influenced international events a great deal.

Although the campaign did not modify opinions significantly, it appears to have been most successful in increasing knowledge on the subject with which it dealt: the Declaration of Human Rights. On the first wave, 8 per cent of the total panel had heard of the Declaration and could describe it. By the second wave this proportion had increased to 32 per cent of the total. This increase is entirely attributable to the campaign, as Table 12 demonstrates.

TABLE 12. Per Cent Who Know of Declaration of Human Rights (By Exposure to the Campaign, Salonica Panel)

	READ BOOKLET	READ ADS	SAW ADS	UNEXPOSED
Both waves	8%	10%	3%	—%
Before campaign only	—	4	2	—
After campaign only	79	43	19	5
Neither time	13	43	76	95
Total	100%	100%	100%	100%
N(100%) =	(24)	(116)	(90)	(55)
Net change	+79	+39	+17	+5

The greatest increase was registered among the most highly exposed, but even among those who merely saw at least one ad without reading any, there was an increase from 5 per cent to 22 per cent in awareness of the Declaration. Among those who had not seen any ads at all, 5 per cent on the second wave were aware of the Declaration—which suggests that some public discussion of the subject reached this group. The increase in knowledge among those exposed was universally high among all elements in the population.[8] (See Table 13.)

TABLE 13. Net Change in Per Cent Who Had Heard of Declaration of Human Rights (By Exposure to the Campaign, Salonica Panel)

	HEAVY EXPOSURE			LIGHT EXPOSURE		
	(BASE N)	INFORMED (ORIGINAL %)	NET CHANGE	(BASE N)	INFORMED (ORIGINAL %)	NET CHANGE
Total	(140)	13%	+46%	(145)	3%	+12%
Men	(107)	12	+46	(96)	2	+17
Women	(33)	12	+49	(49)	2	+4
Young	(53)	16	+45	(45)	2	+18
Middle age	(59)	10	+48	(63)	3	+14
Old	(28)	14	+47	(37)	5	+2
Well-to-do	(25)	24	+36	(16)	6	+44
Middle class	(87)	10	+53	(67)	6	+16
Poor	(28)	11	+35	(62)	—	0

[8] The gradient shown among the lightly exposed is explained by the fact that men, young people and the well-to-do were more apt at least to have *seen* some of the ads.

There was also increased familiarity with the individual democratic rights and freedoms. It is evident from Table 14 that the most exposed could name more rights to begin with, but they also appear to have learned more during the campaign. An increase in information was *also* shown by the unexposed and by those who merely saw but did not read the ads. This may have been due in part to the effect of having been previously interviewed on the same question.

In the mentions of individual rights and freedoms, there was considerable shifting between the two waves. The effect of the campaign was shown most dramatically on the subject of free speech or expression, stressed in the ads. Although in every exposure group there were more mentions on the second wave than on the first, the net increase was greatest among the most heavily exposed (50 per cent for those who read the booklet and 33 per cent for those who read the ads, compared with 20 per cent for the unexposed).

TABLE 14. Average Number of Rights and Freedoms Named (Salonica Panel)

	BASE N	BEFORE	AFTER	INCREASE
Read booklet	(24)	1.2	2.8	1.6
Read ads	(114)	1.5	2.4	0.9
Saw one or more ads	(89)	1.1	2.0	0.9
Unexposed	(54)	1.0	1.8	0.8

The campaign was extremely successful in conveying information about human rights to the people who were exposed to it, in every sector of the population. At the same time our findings indicate that it did not *directly* affect fundamental attitudes. When we examine the shifts in public opinion which took place between Wave I and Wave II, it is evident that those who read the ads and the booklet did not move in a favorable direction to any greater degree than the less exposed respondents. We found no evidence that this was true within any of the subgroups of the population, when information was analyzed separately by sex, age, and social status.

CONCLUSION

Any campaign which sets out to convey ideas may tend to select in its audience a large concentration of persons who are favorable to its objectives, and who expose themselves in order to reinforce their prior opinions. The Greek ad campaign appears to have gotten its *greatest* exposure among people who were somewhat more friendly to the United States to begin with and more articulate in their views. But these people were an important target, precisely because they were drawn from the more articulate and presumably more politically active sectors of the public.

The ads and the booklet won the approval of their readers; they were considered "a good thing" for the U.S. to publish; their execution and subject matter were liked or even admired. It seems likely that this approval was in part a reflection of the initial attitude of approval for America and things American, as well as an expression of the readers' specific reaction to the ads themselves.

What seems more significant is that readers accepted the ads and the booklet at face value. They were interpreted as a genuine attempt to inform people about rights and freedoms, rather than as an attempt to preach at them or to change their views. The fact that the ads and the booklet were not directly perceived as "propaganda" is as important as the fact that the motives behind them were seen as worthwhile or disinterested. Those who said their thinking had been influenced by the booklet or the ads explained this by references to the subjects on which they had become better informed, rather than by references to changes in conviction or point of view.

The comparative findings indicate that the campaign increased public knowledge of the subject on which it was focused, the Declaration of Human Rights, and that it increased familiarity with the individual rights and freedoms enjoyed by citizens in a democracy. This increase in knowledge took place in Salonica but not in the control city, Patras. The gain was greatest among those who were most highly exposed, and it took place among those exposed within every element of the population.

Increased familiarity with the individual rights and freedoms came about through a large number of small increases in the mentions of individual rights (including a number which were *not* stressed in the ads as well as those which were). Had the ads concentrated on a smaller number of rights, with each one being covered in several different ways and several different times, recollection might have been even higher than it was. However, the purpose of the campaign was not to stimulate recall of the individual rights as such, but to build recognition that they exist as an important bond between Greece and the United States. In this respect the campaign was successful, since it heightened awareness and knowledge of the subject.

Experimental studies have repeatedly shown that it is easier to convey information than to change attitudes, even where there is a large amount of room for improvement in attitude change. In the present case, because opinions were so favorable at the outset, there was slight opportunity for favorable change. Of the minority who, at the outset, were not very favorable in their attitude, a certain proportion were probably "hard-core" Communists, and an additional number were politically apathetic and largely beyond reach of the mass media. This left a comparatively small residue of individuals with a neutral, suspicious, or critical view of the United States who might be considered primary targets for a campaign to change attitudes, but who tended to be people who were harder than average to reach through conventional channels.

Careful exploration has yielded no evidence to prove that any change due to the campaign took place in fundamental attitudes. It is important to note that a *simpler* study design might have suggested that major changes took place on a number of points. We have seen that in some cases opinions became more favorable in Salonica (but they also became more favorable in Patras). On the second wave in Salonica, the exposed were more favorable than the nonexposed (but the same individuals were also more favorable to begin with). The use of several methods of control in the design of the study made it possible to rule out such spurious indications of effect.

Only one facet of opinion appears to have been influenced as the direct result of the campaign: it seems to have made people better able to give reasons in support of their existing conviction that the United States wants Greece to remain free and independent. Most particularly it seems to have made more people believe that America's general attitude (and not any self-ish interest) favored such a desire—that America was in effect a country devoted to human rights and freedoms, including the rights of small nations. This interesting development demonstrates how the campaign's effects in conveying information may begin to be translated into attitudes. What happened was not so much an attitude change (attitude was favorable from the beginning on this point). Rather the campaign seems to have confirmed already favorable opinion by giving it a supporting argument.

Changes in public opinion come about slowly, and international propaganda always functions within the context of world events. This survey adds to the already considerable weight of evidence which shows that (apart from political acts) attempts to influence opinion must be carried on consistently and over a period of time before any major shifts are detectable. If, in the long run, what the Greek people *think* of the United States, or of democracy, is a product of what they *know,* then the Salonica test campaign contributed toward the larger purpose of the U.S. information program.

39

A Study of the Effects
of Negro Invasion
on Real Estate Values

Thomas L. Gillette

As long ago as 1920, W. I. Thomas suggested a principle that has become axiomatic in sociology: "If men define things as real, they are real in their consequences." No other selection in this anthology illustrates this principle so vividly as do Gillette's article and the one by Balk (Selection 40). Gillette presents here a study of the effect of Negro invasion: no loss of property value follows. In spite of this finding—confirmed by other scientists—panics continue.

The major purpose of the research discussed in this paper was an attempt to determine the effects, if any, of the invasion of Negroes on real estate values in a selected area of Kansas City, Missouri.[1] There are a number of variables involved in the relationship between such a major change in population and real estate values. As will be noted in the discussion of methodological considerations and research design, an attempt was made to control the effect of some of the more significant variables in order to isolate this one aspect of change.

I. INTRODUCTION TO THE PROBLEM

Like many rapidly growing cities, Kansas City too has felt the tremors resulting from the development and expression in intergroup tensions and feelings of hostility among white and Negro elements of the population. There was little overt evidence of such tension until the late nineteen forties and early nineteen fifties. During the period 1940 to 1950 the Negro population increased by over 15,000, but without a compensating increase in living space.

Reprinted from *The American Journal of Economics and Sociology,* **16,** 2 (January 1957), pp. 151–162, by permission of the publisher and the author.

Thomas L. Gillette is Assistant Professor of Sociology, San Diego State College.

The research which is discussed in this report was made possible through a grant from the University of Kansas City and with the generous cooperation of the Kansas City, Missouri, Mayor's Commission on Human Relations.

[1] A second, and perhaps equally significant problem, was the determination of the changes in the general physical condition of the neighborhood. This paper is devoted to the discussion of the first problem only. The second will be presented in a separate paper.

Expansion was inevitable. As the Negroes began crossing the old social and physical boundaries into white neighborhoods there were ominous rumblings from white residents. "Improvement" committees were organized to withhold the advancing wave of Negroes.[2] Physical and social walls of segregation were being weakened.

A portion of this rising tension culminated on May 21, 1952, in the bombing of the home of the first Negro family to cross the color-bar formed at Twenty-seventh Street and Paseo Boulevard. A second bomb was exploded at the home on September 7, 1952. During this period numerous threats were made against the Negro residents and minor acts of violence occurred.

Some white property owners in this neighborhood justified or rationalized the bombings through arguments based on the feeling that the movement of Negroes southward, into their neighborhood, placed their property in jeopardy.[3] These individuals felt that the invasion by Negroes would result in a decline in real estate and property values and a general deterioration of the neighborhoods undergoing this transition. The Mayor's Commission on Human Relations was quite concerned with the problem and presented it to the University of Kansas City for study. It was out of this setting and this concern that the research evolved.

There are several changes and trends in the city which must be noted in a discussion of this research. During the period 1940 to 1950 the metropolitan area of Kansas City increased by almost 100,000 persons. This was an increase of 14.3 per cent. The Negro portion, in striking contrast, increased by 33.9 per cent. Housing available to Negroes, both standard and substandard, did not keep pace with the population increase during this period, thus making more acute an already overcrowded situation.

In addition to this quantitative lack of housing, the qualitative nature of available housing must be noted. The 1950 Census showed that 8,972 (50.6 per cent) of the 17,735 houses occupied by Negroes were classified as substandard.

This factor must be considered in the light of the economic status of the Negro at this time. Many Negroes were being forced to occupy housing well below the quality which they desired and were in many instances financially able to possess. There has been a sharp rise in the earnings and income of nonwhite families in the United States since 1940, and the trend is continuing today. The nonfarm incomes for nonwhite were nearly three times higher in 1949 than in 1939. This upward trend in economic status of the Negro in Kansas City was quite obvious. Unlike the situation several decades ago,

---

[2] Evidence of the increase in overt intergroup hostility and the formation of these committees may be found in: Thomas L. Gillette, *Santa Fe: A Study of the Effects of Negro Invasion on Property Values* (unpublished Master's Thesis, University of Kansas City, Kansas City, Missouri, June 1954).

[3] This statement is based on the results of informal interviews conducted by the writer with twenty-one owner-residents in this neighborhood. Fourteen expressed themselves as being "strongly in favor of the bombing."

much more of the housing needs of the Negro appeared to represent unmet market demand, due in large measure to improved economic status. Recent gains in higher paying jobs and greater employment security have resulted in an appreciable advancement in the purchasing power of Negro families in Kansas City and have created among them an active and expanding market for not only more housing, but also higher quality housing. There were substantial numbers of Negroes, therefore, able to pay and desirous of paying higher prices for better accommodations than those which they were compelled to occupy.

This observation is strengthened by data obtained from the 1940 census, which show that higher proportions of nonwhite than white families in the relatively high income and rent groups were occupying housing that was deficient in various respects. Economic factors were important considerations in this research. As will be indicated, the invading group in this study represented that portion of the Negro population which possessed the economic power to improve their standard of living in terms of better housing. In fact, it may be that economic factors were of more importance in the invasion than the population gains per se.

Thus, there are three interrelated factors associated with the invasion under consideration in this study: (1) the disproportionately high increase in Negro population; (2) the socioeconomic composition of the invading group; and (3) the lack of an increase in available and desirable housing.

II. CONCERNING THE METHODOLOGICAL PROCEDURE

The primary problem was the determination of the difference, if any, which Negro invasion introduces into residential market values. The basic method was to make comparisons between the sales prices of single-family residences which appeared to differ only in the race of the occupant. The general methodological approach was extended to include collection and analysis of data bearing upon socioeconomic characteristics of the individuals under study, the general condition of the property at the time of purchase, and the kind and amount of repairs made on the property after the individual assumed ownership.

The logic behind this comparative approach is to be found in the assumption that if two neighborhoods which tend to possess comparable major characteristics are studied from the point of view of sales of individual residences, comparable houses in two comparable neighborhoods should sell for essentially the same price. If these two neighborhoods should differ only in race of the owner-occupants and a significant price differential should be found in comparing sales prices, then this price differential may be attributed to some other factor than what are essentially the physical characteristics of the neighborhood.

Certain specific characteristics must possess a high degree of comparability if the results of the comparisons are to be valid. The comparable characteristics sought in this study were: (1) age of neighborhoods; (2) size of dwelling unit; (3) type of construction; (4) original sales prices; (5) area of city; (6) proximity to transportation and shopping facilities; (7) general topography; (8) land-use patterns; (9) relation to central business district; and (10) general physical condition of the neighborhood.

If two areas comparable in these characteristics could be located and one area should experience Negro invasion while the other did not, the author felt that any differential in price must be related to the one major variable, race. This is essentially the same method which Laurenti used in his study in San Francisco, although he emphasized just individual houses, rather than neighborhoods as well as individual houses. The present method appears to be the most satisfactory method of isolating the relation of the racial factor to real estate prices. Other price-determining variables must be held constant if the effect of the racial variable is to be satisfactorily determined.

III. SELECTION OF THE AREA OF INVASION

From a comparison of the census tracts of 1940 with those of 1950, it was possible to locate those areas in the city which had experienced a large increase in Negro population. The majority of these areas were eliminated as possible areas of invasion when it was determined that the numerical increase did not indicate a substantial change in the ratio of Negro to white residents, but merely an increase in areas already classified as nonwhite and accounted for through internal migration and natural increase. It was felt that an area experiencing the relatively recent convulsions of invasion would give the most valid and desirable results. That area in Kansas City known as the Santa Fe District was studied and definitely established as this type area.

A pilot study of the area indicated that invasion was in a very dynamic state and there had been a fairly rapid exchange of property from white to Negro for several years, and this exchange was still continuing.

This area is also quite near the area of the bombings, and possesses many similar physical characteristics. Therefore, it might be possible to apply the results of the study of this area to another area, an area which was on the verge of experiencing the very early effects of such a movement. Thus the Santa Fe District (Area A) became the experimental neighborhood for this research.

IV. DATA COLLECTION IN THE SANTA FE DISTRICT (AREA A)

The residents of the area were the major sources of information. A house-to-house survey was made of the entire area. The author was assisted by several trained interviewers in data collection. Table 1 indicates the degree of success in obtaining interviews and also gives the reader some idea of the approximate degree of progress of invasion in the area. Only Negro residents were interviewed during this part of the study.

TABLE 1. Tabulation of Interviews and Attempted Interviews

Category	N
A. Homes approached	392
B. Home-owners not contacted*	69
C. White-occupied residences	128
D. Negro-occupied residences	194
E. Interviews refused	15
F. Interviews completed	179
G. Vacant residences	1

*The interviewer returned twice if the individual was not at home on the first attempt. After three attempts with no interview obtained the residence was put in this category. If it was definitely established before the third attempt that this was a white-occupied residence, then the unit was placed in category "C" without additional attempts at contact.

One hundred seventy-nine interviews were obtained, and of these twenty-six were eliminated as sources of price data. At the end of this phase of data collection it was established that at least 194 of the 392 homes (or 49.4 per cent) in Area A were Negro-owned and occupied. While this portion of the study was in progress, there were additional white-to-Negro exchanges of property in blocks previously covered by the interviewers. These new owners were later interviewed, making a total of 202 schedules available for study from Area A.

Most Negro respondents exhibited a high degree of cooperation with the interviewers. One cause for this may have been the relatively high educational background of the invading group which facilitated their comprehension of the meaning and purpose of this research.

Another factor in the cooperation of the residents and the resulting validity of responses may be found in the *gemeinschaft* nature of the neighborhood. After several months spent in almost daily contact with the people in the area, it became obvious to all researchers that an intimate "we-feeling" tended to exist among a great number of the Negro residents. They knew they were the object of a study which might, or might not, result in a reduction of intergroup tensions. They realized that they were, in a sense, the spearhead of an invasion, and as such they shared many common sentiments and values. Some blocks had even organized formal "block committees" which reported on the general status quo of that particular section.

Such formal and informal relationships undoubtedly provided for unique channels of communication. It seemed that it was through these channels that knowledge of the research would diffuse throughout the neighborhood prior to the actual call by the interviewer. The results of such a situation appeared to be favorable in terms of number of interviews completed, and validity of responses.

V. SELECTION OF THE CONTROL AREA (AREA B)

With the successful interviewing of a representative sample (93.3 per cent) of the Negro home-owners in Area A, the next phase of the research was concerned with the selection of a neighborhood with a high degree of comparability in the major characteristics already discussed. In addition, this area must be far enough removed from any area of invasion so that proximity to Negroes would not influence market value to any appreciable extent.

After an inspection of housing information made available by the Jackson County Assessor's Office and the City Assessor, several areas were tentatively selected as possible control areas. The majority of these were eliminated after an initial inspection indicated that they lacked the desired degree of comparability. An area was finally selected and cautiously studied to insure the existence of a high degree of comparability. Thorough investigation indicated that the general housing structure was remarkably similar to that of Area A. The majority of houses in both areas could be broken down to several categories, with a large representation of each category in each area.

An inspection of the records at the City Assessor's Office indicated that both areas were originally developed within the same six year period of the city's history (1897–1903). Informal interviews with real estate people familiar with the early development of the city brought out the fact that these areas were designed to appeal to the same general class of people, and homes which we had typed as being comparable in 1953 had actually sold for comparable prices when they were new. As a final step, several individuals quite familiar with real estate in the city were driven through both areas and asked for their opinions as to the degree of comparability. They unanimously agreed that an extremely high degree of comparability existed.

In addition, both areas are equidistant from the central business district and in the same general east-central section of the city. Both have immediate access to several major public service transportation arteries; are adjacent to small shopping districts with the usual supermarkets, drug stores, hardware stores, motion picture theaters, restaurants, taverns, etc.

Both areas appeared to be in the same general physical condition. This observation was confirmed by a representative of a local community research firm, several social scientists from the University of Kansas City, and two disinterested realtors. These people also agreed on the general similarity of the two areas.

VI. SELECTION OF GROUP B

The next phase was the determination of the residents in this all-white area to be selected for interviewing. One variable which must be controlled here was date of purchase of the house. All the houses in this area would not be comparable to those in Area A since the normal rate of exchange in such an area is much slower than in an area of invasion. The majority of sales in Area A occurred January 1, 1949, through June 30, 1953. Thus, sales for Area B must be selected to cover this same period in order to hold the sales period constant. Exact date of sales was secured from records in the Jackson County Assessor's Office. Residents of Area B who purchased their houses during this period were approached and interviewed with the same instrument used in Area A. Ninety-seven interviews were secured in Area B. Of these, eleven were eliminated as sales data for the same reasons as enumerated for elimination of sales data in Area A.

The following measure was taken to insure validity of price data. Sales information is available on the copy of the deed recorded in the Jackson County Court House. Federal tax stamps are affixed to each deed. Each $1.10 of federal stamps represents $1,000.00 of the actual sales price, assuming no seller's mortgage is involved. That is, the seller must pay this amount of tax for each $1,000.00 cash difference involved in the transaction. If a portion of the transaction involves the taking over of the seller's mortgage, no revenue is paid on this mortgage. However, such a mortgage and its amount is indicated on the deed of trust.

Thus, by adding the amount of money represented by the tax stamps to the amount indicated in the mortgage clause, if one should exist, it is possible to have a sufficiently accurate verification of sales data. In only a few cases did sales price data provided by the owner differ from that indicated on the deed. In such an instance, that particular information was eliminated from the study.

VII. DEVELOPMENT OF PRICE COMPARISONS

It was now necessary to set up individual price comparisons between houses in Area A and Area B. A 29 per cent sample of the 179 houses studied (interviewed) in the area of invasion was set up for matching. This sample of fifty-two houses is representative of the general housing in the Santa Fe District. The next step was the selection of a "mate" from Area B for each of these Area A houses. These pairs, with individual members comparable in age, type of construction, number of floors, material utilized in construction, number and size of rooms, date of sale, general condition at time of purchase, and other relevant criteria were set up only after a very careful and intensive inspection of each home in each paired group. This included inside as well as outside inspection.

Sales price data of comparable houses were then compared. If the house in Area A sold for more than the house in Area B, the excess between the two was termed a positive difference. If the reverse were true, the difference was classed as a negative difference. These differences were figured for the fifty-two pairs of houses. These houses appear to be representative of the majority of sales to both whites and Negroes in these neighborhoods.

The results of these comparisons are presented in Table 2 which shows the dollar and percentage differences between the sale prices.

From the study of Table 2, it becomes obvious that substantial differences exist between sales prices of homes deemed to be comparable in all major characteristics. The data here were exposed to an analysis of variance to determine statistical significance of differences. That is, could these differences be a result of chance? The results of the test were: $F = 11.46$, and $F = 17.05$. These F scores indicate the existence of a statistically significant difference on the one per cent level of significance.

TABLE 2. Dollar and Percentage Differences Between Sales Prices of Comparable Homes*

A	B	C	C/A
9,600	8,000	1,600	16.67
6,500	7,000	−500	−7.69
15,500	13,300	2,000	12.90
10,000	8,500	1,500	15.00
6,500	8,000	−1,500	−23.08
10,000	9,750	250	2.50
8,000	7,000	1,000	12.50
12,000	10,000	2,000	16.67
6,000	7,000	−1,000	−16.67
8,500	8,500	0	0
7,700	8,500	−800	−10.39
10,000	8,600	1,400	14.00
7,500	7,500	0	0
7,500	7,500	0	0
10,500	9,500	1,000	9.52
9,500	7,400	2,100	22.11
13,000	12,500	500	3.85
14,000	12,500	1,500	10.71
7,875	8,000	−125	−1.59
8,200	8,750	−550	−6.71
9,500	7,000	2,500	26.32
8,500	6,000	2,500	29.41
9,000	9,300	−300	−3.33
7,000	6,000	1,000	14.29
10,000	9,500	500	5.00
7,500	8,250	−750	−10.00

*Explanation of columns:
Column A is the sales price of the house in Area A.
Column B is the sales price of the house in Area B.
Column C indicates the difference between the sales prices of the two houses.
Column C/A is the percentage expression of Column C, or Column C divided by Column A.

TABLE 2. Continued.

A	B	C	C/A
7,500	7,000	500	6.67
9,000	9,000	0	0
7,500	6,250	1,250	16.67
8,000	9,500	−1,500	−18.75
10,000	9,000	1,000	10.00
10,000	9,675	325	3.25
9,000	9,500	−500	−5.56
7,000	6,750	250	3.57
8,000	7,250	750	9.38
10,000	9,500	500	5.00
10,000	9,000	1,000	10.00
11,050	11,000	50	.45
12,000	12,500	−500	−4.17
11,500	7,500	4,000	34.78
12,000	10,750	1,250	10.42
10,500	10,000	500	4.76
7,400	7,000	400	5.41
11,500	11,250	250	2.17
9,000	8,500	500	5.56
9,500	9,500	0	0
9,250	8,750	500	5.41
10,000	10,400	−400	−4.00
11,500	10,500	1,000	8.70
15,500	12,500	3,000	19.29
9,100	8,500	600	6.59
7,500	6,750	750	10.00

Table 3 shows the distribution of the dollar differences between sales prices of comparable homes. These figures, plus those in Table 2, do not support the hypothesis that Negro invasion must result in the decrement of property values. On the contrary, it appears that the overall result was one of increment. If the hypothesis of decrement were valid, then the results would show a distribution of dollar differences gathered in the below zero area. The distribution is actually concentrated in the above zero area.

TABLE 3. Distribution of Dollar Differences Between Sales Prices of Comparable Homes

POSITIVE DIFFERENCES		NEGATIVE DIFFERENCES	
RANGE	NUMBER OF SALES	RANGE	NUMBER OF SALES
$ $ 0	5	$2499–$2000	0
1– 499	6	1999– 1500	2
500– 999	10	1499– 1000	1
1000– 1499	9	999– 500	6
1500– 1999	3	499– 1	3
2000– 2499	4		
2500– 2999	3		
Total 40		Total 12	

The mean difference is plus $1,135.00 for Negroes and $702.08 for whites (see Table 4). This means that the Negro buyer, on the average, paid slightly above $1,000 over market value for the property. Market value is here assumed to be the price which a white would pay for the same property in an all-white area. This mean difference undoubtedly reflects a "premium" which

TABLE 4. Mean Differences in Sales Price

DOLLARS		PERCENTAGES	
Positive	$1,135.00	Positive	11.20
Negative	702.08	Negative	9.32

the Negro is forced to pay if he wishes to move into the area. What these differences mean, therefore, is simply that Negroes have to pay more for comparable housing than whites.

VIII. CONCLUSIONS

These results indicate that prices in this particular neighborhood were enhanced rather than lowered through Negro entry. This evidence refutes the idea held by many that Negro invasion must result in a drop in property value.

In looking for a possible explanation for this upward trend in market value, one must be cognizant of the socioeconomic status of the groups involved in the transaction. The white owners, in this study, attached a surplus value, an additional margin of profit, to the commodity. The Negroes involved here were capable of absorbing this "levy."

The past fifteen years have seen a tremendous upward movement in overall socioeconomic status of the American Negro. This trend is manifested in Kansas City, as well as the rest of the nation. Between 1940 and 1950, annual earning of nonwhite workers increased threefold, while earnings of white workers rose only 158 per cent. Only 0.1 per cent of Negro families in 1939 earned over $5,000.00 a year. This figure had increased to 5.4 per cent by 1950. This is, in effect, the emergence of a new middle class in the United States. This expansion has been true also for the Negro upper class. As the middle and upper income groups in the Negro population have grown, so has the demand for higher quality housing.

The Negro invaders in this study not only had the demand for improved housing, but also the financial potential to pay the premium levied upon them because of the racial variable.

An analysis of the socioeconomic data reveals the Negro invaders to be members of that group in Kansas City earning well over $4,000.00 yearly. In addition, such factors as occupation, education, and number of family members employed give support to the contention that this group represents the upper-income bracket of Negro families in Kansas City.

In an analysis of the socioeconomic status of both the white and the Negro groups through Warner's Index of Status Characteristics, it was found that the invading group definitely possessed a higher socioeconomic status than that of both the invaded group and the control group. If the invading group had been on a significantly lower socioeconomic plane, the level of prices might not have been elevated. This study does not contend, therefore, that Negro invasion will inevitably result in a price increase, but does indicate that when the invading group is of a higher socioeconomic composition than that of the group being invaded, the resulting trend may well be an increase in property values. This is the result of the demand on the part of the invaders, a demand which appears to exceed the present supply of available housing. The resulting competition *among Negroes* in buying of houses makes possible an "above-market" levy which the Negro buyer is capable of absorbing. This ability is obviously related to the income status of the Negro. Thus, it appears that economic factors may play a more important role than purely sociological factors—e.g., race. That is, the change in market value is directly related to the income status of the individuals involved in the population-property transition.

A question arises here as to the applicability of the results of this research. Can such findings be utilized, for example, in the reduction of intergroup hostility? It seems reasonable to suppose that if property owners in a comparable situation were aware of the fact that they are not going to lose their savings or take a severe loss in selling their property, they will be more rational in reacting to Negro invasion. Another portion of this research was concerned with the attitudes of those whites who did not sell in the face of invasion, but who remained behind and became neighbors with the Negroes. The great majority of these people found their stereotypes of the Negro pleasantly shattered, and were quite surprised to note the overall increase in the physical attractiveness of the area after the Negroes assumed occupancy. It may well be that knowledge of such aftereffects may serve as another factor in reducing the pressure which the white owner may feel is being exerted upon him to sell.

In any consideration of the applicability of these findings, it must be noted that this sample is representative only of this particular population in Kansas City, Missouri. Although it is not unreasonable to assume that other universes may possess the same or similar characteristics, no research was undertaken on this problem and thus the reader should be cautious in making generalizations. Further research is needed in other areas to test the validity of this method and these findings, and to provide a more macroscopic view of the invasion process and its consequences.

40

Confessions
of a Block-buster

Norris Vitchek as told to Alfred Balk

> This article (which should be considered in conjunction with
> the preceding study) tells the story of how "Norris Vitchek" (a
> pseudonym) has deliberately and rationally taken advantage of
> public opinion—in this instance, prejudice—to accumulate a for-
> tune.

Not long ago in an all-white block on Chicago's West Side, a FOR SALE
sign appeared in front of a modest frame bungalow. Immediately a wave of
fear swept across the block. A Negro family already was living several blocks
away. Not far beyond that was the western edge of Chicago's "Black Belt."
Every year its border had been moving closer, enclosing blocks like this one
along the way. Suppose the bungalow came into possession of a Negro? What
would happen to the rest of the block?

All the residents were plainly worried. Among them were a widow who had
been living alone and had no assets but her home, and the parents of four
young children who feared what "change" might mean to the youngsters'
safety. "Relax," said the bungalow owner. "I'm selling this through a white
real estate man. I won't even talk to a Negro."

Imagine their shock, then, when the FOR SALE sign came down and the
new owners moved in—Negroes. And consider the impact of what happened
next. Three more buildings, which were already owned by property speculators,
"turned' immediately. Other Negro families arrived to look at homes in the
block. Real estate men, both white and Negro, swarmed in.

Almost overnight the family with four children sold out at a sizable loss.
So did six other home owners in quick succession. "We'll stay," a few owners
said. "We're broadminded." But the situation was out of their control. Finally
the last of the whites left—whether or not they could afford to move. Like
hundreds of others who have been similarly blitzed, they never really knew
what had hit them.

Originally in *The Saturday Evening Post,* **235,** 27 (July 14–July 21, 1962), pp. 15–19.
Reprinted by special permission of *The Saturday Evening Post.* © 1962 The Curtis
Publishing Company.
Alfred Balk is a free-lance writer.

I knew. I triggered the whole sequence of events by buying the bungalow and quickly selling it to a Negro. I am a block-buster. Another and perhaps slightly less odious name from my craft is real estate speculator.

CORNERING A SHARE OF THE HARVEST

I specialize in locating blocks which I consider ripe for racial change. Then I "bust" them by buying properties from the white owners and selling them to Negroes—with the intent of breaking down the rest of the block for colored occupancy. Sometimes the groundwork—the initial block-busting—has already been done by some other speculator by the time I arrive on the scene. In that case all I have to do is to work on the remaining whites and reap my share of the harvest.

I make my money—quite a lot of it, incidentally—in three ways: (1) By beating down the prices I pay the white owners by stimulating their fear of what is to come; (2) by selling to the eager Negroes at inflated prices; and (3) by financing these purchases at what amounts to a very high rate of interest. I'll have more to say about these techniques later.

Block-busting is a relatively new business—only ten to fifteen years old actually—but already it is a crowded field. Block-busters also operate in Washington, D.C., Baltimore, Philadelphia, New York City, Boston, Cleveland, Detroit, St. Louis, and other cities and in some of their suburbs. Chicago alone has more than 100 of us. Because few Negroes can command the necessary financing to enter this occupation, most of us are white, as I am. Over the past ten years we have helped "change" an average of two to three blocks a week in Chicago. Even now, with the overall housing market rather quiet, we bust a new block in Chicago every four to eight days.

With the nation's Negro population exploding and continuing to concentrate in urban areas, the demand simply never lets up. More than half the citizenry of Washington, D.C., is Negro. Philadelphia is one fourth Negro. In Chicago the Negro population, now one fourth of our citzenry, has nearly doubled in the past ten years and probably will double again in the next thirty, rising to 1,700,000 persons, or half the city's present population. Even its suburbs, now mostly white, are expected to contain nearly 700,000 Negroes by 1990.

AVERAGE CITIZENS, AVERAGE PREJUDICES

If you are an average white citizen, with average prejudices, you may regard all this as the ruin of metropolitan neighborhoods. I think of it merely as more business for what already is a growth industry. My attitude stems from the fact that few white neighborhoods welcome Negroes who can afford to buy there; yet the need for homes for Negroes keeps growing. I assist in the solution of this problem. My function, which might be called a service industry, is to drive the whites from a block whether or not they want to go, then move in Negroes.

You might think it would be difficult to bust a block, especially your block. It isn't really. In most blocks someone almost always is being transferred, wanting a larger or smaller home, or moving away for his health. If I offer enough money I can buy any building I want—if not directly, then through a front. It doesn't matter whether Negroes now live nearby. The shock effect of the block-busting, plus my ready financing, can cave in enough of the block to make my efforts successful.

But I prefer blocks near others where Negroes already live—especially old, middle-class blocks with a mixture of frame homes and walk-up apartments. Whites already there have been conditioned to insecurity by the inexorable march of the color line in their direction. This makes these blocks setups for the quick turnover, large volume, and the large profits I like. The case of a South Side block I busted is typical.

Twenty-five years ago when most of the block's residents moved in and Chicago's population was only 8 per cent Negro, none of the whites imagined they might be "endangered." All this racial business was somebody else's problem. Then one day reality began to dawn on them. All-white streets along which they drove to the Loop suddenly "turned." Fairly distant stores and theaters they had patronized, friends' homes they had visited, or churches they had attended were being swallowed.

"We'll organize," some residents said. "We'll keep the niggers out." But other speculators and I already were buying buildings in adjacent blocks and holding them until we thought the area was ready to be turned for maximum profit.

You can't appreciate the psychological effect of such a color-line march unless you have seen it. First, Negro students begin enrolling in neighborhood schools. Then, churches and businesses in the area quit fixing up facilities as they normally might. Parks which have been all white suddenly become all Negro. A home owner applies to his bank for a home-improvement loan and is turned down. "Too close to the color line," he is told.

Small businesses begin to close. New whites, if they move into the area at all, are apt to be of lower economic class than before, and they are tenants, not owners. Because lending institutions always blacklist an area for regular mortgages when change appears imminent, whites can't buy there if they want to.

So it went in my typical South Side block. But the residents still thought they were safe because everyone had agreed not to sell to Negroes. Hence they weren't too disturbed when a bluff, friendly accountant who was retiring and moving to Florida announced to neighbors that he was listing his three-flat building for sale. As weeks passed, however, and no buyer was found, their suspense grew, and the owner became desperate. "We're stuck," he told his wife. "We told everyone we wouldn't sell them out. But we have to."

Up to this point only a few Negro real estate men rather tentatively had rung doorbells in the block. Now we speculators and brokers, both white and Negro, really went to work. One paid several Negroes with noisy cars to begin driving up and down the street a few times a day. He also paid a Negro mother who drew aid-to-dependent-children payment to walk the block regularly with her youngsters. Another arranged to have phone calls made in the block for such people as "Johnnie Mae." Sometimes calls would consist only of a whisper, a drunken laugh or a warning—such as, "They're coming!"

I didn't participate in these vicious tactics. Few large speculators do. If I operated so crudely, frankly I wouldn't have consented to write this report, even under the fictitious name in the by-line. I just use psychology.

I began my work in this case by sending a postcard to everyone in the block and others in adjacent blocks. The cards said, "I will pay cash for your building." That was all except for my phone number. The word "cash" was the key. It assured home owners they could get out quickly and reminded them that their neighbors could too. Then a canvasser and I headed for the block to repeat the offer in person.

BEST PRICE FOR FIRST BUILDING

My first stop was at the home of the retired accountant who owned the three-flat building. "How much are you asking for your building?" I ask him.

"Twenty-two thousand," he said.

"Well," I said, "you might get that if you wait. But you know what is happening in the neighborhood. If you want a quick cash deal, I'll give you $18,-000." But, knowing that we speculators often pay proportionately more for the first building on a block to go, he would come down only $1000 in price. At that point I got a break. My canvasser, who had been talking with other owners, rang the doorbell and called me onto the porch to tell me something.

"His neighbor in the one-story brick just sold for $14,000," he told me.

"Sorry," I told the accountant. "Negroes will be moving in next door. Eighteen thousand is tops." His quick call to the neighbor confirmed my canvasser's report, and he accepted my offer on the spot.

The moment I make a deal, I always place a "Sold by" sign in front of the building. A few such signs—the gaudier, the better—show that events are moving. So does the ringing of doorbells. And with thirty other real estate men working a block, including regular dealers as well as speculators, those bells ring often.

Changing the rest of this block, as in most other blocks, was easy. After posting my signs, I merely sent a man down one side of the street and up the other punching doorbells.

When a delivery driver who had two young daughters in school said he "probably would leave for the good of the kids," but wanted to think about it, my man discussed the pros and cons in a friendly way. "If you take my quick deal," he concluded, "you'll have no worries about the kids. You can give them a nice yard and have them in a good suburban school next week." The man and his wife, obviously troubled, decided my canvasser was right. They sold at a $2000 loss.

To an elderly couple who hesitated, saying their home and neighborhood were the only ones they had known throughout their marriage and they would "stay around and see what our new neighbors are like," my man said, "I know what waiting has meant to people like you in worry and strain. Waiting never makes it easier. If you take my cash deal while I still can offer it, you can begin looking for a new retirement home tomorrow." They sold too.

FIRST "BREAK" CAN BRING TROUBLE

"No, thanks," several owners told my canvasser. "My own real estate man is finding me a Negro buyer."

Some owners on every block consider this. If they can close a deal directly with a Negro, usually it is for a price close to the property's book value—thus benefiting both. But most whites are reluctant to bargain with a Negro over so large a sum. They know that, in the sixty to ninety days before the closing date, he is more likely than a speculator to have to cancel the deal, despite having earnest money down. Many times, although the owner has listed his property with a neighborhood agent, the real estate man ends up by arranging a deal with me—with the seller not only accepting a depressed price but also having to pay a broker's commission.

And so day by day, week by week, month by month, the block collapses further, until the last white finally moves away.

Now admittedly, although somebody would perform this economic function if I did not, these dealings are not always pleasant. In the first place, the Negro able to buy property usually doesn't want trouble. Yet, being the first to "break" an all-white block, or even second or third, can and often does bring trouble.

For example, there was the case of a Negro salesman who had just been promoted to a supervisory position in his firm. He came to a speculator seeking an income property into which he could move with his family. The speculator told him about a three-flat building he had just bought from whites. "The place we're renting is bad," the Negro said, "but we don't want any trouble. Has the block been busted?" The speculator owned another building there, but the block hadn't been busted, in the sense that Negroes already were living there. However, knowing the three-flat building would be a good investment for the Negro and that he should be able to carry it financially, the speculator told him, "It's OK."

In the first few days after the Negro moved in, a bottle was thrown through his front window, his wife was insulted by several whites who lived in the block, and his two children were harassed on their way home from school.

Few Negroes or whites on Chicago's West Side have forgotten the riots involving thousands, three summers ago, after a speculator's sale of a building to Negroes on West Jackson Boulevard. Luckily only the building got hurt. And, fortunately, any incidents connected with the move-ins I handle are so minor in comparison to what Negroes already have experienced that they soon are forgotten.

"YOU'VE SOLD OUT YOUR OWN RACE"

Actually, block-busting probably is tougher on the whites than the Negroes. Nobody who has lived in a neighborhood for years, seen his children grow up there, remodeled his home exactly to his liking, and become accustomed to nearby school, church, and shopping facilities likes to be uprooted. This is particularly true if it happens so suddenly that he has no new neighborhood in mind, if he has to accept less living space and a higher-interest mortgage than he previously had, and if he must sell his property at a loss. Several elderly persons have died because of the anguish and upheaval involved.

As a result of my business dealings, I have been cursed, called "nigger lover," "vulture," and "panic peddler," had doors slammed in my face and even been chased by an irate woman with a broom. "You're Communist and un-American!" one owner shouted at me. "You've sold out your own race!" others have yelled.

It is hard to forget, too, how even long-time neighbors and friends may become jealous, suspicious, and antagonistic toward one another. After one middle-aged couple had built a suburban home and sold their former home to a speculator—and the speculator had "turned" it—several former neighbors hired a sound truck and drove to the couple's new home. They cruised the block, shouting, "Be sure and meet your new neighbors, the Joneses. They sold out their old block to Negroes."

Once a block has been busted, some white owners simply stare, almost dumbfounded, as we draw up sale papers for them. Others break down and cry. Some say, "It's OK to show the place to Negroes before we move, but we don't want to be in the house to watch it when you do."

But no matter how emotional or awkward some situations may be, there is one compensation for it all—money. Some brokers or investors make a good return only on some deals. I make it on every deal in the three ways I mentioned earlier.

You may believe your home is worth $15,000, for example. If I bust your block, I will expect to buy it for $12,000 cash. The odds are that eventually you will sell for that price, if not to me, then to another speculator. If you and your white neighbors did not run, you probably would gain, rather than lose. More than four fifths of the white neighborhoods into which Negroes move hold their own or enjoy an increase in value, according to a five-year Fund for the Republic study of 10,000 transactions in Northern interracial neighborhoods. But the myth that "Negroes lower property values" persists—so whites run, and we block-busters clean up. Within a few days comes profit No. 2: I advertise and sell it to a Negro not for $15,000, but for $18,000. Financing the deal myself, I will accept $500 to $1500 down, with the remainder on contract. The easy-payment plan, I believe it is called—that is, $150 to $200 a month until the contract is fulfilled. When is that? This is profit No. 3, the big one. The contract is fulfilled when I have been paid principal and interest totaling $36,000.

These terms, I am told, force Negroes to overcrowd and overuse their buildings by renting out part of them, or to skimp on maintenance, starting the neighborhood on the way to blight. (In most Negro neighborhoods in Chicago the population density is five times that of white areas.) The contract burden, I also am told, forces Negro mothers to work, despite the presence of youngsters at home, compels fathers to take two jobs, and can lead to numerous other problems because of the financial strain and anxiety.

Even so, the number of Negro buyers who default on their payments is small. When it does happen in my own business, it is no loss to me, since I retain title to property until contracts are completed. I keep all the payments made until that time, evict the owners, and either rent the building or resell it on about the same terms.

The Urban League of Chicago says we speculators make nearly $1,000,000 a month in our city in "abnormal" profit from Negroes who buy former white property on contract. This could be. I know that I make four times the profit I could for the same amount of effort in all-white real estate: If anybody who is well established in this business in Chicago doesn't earn $100,000 a year, he is loafing.

"A dirty business," you say? One that whites should fight?

White people in dozens of neighborhoods have tried fighting. They have pressured neighborhood banks and savings-and-loan associations to quit blacklisting their areas, resulting in token concessions. They have held block meetings to warn home owners not to deal with those of us who advertise "Quick Cash Sales" in newspapers or the classified phone directory, have passed out leaflets listing speculators' names and have ripped up "Sold by" signs which were of larger size or were posted longer than city ordinance allows. They even won a fraud-and-misrepresentation case against two block-busting brokers in Chicago, thanks to several blunders which no established operator would have made. Despite all such resistance, once a block has been busted, only rarely has its complete breakdown been halted. Too many forces are working for us speculators.

ORDAINING THE "CAVE-IN" METHOD

The Chicago Real Estate Board, an organization of the city's most prominent realtors, all but ordained the "cave-in" method in a policy laid down in 1917: "It is desired in the interest of all that each block shall be filled solidly (with Negroes) and that further expansion shall be confined to contiguous blocks. . . ."

The board, which is all white, no longer makes a copy of this statement available in its office, but the policy never has been rescinded or repudiated. None of the board's 1,700 members violates it. No member, if he deals with Negroes at all, is likely to arrange for a sale to them in a white neighborhood that is not next to a "Negro block." Once a neighborhood begins changing, none will show homes there to whites.

Lending institutions' "no-Negro" or "no-integrated area" loan policies further perpetuate the trend, restricting Negroes to blocks we bust and forcing them to rely mainly on our contract sales for financing.

The City Council and Mayor Richard J. Daley, who, like his two immediate predecessors, comes from the all-white Bridgeport area of the city, also help. They regularly table every request for open-occupancy ordinances, which by opening up any neighborhood to Negroes who could afford to buy there would take the pressure off the few collapsing ones which are open.

The police put down violence promptly in any blocks which are busted in a "permissible" area. Yet, if a Negro is leapfrogged into a home beyond this zone, the protests somehow always get out of hand. In one case a policeman guarding a Negro's new home was seen showing several youths how to make a Molotov-cocktail incendiary bomb.

Some churches accept all this, often serving as rallying points for whites trying to "hold the line." One parish even has acted as an agent in the purchase of twenty-two buildings which normal turnover otherwise might have placed in the hands of speculators. When change begins, most churches then simply close up shop and sell most or all of their property.

RELENTLESS MARCH OF THE COLOR LINE

Neighborhood improvement associations actually are usually "all-white" improvement associations. One, the Back of the Yards Neighborhood Council, has kept its area all white. But it began in the 1930's and has a unique authoritarian control extending through stores, banks, churches, and industry in its stockyards neighborhood. Every other neighborhood, including one in which retail businessmen raised a war chest of $100,000, has "gone" when the color line reached it. And associations which opposed me before any breakthroughs end up happy to cooperate—if I will only "go slow" and not change blocks until association officials say they are "ready." I usually do this to keep their goodwill.

Newspapers, too, help prepare the way. Their only stories in this field usually concern the "panic" aspects. If they print stories about Negroes, it's only in connection with crime or welfare problems or population increases, not with Negro church activity or business and educational success or other aspects of normal life in good Negro neighborhoods.

The Board of Education contributes by writing off a school once it begins to change racially, consigning it to overcrowding, double shifts and supervision by the least experienced and lowest-paid teachers—and by giving it the lowest proportion of counselors.

Then there are my financial sources, which are among the most reputable in the city. My credit is good in almost any bank or savings-and-loan association in town. It also is good with insurance companies, including several Negro firms. Merely by placing an ad in a daily newspaper, I can raise cash by selling my contract paper at a discount to some of the most reputable doctors, dentists, lawyers, and other business and professional men in town.

With forces such as these on my side, why should I feel guilty? Am I really the basic cause of whites' fleeing? Do I depress their property values and inflate prices for Negroes? When a Negro has been turned away from a bank, do I "trap" him into accepting a contract sale?

And what alternative can you provide for my function? Would you try to influence your bank or savings-and-loan association to begin lending to Negroes? Would you help remove the pressure on "busted" areas by welcoming a Negro family into your block? Do you even care that my business operates as it does? Whatever my faults and whatever the social stigma I endure, I don't believe I am hypocritical about all this. Can you honestly say the same?

41

The Simulmatics Project

Ithiel de Sola Pool and Robert P. Abelson

The development of electronic computers and the application of mathematical theory to human behavior has made possible the programing of a computer to predict voting behavior under varying conditions. This model,* produced during the 1960 presidential election campaign, enabled the authors to predict not only the results of subsequent public opinion polls and the election but also "what would happen if . . . " (hence the name Simulator). The fact that such extremely complex phenomena as voting can be predicted by means of a mathematical model underlines the importance of the systematic exploitation of sociological knowledge. Note how the investigators incorporate sociological information such as age, sex, religion, rural or urban residence, and social class.

This is the first report on a program of research conducted for the Democratic Party during the 1960 campaign. The research used a new technique for processing poll data and included computer simulation of likely voter behavior. The immediate goal of the project was to estimate rapidly, during the campaign, the probable impact upon the public, and upon small strategically important groups within the public, of different issues which might arise or which might be used by the candidates.

THE DATA

This study is a "secondary analysis" of old poll results. Students of public opinion are becoming aware that the growing backlog of earlier polls provides a powerful tool to aid in the interpretation of new poll results. Polling has now been routine for three decades, but poll archives are just beginning to be assembled. The main one is the Roper Public Opinion Research Center in Williamstown [Massachusetts], the existence of which made feasible the project here described.[1]

Reprinted from *The Public Opinion Quarterly*, **25**, 2 (Summer 1961), pp. 167–183, by special permission of the publisher and the authors.

Ithiel de Sola Pool is Professor of Political Science, Massachusetts Institute of Technology.

Robert P. Abelson is Professor of Psychology, Yale University.

* *Model:* an organizing image of the phenomena to be investigated. A mathematical model exists when the image (conceptual model) is translated into mathematically manipulatable terms.—Eds.

[1] We wish to express our gratitude to that Center, as well as to the MIT Computation Center, and to the men who originally assembled the data, especially George Gallup and Elmo Roper.

The first step in the project was to identify in that archive all polls anticipating the elections of 1952, 1954, 1956, and 1958. (Preelection polls on
the 1960 contest were added later when they became available.) We selected
those polls which contained standard identification data on region, city size,
sex, race, socioeconomic status, party, and religion, the last being the item
most often missing. Further, we restricted our attention to those polls which
asked about vote intention and also about a substantial number of preselected
issues such as civil rights, foreign affairs, and social legislation. From 1952 to
1958 we found fifty usable surveys covering 85,000 respondents. Sixteen polls
anticipating the 1960 elections were added to this number. The sixty-six
surveys represented a total of well over 100,000 interviews.

PROCESSING THE DATA

To handle such massive data required substantial innovations in analytic
procedures. In essence, the data were reduced to a 480-by-52 matrix. The
number 480 represented voter types, each voter type being defined by socioeconomic characteristics. A single voter type might be "Eastern, metropolitan,
lower-income, white, Catholic, female Democrats." Another might be,
"Border state, rural, upper-income, white, Protestant, male Independents."
Certain types with small numbers of respondents were reconsolidated, yielding the total of 480 types actually used.

The number 52 represented what we called in our private jargon "issue
clusters." Most of these were political issues, such as foreign aid, attitudes
toward the United Nations, and McCarthyism. Other so-called "issue clusters"
included such familiar indicators of public opinion as "Which party is better
for people like you?" vote intention, and nonvoting. In sum, the issue clusters
were political characteristics on which the voter type would have a distribution.

One can picture the 480-by-52 matrix as containing four numbers in each
cell. The first number stated the total number of persons of that voter type
queried on that particular item of information. The other three numbers
trichotomized those respondents into the percentages pro, anti, and undecided
or confused on the issue.

We assembled such a matrix for each biennial election separately and also
a consolidated matrix for all elections together. Thus, it was possible by
comparison of the separate matrices to examine trends.

The reduction of the raw data to this matrix form was an arduous task.
The first step was to identify in each survey those questions which seemed
to bear on any of the fifty-two issue clusters we had listed as relevant to the
campaign. One such cluster was attitude toward domestic communism or, as
we called it for shorthand, McCarthyism. Over the past decade many questions
have been asked on this and related matters in many different polls. One
survey might ask, "Are you in favor of permitting a Communist to teach in
the school system?" Another would ask, "What do you think of Senator

McCarthy?" Another would ask, "Do you think McCarthy has done more good or harm?" The problem was to determine which questions tapped essentially the same attitude, domestic anticommunism. The decision was made by a two-step process. First, questions were grouped together *a priori* on the basis of intuitive judgment, and then this grouping was empirically tested.

The empirical test was conducted as follows: Replies to each question were separately trichotomized. Typically, the replies had previously been coded in up to thirteen categories. Where more than three replies had been coded, the codes had to be regrouped. On the McCarthyism issue, replies were classified as McCarthyite, anti-McCarthyite, and indeterminate. A reply opposing retention of a Communist in the school system would be classified as McCarthyite. In the case of such a question as "How well do you like McCarthy?" for which a scale had originally been used, cutting points had to be set depending on the distribution.

For each pair of questions in the presumed cluster we then correlated the percentage "pro," and separately the percentage "anti," across voter types yielding two correlation matrices. (The voter types for this operation were 15, a reconsolidation of the 480. Since this operation dealt with percentages on questions from single surveys, consolidation was essential to obtain base numbers in each voter type large enough so that the percentages being correlated would be reasonably stable.) Only those questions which showed high correlations with each other were retained in a cluster. Thus, our assumption that a question about Communist teachers in the schools could be treated as equivalent to a question about McCarthy was subject to empirical validation.

In many instances questions which *a priori* seemed alike had to be discarded from the clusters. Some clusters had to be broken up into two or more. Indeed, in the particular example we have been using here, it turned out that replies to the identically worded question "How well do you like McCarthy?" ceased tapping the same attitudes the minute the Senate censured him. Clusters thus represented questions which could be regarded as in some sense equivalent, both on the grounds of political common sense and on the grounds of empirical correlation.[2]

It should be emphasized that empirical correlation was not enough. Such a

---

[2] We should qualify. What has been described is what we started out to do and what we did for most issue clusters. In the end, however, we were forced to compromise on certain foreign-policy clusters. This in itself is an interesting finding. On almost all domestic questions, primarily because they were party-linked or left-right linked, it was possible to validate empirically the equivalence of questions which *a priori* seemed alike. On certain foreign-policy issues this was quite impossible. The political scientist looking at a half-dozen questions about foreign aid or about the UN might conclude that they all should reflect a common underlying attitude toward that matter. However, empirically, in many instances the distribution of replies was highly sensitive to conjunctural influences or shades in wording of the question. Rather than completely abandon the hope of doing any analysis of foreign-policy issues in the campaign, we retained some clusters which failed to meet the correlational test, labeling them *a priori* clusters, not sure of what we would do with them (in fact we did very little), but feeling it better to retain them on the computer tape than to discard the data from the start.

question as "Which party is better for people like you?" and a question about the image of Adlai Stevenson would correlate strongly because they were both party-linked. However, they were not included in a single issue cluster unless they also seemed politically equivalent.

The final step in the preliminary data processing—the step which gave us our matrices—was to take all cards in any one of the 480 voter types for a particular biennial period and tabulate for each issue cluster the number of replies pro, con, and indeterminate, and the number of cards on which such replies appeared. That last number varied for each cluster since some questions (e.g. turnout) were asked on virtually every survey we used, while other questions were asked only occasionally.

PURPOSES OF THE METHOD

The reader may wonder what purposes were served by reorganizing the data into the standard format just described. That handling of the data lent itself to three main uses: (1) A "data bank" was available from which one might draw the answer to any one of a vast number of questions at a moment's notice. (2) The consolidation of separate surveys made available adequate data on small, yet politically significant, subsegments in the population. For example, we wrote a report on Northern Negro voters based upon 4,050 interviews, including 418 with middle-class Negroes. The typical national sample survey contains no more than 100 interviews with Northern Negroes, a number clearly inadequate for refined analysis. (3) The data format and its transfer to high-speed tape facilitated its use in computer simulation of the effects of hypothetical campaign strategies. This aspect of the project is the most novel and is the one to which we shall return later in this article.

THE HISTORY OF THE PROJECT

Before we illustrate those uses of the data, let us detour to examine the history of the project: the fact that it was sponsored and actually used by a partisan group makes the story of its management of some interest to students of public opinion research.

The project was initiated in the early months of 1959 by William McPhee and the authors. Our plan for computer simulation (on a different version of which McPhee had already been working)[3] was presented to Mr. Edward Greenfield, a New York businessman actively engaged in Democratic politics. Through his intervention, a group of New York reform Democrats who had taken major responsibility for raising money for the Democratic Advisory Council became interested.[4] Before this group of private individuals was

---

[3] William McPhee, *A Model for Analyzing Macro-dynamics in Voting Systems* (New York: Columbia University, Bureau of Applied Social Research, undated).

[4] We wish to express our particular thanks to Thomas Finletter, Robert Benjamin, Joseph Baird, and Curtis Roosevelt for encouragement and cooperation.

willing to secure funds, however, they wanted to be sure that the results were likely to be valid and useful. In May of 1959 the project was discussed in Washington at a meeting attended by Mr. Charles Tyroler, Executive Secretary of the Democratic Advisory Council; the members of the Council executive committee; Paul Butler, Chairman of the Democratic National Committee; several other officials of that Committee; Mr. Neil Staebler, Michigan State Chairman; and a number of social science consultants, including Samuel Eldersveld, Morris Janowitz, and Robert Lane. This group was interested but reserved. It was suggested that the project should be supported for four months initially and at the end of this period a further review should be made.

The Williamstown Public Opinion Research Center agreed to permit the use of polls in their archives on two conditions: First, all basic data tabulated by Simulmatics from their cards were to be made available to the Center so the Republican Party would have an equal opportunity to use such data if they wanted them. We provided a print-out * of the data on the computer tape, but not, of course, the programs for simulation nor supplementary data obtained from other sources (e.g. the census) and used in our system. Second, and demanded by both the Roper Public Opinion Research Center and the social scientists engaged in the study, all results could be published for scientific purposes after the election. This article is part of our program to meet that condition.

Given the green light to carry out the project, the principals organized themselves as The Simulmatics Corporation, for although the objective of the project constituted scientific research, it was clear that universities would not and should not accept financing from politically motivated sources or permit a university project to play an active role in supplying campaign advice to one party.

The summer of 1959 was devoted to the data reduction job described above. In October 1959, when the preliminary data processing had been substantially completed, a review meeting in New York was attended by many of the same persons who had been at the Advisory Council meeting in May, plus a number of social science consultants, including Harold Lasswell, Paul Lazarsfeld, Morris Janowitz, and John Tukey. Although the degree of confidence in the basic approach ranged from enthusiasm to doubt, a decision to proceed was quickly reached.

The next step was the development of computer programs, some of which will be discussed below. One objective was to make possible rapid incorporation of new data which might, we hoped, become available during the campaign. Our hope, as we shall see, was only slightly fulfilled.

By June of 1960 we were able to prepare a first report as a sample of the kind of thing which might be done by the Simulmatics process. That was the report on the Negro vote in the North.

---

* *Print-out:* information transferred from punch card or tape by a computer system to a linguistic form—Eds.

Our contractual arrangements with our sponsors ended with the preparation of the process and of this report illustrating it, shortly before the 1960 convention. It was understood that actual use of the service in the form of further reports on specific topics would be purchased by appropriate elements of the party in the precampaign and campaign period at their discretion. In the immediate preconvention period, the National Committee felt that it should not make decisions which would shortly be the business of the nominee. After the convention, the Kennedy organization, contrary to the image created by the press, did not enter the campaign as a well-oiled machine with a well-planned strategy. Except for the registration drive, which had been carefully prepared by Lawrence O'Brien, no strategic or organizational plan existed the day after the nomination. It took until August for the organization to shake down. No campaign research of any significant sort was therefore done in the two months from mid-June to mid-August, either by Simulmatics or by others. In August, a decision was made to ask Louis Harris to make thirty state surveys for the Kennedy campaign. However, because of the late start, data from these surveys would not be available until after Labor Day. On August 11, the National Committee asked The Simulmatics Corporation to prepare three reports: one each on the image of Kennedy, the image of Nixon, and foreign policy as a campaign issue. These three reports were to be delivered in two weeks for use in campaign planning. Along with them we were to conduct a national sample survey which, in the minds of the political decision makers, would serve to bring the Simulmatics data, based as they were on old polls, up to date. (It should be mentioned that one of the most difficult tasks of the Simulmatics project was persuading campaign strategists that data other than current intelligence could be useful to them.) The national survey by telephone was conducted for the project by the Furst Survey Research Center and was indeed extremely useful in guiding the use of the older data. It confirmed the published Gallup finding that Nixon was at that point well in the lead, though we disagreed on the proportion of undecideds (we found 23 per cent). It made us aware that Nixon's lead was due to women. It also persuaded us that voters were largely focusing upon foreign policy at that point in the campaign.

The relationship between the use of such current intelligence and the use of a simulation model developed out of historical data is analogous to the relationship between a climatological model and current weather information. One can predict tomorrow's weather best if one has both historical information about patterns and current information about where one stands in a pattern. While it would be presumptuous to assert that in two weeks of intense activity we approached an effective integration of the two sets of data, that was the ideal we had in mind and which in some limited respects we approximated.

It should be added that the introduction of the national survey data was possible only because of prior preparation for rapid data analysis. The survey was ordered on a Thursday, the field interviewing took place between Saturday and the following Thursday; by Friday morning all cards had been punched, and by Friday night the preprogramed analysis had been run and preliminary results were given to the National Committee.

The three reports that had been ordered on August 11 were delivered on August 25. The speed of the entire operation is, of course, a testimony to the advantages of a high-speed computer system. Nonetheless, such intense pressure is not an optimum condition for research work, even though rapid analysis was one of our objectives from the start. The reader who suspects that under those circumstances clerical errors inevitably occurred is quite right. It was our good fortune that none of those which we have found since in rechecking have turned out to alter any conclusion, but we do not recommend such limited schedules as a normal mode of work. Nevertheless, with well-prepared computerized analysis, it can be done when necessary.

The reader may ask whether the large preparatory investment was justified in terms of the quantitatively limited use of the project. When we planned the project, we—perhaps unrealistically—anticipated active campaign work from the beginning of the summer until about September 15. (Anything done later than that would hardly be useful.) How far the investment was justified by the two weeks of work actually done is a question which we find impossible to answer. An answer depends on an estimate of how much impact the contents of the reports had on the campaign. The reports received an extremely limited elite circulation. They were seen during the campaign by perhaps a dozen to fifteen key decision makers, but they were read intelligently by these talented and literate men.

Despite the contraction of our effort, our own feeling is one of relative satisfaction that the Simulmatics project was able to provide research on demand concerning the key issues at perhaps the critical moment of the campaign. While campaign strategy, except on a few points, conformed rather closely to the advice in the more than one hundred pages of the three reports, we know full well that this was by no means because of the reports. Others besides ourselves had similar ideas. Yet, if the reports strengthened right decisions on a few critical items, we would consider the investment justified.

EXAMPLES OF USE OF THE SYSTEM

Earlier in this article we listed three uses of the method herein described: providing a "data bank," rapidly available; providing data on small, politically significant groups; permitting computer simulation. The first of these advantages has perhaps already been adequately illustrated. Let us turn to the other two.

Our report on Northern Negro voters did not use a computer simulation but rather illustrated the capability of the process to provide information about small subgroups of the population. Compare here a number of quotations from the report with what we could have said working from a single survey containing responses from perhaps 100 Northern Negroes. The report demonstrated, for example, that between 1954 and 1956

[A] small but significant shift to the Republicans occurred among Northern Negroes, which cost the Democrats about 1 per cent of the total votes in 8 key states [a shift which continued in 1958]. In those years, the Democratic Party loss to the Republican Party was about 7 per cent of the Northern Negro vote—enough to cause a one-half per cent loss in the *total* popular vote in the eight key states. In addition, among Northern Negro Independents, only about one quarter actually voted Republican in 1952, but about half voted Republican in 1956, enough of a shift to cause an additional loss of a little less than one-half per cent of the total popular vote in the eight key states.

The shift against the Democrats is more marked among the opinion leading middle class Negroes than among lower-income Negroes.

Anti-Catholicism is less prevalent among Negroes than among Northern, urban, Protestant whites.

The most significant point of all is the fact that the shift is not an Ike-shift: it is a Republican Party shift. It affects Congressional votes as much as Presidential votes.

In addition, the report demonstrated that Northern urban Negroes vote as often as whites of comparable socioeconomic status, and that "there is no sharp difference between Negroes and comparable whites in their feelings about Nixon."

This report was made available to all the leading Democratic candidates, to the Democratic National Committee, and to the drafters of the Democratic platform. Probably no one can say what influence, if any, it had upon them. Those men themselves would not know which of the many things they read or heard shaped their decisions. As outside observers, we can assert only that the report was placed in the hands of the platform framers in the ten days preceding the drafting of the problem, and was read.

The most dramatic result, however, was, as indicated above, the finding that Eisenhower had not generated among Negroes the kind of personal following that he had among most white voter types. This suggested that the Negro vote presented far more of a problem to the Democratic campaign than appeared at first glance; it could not be assumed that the losses in recent years would be recovered with Eisenhower out of the picture.

SIMULATIONS

We turn now to what was perhaps the most novel aspect of the study—the use of computer simulations. We describe, first, how we simulated state-by-state results and, second, how we simulated the impact of the religious issue.

One of the benefits gained from the large number of interviews we used was the possibility of approximating state-by-state results. A national sample survey—even a relatively large one—has too few cases from most states to permit any significant analysis of state politics. The same would have been true, however, even for our voluminous data if we had attempted to do a state-by-state analysis in a simple way. We had an average of about 2,000 interviews per state, but that is a misleading figure. In a small state there might have been no more than 300 or 400 interviews, and on a particular issue cluster that had occurred, for example, in only only one tenth of the surveys, there would be too few cases for effective analysis. We therefore developed a system for creating synthetic, or simulated, states.

By an elaborate analysis of census, poll, and voting data—made more difficult because 1960 census results were not yet available—we developed a set of estimates on the number of persons of each voter type in each state. (Note that since *region* was one of the defining characteristics for the 480 voter types, there were at most only 108 voter types in any given state.) It was assumed that a voter of a given voter type would be identical regardless of the state from which he came. A simulated state therefore consisted of a weighted average of the behaviors of the voter types in that state, the weighting being proportional to the numbers of such persons in that state. For example, we thus assumed that the difference between Maine and New York is not truly a difference between New Yorkers and inhabitants of Maine as such, but a difference in the proportions of different voter types which make up each state. We assumed that an "upper-income Protestant Republican rural white male" was the same in either state, and that a "small-city Catholic Democratic lower-income female" was also the same in either. This assumption enabled us to use all cases of a voter type from a particular region in arriving at a conclusion for a state.

We do not assert that the assumptions on which this simulation is based are true. On the contrary, we can be sure that they are partly false. The interesting question intellectually is how good were the results obtained with these partially true assumptions. The test is, of course, how far state-by-state predictions made on these assumptions turn out to correspond to reality. To the extent that they do, they suggest that the essential differences between states in a region are in distributions of types rather than in geographic differences, even within a voter type.[5]

Upon this simulation of states was built a second and more interesting simulation, one which attempted to assess the impact of the religious issue. Since the one simulation rests upon the other, the effectiveness of the state simulation is simultaneously tested by examination of the religious simulation. The latter, the main simulation actually carried out during the campaign,

---

[5] The states where the simulation was most notably off included Arizona, Nevada, New Mexico, Idaho, and Colorado, states mostly of small population, and states which, in the absence of a "Mountain Region" in our classification, we attempted to treat as Western or Midwestern. Clearly, the assumption of regional uniformity was misleading as applied to them.

represented a hypothetical campaign in which the only issues were party and Catholicism. Our report of this simulation was limited to the North because of the peculiar role of party in the South. The outcome was a ranking of thirty-two states ranging from the one in which we estimated Kennedy would do best to the one in which we estimated he would do worst. The ranking was

1. Rhode Island	17. Pennsylvania
2. Massachusetts	18. Nevada
3. New Mexico	19. Washington
4. Connecticut	20. New Hampshire
5. New York	21. Wyoming
6. Illinois	22. Oregon
7. New Jersey	23. North Dakota
8. California	24. Nebraska
9. Arizona	25. Indiana
10. Michigan	26. South Dakota
11. Wisconsin	27. Vermont
12. Colorado	28. Iowa
13. Ohio	29. Kansas
14. Montana	30. Utah
15. Minnesota	31. Idaho
16. Missouri	32. Maine

The product-moment correlation over states between the Kennedy index on the simulation (not strictly speaking a per cent) and the actual Kennedy vote in the election was .82.* It should be emphasized that this satisfying result was based upon political data not a single item of which was later than October 1958. Surveys on the 1960 election were not available soon enough to be incorporated into this analysis.

The basic method in this simulation was a fairly straightforward application of the cross-pressure findings of earlier election studies.[6] These findings enabled us to improve our estimate of how a particular voter will behave if we know the cross-pressures he is under. With such knowledge, an analyst should feel more comfortable making guesses about how voters under particular kinds of cross-pressure will shift in an election than he would about making an overall intuitive guess at the outcome. The method of this simulation was to make a series of such detailed estimates and then let the computer put them together to give an overall outcome.

---

* Perfect prediction is a correlation of 1.00, pure chance would yield a correlation of .00, results exactly the opposite of the prediction would show a correlation of −1.00.— Eds.

[6] Bernard R. Berelson, Paul F. Lazarsfeld, William N. McPhee, *Voting: A Study of Opinion Formation in a Presidential Campaign* (Chicago: University of Chicago Press, 1954).

To make these detailed estimates we classified our set of 480 voter types into 9 possible cross-pressure subsets arising from a 3-by-3 breakdown on religion and party: Protestants, Catholics, and others; Republicans, Democrats, and Independents. For each of the nine resulting situations we made a prediction. For example, take the Protestant Republicans. They were not under cross-pressure. Since our data had revealed no substantial dislike of Nixon as an individual among such voters, we saw no reason why their vote in 1960 should differ substantially from their vote in 1956, even though Eisenhower was not running. Thus for them we wrote two equations:

$$V_k = P_{56}(1 - P_{35})$$

$$V_n = Q_{56}(1 - P_{35})$$

meaning that the predicted Kennedy percentage (V_k) in any voter type of this Protestant-Republican sort would be the percentage of persons in that voter type who had indicated a preference for Stevenson in the 1956 polls (P_{56}), reduced by the nonvoting record of that voter type $(1 - P_{35})$.[7] The equation for the expected Nixon percentage (V_n) was the same except that it used the 1956 Eisenhower supporters (Q_{56}).

The above was the simplest set of equations used. Let us now turn to a more complicated set, that for a group under cross-pressure—Protestant Democrats. First, we decided that, barring the religious issue, 1958 vote intentions would be a better index of the Protestant Democrats' 1960 vote than would their 1956 vote intentions. Too many of them were Eisenhower defectors in 1956 for us to believe that 1956 was a good indicator of normal behavior. On the other hand, 1958 polls would overestimate their Democratic vote, since many of them would defect again against a Catholic. However, it would not suffice merely to subtract the percentage who gave anti-Catholic replies on poll questions, for perhaps those very Democrats who were anti-Catholic were the ones who in practice voted Republican anyway. In short, the question was: Were the bigot defectors right-wingers whose vote the Democrats would lose even without a Catholic candidate? Our system could not give us that information for each respondent incorporated into our data. While respondent in a voter type might have been polled in a survey in 1958 about his vote intentions, another man of the same voter type, on a different survey, might have been polled on whether he would vote for a Catholic for President. To estimate the correlation between these two variables we had to find one or more surveys on which both questions appeared. We then ran anti-Catholicism by 1958 vote for each of the more numerous Protestant Democrat voter types. We found that among them the ratio ad/bc in the

[7] Since we trichotomized results, $P_{56} + Q_{56}$ do not add up to 100 per cent. The reader may wonder why a turnout correction is added: are not the residuals the nonvoters? The answer is that a turnout correction is needed because many more persons express a candidate preference on a poll than actually turn out to vote.

following fourfold table averaged about .6. With that information we could estimate how many of the anti-Catholics were hopeless cases anyhow (i.e. had gone Republican even in 1958) and how many would be net losses only in a campaign dominated by the religious issue.

1958 VOTE INTENTIONS	ANTI-CATHOLIC	NOT ANTI-CATHOLIC
Democratic	a	b
Republican	c	d

It should be added here that we decided to take poll replies on the religious issue at face value. We were not so naïve as to believe that this was realistic, but since we were not trying to predict absolute percentages, but only relative ones, all that mattered was that the true extent of anti-Catholicism, voter type by voter type, should be linearly related to the percentage overtly expressed. Even this could only be assumed as a promising guess.

Finally, in predicting the vote of the Protestant Democrat voter types, we took account of the established finding that voters under cross-pressure stay home on election day more often than voters whose pressures are consistent. Therefore, for our 1960 estimate we doubled the historically established non-voting index for these types.

Thus we arrived at equations applied to each Protestant Democratic voter type:

$$V_k = (P_{58} - a)(1 - 2P_{35})$$
$$V_n = (Q_{58} + a)(1 - 2P_{35})$$

The estimate of anti-Catholic 1958 Democratic voters (i.e. persons in cell a in Table 1) was arrived at by the computer, given that

$$a + b = P_{58} \qquad a + c = P_{14}(P_{58} + Q_{58})$$

$$P_{14} = \text{per cent anti-Catholic} \qquad \text{and} \quad \frac{ad}{bc} = .6$$

Space precludes a similar examination of each of the other of the nine conditions.[8] Suffice it to say that one other set of serious guesses had to be

---

[8] With the above information, the remaining equations should be decipherable and are reported here for the record:

Protestant Independents, same equations as Protestant Democrats.
Catholic Democrats and Catholic Independents:

$$V_k = (P_{58} + \frac{Q_{58}}{3})(1 - P_{35})$$

$$V_n = \frac{2Q_{58}}{3}(1 - P_{35})$$

Catholic Republicans:

$$V_k = (P_{58} + \frac{Q_{58}}{3})(1 - 2P_{35})$$

$$V_n = \frac{2Q_{58}}{3}(1 - 3P_{35})$$

made, namely what proportion of those Democratic Catholics who had voted Republican in 1958 would switch back to their party to vote for Kennedy and what proportion of Republican Catholics who had voted Republican in 1958 would also switch to Kennedy. After an examination of the trial-heat data from polls which asked about Kennedy vs. Nixon, we decided to use one third as the proportion in each case, and to use that figure also as an estimate of the proportion of Catholic Independents who would be won back by the religious issue.

The simulation required that the computer make 480 separate calculations, each one using the appropriate set of equations from above. During each of the 480 calculations, the computer put into the equations values for turnout record, 1958 vote intention, 1956 vote intention, and anti-Catholicism, derived from the data which had been assembled about that particular voter type. This gave a 1960 vote estimate for each voter type for the particular hypothetical campaign being investigated. Weighted averages of these gave the state-by-state estimates.

These estimates, as we have already noted, turned out to be close to the actual November outcome. They were not intended to be predictions. Or, rather, they were *contingent* predictions only. They were predictions of what would happen *if* the religious issue dominated the campaign. We did not predict that this would happen. We were describing one out of a set of possible types of campaign situation. But by August, when we took our national survey, comparison of our simulation and the survey results showed that this situation was actually beginning to occur. And the closeness of our contingent prediction to the final November result suggests that, indeed, the religious issue was of prime importance.

How close was the religious-issue simulation to the actual outcome compared to alternative bases of prediction? A full exploration of this remains to be made. We must, for example, further vary the parameters * used in the

---

All others:

$$\frac{ad}{bc} = .6$$

$$a + b = \frac{P_{58} + P_{56}}{2}$$

$$c + d = \frac{Q_{58} + Q_{56}}{2}$$

$$a + c = P_{14} \frac{(P_{58} + Q_{58} + P_{56} + Q_{56})}{2}$$

$$b + d = (1 - P_{14}) \frac{(P_{58} + Q_{58} + P_{56} + Q_{56})}{2}$$

$$V_k = \left(\frac{P_{58} + P_{56}}{2} - a\right)\left((1 - 2P_{35})\right)$$

$$V_n = \left(\frac{Q_{58} + Q_{56}}{2} + a\right)\left((1 - 2P_{35})\right)$$

* Parameters: numbers—i.e., means, proportions, etc., based upon a population, not a sample.—Eds.

simulation to determine which ones affect the results most critically and which values of those give the best prediction. For the present we look only at the one set of values and equations on which we relied during the campaign and which has already been described. (A few variations were tried and dismissed during the campaign, but none that made much difference.) How did this one simulation compare with other predictive data?

An obvious comparison is with the Kennedy-Nixon trial heats on polls taken at the same time as the latest polls used in the simulation. The correlation between the state-by-state result of these polls and the actual outcome is but .53 as compared to .82 for the simulation. The simulation, in short, portrayed trends which actually took place between the time the data were collected and election day. The uncorrected polls two years before the election explained but one fourth of the variance in the real results, while intelligent use of them taking into account the cross-pressure theory of voting behavior allowed us to explain nearly two thirds of the variance.

A more stringent comparison would be with Kennedy-Nixon trial heats run in August 1960, when the simulation was run on the computer. Such a comparison would answer the question of whether the Democratic Party would have gotten as good information at that date by the conventional means of up-to-the-minute field interviewing as it got by reanalysis of old data. Very likely it could have, if it had chosen to invest in a large enough national sample survey to give it state-by-state results, for as far as we can now tell the Catholic issue exerted most of its impact by shortly after the conventions. However, until poll data for that period becomes available we can only speculate. We wish to emphasize, however, that at some point in the history of the campaign, poll data certainly came into close correlation with the November election results and thus with our simulation. The date the raw poll results became as or more predictive than the simulation would be the point in the campaign at which mechanisms of voter behavior anticipated in the simulation became reality.

Besides simulation and polls, what other indices might have forecast long in advance the state-by-state order of voting in 1960? Results of previous elections would be one such index. Perhaps the rank order of the states in a previous election is a good forecast of rank order in future ones, even if the electoral outcome changes. (The whole country could move one way or the other, leaving the order of the states much the same.) But, if one is to use this device, which election should one use? The year 1956 was a presidential election year, as was 1960, but in 1956 the Eisenhower phenomenon was operating. 1958, although more recent and less affected by Eisenhower's idiosyncratic appeal, was a Congressional election year. In our simulation, too, we faced this problem. We resolved it for some voter types one way, for some another. But what happens if one relies on a single simple overall assumption of continuity between elections? The result is not very good, though slightly better using 1956 than 1958. The product-moment correlation of Northern results between 1956 and 1960 was .39, between 1958 and 1960, .37. The multiple correlation using both earlier years was .44 with the 1960 election. So far our simulation clearly was superior as a forecast. . . .

The test of any new method of research is successful use. The outcome of the present study gives reason to hope that computer simulation may indeed open up the possibility of using survey data in ways far more complex than has been customary in the past. The political "pros" who commissioned this abstruse study were daring men to gamble on the use of a new and untried technique in the heat of a campaign. The researchers who undertook this job faced a rigorous test, for they undertook to do both basic and applied research at once. The study relied upon social science theories and data to represent the complexity of actual human behavior to a degree that would permit the explicit presentation of the consequences of policy alternatives.

This kind of research could not have been conducted ten years ago. Three new elements have entered the picture to make it possible: first, a body of sociological and psychological theories about voting and other decisions; second, a vast mine of empirical survey data now for the first time available in an archive; third, the existence of high-speed computers with large memories. The social science theories allow us to specify with some confidence what processes will come to work in a decision situation. The backlog of survey data permits us to estimate the parameters of these processes with fair precision and great detail for each small element of our national population. The computer makes possible the handling of this mine of data. More important still, it makes possible the precise carrying out of long and complex chains of reasoning about the interactions among the different processes. In summary, we believe that conditions now exist for use of survey data in research far more ambitious than social scientists are used to. If it is possible to reproduce, through computer simulation, much of the complexity of a whole society going through processes of change, and to do so rapidly, then the opportunities to put social science to work are vastly increased. It is our belief that this is now possible, which was put to a test by the campaign research reported here.

Chapter Ten

Population and Ecology

ALTHOUGH THE TERMS *population* and *ecology* are not, technically speaking, concepts, they have been utilized as tools of analysis in the same way as the other concepts considered in this anthology. Population study, or *demography,* centers upon the characteristics of a population (such as age and sex distribution) and the factors relevant to its growth or decline. *Ecology* is also treated as a concept, for example by Young and Mack in their definition: "Human ecology deals with the spatial distribution of populations and their culture as these are affected by invasion, succession, segregation, centralization, and related processes." [1]

The numbers and distribution of people have become an area of increased interest, if not concern, to laymen as well as sociologists. In this chapter the first two articles are primarily concerned with the effect of an increased population size: Selection 42 on the facilities of a state prison system; Selection 43 on the need to establish new church congregations. The last four articles (Selections 44–47) are primarily concerned with the spatial aspect as it affects the location of factories, intergroup relations, health, and crime.

[1] Kimball Young and Raymond W. Mack, *Sociology and Social Life* (New York: American Book Co., 1962), p. 491.

42

Predicting the Population in Institutions for Delinquent Children and Youth

Arnold M. Rose and George H. Weber

Administrators of every public correctional institution are plagued by the question, "What ten-years-hence population must we plan for?" The authors show how they tried to answer the question for Minnesota through techniques of demographic analysis.

The rapid increase in the youthful population and the changing character of juvenile delinquency make it highly important for state authorities to make predictions of the number of committed young people they will have to handle in the foreseeable future. Educational institutions, especially the universities, have been devoting a considerable amount of effort and money to estimating the population they will be serving in the coming years.[1] For the same reasons, those responsible for penal institutions would be well advised to do likewise. Partly to meet a request of the State Legislature's Interim Commission, but mainly because it felt the need for a predictive study to accomplish its own planning, the Youth Conservation Commission of Minnesota asked us to do a statistical study which would be the basis of a prediction of needs for institutional facilities for delinquents up to 1970. The techniques of this study are reported in the present article, and they would probably be directly applicable for any other state.[2] The article will be largely based on excerpts from the original report, showing trends in Minnesota but eliminating all of the detailed statistics.

A prediction of the number of delinquent youngsters[3] committed to institutions must be based on two sets of factors: (1) changes in the popula-

Reprinted by special permission of the *Journal of Criminal Law, Criminology and Police Science*, Vol. 50, No. 2 (July–August 1959), pp. 124–131 (Copyright © 1959, By Northwestern University School of Law). Also, by permission of the authors.

Arnold M. Rose is Professor of Sociology, University of Minnesota.

George H. Weber is Director of Berkshire Farm Institute for Training and Research; Senior Research Associate, Youth Development Center, Syracuse University.

[1] See, for example, William T. Middlebrook, *How to Estimate the Building Needs of a College or University* (Minneapolis: University of Minnesota Press, 1958).

[2] The full report is available only in typewritten form in the offices of the Youth Conservation Commission in St. Paul, Minnesota.

[3] "Children" or "juveniles" refers to those under 18 years of age; "youth" refers to those 18–21 years of age; "youngsters" or "young people" are nontechnical terms used to refer to both children and youth.

tion under 21 years of age and the proportion of it becoming delinquent; (2) administrative changes in commitment, probation and parole policy. Our method attempts to predict both sets of these changes by extrapolation of present trends, but the two sets of predictions should be understood as having differing validity. Barring catastrophic killing off of a significant portion of the population or drastic economic upheaval which forces unusual migration, it is possible to predict fairly accurately the number of youngsters in the state of Minnesota up to 1970 who will be in the ages when most delinquent acts are committed (12–21 years). It is even possible to predict with a fairly high degree of accuracy, by means of extrapolation of current trends, the proportion of these youngsters who are likely to be arrested for delinquent acts, as changes in the tendency to commit delinquent acts are functions of a host of social conditions which are changing at a fairly steady rate and are not likely to modify their direction of change all at once—barring major social upsets and changes in police policy.

Administrative policy concerning the treatment of juvenile delinquents and youthful offenders is a function of law and of the climate of opinion that are subject to significant change at almost any time. For example, a report to the 1957 Legislature by the Commission on Juvenile Delinquency, Adult Crime, and Corrections calls for immediate expansion of probation and parole services. If this should be done, it might reduce the number of delinquents committed at any one time to an institution. It is not possible to predict whether there will be legislation that significantly increases the probation and parole services, and it is not even possible to predict whether such an increase —if provided for in law—would significantly keep delinquents out of institutions. The study is based on an extrapolation of current trends, using existing statistics and reasoned guesses, and it is only as reliable as the data are accurate, as the reasoning is logical, and as current trends remain the same.

But there is no necessary reason why many of the relevant trends should remain the same: changes in the policies and practices of the legislature, the judges, and of those who handle delinquents can make significant changes in the future number of institutionalized delinquents that cannot be predicted. However, the study ought to provide a base line from which the effects of any future change in policy or practice can be partially estimated. Thus, it is highly unlikely that the number of juvenile delinquents and youthful offenders that will be predicted here as likely to be committed to state institutions in 1970 actually will be there at that time. But the study ought to help make it possible to recognize factors that will create a discrepancy when they occur or are inaugurated. Further, the study provides some basis for judging the needs for institutions in the coming years, unless new policies and practices are inaugurated.

Prediction is made by straight-line projection of recent trends. What constitutes "recent" is a matter of arbitrary definition, of course. Extending back the number of years from which data are used increases the stability of the projection but also allows consideration of earlier periods when administrative practices were quite different. For this study, data from 1952 or 1953 begin each series (except that for total population). There are several ways of projecting data; in this report the method of average change from year to year will be used for all arrest, court, institutional, probation and parole data.

Throughout this study, girls are kept statistically separated from boys because each institution for delinquents serves only one sex. In so far as possible also children under the age of 18 will be kept separate from those 18 to 21 years of age, for a similar reason. For some purposes, children under the age of 12 will be ignored as they constitute only a tiny proportion of the institutionalized delinquent population. This study is primarily concerned with delinquents committed to Youth Conservation Commission (YCC) institutions, but it will occasionally be necessary to refer to other state institutions for delinquents run by the Welfare Department. Under Minnesota law,[4] children under 18 can be committed to the YCC only by Juvenile Court (in three metropolitan counties) or Probate Court (in the 84 other counties), except when the juvenile or probate courts transfer a case to District Court. Youthful offenders can be committed to the YCC only by a District Court, either through direct jurisdiction or through transfer from a lower court. Children and youthful offenders can be committed to state institutions only by the YCC, except in the case of those convicted of 1st or 2nd degree murder who can be sent directly to the state prison.

A. PREDICTING POPULATION CHANGES

The first factor of change to be considered is that of population. With the rise in the birth rate beginning in 1940, the child and youth population has increased rapidly and has been creating heavier burdens for all child- and youth-caring institutions. Since the children who will be entering the delinquency age of 12 years in 1970 are born in 1958, it would seem fairly simple to apply the current death rates to them and estimate how many will be left by 1970. The matter is complicated, however, by in-migation to and out-migration from the state. The technique that will be used for predicting the youth population up to 1970 in Minnesota is as follows:

To the child population for 1957,[5] age specific death rates can be applied to reduce the population year by year. To this can be added an estimate of the current in-migration and subtracted an estimate of the current out-migration. The latest age specific death rates are those for 1955, and while these may be slightly too high for the future considering the trend toward decline in the death rate of youth, they are low enough not to create too much error. The State Statistician has calculated a net in-migration into Minnesota of 5,470 persons during the year April 1956–April 1957. This we have allocated to

4 The law is not always followed in original commitment; but when it is not, the case is subject to review by the appropriate court.

5 Population estimates for 1957 have been kindly provided by the State Statistician for Vital Statistics, *Mr. Emerson W. Storey.*

the youth population according to their proportion in the population. This is probably not quite sufficient for the future as the net in-migration to Minnesota has been increasing slightly.

Thus our estimates are quite conservative, tending to underestimate the size of the future youth population. Projected estimates made by the U.S. Bureau of Census are not broken down by age and sex, as are required for the purpose here, but comparing our total estimates with theirs suggests that ours tend to underestimate the future youth population slightly. For example, our prediction for the total Minnesota population up through 18 years of age in 1960 is 1,221,700 persons, whereas the four estimates made by the U.S. Census Bureau are (1) 1,226,000 (2) 1,255,000 (3) 1,244,000 and (4) 1,279,000.

Delinqency statistics generally show higher rates for city youngsters than for country youngsters, although the question has been raised as to whether this represents a true differential in delinquency or merely a different procedure for handling delinquency. Even if the latter should be the fact, state institutions for young offenders receive a disproportionate share of city dwellers, and this is what is important for our analysis. City dwellers (including suburbanites) have been increasing and farm dwellers have been decreasing, especially since 1940, although rural nonfarm population (mostly in small towns and villages) has been increasing rapidly also.

Extrapolating the decrease in farm population from 1957 to 1970, we might estimate that the farm population will have fallen a further 40 per cent and the metropolitan population will have risen another 40 per cent during this period. Such extrapolations are perhaps particularly hazardous, but they suggest a continuing large shift from farm to urban population. The present urban-rural differential in the rate of juvenile and youthful commitment to state institutions will not be maintained in the face of these population shifts, however, as most of the metropolitan increase is in suburban areas (which have a relatively low commitment rate) and the farm population increasingly includes Indian and Mexican-born farm laborers whose youngsters contribute disproportionately to the commitment rate. In sum, these data on rural-urban shifts suggest that the increase in the number of commitments due to changes in the population will rise faster than the increase in the minor population itself. But little can be said as to exactly how much this will be, and the data to be subsequently presented on trends in arrests and commitments include both the increase in the population and the rural-urban shift.

B. PREDICTING THE NUMBER OF ARRESTS

The number of arrests is a function both of the number of delinquencies and of police practices regarding the arrest of youngsters believed to have engaged in delinquent behavior. These two factors cannot be separated in any prediction, and it should be understood that the prediction is for a combination of them. Reliable data are available only for Minneapolis and St. Paul, but trends were extrapolated to the whole state. The data show that the number of arrests is increasing faster than is the child and youth population, at least in the Twin Cities. Considering changes in the number of arrests only, the population of institutions for delinquents can be expected to increase 131 per cent among males up to 18 years of age by 1970, 65 per cent among males 18 to 21 years of age, and 62 per cent among females up to 18 years of age. The trend for arrests of females 18–21 years of age seems to be downward, but considering the rise in the female youth population, it would probably not be meaningful to project the downward trend in arrests.

C. PREDICTING THE NUMBER OF COURT CASES

As to cases brought before the juvenile courts, the percentage increases are greater than those for the child population in general and for the number of arrests of accused juveniles. The data also show a projected increase of 39 per cent in the number of males 18–20.9 years of age brought before all district courts in Minnesota between 1957 and 1970, and a projected increase of 177 per cent in the number of females of these ages. The increase for males is quite comparable to that for the growth of the population as a whole (39 and 31 per cent increase, respectively) but the increase for females aged 18–20.9 years who appear in district courts promises to increase much more than the comparable population growth (177 and 32 per cent increase, respectively). At the same time, there seems to be a trend for juvenile and probate courts not to transfer children to district courts but to judge them themselves. But the number of children appearing in district court has been very great— ranging between 40 and 61 males and between 6 and 16 females in recent years—so that their gradual disappearance from district courts cannot relieve those courts very much nor change significantly the trends in total number of children appearing in any court.

D. PREDICTING THE DIFFERENT KINDS OF DISPOSITIONS BY COURTS

A young offender may be given "probation" in three sorts of ways in Minnesota, and probation itself is to be distinguished from parole. Theoretically, probation is given in place of commitment to an institution, while parole is given upon release from an institution. Actually, all three types of probation generally follow lock-up in some kind of local jail,[6] and the third kind of probation—from a YCC reception center which is physically located at the same place as the regular YCC institution—generally does not take place until

---

[6] The law requires that young offenders be segregated from adult offenders; the large cities have special facilities for temporary incarceration of young offenders.

after the offender has been incarcerated for some weeks. The first kind of
"probation"—not officially called that but often followed up by some sort of
observation as in the case of the other forms of probation—is by the Intake
Division of the Court Services Department (or its equivalent with another
name in the three metropolitan counties). It is impossible to tell how many
arrested cases released without being brought formally to court are followed
up by the social workers in the various public and private agencies, so no
effort will be made here to predict trends for this kind of informal "probation."

The second kind of probation is that ordered by the courts. The projected
prediction is a 133 per cent increase by 1970 for the Hennepin County
Juvenile Court, 106 per cent increase for Ramsey County Juvenile Court, but
a decrease of 31 per cent for all the district courts in the state. The figures
for the two juvenile courts are almost the same as for the increase in juvenile
court case load. The district courts are increasing commitments to the YCC,
and decreasing most other kinds of disposition, including probations.

Trends in dismissals by courts are considered next. If Ramsey County
experience be taken as typical for all juvenile court jurisdictions, there was
a fairly stable number of dismissals from 1953 to 1956, but a jump upward
of over 100 per cent from 1956 to 1957 that suggests a higher number in
the future. A projection up to 1970 suggests a 48 per cent increase over 1957.
The number of dismissals by district courts has always been small, and is
tending to decline.

The courts' tendencies to commit child and youth offenders to institutions
other than YCC are then taken up. The prediction for 1970 is for almost 200
per cent increase in males so committed by juvenile courts in the two largest
counties. For females the percentage increase predicted is almost as large—
148 per cent. Cases so committed by district courts in Minnesota are so few as
to make any prediction meaningless.

Commitments to YCC institutions for the two largest counties show that a
146 per cent increase over 1957 figures can be expected by 1970 for the
male juveniles. For female juveniles the prediction is for only a 76 per cent
increase. The increase predicted for juvenile offenders from the other 85 counties (including the metropolitan St. Louis county) is only slightly smaller.
For male youthful offenders the percentage increase is expected to be 65
per cent by 1970. The number of female youthful offenders committed by district courts is too small to permit of reliable prediction as to trends affecting
the committed population. It is to be noted that the increases predicted for
commitments to YCC institutions are considerably higher than the increases
predicted for the child and youth population generally. They are at least as
high as the increases predicted for number of arrests, and possibly higher
than the increases predicted for the number of cases appearing in court (because the courts are becoming less inclined, relatively speaking, to dismiss a
case presented before them).

E. PREDICTING YCC DISPOSITIONS, LENGTH OF STAY, AND RETURNS

The YCC reception centers are physically located at the state institutions but the offenders are kept apart, given a different treatment, and there is possibly a psychological difference for a child who may have been at an institution but was not actually committed to the institution. The YCC may decide to grant probation to a child or youth committed to its care. The trends in probations granted from each of the YCC reception centers show that the increase is greatest for the younger boys sent to Red Wing probably because the facilities there are greatly overcrowded: 165 per cent increase is predicted for 1970 for boys from the three metropolitan counties (Hennepin, Ramsey, and St. Louis) and 109 per cent increase for boys from the other 84 counties. For girls sent to Sauk Centre, there is a trend toward increase in probations granted to those from the three metropolitan counties, but no change for those from the other 84 counties. For the older boys sent to St. Cloud, there is a slightly increasing trend in probation for those from the nonmetropolitan counties. (There were too few older girls put on probation from the Shakopee Reception Center to report.)

After deciding not to grant probation to a child or youthful offender, the YCC orders him or her to one of its regular state institutions. But the strain on the facilities at the reception centers and institutions is not to be measured solely by the commitment rate. One additional factor is the variation in the number of commitments, day by day and week by week. In many respects the strain on facilities (such as beds) and personnel at the installations is better measured by the peak population than by the average population. On the average, the peak population is 40.1 per cent greater in 1956–57 than the average daily population at all YCC installations. In general, the peak is reached in April or May at the institutions for juveniles, as there is a tendency to let children close to being paroled to be held until they finish a school year.[7] There is a very slight relief created by the inactive population—that is, those hospitalized, those on home visits, and runaways. The average inactive population is only 4.4 per cent of the peak population, and 6.2 per cent of the average daily population in 1956–57, for all institutions taken together. But there is practically no correlation between the inactive population on any given day and the daily size of the active population, so the inactive population creates practically no relief to the problems created by peak load.

Another factor affecting use of YCC facilities and personnel is the duration of stay under YCC supervision. Naturally, the length of stay in an institution is greater for violators of probation or parole, and the length of stay on probation is greater for nonviolators. Two different sets of YCC personnel handle the installations and the probation and parole supervision, so that when

---

[7] Statement by R. E. Farrell, Superintendent of State Training School for Boys, July 5, 1957.

projection of trends are made for either number of commitments or length of stay, the separate effect on these two divisions of personnel must be considered.

For the younger boys (at Red Wing) who do not violate probation or parole, the length of stay in the installations and on probation and parole is sharply downward. This is probably as it should be, but two observations need to be made: (1) The length of stay in an installation will reach a natural minimum true for the Training School at present. For the Reception Centers the length of time could be reduced if there were adequate professional staffs to study the boys. Under better staffing, they could be "processed" in six weeks whereas now the study averages 10–12 weeks. This, however, would not reflect itself in a direct reduction of population because many of the Reception Center cases are transferred to the Camp or institution anyway. Observation, testing, and processing require some time and cannot be expected to go down indefinitely so that some of the savings in space and personnel now being made cannot be extended much more. (2) Even when a boy has been "cured" of delinquency, he must be helped and observed on probation or parole, so that a certain time on probation or parole is desirable even for the better "risks"; for this reason, the "savings" of YCC personnel working with boys on probation or parole probably cannot, or should not, be extended much more than they already have been.

The observations just made may help to explain why length of stay in installations or on probation or parole is not moving down for all children and youthful offenders who do not violate probation or parole: The length of stay may already have reached its natural or desirable limit, and is now turning upward in correction of excessive "cutting."

For those who do violate probation and/or parole a downward trend in length of stay at a reception center is probably indicated as not desirable and an upward trend in length at an institution may be desirable, in terms of doing something for the offender and in protecting the public from offenders. The fact is that there is a downward trend in length of stay at the reception centers. The trend toward a shorter stay on probation for all categories of offenders reflects the increasing tendency toward delinquency (those who violate probation now are violating sooner). Or, it reflects the growing pressure on YCC authorities, who seem to be increasingly placing offenders on probation who are not good risks (probably in an effort to avoid excessive overcrowding in institutions). In either of these cases, the downward trend in length of stay on probation, for those who violate probation, is not a good thing; it also does not relieve the burden of work on YCC personnel as it shifts the burden to those who work in institutions or with parolees. A third possibility is that the trend toward a shorter stay on probation is due to the recent increase in the number of parole agents, who thus are probably more quickly aware of probation violations.

The upward trend in length of stay on parole, for those who violate probation or parole, may simply reflect what has just been said: When offenders more rapidly and increasingly violate probation, they have to be watched a longer time on parole. Since all institutionalized offenders leave their institutions by way of parole, it can be seen from these data on increasing length of stay on parole that the future is likely to bring an increasingly heavy burden on parole officers. The extent of future burden is suggested by the ratios of the projected figure for 1970 over the actual figure for 1957.

It is not possible to say with any strong basis in factual knowledge just how long a commitment should be. Experts differ in their opinion. But the following considerations should be borne in mind when considering the question:

1. Those committed to YCC and other state institutions are usually the more difficult cases, although judges differ in their tendencies to commit to the YCC. As we have noted in the course of this report, there is a peeling off from the total number of those who violate the law at the time of arrest by the police, at the time of consideration as to whether a violator should be brought into court by the county attorneys and the social workers in the departments of court services, at the time of judgment by the judge, at the time of transfer out of the reception centers by the YCC and its recommending personnel. Those who "pass" through all these peeling-off processes are likely to be the "more serious" cases, in terms of prognosis for their recidivism and seriousness of their offense.

2. The YCC—both the commission and the professional personnel—have to keep in mind two separate but related interests: how to do most for the child or youth so that he will not commit delinquent acts again, and how to protect the general public from offenders. The YCC has not only the power to segregate the offender from the public and to "punish" him, but also some opportunity to "cure" him. YCC personnel include trained social workers and psychologists as well as teachers, and they have recourse to studies made by sociologists, psychiatrists, and psychologists. Often they can do something for the children and youth in their charge, if they have enough time to put their techniques into full operation.

3. YCC installations have places for only so many inmates, and only so much flexibility is possible through putting additional beds in corridors, by building new dormitories or cottages. There is only so much money for personnel, and qualified personnel often cannot be readily hired. The YCC cannot control the number committed to its charge; it can adjust to the number of its facilities and personnel only by modifying length of stay and by varying the number of probations and paroles it grants in any given period.

The average length of stay for all boys in the State Training School at Red Wing was about eight months. After stating that no definite answer could be given to the question concerning an optimum average length of stay, the superintendent of the school wrote:

I believe an average stay from 12 to 14 months would be needed to give each boy the help he may need. I do not want to indicate that all boys should be here that length of time; however, most, if not all, boys coming here are in need of some type of treatment, and many if not most of them have long and established patterns of behavior. It is foolhardy for us to even think we can change these well-established behavior patterns in 6 or 7 months.[8]

The acting superintendent of the Home School for Girls at Sauk Centre reported that the average length of stay

is becoming shorter as the institution population increases. In my opinion, this trend should be reversed if anything. The individual treatment certainly suffers when the population increases without a corresponding increase in staff members. Perhaps a longer period of time would offset this somewhat.

In opposition to this, I have a definite feeling that there is a time when the girl should go out regardless of progress and that commitment beyond this point is harmful.

I believe then that the present flexibility is good but that the administration should not have to think in terms of bed and classroom space in determining the length of stay.[9]

This article has already taken up the trends in the number of probations granted from YCC reception centers. Work with probationers and parolees is handled by the same division within the YCC, and in order to get a prediction of its future work load, the trends in the number of paroles granted from YCC institutions need to be examined. The increase in parolee load is greatest in the case of the younger boys: The prediction for 1970 is that they will be increased about 150 per cent over the number for 1957 (the increase is about the same for the two groups of counties). For the younger girls the projected increase is only 12 per cent by 1970 for those from the three metropolitan counties and only 38 per cent for those from the 84 other counties.

The question may next be raised as to whether the increasing number of commitments to YCC installations, and the incomplete expansion of facilities and nonproportionate addition of personnel which means a relative reduction of space and services for the offenders, has meant that too many probations have been granted and that parole has been granted too early. In other words, is there any factual basis for the belief that space and personnel considerations are outweighing the best interests of the public and the offenders? Evidence on this point is that the trend in the proportion of offenders violating YCC probation is sharply upward for the younger boys—with a projected prediction of a 109 per cent increase in the proportion of violators by 1970. The trend is also sharply upward for the older boys, and the present figure of 50 per cent violation promises to become 100 per cent violation by 1970 (although here the number of cases on which the percentage is based is too small to be reliable). On the other hand, the trend is downward for the younger girls, so that one-fourth fewer girls may be expected to violate probation by 1970. (There are not enough cases to justify any prediction for older girls.)

---

[8] Unpublished communication from R. E. Farrell, March 26, 1958.
[9] Unpublished communication from Roy Palm, March 29, 1958.

The situation is only slightly less serious in the case of parole. The percentage increase by 1970 over 1957 in percentage violating parole is expected to be 59 per cent for the younger boys, 46 per cent for the younger girls, 83 per cent for the older boys, and several hundred per cent for the older girls.

The figures reported here are expected percentage changes in percentage violating probation or parole. Another technique for examining the same data is to consider the expected percentage changes in the raw number of those violating probation or parole. The changes predicted for 1970 by this technique are in the same direction and approximately the same relative order as for the first technique, although the specific figures differ.

F. SUMMARY AND CONCLUSION

The factors to be considered in predicting the future needs for space and personnel of state institutions are so numerous, and their interrelationships so complex that it is impossible to arrive at a single figure that will predict the needs of 1970. The cautions suggested at the beginning of this paper, concerning the validity of projections, should be reviewed. A summary glance at the major findings of this report, however, will help us in arriving at a synthesis.

1. There is highly likely to be a population increase of those under 18 years of about 50 per cent by 1970, and of those 18–21 years of about 31 per cent. Pertinent to a prediction of delinquency, however, is the second demographic fact that the urban (particularly the suburban) population is continuing to increase rapidly and the farm population to fall rapidly; this will tend to rise the commitment rate as urban areas have more commitments.

2. For the Twin Cities alone, male juveniles arrested are increasing to the extent that an increase of 131 per cent is predicted by 1970. For female juveniles, the figure is 62 per cent, and for male youths 65 per cent. Thus the predicted increase in urban arrests is higher than the predicted increase in population.

3. Court cases are also bounding upward: if the present trend continues until 1970, the prediction is for a 152 per cent increase for Hennepin County male juveniles, 144 per cent increase for Hennepin County female juveniles, a 79 per cent increase of the juveniles in Ramsey County, a 39 per cent increase for all Minnesota older boys and a much larger increase for the older girls.

4. Probations ordered by court are increasing at about the same rate as the increase in court cases. Outright dismissals, however, are much lower. Commitments to non-YCC institutions (data from juvenile courts in the two largest counties only) are increasing most rapidly of all.

5. Commitments to YCC institutions are going up at a rate more rapidly than population, and about as rapidly as the rate of arrests or court cases. For the two largest counties, the juvenile court commitments are tending toward a 146 per cent increase for males by 1970, 67 per cent for females. For the other 85 counties, the expected increase will be 101 per cent for males and 59

per cent for females by 1970. For the youthful offenders 18–21 years of age, the increase is 65 per cent by 1970.

6. The YCC is granting probation from its reception centers and parole from its institutions at about the same increasing rate as it is taking in committed juveniles (for youthful offenders, the probation and parole rate increase is somewhat lower).

7. The peak population for all YCC installations is about 40 per cent higher than their average daily population. This peak usually occurs in spring. The inactive population is only about 4.4 per cent of the peak population.

8. Probably under the pressure of increasing commitments and of not-so-quickly expanding facilities and personnel, the length of stay at most YCC installations is falling, as is the length of stay on probation, especially for those who do not violate probation or parole. The length of stay on parole is moving upward in most categories of those who have violated probation or parole. These trends predict relatively greater burdens on the YCC in the future.

9. Violation of probation and parole is increasing considerably, except in the case of the younger girls (for whom violations are decreasing). The upward trend may well reflect the progressive insufficiency of the facilities and personnel of the YCC.

It is understood that any change of practice or policy—for example, in committing or assigning to probation—will necessarily change these predictions. Looking at the facts together, one cannot but arrive at the conclusion that the burden on the YCC will increase considerably during the coming years. To maintain facilities and personnel at their present quality [10] the YCC must double itself by 1970. No significant further relief can be expected from a policy of increasing the proportion put on probation, for probation is already increasing at about the same rate as commitments, and violations of probation are going upward (except for the girls under 18 years of age). It may be that some significant new treatment or procedure in handling delinquents will possibly reduce future costs—such as the already promising work camps at Willow River and Thistledew or as conceivable local centers which "commit" the more reformable delinquents only during evening and night hours. But these are only possibilities. If there is to be a serious effort to protect the public and to reform at least the more "reformable" delinquents, facilities and personnel will have to be kept at least to their present level— which means a doubling of real costs by 1970.

---

[10] In considering "present quality," it must be recognized that some of the installations are grossly overcrowded and significantly understaffed for the present population, as pointed out by the *Legislative Interim Commission Report to the 1957 Minnesota Legislature (op. cit.).*

43

Religion and Ecological Change in Eastern Florida

Frederick A. Shippey

Social change and ecological change are inextricably interwoven. A change in the population distribution brings about changes in social relationships; a change in the social structure induces changes in the population composition and distribution.

Changes in society ranging from modification of retirement practices to space-age technology have brought about changes in the composition and distribution of population in eastern Florida. The church, like any other social institution, must adapt itself in order to meet new demands effectively. The author of this selection was consulted by the officials of one religious denomination about what changes in the church program should be made to adapt to the new population movements. As a result of his research and recommendations, twenty new churches were organized within four years. Unlike all too many projects in social research, this one was followed by action based on the sociologist's recommendations.

Where significant social change occurs, religion is compelled to reconsider its contemporary institutional and spiritual efforts.[1] Drastic change often demands major reassessment and adjustment. In terms of strategy, the church may need to cope with a new set of problems or to be brought up-to-date. Since World War II, an enormous expansion of suburbia has occurred in the United States. Citrus orchards, fields and forests, literally have been supplanted by hundreds of new communities. Moreover, many reluctant old places have become inundated by the swift advancing tide of new residential construction. Throughout America this dual-pronged change is a widely-acknowledged phenomenon. One fourth of the nation now resides under suburban conditions. By 1980 the figure is expected to rise to one person out of three. Clearly the suburban trend is one of the remarkable social changes of our time.[2]

Frederick A. Shippey is Professor of Sociology of Religion, Drew University, Madison, N.J. This article was written especially for this volume.

[1] For detailed discussions consult F. Boulard, *An Introduction to Religious Sociology* (London: Darton, Longman and Todd, 1960); Gabriel LeBras, *Études de sociologie religieuse,* I et II (Paris: Presses Universitaires de France, 1956); Frederick A. Shippey, "The New Rapprochement Between Theology and Social Sciences in France," *Religion in Life,* **32,** 1, pp. 95 ff.

[2] *Vide* Bennett M. Berger, *Working-Class Suburb* (Berkeley: University of California Press, 1960); William Dobriner (ed.), *The Suburban Community* (New York: Putnam,

This population explosion demands new public schools, new fire stations, expanded health facilities, new streets, and huge new shopping centers. Moreover, it calls for numerous new synagogues and new churches. Thousands of brand new religious congregations have been established in suburbia since World War II.[3] Many received constructive guidance from social scientists. Continuing large scale social change around the periphery of cities has led harassed religious leaders to request sociological research projects on manifold crucial questions. This interdisciplinary approach is not completely new. According to the extensive literature, religion in the United States has placed considerable reliance [4] during the past fifty years upon social science for a technical understanding of change in American society. Religious work among ethnic minorities, migrants, the urban poor, and kindred subcultural groups can be listed among the questions explored. As a whole, the relationship has proved mutually stimulating.

SOCIAL CHANGE IN EASTERN FLORIDA

Thus when conspicuous suburban change manifested itself in eastern Florida, the church turned to sociology for assistance. The appearance of vast new residential subdivisions covering many acres of land and the rapid expansion of old towns and cities led a particular Protestant leader to seek an analysis of changed conditions. He sought answers to three questions. *What are the major implications now for The Methodist Church? Are the changes sufficiently drastic to demand the establishment of new congregations in the new subdivisions? If so, where and how soon?*

One of Florida's areas of conspicuous suburban population change was the fifty-mile wide strip of coastal territory, beginning at Fort Lauderdale and extending northward to the launching pads of Cape Kennedy. It consisted of five complete counties and part of six others, comprising approximately 2,500 square miles. As Florida goes, this section of the state proved to be an area of late development. But when it started, a boom was on. The recent advent of a Pratt and Whitney manufacturing plant in Palm Beach County and of other industrial concerns situated in adjacent counties accelerated the residential growth patterns so phenomenally that religious leaders were overwhelmed by the change. Hence the aforementioned, beleaguered church

1958); Seeley, Sim, and Loosley, *Crestwood Heights* (New York: Basic Books, 1956); Robert C. Wood, *Suburbia—Its People and Their Politics* (Boston: Houghton Mifflin, 1959); and other works.

[3] Lewis W. Bloede, "Development of New Congregations in the United States and Canada by the Evangelical United Brethren Church" (unpublished Th.D. Thesis, Boston University, 1960); Bonneau P. Murphy, *The Call for New Churches* (New York: The Methodist Church, 1961); Dwight H. Shelhart, *A Church Is Born* (Philadelphia: Muhlenberg Press, 1947); and additional studies.

[4] Consult especially the writings of M. Martina Abbott, H. Paul Douglass, Joseph H. Fichter, Albert I. Gordon, Gerhard Lenski, Murray H. Leiffer, David Moberg, Liston Pope, Ross Sanderson, Joseph B. Schuyler, Frederick A. Shippey, J. Milton Yinger.

administrator sought a sociological research study in the late 1950's. He wanted to familiarize himself with the local facts, trends, processes, and their implications.

Growth patterns in eastern Florida were phenomenal. Virtually every community, large and small, doubled, tripled, or quadrupled in population size since World War II. Belle Glade, Boca Raton, Boynton Beach, Delray Beach, Eau Gallie, Fort Lauderdale, Fort Pierce, Greenacres City, Lake Worth, Lantana, Melbourne, Oakland Park, Pompano Beach, Riviera Beach, Stuart, Vero Beach, West Gate, and West Palm Beach are among the communities showing sensational gains in population. Many places were even too new to be found on the maps. No matter in what direction one turned, extensive new subdivisions were opening up fast. Residential development, far from being sporadic, was astonishingly dynamic and purposeful. County population tripled in slightly over a decade. This amazing increase put a heavy strain on all community institutions (religious, educational, political, et cetera), as well as on roads, fire, and police protection. Indeed, in both the best and worst senses, it was boom times! [5]

RELIGIOUS ASSUMPTIONS AND CRITERIA

Certain assumptions were necessary in order to carry out the proposed field research project. These can be summarized briefly. Protestant Christianity relates itself to American society in such manner that the faith's institutional fortunes are somehow entangled with those of the secular world. Methodism is capable of making adequate use of knowledge about drastic social change, particularly current population shifts of noteworthy magnitude. "Inside" studies [6] made by persons who are both trained sociologists and active participants in religion prove reliable provided the researcher fulfills the exacting requirements of the academic discipline. Persons of faith can understand and utilize data on population change provided such information bears directly upon critical but unresolved problems.

Moreover, several criteria of a phase of Protestant church work underlie the present research project. In determining the adequacy of a site for a new Methodist congregation certain basic value judgments are relevant, being derived from the experience and insights of specialists. [7] The basic principle stressed is that of *indigenization*. Local really means local. Members for a proposed new congregation will be recruited normally from the residences within one mile of the site. A suitable church location is one which allows

[5] Havighurst and Morgan, *Social Life in a War Boom Community* (New York: Longmans, Green, 1951). Describes the impact of social change upon organized religion.

[6] Cf. Joachim Wach, *Sociology of Religion,* Chaps. I and IX. Stresses "inside" studies.

[7] Specialists referred to here include Lewis W. Bloede, B. P. Murphy, Dwight H. Shelhart, and others. See Frederick A. Shippey, *Church Work in the City* (New York: Abingdon Press, 1952), Chap. VII.

parish cultivation to extend outward in all directions unimpeded by primary barriers (e.g., rivers, irregular terrain, industrial installations, railroad tracks, etc.). The contemplated site should be spaced at least one and a half to two miles distant from the nearest Methodist church in any direction. It is desirable to select several possible sites (arranged in order of priority) in each community lest first choice property not be available. Finally, approximately one hundred interested adults or seventy-five families are needed initially to launch a new Protestant congregation, plus, of course, adequate potential for future growth. These value judgments underlie the present study, informing its methodology and influencing the research design.

Both assumptions and criteria are relevant. As such, they are not under investigation here. Rather they serve as important bridges reaching across between social science and religion. The researcher notes that "inside" knowledge is essential here to an understanding of the functional reality of religious institutions. Let a single illustration suffice. Respecting the pattern of door-to-door interviews, a *center point* was established (based upon the criteria noted above) in each neighborhood under consideration for possible Methodist church extension. Usually this point of focus turned out to be either a shopping center or an elementary school. The religious census began here, proceeding in a spiral fashion, round and round, until the canvassers had contacted at least five hundred families or had reached a perimeter of one mile radius from the center, whichever came first. Subsequently the interview materials were tabulated, showing by small geographical units the religious composition of the neighborhood. After an examination of the evidence, a decision could then be made whether or not it was a territory of promise for Methodism. Thus the aforementioned "inside" knowledge had an effect upon the research design without interfering with the proper function of social science.

NATURE AND SCOPE OF THE RESEARCH

Certain major delimitations are readily seen. It has already been noted that geographically, this project embraces a portion of the northeastern coast of Florida; temporally, it covers the period since World War II; topically, it touches new residential subdivision development; focusing upon certain demographic data and some problems of church extension locally for The Methodist Church. At least fifty hamlets, villages and towns of the survey territory did not have a Methodist church within their boundaries although the denomination is matched only by the Baptists for its ubiquity in Florida. Why? To what extent had social change caused Methodism to lag behind in the normal expansion of its work?

The empirical study comprised five elements: (1) an examination of the land-use patterns, local zoning codes, and kindred morphological data; (2) an evaluation of the socioeconomic levels of the new communities; (3) the rate of population growth as evidenced in trend patterns and in the pace of new residential construction; (4) an inventory of existing churches, noting especially the location and adequacy of these congregations; and (5) the religious composition (by faith, by denomination) of selected neighborhoods. Since these elements actually are inextricably bound together in the empirical reality, the underlying wholeness was scrutinized closely in order to discern answers to crucial questions on church extension. Here sociology contributed a scientific perspective, reliable research methods and a technical understanding of group phenomena in the changing situation.

Extensive use was made of pertinent *secondary* data [8] already on file in the offices of city planners, engineers, public school officials, building inspectors, and others. Academic theses and professional studies were perused also. Indeed, all available sources of reliable information were explored in order to achieve an understanding of the nature and extent of the territory's metamorphosis during the trend period since the end of World War II.

In addition, certain *primary* data were gathered: materials disclosing the scope and adequacy of Methodist churches currently situated within the survey territory; information on real estate properties (parcels of land) strategically located for possible new church sites; and detailed knowledge of the religious composition of neighborhoods selected for intensive study. The procurement of such primary data required special empirical investigations. Visits to the field, plus extensive door-to-door interviews were utilized. Where relevant, information was gathered in the categories utilized by the United States Bureau of Census. Thus sociology examined a problem confronting organized religion without jeopardizing its own methodological and substantive integrity.

TABULATION AND ANALYSIS OF MATERIALS

Relevant demographic materials were brought together for forty-five places and for every important new subdivision in the survey territory. Population composition, trends, housing value, land-use, and kindred materials were evaluated, town by town, city by city, subdivision by subdivision. From each local Methodist church materials were assembled to show the places of residence of church members and church school enrollees (parish maps), to disclose the occupations of all gainfully employed members, to report membership and church school trends since 1945 by individual congregation, to provide the geographical location of each Methodist church edifice, and kindred data. Moreover, door-to-door religious census information was gathered from more than 1,500 new households. Materials were procured in categories showing adults and children by faith and by denomination. Faith

---

[8] For an account of materials sought and the methodology utilized, consult P. V. Young, *Scientific Social Surveys and Research,* Chaps. VII, IX, and XVI; Frederick A. Shippey, *Church Work in the City,* Chaps. II, III, and VII.

breakdown in terms of percentages for selected subdivisions is shown in the
accompanying Table 1. As a southern state, Florida reflects the region's

TABLE 1. Door-to-Door Religious Census Results

New Subdivision	Protestant	Roman Catholic	Jew	Total
Belvedere suburb	73.1%	24.8%	2.1%	100.0%
North Andrews	59.5	39.9	0.6	100.0
Indialantic	83.1	15.3	1.6	100.0
Riverland Road	74.0	24.4	1.6	100.0
Melbourne suburb	82.1	17.9	—	100.0

predominant faith—Protestantism. Among Protestants, Methodists, plus persons interested in a new congregation, ranged as high as one resident out of three in the subdivisions. Only Baptists consistently rivaled the Methodists in numerical strength. Out of a mountain of interesting data were sifted pertinent insights which related to the crucial problems under investigation.

Tabulation and analysis yielded *twenty-six communities* which *emerged as new church possibilities*. Other places carefully studied were dropped from consideration. These included neighborhoods which already possessed sufficient churches. The religious potential for The Methodist Church was assessed through numerous door-to-door interviews. The rate of population growth was studied and the additional number of persons who might take up residence in each community within the foreseeable future was conservatively estimated. When all of the relevant data were combined respecting future development, a tentative judgment was formed respecting the "readiness" (how soon a new church should be started) of the closely studied territories in terms of a time table. Each territory revealing possibilities for a new congregation was assigned an appropriate year over a designated time schedule, 1957–1963.

Accordingly, the twenty-six promising territories were identified and arranged as follows:

1. 1956–7:   North Broward and Belvedere.
2. 1957–8:   North Andrews, Indialantic, and West Vero.
3. 1958–9:   Lake Osborne, Riverland Road, and Rolling Green Ridge.
4. 1959–60: Coral Ridge, North Palm Beach Village, and Jensen.
5. 1960–1:   Forrest Hill Boulevard, Hobe, and South Fort Pierce.
6. 1961–2:   Indian Town, Oslo, and South Boynton.
7. After 1962: Southside, Deerfield, Highland, Juno, Salerno, North Fort Pierce, Loxahatchee, Mintons Corner, and Indian River Shores.

This recommendation properly was accompanied by a caveat, pointing out that such forecasts for action normally are predicated upon the continuance of existing conditions. Of course, it is unlikely that such conditions would persist indefinitely. Thus each territory should be kept under surveillance, watching for important modifications of trends. Priorities can change significantly within several years.

This brief account of a sociological study embracing some aspects of the territory on the eastern Florida coastline can provide the reader a glimpse of the impact of social change, the intelligent concern of a religious leader, the nature of the sociological analysis rendered, and the concrete suggestions for action submitted to The Methodist Church. Of further interest to the reader is a report on the implementation which followed the present research study. Here is where considerable light is thrown upon response to drastic social change in terms of institutional adjustment and the deployment of religion's resources. Though not explored here, it also carries implications for subsidiary groups, relationships, processes, and voluntarism.

RESEARCH AFTERMATH

The sociological study of eastern Florida was completed and its findings presented to the harassed church administrator. Soon the social scientist would learn whether the report would be received politely, perused cursorily, and then laid aside to gather dust. Such often is the fate of research reports. However, this case proved to be an exception. Dominant and ubiquitous social change led to quick action. With the master priority list of the twenty-six neighborhoods in hand, the Methodist leader commenced negotiations simultaneously for land for several new church sites. Moreover, a capital funds campaign was launched at once and the needed additional clergymen for the proposed new congregations were procured. Because the research was born in suburban crisis and the findings derived from sound sociological analysis the project had a ring of reality in it. Apparently church leaders took seriously the practical implications of the study. They began with a problem and ended with a course of action.

Just exactly what results were obtained? During the first four years following the completion of the sociological research study, *twenty new Methodist congregations were organized* within the survey territory. (Additional new churches have been established at the rate of two per year since then.) All were established, making maximum use of the findings of the research study. The accompanying Table 2 identifies the new congregations and provides some interesting current statistics. On the accompanying Figure 1 may be noted the geographical locations as well as proximity to older Methodist churches. In terms of data shown in Table 2, the new congregations averaged more than 200 members in size in 1963 and aggregated 4,126 affiliated persons. The church school averaged 161 enrollees and yielded a total of 3,216 children and adults. To date these new churches have contributed more than $30,000 to missionary and humanitarian causes beyond the boundaries of the local community. When one realizes that it costs approximately $100,000

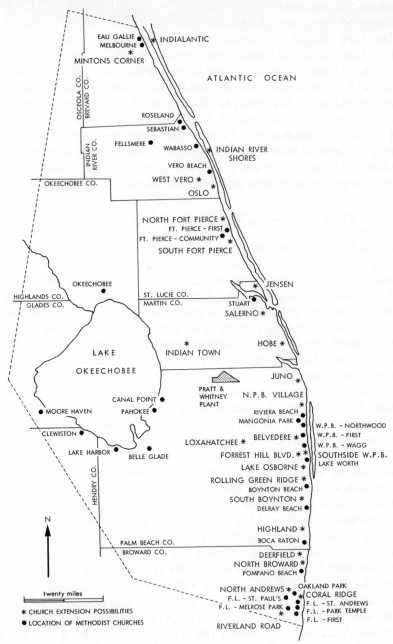

FIGURE 1. Eastern Florida survey territory, showing present Methodist churches and extension possibilities.

to start a new congregation, the implementation of research here is truly re-markable. Methodism in Florida spent $2 million on the basis of the results of this research.

TABLE 2. Twenty New Congregations in Four Years

PLACE AND NAME OF NEW CHURCH	NUMBER OF CHURCH MEMBERS	CHURCH SCHOOL ENROLLMENT
Boynton Beach–St. Johns	96	107
Fort Lauderdale–Aldersgate	139	88
Fort Lauderdale–Christ	599	294
Fort Lauderdale–Plantation	421	395
Fort Lauderdale–Wesley Chapel	100	92
Indialantic–St. Marks	309	165
Indiantown	68	78
Jensen Beach	71	22
Juno Beach	217	137
Lake Worth–Lakeside	436	331
Lake Worth–St. Lukes	104	113
Margate–Cokesbury	152	129
Okeechobee–Fort Drum	33	50
Palm Bay	165	104
Pompano Beach–Trinity	485	199
Port St. Lucie	179	112
Vero Beach–Asbury	228	267
Vero Beach–Lakewood Park	34	18
West Palm Beach–Grace	225	454
White City	65	61
Totals	4,126	3,216

44

The Great Factory Sweepstakes

Stanley Frank

In this article, the author describes the analysis of the problems and prospects of locating a business in a new community. Careful investigation and planning can obviate many future difficulties, whereas haphazard guessing can be ruinous in a highly competitive situation. Communities, too, should become sharply aware of the conditions that favor industrial development if they wish to be in on the "gravy." Indeed, many communities have already established organizations or committees. Note that the successful bid is seldom the result of one individual's work, but rather of the collective spirit of the community. It may be predicted that success will increasingly come less to those who work hard than to those educated in social engineering.

Though the founder of the location consultant firm described in this article is not a professionally trained sociologist, he does, as the author observes, operate like one. The questions he raises and the investigative techniques he employs illustrate applications of the sociological methods to this phase of business and community planning.

Celebrities visit Hillsboro, Ohio, so infrequently the 5,400 residents had not given a V.I.P. the red-carpet treatment since the 1956 Presidential campaign, but they reacted like veteran civic boosters when Leonard Yaseen arrived in town last February. Everyone knew that Yaseen, a specialist in selecting new factory sites, had come to investigate local facilities for a metal-plating plant employing 400 people, a project that would almost double the community's industrial jobs. Long experience with quaint native customs braced Yaseen for a relentless barrage of hospitality Hillsboro was certain to shower on him to make a more favorable impression than did the seven other towns competing for the plum.

The schedule followed a ritual as fixed as the protocol for presenting diplomatic credentials at the Court of St. James's. First there was a guided tour of the town and the lovely countryside blanketed under three inches of snow, then a round of social functions sponsored by leading citizens. Finally the Committee for Industrial Development made its big pitch fortified with charts and statistics plugging the unique advantages that Hillsboro offered new busi-

Originally in *The Saturday Evening Post*, **223,** 17 (October 22, 1960), pp. 34, 142, 144, 147, 148. Reprinted by special permission of *The Saturday Evening Post.* © 1962 The Curtis Publishing Company and the author.

Stanley Frank is a free-lance writer.

ness. After listening to a Niagara of fervent adjectives for an hour, Yaseen casually asked a committee member, "How many days were you permitted to water your lawns last summer?"

The man bolted with surprise, "As often as we pleased," he answered. "There were no restrictions." He looked at Yaseen quizzically. "That's an odd question to ask in the dead of winter."

"My client must have an unlimited supply of water, and I want to make sure your resources are adequate even at the lowest ebb," Yaseen said. "You've just told me more about the water situation here than all the fancy statistics whipped up by your group." On June twenty-third, the Moore Drop Forging Company awarded its new plant to Hillsboro.

During the last quarter century disarming questions asked by Yaseen, an urbane, forty-eight-year-old Chicagoan, and his staff have been instrumental in determining where more than 1,000,000 industrial workers earn livings and rear families. Astronomical figures are bandied so indiscriminately nowadays that the reference to an army of 1,000,000 workers makes merely a glancing impact on the eye. Expressed in more concrete terms, it is equivalent to the combined factory personnel of Pittsburgh, St. Louis, Baltimore, and Houston—but Yaseen's Fantus Factory Locating Service never had recommended an installation in those four great industrial complexes.

In fact, Yaseen consistently has advised his 1,800 clients to bypass every metropolitan area but Los Angeles, an exception because the Rocky Mountains isolate the Pacific Coast from cheaper centers of distribution. Through the years, 90 per cent of the sites chosen by the Fantus organization have been in towns with populations of less than 20,000.

In a country as vast and dynamic as the United States, one man cannot trigger the massive population shift disclosed recently by the 1960 census. The overwhelming majority of the nation's large cities lagged behind our overall population increase of 18.6 per cent during the 1950's, a reversal of a century-old pattern directly related to the decentralization of industry. The trend would not have been affected in the slightest degree had Yaseen elected to pursue a career as a jazz pianist, but no one made a more accurate prognosis of the forces revamping the face of America.

Although the proper label for Yaseen's field is economic geography, he operates more like a sociologist. "The psychological climate of a community is the key factor in locating a plant because it exerts a strong influence on an employee's productivity," he explained at our first session. "Performance on the job reflects the satisfaction he derives from his work, and it's not always predicated on his pay. He may be better off in the long run earning less where the tempo of spending is slower than it is in a section with a higher wage scale. Here, look at this."

He produced a bulletin issued in June 1960 by the United States Department of Labor giving the average weekly industrial salary by states. In North Carolina it was $61.29, in Indiana $100.23.

"Regional differences in status symbols and the size of the skilled labor force account for that tremendous wage spread," Yaseen went on. "A worker in Indiana is conditioned to a more sophisticated standard of living than a native North Carolinian holding a similar job. He demands more money to maintain a more expensive home and car. His family spends more on clothes, entertainment, vacations, and personal services. The social rat race is a lot less intense in North Carolina. The relaxation of pressures promotes labor stability, the most important consideration to a manufacturer today because it's so hard to find.

"There are many technical elements in deciding on a factory site—transportation and power rates, state and local taxes, labor laws, availability of raw materials. Conditions vary so greatly with each industry that it's impossible to generalize about them. The one common factor in all situations is the labor force. Interpreting its attitudes is the toughest, but the most interesting, phase of an assignment."

Yaseen was asked to give a few typical gambits showing how he makes such evaluations.

"You can get a good idea of a town's tempo of spending by asking the owner of the leading department store the price range in which the majority of ladies' slips are sold. When workers' wives habitually buy top-quality merchandise, it's a danger signal to a prospective employer that wages are on a rising spiral. It's not unusual to find towns only thirty miles apart with conflicting shopping patterns. In one, cheaper goods are the best sellers. In the other, those items die on the shelf.

"A reliable tip-off on the character of a community is the number of traffic tickets handed out to transient drivers. Some small towns are notorious speed traps and impose stiff fines on tourists to cut down local taxes for schools and public services. A town that chisels on its responsibilities is infested with poor morale that invariably spreads to a plant.

"I also make it a policy to stay out of a place with a history of violence. We keep a record of disturbances in labor and race relations throughout the country. A quick way to find out whether an ugly situation has been corrected is to ask the mayor, 'What happened to so-and-so, that cop who beat up a picket here seven years ago?' A town that condones police brutality by keeping strong-arm goons on the force has little respect for life and property. I want no part of it."

Unforeseen headaches constantly plague location consultants—and their clients. Two years ago the Kenyon Instrument Company built a new branch at Brewster, New York, expecting to draw on a large pool of skilled labor in Danbury and Stamford, in nearby Connecticut. Workers rejected good jobs, however, refusing to pay the New York state income tax on their earnings. (Connecticut does not have a similar tax.) Kenyon raised wages twenty-five cents an hour above the going rates in Connecticut, an increase that more than compensated for the New York state assessment. The jobs are still going begging. The company has filled only 130 of the 200 positions needed for full production and has to farm out some operations to subcontractors, an expensive proposition that cuts heavily into profits.

"It's fortunate we didn't have the Kenyon account because I might not have anticipated such violent opposition to the tax," Yaseen admits. "New Englanders evidently can be awfully stubborn when they get riled up over a principle. When we case an area near a state line now, we do a double check to make sure we don't get caught in the same jam."

All sorts of new complications in plant location are posed by the increasing preference for female employees in many manufacturing processes. Women have more manual dexterity than men in making and assembling small parts, and they bear up better under monotonous jobs involving simple, repetitive skills. Then the women's wage scale generally is lower than the men's, despite state laws designed to end such discrimination.

Special requirements necessary to hold women workers rule out sites that ordinarily are thoroughly acceptable. The girls will not stick to a job unless it is near a shopping center where they can browse to their hearts' content during lunch periods. Since national prosperity has not yet put two cars in every working family's garage, a factory with a large complement of women must be on a public-transportation system. The trickiest qualification is the surrounding neighborhood.

"Women are understandably afraid to walk through slums, but their emotional reaction is just as strong if they see evidence of luxurious living on their way to work," Yaseen comments. "Every woman who takes a factory job has to supplement her family's income. She accepts the situation as long as she isn't reminded daily that there are women in a more enviable position. Passing their comfortable homes arouses her subconscious resentment of wives who can sleep late and live it up socially, and she transfers her hostility to her job. Morale always is better when the approach to a plant is through a respectable, low-income neighborhood."

An expatriate out of touch with the American scene since World War II could catch up on the social and economic trends that have effected enormously significant changes in the country by reviewing the developments in Yaseen's field. He graphically illustrated the highlights on a map in his New York office by placing the heel of his hand on the New England states, with his outstretched fingers pointing south and west.

"Forty years ago half the population and more than three quarters of our industry were concentrated in the sixteen states covered by the palm of my hand," Yaseen said. "The northeastern sector bounded by Illinois and Wisconsin and extending due east to the Atlantic Ocean was the traditional manufacturing belt. In those days executives thought you were crazy if you suggested building a factory elsewhere. They argued that virtually all the skilled labor and the bulk of the purchasing power was in the traditional belt, a view that prevailed until the end of the Second World War.

"You know what happened then. Housing shortages in metropolitan centers, the exploding birth rate and returning servicemen looking for new opportunities touched off a mass movement of people. They could expand only in the direction of my fingers toward the peripheries of the country—to Florida, Texas, and the West Coast. Industry had to follow consumers when drastic increases in distribution costs made it uneconomic to ship products from the Northeast.

"As a result, the West and South employ as many industrial workers as the traditional belt. New markets have been created in rural areas that were exclusively agricultural only ten years ago. That, in a nutshell, is the story of decentralization in industry."

How can recently industrialized sections meet the demand for competent labor, the critical factor mentioned earlier by Yaseen?

"I need another nutshell," he conceded. "Automation and more efficient machinery have simplified the problem. A good deal of the equipment in modern plants can be operated by semiskilled workers with a few months of training. The blunt truth is that technological advances have superseded the old-time craftsmen who had to go through long apprenticeships to learn a wide range of skills.

"We'll be in a bad fix in a decade if vocational schools don't turn out more mechanics who really know their trades. In the last two generations the labor force has increased 75 per cent, but the ratio of skilled industrial workers has remained steady at about 14 per cent. The trouble is that unskilled labor receives disproportionately high wages. There's no incentive today for a kid to spend four or five years learning to qualify as a tool and die maker at two dollars and seventy-five cents an hour when he gets two dollars and forty cents on a job he can knock off with one hand tied behind his back.

"There's a bright side to the picture, though. We've discovered that people with limited mechanical experience have a much greater aptitude for acquiring skills than anyone ever suspected. Intricate techniques that once were confined to one small section, even one town, are popping up all over the place. Musical instruments and telephone switchboards are made in Mississippi, electric transformers in Georgia, precision meters in North Carolina, electronic devices in Florida and chemicals in Texas."

The $13,000,000,000 American industry spends annually on new plants and equipment has stimulated frantic competition for the payrolls that pump vitality into communities. No hamlet is too small to enter the great factory sweepstakes. The 2,901 residents of Audubon, Iowa, in the heart of the corn belt, raised $50,000 in May to attract industry. Every state and practically every sizable town is pouring money into advertising and promotion campaigns beamed at manufacturers. Many offer astonishing inducements to push their bids.

Virginia has a special fund to build access roads from highways to new plants. Madison County, Alabama, donates the use of its road-building equipment to grade and improve sites. North Carolina sacrificed $7,000,000 in annual revenue by slashing corporate income taxes in 1957, but has more than made up the deficit in receipts from new business. Innumerable towns underwrite the construction of factories and give tenants long-term leases at rock-bottom rentals. A widely adopted measure that always interests a company is a municipally financed vocational program designed to its specific requirements for trained employees.

Classes are held during the day for high school students and at night for adults already working at other jobs. Meridian, Mississippi, supports an outstanding curriculum that includes two free years of junior college for technicians and white-collar workers. Laurinburg High School, in North Carolina, prepares residents for jobs with the Ingraham clock company; Radford, Virginia, specializes in craftsmen; Jackson, Mississippi, features courses in metalworking; a steady stream of pretrained employees has enabled the South to supplant New England as the center of the textile industry.

The deep South, surprisingly enough, is the most enterprising section in bidding for industry. "Business leaders know they entered late in the race, but they're moving up fast and giving management fine cooperation," Yaseen says. "The Middle West is spotty, progressive in some places, backward in others. The Far West is showing initiative in maintaining the momentum of its rapid growth. The worst section is the East. New England has been jolted out of its complacency, but the big cities in other Northeastern states are doing little to check the dry rot that has been driving firms out of their industrial slums for the last twenty-five years."

Has the integration controversy deterred companies from moving to the South?

"It did for a while after the schools were closed in Little Rock three years ago, but no client has expressed any uneasiness over the situation in the last six months. Actually there have been few incidents between Negroes and whites working side by side. Now, I don't want to oversell industry's influence, but I think it's helping to solve the racial problem. We know that prejudice feeds on poverty and frustration. Segregationists are gradually moderating their attitudes as they see improved standards of living industry is bringing to the South."

The Fantus Company is a prime target, of course, for the blizzard of brochures turned out by local and regional publicity mills. The ads are cluttered with so many clichés and exaggerated claims that they generally land in the wastebasket. Some years ago Rockland County, New York, told employers its population of 70,000 assured an ample supply of labor. An analysis of the figures revealed that 11,000 residents were inmates of prisons and mental institutions. Fantus has such extensive, authoritative records it can paraphrase the old show-business gag and tell the propaganda boys, "Don't call us—we've got your number."

The Fantus offices in New York and Chicago are lined with filing cabinets containing surveys of every town in the United States with a population exceeding 2,500. In each town's folder is a digest of its public-service facilities, educational system, labor background, tax and debt structure, and the composition of its population. A cross-index is kept on new markets and technical developments in 550 basic industries and the wage differentials and sources of materials in geographical areas. Another catalogue gives pertinent data on the major companies in every industry.

With that mass of information at his fingertips, Yaseen has picked from the files towns he never has seen as likely locations for plants. In 1953 the General Time Corporation retained Fantus to find a site for a clock factory. After studying the potentials of a dozen communities, Yaseen decided Athens, Georgia, was the best bet. The seat of Clarke County and the University of Georgia, Athens could draw workers from an untapped population of 200,-000 in eight counties within a twenty-mile radius. The adjacent counties had been losing inhabitants since 1920, for an obvious reason. The largest factory in the area employed 461 workers. Young people had to pull up stakes and look for jobs elsewhere.

Yaseen made an unsolicited visit to Athens, and his first impression was disappointing. Homes were unpainted, the downtown center was deteriorating, and civic pride was almost nonexistent. His dim view changed abruptly as soon as local officials and businessmen learned the purpose of his trip. Dr. Omar C. Aderhold, president of the university, volunteered to set up a vocational program. The Chamber of Commerce assured Yaseen full cooperation in clearing up any problems General Time might encounter.

The upshot was that Yaseen recommended Athens for the factory, and the town delivered so well on its promises that he subsequently advised Westinghouse Electric and Anaconda Wire and Cable to open plants there. The 2,000 jobs created by the three companies underscore industry's revitalizing impact on a community. In six years Athens' population has jumped from 28,000 to 42,000, retail sales have increased 75 per cent, two medical centers have been built, school-bond issues of $1,250,000 have been approved, and the university has launched a $15,000,000 expansion program. Tupelo, Mississippi, was so grateful for its economic pickup that a street was renamed Fulton Drive in honor of Maurice Fulton, Yaseen's partner in Chicago.

A Fantus report generally takes four months of research and costs $20,-000. The elaborate procedure begins with a company's executives answering questionnaires that reveal the special aspects of the business. The Fantus staff then decides whether a plant should be oriented toward labor, a market, or raw materials. For example, the primary consideration for a machinery manufacturer is a pool of skilled labor, for a bottling plant it is proximity to a local market, and for a paper mill it is sources of raw materials. Having narrowed the search to an area, the staff looks through the files for towns that match the client's requisites.

This screening is not as formidable as it appears, since 70 per cent of the towns listed are unsuitable for new industry by Yaseen's standards. He rules out communities near resorts (workers tend to quit for high-paying seasonal jobs) and ports (they attract migrants who disrupt the stability of a labor force). The suburbs of large cities also are avoided by Yaseen because their booming populations are comprised mainly of white-collar workers who refuse to take industrial jobs. In one out of every thirteen surveys a company is advised to remain where it is because the marginal advantages of another town do not justify the cost of moving.

When the field has been reduced to a half dozen or so possibilities, a crew of four men examines each remaining town's facilities—and, more importantly, its psychological climate. The appraisal is based on conversations with merchants, the appearance of homes and streets, the caliber of protective services, recreational programs for adolescents. The school budget gets close attention. If a town has been skimping on its per-capita expenditure for education, a new employer eventually will be soaked for a tax boost when classroom congestion becomes intolerable.

"I ask officials how they plan to cope with the heavy strain a new factory puts on housing, schools, hospitals, and parking," says Clinton Hoch, a Fantus vice president. "If they can't give good answers, they're not ready for the factory."

The next step often is the payoff. Established manufacturers are interviewed to get a cross section of their experiences and opinions of the town's attitude toward industry. "We assure them everything told us will be held in the strictest confidence, and they're surprisingly honest with us," Yaseen remarks. "Occasionally a guy paying substandard wages tries to scare off competition with distorted stories, but most people realize it's to their advantage to tell us the truth.

"The interviews give valuable hints of the treatment our client is likely to receive. A town recently was crossed off our list after a candy manufacturer told us it reneged on a promise to pave a street outside his plant, then ignored complaints that dust was ruining his product. The man finally had to pave the street at his own expense. A company is bound to have trouble if a town does nothing about a legitimate gripe like that."

The final report runs 350 pages and is a group effort written by a battery of industrial engineers who hold postgraduate degrees in economics. Now and then a client opposes a recommendation, but the flat rejections of sites chosen by the Fantus staff can be counted on the fingers of one hand since Yaseen's first assignment.

That was in 1935, the depths of the depression, when manufacturers scrambling desperately to keep solvent had no time for a young nut peddling a ridiculous scheme for scientific selection of factory locations. Yaseen had been graduated from the University of Illinois with a degree in business administration, but he was more fascinated with earning a living as a jazz pianist. Life became real and earnest, however, when he married the daughter of Felix Fantus, an industrial-real-estate broker in Chicago, and he went with the outfit as a salesman. Fantus dabbled in the rudiments of plant location by directing manufacturers to suitable vacant buildings, and Yaseen suggested that his father-in-law charge a fee for his advice. Fantus doubted anyone would pay for the service, but Yaseen was so convinced the idea was sound that he struck out on his own in New York.

After canvassing the field for a year Yaseen finally was retained by the American Machine and Foundry Company to survey future sites. He survived another lean year by making a $5,000 commission on the sale of a building in Waycross, Georgia, to a shoe company forced out of New York by rising costs. To occupy his time he tackled his first research project, a complete record of labor strikes and agitation in every town since 1917.

"That data led to the formulation of a basic policy," he says. "It taught me that what has happened in the past is likely to recur. Labor attitudes follow a pattern peculiar to a locality. A town with a history of unrest figures to give management a hard time."

Yaseen's surveys paid handsome dividends during World War II, when adequate sources of manpower, water, and transportation were vital for all-out production. Felix Fantus tacitly admitted his earlier error by getting out of real estate and merging with his son-in-law. "The Fantus name was kept for prestige," Yaseen says, "but we gave up handling real estate, to maintain our complete objectivity. We believe a better job can be done for a client when you have no financial interest in a site."

The postwar boom gave added impetus to the techniques of economic geography. Many large corporations have their own departments scouting new locations, but the Fantus Company gets the lion's share of the work given to some sixty private consultants. Last spring the firm expanded its operations to Europe, with headquarters in Brussels.

There is an amusing conflict between Yaseen's personal preferences and his professional activity. A man of cosmopolitan tastes, he amiably admits he would go out of his mind if he lived and worked in the rural atmosphere he advocates for clients. He commutes daily between Larchmont, a suburb in Westchester County sometimes described as a split-level extension of Park Avenue with crabgrass, to his office in the Empire State Building. Yaseen's restless drive does not permit him to settle down in one recreation, much less one place, for long. He takes impulsive whacks at tennis, golf, boating, and jazz piano lessons with Teddy Wilson, who plays with Benny Goodman. Three years ago, when the merry-go-round palled on him, he took a trip around the world with his wife and grown children, Barbara and Roger. Their itinerary featured excursions to ancient cultural centers in the Far East well off the beaten tourist track.

"You're a confirmed big-city boy temperamentally," I observed. "Why are you so hipped on small towns for industry?"

"That's where management gets the best break," he retorted. "I want to make it clear I mean only in manufacturing. There's no question the excitement of a big city stimulates people in creative work. I've advised many publishers and service businesses against leaving New York and Chicago, but I wouldn't dream of putting a factory there or in any other metropolis.

"Look, a company doesn't go on my say-so and invest a couple of million dollars in a building a hundred miles from nowhere without proof that I'm right. Here it is."

He took a mimeographed sheet out of his desk comparing in twenty-two industries the sale value of products per payroll dollar expended in cities with populations of more than 500,000 and towns with less than 10,000 inhabitants. The figure showed that productivity is, on the average, 45 per cent higher in small towns. Just to cite a few examples, a worker in a rural pharmaceutical plant turns out products worth $4.89 for each dollar he receives in wages. In an urban plant a manufacturer gets a return of only $2.97 on the dollar. The comparative figures for plastics are $4.70 in small towns and $2.55 in large cities.

Location alone is not an automatic guarantee this huge differential will be obtained, however. Experience has taught Yaseen that some agonizing decisions must be made by employers when moving from big to small communities. The most difficult policy involves workers who have been with the company for a long time.

"I advise clients to leave them behind," Yaseen says. "I hate to draw this analogy, but it's a harsh fact that old personnel becomes obsolete like old machinery. Morale also suffers when outsiders with union seniority block the promotion of local people. Then, big-city attitudes often clash with rural customs. Right now, old, displaced workers can get jobs in urban areas, but it's not pleasant to think what will happen if there's a recession. I wish there were another solution to the problem."

Executives, surprisingly, are more amenable to shifts than factory workers. "Their salaries go so much farther in a small town that the added security is a compensation for being out of the thick of things," Yaseen explains. "Whenever there's dissatisfaction with a transfer, it usually can be traced to wives. Women don't adjust to the new environment as quickly as men. They miss the social and cultural refinements of urban living. They worry that their children won't get into Ivy League colleges from rural schools or make desirable marriages. In a family-owned business a wife's opposition can keep a factory in an unprofitable location."

Yaseen recently showed four brothers they could clear $1,000,000 more annually on a gross of $9,000,000 by moving from New York to the South. The brothers enthusiastically favored the shift. Their wives firmly vetoed the idea. The factory remained in New York.

Foibles of human nature are not the only booby traps in plant location. Failure to make exhaustive checks on physical conditions can lead to serious mistakes. In 1952 the United States Steel Corporation built the Fairless Works on the Delaware River at Morrisville, Pennsylvania, to receive iron ore shipped from Venezuela, thereby effecting tremendous savings on rail transportation costs. The forty-mile stretch of river above Philadelphia was not deep enough for heavily laden vessels, but the Government tentatively agreed to spend $55,000,000 for the necessary dredging.

Engineers found that saline seepage from the dredging would ruin the water supply of towns on the river. The project was abandoned—but the plant already was in construction. As a result, some ore has to be unloaded at Philadelphia so that the ships can negotiate the channel to Morrisville, an operation that cancels out at least some of the anticipated savings.

Small firms have been put out of business by careless oversights. A company unwittingly built a factory a few blocks outside the free pickup and delivery freight zone of a city, a blunder that added $40,000 to the annual overhead. Fantus saved a chemical outfit from bankruptcy by checking on the temperature of the water at a site in southern Texas selected by the production department. It was eighty-five degrees, which would have required the installation of an exorbitantly costly cooling system. The plant was shifted to Kansas, where the water was sixty-three degrees. A few months ago an electric-appliance plant with 2300 employees was closed in Central Pennsylvania because shipping costs to major markets had been miscalculated. Although the town was suitable for a Fantus client, Yaseen passed it up.

"The scars left in a town after a plant closes don't heal for a long time," he declares. "There is a backwash of bitterness that makes people hostile to a new company. The sharp decline in retail sales ruins the credit ratings of merchants. I know this sounds like a plug for my business, but the social and economic repercussions are so damaging in a small community when a site has been chosen haphazardly that industry must adopt more responsible policy in its expansion.

"Anything that disturbs the stability of a community should be avoided. It's bad to transform a rural village into a boom town by pouring in a thousand workers overnight. A gradual increase in the labor force is better for the community and the company. I never go into a low-wage area with an industry that pays a high scale. You're a hero to a few hundred people, but you make thousands of enemies who don't share in the gravy."

Further decentralization of industry is sure to bring sweeping changes in our social structure, but the situation is so fluid Yaseen refuses to gaze into the crystal beyond 1965. "That," he went on, "was to be the beginning of a critical period, with high schools graduating four million youngsters every year. Half of them will go on to college, but the other two million will have to be integrated in the labor force without dislocating mature workers. Fortunately the majority of the kids will be distributed in the right places. Industry is moving out of cities with relatively static populations into outlying areas where labor is needed.

"I will make one prediction. Provincialism will disappear, and there will be broadening of culture as industry branches out, providing more money for rural schools and raising the standard of living. There won't be any yokels in another decade."

Even the grumpiest backwoods denizens are submitting to the invasion of industry. Last April Jack Klingle, Fantus fieldman, was prowling through the Blue Ridge Mountains near Leesville, Virginia, on a survey for the Norfolk and Western Railway. He climbed over a rock and found himself looking into the muzzle of a very large, disgruntled bear.

"That was one predicament they never prepared us for at the Harvard Business School," Klingle relates. "I knew the bear could run and climb a tree faster than I, so I just stood there paralyzed with fear. The bear stared at me, then shambled away, as though it was reconciled to the march of progress."

45

Neighborhood Reactions to Isolated Negro Residents: An Alternative to Invasion and Succession

Arnold M. Rose, Frank J. Atelsek, and Lawrence R. McDonald

Folk knowledge runs rampant on the question of interracial housing. In Chapter Nine, two articles (39 and 40) related to interracial housing. This selection provides theoretical insights that are of value for future action programs.

The maintenance of residential segregation under a caste or semicaste social system has resulted in a now familiar pattern of change when the minority group expands its numbers due either to immigration or to natural increase.[1] The process begins when the area of minority dwelling increases its population density much beyond that of adjacent areas of majority dwellings.

Reprinted from the *American Sociological Review*, **18**, 5 (October 1953), pp. 497–507, by permission of the publisher and the authors.

Arnold M. Rose is Professor of Sociology, University of Minnesota.

Frank J. Atelsek is Program Officer, Economic Planning, Area Redevelopment Administration, United States Department of Commerce.

Lawrence R. McDonald was at the University of Minnesota when this article was originally published. He is now scientific director for a market research firm in Minneapolis.

[1] The process has been documented by several researchers. See, for example: Herman H. Long and Charles S. Johnson, *People vs. Property* (Nashville: Fisk University Press, 1947); Robert C. Weaver, *The Negro Ghetto* (New York: Harcourt, 1948).

Since relatively little new building goes on in the old areas where minority groups live, the process of increase in population density occurs by means of doubling up of families in existing dwellings and conversion of older large units into several smaller ones. The one-room kitchenette apartment is the characteristic end point of this conversion process in the "Black Belt" of large Northern cities where large-scale immigration of Negroes from the South has been going on for several decades. Because of other aspects of the caste system, most members of the minority group have relatively low incomes and are not able to pay for new buildings or for complete and adequate conversion of old ones. The splitting up of large old apartments or large old houses in segregated minority areas provides small units at moderate prices for the largest possible number of people.

In this situation several economic factors combine to start the process of movement into adjacent areas then inhabited solely by whites. (1) Population density reaches a natural limit within the minority area; there are no more houses or apartments available for conversion, and people with money to spend on rent have no place to live. (2) While the rent for the one-room kitchenette is relatively low per family, it provides an unusually high income for the owner of the apartment or building because of the small amount of space a unit requires. For example, a large apartment which originally rented for 50 dollars a month, when split into five apartments each renting for 20 dollars a month, nets a total rental twice as high after conversion as it did before. It therefore becomes highly profitable for potential landlords to seek other large units still available for conversion; these are to be found only in areas occupied by members of the majority group. (3) Because the minority group areas are old and heavily overpopulated, they have a slum character. Some members of the minority group, not many but enough to have an economic influence, have sufficient incomes to afford much better housing in better areas if they were in free market competition.

The movement of minority persons into adjacent majority group areas usually begins when some member of the majority group, planning to move anyway, finds it highly profitable to sell to a member of a minority group, or a third person, a real estate agent usually, purchases in his own name a piece of property in the majority group area and turns it over at a very large profit to a member of the minority group. If all the members of the majority group are highly cohesive they are sometimes able to eject the sole minority group family, but generally there are some persons who either believe that a trend toward minority group movement invasion is inevitable and are willing to sell out to other members of minority groups in order to leave the area, or become panicky and think their property will become nearly worthless unless they sell quickly, or are willing to take advantage of the still-high prices for sales to minority persons. After two or three houses are sold to members of the minority group the property begins to change hands rapidly as the resistance of the majority group crumbles. For a brief period, ranging from a few weeks up to a year or so, the property of the area may be sold very cheaply. Quite often members of the minority group seeking housing do not have sufficient cash available to buy these cheap properties but they are sold to real estate agents or other people who intend to make money out of real estate through conversion or resale. After the scare selling period the prices of property in the area of transition go up sharply until they reach the high level prevalent in the old minority group area and are considerably higher than those in equivalent areas occupied by the majority group.[2] And so the solidly ethnic Black Belt, or the ghetto, or the Mexican district, expands.

In the last few years, however, new factors have entered the situation which are changing this pattern of "invasion and succession."[3] One factor is the change in attitude toward living near members of a minority group. Partly as a result of an organized effort to reduce prejudice and discrimination, and partly as a result of the housing shortage, more people are "willing" to live next door to members of minorities than was formerly the case. The second new factor is a Supreme Court decision of 1948 which removed the legally enforceable basis of the restrictive covenant, which has hitherto been the most powerful legal device used to prevent members of the minority groups from buying or renting in majority group areas. Since 1948, in most Northern

---

[2] Studies on the racial factors in property value movements include: Elsie Parker, "Both Sides of the Color Line," *The Appraisal Journal* (January 1943), pp. 27–34; (July 1943), pp. 231–49. George W. Beehler, Jr., "Colored Occupancy Raises Values," *The Review of the Society of Residential Appraisers* (September 1945), pp. 3–6, 12. Paul F. Cressey, *The Succession of Cultural Groups in the City of Chicago* (unpublished Ph.D. thesis, University of Chicago, 1930). Oscar I. Stern, "The Long Range Effects of Colored Occupancy," *The Review of the Society of Residential Appraisers* (January 1946), pp. 4–6. Homer Hoyt, *One Hundred Years of Land Values in Chicago* (Chicago: University of Chicago Press, 1933). Richard Marks, "The Impact of Negro Population Movement on Property Values in a Selected Area in Detroit," unpublished study made for the Mayor's Interracial Committee of the City of Detroit, 1950. Egbert F. Schietinger, *Real Estate Transfers During Negro Invasion: A Case Study* (unpublished M.A. thesis, University of Chicago, 1948), 118 pp. Belden Morgan, "Values in Transition Areas: Some New Concepts," *The Review of the Society of Residential Appraisers* (March 1952), pp. 5–10. Luigi M. Laurenti, "Effects of Nonwhite Purchasers on Market Prices of Residences," *The Appraisal Journal,* **20** (July 1952), pp. 314–329.

[3] These are terms borrowed by Robert E. Park from plant ecology to describe the analogous human process we are considering. Robert E. Park, "Human Ecology," *American Journal of Sociology,* **42,** (July 1936), pp. 1–15; "Succession, An Ecological Concept," *American Sociological Review,* **1** (April 1936), pp. 171–179. Also see: Bessie McClenahan, *The Changing Urban Neighborhood* (Los Angeles: University of Southern California, 1929), pp. 5, 26–29, 83–89. While Park used the term "invasion" in an ecological context of competitive relationships, the term is an unfortunate one since its popular meaning has a strong connotation of conflict. In its use by realtors, newspaper writers, and other nonsociologists—although they have learned the term from sociologists—"invasion" has a moral connotation of unrighteous seizure of property from unwilling sellers. The term has probably helped transform a competitive process into a conflict process.

cities and some Southern cities as well, Negroes have been moving into many white neighborhoods which under the old system would have taken them decades to penetrate, if ever they could have gotten in at all. There are now a large number of otherwise white neighborhoods into which one or two Negro families have moved. Mixed housing seems to be becoming the dominant pattern in at least the Northern cities.

What are the social consequences of this new pattern of Negro-white living in American cities? How do the whites react to Negro neighbors? One answer comes from studies of government-subsidized housing projects in which apartments are made available only on an unsegregated basis.[4] This type of study, however, was not designed to answer our questions. While suggestive, it has certain defects in indicating the social consequences of a general breakdown in residential segregation because (1) the people involved are drawn mainly from the lower income classes; (2) the situation is one in which all of them are placed simultaneously in the neighborhood rather than one in which whites see a few Negro families entering "their" neighborhood; (3) there is a much more obvious source of pressure for unsegregated living in the projects, since there is government subsidy and government direction, whereas in an ordinary community the unsegregated living seems much more voluntary—being limited only by such impersonal factors as the housing shortage and inertia against moving.

Another type of research which would aid in determining how whites react to Negro neighbors in the newly developing pattern of mixed housing is a study of communities where one or two Negro families have been living for some time among a much larger population of whites. Such communities are found in Minneapolis, where our study was conducted. Minneapolis has otherwise a pattern of race relations not perceptibly different from that prevailing in other Northern cities. The one significant way in which Minneapolis differs from other Northern cities is in its proportion of Negroes: Only 1.3 per cent of the population of Minneapolis is Negro, as compared to 13.6 per cent in Chicago, 16.2 per cent in Detroit, 9.5 per cent in New York, and 18.1 per cent in Philadelphia. Other Northern cities have smaller proportions of Negroes. Whether this small proportion in Minneapolis makes it noncomparable with other cities is not known, but it needs to be stressed that in every other aspect of race relations Minneapolis does not differ from other Northern cities. There is a small "Black Belt" in Minneapolis, but a few Negro families have managed to obtain residences in most other parts of the city. Some moved into the otherwise white neighborhoods many years ago,

---

[4] A carefully designed research of this type, involving comparison of housing projects that are completely unsegregated with projects that have Negroes living in segregated sections, is that of Morton Deutsch and Mary Evans Collins, *Interracial Housing* (Minneapolis: University of Minnesota Press, 1951). This study has been followed up and its results are confirmed in a study by D. M. Wilner, R. P. Walkley, and S. W. Cook, "Residential Proximity and Intergroup Relations in Public Housing Projects," *Journal of Social Issues*, **8** (1st issue, 1952), pp. 45–59.

while others moved in fairly recently, and we shall compare these two types of neighborhood. In nearly every case there was some opposition to the Negro family moving in, and in one or two cases there was actual violence. But in all the cases we shall consider, the Negro family stayed and so did most of the whites (those whites who moved out were replaced by other whites). Other Negro families did not follow the first one into the neighborhood, since the pressure on Minneapolis Negroes to secure living space was not nearly as great as elsewhere, and consequently there was no process of "invasion and succession." This now seems to be becoming the new pattern for other large cities, at least in the North, as Negroes find it increasingly possible to move where they wish to, and not only into a Black Belt.

The data were collected by means of interviews, using a schedule with mainly checklist answers, conducted by volunteer students specially trained for the purpose. Interviews were conducted in the spring of 1951 in eight neighborhoods, chosen because they had only one Negro family (in one case, two Negro families) living in what was otherwise a white residential neighborhood. In four of the neighborhoods the same Negro family had been resident for at least ten years, while in the four others the Negro family had been resident less than two years. In each group of four neighborhoods, two were chosen as lower-income areas, and the two others as middle-income areas. The neighborhood was defined in terms of distance from the Negro's home and divided into a primary and a secondary zone: in the primary zone, consisting of the homes on both sides of the street within one block of the Negro's dwelling, one adult was to be interviewed within every home; in the secondary zone, containing all second blocks from the Negro's home on the same street, as well as one block on all adjacent streets, every other dwelling was included in the sample. Deviations were made from this plan because of odd block structures, the presence of factories and railroad tracks, and other neighborhood barriers. A total of 545 interviews was obtained; of the total original sample 9.6 per cent was lost because no person could be found at home after repeated visits or because of refusal to be interviewed. Information was obtained on the personal characteristics of the white and Negro families, but these data can only be used to explain apparent exceptions in the attitude and behavior patterns, since not enough neighborhoods were studied to make comparisons between types of neighborhoods in terms of the personal characteristics of the residents.

Before the study began, a number of hypotheses were set forth and used to formulate the questions in the schedule. They fell into the following subject-matter areas: (1) satisfaction with and participation within the neighborhood; (2) attitudes toward and knowledge about the Negro residents; (3) the extent and kinds of relationships with the Negro residents; (4) general endorsement of interracial housing and association. The specific hypotheses will now be presented with the relevant data.

1. The closer neighbors have more contact with the Negro family and

are more willing to approve of the general idea of mixed racial housing and association than are those persons who live at a greater distance from the Negro family. For all neighborhoods where Negroes had been living for at least ten years, 63 per cent of the white respondents in the primary zones speak with members of the Negro family, while in the secondary zones only 23 per cent have a speaking acquaintance with the resident Negroes. For neighborhoods where Negroes have been living for less than two years, 36 per cent of the whites living in primary zones speak with members of the Negro family as compared to 30 per cent in the secondary zones. This finding is consistent with that found in studies of areas that are racially homogeneous, that closer neighbors have more neighborly contacts than do relatively distant neighbors.[5] The measurement of approval of mixed racial associations was made by three questions whose answers were found to scale according to Guttman criteria.[6] These questions asked whether the respondent thought Negroes should be permitted to live in the same building,[7] to live in the same block, to go to the same school, as whites.[8] Table 1 shows that for areas where Negroes have been living for at least ten years, respondents who live in the primary zones include a larger proportion in favor of interracial association than respondents who live in secondary blocks, but that for areas where Negroes have been living for less than two years there is no significant difference between those living in primary and secondary zones. When the question is raised concerning getting along with the Negro family the results are mixed. On the one hand, a significantly greater proportion of the primary zone population said that their relationships with the Negro families were very good (43 as compared to 10 per cent in areas where Negroes have been living at least ten years; 17 as compared to 11 per cent in areas where Negroes have been living less than two years); on the other hand the very few respondents who said they did not get along well were mostly also in the primary zone (3 per cent as compared to less than 1 per cent in both types of areas). The latter cannot be said to go against our hypothesis, since not getting along well with a specific family might reflect a reaction to a particular family rather than a reaction to Negroes in general.

2. Those who have more contacts with their Negro neighbors are also those who are more favorable to interracial association and who have a more favor-

---

[5] L. Festinger, S. Schachter, and K. Back, *Social Pressures in Informal Groups* (New York: Harper, 1950); T. Caplow and R. Forman, "Neighborhood Interaction," *American Sociological Review,* **15** (June 1950), pp. 357–366.

[6] Louis Guttman, in S. A. Stouffer *et al., Measurement and Prediction* (Princeton, N.J.: Princeton University Press, 1950), pp. 46–90.

[7] Living in the "same building" is an ambiguous matter, since some respondents live in duplexes and apartment buildings, while most live in single-family homes.

[8] The exact wordings were: "Do you think that Negroes should be permitted to live in the same building with white persons?" "Do you think Negroes should be permitted to live in the same block with white persons?" "Would you object to Negroe and white children going to the same school?" The answers permitted were simply "yes" and "no."

TABLE 1. Attitude Toward Interracial Association in Primary and Secondary Zones

THOSE LIVING IN	NUMBER RESPONDING TO ALL 3 QUESTIONS	PERCENTAGES TAKING EACH OF FOLLOWING POSITIONS WITH RESPECT TO INTERRACIAL ASSOCIATION				MEAN SCORE
		0 SCH., BLK., BLDG.— No	1 SCH.— YES; BLK., BLDG.— No	2 SCH., BLK.— YES; BLDG.— No	3 SCH., BLK., BLDG.— YES	
Areas where Negroes have been living at least 10 years:						
Primary zones	(79)	4	35	30	30	1.85
Secondary zones	(174)	14	40	23	22	1.52
Areas where Negroes have been living less than 2 years:						
Primary zones	(90)	13	37	17	33	1.70
Secondary zones	(159)	18	30	20	32	1.66

able opinion of their Negro neighbors.[9] Some of the data already presented support this hypothesis. Whites who live in areas where a Negro family has been living for at least ten years, and live in primary zones close to the Negroes, both have more contact with their Negro neighbors and are somewhat more likely to be favorable to them specifically, and to interracial association generally, than are whites who live in areas where a Negro family has been living for less than two years. Whites who live in primary zones (i.e. closer to their Negro neighbors) are more acquainted with their Negro neighbors than are whites who live in secondary zones, and also tend to get along with them better. Primary zone whites are more favorable to interracial association generally, however, only if the Negroes have been living in the neighborhood for a considerable length of time. Our direct correlational evidence also gives support to the hypothesis. While correlational evidence does not, by itself, indicate the direction of causation, in the light of the above-mentioned considerations it seems reasonable to assume that the contact is the "cause" and the attitude toward interracial association the "effect." There is a more serious limitation of our data, however, due to the actually limited character of "neighborly" contact in a large city: There were so few kinds of contact with Negro neighbors (with other white neighbors also, in most cases) that, among the various questions on contacts we asked, the only one eliciting enough positive answers to permit a significant cross tabulation was the contact of "speaking with" the Negro neighbor. Table 2 shows the relationship

[9] This hypothesis gets support from many other studies, with certain qualifications. See Stuart W. Cook, "Contact and Intergroup Attitudes: Some Theoretical Considerations," Presidential address to Society for the Psychological Study of Social Issues, September 1952.

between this contact and evaluation of Negro neighbors and approval of interracial association. The differences showing the relationships are all consistent and all statistically significant at the 5 per cent level at least, but they are not very great.

TABLE 2. Relationship of Contact with Evaluation of Negro Neighbors, and with Attitude Toward Interracial Association

| | | PERCENTAGE EXPRESSING INDICATED ATTITUDE AMONG THOSE WHO,* IN AREAS WHERE NEGROES HAVE BEEN LIVING | | | |
| | | AT LEAST 10 YEARS | | LESS THAN 2 YEARS | |
QUESTION	ANSWER	SPEAK WITH NEGRO NEIGHBOR	DO NOT SPEAK WITH NEGRO NEIGHBOR	SPEAK WITH NEGRO NEIGHBOR	DO NOT SPEAK WITH NEGRO NEIGHBOR
"Disregarding their race, how well do you think this family compares *as neighbors* with the other families in this area?"	Better	16	6	19	8
	About the same	81	85	72	79
	Not as well	3	9	9	13
Number of cases		(92)	(89)	(67)	(109)
Scale of attitude tward interracial association	0 Sch., blk., bldg.—no	4	14	7	21
	1 Sch.—yes; blk., bldg.—no	32	44	23	35
	2 Sch., blk.—yes; bldg.—no	38	19	28	16
	3 Sch., blk., bldg.—yes	26	23	42	28
Number of cases		(92)	(154)	(72)	(153)

*Persons who indicate that they don't know their Negro neighbors are excluded from the top half of this table.

3. The third hypothesis is that areas which are more integrated, and individuals within any area who are more integrated into it, will display a greater degree of unity in their response to the Negro family and to interracial association in general. To measure integration, a scale was formulated in the pattern of a social distance scale,[10] except that social distance was expressed toward a neighbor rather than toward minority groups. When comparisons were made between areas with highest and lowest average scale scores, and between individuals with high and low scale scores within all primary areas, on several indices of association with the Negro family and with attitude toward interracial association generally, no consistent or statistically significant differences in variation appeared. Thus the hypothesis is not supported by our data.

4. The fourth hypothesis is that those who are more integrated into the

---

[10] The principles underlying social distance scales have been formulated by Emory J. Bogardus. See his "Measuring Social Distance," *Journal of Applied Sociology,* **9** (1925), pp. 299–308; and "A Social Distance Scale," *Sociology and Social Research,* **17** (1933), pp. 265–271.

neighborhood, or who have a stronger "stake" in the neighborhood, are more inclined to accept the specific Negro family, where the Negro family has been living for a long time. The several relevant items of data in our study support this hypothesis. (a) A comparison was made of people with different scores on the general social distance scale, for people who live in the primary zones of areas where Negroes have been living for at least ten years. It shows that people who are less socially distant from their neighbors in general are slightly more likely to know their Negro neighbors, and this acquaintanceship is more likely than not to take the form of a friendly relationship. The difference is not great (52.5 per cent among the socially distant who get along "very well" or "fairly well" with the Negro family, as compared to 61.6 per cent among the less socially distant) and the cases are so few (40 and 48, respectively) that the difference cannot be considered statistically reliable (at the 30 per cent level). (b) Ownership of property represents another index of integration into the neighborhood, and data relating ownership to acceptance of the Negro family are presented in Table 3. A larger proportion of owners than of renters are acquainted with the Negro families, and are as likely to evaluate them favorably as neighbors. In areas where Negroes have been living for at least ten years, there is no difference between the proportions of owners and renters believing that the presence of the Negro family lowers property values in the neighborhood, although a differential appears in areas where Negroes have been living less than two years. Owners are, of course, the ones directly affected by lower property values, and the fact that no more of them—in areas where Negroes have been living for ten or more years—believe that the presence of the Negro families decreases property values is undoubtedly a reason why they are as willing as renters, to accept the Negro families.

TABLE 3. Comparison of Owners and Renters in Acceptance of Negro Neighbors and in Belief That Presence of Negroes Decreases Property Values

| | | PERCENTAGES GIVING INDICATED RESPONSE AMONG: | | | |
| | | IN AREAS WHERE NEGROES HAVE BEEN LIVING FOR AT LEAST 10 YEARS | | IN AREAS WHERE NEGROES HAVE BEEN LIVING FOR LESS THAN 2 YEARS | |
QUESTIONS	ANSWERS	OWNERS	RENTERS	OWNERS	RENTERS
"Do members of this family ever talk to you or your family?"	Yes	34	23	30	27
"Disregarding their race, how well do you think this family compares *as neighbors* with the other families in this area?"	Better	8	3	8	10
	Same	55	51	52	45
	Not as well	4	3	10	3
	Don't know them	33	43	30	42
"Some time ago a Negro family moved into this neighborhood. Do you think this hurt property values in the neighborhood?"	Yes	34	34	51	30
	No	36	32	32	41
	Don't know	30	34	17	30
Number of cases		(213)	(35)	(190)	(62)

5. Complementary to the preceding hypothesis that the more integrated people in the neighborhood are more likely to accept the specific Negro family is another hypothesis that they are more likely to resist a more general interracial association. Using the respondents of the primary zones only, we find that the average score on the scale of interracial association for the more socially distant people is 1.92, whereas for the less socially distant people it is 1.88 (based on 40 and 48 cases, respectively). This is not a statistically significant difference, but it is in the expected direction. Table 4 shows a more conclusive and more interesting comparison between owners and renters. On the mean score, in areas where Negroes have lived at least ten years, owners are slightly less favorable to interracial association in general than are renters. The difference is in the direction which confirms our hypothesis, but is not large enough to be statistically significant. In areas where Negroes have been living less than two years, the difference between owners and renters is sharply in the expected direction and is highly significant. The specific responses of those dwelling in areas where Negroes have been living at least ten years show that the owners are more likely than renters to be more favorable as well as less favorable to interracial association in general. This is possible because owners are more likely to take the position that Negro children should be allowed to go to the same school as white children go to, but that Negro families should not be allowed to live in the same block or building that white families live in. Thus owners express both their friendliness to Negroes—which we suggest arises from their satisfactory relations with their Negro neighbors—as well as their concern about the value of their property.

TABLE 4. Comparison of Owners and Renters in Attitude Toward Interracial Association

POSITION ON SCALE OF ATTITUDE TOWARD INTERRACIAL ASSOCIATION	IN AREAS WHERE NEGROES HAVE BEEN LIVING 10 OR MORE YEARS, PERCENTAGE EXPRESSING INDICATED ATTITUDE AMONG:		IN AREAS WHERE NEGROES HAVE BEEN LIVING LESS THAN 2 YEARS, PERCENTAGE EXPRESSING INDICATED ATTITUDE AMONG:	
	OWNERS	RENTERS	OWNERS	RENTERS
0 Sch., blk., bldg.—no	10	19	18	9
1 Sch.—yes; blk., bldg.—no	43	25	36	22
2 Sch., blk.—yes; bldg.—no	24	28	18	19
3 Sch., blk., bldg.—yes	23	28	28	50
Mean score	1.59	1.65	1.56	2.10
Number of cases	(213)	(35)	(190)	(62)

6. Children in a family create for their parents both a stronger relationship to the neighborhood—including Negro neighbors—and at the same time an anxiety about the effect of Negro neighbors on the children. Therefore we hypothesize that respondents with young children—who would create anxiety but are too young to create relationships—will be more distant from the Negro

neighbors than are respondents without children, but that respondents with older children have counteracted their anxiety because of the increased relationship with the Negro neighbors for which the children were responsible. Table 5 provides striking confirmation of this hypothesis for areas in which Negroes have been living for at least ten years. Respondents with children of preschool age are least likely to have relationships with the Negro neighbors and most likely to be hostile to interracial association in general, whereas respondents with older children are much more likely to have contact with the Negro family and less hostility toward interracial association. Respondents with school age children, as compared to respondents without children, include a slightly larger proportion hostile to all three types of interracial association as well as a larger proportion not hostile to any of the three types. In areas where Negroes have been living for less than two years, the hypothesis does not hold up at all. There are no significant differences in percentage of families speaking with members of the Negro family, and the major difference in attitude toward interracial association generally is that whites with preschool age children are more favorable than any other group. We might hazard the guess that the state of attitudes predicted in our hypothesis has not yet had a chance to take form in the short time Negroes have been living in the neighborhood.

TABLE 5. Relationship Between Presence of Children in the Family and Contact with Negro Neighbors, and Attitudes Toward Interracial Association

In Areas Where Negroes Have Been Living at Least 10 Years	Percentage of Respondents Giving Indicated Answers Among Those with:			
	No Children	Preschool Children	School-Age Children	Children 19 and Over
Percentage speaking with members of Negro family	31	12	39	43
Position on scale of attitude toward interracial association				
0 Sch., blk., bldg.—no	8	23	13	16
1 Sch.—yes; blk., bldg.—no	41	53	31	40
2 Sch., blk.—yes; bldg.—no	27	13	22	20
3 Sch., blk., bldg.—yes	24	10	33	24
Mean score	1.66	1.10	1.76	1.52
Number of cases	(118)	(34)	(56)	(28)
In Areas Where Negroes Have Been Living Less Than 2 Years				
Percentage speaking with members of Negro family	24	28	27	22
Position on scale of attitude toward interracial association				
0 Sch., blk., bldg.—no	15	7	24	28
1 Sch.—yes; blk., bldg.—no	42	33	34	24
2 Sch., blk.—yes; bldg.—no	16	24	13	20
3 Sch., blk., bldg.—yes	27	35	29	28
Mean score	1.55	1.86	1.47	1.48
Number of cases	(86)	(57)	(40)	(27)

7. Our seventh hypothesis is one that has several times been confirmed in earlier studies.[11] It is that the more educated the person the more likely he is to be favorable to interracial association, but the less likely he is to have had contact with his Negro neighbor. Table 6 gives direct confirmation of this. Especially in attitudes toward interracial association there are striking differences between respondents of different educational levels.

TABLE 6. Relationship Between Education and Contact with Negro Neighbors and Attitudes Toward Interracial Association

In Areas Where Negro Family Has Been Living for at Least 10 Years	Indicated Responses Among Persons with Educational Attainment at Level of:			
	Grade School Only	High School Only	Some College	College Graduation
Mean score on scale of attitude toward interracial association	1.40	1.74	1.97	2.04
Percentage who speak with Negro neighbor	36	36	29	29
Number of cases	(64)	(125)	(36)	(23)
In Areas Where Negro Family Has Been Living Less Than 2 Years				
Percentage who speak with Negro neighbor	1.43	1.59	1.83	2.31
Mean score on scale of attitude toward interracial association	30	35	24	40
Number of cases	(57)	(113)	(46)	(22)

8. We had no hypothesis about the relationship between religious affiliation and attitudes toward interracial association, but a comparison of scores of different religious groups on the scale of attitude toward interracial association shows that the religious groups are not very far apart. For areas in which Negroes have been living at least ten years, the score of Catholics (52 cases) was 1.59, of Lutherans (106 cases)—1.55, of members of the other large Protestant denominations (51 cases)—1.55, of the fundamentalist Protestants (16 cases)—1.50, and of those who said they had no religious affiliation (29 cases)—1.73. For areas in which Negroes have been living for less than two years, the score of Catholics (62 cases) was 1.46, of Lutherans (97 cases)—1.72, of members of the other large Protestant denominations (38 cases)—1.92, of the fundamental Protestants (12 cases)—1.84, and of those who said they had no religious affiliation (26 cases)—1.63.

[11] See the summary contained in Arnold M. Rose, *Studies in Reduction of Prejudice* (2nd ed., Chicago: American Council on Race Relations, 1948), pp. 19–24.

CONCLUSION

The evidence of this survey of eight neighborhoods of Minneapolis where a single Negro family lives in an otherwise white neighborhood indicates that there is a tendency to accept or to accommodate to the Negro as a neighbor.[12] Those who live close to the Negro neighbors have more contact with them and are more favorable to them and to interracial association generally than those who live farther away. This is especially true in neighborhoods where Negroes have been living for a long time. Those who have more contacts with their Negro neighbors are more favorable to them specifically and to interracial association generally. Those who live in neighborhoods where Negroes have been living for at least ten years, and live close to the Negroes, are somewhat more likely to have contact with their Negro neighbor and to be more favorable to them and to interracial association generally than whites who live in neighborhoods where Negroes have been living less than two years. Those who are more integrated into the neighborhood and who have a stronger "stake" in it are more inclined to accept the Negro family, although not to be more favorable to interracial association generally. We used home ownership—as opposed to renting—as an index of "stake in neighborhood" and it is significant that the owners—in areas where Negroes have been living ten or more years—were as favorable toward, probably because they were more acquainted with, the Negro family, and no more inclined to believe that the presence of the Negro family hurt property values. Renters are slightly more likely to be favorable toward interracial association in a neighborhood, however, while owners are slightly more likely to be favorable toward interracial association in the schools, in areas where Negroes have been living at least ten years. In areas where Negroes have been living less than two years, owners are less likely than renters to be favorable to interracial association and more likely to believe that Negroes hurt property values. Well-educated whites are much more likely to be in favor of interracial association, but not more likely to have actually had contact with their Negro neighbors, than are poorly educated whites. In areas where Negroes have been living for a long while, families with school age children are more favorable to interracial association than are families with preschool age children. This pattern has not developed, however, in areas where Negroes have been living less than two years. The dominant religion of the whites in a neighborhood does not seem to affect any of the above patterns, although data not presented suggests that the more heterogeneous the population, in terms of religion and national origin, the more favorable is the area toward Negroes.

---

[12] In Duluth, virtually all Negroes live in neighborhoods that are predominantly white, and a survey by Turbeville reports that "over 82 per cent of the heads of households stated that they had not been victims of neighborhood discrimination because of their race." Gus Turbeville, "The Negro Population in Duluth, Minnesota, 1950," *Sociology and Social Research,* **36** (March–April 1952), pp. 231–238.

In so far as the limited data of this survey of Minneapolis can be generalized, if the residential pattern of Northern cities takes the form of a scatter-
ing of Negro families living in predominantly white areas, the prognosis is that
this would tend to increase the acceptance and accommodation of Negroes by
whites.

46

Sociology and Staphylococcus

Helen G. Tibbitts, Nicholas J. Demerath, and Albert F. Wessen

> This call for help introduces an interesting recognition of the
> utility of cooperation between the medical profession and sociolo-
> gists. Though the reader may already have envisioned some re-
> lationship between sociology and medicine, he may be unaware
> of the value of sociology in the actual combatting of disease.

The attention of sociologists is invited to a perplexing problem of infection
in hospitals. Staphylococcus infections, of clinical interest for some time, have
become a problem of public health importance since 1952. Numerous and
costly measures of control of a physical or chemical sort have been taken with
little result. At the same time, knowledge of some aspects of the infectious
process, especially the problem of resistants, is so primitive that effective measures of control can scarcely be expected. In August, 1958, the United States
Public Health Service held a conference to consider what new or additional
research should be undertaken, from which issued suggestions posing problems
that, in varying degrees, may interest sociologists.

In June, 1958, the National Library of Medicine published a bibliography
on staphylococcus infections covering the English, French, and German literature of 1952–58. More than five hundred reports are listed, only ten of which

Reprinted from *American Journal of Sociology,* **65,** 3 (November 1959), pp. 299–300,
by permission of The University of Chicago Press and the authors.

Helen G. Tibbitts is Scientific Administrator, Executive Secretary, Nursing Research
Study Section, Division of Research Grants, United States Public Health Service.

Nicholas J. Demerath is Professor of Sociology, Washington University.

Albert F. Wessen is Chairman, Department of Sociology-Anthropology, Washington
University.

were published in 1952. Until 1957 the majority of the articles were reports of a case or cases caused by antibiotic-sensitive or antibiotic-resistant staphylococci. In that year reports of staphylococcal infection in the hospital (epidemiological studies, or studies dealing with occurrence or prevention) received major attention in the literature, perhaps as an aftermath of a few epidemics in either a nursery, a maternity ward, or a surgical ward. A few scattered reports state the condition to exist also in the home, the school, and the community.

The staphylococcus is normal to the flora of man and is found on the skin, in nasopharyngeal passages, and in the gastrointestinal tract. It appears that staphylococcus may be transmissible by ventilation systems as well as by personal contact. Only under certain circumstances, possibly host-determined, is it pathogenic. Many strains have been identified, most of which can produce disease when the host's defenses are lowered. Some strains have acquired resistance to antibiotics; these strains are isolated most frequently in outbreaks. The organism is characterized by a very large gene pool and hence is highly variable biochemically; new variants constantly are emerging.

Epidemiological investigations conceivably could yield clues to the solution of some of the riddles of this infection. Such investigations search for the characteristics of the host and his environment which are associated with the occurrence of different manifestations of the disease. Here is an opportunity for sociologists to collaborate with epidemiologists. Pertinent social variables could include demographic characteristics of the affected population; incidence in the social space of family, community, or hospital, with consideration being given to positions, quality of the social relations, hygienic practices, and values and attitudes of individuals or social categories which are affected. Because of the ubiquitous character of the organism, it might be highly profitable to study differences within social groups between individuals who are and are not stricken, given common exposure, as nearly as this can be determined.

In collaboration with hospital administrators, sociologists might explore differing perceptions of the staphylococcal problem as between nurses and physicians, surgeons and nonsurgeons, and administrators, supervisors, and others in hospital organizations. These might pertain to the sources-of-control ideas, the kind of control measures considered and adopted by hospital administrators and the more and less likely sources and mechanisms of infection. It might be revealing to explore the relation to infection rates of structures of authority and influence or of the correspondence between formal and informal patterns of communication. The effectiveness of a hospital committee on infections could be studied in relation to the composition of the committee. Of particular interest might be the correspondence between such a member's positions in the hospital power structure, in interaction in the committee, and as practitioners in the community.

Another research project would be the impact on the hospital of programs of staphylococcus control in terms of cost, the adoption of new procedures, and the development of permissive ideologies, such as free visiting on isolation and maternity wards, "rooming-in," etc.

It should be noted that these are opportunities in the making, and they apply to the epidemiology and control of other communicable diseases, as well as to staphylococcal infection. To exploit these opportunities, sociologists will need to associate themselves with medical and hospital people who have sufficient interest and insight to collaborate fully and responsibly.

47

The Chicago Area Project—
A 25-Year Assessment

Solomon Kobrin

All too frequently, delinquency prevention programs are initiated with compassion and dedication but with little if any understanding of the causes of delinquency. The Chicago Area Project was developed through the efforts of a sociologist, Clifford Shaw, concerned with linking sound theory and practice. The Kobrin article describes and evaluates this program twenty-five years after its inception.

Note that although many concepts are involved (socialization, social control, and so on), the key concern of this article is the natural area concept—the ecological unity of a section of a city. Cole defines the concept of natural area as ". . . clusters of people, institutions, and interests. . . . They have developed 'naturally,' the result of people seeking adjustment with one another, and of social systems and social institutions seeking adjustment with one another." †

The Chicago Area Project shares with other delinquency prevention programs the difficulty of measuring its success in a simple and direct manner. At bottom this difficulty rests on the fact that such programs, as efforts to intervene in the life of a person, a group, or a community, cannot by their very nature constitute more than a subsidiary element in changing the fundamental

Reprinted from The *Annals* of the American Academy of Political and Social Science, **322** (March 1959), pp. 19–29, by permission of the publisher and the author.

Solomon Kobrin is Research Sociologist, Institute for Juvenile Research, Chicago.

† William E. Cole, *Urban Society* (Boston: Houghton Mifflin, 1958), p. 157.

and sweeping forces which create the problems of groups and of persons or which shape human personality. Declines in rates of delinquents—the only conclusive way to evaluate a delinquency prevention—may reflect influences unconnected with those of organized programs and are difficult to define and measure.[1]

For two reasons the simple and satisfying laboratory model of the controlled experiment is difficult to achieve in measuring the effects of a program. First, it is virtually impossible to find groups which are identical in all major respects save that of participation in a given program. Second, there exists a widespread and understandable reluctance to deny to systematically selected segments of homogeneous groups the putative benefits of programs, a procedure which does produce an approximation to a control group.[2]

The present assessment of the Chicago Area Project will have to rest, therefore, on an appraisal of its experience in carrying out procedures assumed by its founders and supporters to be relevant to the reduction of delinquency. To this end, the theory of delinquency causation underlying the Area Project program will be presented. This will be followed by a description of the procedures regarded as essential to the modifications of conditions which produce delinquency. Finally, the adaptations and modifications of these procedures will be described and evaluated.

CONCEPTION OF THE DELINQUENCY PROBLEM

A distinctive feature of the Area Project program is that at its inception it attempted explicitly to relate its procedures in a logical manner to sociological postulates and to the findings of sociological research in delinquency. Under the leadership of the late Clifford R. Shaw, founder of the Area Project and its director during virtually all of its existence, a series of studies completed between 1929 and 1933 brought to the investigation of this problem two heretofore neglected viewpoints: the ecological and the sociopsychological. The first was concerned with the epidemiology of delinquency in the large city; the second with the social experience of the delinquent boy in the setting of his family, his play group, and his neighborhood.[3]

---

[1] For example, rates of delinquents among nationality groups whose children at one time figured prominently in juvenile court statistics declined as these groups improved their economic and social position and moved out of neighborhoods of high rates of delinquents. See Clifford R. Shaw and Henry D. McKay, *Juvenile Delinquency and Urban Areas* (Chicago: University of Chicago Press, 1942), pp. 151–157.

[2] See Edwin Powers and Helen Witmer, *An Experiment in the Prevention of Delinquency* (New York: Columbia University Press, 1951), as a distinguished and solitary example of one program which, in the interest of advancing knowledge, denied hypothesized benefits of a program to a control group.

[3] Studies in the first category include Clifford R. Shaw and others, *Delinquency Areas* (Chicago: University of Chicago Press, 1929); certain sections of Clifford R. Shaw and Henry D. McKay, *Social Factors in Juvenile Delinquency* (Washington, D.C.: U.S. Government Printing Office, 1931); and a final volume in which the geographic distribu-

With respect to the first problem, it was found that certain areas of the large city produced a disproportionately large number of the delinquents. The high rate areas were characterized as "delinquency areas" and subsequently an effort was made to define their major social features. In the American city of the period, the populations of these communities were made up of predominantly recent migrants from the rural areas of the Old World. As a group they occupied the least desirable status in the economic, political, and social hierarchies of the metropolitan society and in many ways showed an acute awareness of their position. Their efforts to adapt their social institutions to the urban industrial order were at the most only partly successful. The generation of immigrants, in their colonies in the decaying heart of the city, adapted with moderate success only those institutions which preserved customary forms of religious practice, mutual aid, and sociability.

However, the immigrant generation was notably unable to preserve the authority of the old institutions, including the family, in the eyes of the rising generation and was quickly confronted with a problem of conflict with their children. Disruption of cross-generational control produced the conditions for the emergence of a variant species of youth subculture in these communities marked by a tradition of sophisticated delinquency. At the same time this tradition was sustained and fostered by the anonymity of much of the population of slum areas, by the presence of a young adult element which engaged in crime both as an occupation and a way of life, and by the extraordinary harshness of the competitive struggle which arises when the controls of social usage decay. The distribution of official delinquents pointed firmly to the conclusion that the high-rate areas constituted the locus of the city's delinquency problem, both as to number of delinquents and seriousness of offenses.

THE DELINQUENT AS A PERSON

With respect to the second problem, these investigations suggested that, given the conditions of social life in the delinquency areas, delinquency in most cases was the product of the simple and direct processes of social learning. Where growing boys are alienated from the institutions of their parents and are confronted with a vital tradition of delinquency among their peers, they engage in delinquent activity as part of their groping for a place in the only social groups available to them. From investigations of the type reported in

tion of rates of delinquents in a number of American cities was analyzed in great detail, Clifford R. Shaw and Henry D. McKay, *Juvenile Delinquency and Urban Areas.* While the last volume was published a decade after the earlier ones much of its data were available to the authors at the time of the founding of the Area Project. Studies of the social experience of delinquent boys include Clifford R. Shaw, *The Jack-roller* (Chicago: University of Chicago Press, 1930); Clifford R. Shaw, *The Natural History of a Delinquent Career* (Chicago: University of Chicago Press, 1931); and Clifford R. Shaw, Henry D. McKay, and James F. McDonald, *Brothers in Crime* (Chicago: University of Chicago Press, 1938).

The Jack-roller, Natural History of a Delinquent Career, and *Brothers in Crime,* the conclusion was drawn that with significant frequency, delinquency in the slum areas of our cities reflects the strivings of boys in a social rather than an antisocial direction. These studies focused attention on the paradoxical fact that no matter how destructive or morally shocking, delinquency may often represent the efforts of the person to find and vindicate his status as a human being, rather than an abdication of his humanity or an intrinsic incapacity to experience human sentiment.

This view formed something of a contrast to notions of human nature and delinquency which were, and still are, somewhat more widely accepted. These beliefs, which generally represent delinquent conduct as a manifestation of pathology or malfunction of personality, rest implicitly on an image of man as quick to lose his distinctively human capacities under adverse conditions. The image implied in the Area Project conception of the delinquency problem is that man tends always to organize his behavior in the service of his human identity. To what extent this view is supported by the research of Shaw and his associates, and to what extent the research proceeded from this view is, of course, a difficult question to answer. The fact remains, however, that from the beginning the Area Project program rested on a conception of human nature which was optimistic concerning the prevention of delinquency and the rehabilitation of the delinquent. Delinquency was regarded as, for the most part, a reversible accident of the person's social experience.

Thus, the theory on which the Area Project program is based is that, taken in its most general aspect, delinquency as a problem in the modern metropolis is principally a product of the breakdown of the machinery of spontaneous social control. The breakdown is precipitated by the cataclysmic pace of social change to which migrants from a peasant or rural background are subjected when they enter the city. In its more specific aspects, delinquency was seen as adaptive behavior on the part of the male children of rural migrants acting as members of adolescent peer groups in their efforts to find their way to meaningful and respected adult roles essentially unaided by the older generation and under the influence of criminal models for whom the inner city areas furnish a haven.

SOCIALIZATION AND COMMUNITY ACTION

Research in the problem of delinquency formed one of two major sources of suggestion for the Area Project program. The second was furnished by what may best be regarded as a set of sociological postulates concerning, first, the processes by which persons come under the influence and control of social groups and take over their values; and, second, those affecting communal or collective action in the solution of social problems.

It is a commonplace of sociological observation that the source of control of conduct for the person lies in his natural social world. The rules and values having validity for the person are those which affect his daily nurturance, his place in primary groups, and his self-development. He is responsive as a person within the web of relationships in which his daily existence as a human being is embedded.

The inference seemed unavoidable, therefore, that to succeed delinquency prevention activities must somehow first become activities of the adults constituting the natural social world of the youngster. Or, put another way, a delinquency prevention program could hardly hope to be effective unless and until the aims of such a program became the aims of the local populations. Thus, an indispensable preliminary task of delinquency prevention is to discover effective methods of inducing residents of the disadvantaged city areas to take up the cause of prevention in a serious manner. The disposition of the founders of the Area Project was to regard this element of the program as so indispensable that if these populations proved unable to act in relation to the problem, the prevention of delinquency was a lost cause.

A second postulation concerned the problem of developing collective action toward delinquency. Here another commonplace of sociological observation suggested that people support and participate only in those enterprises in which they have a meaningful role. The organized activity of people everywhere flows in the channels of institutions and organizations indigenous to their cultural traditions and to the system of social relationships which defines their social groups. Consequently one could not expect people to devote their energies to enterprises which form part of the social systems of groups in which they have no membership. The relevance of this observation is that there had always existed an expectation that people residing in the high delinquency rate areas could somehow be induced to support the welfare agencies established there. A basic assumption of the Area Project program was that under prevailing conditions it was illusory to expect this to happen.

Thus, in view of the primacy of the local social life in the socialization and control of the young person, all effort, it was felt, should be devoted to helping residents of high delinquency rate areas to take constructive action toward the problem. The interest of the wider society in winning the rising generation of these communities to orderliness and conformity had first to become a vital interest of the local society.

ORGANIZATION OF THE DELINQUENCY AREA

A final assumption necessary to the rationale of the Area Project program had to do with the social and institutional organization of the high delinquency rate neighborhood and with the related issue of the capacity of residents of these areas to organize and administer local welfare programs. It was observed that despite the real disorder and confusion of the delinquency area, there existed a core of organized communal life centering mainly in religious, economic, and political activity. Because the function of the slum area is to house the flow of impoverished newcomers and to furnish a haven of residence for the multitudes who, for various reasons, live at the edge of respectability, the nucleus of institutional order actually present is sometimes difficult to discern. There seemed further to be strong evidence that the residents most active in these local institutions were, in terms of interest, motivation, and capacity, on their way up the social class ladder. With respect to these elements of the population it was assumed, therefore, that they represented forces of considerable strength for initiating delinquency prevention activities.[4] There being no evidence of a deficiency of intelligence among them, it was taken for granted that with proper guidance and encouragement they could learn how to organize and administer local welfare programs.

In summary it may be said, then, that the Area Project program regards as indispensable to the success of welfare activity in general and delinquency prevention in particular the participation of those who form a significant part of the social world of the recipients of help. This is seen not as a prescription or a panacea, but as a condition for progress in finding a solution. The program has remained experimental in the sense that it has continued to explore the question: What kind of participation is necessary on the part of which kinds of persons in terms of social role in the local society? But it has rested firmly and consistently on the conviction that no solution of a basic and lasting character is possible in the absence of such participation.

PROCEDURES IN NEIGHBORHOOD ORGANIZATION

It follows that the basic procedure in the program is the development of local welfare organization among residents of high delinquency rate neighborhoods. This undertaking called for skill in the organizer in identifying the residents holding key positions of influence and the ability to arouse their interest in youth welfare activities. The first phase requires a knowledge of the local society; the second a capacity for sympathetic identification with the local resident. Knowledge of the local society implies familiarity with its culture and history, in the case of ethnic groups; with the local institutions; with the structure of power through which decisions are made and executed; and with the conflicts and cleavages which orient and align the population.

Initial organization in several of Chicago's delinquency areas was undertaken by sociologists employed jointly by the Behavior Research Fund, now dissolved, the Chicago Area Project, and the Illinois Institute for Juvenile Research. The Institute, an agency of state government, until recently has furnished a major share of the salaries of the staff engaged in this program.[5]

---

[4] It should be observed in passing that some of the economic and political leadership of these communities did not always fit philistine specifications of respectability, and that on this score the Area Project program came under criticism during its early days.

[5] A recent reorganization of these services shifted much of this staff to the administrative jurisdiction of the Illinois Youth Commission.

It became quickly evident, however, that, for cogent reasons, the employment of qualified local residents offered advantages in the establishment of such programs. In the first place the indigenous worker usually possessed a natural knowledge of the local society. Second, he was hampered by none of the barriers to communications with residents for whom the nonresident, especially those identified with "welfare" enterprise, tended to be an object of suspicion and hostility. Third, his employment was a demonstration of sincere confidence in the capacity of the area resident for work of this sort. Fourth, he was more likely than the nonresident to have access to the neighborhood's delinquent boys and therefore to be more effective in redirecting their conduct. Fifth, his employment represented a prime means of initiating the education of the local population in the mysteries of conducting the welfare enterprise. Hence, virtually from the first, one of the most distinctive features of Area Project procedure was the employment, in appropriate categories and under the tutelage of staff sociologists of the Institute, of local residents to aid in the organization of the approximately dozen community or civic "committees" which were established in Chicago over the course of two decades.[6]

A second major procedural feature of the Area Project program is represented by efforts to preserve the independence of the neighborhood groups after they become established as functioning units. This turned out to be mainly an exercise in self restraint, for the easier and in many ways more natural course would have been to maintain a close supervision and control of their activities. However, since it was the aim of the program to foster the development of knowledge and competence in the conduct of youth welfare activities and to encourage among residents of delinquency areas confidence in their own capacities to act with respect to their problems, the policy was followed of insisting upon a formal, structural autonomy of the organization. The problem in this connection was to maintain full support and help without rendering the independence of the group an empty formality.

MAINTAINING AUTONOMY

Three devices were found to be useful in dealing with this problem. First, neighborhood groups either exercised the power of veto in the assignment of Area Project staff to function as their executives; or, more frequently, nominated a qualified local resident as their executive who was then employed as an Area Project staff member. Second, staff members were required to function as representatives and spokesmen of the local groups rather than as rep-

---

[6] Sharp question has been raised by leaders of the social work profession regarding the competence of such persons, whose qualifications rested on assets of character and personal trait rather than on formal training and education. Leaders of the Area Project have always encouraged talented workers in this field to obtain as much training in the group work and social work fields as they could. However, they have regarded the talent for this work as the primary value.

resentatives of the Area Project central office or of the Sociology Department of the Institute for Juvenile Research. This served to foster an identification of the worker with the point of view and the needs of the local group. Third, policy decisions of neighborhood groups which appeared to Area Project staff to be unsound were nonetheless accepted and acted upon by them. Since staff members exercised much informal influence with the groups to which they were assigned, this problem arose infrequently. However, when it did arise, the autonomy of the neighborhood group was scrupulously respected.

These, then, are the procedural principles of the Area Project program: development of youth welfare organizations among residents of delinquency areas; employment of so-called indigenous workers wherever possible; and the fostering and preservation of the independence of these groups.

TYPES OF NEIGHBORHOOD GROUPS

Before moving to an evaluation of the Area Project as a delinquency prevention program, some indication ought to be made of the specific activities and forms of organization found among these neighborhood groups. The founders of the Area Project were always mindful of variety in the forms of social life and of the necessity, therefore, of adapting the approach to problems of organization as well as the content of program to conditions existing in each work location. In consequence each neighborhood organization within the Area Project differs somewhat from the others in both these respects.

Generally these differences are related to the patterns of social organization existing in their areas of operation and to the degree of unity and coordination among local institutions. On this axis, delinquency areas may be classified as structured and stable, structured but unstable, and unstructured and unstable.[7]

In the structured and stable communities, Area Project neighborhood organizations reflect a direct expansion in interests and functions of established neighborhood institutions. In some cases in this category, the dominant local church sponsors the organization, encouraging influential lay leaders to assume responsibility in the development of its program. However, there are few urban neighborhoods in which a single institution exercises complete dominance of the life of the residents. The more usual case in this class is represented by the local organization in which a number of important neighborhood institutions participate. These may include one or more churches, local political bodies, businessmen's groups, and lodges and fraternal groups. However, the representation is always informal, and membership belongs to participating persons as individuals. This informal mode of representation has come to be preferred, probably because it permits the inclusion of important

---

[7] These terms are relative. From the vantage point of an orderly and integrated middle-class residential community the structured and stable delinquency area might appear to be both excessively disorderly in terms of delinquency, crime, and other social problems and excessively controlled and dominated by religious or political organizations.

groups which are not formally constituted. Such, for example, are extended kinship groups, friendship cliques, and aggregations of persons temporarily unified around specific problems or issues. In unstructured or unstable communities the member usually represents only himself.

REASONS FOR JOINING GROUPS

Differences of this order among Area Project groups seem also to be accompanied by differences in motivation for participation. Members of all Area Projects groups share a responsiveness to slogans of youth welfare. However, members of groups operating in the relatively well-organized neighborhoods tend to find in this activity a means for realizing their aspiration for upward mobility. A related need is served in those communities where the framework of institutional life fails to furnish a satisfactory place for certain age or sex groups. In these situations young adults and women, for example, may find in the Area Project neighborhood organization a means of gaining recognition.

The second major motivation is found most frequently in communities with few or no organizations (unstructured), and in those that have no fixed pattern of integration of the activities of organizations which may exist (unstable). Here the dominant motives for participation in the Area Project group are, first, a simple concern with the tragedies attending youthful law violation; and second, a desire to break down social isolation through organized contact with neighbors. These constitute the motivations most frequently sanctioned in official representations of Area Projects doctrine because they are most apt to evoke a positive response to promotional appeals.

VARIETY IN PROGRAM CONTENT

Area Project neighborhood organizations all include, with varying emphasis and elaboration, three elements in their programs. The first is the sponsorship of a standard kind of recreation program for the children of the neighborhood, including in some instances programs of summer camping of considerable scope. Such recreation programs are likely to have two distinctive features: the use of residents, usually active members of the Area Project group, as volunteers assisting in carrying on the recreation program; and the improvisation of store-front locations or unused space in churches, police stations, and even basements of homes for recreational use.

The second element of the program is represented by campaigns for community improvement. These are usually concerned with such issues as school improvement, sanitation, traffic safety, physical conservation, and law enforcement.

The third element of the program is reflected in the activity directed to the delinquent child, gangs of boys involved in delinquency, and, in some cases, adult offenders returning to the neighborhood from penal institutions. The activity includes helping police and juvenile court personnel develop plans for the supervision of delinquent youngsters; visiting boys committed to training schools and reformatories; working with boys' gangs in the informal settings of the neighborhood; and assisting adult parolees in their problems of returning to the community.

Specific program content in each of the local groups varies in relation to a number of factors. Among these are the facilities available for recreation or camping; the character and intensity of problems of safety, physical maintenance, or law enforcement in the area; and the staff's ability to arouse enthusiasm and effort from the leaders of the local organization in carrying on direct work with delinquents. Some groups are committed to an extensive program of recreation, including the development and operation of summer camps. Others, located in neighborhoods well equipped with such facilities, carry on no recreation work at all.[8] Some have labored strenuously in programs of neighborhood conservation; others have not concerned themselves with such issues. All have been continuously encouraged and helped by state employed Area Project staff to maintain direct work with delinquent children and with street gangs, and with virtually no exception all local groups have done so.

ACHIEVEMENTS OF THE AREA PROJECT

The achievements of the Area Project may best be assessed in relation to its theory of delinquency causation in the social setting of the high-rate neighborhoods: In this theory, delinquency is regarded as a product of a local milieu (a) in which adult residents do little or nothing in an organized public way to mobilize their resources in behalf of the welfare of the youth of the area; (b) in which the relative isolation of the adolescent male group, common throughout urban society, becomes at its extreme an absolute isolation with a consequent absolute loss of adult control; and (c) in which the formal agencies of correction and reformation fail to enlist the collaboration of persons and groups influential in the local society. Leaders of the Area Project assume that progress in the prevention of delinquency cannot be expected until these three problems are well on their way to solution. Since progress in the solution of these problems comes only slowly, permanent declines in delinquency are not expected even after years of effort.

First among the accomplishments claimed by the Area Project is its demonstration of the feasibility of creating youth welfare organizations among residents of delinquency areas. Even in the most unlikely localities capable persons of good will have responded to the challenge of responsibility and have, with help and guidance, operated neighborhood programs. On the whole these

---

[8] Contrary to popular impression those of our big city neighborhoods which have been centers of social problems, including delinquency, for many decades sometimes acquire more than a just share of recreational facilities. This has resulted, quite simply, from their long-time status as objects of society's solicitude and philanthropy.

organizations have exhibited vitality and stability and have come to represent centers of local opinion regarding issues which concern the welfare of the young. Above all, they have justified the assumption made by Clifford Shaw and his associates that persons residing in these localities have the capacity to take hold of such problems and contribute to their solution.

The Area Project has made an equally distinctive contribution respecting the problem of the isolation of the male adolescent in the delinquency area. From the beginning it called attention to the fact that the recreational and character-building agencies in these areas were unable, through their established programs, to modify the conduct of boys caught up in gang delinquency. In all probability the Area Project was the first organized program in the United States to use workers to establish direct and personal contact with the "unreached" boys to help them find their way back to acceptable norms of conduct. The adoption of this pattern in many cities during recent years may be regarded as in part, at least, a contribution of the Area Project to the development of working methods in the delinquency prevention field. At the same time, it should be indicated that from the viewpoint of Area Project assumptions and procedures such work, to be effective, must be carried on as an integral part of a more general program sponsored by residents of the locality.

Finally, the Area Project has pioneered in exploring the problem of tempering the impersonality of the machinery which an urban society erects to control and correct the wayward child. Leaders of the Area Project have tended to regard the procedures of juvenile courts, school systems, police departments, probation and parole systems, training schools, and reformatories as inescapably bureaucratic. That is, the procedures of these organizations tend to become set ways of dealing with persons as members of categories. While it is both rational and efficient as a way of processing human problems, of doing something about and hence disposing of cases, this mode of operating results in serious loss of control of the conduct of the young person. The young person in particular is regarded as responsive mainly to the expectations of his primary groups. Thus, to enhance the effectiveness of the corrective agencies of society, it is necessary to enlist the disciplining power of such groups. This is a difficult and complex undertaking, since the customary primary groups for the child, namely family and peers, are often, in the disorder of the delinquency area, unable or undisposed to exercise the needed discipline.

However, it has been found that in no area is the disorder so unmitigated as to be devoid of persons, whether residents or staff employees of the local organization or both, who staunchly represent the values of conformity, many of whom have or can gain the trust of the wayward. Such relationships capture the essential element of the primary group. The Area Project effort has been to discover an effective pattern through which the good offices of these persons may be used by teachers, police, social workers, and court officials to formulate and execute for the supervision of delinquent children jointly conceived plans designed to meet the specific problems and needs of the person. In this exploration the Area Project has found that there are natural primary relationships with delinquents which may be used effectively for delinquency prevention and that they are best utilized in collaboration with the agencies having formal responsibility for the welfare of the children and the protection of the community.

CONCLUDING OBSERVATIONS

In all probability these achievements have reduced delinquency in the program areas, as any substantial improvement in the social climate of a community must. However, the extent of the reduction is not subject to precise measurement. The effects of improvement in the environment of children are diffuse, cumulative, and intertwined with trends and forces which have their origin outside of programs of this character. In the final analysis, therefore, the Area Project program must rest its case on logical and analytic grounds.

No assessment of this program can be complete without defining its historically unique character. The genius of its founder, Clifford Shaw, lay in his sharp perception of delinquency as human behavior and in his sense of the naturalness or inevitability of violative activity in the youngster who, whether singly or in groups, is neglected, despised, or ignored as a person. This is the spirit which has animated the Area Project program and which has made it distinctive among delinquency prevention programs. This image of the delinquent and this notion of the delinquency-making process have led to the program's insistence on centering the operation within the milieu directly productive of delinquency, upon drawing into the operation as many as possible of the persons involved in the basic socializing experiences of youngsters, and upon dealing with delinquents or incipient delinquents as persons worthy of consideration and respect.

Not uncommonly, programs of prevention, whatever their initial intention or resolve, understandably tend to move away from direct contact with the delinquent and his milieu. Distance is achieved by interposing institutional forms between workers and delinquents as in programs of formal and official treatment, or by dealing with the delinquent as a person arbitrarily abstracted from his social environment, as in programs based on individual therapy. This kind of evolution is comprehensible in the former type of retreat because the delinquent arouses anger and resentment in the law-abiding person, who consequently is hard put to form a sympathetic identification with him. Retreat from the milieu of the delinquent is even more understandable, for nothing would seem more unrewarding than to attempt to put aright the social disorder of the delinquency area.

It may well be that in perspective the Area Project's distinctive contribution to delinquency prevention as a field of practice and technique will be seen in its development of a method designed to keep preventional work focused upon its proper object, the delinquent as a person in his milieu. Central to this method is not only a view of the problem which stubbornly refuses to uncouple the delinquent from the social world which has created him, but a set of procedures which have demonstrated a capacity to draw into the preventional process itself the inhabitants of this world.

Chapter Eleven

Epilogue: Prospects
and Problems
of Applied Sociology

THIS ANTHOLOGY has been designed to acquaint the beginning student with the utility of sociology and the concepts central to it. It closes by examining some aspects broader in scope than any single field of sociology, and too important to be disregarded.

By intention this book has concentrated upon utility, a value dear to the majority of our society. Throughout, the editors have attempted to demonstrate to the student the worth of sociology in a variety of facets of life—in business, in medicine, in religion, in community living. Now we might do well to pause and raise the question of values. We know a good deal about human behavior and shall, through future research, learn a great deal more. What can we do with this knowledge?

In the first article (Selection 48), Dr. Alpert provides us with one answer: we can and we shall use this knowledge. The start has been slow and the course littered with suspicion, fear, and misunderstanding. Social scientists appear to be emerging on a smoother stretch, with growing recognition and encouragement to increase their efforts. The increase in knowledge depends to a great extent, of course, upon the competence of social scientists; but perhaps even to a greater degree it depends on how much our society wants to abandon outmoded folk knowledge and give social scientists the kind of support that physical and biological scientists have had.

With this encouragement, will the social scientist stay on course? What god or gods will he serve? Dr. Rose (Selection 49) suggests that society would do well to integrate the social scientist into the general fold of acceptability. To look upon his research with anything other than respect is folly. The informal controls provided by recognition will serve to ensure that the social scientists will hold a system of values consistent with that of his society.

Finally, should society use social science to formulate new values for itself? Is it sufficient for the social scientist, or any one for that matter, to plead objectivity and hide behind a shield of relative values and social norms? On what basis should policy makers construct their programs? Dr. Bain (Selection 50) may not tell us what we want to hear—indeed, some might consider his views extreme—but his message deserves careful consideration.

48

The Government's Growing Recognition of Social Science

Harry Alpert

If science is to flourish in any nation prerequisites must be met. Among these, two appear vital: (1) an atmosphere of freedom to pursue the truth, reasonably unfettered by immediate financial concerns, with all necessary equipment and other resources the society can provide; and (2) recognition of achievement by the people, often presented through a grateful government. The extent to which these needs of social scientists are beginning to be met is discussed by Dr. Alpert, with examples to document the progress.

"They never had it so good." This vernacular phrase may startle grammarians, but it describes accurately the present position of the social sciences with respect to support and interest by the federal government. As the result of important new developments which have served to consolidate the standing of the social sciences in the federal government, there is every likelihood that the ten years from 1950 to 1960 will be viewed as the "March" decade of the social sciences. March, according to folk weather lore, comes in like a lion and goes out like a lamb. Similarly, the nineteen-fifties may be said to have come in with a roaring antipathy to the social sciences and to be departing with attitudes of positive interest and quiet acceptance.

That it has taken so long for the federal government to develop a *modus vivendi* with the social sciences is quite ironical, for its involvement in social research was written into the United States Constitution. By providing for a decennial census and making this count of the population the basis for representation in Congress, our founding fathers made a social science activity the ultimate basis of political power.[1] In fact, the gathering, analysis, and dissemination of social and economic statistics has continued to be one of the three major ways in which the federal government relates itself to the social sciences. The other two are exploitation and utilization of the findings and

Reprinted from The *Annals* of the American Academy of Political and Social Science, **327** (January 1960), pp. 59–67, by permission of the publisher and the author.

Harry Alpert is Dean of the Graduate School, University of Oregon.

[1] See Don K. Price, *Government and Science* (New York: New York University Press, 1954), p. 5.

results of social research; and direct support of social sciences through the intramural conduct of social science research in the federal government's own research laboratories and units or through contracts and grants for extramural social science studies at colleges and universities, other nonprofit organizations, and business and commercial establishments.

PRE-WORLD WAR II STATUS

Up to World War II, the role of the federal government in the social sciences consisted largely of the first two of these functions, namely, producing mass statistical series and exploiting social science findings produced outside of the government. During the nineteenth century, the social sciences played a modest but effective role in the development of government powers and programs. Don K. Price has called attention to the contribution of economic and statistical series in the growing development of the regulation of business, as well as to the impact of John R. Commons' institutional economics on labor legislation and of Charles Francis Adams' studies on the regulation of railroads.[2]

Even as late as 1940, the government's direct activities in the social sciences were still predominantly confined to the collection and analysis of statistical information.[3] However, the roots of later developments in the government's social science programs were discernible in the 1920's. The appointment by President Hoover of a research committee on recent social trends provided significant White House endorsement of a major social science enterprise. Further impetus for governmental support of the social sciences came in the thirties from the practical programs of the New Deal. An outstanding example was the Department of Agriculture's Division of Program Surveys which assumed the leadership in introducing the sample interview survey as a basic social science tool and as an instrument of governmental policy.

IMPACT OF WORLD WAR II

But the defense mobilization period and World War II itself were undoubtedly the major catalytic events leading to the expansion of the federal government's programs of social science research. The events of the war on both the military and civilian fronts and the problems of postwar adjustment as they affected the nation and the individual provided the social sciences with dramatic opportunities to demonstrate their practical value and essential role in modern society. A brief review of illustrative uses of social science during World War II lists eight examples of problem areas in which important social

---

[2] *Ibid.*, pp. 11–12.

[3] The several paragraphs which follow are adapted from the author's chapter on "The Growth of Social Research in the United States" in Daniel Lerner (ed.), *The Human Meaning of the Social Sciences* (New York: Meridian Books, 1959), pp. 73–86.

science research accomplishments were achieved: soldier orientation and morale; analysis of command problems, particularly among Negro troops; more efficient use of psychiatry; venereal disease control; analysis of the American soldier's problems of adjustment, combat performance, and response to mass communications; evaluation of Japanese morale; estimation of war production requirements; and regulation of prices and rationing.[4] To this list may be added the media analysis activities of the Office of War Information and the Foreign Broadcast Intelligence Service; the propaganda studies of the Library of Congress, Department of Justice, and various intelligence agencies; the surveys of war bond purchases and other evaluations of the effectiveness of drives; the testing of the public comprehension of governmental information materials; and research on national character and other problems related to a better understanding of the behavioral characteristics of foreign peoples.

POSTWAR DIFFICULTIES

The immediate postwar period of demobilization witnessed the dismantling and disappearance of many of these wartime programs. Dissatisfaction with the limited accomplishments of some of these social science activities was expressed, largely as the result of the disillusionment which set in when excessive promises of achievement were unfulfilled. Social scientists became their own worst enemies by promising too much, too fast, and accepting funds in excess of what could be effectively expended. Moreover, the social sciences have suffered from their minority group status among the scientific disciplines. Like minority groups on the labor market, they are subject to the rule of "last hired, first fired." Thus, many social science programs were speedily demobilized because of their relatively low priority and because of a failure to appreciate their long-range implications and future contributions.

Nevertheless, significant efforts were made to continue programs which had demonstrated their effectiveness during the war. The Office of Naval Research, created shortly after World War II, supported research on manpower problems, personnel and training, group morale, organizational structure, and related social psychological areas. The Army continued, in abbreviated form, its studies of opinions and attitudes of American soldiers. The new Department of the Air Force, proud of the accomplishments of the Aviation Psychology Program, organized units to undertake and support research in problems of selection and training, manpower, leadership, human relations and morale, and psychological warfare. When the Research and Development Board was established in the Department of Defense it included a Committee on Human Resources.

However, the skepticism and disenchantment which many of these pro-

---

[4] Russell Sage Foundation, *Effective Use of Social Science Research in the Federal Services* (New York: Russell Sage Foundation, 1950).

grams engendered did not provide a favorable environment for their persistent growth and development. There set in, consequently, a period of recurring ups and downs, of "acute, and sometimes critical fluctuations," as Leonard S. Cottrell, Jr. has described it.[5] A "starts and fits" pattern became evident: an activity got started and then was curtailed or discontinued when some congressman or general threw a fit. The Division of Research of the Housing and Home Finance Agency, the excellent survey research unit of the Veterans Administration, the Air Force's Human Resources Research Institute at Maxwell Field and its Personnel and Training Center at Lackland Air Force Base were but a few of the research units which experienced difficulty.

Despite the "on again, off again" character of some of these programs, the long term trend was toward increasing appreciation of the social sciences as valuable national assets. As the postwar pattern of extramural support developed, the social sciences, too, received encouragement, although not at the same rate and magnitude as the physical and life sciences.

THE "MARCH" DECADE

The "March" decade, 1950–60, will perhaps be viewed historically as the turning point in federal government recognition of the social sciences. The full measure of the change from the "lion" to the "lamb" phase of this decade may be observed in comparing the National Science Foundation Act of 1950 with the National Defense Education Act of 1958. In the former legislation, the social sciences are included only on a permissive basis and are referred to only as "other sciences." In the 1958 act, the section dealing with graduate fellowships mentions no limitations whatsoever with respect to disciplines. Moreover, a separate title provides for research and experimentation in more effective utilization of television, radio, motion pictures, and related media for educational purposes. This act also recognizes the importance of improving statistical series in the field of education.

Note must be taken, also, of other evidences of changing attitudes toward the social sciences, such as the establishment, in December 1958, of an Office of Social Sciences within the National Science Foundation; the appointment, in the spring of 1959, of a sociologist, President Logan Wilson of the University of Texas,[6] as a member of the National Science Board; and the expansion of the social science research activities of the Department of Health, Education, and Welfare.

In the vernacular of the boxing ring, it may be said that the social sciences were, for several years, definitely "rocky and punch drunk," but were still on their feet when the fight was over. They have survived Cox Committee and

---

[5] Leonard S. Cottrell, Jr., in Foreword to Morris Janowitz, *Sociology and the Military Establishment* (New York: Russell Sage Foundation, 1959), p. 5.

[6] Dr. Wilson was subsequently required by Texas law to give up his membership on the National Science Board.

Reese Committee investigations. They have endured pariah status and innumerable reorganizations. They have weathered appropriation storms which threatened to cut off funds for studies of child-rearing practices, mother-love among lambs, population dynamics, message diffusion, and other projects which became the pet peeves of individual legislators.

MAJOR DYNAMIC FACTORS

In attempting to assess the major factors that account for the more favorable position in which the social sciences find themselves at the end of this decade, I am able to identify five important considerations: (1) changing congressional attitudes; (2) acceptance of the social sciences at the White House level; (3) inclusion of the social sciences as part of broad umbrella definitions of scientific disciplines; (4) the general post-Sputnik interest in American education; and (5) the concern with redressing the imbalances in education which stemmed from the earlier almost exclusive emphasis on natural science and mathematics. Brief comments on each of these five factors follow.

CHANGING CONGRESSIONAL ATTITUDES

In his report on the crucial Senate debate in 1946 which preceded the vote to exclude from the then pending bill to establish a National Science Foundation the specific provision which created a Division of Social Sciences, George A. Lundberg concluded that the Senate thought of the social sciences as at best "a propagandist, reformist, evangelical sort of cult." [7] The unfortunate phonetic confusion of social science with socialism reinforced such viewpoints. Just a few years later, however, more positive attitudes were being expressed. In 1953, the Cox Committee, in its "Final Report," noted the special importance of the social sciences in the contemporary world. It stated:

It is entirely possible that in a time when man's mastery over the physical sciences threatens him with possible extermination the eventual reward from the pursuit of the social sciences may prove even more important than the accomplishments in the physical sciences.[8]

Other important turning points in congressional expressions toward the social sciences were the vigorous statements by Senator Estes Kefauver's Subcommittee on Juvenile Delinquency in 1955, 1956, and 1957; the 1955 recommendations of Representative Richard Bolling's Subcommittee on Economic Statistics of the Joint Committee on the Economic Report; Senator Hubert Humphrey's report to the Senate in 1957 of his experiences in the Middle

---

[7] "The Senate Ponders Social Science," *The Scientific Monthly,* **64,** 5 (May 1947), p. 399.

[8] "Final Report" of the Select Committee to Investigate Foundations and Other Organizations, 82nd Congress, 2nd Session, House Report No. 2514, Union Calendar No. 801 (Washington, D.C.: U.S. Government Printing Office, January 1, 1953), pp. 9–10.

East; and speeches by Senator Wayne Morse, Representative Charles O. Porter and others.[9] This year neither house of Congress raised any objections to the National Science Foundation's request for $2,000,000 for support of basic research in the social sciences in fiscal year 1960, even though this represented a considerable increase over the $850,000 appropriated for this purpose for fiscal year 1959. (The actual budgetary allowance for social science research in the National Science Foundation for fiscal year 1960 is $1,600,-000.)

This is an encouraging picture, indeed. But congressional confusion regarding social science has by no means been completely eliminated. Negative attitudes still persist and need to be reckoned with.[10]

WHITE HOUSE INTEREST

The White House, too, has shown increasing interest in the support of the social sciences. In his State of the Union message delivered on January 9, 1959, President Eisenhower expressed his desire to undertake a systematic study of American values, goals, and social trends, comparable to the earlier Hoover Committee study.

The objective, President Eisenhower said, would be "the establishment of national goals that would not only spur us on to our finest efforts but would meet the stern test of practicality." He hoped that this new study would be concerned, among other things, "with the acceleration of our economy's growth and the living standards of our people, their health and education, their better assurance of life and liberty and their greater opportunities." He noted that the report of Hoover's Recent Social Trends Committee "has stood the test of time and has had a beneficial influence on national development." Here, indeed, is a significant compliment to social science.

An in its report on "Strengthening American Science," issued December 27, 1958, the President's Science Advisory Committee included social psychology among the scientific disciplines for which a strong case could be made for intensifying the nation's scientific effort. The Committee stated, "And advances in social psychology might help to reduce tension and conflict at every level of human intercourse—in our communities, in business and industry, in Government, and even among nations." [11] Furthermore, as previously noted, President Eisenhower has appointed a social scientist to the National

---

[9] For details and references, see Harry Alpert, "Congressmen, Social Scientists, and Attitudes Toward Federal Support of Social Science Research," *American Sociological Review*, 23, 6 (December 1958), pp. 682–686.

[10] See, for example, *Independent Offices Appropriations For 1960*. Hearings Before the Subcommittee of the Committee on Appropriations, House of Representatives, 86th Congress, 1st Session (Washington, D.C.: U.S. Government Printing Office, 1959), p. 527. For a discussion of persisting negative attitudes, see Harry Alpert, *op. cit.*

[11] *Strengthening American Science:* A Report of the President's Science Advisory Committee (Washington, D.C.: U.S. Government Printing Office, 1958), p. 4.

Science Board. This policy-determining body for government science on January 23, 1959, adopted the following statement:

The National Science Board recognized the importance, as well as the complexity and difficulty, of research in the social sciences. It is clear that the intellectual, economic, and social strength of our Nation requires a vigorous approach to social problems, with scientific techniques of study making their maximum contribution.[12]

PROTECTIVE UMBRELLAS

The social sciences have prospered best in the federal government where they have been included under broad umbrella classifications of the scientific disciplines such as agricultural sciences, military sciences, medical sciences, and health sciences. Under such umbrellas and in close company with scientific areas which enjoy the prestige and status of biological or physical sciences, the social sciences have enjoyed a protection and nourishment which they normally do not have when they are identified as such and stand exposed, "naked and alone."

Agricultural research has been heavily supported by the federal government from its very inception. Quite early the concept of agricultural sciences was broadened to include not only biological research but agricultural economics and rural sociology as well. In fact, for many years the Department of Agriculture's Bureau of Agricultural Economics was internationally famous for its leadership in significant areas of social and economic research. Although from time to time specific social science projects of the Department of Agriculture have suffered congressional attack, there has been little question of the legitimacy of the inclusion of social research in the scientific program of the Department. In fact, one appropriation committee, with remarkable indifference to the distinction between biological and social science research, once included, in a list of fields for which research funds were not to be expended, the orchids of Guatemala, the flora of Dominica, child-rearing practices, research methodology, and population dynamics.

The Medical Sciences and Health Sciences rubrics have also provided generous hospitality to the social sciences. Social science research projects are given careful and sympathetic consideration by at least five study sections of the National Institutes of Health: Behavioral Sciences, Hospital Facilities Research, Mental Health, Nursing Research, and Public Health Research. Social scientists serve as members of these study sections as well as on several other committees of the National Institutes of Health. The National Institute of Mental Health's Laboratory of Socio-Environmental Studies is outstanding in the quality of its research program.

Research undertaken by the military establishment in relation to the defense

---

[12] Reproduced in *Congressional Record* by Representative Charles O. Porter, March 10, 1959, pp. A 1969–70.

needs of the nation develops strong immunities to congressional or other attacks if military authorities certify its importance to the mission of the Department of Defense. Despite the ups and downs previously referred to, the Army, Navy, and Air Force have arrived at a realization of the importance of basic research in the social sciences. The Office of Naval Research includes a Psychological Sciences Division. The Air Force has established a Behavioral Sciences Program in its Office of Scientific Research. And here is the testimony of an Army General presented recently before an appropriations committee:

> We can never afford to neglect basic research and the Army wants to do more of it whenever we find applicable projects to further this increase of scientific knowledge. Such research is not confined to the physical sciences. Investigation of the social sciences to help us to utilize more effectively our manpower and insure man-machine compatibility with complex engines of war being developed is vital. Should we neglect these important considerations we only aggravate the trend in which the physical sciences are outstripping the social sciences and may, in time, reach a point where the machine may destroy its maker.[13]

These are the words of Lieutenant-General Arthur G. Trudeau, Chief of Research and Development, Department of the Army.

Another important umbrella for the social sciences is Operations Research. The various operations research units supported by the federal government have invariably included a social science component.

IMPACT OF SPUTNIKS

The social sciences have not been indifferent to the whir of the Russian Sputniks and have directly felt the impact of these successes in space technology. It was recognized that Soviet Russia's accomplishment was not only the result of advances in science and engineering but also the consequence of a social system that was capable of making and carrying out significant decisions. Interest developed in studies of the social, economic, and political implications of the space age. It became imperative that we keep ahead of the Russians in the social science fields. For this reason, Vice-President Richard M. Nixon encouraged the formation of a committee on National Support for Behavioral Science which reported on social science needs to the President's Scientific Advisory Committee. Substantially increased appropriations were made available to the National Science Foundation, and in the National Defense Education Act of 1958, Congress officially declared as national policy the doctrine that the defense of this nation depends upon the mastery of modern techniques developed from complex scientific principles, and, as well,

---

[13] *Department of Defense Appropriations for 1960.* Hearings Before the Subcommittee on Appropriations, House of Representatives, 86th Congress, 1st Session (Washington, D.C.: U.S. Government Printing Office, 1959), p. 339.

upon "the discovery and development of new principles, new techniques, and new knowledge." [14]

REDRESSING IMBALANCES

For a time, it looked as if only the natural sciences and mathematics would be the beneficiaries of the increased responsibilities of the federal government toward research and education. Programs were quickly organized to improve the quality of science teaching, to train more scientists and engineers, and to intensify the pace of research in the physical, mathematical, and biological sciences. It became evident, however, that the neglect of other areas of scholarship and learning would spell national disaster. The government's difficulties in international relations led to intensified interest in language study. Soon voices were heard calling attention to the need to redress the imbalances in American education which a predominant concern with the natural sciences and engineering was creating.[15] Cognizance of this requirement is found in the newly released report of the President's Science Advisory Committee on "Education for the Age of Science." This report stresses the fact that, "Today in America we need a very wide variety of human talents." [16] It goes on to urge that "a proper balance be maintained in our educational offerings." [17] To achieve such a balance we must encourage intellectual leadership in the humanities and social sciences as well as in the natural sciences and mathematics.

HEALTHY PROGNOSIS

The social sciences thus face the nineteen-sixties in an atmosphere of encouragement and with the active support of influential well-wishers. Research funds are becoming more plentiful. The federal government alone will soon be spending in the neighborhood of $60,000,000 a year in support of the social sciences. This estimate does not include the $100,000,000 or so that the Decennial Census of 1960 will cost.

MORE FELLOWSHIPS NEEDED

A major problem, however, remains. The most urgent need of the social sciences is expansion of the pool of available trained, specialized manpower. Recent studies have indicated that the length of time required to obtain the

---

[14] Public Law 85–864, Section 101.

[15] See, for example, statements by Pendleton Herring and Harry Alpert, *The Saturday Review*, **41**, 5 (February 1, 1958).

[16] "Education for the Age of Science." *President's Science Advisory Committee* (May 24, 1959), p. 3.

[17] *Ibid.*, p. 6.

Ph.D. degree is strongly influenced by the availability of financial support to graduate students in the form of assistantships and fellowships. It is here that the social sciences, and humanities, too, are most seriously disadvantaged vis-à-vis the natural sciences. The major bottleneck in the advancement of the social sciences is not research funds, but fellowship and scholarship opportunities for basic and advanced training. If the social sciences are to fulfill the general public's expectations of them, they must double, at least, the number of trained practitioners. To make the training process more productive and more effective, however, additional fellowships and other types of financial support for training are an imperious and critical necessity. Title IV of the National Defense Education Act has been extremely helpful in this regard. Almost a fourth (23 per cent) of the first 1,000 graduate fellowships were awarded in the social sciences. The various training programs of the National Institutes of Health also provide valuable opportunities for social science education. But more needs to be done. The National Science Foundation, for example, has the basic legislation to include the social sciences within its "Education in the Sciences" program. It also has reasonably adequate funds for training and education. It has broadened its conception of the social sciences in its research support program. Only administrative nearsightedness prevents it from giving the social sciences, broadly conceived, their deserved place within the various program activities of its Division of Scientific Personnel and Education.

COMPLACENCY TO BE AVOIDED

We can be proud of the achievements of the social sciences in government, but we cannot afford to be complacent. Certain past mistakes must be avoided: premature promises, excessive expectations, hasty growth, disastrous indifference to the political process, unwarranted impatience with the administrative processes of justification and review, and lack of concern with the public image of the social sciences. By careful planning and effective operations a solid basis can be established for future growth.

Advance in the social sciences will depend most immediately on what in fact social scientists do: how well they teach at the undergraduate level, how well they communicate with the general public, how effectively they respond to calls from industry and government for help in resolving practical problems, and how much they devote to fundamental research. It depends also on their willingness to cultivate patience and humility.[18] Charles Dollard has well defined the problem: "The long-term contract of the social scientist with society is not to perform miracles but to bring to the study of man and his problems the

---

[18] See *The Saturday Review*, **41**, 5 (February 1, 1958), p. 38 and *The Saturday Review*, **42**, 14 (April 4, 1959), p. 64.

same objectivity and the same passion for truth which have in the past given us some understanding and control of the physical world." [19]

[19] "Strategy for Advancing the Social Sciences," in Social Science Research Center of the Graduate School, University of Minnesota, *The Social Sciences at Mid-Century* (Minneapolis: University of Minnesota Press, 1952), pp. 19–20.

49

The Social Responsibility of the Social Scientist

Arnold M. Rose

Knowledge is power. How will this power be used? Although many scientists consider pure and applied research sufficiently separated so that no overlap exists, recent events (for example, the social consequences following from the harnessing of atomic energy) demand that this position be questioned. Does the increasing knowledge in the social sciences mean little more than refinements in the ways we are to be manipulated? In this article Dr. Rose examines the consequences of social research and the ends to which its results are applied.

The increase of knowledge about the control of the physical world has raised in the minds of informed citizens the question as to whether society will be able to control this knowledge. The problem has demanded a more immediate solution with the invention of the atomic bomb. The question used to be raised as to how we can prevent the machine from enslaving man; the one now more frequently raised is how we can prevent atomic energy from destroying man and his civilization. How can our society gain the wisdom, the good will, and the commonness of purpose to control this and other inventions?

For many social scientists the question has become one of discovering enough about society so that society can, if it wishes to use this knowledge, control the use of physical knowledge. Hornell Hart, for example, poses the problem in these words:

Reprinted from *Social Problems,* **1,** 3 (January 1954), pp. 85–90, by permission of the publishers and the author.
Arnold M. Rose is Professor of Sociology, University of Minnesota.

the fact of technological acceleration means that the problems of the future will keep on compounding and expanding until they wreck our world, or until organized intelligence applies science effectively to mastering the social problems which technological acceleration creates.[1]

The social scientist usually stops here, and does not inquire further. He seldom raises the logically next question: once the social scientists gain the social knowledge which can be used to control physical knowledge and to control society, how will this social knowledge be controlled? What is to prevent a social scientist from using social knowledge to expedite the enslavement or destruction of society? What is to prevent the social scientist from selling or giving his knowledge to one group in society for the purpose of controlling another group? Of course, many social scientists feel that these questions are a little premature. After all, they say, the knowledge we produce is so trivial that it is no possible threat to society in the way that knowledge produced by physical scientists is. But the belief that social science knowledge has not yet developed to a point where it influences society is not correct, and the attitude that social scientists should not be concerned with their own influence on society is not consistent with their frequently expressed concern about developing social science knowledge that will aid in controlling physical science knowledge. If we are striving toward the control of physical science knowledge, should we not also consider the control of the potential social knowledge that is to control the physical knowledge?

There are many evidences that we are acquiring some potentially dangerous social knowledge, that we are developing social "atomic energy," to speak figuratively. For example, we have witnessed the power of propaganda and other "mass persuasion" and mob-incitement techniques to control people, destroy political enemies, and seize power. Even though Hitler may have derived his knowledge largely from brilliant intuition, social scientists can analyze the patterns of his successes and failures, and from them draw conclusions as to how masses of people can be incited and controlled in the future. There have been books on the "governing of men," "mass persuasion," and on a wide range of techniques of psychological warfare, stating a number of tested principles for controlling the minds of men.[2]

We can eliminate some value judgments from the conclusion by saying in a factual way that knowledge about society can be used by one group to enhance its power at the expense of another group. Expressed thus, we are simply restating the old truism that knowledge is power. In the case of the social scientists' knowledge, it is political and economic power with which we are

[1] Hornell Hart, "Technological Acceleration and the Atomic Bomb," *American Sociological Review*, **11** (June 1946), p. 291.

[2] For example: Alexander Leighton, *The Governing of Men* (Princeton, N.J.: Princeton University Press, 1945); Paul M. A. Linebarger, *Psychological Warfare* (Washington, D.C.: Infantry Journal Press, 1948); Robert K. Merton, *Mass Persuasion* (New York: Harper, 1946); Dorwin Cartwright, "Some Principles of Mass Persuasion," *Human Relations*, **2** (1949), pp. 197–292.

concerned. Wirth has stated the proposition in even more general terms: "Every assertion of a 'fact' about the social world touches the interests of some individual or group." [3]

Some questions are in order as to what kinds of persons these social scientists are who are acquiring this knowledge and potential power. Are they the sort of persons who will use their knowledge for their own gain or the gain of a minority within society whom they happen to favor? The answer to this question involves a systematic study of the social backgrounds, the personality traits, and the attitudes of the social scientists. Until such a study is made, we cannot begin to answer the fundamental question about what the social scientists will do with their knowledge. We can, however, give a partial answer to an allied question: Are there any tendencies observable among social scientists which might lead them to use their knowledge for ends dangerous to society as a whole or to large segments of society? Even a hasty examination of the processes by which social scientists get trained and do their research would lead one to answer tentatively in the affirmative.

In the first place, social scientists have a not-too-far-from-average number of human frailties and there are none but the ordinary controls prevalent in our society to prevent a social scientist's frailties from directing his knowledge toward ends dangerous to society. For instance, he may be selfish and callous of others. Such an attitude may have been stimulated by the shortage of opportunities available to satisfy his aspirations, especially during the war boom.

Few would deny that some American social scientists have been "bought" when the purchase has been made under certain rules of "good taste." An economic depression which accentuates the competition among social scientists, or an increase in the monetary or prestige rewards to be striven for, could demoralize a significant proportion of social scientists.

A second fact to be noted is the low prestige of the social sciences and the consequent frustration of the social scientist. Intellectuals generally have never had as high prestige in the United States as they enjoy in most European countries, and education derived from being the most important determinant of social status. Social scientists have a lower status than do physical and biological scientists, not only in the minds of the general public but frequently in their own minds as well. Many social scientists feel inferior to natural scientists in the possession of specialized knowledge and in the possession of techniques for acquiring new knowledge. The press campaign to discredit social scientists during the New Deal era, which was part of a larger political campaign, did not increase the self-respect of the social scientists. They do not hold their discipline in the highest esteem, and that results in a sense of personal insecurity for many of them. Outward evidences of this are seen in

---

[3] Louis Wirth, Preface to Karl Mannheim, *Ideology and Utopia* (New York: Harcourt, 1936), p. xvii.

movements within the disciplines of psychology and sociology to ape the techniques of the physical sciences, even at the sacrifice of some of the subject matter of their own disciplines. It is seen even more sharply in the number of social scientists who escape academic life for business or government work when the opportunity offers itself. These people are not so devoted to the pursuit of knowledge as they claimed to be. The statement of this fact should not be taken as an accusation, or an attempt to fix blame, but as an evidence of the relatively low prestige of the academic pursuit in the social sciences.

The implication of these remarks is that social scientists experience enough frustration in the pursuit of social knowledge so that they might be willing to to offer their services to anybody who could pay a high price for them. There is a deep desire in every social scientist to tell the world "I told you so" after all the questioning gibes about the value and significance of his work.

Even if the social scientist never sells his knowledge for personal profit or prestige, he has some tendencies which will allow him to give it away without regard to whom he gives it. Some social scientists believe that knowledge has no relation to social action, that conscious ideas and the possession of factual information cannot effect social change. We cannot debate this issue here, but suffice it to say that *if* social scientists believe there is a lag between the invention of material objects and the invention of social wisdom to control these material objects, there is logically implied in this contention the belief that social knowledge can be used to change the course of society. However, if social scientists believe that their knowledge can have no social influence, they are likely to give away their knowledge without much concern as to where it is going.

It would be a mistake to give the impression that scientists have been completely unaware of the dangers they create for society. The natural scientists never had to worry too much prior to 1940 about the possibly harmful social effects of their discoveries, as the overwhelming proportion of their discoveries seemed to increase the health, standard of living, and opportunities of people. Of course, the broader social implications of certain discoveries were ignored—such as whether the creation of leisure time due to productive efficiency was really conducive to happiness—because there was unconscious acceptance of the notion that "progress" would eliminate these "cultural lags." When the few discoveries were made that seemed to have direct potentialities for human harm, the natural scientists were usually upset. For example Alfred Nobel, the inventor of dynamite, set up the Nobel peace prize. David Lilienthal, head of the Atomic Energy Commission, wrote:

it is by no manner of means inevitable that scientific research and technology will work for good. It is equally possible that they may yield a harvest of bitter fruit. When those speak who imply that our problem is only one of securing more and more funds for more and more scientific workers in private or public research, we need constantly to remind ourselves that, in terms of human happiness and freedom, such a conclusion is far from true. Unless research and technology are consciously related to a central purpose of human welfare, unless research is defined and directed by those who believe in and who have faith in people and in democratic ends and means, it may well be that the more money we spend on research the further we miss the mark. It is like trying to reach your destination in an automobile that is going in the wrong direction; the faster you drive the farther away from your goal you will be.[4]

This writer would guess that most physical scientists were shocked when, after the invention of the atomic bomb, several social scientists and philosophers claimed that science is amoral. Many physical scientists began to urge social scientists to develop social means of control over atomic energy, and they asked us for effective techniques of communicating to the public some of the dangerous implications of the recent discoveries. They set up organizations to disseminate information on the potential social influence of the discovery of how to tap atomic energy. Some social scientists have also expressed awareness of the possible harmful social implications of social science knowledge.

Another socially dangerous tendency is for educated people, generally, to identify themselves with the upper classes and to separate themselves from the poorly educated. The snobbery of family background in Europe is almost matched by the snobbery of education in America. A certain amount of separation, based on differences of interest, is natural. The problem is that the division is so complete that educated people, while retaining their respect for wealth, lose their respect for the more common values. The isolation is physical as well as social, since the universities, their faculties, students, and hangers-on frequently form distinct communities. It would be no more desirable for social scientists to identify with the lower classes than with the upper classes. What is desirable for scientific purposes is to have the "free-floating" objectivity that Karl Mannheim spoke of and to have contact with all sectors of society. Also, some social scientists allow their attitudes from their role as scientists to be carried over into their role as citizens. They believe they are exempt from social responsibilities, and they have the tendency of educated persons generally to regard themselves as superior to the common herd. When social knowledge is discovered that can control the majority of the people, it can become dangerous to that majority because of these attitudes of the holders of the social knowledge.

There is possibly also less use of rigorous procedure and less certainty of the reliability and validity of conclusions in the social sciences than in the natural sciences. The criteria of scientific method are much clearer, and the tests for reliability and validity much simpler in the natural sciences than in the social sciences, and therefore it is much easier to be rigorous and unswerving in the former fields. A survey of replicated studies in the social sciences shows a high proportion that fail to reach the same conclusion as

---

[4] David E. Lilienthal, "Research Has a Moral Responsibility," *The Christian Century*, **62** (July 4, 1945), pp. 786–787.

the original study.[5] Social scientists may thus be aware that sometimes they are merely satisfying a propagandist's need rather than producing valid knowledge.

To the extent that the above statements are true, and admittedly they require further evidence before they can be regarded as of high validity, certain actions are incumbent upon social scientists if they are not to be dangerous to our society. One approach is to demand that social scientists engage only in "pure science," as opposed to "applied science," and it is likely that one reason for the popularity of this demand is a deep-seated but inhibited concern about the social responsibility of the social scientist. Some of those who are engaged in the most utilitarian of studies, for business or government, are perhaps for that reason those who cry the loudest for "basic research" and "pure science." The points made in this paper however, indicate that "pure science" and a profession which aims at "pure science" cannot avoid having some kind of social influence. Knowledge is power, and if we— as social scientists—wish to avoid the misuse of the power we produce, we shall be obliged to take certain more positive steps. I cannot presume to offer a solution, as the problem is too difficult, and too little thought has thus far been concentrated on it.

In general, my suggestions would follow the sociological principle that the way to increase informal social control over an individual is to increase his integration into the society, develop his sense of social responsibility toward the society, and to give the society a greater understanding of his activities. The individual in this case is the social scientist, and it is deemed necessary to increase informal social controls over him because he is on the verge of discovering knowledge that could lead to a redistribution of power relations in the society. If the latter happens, society as a whole or some sector of society will be hurt, or society may check the redistribution of power in time and clamp down formal social controls over the social scientist. Any of these prospects is dangerous to democratic society and to science. While science formerly thrived under monarchies, even absolute ones (possibly because the rulers were not concerned with science), the evidence from modern *totalitarian* dictatorships is that they distort science even as they exploit it.[6] Solutions must be sought in the direction of increasing the chances that the social scientist's activities are an asset to democratic society. Social scientists, either

---

[5] Arnold M. Rose, "Generalizations in the Social Sciences," *American Journal of Sociology*, 59 (July 1953), pp. 49–58.

[6] Two studies of how Hitler's government turned scientists into propagandists and distorted science itself are (1) Max Weinreich, *Hitler's Professors* (New York: Yiddish Scientific Institute, 1946) and (2) H. L. Ansbacher, "Testing Management and Reactions of Foreign Workers in Germany During World War II," *American Psychologist*, 5 (1950), pp. 38–49. Similar reports for the Soviet Union are the following: (1) Stuart A. Rice, "Methodology Conference of the Central Statistical Administration, USSR," *The Scientific Monthly*, 75 (August 1952), pp. 71–78; (2) E. Ashby, "Marxism Versus Science," *New York Times Magazine* (January 6, 1952), p. 12 ff.; (3) Evsey D. Domar, "The Varga Controversy," *American Economic Review*, 40 (1950), pp. 132–151.

as individuals or as a group, are by no means in complete control of the situation, because knowledge produced for "its own sake" or for "good" purpose may be perverted to other purposes. But social scientists can make use of those degrees of freedom that the larger society permits.

50

Natural Science and Value Policy

Read Bain

The probability that sociology is not yet sufficiently developed to be generally used in policy making is one factor Dr. Bain does not emphasize. But surely his statement about our nation's social thinking—"It is in what Comte called the 'metaphysical stage.' Much of it is still crudely theological and mythic"—bears thoughtful consideration.

No final statement can be made regarding the relations between science and policy-making. Knowledge, values, and techniques are interrelated, cumulative, and constantly changing. They are derived from man's responses to the complicated interactions between physical, biological, and cultural phenomena. Final answers are impossible because the answers themselves are part of the world and therefore are factors in changing it. We see through a glass darkly, whether it be the giant glass of Palomar or the eyepiece of the electron microscope.

The more we learn, the more we realize how little we know. We shall learn more and more, but it is unlikely we ever shall be able to answer all logically legitimate questions. New phenomena (things and relations) constantly are coming into existence. Some of these eventually will be known; perhaps most of them will not. Man must run fast to keep abreast of change.

Reprinted from *Philosophy of Science*, **16,** 3 (July 1949), pp. 182–192, by permission of the publisher and the author.

Read Bain is Emeritus Professor of Sociology, Miami University, Oxford, Ohio.

Dr. Bain's acknowledgments for this article are as follows: "I am indebted to the following friendly critics: Robert Bierstedt, sociology and philosophy, University of Illinois; Fred Cottrell, sociology and government, Miami University (Oxford, Ohio); David French, anthropology, Edwin Garlan, philosophy, and Frank Munk, political science, all of Reed College (Portland, Oregon); Oscar Winter, history, Indiana University. The comments of Mr. Bierstedt and Mr. Garlan were especially helpful to me."

Man, the knower and predictor, is a creature of change in a changing world. He appears to be an increasingly effective agent of change but it is difficult to foresee how man-made changes may affect a long-run human welfare. Man's life is precarious and problematic, as John Dewey is so fond of saying. This is true, whether man be defined as a person or a species.

Sound policy may be defined as the attempt to minimize those factors in experience which are, or are thought to be, adverse to long-run human welfare. Since science and its applications make man an increasingly powerful agent of change, it seems reasonable to consider the possibility of using science both in the formulation and implementation of sound policy. The physical and biological sciences are mainly concerned with devising effective means to achieve chosen ends. Many people believe the most useful application of science to policy-making will come from the development of the social sciences along the same general line that has characterized the biophysical sciences. The social sciences are becoming increasingly useful as means to ends, but they also have the possibility of being used in the definition of ends. Needless to say, in this general task, the normative sciences such as ethics, esthetics, and social philosophy, will become increasingly important as they orient themselves more closely to the methods and findings of the natural sciences, in which, of course, I include the social sciences.

The findings of the natural sciences, and especially the thoughtways that have produced them, compel the conclusion that man's behavior and the universe in which he acts are unpredictable in any final and absolute sense. All the events in the universe, among which man's responses must be included, are essentially unique and unrepeatable. Man, the predictor, is changing constantly. So are all the experienced phenomena he attempts to describe and predict. The apparent permanence and identity of sensory experiences, even when aided by instruments, are really transient and different.

What one "sees" is a blotch of something that is conceptualized into an entity called "blue." When the generalized abstraction appears to be immediately observable, or to be abstracted from immediate sense experience, F. S. C. Northrop calls it a "concept by intuition." This is the "blue" of commonsense. The blue of the physicist, on the other hand, is number on a frequency scale of light waves or quanta. We never "see" the vibrations, the waves, or the quanta. We infer them. This he calls a "concept by postulation."

This may be a useful dichotomy of concepts but it seems to me that all concepts are based upon concepts by postulation. Among these are the primitive ideas that something is "there" to be perceived and that communication of what is perceived is possible. In short, all concepts of being and knowing are really radical concepts by postulation. What Northrop calls "concepts by intuition" are merely those which take for granted the implicit concepts by postulation. Concepts by intuition lead to the naive belief that we know the *real* world directly through immediate sensory contact with it. The findings of modern science certainly make such a conclusion untenable. We are forced to the conclusion that all knowledge is dependent upon "taken" rather than "given" frames of reference, as John Dewey has been insisting for over a half a century. Hume's analysis seems to make this conclusion necessary. Modern science seems to confirm it. The "quest for certainty" thus appears paradoxical in a world of uncertain flux in which each sense experience is unique and each object that is sensed is equally fluid and impermanent.

A possible, practicable, and perhaps necessary resolution of the apparent paradox is found in the fact that the frames of reference man can "take" or construct are limited by human nature (culture) and biophysical nature, both of which to some unascertained degree are constructs of that class of natural phenomena called "mind." Perhaps the most significant factors in determining "takens" and "takeables" are the concepts of natural science, the technologies derived therefrom, and the ways of thinking and acting which produce science and are modified by it and its applications. These factors probably will become more coercive as science-based culture cumulates and accelerates, which in turn will diminish the role of supernatural and other fantasy-based concepts.

Experience shows that some predictive generalizations can be formulated which have great usefulness within designated limits of time and space. This is notably true of biophysical science, and to a lesser degree, of social science also. As observational and logical (which includes mathematical) techniques have improved, the limitations on possible frames of reference have become much less restricted than was the case at the end of the nineteenth century. Until the beginning of the present century, man's "mind" was in such bondage to the postulates of supernaturalism and natural law that, with a few notable exceptions, he was not "free" to take the points of view, to make the postulates, which the empirical findings of science and their applications made possible and logically necessary. This condition has largely disappeared so far as biophysical science is concerned. Both the scientists and the public are ready to accept any concept which seems useful for research and "explanation" even though it appears contrary to commonsense and previously accepted scientific theory.

This is much less true in the realm of social thinking. It is still largely in what Comte called the "metaphysical stage." Much of it is still crudely theological and mythic.[1] It is hortatory and epithetic rather than scientific. It believes in the magic of words rather than the logic of empirical facts. In support of this, one need only consider political campaigning, Un-American Committees, advertising, the press, and the radio. Candor also compels the observation that many so-called social scientists aid and abet those who would explain and guide social behavior by means of a set of concepts which antedate and are logically different from those which have emerged with the development of natural science.

As supernatural and natural law concepts of social phenomena lose their

---

[1] Read Bain, "Man, the Myth Maker," *The Scientific Monthly* (July 1947), pp. 61–69.

constrictive power, the constructive power of social scientists and the ability of the public to accept and use social science knowledge will doubtless increase. Greater freedom will be gained to make new postulates and formulate testable theorems. New research techniques and findings will make it possible to construct more powerful concepts by postulation which in turn will react upon empirical research as has been the case in the physical and biological sciences. This is the inevitable result of taking seriously the concept that social phenomena are natural phenomena and are therefore amenable to ordering by the logic and methods which prevail in the other natural sciences.

One should be wary of a priori assertions that any proposed postulate, hypothesis, or frame of reference is useless or unworthy of serious examination. It is wiser to affirm man's most fruitful freedom—the freedom to think, the freedom to push intelligence to its utmost limits, to use the mind as spontaneously, creatively, and courageously as possible. It is certain that most "new ideas" will be false, but many false hypotheses have been useful in extending man's knowledge and control.

The important thing is that nothing should impair the inalienable right to use intelligence to its limit—and thus extend the limit. The major difference between the postulates of animism and the postulates of science is that the former denied, derogated, and restricted the free play of intelligence; the latter honors and encourages it and relies upon it for whatever future man may have. This is particularly pertinent to the problem of science and policy, which is really the question of the relation between means and ends, between scientific description and prediction, and man's desires, goals, and ultimate values.

Most scientists now regard the universe as an equilibrating energy system rather than a fixed and final equilibrium. As a recent writer says, in speaking of the cosmological assumptions underlying Einstein's theories: "The universe is not a rigid and immutable edifice where independent matter is housed in independent space and time; it is on the contrary an amorphous continuum, without any fixed architecture, plastic and variable, constantly subjected to change and distortion. Wherever there is matter and motion, the continuum is disturbed. Just as a fish swimming in the sea agitates the water around it, so a star, a comet, or a galaxy distorts the geometry of the space-time through which it moves." [2]

This is equally true of a man moving down the street, moving a resolution in the United Nations, or moving a hypothesis before a learned society. He may disturb *social* space-time more than he does physical space-time, but he certainly affects both.

It is more accurate to say that man knows about his universe only through his senses (aided by instruments) and whatever logical inferences, whether by

---

[2] Lincoln Barnett, "The Universe and Dr. Einstein," *Harper's Magazine* (June 1948), p. 532.

"intuition" or "postulation," he may draw from his generalizations about sensory experience. One present postulated conclusion is that the world is a series of energy transformations. It is dynamic, not static. Concepts of it are probably no more systematic and well ordered than the events which are observed. The events are essentially unique, but the act of observing them gives them an apparent order and at least a partial and transient stability or fixity.

The foregoing concept of nature tends to eliminate belief in theistic and deistic gods and mechanistic natural laws. It makes man an integral part of a universe which consists of relatively stable, interactive physical, biological, and cultural energy-systems. In such a changing and changeable world, man feels freer to make effective choices and feels more morally responsible for them. He *finds* no purposes in the world; he himself *makes* purposes. He has the frightening and challenging consciousness that his destiny is in his own hands to the degree that he can control natural phenomena and adapt himself to those aspects of nature which he cannot control. He no longer feels that he is the prey or pet of personal or impersonal powers which he can neither control nor to which he can make any effective adaptation. He no longer can regard himself as the crown of creation or the "reason" for the existence of the universe but he can try to understand it and use it for what he regards as his best interests. He strives to diminish his limitations and increase his capacities.

Theoretically, the systems man can construct to describe and control his universe are limited only by his sense, his symbol systems, and the nature of the world plus experience. Few thoughtful men are wise—or foolish—enough to state with much finality or in great detail just how these factors limit man's ability to deal with his world. Those who are competent to discuss the question at all are likely to be more modest than certain. It is evident that man is not yet what he may become. It is equally evident that what he may become, what his cultural potentiality is, will be largely the result of the interaction between science and policy.

Biophysical phenomena are precarious, problematic, and afflicted by flux in the "amorphous continuum of space-time." These characteristics are even more obviously true of those natural phenomena called "cultural." Of course, all man's responses to the biophysical world are strongly conditioned by culture, by the symbol-mediated responses of his senses, and by logical inferences therefrom. However, the following discussion is directed toward those aspects of culture commonly called "social" rather than toward man's culturally conditioned responses to physical and biological phenomena. We are concerned mainly with those natural phenomena called personal, groupal, and institutional; with values and social structures.

Compared to many physical and biological phenomena, though by no means to all, social phenomena are highly unstable, varied, and variable, difficult to observe and classify, and still more difficult to reduce to predictive generalizations. This difference between biophysical and cultural phenomena is largely a matter of degree and has been greatly exaggerated by those who deny that social phenomena are natural and by those who assert they are "natural" but "basically different" from biophysical phenomena. When concepts by postulation take precedence over concepts by intuition, as they must, if deductively formulated social sciences are to be constructed, it becomes very difficult to show what this alleged basic difference is. The problem of knowing social phenomena is epistemologically identical with that of knowing biophysical phenomena.*

It is unnecessary to argue this point. It is necessary to recognize the fact that many matters which seriously concern mankind present a kaleidoscopic mass of data which is in a highly unsatisfactory state of generalization. Among these are such things as the rise and fall of civilizations; the role of leaders; the variety and change in values, ideologies, and technologies; the origin and development of social structures; the relations between ideas and actions, words and things, desires and deeds; differences between adjacent culture areas; differences within particular cultures; the relation between population and natural resources, climate, and the state of the industrial arts; social class and ethnocentric phenomena; and so on almost endlessly. It is probable that there is some relationship between the lack of scientific knowledge about social phenomena and the existence of widespread social conflict and confusion, waste, cruelty, and catastrophe. It is neither a snug nor a pretty world.

It is easy to see why the concept of relativity first emerged from the study of social rather than physical phenomena and why the social sciences are at present more ideograhic than nomothetic.† However, cumulative study of social phenomena has revealed more relatively stable uniformities than formerly was suspected. An increasing number of useful descriptive and predictive generalizations are appearing. Social phenomena gradually are being incorporated into the theoretical framework of science.

Partly as a result of incorporating the concept of relativity into the theoretical framework of physics, there is now emerging an attempt to construct a unified field theory which shall be of sufficient generality to serve as a theoretical framework for all the physical, biological, and social sciences. The most promising method of unifying all the sciences seems to be mathematical logic. All the natural sciences increasingly use hypotheses which postulate objects and relations not immediately observable. Such hypotheses are assumed to be true if supported by sufficient empirical evidence. To assert the truth of such a theorem is not permissible in strict logic. Only "probability-truth" can be claimed. Statistics and logic are the means of testing the degree of probability.

This combination of theoretical analysis and empirical testing has paid big

---

* That is, problems of establishing the truth or reliability of statements about social phenomena are the same as those for statements about physical phenomena.—Eds.

† That is, at present the social sciences produce broad descriptions, but do not offer statements sufficiently general to be considered as theoretical laws.—Eds.

dividends in the actual advancement of scientific knowledge, especially in mathematical physics and modern biology. Even though this involves "affirming the consequent," which is not really the case, since probability, not certainty, is all that is affirmed, it has the great practical advantage of keeping open the question of what is "proper" postulation. Any postulation is permissible that generates testable theorems. This increases the ease with which unsatisfactory postulates may be revised or discarded. It reduces the danger of reifying concepts which was one of the greatest barriers to the free play of intelligence so long as man's thinking was dominated by postulated supernatural beings and "forces."

Thus, all modern science is the resultant of the reciprocal interaction between induction and deduction. By adequate preliminary theoretical analysis, the scientist will save himself much work in the laboratory and in the field. He can make his head save his feet and hands. In fact, empirical research is impossible until proper theoretical work has been done and the significance of empirical findings is not evident until the new knowledge has been incorporated into the deductively formulated system of scientific theory. One of the most meaningful symbols of modern science is Einstein with a pencil and a sheet of paper. Cyclotrons and transgalactic telescopes rest on scraps of paper, but the Einsteins are helpless and the scraps of paper remain blank except for the work of observers, engineers, artisans, and men with measuring instruments. This is equally true of research in the social sciences. If descriptive, empirical, and systematic social science were not emerging, if there were no predictable sequences in the occurrence of social phenomena, it would be pointless to talk about the relations between social research and policy-making.

Policy-making implies values. These values are of at least two kinds: those of the policy-makers and those of the people affected by the policies. Policy also implies an objective. There is no problem of policy unless at least two, and usually there are more, alternative courses of action are recognized and are possible. When there is no conflict of values, usually there are alternative methods by which a given objective could be accomplished. Choosing proper methods is an important aspect of policy-making but it is in an entirely different category from policy choices which involve conflicting values.

The policy-maker differs from other people in that he is responsible for outcomes. He is a risk-taker. Those closely associated with him are also risk-takers, of course, though they are relatively passive and helpless. If the policy fails, they, along with the responsible policy-maker, may lose their jobs or their heads. Therefore, it is important to keep these two types of policy separate in thought, even though they are interdependent in practice: those which involve value-choices and those which involve method-choices to implement a value-policy already chosen.

Applied social science is being used chiefly at the method-policy level at the present time. This is proving to be increasingly useful for "practical" purposes, but the use of science in formulating value-policy is likely to be much more important to long-run human welfare. This question deserves much more scientific study than it has received or is now receiving. To what extent can science aid in the formulation of value-policy? The degree to which the policy-maker will use science, whether he is concerned with method-policy or value-policy, depends upon the amount of confidence he has in its adequacy. This, in turn, depends upon the adequacy of his knowledge of the science in question and its demonstrated success in solving the kinds of problems with which he is faced.

To an appalling degree, most policy-makers are ignorant of the social sciences and therefore have a negative attitude toward them even in connection with method-policy. The very concept of value-policy is almost foreign to their minds, and the idea that social science might be of use in defining goals and predicting results is beyond their comprehension. They have a great and childlike confidence in physical and biological science but where social science is concerned, they are men of little faith. Consequently, much available social science knowledge is not used in policy-making, even at the method level. When it is used, it often is misused so far as public welfare is concerned. It is little used at the value-policy level where it is indispensable for sound long-run policy. Applied social science is chiefly used to implement method policies in business, politics, education, war, etc., the value aspect of which is naively taken for granted. The result is often catastrophe soon or late— and too often, too soon. Can science be used in value-policy making, and if so, how? This is the most crucial question that one can ask about the relation of science to policy-making.

Most so-called "policies" deal with immediate questions of the practicality, cost, and probable success of programs based on the naively held values of the policy-maker, or those of his social class, or those of the organization that employs him. Science is seldom used to test these values in terms of the long-run welfare of the community or even that of the social class or organization to which the policy-maker belongs. If research is used at all, it is likely to be directed toward the solution of method-policy problems—how best to effectuate the taken-for-granted values. In such a situation, the researcher is merely another technician like a carpenter or a salesman. He sells his services to carry out a policy he has had no responsible part in making. He surrenders his moral integrity and thus abandons his role and status as a professional man. All too often there is a dubious quality about the usually short-run policies implemented by such research. They are mainly method-policies designed to sell goods at the highest possible profit; to get elected; to promote a vested interest; to control quality; to measure costs; to explore and control the market; or to gain public support for some ill-defined policy which may be detrimental to public welfare. Research is seldom used to ascertain or influence the long-run effects of the policy on the welfare of the community or even the organization that is sponsoring the program. This would require intensive value-policy research.

When applied science is used for method-policy research, it indirectly improves pure science, which of course improves applied science.[3] This is fortunate since the findings and methods of both pure and applied science must be employed to the limit for a successful attack upon the problem of value-policy. That more such knowledge is now available than is currently used should not blind us to the crying need for a vast and rapid increase of all types of social science knowledge.

Take a simple case—building a bridge. At the method-policy level, engineering science is used as necessary routine. Some applied social science may also be used: in persuading the community to pay for the bridge; ascertaining the reliability of contractors; managing personnel; etc. However, much social science knowledge could be used at the value-policy level though this is seldom done. Should the bridge be built? Who will use it? What kinds of traffic and how much? How will it affect the lives of the people and the structure of the community? Will it be adequate in twenty years? Can beauty and utility be combined?

To answer these and other value-policy questions properly, the general principles of social science must be applied by research into the ecology of the area where the bridge is contemplated. Population trends, business trends, educational and health and policing and sanitation needs must be considered. A hundred other factors must be dealt with if the bridge is to promote the long-run welfare of the community. Sound value-policy is impossible unless it is formulated in accordance with a long-range community plan based upon local research and all applicable scientific knowledge. This is a sound principle whether one is building a bridge, a nation, or a world community.

Value-policy deals with what man thinks ought to be done with his immediate and ultimate objectives. If man's "ought" is based upon a false or inadequate conception of his own nature, or the nature of the biophysical world, his action to achieve his desires will be futile, wasteful, or destructive. If he accepts the equally fatal view that nothing can be done, that what is, is, and what will be will be, his behavior may be apathetic resignation. Sometimes he indulges in vague verbal fantasies of what he wishes might be; he even deludes himself into believing that "wishing makes it so." The nonrealistic contradiction between what is, or is reasonably possible, and value-policy often leads to aggressive conflict, with fantasy, or regressive resignation and inaction. In either case, no sanctioning moral standards and hence no effective moral responsibility is possible. Man tends to become a nonmoral monster, or a passive accepter, or a cynical, superficial exploiter of the moment.

---

[3] Read Bain, "Sociology and the Other Sciences," *The Scientific Monthly* (November 1941), especially, pp. 449–453.

As more people find it impossible to accept the hypothesis of capricious supernatural beings, as they lose faith in the concept of natural law as a basis for moral values, as they come to reject metaphysical ultimates such as race-soul, national destiny, dialectic Marxism, private-profit capitalism, and so on, they are forced into moral anarchy and subjective moral atomism, or they are forced to find or construct a new moral sanction.

This has led some people to postulate logical consistency between natural science knowledge and normative values. They believe that the final moral sanction, and therefore the logical basis for moral responsibility, can be grounded in this relationship; that it is possible to measure what ought to be by what is, and is possible, according to the findings of science. Northrop has expressed this view as follows: "Clearly, that philosophy of culture is the more scientifically correct and adequate one which can take care of the widest range of facts concerning nature and the natural man." [4] By "natural man," I assume he means substantially what I mean by "cultural man," since culture is natural.

This view provides a simple test of sound value-policy. The validity of an "ought," a normative value, is measured by what is, and what is possible, according to extant scientific knowledge and technology. It is immoral to desire, promote, or value what is in clear contradiction to what is possible. This view also provides a moral tentativeness for many types of desired things because it is not always clearly evident just what *is,* or is possible. However, for *some* types of behavior, a clear moral sanction is given. A logical basis is also given for what in fact actually occurs—changes in normative values. Man learns what to value and devalue as his knowledge and skill increase. The changing state of scientific knowledge and technology implies, and brings about, corresponding changes in normative theory and sought-for ends.

However, despite the fact this view is consistent with moral relativity, and logically implies it, there is a considerable number of values which are relatively stable and common to all mankind. Among these are the desire to live as long and be as healthy as possible; to have adequate food, shelter, and clothing; to enjoy security of person and property; to have recreational and artistic opportunities; to study, think, and communicate findings of fact and theory; to play an effective part in determining public policy; to gain status and recognition; to satisfy sexual needs and to rear children according to the standards of one's community; to worship whatever gods one thinks may exist; to promote "sacred" values and demote what one regards as evil; and so on. These relatively common aims probably contain the only rational basis for the creation of a world community. Basic research is needed to find out how many, how widespread, and how intense such common values are.

---

[4] F. S. C. Northrop, *The Logic of the Sciences and the Humanities* (New York: Macmillan, 1947), p. 340. See especially Chap. 21, "Normative Social Theory."

Obviously, these values vary in time and place, both within and between various social aggregates: nations, regions, and social classes. However, there is a basic core of persistent similarity between them in all cultures. This tends to increase as the cultures come more and more under the sway of nature science. The hierarchies of moral values tend to assume a somewhat similar ordinal relation in science—based cultures. This also calls for basic research. People put first things first in values when we judge them by their behavior rather than by their words. More research needed here.

All values, however defined and ordered, involve costs. A value-policy maker who wishes to formulate valid programs will use all means of research to ascertain the relative worth of the relevant values to the people who will be affected by his policies. He must know value-facts and trends as well as method-facts. To know what "is," and therefore what "ought to be" (what is possible), he must know what people want and the order and intensity of their desires. This means he must know what they are willing to pay in time and effort to actualize their goals.

Most current research in connection with policy-making is method-research to implement a value-policy which has been adopted with little or no reference to extant natural science knowledge and with no value-research focused on the specific problem. The problem itself is frequently not well understood. Northrop emphasizes this in the volume quoted above. The values involved usually are taken for granted. They are the values imposed on the policy-maker, or accepted by him, due to the nature of his function, whether he be a public or private functionary. His own socioeconomic position, his age, race, sex, religion, politics, and other status attributes may determine what values he chooses to support or oppose by his policies. He may assume these values are equally valued by others. He may seek or produce research findings to induce them to accept the value-policy he proposed and then formulate the method-policy research by which the adopted policy can best be carried out. The result is often harmful, unworkable, wasteful, and contradictory policy decisions.[5]

The greatest contribution to value-policy research is likely to be made by the social scientists. They must develop a large body of factual, empirically valid knowledge about the structure and functioning of social aggregates. They must formulate methods of evaluating values. They must arrive at normative concepts which are the logical implications of the deductively formulated theory of social phenomena. They must be able to show the limits within which various policies are possible and the costs of attaining a specified approximation to these limits. They must show the probable results of adopting, or not adopting, specific policies. They must specify the order of preference for various value-policies in designated segments of the population. They also

---

[5] See Stuart Queen's discussion of Francis E. Merrill's paper, "The Study of Social Problems," *American Sociological Review* (June 1948), pp. 261–262.

must show the rates and direction of change in these various value-preferences as they are modified by the impact of science and technology. They must indicate the logical contradictions between various values and also the discrepancies between them and what is possible in view of the existing factual limits imposed by physical, biological, and cultural factors. This is only a brief indication of the scope of research which is necessary for adequate decisions regarding value-policy.

Much scientific knowledge is now available which could be used in formulating value-policy. More is accumulating all the time. However, the need for special value-policy research always will exist when any specific areal policy is under consideration. This should be as much a matter of routine as the method-policy research involved in building a bridge. In all cases, it is indispensable. No specific policy involving considerable numbers of people and large sums of money should be undertaken without adequate value-policy and method-policy research.[6] This includes relevant physical and biological research as well as social research. All three are involved in most specific problems.

Until such a general policy is adopted for policy-making, we shall continue to have guess, special interest, exploitation, ignorance, waste, and confusion exhibited by those whom we now erroneously call policy-makers—those blind leaders of the blind. Contradictory, impossible, inadequate, detrimental, too costly, controversial, and often tragic programs will continue to be set in motion by irresponsible people in high places until policy-making is conceived as a by-product of natural science knowledge and value-policy is regarded as more important than method-policy. Pure and applied social science holds the greatest promise of greatest usefulness for sound overall policy-making.

However, it cannot develop its greatest usefulness until it is used and it should not be used until it is more useful than common sense which often is nonsense in a rapidly changing and increasingly interdependent world society. This apparent paradox is not a real one. Modern social science has produced a great body of scientific knowledge which could profitably be used in the formulation of both method-policy and value-policy. What is more important, it knows how to get approximate answers to many questions socially intelligent policy-makers should be asking. If policy-makers would now use all the available social science knowledge, both the methods of getting factual data and transforming them into deductively formulated theory (pure science) would rapidly improve.

This is happening, of course. The most pressing question is whether it is happening fast enough to provide the knowledge and techniques which can save mankind from more serious catastrophes than he has suffered up to now.

---

[6] See Robert Bierstedt, "Social Science and Social Policy," *American Association of University Professors Bulletin* (Summer 1948), pp. 310–319, for a stimulating discussion of this whole question.

There is presumably a limit to the number and kinds of catastrophes man can experience and still survive. We may now be approaching that limit. Thus far, man has learned the hard way. Perhaps he eventually will learn how to learn the easy way, that is, by relying upon his intelligence as it manifests itself in natural science, by trusting his reason more and his impulses less, by ceasing to rely upon the goodness of hypothetical gods, the beneficence of metaphysical reifications, and the leadership of people whose paranoid certainty parades as wisdom and knowledge.

If he learns to form his norms and formulate his policies according to the logic of natural science, he may survive as long as the solar system retains its present rate of radiation. If he continues his present course, his future appears to be nasty, dim, and brief—say 50,000 years, if you are optimistic.

Topical Index

COMMUNITY

CONFLICT

COOPERATION

CRIME AND DELINQUENCY

CULTURE

ECOLOGY

SOCIAL RESEARCH—Continued

SOCIALIZATION